D0893441

HANDBOOK OF CAREER PLANNING
FOR STUDENTS WITH SPECIAL NEEDS

HANDBOOK OF CAREER PLANNING FOR STUDENTS WITH SPECIAL NEEDS

THIRD EDITION

Edited by
Thomas F. Harrington

8700 Shoal Creek Boulevard
Austin, Texas 78757-6897
800/897-3202   Fax 800/397-7633
www.proedinc.com

An International Publisher

1982, 1997, 2004 by PRO-ED, Inc.
8700 Shoal Creek Boulevard
Austin, Texas 78757-6897
800/897-3202   Fax 800/397-7633
www.proedinc.com

All rights reserved. No part of the material protected by this
copyright notice may be reproduced or used in any form or by
any means, electronic or mechanical, including photocopying,
recording, or by any information storage and retrieval system,
without prior written permission of the copyright owner.

Library of Congress Cataloging-in-Publication Data

Handbook of career planning for students with special needs / edited by Thomas F.
Harrington.—3rd ed.
    p. cm.
    Includes bibliographical references and index.
    ISBN 0-89079-965-2
    1. People with disabilities—Vocational guidance—Handbooks, manuals, etc.   2. Students
with disabilities—Vocational guidance—Handbooks, manuals, etc.   I. Harrington, Thomas F.

HV1568.5.H36 2003
362.4'0484—dc21
                                                                    2002036821

This book is designed in Goudy.

Printed in the United States of America

1 2 3 4 5 6 7 8 9 10   07 06 05 04 03

to Joan,

a caring wife

CONTENTS

CONTRIBUTORS

Shirley K. Chandler, PhD
Department of Rehabilitation Studies
Division of Human Services
Thomas University
1501 Millpond Road
Thomasville, GA 31792

Mary E. Cronin, PhD
Department of Special Education
University of New Orleans
New Orleans, LA 70148

Timothy Gray Davies
Community College Leadership Program
Colorado State University
Fort Collins, CO 80524

Richard W. Feller, PhD
Colorado State University
School of Education 222
Fort Collins, CO 80524

Neeta P. Fogg, PhD
Center for Labor Market Studies
315 Holmes Hall
Northeastern University
360 Huntington Avenue
Boston, MA 02115

Andrea G. Gurney, MSEd
Brazelton Touchpoints Center
Boston Children's Hospital
1295 Boylston Street, Suite 320
Boston, MA 02215

Paul E. Harrington, EdD
Center for Labor Market Studies
315 Holmes Hall
Northeastern University
360 Huntington Avenue
Boston, MA 02115

Thomas F. Harrington, PhD
Department of Counseling and Applied
  Educational Psychology
203 Lake Hall
Northeastern University
360 Huntington Avenue
Boston, MA 02115

David K. Hollingsworth, PhD
Department of Psychology and Sociology
Our Lady of Holy Cross College
4123 Woodland Avenue
New Orleans, LA 70131

Louis J. Kruger, PsyD
Department of Counseling and Applied
  Educational Psychology
203 Lake Hall
Northeastern University
360 Huntington Avenue
Boston, MA 02115

Robin H. Lock, PhD
Department of Special Education
Texas Tech University
388 Education Administration Building
Lubbock, TX 79409-1071

Ross K. Lynch, PhD
Professional Rehabilitation Services, Ltd.
559 D'Onofrio Drive, Suite 100
Madison, WI 53719

Ruth Torkelson Lynch, PhD
Department of Rehabilitation
Psychology and Special Education
University of Wisconsin–Madison
432 North Murray Street, Room 431
Madison, WI 53706

Barbara F. Okun, PhD
Department of Counseling and Applied
Educational Psychology
203 Lake Hall
Northeastern University
360 Huntington Avenue
Boston, MA 02115

James R. Patton, EdD
PRO-ED, Inc.
8700 Shoal Creek Boulevard
Austin, TX 78757-6897

Mary Reinke-Scorzelli, PhD
19 Adella Avenue
West Newton, MA 02165

Salvatore J. Rizzo, PhD
Collaborations in Clinical Care
275 Turnpike Street, Suite 105
Canton, MA 02021

William Sanchez, PhD
Department of Counseling and Applied
Educational Psychology
203 Lake Hall
Northeastern University
360 Huntington Avenue
Boston, MA 02115

James F. Scorzelli, PhD
Department of Counseling and Applied
Educational Psychology
203 Lake Hall
Northeastern University
360 Huntington Avenue
Boston, MA 02115

David Shriberg, MS
Carlisle Public Schools
83 School Street
Carlisle, MA 01741

Kim E. Simmons, MS
Vocational Rehabilitation Services
Georgia Department of Labor
Savannah, GA 31410

Dawna M. Thomas, PhD
Law, Policy, and Society Program
305 Cushing Hall
Northeastern University
360 Huntington Avenue
Boston, MA 02115

Pamela H. Varrin, PhD
Cotting School
Lexington, MA 02421

USING THIS BOOK

Professionals and paraprofessionals from many disciplines are involved in preparing individuals for careers. Many of these professionals enter career planning practice without having in place the competencies for effective service delivery that are set forth in this book. The delivery of career development services requires age-appropriate accommodations for children as well as adaptations to address remedial developmental issues of adults that arise when an individual is laid off due to organizational downsizing. Because both students and adults want to participate in their own career planning, persons who are helping them must be creative and flexible to accommodate the needs of all individuals.

The following definitions clarify some generic terms used by the authors.

- **Helper:** A generic term inclusive of a variety of professionals and nonprofessionals with different occupational titles who provide career development services (e.g., teacher, counselor, career counselor, college counselor, job developer, employment interviewer, career resource room technician, career paraprofessional, practitioner, social worker, nurse, parent)

- **Client:** A generic term to indicate any recipient of career development services (e.g., student, adult, parent or guardian, helpee)

- **Student with special needs:** Occasionally referred to as a person with a disabling condition

- **Communication skills:** Consistent with such terminology as counseling process, helping relationship, or interpersonal skills

The content of career counseling differs conceptually and strategically according to the client's specific developmental stage. Drummond and Ryan (1995) detailed developmental theories for kindergarten through Grade 5 and goals and strategies appropriate to middle or junior high school students; high school students; community and senior college students; and young, middle-age, and older adults. A survey of members of five national professional associations by the National Occupational Information Coordinating Committee (NOICC) (1995), which was conducted by the Career Development Training Institute at the University of South Carolina, revealed that the career development needs of middle school students are frequently neglected in master's level counseling and guidance degree programs. In addition, data indicated that discussion of these needs by elementary school–age children may be excluded from nearly 80% of the courses in these programs. These younger students need to be building a foundation of competencies that will form an important basis for future career planning. Perrone, Perrone, Chan, and Thomas (2000) reported that a substantial difference in rankings of the most important career counseling competencies occurred between school counselors and a panel of counselor educators and state Department of Public Instruction consultants. Differences in counselors' self-efficacy ratings for these competencies also occurred. The study used NOICC/National Career Development Association competencies. The school counselors were from a very large sample of midwestern high schools, middle schools, and elementary schools; however, no analysis of differences among the three groups was made. The competencies for elementary school, middle school, and high school students and adults, which were published by NOICC (1996), are reprinted at the end of the book in Appendixes A through D.

Examination of the elementary competencies (Appendix A) reveals that group guidance or classroom strategies are effective delivery systems. Further examination indicates that many of these competencies could be integrated by teachers into their normal instructional activities, albeit not without some additional training. This book describes how the career development specialist might work collaboratively with teachers and administrators to design a curriculum that achieves the enumerated competencies. The middle school competencies (see Appendix B) call for a staff person with specific career expertise. The strategies presented in this book are adaptable to elementary school and middle school youth if age-appropriate language, materials, and exercises provided in this book are employed. The competencies for high school (see Appendix C) bring students to preemployment levels and ready them for further postsecondary education. The competencies for adults (see Appendix D) address issues of adapting, coping with stress, and assuming additional life roles.

Unfortunately, many people reach adulthood without the opportunities and experiences necessary to acquire self-knowledge. The deficits in this competency, which most individuals begin developing in elementary school, often do not come to light until young adulthood. Some adults also suffer from a lack of career awareness, which may become a necessary competency during this economic period of layoffs and industrial and governmental downsizing. Because this competency currently is developed by many middle or junior high schools, helpers need to make developmental adjustments to work with older clients. Typical adjustments include use of age-appropriate language; use of materials and exercises relevant to the person's age and learning style; and helper adaptability in order to meaningfully integrate a person's experience into the achievement of a developmental task and specific career skill.

This book covers the 13 competencies identified by NOICC (1995) as basic to effective performance by career development practitioners:

1. Career development theory

2. Decision-making skills

3. Consultation skills (referred to as team building in Chapter 14)

4. Assessment

5. Labor market information

6. Career counseling skills

7. Working with special population skills

8. Collaborative approaches

9. Research and evaluation

10. Career services ethics

11. Group guidance approaches

12. Computer software and information systems

13. Development, management, and implementation of programs and public information and marketing

The NOICC survey revealed that only the first 5 of these 13 competencies (as listed above) were included in master's level degree programs in guidance and counseling. The remaining 8 competencies were not addressed in these preemployment training courses. The NOICC *National Career Development Guidelines* were revised and updated and are now available in the kindergarten through adult handbook (Kobylarz, 2001). Today those guidelines are being used in at least 40 states to deliver comprehensive counseling programs. In addition, Real Game (Barry, 2001), uniquely geared to six age levels from Grades 3 and 4 up to adults, provides curricula that link student life roles, work roles, and personal career aspirations to subjects. Real Game is a series of group activities forming a career development program for youth and adults. It includes specific lessons for all group sessions in the curricula, with measurable performance indicators matching the *National Career Development Guidelines*.

This book attempts to address all of these competencies, some in greater detail than others. Some competencies are identified by chapter title; others may be integrated within text that is focused on broader content. The contributors to this book hope that the information they provide will help persons achieve the 13 competencies. Readers also should be able to apply the rich material in the book to their cases, thereby developing skills and moving theory into practice.

References

Barry, B. (2001). *Real game*. Memramcook, New Brunswick, Canada: National Life/ Work Center.

Drummond, R., & Ryan, C. (1995). *Career counseling: A developmental approach*. Englewood Cliffs, NJ: Prentice Hall.

Kobylarz, L. (Ed.). (2001). *National career development guidelines: K–adult handbook*. Des Moines, WA: National Training Support Center.

National Occupational Information Coordinating Committee. (1995, October). *Survey of career development educators*. Washington, DC: U.S. Department of Labor.

National Occupational Information Coordinating Committee. (1996). *The national career development guidelines project*. Washington, DC: U.S. Department of Labor.

Perrone, K. M., Perrone, P. A., Chan, F., & Thomas, K. R. (2000). Assessing efficacy and importance of career counseling competencies. *The Career Development Quarterly, 48*, 212–225.

CAREER THEORY AND PROCESS

C H A P T E R

CAREER DEVELOPMENT THEORY
Thomas F. Harrington

This chapter is a primer of the most important concepts, language, and definitions of the major career development theories. Learning this information will foster an understanding of the uniqueness and differences of the various theories. Short quotes are used to give the reader some familiarity with the theory author's style of expression. Because of its importance, a linkage between theory and practice is attempted despite the brevity of this primer. No doubt readers will want to learn more about a specific theory from reading the theorist's original work or compilations such as Brown's (2002) *Career Choice and Development* (4th ed.) or Sharf's (2002) *Applying Career Development Theory to Counseling* (3rd ed.).

The second edition of this handbook was written at a time when the field attempted to converge or reduce the number of unique theories to four. In addition, at that time, I included two separate sections because of theoretical deficiencies — the role of cultural context in career development and the career development of women. This third edition gives greater coverage to these very important areas by incorporating the topics into specific theories where most appropriate. More theories are also covered in this chapter. Several concepts, such as a developmental approach and self-efficacy, are covered by two theorists. When this happens, the more current version is treated more comprehensively, including referencing it to a relevant chapter in the handbook. The intent is to provide the reader with an historical as well as a more in-depth perspective.

Note. I appreciate the assistance of Susan Connell in writing this chapter.

Overall, the theories presented here are generic enough to apply to all people who plan to work in the United States, but they possess a definite Western cultural bias. I contend that individuals with special needs should be accommodated within existing theoretical frameworks to help eliminate myths about disabling conditions and discrimination. The criteria that make these theories useful are (a) their authors have delineated key constructs about career planning and presented supporting research data, and (b) each theory has a distinctive orientation and capacity for practitioner operationalization.

Career development theories provide general explanations of why and how people make career plans and choices. Theories differ because the authors are attempting to achieve different objectives. One theorist seeks to explain why an individual chooses a specific career over other careers, whereas another theorist is more concerned with explaining the development of an individual's career path over a lifetime. The reader is therefore encouraged to examine, compare, and contrast the assumptions of the theoretical orientations. This examination is intended not to teach the helper to choose the "best" theory but to identify conditions under which one theory may be more appropriate than another. Theory can be a pragmatic helping strategy. With little experience, no models to organize large quantities of information, and no paradigms to help suggest relationships between seemingly unrelated data, the inexperienced or nontheoretical helper is a long way from being professional in practice.

Many practitioners working with students with special needs lack a background in vocational development theory. Their failure to use systematic theoretical approaches to career planning can have a severe impact on their clients' personal development. If an individual's career development does not mature, it can affect his or her self-concept, future career position, and eventual economic status. Nontheoretical approaches to vocational development frequently minimize self-awareness and career exploration, resulting in the consideration of a narrow or truncated spectrum of available work options. A theoretical orientation fosters self-awareness, career awareness, and career exploration to prevent premature closure of job choice and espouses the maximization of self-determination. Full individual participation in goal setting and an emphasis on self-direction reduce dependency, increase self-responsibility, and minimize possible underutilization of talents.

Super's Life-Span, Life-Space Developmental Theory

Donald E. Super is the most established of the theorists discussed in this chapter, having begun his influential writings in 1942. His theory of careers is a comprehensive synthesis of diverse popular counseling beliefs. Super contended that people are capable of achieving success in a number of jobs, and his developmental viewpoint emphasized a focus on the whole process.

According to Super's theory, individuals choose occupations that will allow them to function in roles consistent with their self-concepts. Super identified career development tasks for five life stages, and he contended that although the content of decisions differs, decision-making principles are the same at any age and any life stage. An understanding of career life stages gives individuals an awareness of the issues, roles, and conflicts with which most people will need to cope during their lifetimes and provides a longitudinal perspective of career maturation. One of Super's basic premises is that because people are both rational and emotional, "the best vocational counseling is a combination of the two, somewhere between the theoretical extremes" (Super, 1951, p. 91). "It is not so much counseling concerning choice, as counseling to develop readiness of choice, to develop planfulness. It involves helping (the client) to understand the personal, social, and other factors which have a bearing on the making of educational and vocational decisions" (Super & Overstreet, 1960, p. 147).

The Theory

Super's theory of vocational development has been categorized as a developmental theory. However, Super (1994) preferred the description of his approach as differential–developmental–social–phenomenological psychology and believed that a comprehensive theory must use all of these fields, including aspects of sociological and economic theories. The following description of the theory includes the contributions from these various disciplines.

Differential Psychology

Super referred to his theoretical orientation as *differential psychology*, a psychology based on individual differences. People vary in their abilities, interests, and personalities. These characteristics can be assessed to attain self-knowledge through interviews, self-reports, inventories, and tests, which are the embodiment of trait-and-factor theory. Super also believed that individuals' interests and abilities are more likely to fit some occupations than others and that people will be more satisfied when their chosen occupations match their abilities and interests. In any given occupation, however, some variety exists in workers' personal traits. Super believed that people have the potential to be qualified for a variety of occupations. Differential psychology is significant in its emphasis on creating self-knowledge and having the capability to describe the self as well as to identify one's differences of self from others.

Developmental Psychology

Super disavowed the idea that job selection is a one-shot event, ending when a person is matched with a job. His psychology of careers used the evolutionary principle of human development. Life career planning is founded upon the concept that people progress through developmental periods in their careers. The whole cycle of developmental stages and series of experiences and jobs must be observed to fully comprehend a person's vocational life. Individuals' self-concepts, vocational preferences, competencies, and work and life situations change with time and experience, making career choice and adjustment a continuous process. Using a developmental psychology framework, Super described in a ladder analogy the vocational tasks and decisions for each of five life stages: growth, exploration, establishment, maintenance, and decline. The first two life stages are the primary focus of this chapter. (See Table 1.1 for elaboration of the substages and developmental tasks associated with each life stage.)

Social Psychology

An individual is portrayed as having eight typical role functions, each of which interacts with the others during his or her life span — child, student, leisurite, citizen, worker, spouse, homemaker, and parent. Life is viewed as a theater in which individuals act out their respective roles. Super (1994) specified the roles and their approximate time of onset. It is expected that each individual will define these roles differently. The theory's implicit belief is that each person has choices in accepting or rejecting each role. Everyone has the capacity for self-determination and can shape the roles within the constraints of his or her environments, for example, differing role expectations for sons and daughters, spouse and parent roles, and conflicting expectations between the worker role and the family role.

Readers frequently debate designated developmental ages as personally inapplicable. To demonstrate date relativity and the impact of local customs and different cultural groups' practice, I have included the 1994 Super reference to contrast it with the altered dates Super, Savickas, and Super presented in 1996. For some individuals, entry into the student role is earlier than age 5, as some children now are enrolled in a variety of preschool activities; for many people, higher education now expands to age 24. Super et al. (1996) put the full-time work entry age at 27 years. Super et al. changed the onset of the homemaker role from age 25 to age 30. For many people, the parent role is beginning later than age 27, and they dropped the spouse and parent roles in 1996. The leisurite role starts earlier now, at age 10, and the citizen role has been moved back to age 21. The key point is that people enter and exit different roles in patterns

TABLE 1.1
Super's Conception of Life Stages and Developmental Tasks

Growth	Exploration	Establishment	Maintenance	Decline
Birth	*14 years*	*24 years*	*44 years*	*64 years*
Self-concept develops through identification with key figures in family and school; needs and fantasy are dominant early in this stage; interest and capacity become more important with increasing social participation and reality testing; learn behaviors associated with self-help, social interaction, self-direction, industriousness, goal setting, persistence.	Self-examination, role try-outs, and occupational exploration take place in school, leisure activities, and part-time work.	Having found an appropriate field, an effort is made to establish a permanent place in it. Thereafter changes that occur are changes of position, job, or employer, not of occupation.	Having made a place in the world of work, the concern is how to hold on to it. Little new ground is broken, continuation of established pattern. Concerned about maintaining present status while being forced by competition from younger workers in the advancement stage.	As physical and mental powers decline, work activity changes and in due course ceases. New roles must be developed: first, selective participant and then observer. Individual must find other sources of satisfaction to replace those lost through retirement.
Substages:	**Substages:**	**Substages:**	Tasks:	**Substages:**
Fantasy (4–10 years) Needs are dominant; role-playing in fantasy is important.	*Tentative* (15–17) Needs, interests, capacities, values, and opportunities are all considered; tentative choices are made and tried out in fantasy, discussion, courses, work, etc. Possible appropriate fields and levels of work are identified. Task: Crystallizing a vocational preference.	*Trial-Commitment and Stabilization* (25–30) Settling down. Securing a permanent place in the chosen occupation. May prove unsatisfactory, resulting in one or two changes before the life work is found or before it becomes clear that the life work will be a succession of unrelated jobs.	Accepting one's limitations. Identifying new problems to work on. Developing new skills. Focusing on essential activities. Preserving achieved status and gains. Variation or complete cessation of work or shift to part-time or volunteer activities.	*Deceleration* (65–70) The pace of work slackens, duties are shifted, or the nature of work is changed to suit declining capacities. Many men find part-time jobs to replace their full-time occupations.

(continues)

TABLE 1.1 Continued.

Growth	Exploration	Establishment	Maintenance	Decline
Birth (*continued*)	**14 years** (*continued*)	**24 years** (*continued*)	**44 years** (*continued*)	**64 years** (*continued*)
Interest (11–12 years) Likes are the major determinant of aspirations and activities.	*Transition* (18–21) Reality considerations are given more weight as the person enters the labor market or professional training and attempts to implement a self-concept. Generalized choice is converted to specific choice.	*Advancement* (31–44) Effort is put forth to stabilize, to make a secure place in the world of work. For most persons these are the creative years. Seniority is acquired; clientele are developed; superior performance is demonstrated; qualifications are improved.	Tasks: Developing nonoccupational roles. Finding a good retirement spot. Doing things one has always wanted to do. Reducing working hours.	*Retirement* (71 on) Variation on complete cessation of work or shift to part-time, volunteer, or leisure activities.
Capacity (13–14 years) Abilities are given more weight and job requirements (including training) are considered.	Task: Specifying a Vocational Preference			Tasks: Deceleration, disengagement, retirement.
Tasks: Developing a picture of the kind of person one is. Developing an orientation to the world of work and an understanding of the meaning of work.	*Trial-Little Commitment* (22–24) A seemingly appropriate occupation having been found, a first job is located and tried as a potential life work. Commitment is still provisional, and if the job is not appropriate, the person may reinstitute the process of crystallizing, specifying, and implementing a preference.	Tasks: Finding the opportunity to do desired work. Learning to relate to others. Consolidation and advancement. Making occupational position secure. Settling down in a permanent position.		
	Tasks: Implementing a vocational preference. Developing a realistic self-concept. Learning more about opportunities.			

Note. From *Career Guidance Through the Life Span: Systematic Approaches,* by E. L. Herr and S. H. Cramer, 1988, Boston: Little, Brown. Copyright 1988 by Edwin L. Herr and Stanley H. Cramer. Reprinted with permission of Little, Brown and Company.

that necessitate readjustments and new thinking. Other recent changes include the adoption by Super et al. of the category of *child* as a replacement for the son and daughter roles. (My observation is that roles are gender dependent for some, and denying it ignores cultural diversity.) Note that the role of spouse in today's world might be expanded to include same-gender partners. Their elimination of an earlier annuitant or retiree role also appears to deny the long-desired goal of many individuals for entry into a period of redefining one's life. This is not to deny that early retirement has been altered from the traditional age of 65 and that part-time jobs, which employ many women, have no officially recognized retirement period. People simply stop working for varied reasons, and a clear retiree description role is difficult, partly because downsizing companies force people to seek jobs, increasingly in part-time work, for economic survival. As people age, however, they do enter into a new phase of their lives with different expectations and roles.

Social psychology's significance lies in its contention that, regardless of what role a person assumes as a worker, he or she will continue to fulfill other roles. The need to juggle and prioritize roles, especially in the early stages of adulthood, is seen vividly in stressful role conflicts among worker, spouse, parent, and time for self. Time commitments to roles also vary, depending on whether difficulties occur within a particular role.

Super's beliefs eventually evolved into a life-span, life-space theory of career development. Writing after Super's death, Herr (1997) saw the movement toward this approach as an improvement that replaced the self-concept dimension with a social–constructionist framework: "His life-span, life-space approach advanced the notion that the work is not the only role to which career scholars or counselors need to attend. Rather, persons live in multiple-role environments in which work role, family roles, educational and community roles vary in their demands on and significance for different persons and within different development periods" (p. 239). Herr also noted that Super's approach has been the primary interpretation of a developmental approach to career development used in the United States, Europe, Japan, and other countries in the industrialized world.

Phenomenological Psychology

The phenomenological viewpoint of personality is that the self is a flexible and changing perception of personal identity that emerges from a person's total subjective experience or reality. People are viewed as having not one self-concept but constellations of self-concepts (e.g., a person may perceive himself or herself as a good student, a poor speaker, and a fantastic runner). In 1951, Super was one of the first vocational psychologists to write about implementing a self-concept through work. In 1969, he described vocational growth as the development and implementation of a self-concept within the context of the world of work. The assumption is that individuals are self-determining beings who modify concepts of themselves and their environments as a result of experience.

According to Super (1969), the development of self-concept involves three processes: *formation, translation* into occupational terms, and *implementation*. Formation "includes exploration of the self and of the environment, the differentiation of the self from others, identification with others who can serve as models, and the playing of these selected roles with more or less conscious evaluation of the results" (p. 7). The translation of self-concepts into occupational terms occurs when the general self-concept is further defined through the tentative searching and feedback gained through experience in a role and the learning of occupational skill proficiencies. The implementation process involves the commitment to obtain the needed training and preparation and the effort to seek work in the field. Modification and adjustments are expected after entry into the field. Super thus viewed vocational self-concept formation as a continual, dynamic, and fluid process, which other theorists such as Gottfredson and Lent, Brown, and Hackett developed further (discussed later in this chapter). Self-concept is very important, given that some children with special needs live in a world radically different from the world of individuals without disabilities, and the former's physical or mental disabling conditions often impose sharp constraints on the ways in which they gain experience and define themselves. The practitioner's objective is to stress positive thinking and adaptability early on in order to gain experiences and feedback versus waiting until the person is 17 or 18 years of age, nearing graduation, and seeking work situations that might offer little chance of advancement.

The Archway Model

Super (1990) developed the archway model to visually depict the synthesizing of various segments of the self that compose the broadly conceived life-span, life-space theory. Beginning at the base of the arch, which represents the person's genetic origin, the model shows personal development reflecting needs, values, aptitudes, and interests, culminating in an achievement level and personality. These segments interface simultaneously with community, family, educational system, and peers, all of which are influenced by social policy and the economy. The culmination at the top of the arch is an idiosyncratic definition of self as the result of progressing through stages and developing diverse self-concepts within various life roles. The model in Figure 1.1 graphically illustrates the complexity of career development and illustrates Super's inclusions

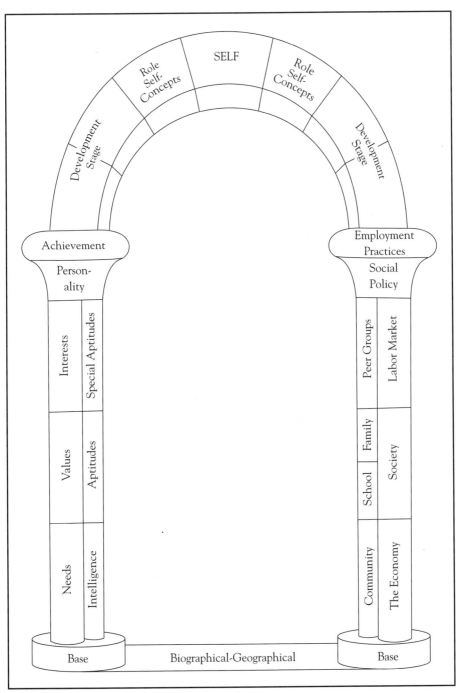

Figure 1.1. A segmental model of career development. From "A Life-Span, Life-Space Approach to Career Development," by D. Super, 1990, in *Career Choice and Development: Applying Contemporary Theories to Practice* (2nd ed., p. 200), by D. Brown, L. Brooks, & Associates (Eds.), San Francisco: Jossey-Bass. Copyright 1990 Jossey-Bass, Inc. Reprinted with permission.

from differential, developmental, social, and phenomenological psychology, as well as contributions from the disciplines of sociology and economics.

Savickas (1997) proposed the construct of adaptation for integrating or bridging different aspects of the archway model — individual differences and developmental, self, and contextual segments in life-span, life-space theory. *Adaptation* may be defined as "making more congruent or fitting" and thus corresponds to the central construct of person–environment theory. When viewed as receptive to feedback, adaptation also is compatible with a developmental view. Without the negative connotation of adjusting, accommodating, or conforming, adaptation reflects a positive perspective of being open to and flexible regarding change. This also shifts the perspective from one that is solely individualistic to "individual-in-situation," which is in agreement with multicultural viewpoints.

Vocational planning is the examination of self-concept expressed in occupational terms. In the planning process, it is important to explore the impact of a decision to select a particular job and the effect it will have on future roles and life stages. Too great an emphasis frequently is placed on job choice, whereas too little, if any, attention is given to the effect a current job decision can have on an individual's life at a subsequent developmental stage. (Chapter 10 vividly shows the role education can play in achieving a satisfying economic life position.)

Of the 14 theoretical propositions that underlie the vocational development theory (Super et al., 1996), four appear to be critical to career planning for people with special needs:

1. Vocational preferences and competencies, the situations in which people live and work, and hence their self-concepts change with time and experience, although self-concepts, as products of social learning, are increasingly stable from late adolescence until late maturity, providing some continuity in choice and adjustment.

2. The process of career development is essentially that of developing and implementing occupational self-concepts. It is a synthesizing and compromising process in which the self-concept is a product of the interaction of inherited aptitudes, physical makeup, opportunity to observe and play various roles, and evaluations of the extent to which the results of role playing meet with the approval of superiors and fellows (interactive learning).

3. Work satisfactions and life satisfactions depend on the extent to which the individual finds adequate outlets for abilities, needs, values, interests, personality traits, and self-concepts. Satisfaction depends on establishment in a type of work, a work situation, and a way of life in

which one can play the kind of role that growth and exploratory experiences have led one to consider congenial and appropriate.

4. The degree of satisfaction people attain from work is proportional to the degree to which they have been able to implement self-concepts.

Ginzberg (1972), another developmental theorist, used the term *optimization* instead of Super's *compromise*. Although everyone compromises, some individuals think that persons with disabling conditions do so more often. For example, beginning workers usually start in a job that is less than ideal and find a great difference between their dreams and aspirations and the realities of their present (and anticipated future) work setting. In the optimization process, workers believe they can change and adjust to the work setting so that it comes closer to their aspirations rather than deferring or realigning their ideal. More time in supportive environments may be necessary to developmentally achieve one's goals. The Americans with Disabilities Act of 1990 fits more closely into the optimization perspective.

Gottfredson's Theory of Circumscription and Compromise

In 1981, Linda S. Gottfredson set forth the core beliefs of the theory of circumscription and compromise of vocational aspirations, which hypothesized that adolescents may unnecessarily delimit their career options because of gender role stereotyping. Gottfredson (2002) expanded her focus to why people differ based on behavioral genetics and how people possess the power to create themselves. The reason the theory is positioned after Super's is its concern with developmental and self-concept issues.

Self-concept is one's view of self. Like Super, Gottfredson believed self-concept is multidimensional, with some elements, such as appearance, abilities, personality, gender, and place in society, being more important than others. Self-perceptions may or may not be accurate, and sometimes a self-description and its expression can be difficult: "The self-concept is the object of cognition (the 'me'), but it also reflects the person as actor (the 'I')" (p. 88). Gottfredson thus believed in personal agency or acting on one's own behalf to create one's self.

The cognitive map of occupations is a way of distinguishing occupations on three dimensions — masculinity/femininity (sex type), occupational prestige level (their overall desirability), and field of work. Gottfredson assumed that

Americans overall view images of occupations comparably as well as the prestige levels of workers in the jobs.

Circumscription involves youth progressively eliminating "unacceptable alternatives in order to carve out a social space (their zone of acceptable alternatives) from the full menu that a culture offers. Choosing one particular occupation is but the end of a long process in which youngsters have greatly constrained that final choice, knowingly or not" (Gottfredson, 2002, pp. 92–93).

Compromise involves relinquishing more preferable options for lesser compatible ones because they are seen as more accessible. It may mean reversing choices and selecting less preferable choices that earlier they rejected: "Compromise can occur either in anticipation of external barriers (anticipating compromise) or after they are encountered (experiential compromise)" (Gottfredson, 2002, p. 93).

Gottfredson's work can be seen as an expansion of Super's developmental and self-concepts work. She set forth in four stages of circumscription the development of self-images and occupational aspiration. The first stage is from ages 3 to 5 and is called Orientation to Size and Power, or adults as big and powerful images. In this stage, children dismiss their fantasy images of animals or princesses and recognize occupations as adult roles. The second circumscription stage, Orientation to Sex Roles, is when children ages 6 to 8 actively reject cross-gender behavior, effectively ruling out some jobs as inappropriate because they are the wrong sex type. By ages 9 to 13 — or Grade 8 — the third stage, Orientation to Social Valuation, involves children ranking occupations by prestige (the visible benefits of jobs) in the same way as adults, for example, as low-status or high-status careers. In the fourth stage, Orientation to the Internal, Unique Self, children at ages 14 and up adopt a personal sense of self, are able to think abstractly, and are able to sense internally desired goals. These developmental stages are described more in-depth, with cultural differences added, in Chapter 4.

The following quotes offer an example for contrasting the principles of compromise with the stages of circumscription: "Severe threats to sextype will be warded off before severe threats to either prestige or interests because a 'wrong' sextype is usually the greater threat to self concept" (Gottfredson, 2002, p. 104). Women also are believed to be more tolerant of cross-gender work than men, according to Gottfredson: "Overall satisfaction with one's occupation will depend on the degree to which compromise allows one to implement a desired social self concept, either through the work itself or the lifestyle it allows self and family" (2002, pp. 106–107).

Gottfredson is the first theorist I have read to present so comprehensively a biosocial perspective of career counseling. She presents research to refute longstanding socialization theory. She presents facts in support of nature–nurture partnership theory that might lead to the creation of new approaches to career theory. Her forthright declaration of fact is that we cannot change individual differences in such traits as intelligence and personality. For example, Gottfredson notes that the administration of treatments on highly general tendencies of cognition and personality will have no lasting effect: "So although we cannot eradicate the unfavorable ones (extreme impulsivity, aggressiveness, timidity, low intelligence), we may be able to suppress, mute, constructively channel, or even disguise them, just like we can highlight, train, and capitalize on the more favorable elemental traits (gregariousness, high quantitative ability, conscientiousness)" (Gottfredson, 2002, p. 135).

Holland's Career Typology Theory

The earliest theory of vocational counseling was trait-and-factor theory. This approach fell into professional disfavor years ago when the humanitarian, personal development perspective advocated by Carl Rogers, among others, came into vogue. Even though it is grossly inadequate, trait-and-factor theory survives in practice and is the orientation most frequently used because it provides answers quickly (Krumboltz, 1994). Trait-and-factor theory is often associated with an emphasis on diagnosis; an overreliance on tests; the nonglamorous task of educating people about occupational information; and a rational, directive, and authoritarian orientation. John L. Holland developed a modified trait-and-factor methodology and addressed some of these earlier criticisms by constructing a simulation technique of vocational counseling that emphasizes self-responsibility and self-direction. His theory (Holland, 1997) easily translates into a practical technique, accounting for its present widespread acceptance by practitioners. Holland's work is currently the most researched of all vocational development theories.

First, the theory offers a structural model that links individuals and their personalities with jobs. This methodology fosters a comprehensive exploration of the world of work. Second, the theory places responsibility on the individual to assess both self and career. The process requires a self-searching that fosters self-awareness and career awareness in an educational manner without tremendous professional help. Third, the approach quickly teaches people a process that creates less dependence on the helper, fostering independent behavior. The same vocabulary is used both in an individual's assessment and in the occupational classification scheme that organizes jobs according to the psychological types and similarities of workers. Some writers have described the theory as a person–environment (P-E) model, where a personality type fits or matches an environment. Fourth, the theory's orientation is one of self-development. The procedures create multiple options. The process stresses the positive, and the theory does not use any references to negative factors or limitations. Fifth, users gain (a) information about and an understanding of the relationships among leisure and recreational activities, competencies, and interests and (b) knowledge about the skills involved in occupations. Career choice is believed to be an extension of personality, which people seek to implement in compatible work environments.

The Theory

Holland's theory maintains that people can be characterized by their resemblance to each of six personality types: realistic, investigative, artistic, social, enterprising, and conventional. Most people will have one predominant personality type, with a second or third type contributing to their overall approach to coping with their environment. The more a person resembles any given type, the more likely he or she is to manifest some of the behaviors and traits attributed to that type. Due to the complexity of personality, a person can resemble different types in varying degrees. A type is a theoretical model against which each person can be compared. According to Holland (1997), the development of typological predisposition within an individual proceeds as follows: "A child's special biology and experience first lead to preferences for some kinds of activities and aversions to others . . . increasing differentiation of preferred activities, interests, competencies, and values — create a characteristic disposition or personality type that is predisposed to exhibit characteristic behavior and to develop characteristic personality traits, attitudes, and behaviors that, in turn, form collections of skills and coping mechanisms" (p. 18).

There are also six types of occupational environments, with the same names as the personality types, which also can be described by certain characteristics. Environments are characterized by the people who occupy or work in them. Holland hypothesized that people seek out environments compatible with their personality types. People usually prefer to associate with others who share common viewpoints, interests, and competencies; for example, investigative personality types seek out and tend to be more satisfied with investigative environments. The level to which a person aspires within the environment is affected by the individual's intelligence and self-evaluations.

The six personality types and six environments with associated characteristics (Holland, 1997) are described below. The letters following the personality type names are frequently combined — RIASEC — and used to name the theory.

1a. *Realistic personality types* (R) express an interest in mechanical activities that often involve building things. They prefer working with tools and objects rather than with words and people. They are practical, are physically agile, and often avoid social situations.

1b. *Realistic environments* stress mechanical skills, practicality, persistent behavior, and physical movement. Typical jobs in this type of environment are farmer, automotive mechanic, carpenter, and truck driver.

2a. *Investigative personality types* (I) value mathematics and scientific phenomena and enjoy problem-solving and intellectual activities. They tend to be curious, creative, introspective, theoretical, and studious, and they often prefer to work by themselves.

2b. *Investigative environments* involve the use of abstract and rational analytical abilities rather than strong social orientations. Typical jobs in this type of environment are mathematician, physician, and physicist.

3a. *Artistic personality types* (A) are interested in creative activities. They often exhibit sensitivity, independence, and self-expressive behaviors.

3b. *Artistic environments* stress the expressive and imaginative use of art forms. Common jobs are writer, musician, artist, actor, singer, and dancer.

4a. *Social personality types* (S) are interested in the well-being of others. They are generally friendly, responsible people who get along well with others and can express themselves well.

4b. *Social environments* typically involve the ability to understand and change human behavior. Social types show an interest in caring for and dealing with other people. Common jobs are social worker, teacher, counselor, nurse, and recreation leader.

5a. *Enterprising personality types* (E) are often self-confident, energetic, enthusiastic, and assertive. They see themselves as verbally persuasive and are attracted to opportunities to lead others and to convince them to think the way they do.

5b. *Enterprising environments* demand verbal skills to direct and persuade other people. Common jobs are banker, small business owner, salesperson, manager, and business executive.

6a. *Conventional personality types* (C) have a preference for situations where duties are clearly defined. They typically enjoy organized tasks and have mathematical ability. They tend to be orderly, systematic, and dependable. They often place a high value on financial success and status.

6b. *Conventional environments* require systematic, concrete, and routine processing of verbal and mathematical information. Typical jobs are bank teller, secretary, accountant, and computer operator.

Holland proposed five assumptions, described in the following paragraphs.

1. *Consistency.* Within a person or an environment, some pairs of types are more closely related than others. For example, realistic and investigative types have more in common than conventional and artistic types. Consistency is the degree of relatedness between personality types or between environmental models. Degrees of consistency or relatedness are assumed to affect vocational preference. For instance, a person who most resembles the realistic type and next most resembles the investigative type (a realistic–investigative person) should be more predictable than a realistic–social person.

2. *Differentiation.* Some persons and environments are more clearly defined than others. For instance, a person may closely resemble a single type and show little resemblance to other types, or an environment may be dominated largely by a single type. In contrast, a person who resembles a number of types or an environment characterized by several types is undifferentiated or poorly defined. The degree to which a person or environment is well defined is the degree of differentiation.

3. *Identity.* This concept provides an estimate of the clarity and stability of a person's identity or the identity of an environment. Personal identity is defined as the possession of a clear and stable picture of one's goals, interests, and talents. Environmental identity is present when an environment or an organization has clear and integrated goals, tasks, and rewards that are stable over long time intervals.

Identity, consistency, and differentiation are all concerned with the clarity, definition, or focus of the main concepts — personality types and environmental models. They probably represent three techniques for assessing the same concept.

4. *Congruence.* Different types require specific environments. For instance, realistic types flourish in realistic environments because such environments provide the opportunities and rewards that a realistic type needs. Incongruence occurs when a personality type lives in an environment that provides opportunities and rewards foreign to the person's preferences and abilities — for instance, a realistic type in a social environment.

5. *Calculus.* The relationships within and among personality types or environments can be ordered according to a hexagonal model in which the distances between the personality types or environments are inversely proportional to the theoretical relationships between them (see Figure 1.2). This spatial arrangement provides explicit definitions of both consistency of a person or an environment and congruence of person and environment. In this way, the internal relationships of the theory are defined and organized by a single geometric model.

In a very large study, Day and Round (1998) offered support for the universality of this RIASEC vocational interest structure among racial and ethnic minorities. They found that "Men and women in the U.S. describing themselves as Caucasian, Native American, Asian American, Mexican American, and African American, all responded to activities in the same patterns, expressing likes and dislikes for pursuits grouped by Holland type" (pp. 734–735).

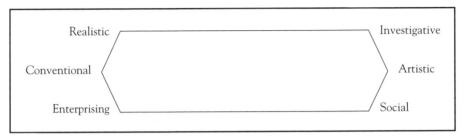

Figure 1.2. Holland's hexagonal model of the six types of personality and environment. From *Making Vocational Choices: A Theory of Vocational Personalities*, by J. L. Holland, 1985, Odessa, FL: Psychological Assessment Resources. Reproduced by special permission of the publisher, Psychological Assessment Resources, Inc., from *Making Vocational Choices*, copyright 1973, 1985, 1992, by Psychological Assessment Resources, Inc. All rights reserved.

Thus, if a person uses the *Self-Directed Search* (SDS; Holland, 1994), an instrument (described later) that operationalizes this theory, and receives a high score on one personality type and much lower scores on the five other types, this well-defined profile is referred to as being differentiated. When the individual's preferences are more crystallized, an eventual career focus is more predictable. Individuals with differentiated profiles may have had more career exploration opportunities or experiences that better enable them to realistically identify their skills.

One concern about this theory is its appropriateness in a dramatically changing world where new jobs require different skills and knowledges. Patterson and Allen (1996) noted that it is an error to view the world as unstable or unpredictable based on changing jobs, because in reality, the majority of occupations change very little. In an analysis of employment data collected by the U.S. Census Bureau in 1960, 1970, 1980, and 1990, Reardon, Vernick, and Reed (2001) concluded there was considerable stability in the nature of occupations with respect to Holland codes. In one of the few long-term predictive validity studies of interest inventories, Harrington (2002) used the Holland-based *Career Decision-Making System* (CDM) scales and found that 61% of students who took the CDM as high school sophomores in 1981 were in occupations in 2001 suggested to them 20 years earlier. In one of the longest follow-up studies ever completed, Harrington concluded that the research offered practitioners practical support for the predictive validity of RIASEC and the person–environment matching theoretical model.

The Self-Directed Search

The SDS is the most popular of Holland's instrumentations and the methodology that implements the theory. The SDS is a simulated counseling experience with which users interact on their own. It teaches individuals a process that links them with jobs. The user learns how to translate personal characteristics, interests, and abilities into appropriate occupational titles.

The SDS is self-administered, self-scored, and self-interpreted. Form R is appropriate for high school students and the SDS Career Explorer is for middle school students. Form E is available for adults and older adolescents with limited reading ability. The SDS assessment booklet contains five sections that solicit self-reports and self-estimates. From the areas assessed — occupational daydreams, preferences for activities, statements of competencies, preferences for kinds of occupations, and self-estimates of abilities — the user receives a total score for each of the six personality types. For a user of Form R, a three-letter summary code is developed from the three highest scores. For a Career Explorer or Form E user, a two-letter summary code is developed from the two highest scores. The user is then directed to the Occupations Finder to identify occupations with the identical three-letter code. Users are encouraged to expand their career exploration by reordering the three highest code letters to identify additional codes and jobs. The Career Explorer uses a simpler two-code summary to identify related occupations.

The Occupations Finder, an integral part of the SDS, contains Holland's occupational classification system, which codifies occupations by environmental types. Holland's research demonstrated that all occupations in the U.S. Department of Labor's *Dictionary of Occupational Titles* (now in its revised fourth edition, 1991) can be defined by a three-letter code. It has been shown empirically that samples of employed accountants, for example, have an SDS profile of CRS. Conventional (C) is the highest personality type score for accountants, followed by Realistic (R) and Social (S). These codes then provide a brief description of the predominant behaviors characterizing individuals within the given occupation. For example, accountants have a preference first for orderly and systematic tendencies, followed by technical and practical applications, and then working and interacting with people.

The occupational classification system provides a link by which people can explore congruence or incongruence between themselves and their personal characteristics and occupations. Once the person understands the use of the materials, he or she has an opportunity to fully explore all jobs and learn the characteristics of the people who typically work in these jobs. The Occupations Finder lists the job codes of all of the most common occupations in the United States.

My observations about Holland's theory are as follows:

1. *People will define themselves in positive terms if only positive alternatives exist.* Holland's theory does not use the concept of weaknesses. The introduction of weaknesses or limitations into the planning process, especially at the beginning, may limit options.

2. *Early prevocational explorations will permit the examination of an individual's occupational daydreams, competencies, activities, job preferences, and abilities.* The SDS materials are referred to as an open system, because people can readily see the abilities, skills, and interests related to each personality type. By showing individuals actual career requirements, this exploratory process works toward the elimination of fewer experiential opportunities for those with disabling conditions.

3. *Adaptations in the use of SDS for individuals with special needs can be created.* For example, for students who are distractible or have limited reading skills, the instrument can be administered orally by an adult.

4. *Teaching methodologies exist for self-assessment and examination of work requirements.* Unlike individual interpretation, sharing and group discussion of SDS results and views about jobs, talents, and interests permit an enrichment of perspectives. Everyone has some biases, but small-group interactions help introduce greater reality testing because they have the potential for exposing stereotypic thinking and narrowness of perspective.

5. *Realistic occupational choices need examination.* Can a person who is blind be a physician in the United States? There are practicing physicians who are blind. As people challenge traditional practices, choices previously considered unrealistic become future possibilities.

The Cognitive Information Processing Theory

The cognitive information processing theory (CIP) highlights the acquisition of career problem-solving and decision-making skills (Peterson, Sampson, Reardon, & Lenz, 1996). In brief, the pyramid of information processing, the CIP's theoretical model, consists of three levels of knowledge domains. The first, or bottom, level consists of two parallel knowledges — self- and option-knowledges. *Self-knowledge* consists of explorations of one's own values, interests, and skills. *Option-knowledge* can focus on occupations, programs of study, or jobs. Occupational knowledge involves researching a few occupations in depth; exploring typical entry patterns; skills used; employment forecasts, including those for women and minorities; how jobs are posted; effect on lifestyle; and education, training, and licenses needed. The second level of the pyramid consists of decision-making skills, which involve a process following six steps: knowing I need to make a choice, understanding myself and my options, expanding and narrowing my list of options, choosing an occupation or college major, implementing my choice, and knowing I made a good choice. The top level, or the apex, of the pyramid involves the executive processing domain, which covers one's thinking about his or her thoughts, such as self-talk, self-awareness, and managing the decision-making process as it unfolds in the previous level. For some individuals, this task can be overwhelming because of feelings of anxiety or fear of deciding. The theory's authors developed an instrument, the *Career Thoughts Inventory* (CTI; Sampson, Peterson, Lenz, Reardon, & Saunders, 1996), to assess dysfunctional thoughts people might have at this stage. The CTI has three scales — Decision-Making Confusion, Commitment Anxiety, and External Conflict. Test assessment results are used in conjunction with a cognitive exercise workbook. Through a cognitive restructuring approach, exercises help users to reframe negative CTI statements into more positive statements.

The CIP theory thus involves the following key concepts. You begin with a problem that is a gap or the difference between where a person is and where he or she wants to be. Problem solving is the process of removing the gap between the current situation and a desired state by means of using information and learning cognitive strategies. The outcome of the problem-solving process is a choice presented to the individual that has a reasonable probability for narrowing the gap. "Decision-making involves transforming the choice into specific action steps" (Sampson, Lenz, Reardon, & Peterson, 1999, p. 5). The previously mentioned six decision-making steps are referred to by the authors as the CASVE cycle, with specific goals for each phase. The Communication (C) phase involves recognition of "I have a problem," or the awareness of the gap. The Analysis (A) phase involves working with the first level of the knowledges in the pyramid of information processing, addressing "Who am I?" and exploring options that can satisfy needs. According to Sampson et al. (1999), "During the Synthesis (S) phase, individuals expand (elaborate) and narrow (crystalize) the options they are considering" (p. 6). The Valuing (V) phase is a prioritizing process, where different options are evaluated as more satisfactory because of such things as cost and benefits, thus leading to the identification of the most beneficial preference. The Executive (E) phase involves creating a plan and expressing a commitment to follow through with the plan. The benefit of the CASVE cycle is the ability to monitor where each person is in the decision-making process and, if he or she is "stuck," to supply coaching strategies to move the individual along.

Reardon and Wright (1999) applied Holland's theory combined with the cognitive information processing theory in career counseling, especially in the self-knowledge domain. Searching for sources of gender differences in decision making, Gati, Osipow, and Givan (1995) also studied the baseline self- and option-knowledges in the CIP model. Their results indicated that in spite of the observed differences, the similarities between the genders are greater than previously believed. On the other hand, the authors noted that the differences that were found are meaningful and deserve further theoretical attention, for example, to determine whether there is a need for a distinct theory to deal with the unique characteristics of women's career decision making.

The CIP authors have addressed what they perceive as a limitation of career development theories — that they address how people make choices and develop goals but do not describe how one goes about finding a job. Sampson et al. (1999) applied the CIP theory to strategies for seeking employment and to a theoretical linkage to job-search strategies.

In a review of the effectiveness of 40 different career-planning courses in institutions of higher education from 1976 to 2000 involving 16,320 students, Folsom and Reardon (2000) identified 36 career course outputs. Eighty-two percent of the students reported positive gains, such as "career thoughts, career decision-making skills, career decidedness, and vocational identity which are theoretically related to outcomes of career interventions such as persistence (retention) in college, and job satisfaction, or satisfaction with field of study" (Folsom & Reardon, 2000, p. 2). These studies offered a very optimistic view of CIP theory, which also can demonstrate cost-effective data for its approach. This is where research is needed to show if a theory is applicable to certain populations, such as students with special needs. Young and Chen indicated how the profession and theorists are now involved in "catching up" in regard to dealing with all the constituents of career development: "One of the major themes emerging from the 1998 literature was the attention given to the topic of career enhancement for people with disabilities, including studies that addressed student career development issues in the workplace, and counseling and career services" (Young & Chen, 1999, p. 106). These authors' impressive review covered 21 books and 259 articles from 24 career development and counseling journals and 34 psychology and social and behavioral sciences journals.

Krumboltz's Social Learning Theory

John D. Krumboltz's social learning theory applies behavioral concepts and Bandura's learning theory (1977, 1986) to career development. Social learning theory offers a more explicit understanding of how a person enters one career area versus another and suggests interventions that can help in decision making. Prior to development of the formal theory in 1975, Krumboltz and his colleagues researched the application of behavioral techniques, such as verbal reinforcement and social modeling theory, to educational and occupational issues. In social learning theory, the focus is on explaining how educational and vocational preferences and skills are acquired and taught, and how choices are made in these two areas of life.

Distinctive Features

The theory's distinctive features were summarized by Unruh (1979), who cited six advantages of social learning theory over existing theories:

1. Human behavior is under the control of the individual as well as the environment; the individual can assert some control over the various alternatives and consequences.

2. Sources of reinforcement, both internal and external, act as motivational and informational sources to produce an integration of past experiences with anticipated events, making the learning process easier.

3. The theory is comprehensive, including economic and sociological factors as well as psychological influences such as experiences, aspirations, and skills.

4. Constructs such as self-concept are stated in testable form; thus, "Experiences can be traced through the analysis of input and output variables and cognitive mediating responses" (p. 17).

5. The model describes processes and interactions in operational terms and demonstrates how they fit into a comprehensive framework.

6. The model deals with observable causes and effects, making research and intervention easier.

The uniqueness of the theory in comparison to the theories already presented is its focus on learning and teaching techniques such as career decision making. Much human behavior is learned by watching others. A person watches how other people behave, remembers it, and later uses the information as a model for his or her own actions. In later chapters, authors discuss how the modeling of successful performance by one individual with a disabling condition can open up new learning experiences for other students with special needs and motivate them to continue in their career exploration.

The Theory

The authors Mitchell and Krumboltz (1996) emphasized the importance of learning experiences and their effect on career choice. Each individual has a set of inherited attributes and lives in an environment that affords a specific set of experiences and conditions or learning histories. Learning experiences either are provided by the environment or are self-initiated. They result in generalizations about the self, the development of skill sets to cope with the environment, and the initiation of career-related behaviors such as selecting an educational program or training institution. More specifically, the interaction of the following four factors is believed to be influential in determining an individual's career selection (Figure 1.3 presents a case to illustrate how some of these factors relate to a specific person's career path):

1. *Genetic endowment*, such as race, gender, physical appearance (including disabilities), intelligence, muscular coordination, and special abilities such as artistic and athletic talents.

2. *Environmental conditions and events*, including the school system, the number and nature of job and training opportunities available, social policies and procedures for selecting trainees and workers, financial and nonfinancial rewards for various occupations, union rules, technological developments, labor market conditions, events such as drought, family and neighborhood influences, and political stability.

3. *Learning experiences*, which consist of three types. *Instrumental learning experiences* occur when a person acts on the environment in such a way as to produce certain consequences (e.g., antecedents, overt and covert behaviors, and consequences). This sequence of events enables the individual to master skills necessary for educational and occupational performance and is in the direct control of the person. *Associative learning experiences* occur when a person responds to external stimuli (e.g., responds to a neutral situation with a positive or negative response). Associative learning includes observational learning (learning by observing a model) and classical conditioning. Associative learning is not directly initiated by an individual, but results in outcomes. (In Figure 1.3, this concept is represented by a circle.) *Vicarious learning* is random accidental learning; that is, a person just happens to be in a location where he or she experiences something that may result in a new acquisition or conclusion.

4. *Task approach skills*, which are the skills, values, work habits, cognitive processes, and emotional responses that both influence outcomes and are outcomes themselves. They include problem-solving skills to cope with daily living, as well as the ability to estimate one's emotional capacity to deal with a specific task. (In Figure 1.3, this concept is represented by a parallelogram.)

Every individual has a unique and varied set of experiences, influenced by the factors listed previously, that lead to the following types of outcomes:

1. *Self-observation generalizations* are overt or covert self-statements that evaluate one's own actual or vicarious performance or assess one's own interests and values (Mitchell & Krumboltz, 1996, p. 244). For example, people with little practice at dancing make self-judgments that they are not good dancers and conclude that they do not

like dancing. These are self-views that each person learns from experience about his or her own efficacy. (In Figure 1.3, this concept is represented by a triangle.)

2. *World-view generalizations* result from learning experiences and observations made about the environment. These observations are generalized and are used to predict the future and what will happen in other environments. For example, if a child observes his or her father and other fathers as not caring for their children, the child may generalize that men are not caring people.

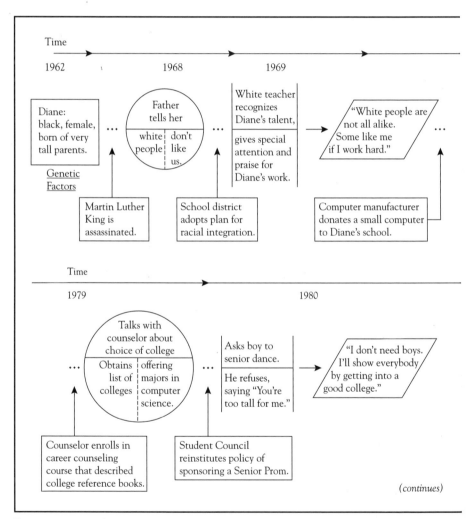

Figure 1.3. Sample career path sequence of factors affecting occupational selection. From "Social Learning Approach to Career Decision Making: Krumboltz's Theory," by L. Mitchell and J. D. Krumboltz, 1990, in *Career Choice and Development: Applying Contemporary Theories to Practice* (2nd ed., pp. 162–165), by D. Brown, L. Brooks, & Associates (Eds.), San Francisco: Jossey-Bass. Copyright 1990 by Jossey-Bass, Inc. Reprinted with permission.

3. *Task approach skills* are "cognitive and performance abilities and emotional predispositions for coping with environments, interpreting [an event or decision] in relation to self-observation generalizations, and making covert or overt predictions about future events" (Mitchell & Krumboltz, 1996, p. 240). Work habits, performance standards, career decision-making skills such as goal setting and planning, and emotional responses to each new task are examples of task approach skills. They represent overt steps in career advancement, such as applying for a particular job or school program,

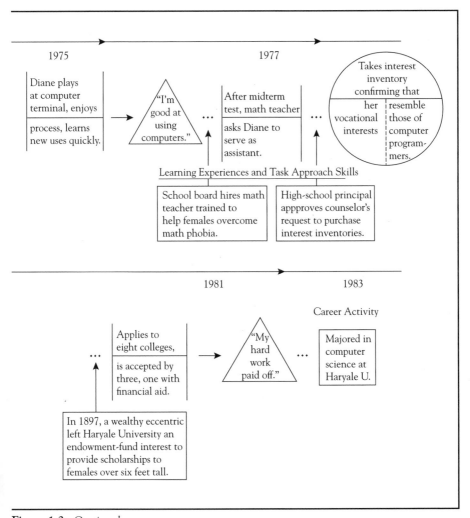

Figure 1.3. *Continued.*

developing new skills, learning about one's likes, and selecting a learning experience for future actions.

Beliefs about one's self or one's environments exert a powerful influence over one's actions. They ultimately influence one's approach to learning new skills and affect one's aspirations. They can be problematic and affect an individual's development. Krumboltz (1988) developed his *Career Beliefs Inventory* to identify many presuppositions that can block individual achievement of career goals. Individuals using this inventory rate the degree to which potential barriers would hinder their career progress.

Krumboltz, Mitchell, and Jones (1978) set forth a series of propositions that are still relevant to explain how the theory operates and how particular self-observation and world-view generalizations and task approach skills are acquired. Based on learning experiences and reinforcement theory, the propositions are hypothesized as positive or negative influences that will either facilitate or limit behavior. I have condensed the propositions to explain how self-observation generalizations are acquired. These are definite strategies that job coaches and mentors apply.

1. Individuals are more or less likely to prefer or reject a course of study, an occupation, or tasks and consequences of a field of work depending on

   - whether the persons are positively reinforced, punished, or not reinforced for engaging in activities they have learned are associated with successful performance of that course, occupation, or field of work.

   - whether individuals observed a valued model being reinforced, punished, or not being reinforced for engaging in activities they have learned are associated with successful performance of that course, occupation, or field of work.

2. Words of encouragement and grades are typically good reinforcers. Seeing one's best friend or admired brother or sister get good results or even having them talk about their experiences are other sources of learning and reinforcement.

The theory acknowledges the complexity of the development of career aspirations and provides an explanation for how the individual can learn to control influencing factors.

Many people debunk the mechanistic diagrams of learning and the structured sequences of decision making as unnatural, claiming that a person takes advantage of what comes along or follows what feels "right." Krumboltz (1998) stated that professionals needed to give credence to unplanned events and to depart from typical lock-step approaches when appropriate. Krumboltz offered three perspectives:

1. Think of individuals in positive terms, such as being open-minded rather than indecisive when they are reluctant to make a commitment about an unpredictable event.

2. View unplanned events as normal and expected in career planning.

3. Making people more aware of how past unplanned events in their lives came about and having them reflect on their outcomes and how they were dealt with can turn these situations into teaching events for learning coping behaviors.

Self-Efficacy

Simply stated, the concept of self-efficacy is as follows: If you think you can, you try, or when you see an opening, you take it (Spokane, 1994). Although self-efficacy concepts grow out of social learning theory, recently self-efficacy, as well as social learning theory itself, has been shown to cut across theoretical boundaries. According to Walsh and Chartrand (1994), for example, social learning theory can operationalize concepts in other theories; it "can be the cement that bonds the structural components of Holland's and Super's theories" (p. 188).

Self-efficacy theory maintains that rather than a person's holding a single generic conceptualization regarding self-efficacy, the person believes that his or her performance capabilities can be strong in some areas, such as athletics and language skills, but weak in other specific areas, such as mathematics. Osipow and Fitzgerald (1996) described two dimensions: "The level of self-efficacy expectations refers to the difficulty of the tasks one aspires to achieve, while the strength of self-efficacy refers to the confidence one has in one's ability to perform a task" (p. 171). Self-efficacy research has focused on performance, aptitudes, interests, decision making, fear, and many other areas.

There are two perspectives regarding self-efficacy. The work of Krumboltz and Bandura is based on cognition affecting behavior and accounts for the relationships between past and future behaviors. Lent and Hackett (1994), however, maintained that social learning theory assigns a relatively minor role to self-efficacy and reflects a largely mechanistic view of human functioning. They advocated for a social cognitive theory that emphasizes a cognitive constructive approach: "Constructive theories emphasize cognitive feed-forward mechanisms highlighting the importance of anticipation, forethought, and active construction of meaning, in interaction with environmental events. Such theories view people as proactive shapers of the environment, not merely as responders to external forces" (p. 95). Individuals with disabling conditions may benefit from a social cognitive approach supporting self-efficacy as an independent predictor. This perspective contrasts with Mitchell and Krumboltz's (1996) position that "self efficacy expectations are dependent variables — the outcomes of numerous learning experiences — not independent variables" (p. 267).

Social Cognitive Career Theory

The relatively new social cognitive career theory (SCCT; Lent, Brown, & Hackett, 1994, 1996) is based on Bandura's (1997) social cognitive theory, which claims self-efficacy expectations are a major mediator of behavior and behavior change. Lent et al. (1996) proposed their model to explain how vocational interests develop and how these are related to career choice: "SCCT asserts that people form enduring interest in an activity when they see themselves as competent at it and when they anticipate that performing it will produce valued outcomes" (p. 383).

Today, however, in SCCT the expanded focus is on how self-efficacy beliefs affect outcome expectations in shaping interests, personal actions, and performance. The theory's three central constructs are *self-efficacy*, *outcome expectations*, and *personal goals*. Self-efficacy is portrayed as a belief in one's ability to perform a behavior. Outcome expectations are beliefs about the outcome of behaviors, such as, "If I do this, that will happen." The perceived importance or determination of the behavior, the goal, and anticipated results relate to the interest in performing the behavior. Interest in an area leads to choosing actions and eventual performance (Lent et al., 1994). The authors noted, however, the recent lack of attention to another part of the theory — contextual supports and barriers. More specifically, social cognitive career theory "emphasizes cognitive-person variables that enable people to influence their own career development, as well as extra-person (e.g., contextual) variables that enhance or constrain personal agony" (Lent, Brown, & Hackett, 2000, p. 36). The authors are currently recommending research using SCCT theory to study career barriers, such as workplace discrimination and disapproval of a career goal by a significant other, which are examples of extraperson variables.

Smith and Fouad (1999), without concern for definition, explained the above constructs as follows:

Self-efficacy is an individual's belief that she or he can accomplish a task; outcomes expectancies are literally the outcomes expected from doing the task. Individuals' confidence to perform tasks (self-efficacy) mediates between their skills and their performance. Sources of self-efficacy are previous accomplishments, vicarious learning, physiological arousal, and verbal persuasion. Confidence that one can accomplish a task is distinct from the expectations one has about the result of such behavior; each is also different from the intent to perform such behavior. (p. 461)

Although this theory is conducive to developing studies and has generated a large amount of research, study results also have led to a tentativeness about the theory. For example, conflicting results such as Tracy's (1997) finding that interest and self-efficacy measures are redundant were later disproven by Donnay and Borgen (1999), who found that a vocational self-efficacy measure is distinct from interests, and they cited evidence to suggest an incremental validity for vocational self-efficacy. Does this latter study, however, prove Bandura's 1997 assertion "that social cognitive theory posits a reciprocal but asymmetric relationship between efficiency and occupational interests, with efficacy playing the stronger determinant role"? (p. 424). Because of the personal agency aspect of social cognitive theory, how the sociopolitical and cultural differences of racial and ethnic groups influence the self-efficacy career-related constructs also have now been called into question (Gloria & Hird, 1999).

Working on self-efficacy beliefs represents a major personal development issue for most people, which is a central tenet of this theory. A major goal for some helpers working with individuals with disabling conditions is to break a chain of events that impair self-fulfillment. Thus, SCCT theory seems a logical theoretical resource for helpers.

Theory of Work Adjustment

Work adjustment theory is a sophisticated, trait-oriented theory developed by Lloyd Lofquist and Rene Dawis in 1969 and currently set forth by Dawis (2002). The theory is based on the belief that specific jobs can offer satisfaction or dissatisfaction for different configurations of personal attributes common to everyone, such as abilities, skills, needs, and values. Lofquist and Dawis (1969) reported extensive use of the theory in the Minnesota Division of Rehabilitation's Vocational Assessment Program during their early work and found client satisfaction with their approach. The uniqueness of this theory is its focus on the actual performance of the job.

Implementation Instruments

Two instruments are used to implement the theory of work adjustment. *The Minnesota Importance Questionnaire* (MIQ; Weiss, Dawis, & Lofquist, 1975) is designed to assess the needs and values of individuals 16 years of age and older. *The Minnesota Satisfaction Questionnaire* (MSQ; Weiss, Dawis, England, & Lofquist, 1977) is designed to measure an employee's satisfaction with his or her job environment. Occupational reinforcer patterns are available to predict job satisfaction in specific work environments. Zytowski (1994) noted, however, that the MSQ used in implementing the "well-conceived theory" should be evaluated cautiously. Although Brooke and Ciechalski (1994) had psychometric concerns about the MIQ, they concluded that it may be useful in career counseling.

I believe that adjustment to work and job satisfaction are important concepts for everyone to explore. The theorists believe that satisfaction is a key indicator of work adjustment. Although this theory is more applicable for adults than for younger students, exploration of the concepts of job satisfaction and work adjustment needs to occur early.

The Theory

All people have abilities they use to perform work. In addition, people have specific needs that they expect to be satisfied by their work. Likewise, jobs or work environments have ability requirements and the potential to satisfy certain needs. The work adjustment theory is a person–environment-correspondence fit theory (P-E). Personal satisfaction, a self-identified concept, occurs when the P-E match fits, resulting in correspondence or reinforcement; a poor match results in dissatisfaction. Some of the specifics of this abbreviated theoretical synopsis can be gleaned from an examination of the theory's four basic psychological concepts: *ability, reinforcement, value satisfaction,* and *P-E correspondence*.

Abilities are conceived in skill-level terms, as well as in the more typical comprehensive manner. According to Dawis (1994), "Having a particular skill implies having the prerequisite abilities, having the requisite abilities does not necessarily imply having the particular skill. People with the same abilities may not have the same skills if their experience and learning are different" (p. 34). This idea of a more detailed ability definition reinforces the contribution of an individual's self-esteem as he or she builds new skills. In addition to skills and abilities, needs and values are key components in the theory.

Needs reflect a person's requirements for a certain reinforcement value. The importance of the need is inferred from a person's preferences for reinforcers;

however, needs reflect values and values inform needs. Skills and needs are more variable reflections of a person, but abilities and values are portrayed as more foundational and stable personality characteristics. On the surface, therefore, when there is a correspondence or fit between the person and the environment, satisfaction is predicted. Also, although the organization can shape the individual, reciprocity can likewise occur in that individuals can redefine an organization. Satisfaction is also defined as the affect — the feeling or emotion, whether positive or negative — that results from one's evaluation of a situation. A person or an environment thus can experience satisfaction with the other. The concept of *satisfactoriness* occurs when the employer is satisfied with the employee's performance. A person who has a certain value priority can feel dissatisfied with the match when, on the surface, it appears to be an obvious fit to others. Alternatively, a person with specific skills can feel satisfied with what seems a bad match because his or her needs are being met. Satisfaction is self-defined. Work adjustment occurs when the individual is satisfied with the environment and the environment is satisfied with the individual. Measures of job satisfaction and satisfactoriness are job productivity, employee turnover, morale, absenteeism, and tardiness.

People with the same skills and needs nevertheless differ because of their personality styles, described by the theory as comprising celerity, pace, rhythm, and endurance. *Celerity* is an individual's speed of response in interacting with the environment. *Pace* is the amount of energy or activity the individual uses in the interaction. *Rhythm* is the consistency of the pace, such as steady performance, stops and starts, or multiple starts. *Endurance* is persistent and sustaining interaction with the environment. Students with special needs may have to consider these components of personality style, as they are often embedded within their diagnosed problems, for example, the need for more time to perform a task.

Work adjustment is characterized by different styles: flexibility, activeness, reactiveness, and perseverance. *Flexibility* refers to tolerance for a poor P-E fit, whereas *perseverance* is the amount of time a person puts up with the mismatch. *Activeness* is the commitment a person gives to improving the P-E and personal style fit. *Reactivity* is described as a change made in one's work personality to accommodate the work environment. Work adjustment theory illustrates that career planning involves preparing people to be both proactive in creating their environment and reactive in making adjustments.

Hershenson (1996) preferred to focus on work adjustment, which he pointed out involved a greater proportion of a person's life, rather than to concentrate on issues of career choice. His model of work adjustment is different from Lofquist and Dawis's work adjustment construct, which consists of two components — satisfactoriness and satisfaction. Hershenson used three components — work personality, work competencies, and work goals. Hershenson's focus was definitely developmental, including childhood years, whereas Lofquist and Dawis focused primarily on the adult level. *Work personality* consists of one's self-concept that develops during preschool years under the influence of family. *Work competencies* consist of work habits and physical, mental, and social skills that develop during school years and are shaped by feedback on one's strengths and limitations. Last, *work goals* are influenced by one's peer group as one leaves school.

A value of the work adjustment theory is identifying concepts, topics, or issues not previously identified, such as motivation variables leading to job satisfaction or dissatisfaction and job adjustment. The reality is that some work may offer little in terms of personal satisfaction, other than a salary, which is linked to economic survival. Individuals also need to be prepared for the expectations of the work environment, whether these are demands of an employer or of a particular job. The theory of work adjustment helps individuals deal with these components with which most everyone has to learn to cope.

A Model of Career Decision Making

Choosing a career involves decision making. Because the two most prominent career development theorists, Super and Holland, did not incorporate a model of decision making into their work, this model needs to be explained. Decision theory belongs to no single discipline. It is an integral part of economics, business, mathematics, psychology, and gambling. Its use in explaining career choice began in the early 1960s.

One of the distinctive features of decision making is that people learn they have options from which to choose. Second, the model satisfies the goal of many practitioners to make career development a more systematic and understandable process, with the locus of control remaining with the individual. Third, the steps of decision making can be concise, clear, and easily communicated and taught. Fourth, the person's active involvement in the implementation of the process creates a feeling of individual freedom and independence. Fifth, parents and adults value the approach because they understand the model's practical application in the business world; however, herein lies one of the biggest issues for participants. Who is the decision maker — the individual, a parent, or a significant other? Some parents of students with special needs have difficulty letting their children assume full decision-making responsibility.

The Model

The decision model is based on the concepts of value and probability. *Value* refers to the desirability of an object or an outcome, which can be either positive or negative. A negative value means that a given object or event is undesirable. (This concept of value closely resembles the behavioral concepts of positive and negative reinforcement.) *Probability* refers to the likelihood that a given event will occur. Because words are too imprecise to describe probability, the concept is typically described in symbolic mathematical language. The probability of an event, from certain occurrence to nonoccurrence, is presented on a numerical scale bounded by the points of 1 and 0. Probability is related to risk. Risk ranges from no risk, where the outcome is known and certain, to risky, where the outcome is known but has a specified probability factor, to uncertainty, where the chances of the outcome's occurring are unknown and uncertain.

The process of deciding is often cyclical in nature. At the conclusion of the process, the person may decide to get more information and continue the process until a terminal decision is made. This is a critical point. First, the person may not yet be clearly focused on his or her aims or goals; second, the information learned in the deliberation process may reveal that the initial goal was truly not a desired one; and third, the statement of a new goal can now be made with greater certainty. The process, therefore, recycles to the first step of stating a goal, with examination of new options, probabilities, and possible outcomes, and the eventual selection of a choice. Acquired information along with knowledge of the process usually makes proceeding through the process faster the second time around. The need to recycle should not be viewed as an error or a failure but as a possible desirable outcome of the decision-making process.

The decision-making process was described by Krumboltz and Baker (1973) in a step sequence:

1. Solicit the client's goals and define the problem.

2. Mutually agree to achieve the goals set forth.

3. Generate alternative solutions to the problem.

4. Collect information about alternatives to the situation.

5. Examine the consequences of the options.

6. Reevaluate the goals, alternatives, and consequences.

7. Make the decision or tentatively select an alternative based on new developments and opportunities.

8. Generalize the decision-making procedure to other problems.

9. Establish a plan to implement the decision.

Implementation

Decision making at different life stages can also be viewed as a developmental procedure of acquiring and processing information. Confronting decisions offers people new learning situations and potential for growth, but the process is accompanied by anxiety. Katz (1963) noted, "An individual either does not know what information he needs, does not have what information he wants, or cannot use what information he has. Thus, the pressure of making a decision creates a discrepancy between the individual's present state of knowledge (or wisdom) and the state that is being demanded of him" (p. 25).

Tiedeman and Miller-Tiedeman (1979) stressed the importance of both the choice process and the decision process and distinguished between the two concepts. In fact, choosing to decide is believed to be a prerequisite to conscious use of choice. Both choice and decision making must be integrated into the decision process. It is obvious that the choice process is more difficult to learn: "We have found that adolescents can master the decision process used in momentary decisions fairly readily in about 10–12 weeks of daily instruction. But what takes extensive attention and repeated help is comprehension of development in the decision and choice processes" (Tiedeman & Miller-Tiedeman, 1979, p. 178).

Tiedeman and Miller-Tiedeman defined choice as "a preference" that involves the processes of selection and election from specific options. On the other hand, decision is seen as "a conclusion" that involves the processes of forming and acting upon an opinion. Although a casual reading might suggest that these theorists are involved in a semantic harangue, in the case of some students with special needs, the difference between a choice and a decision could be very significant. Some people have contended that many individuals with disabling conditions are dependent and consequently will not choose for themselves. In other words, people have to first be encouraged to choose to decide. A more fundamental task for these individuals thus is to help them understand that they truly have choices in their lives. Decision making can then be mastered, perhaps with greater ease.

So after becoming aware that he or she needs to or "should" decide, a person often reflects on his or her past experiences in selecting, choosing, or deciding. Possible images arise: "I am a worrier," "I like to know as much information as possible," "I start off being very careful to details, then I throw my hands up and rush to a conclusion," or "I don't care, you decide." Helpers have to respond to their clients' emotional reactions. They may affect a person's conclusion regarding having made a good choice. Some researchers believe that if a person follows a conscientiously systemic approach, then it is a good decision. Others feel that a good decision is assessed only if the results are a desirable outcome. In general, the better the information a person has when making a decision, the clearer the risks; however, he or she needs to communicate whether the outcomes are being judged subjectively or objectively.

Often when decisions are being made, the issue arises as to whether people are being realistic in their expectations. Because the steps have a concrete quality, the decision-making perspective helps separate emotional beliefs, which will be confronted separately during the reality-testing process of achieving a goal or selecting the best outcome, given the circumstances. Because making decisions is part of everyday living, decision making is considered a basic skill.

Family Influence Theories

The position of this theory, as the last in the sequence, is no reflection of its importance or value. Regarding the sociological model developed in this section, which is not new, Hotchkiss and Borow (1996) wrote, "Few models in social research have held up so well under such extensive scrutiny" (p. 288). Unlike the previous theories, this theory does set forth influencers external to the person that have a direct impact on the individual, namely, the family and social context in which one lives. Personally having visited over 75 countries and having lived on different continents, I observed the power, control, and influence families have over their children. The freedom of individual choice suggested in previously presented theories is not applicable worldwide. Helpers must keep this in mind as they function in a diversified society.

Status attainment theory has its roots in sociology, a different academic discipline from most of the earlier psychologically based theories. Its central tenet is that the social status of one's parents affects the child's amount and quality of education received, which in turn affects the educational and occupational levels one achieves. Parental status is assessed by the father's occupation and education. Educational attainment is the number of years of schooling completed. Occupational attainment is one's first job, which can be measured by its prestige level or socioeconomic level. Later developments to the model added the ability of the individual, such as mental ability, test scores, and school grades, as having an equal weighting to family status in influencing the eventual outcome. Social psychological processes, such as the individual's aspirations, encouragement by parents and teachers to attend college, and one's immediate peers' influence regarding attending college, are also recognized.

Hotchkiss and Borow (1996) summarized this theory as follows. "Parental status affects the occupational level of their offspring through the following path of influences: from parental status to significant others' attitudes about appropriate levels of education and occupation to career plans to schooling to occupational level. Expanded versions of the model incorporate earnings as the last step in the process, as directly dependent on occupation" (p. 287).

The National Center For Educational Statistics (2001) offered support for this theory. Eighty-two percent of high school graduates in 1999 whose parents had a bachelor's degree or higher enrolled in college after finishing high school. This compared with 54% of graduates whose parents did not go beyond high school and 36% of graduates whose parents did not earn a high school diploma. The study focused on "first-generation" college students, or those whose parents did not go to college. Parents who did not attend college themselves did not know how to negotiate college deadlines, the application process and forms, and financial aid. The children of these parents were often left to do the tasks themselves, and it was noted that high school guidance counselors were not available to help.

Attachment theory and its empirical psychological literature were reviewed by Bluestein, Prezioso, and Palladino Schultheiss (1995). This theory is relevant to an examination of the influence of families in career development. The authors noted that attachment relationships refer to "the 'close affectional' ties that serve to provide the experience of felt security" (p. 416). This feeling derives from regular interactions with caregivers. For example, the authors stated,

> For those clients who are struggling with the exploration and commitment processes, it may be helpful to expand the scope of the treatment contract (with the clients' explicit approval) to explore the nature of the child-caregiver attachment relationship. As we have argued, the absence of felt security may curtail such anxiety-provoking activities as self-exploration, the exploration of the world of work, decision making, and commitment. To the degree that unresolved issues related to familial attachment relationships are effectively addressed within the context of counseling, individuals may engage more effectively in the pre-implementation career development tasks that entail anxiety and risk. (p. 428)

Family system therapy, which has been applied to career counseling issues, is discussed fully in Chapter 13. Two types of families, enmeshed and disengaged, will be fully explained there; however, so that research results can be presented here, the following brief definitions are given. *Enmeshed families* are families in which rules and who participates in setting boundaries and responsibilities are unclear. *Disengaged families* could be described as having an authoritarian parent and children who "know their place and role." The boundaries are rigid and typically prevent communication for effective problem solving. Penick and Jepsen (1992) found that family functioning is a stronger predictor of career development than gender, socioeconomic status, or educational achievement. Their research suggested that "adolescents from enmeshed families may have difficulty mastering career development tasks because they are unable to distinguish their own from parental goals and expectations . . . . Adolescents from disengaged families may lack familial support and interaction, resulting in limits on self-knowledge and task orientation that interfere with mastery of career development tasks" (p. 220).

Without any question, parents and other family members affect the children in the family. I deliberately have made no specific reference to parents of students with special needs because any family can have a parent where attachment relationships are not nurturant and do not foster a sense of feeling secure, which can create life-long problems. Any practitioner who neglects the fact that parents directly or indirectly influence their children's decision is avoiding a significant piece of the career puzzle. Personally and minimally, I will ask a client, "Is this your decision, or have others suggested what the best choice is?" I want to know who my client is because it has a bearing on how I proceed.

Eclecticism

No theory is applicable to all the people that a practitioner encounters. Hackney and Cormier (2001) reported that 37% of counselors, 40% of counseling psychologists, and 53% of psychologists consider themselves eclectic. Lazarus and Beutler (1993) wrote that it is techniques, not theories, that counselors use with people. Practitioners use the techniques that work, and few techniques are the sole property of any theory. *Webster's New World Dictionary* (Guralink, 1986) defined eclectic as "selecting from various systems, doctrines or sources" (p. 441) of what appears to "work best." Many practitioners thus will find themselves using several of the theories presented in this chapter as they counsel individuals.

It is all right for helpers to use an eclectic counseling approach. One should remember, however, that the philosophical underpinnings of various techniques may be different and thus could be contradictory if they all were put into one theory. Eclecticism typically involves selecting the theoretical approach that matches an individual's need at a given time and situation and then using that theory intact. In practice, when the person's goals change and another theoretical approach is more suitable, the helper needs to communicate that he or she is changing to another technique, strategy, or intervention. This does not need to be a long dialogue about using a different theoretical approach.

Summary

The format of this chapter was that of a primer; that is, it presented the concepts, definitions, and language of the major career theorists. Reflecting the trend in the career counseling field, in this edition I doubled the number of theories presented in the second edition, adding cognitive information processing, circumscription and compromise, social cognitive, family influence theories, and eclecticism. The number of references increased substantially, reflecting the need for practitioners to keep up with the professional literature to see these theories in action and application and also to see their effectiveness. Professionals have been addressing issues neglected by theorists, such as gender, gender orientation, race, and ethnicity. Last, although individual theorists have not specifically addressed special needs populations, I commented upon each theory as to its unique contribution to individuals with special needs or issues.

These expanded concepts, with their unique strategies, are necessary for addressing the separate goals and competencies of elementary, middle, and high school children and adults, especially given the diversity of the clients whom career counselors serve.

References

Bandura, A. (1977). *Social learning theory*. Englewood Cliffs, NJ: Prentice Hall.

Bandura, A. (1986). *Social foundations of thought and action: A social cognitive theory*. Englewood Cliffs, NJ: Prentice Hall.

Bandura, A. (1997). *Self efficacy: The exercise of control*. New York: Freeman.

Bluestein, D., Prezioso, M., & Palladino Schultheiss, D. (1995). Attachment theory and career development: Current status and future directions. *The Counseling Psychologist, 23*, 416–432.

Brooke, S., & Ciechalski, J. (1994). Minnesota importance questionnaire. In J. T. Kapes, M. M. Mastie, & E. A. Whitfield (Eds.), *A counselor's guide to career assessment instruments* (3rd ed., pp. 220–225). Alexandria, VA: National Career Development Association.

Brown, D. (Ed.). (2002). *Career choice and development* (4th ed.). San Francisco: Jossey-Bass.

Dawis, R. V. (1994). The theory of work adjustment as convergent theory. In M. L. Savickas & R. W. Lent (Eds.), *Convergence in career development theories: Implications for science and practice* (pp. 33–43). Palo Alto, CA: CPP Books.

Dawis, R. V. (2002). Person–environment-correspondence theory. In D. Brown (Ed.), *Career choice and development* (4th ed., pp. 427–464). San Francisco: Jossey-Bass.

Day, S., & Round, S. (1998). Universality of vocational interest structure among racial and ethnic minorities. *American Psychologist, 53,* 728–736.

Donnay, D., & Borgen, F. (1999). The incremental validity of vocational self-efficacy: An examination of interest, self-efficacy, and occupation. *Journal of Counseling Psychology, 46,* 432–447.

Folsom, B., & Reardon, R. (2000). *The effects of college courses on learner outputs and outcomes* (Tech. Rep. No. 26). Tallahassee: Florida State University, University Center, The Center for the Study of Technology in Counseling and Career Development.

Gati, I., Osipow, S., & Givan, M. (1995). Gender differences in career decision making: The content and structure of preferences. *Journal of Counseling Psychology, 42,* 204–216.

Ginzberg, E. (1972). Toward a theory of occupational choice: A restatement. *Vocational Guidance Quarterly, 20,* 169–176.

Gloria, A., & Hird, J. (1999). Influences of ethnic and nonethnic variables on the career decision-making self-efficacy of college students. *Career Development Quarterly, 48,* 157–174.

Gottfredson, L. S. (1981). Circumscription and compromise: A developmental theory of occupational aspirations [Monograph]. *Journal of Counseling Psychology, 28,* 545–579.

Gottfredson, L. S. (2002). Gottfredson's theory of circumscription, compromise and self-creation. In D. Brown (Ed.), *Career choice and development* (4th ed., pp. 85–148). San Francisco: Jossey-Bass.

Guralink, D. B. (Ed.). (1986). *Webster's new world dictionary.* Englewood Cliffs, NJ: Prentice Hall.

Hackney, H., & Cormier, L. S. (2001). *The professional counselor* (4th ed.). Needham Heights, MA: Allyn & Bacon.

Harrington, T. F. (2002, January). *A 20-year predictive validity study of the Harrington-O'Shea Career Decision-Making System.* Paper presented at the University of Wisconsin–Madison's Center on Education and Work Career Conference.

Herr, E. L. (1997). Super's life-span, life-space approach and its outlook for refinement. *Career Development Quarterly, 45,* 238–246.

Herr, E. L., & Cramer, S. H. (1988). *Career guidance through the life span: Systematic approaches*. Boston: Little, Brown.

Hershenson, D. (1996). Work adjustment: A neglected area in career counseling. *Journal of Counseling & Development, 74,* 442–446.

Holland, J. L. (1994). *Self-directed search*. Odessa, FL: Psychological Assessment Resources.

Holland, J. L. (1997). *Making vocational choices: A theory of vocational personalities and work environments* (3rd ed.). Odessa, FL: Psychological Assessment Resources.

Hotchkiss, L., & Borow, H. (1996). Sociological perspectives on work and career development. In D. Brown, L. Brooks, & Associates (Eds.), *Career choice & development* (3rd. ed., pp. 281–334). San Francisco: Jossey-Bass.

Katz, M. (1963). *Decisions and values*. New York: College Entrance Examination Board.

Krumboltz, J. D. (1988). *Career beliefs inventory*. Palo Alto, CA: Consulting Psychologists Press.

Krumboltz, J. D. (1994). Improving career development theory from a social learning perspective. In M. L. Savickas & R. W. Lent (Eds.), *Convergence in career development theories: Implications for science and practice* (pp. 9–31). Palo Alto, CA: CPP Books.

Krumboltz, J. D. (1998). Serendipity is not serendipitous. *Journal of Counseling Psychology, 45,* 390–392.

Krumboltz, J. D., & Baker, R. D. (1973). Behavioral counseling for vocational decisions. In H. Borow (Ed.), *Career guidance for a new age* (pp. 235–284). Boston: Houghton Mifflin.

Krumboltz, J. D., Mitchell, A. M., & Jones, G. B. (1978). A social learning theory of career selection. In J. M. Whitely & A. Resnikoff (Eds.), *Career counseling* (pp. 100–127). Monterey, CA: Brooks/Cole.

Lazarus, A., & Beutler, L. E. (1993). On technical eclecticism. *Journal of Counseling & Development, 71,* 381–385.

Lent, R. W., Brown, S. D., & Hackett, G. (1994). Toward a unifying social cognitive theory of career/academic interest, choice, and performance [Monograph]. *Journal of Vocational Behavior, 45,* 79–122.

Lent, R. W., Brown, S. D., & Hackett, G. (1996). Career development from a social cognitive perspective. In D. Brown, L. Brooks, & Associates (Eds.), *Career Choices & Development* (3rd ed., pp. 373–421). San Francisco: Jossey-Bass.

Lent, R. W., Brown, S. D., & Hackett, G. (2000). Contextual supports and barriers to career choice: A social cognitive analysis. *Journal of Counseling Psychology, 47,* 36–49.

Lent, R., & Hackett, G. (1994). Sociocognitive mechanisms of personal agency in career development: Pantheoretical prospect. In M. L. Savickas & R. W. Lent (Eds.), *Convergence in career development theories: Implications for science and practice* (pp. 77–101). Palo Alto, CA: CPP Books.

Lofquist, L. H., & Dawis, R. V. (1969). *Adjustment to work.* New York: Appleton-Century-Crofts.

Mitchell, L. K., & Krumboltz, J. D. (1996). Krumboltz's learning theory of career choice and counseling. In D. Brown, L. Brooks, & Associates (Eds.), *Career choice & development* (3rd ed., pp. 233–280). San Francisco: Jossey-Bass.

National Center For Educational Statistics. (2001). *The condition of education 2001.* Washington, DC: U.S. Department of Education.

Osipow, S., & Fitzgerald, L. (1996). *Theories of career development* (4th ed.). Needham Heights, MA: Allyn & Bacon.

Patterson, V., & Allen, C. (1996). Occupational outlook review: Where will the jobs be in 2005? *Journal of Career Planning and Employment, 56*(3), 32–35.

Penick, N. I., & Jepsen, D. A. (1992). Family functioning and adolescent career development. *Career Development Quarterly, 40,* 208–222.

Peterson, G. W., Sampson, J. P., Jr., Reardon, R. C., & Lenz, J. G. (1996). A cognitive information processing approach to career problem solving and decision making. In D. Brown, L. Brooks, & Associates (Eds.), *Career choice & development* (3rd ed., pp. 423–475). San Francisco: Jossey-Bass.

Reardon, R., Vernick, S., & Reed, C. (2001). *A Holland perspective on the U.S. workforce* (Tech. Rep. No. 33). Tallahassee: The Florida State University, Center for the Study of Technology in Counseling and Career Development.

Reardon, R., & Wright, L. (1999). The case of Mandy: Applying Holland's theory and cognitive information processing theory. *Career Development Quarterly, 47,* 195–203.

Sampson, J. P., Lenz, J. G., Reardon, R. C., & Peterson, G. W. (1999). A cognitive information processing approach to employment problem solving and decision making. *Career Development Quarterly, 48,* 3–18.

Sampson, J. P., Peterson, G. W., Lenz, J. G., Reardon, R. C., & Saunders, D. E. (1996). *Career thoughts inventory manual.* Odessa, FL: Psychological Assessment Resources.

Savickas, M. (1997). Career adaptability: An integrative construct for life-span, life-space theory. *Career Development Quarterly, 45,* 247–259.

Sharf, R. (2002). *Applying career development theory to counseling* (3rd ed.). Pacific Grove, CA: Brooks/Cole.

Smith, P., & Fouad, N. (1999). Subject-matter specificity of self-efficacy, outcomes, expectancies, interests, and goals: Implications for the social-cognitive model. *Journal of Counseling Psychology, 46,* 461–471.

Spokane, A. (1994). The resolution of ingruence and the dynamics of person–environment fit. In M. L. Savickas & R. W. Lent (Eds.), *Convergence in career development theories: Implications for science and practice* (pp. 119–137). Palo Alto, CA: CPP Books.

Super, D. (1951). Vocational adjustment: Implementing a self concept. *Occupations*, 30, 88–92.

Super, D. (1969). Vocational development theory: Persons, positions, and processes. *The Counseling Psychologist, 1*, 2–14.

Super, D. (1990). A life-span, life-space approach to career development. In D. Brown, L. Brooks, & Associates (Eds.), *Career choice and development: Applying contemporary theories to practice* (2nd ed., pp. 197–261). San Francisco: Jossey-Bass.

Super, D. (1994). A life-span, life-space perspective on convergence. In M. L. Savickas & R. W. Lent (Eds.), *Convergence in career development theories: Implications for science and practice* (pp. 63–74). Palo Alto, CA: CPP Books.

Super, D., & Overstreet, P. (1960). *The vocational maturity of ninth grade boys.* New York: Teachers College Bureau of Publications.

Super, D. E., Savickas, M. L., & Super, C. M. (1996). The life-span, life-space approach to careers. In D. Brown, L. Brooks, & Associates (Eds.), *Career choice and development* (3rd ed., pp. 121–178). San Francisco: Jossey-Bass.

Tiedeman, D. V., & Miller-Tiedeman, A. (1979). Choice and decision processes and career revisited. In A. M. Mitchell, C. B. Jones, & J. D. Krumboltz (Eds.), *Social learning and career decision making* (pp. 160–183). Cranston, RI: Carroll Press.

Tracy, T. J. G. (1997). The structure of interests and self-efficacy expectations: An expanded examination of the spherical model of interests. *Journal of Counseling Psychology, 44*, 32–43.

Unruh, W. R. (1979). Career decision making: Theory construction and evaluation. In A. M. Mitchell, G. B. Jones, & J. D. Krumboltz (Eds.), *Social learning and career decision making* (pp. 5–18). Cranston, RI: Carroll Press.

U.S. Department of Labor. (1991). *Dictionary of occupational titles* (4th ed.). Washington, DC: U.S. Government Printing Office.

Walsh, W. B., & Chartrand, J. M. (1994). Emerging directions of person–environment fit. In M. L. Savickas & R. W. Lent (Eds.), *Convergence in career development theories: Implications for science and practice* (pp. 187–195). Palo Alto, CA: CPP Books.

Weiss, D. J., Dawis, R. V., England, G. W., & Lofquist, L. H. (1977). *Minnesota satisfaction questionnaire.* Minneapolis: University of Minnesota, Vocational Psychology Research.

Weiss, D. J., Dawis, R. V., & Lofquist, L. H. (1975). *Minnesota importance questionnaire.* Minneapolis: University of Minnesota, Vocational Psychology Research.

Young, R., & Chen, C. (1999). Annual review: Practice and research in career and development–1998. *Career Development Quarterly, 48*, 98–141.

Zytowski, D. (1994). Minnesota satisfaction questionnaire. In J. T. Kapes, M. M. Mastie, & E. A. Whitfield (Eds.), *A counselor's guide to career assessment instruments* (3rd ed., pp. 226–230). Alexandria, VA: National Career Development Association.

CHAPTER

DEVELOPING COMMUNICATION SKILLS
Barbara F. Okun

Effective communication skills are not only the underlying core of any helping relationship but also a major factor in any type of interpersonal relationship. Effective communication involves the capacity to listen, pay attention, perceive, and respond (rather than react) verbally and nonverbally in such a way as to demonstrate that one has attended, listened, and accurately perceived.

Most interpersonal difficulties at home, in school, or at work evolve from faulty communications. Both employers and employees report that a large proportion of job dissatisfaction and failure results from some type of interpersonal difficulty in the workplace. These interpersonal difficulties may arise among coworkers, between worker and supervisor, and between worker and customers or clients. The development of communication skills therefore is a vital aspect of the vocational planning process. Because communication skills are necessary for both successful interpersonal relations and employment interviews, the implementation aspect of the vocational planning process must focus on the teaching of these skills.

Helpers must use effective communication skills to establish a trusting relationship with clients, which is conducive to their learning to make choices and decisions. Helpers must also teach these basic skills to clients. The general goal of such teaching is to help clients improve their communication skills with their friends, family members, teachers, coworkers, supervisors, and others. A more specific goal is to teach clients to apply effective communication skills to the job interview situation.

45

Communication, as used in this chapter, refers to all verbal and nonverbal behaviors that occur between two people. All interactive behavior is communicative because it is impossible not to communicate (send out and receive some type of message) when with another person. Faulty communications may involve not being able to send out clear verbal messages that are consistent with nonverbal messages and/or not hearing the messages that others send out. In other words, faulty communications may take the form of distorting or blocking what has or has not been communicated.

Most people learn basic communication (verbal and nonverbal) behaviors and patterns as children from their families and significant others; however, individuals with special needs may not have had the same opportunities to develop effective communication and social skills as have individuals without disabilities. They may have had a more limited range of community exposure and experiences, as well as fewer opportunities for volunteer and part-time jobs, for helping around the house and school, and for socializing with a variety of people in different situations and settings. In addition, they may have special burdens, such as experiencing a larger amount of frustration and difficulty in communication attempts and encountering many situations of nonacceptance, prejudice, and evaluation. These special burdens can result in problems concerning self-concept, body image, expression of frustration and anger, and ability to deal with dependency and motivation. These types of problems can impede interpersonal relationships, perhaps leading individuals to behaviors such as avoidance, withdrawal, or excessive defensiveness.

One of the first considerations for helpers is attention to their language. For example, when speaking of individuals with special needs, words such as *handicapped* or *disabled* perpetuate stereotypes that ignore an individual's personal characteristics. Accepted terminology today places emphasis on the disability as an attribute of the individual rather than as a descriptor of the whole person (e.g., "person with special needs" or "person with disabling condition"). Helpers' language should facilitate empowerment, so that helpers and clients are focusing as much on identifying and promoting requisite environmental modifications in the workplace as on individual adaptation to the traditional work environment. Humes, Szymanski, and Hohenshil (1989) recommended that counselors (a) avoid using disabling language, (b) always consider the effects of environment(s) and individual perceptions (including expectations) in educational and vocational planning, (c) emphasize abilities rather than limitations, and (d) recognize the complexity of disability and consult with specialists when necessary.

Gender, race, ethnicity, and class also have significant influence on communication styles and processes (Okun, Fried, & Okun, 1999; Sue & Sue, 1999). Helpers must develop sensitivity to the nuances and implications of cultural variables. For example, they need to remember that cultural differences exist in the ways groups express empathy; in other words, what may be empathic behavior for one client (i.e., direct eye contact, touching) may not be for another. It is also important to study an individual and his or her family's meaning-making and experience of special needs within the context of their cultural value system. Cultural sensitivity and awareness allow helpers to be able to communicate accurate empathy and understand how clients' expectations and attitudes are affected by status, gender, class, ethnicity, and race.

Chapter Purpose

I have two major purposes in this chapter. One is to present a model of responsive listening that identifies the key skills inherent in effective communication and provides exercises (for both the helper and the client) and examples for learning these skills. The second is to highlight communication skills essential for job interviews and to provide specific suggestions and strategies for teaching these skills to clients and students.

The responsive listening model is viewed as a cornerstone for helping persons in establishing a trusting, helping relationship to facilitate the development and implementation of plans for change and growth. Helpers need to practice these skills to facilitate the vocational planning process and to model and teach them to clients for improved interpersonal relations and employment interviews. By modeling and actively teaching these communication skills during the actual vocational planning process, helpers can provide opportunities for students and clients to enhance their communication skills and improve their interpersonal relationships.

In this chapter, I address (a) research on communication skills, (b) the responsive listening theoretical model of communication, (c) the helping person's own communication behavior, (d) teaching communication skills to clients, and (e) relating verbal and written communication skills to applications in interpersonal relationships and implementation of vocational planning, namely, employment interviews.

Process Research on Communication Skills

Early research in the 1960s and 1970s (Anthony & Carkhuff, 1977; Barrett-Lennard, 1962; Condon, 1975; Ekman, Friesen, & Ellsworth, 1972; Ivey & Authier, 1978; Labov & Fanshel, 1971; Mayo & LaFrance, 1973; Strupp, 1977; Toukmanian & Rennie, 1975; Truax & Mitchell, 1971) concentrated on identifying the variables potentially important in producing positive outcomes from the helping relationship. They attested to the importance of attending behavior on the part of the helper and its concomitant nonverbal aspects in the helping process (i.e., eye contact patterns, body language, vocal tone, and verbal responsive listening). Over the years, data from various studies (Brammer & McDonald, 1996; Combs, 1989; Corey, 2001; Cormier, 1998; Egan, 1998; Gerber & Purkey, 1999) consistently have suggested that certain key qualities, such as empathy, nonjudgmental acceptance, genuine concern and caring, immediacy, and concreteness, underlie all effective helping or counseling interviews, even though different theoretical orientations may use these qualities in different ways. In sum, it appears that the qualitative dimensions of empathy and the attending behaviors are constants in the helping process, whereas skills and theoretical orientations may vary according to the individual helper.

People who receive basic communication skills training can apply these skills to all types of populations and settings. Ivey (1991) and Okun (2002) have administered this training to a variety of helpers and found that it facilitates interpersonal relationships.

Most researchers agree that helper approaches to working with students with special needs are more similar to than different from approaches with students without disabilities (Vandergriff & Hosie, 1979). Specific training and information are needed, however, to deal with the complex problems of individuals with special needs. Students with special needs require specific training to communicate self-advocacy skills, including the ability to communicate understanding of one's own disability (strengths and weaknesses), knowledge of individual rights under the law, and accomodations needed (Merchant & Gajar, 1998). Helpers must be creative and flexible in their communication skills so as to modify them appropriately for specific clients. Expressive and receptive sign language is necessary to communicate with individuals who are deaf, verbal and touching communications are effective with individuals who have visual impairments, and handshaking may not be appropriate for people with certain types of disabilities. Clients with communicative disorders may require a different type and modality of communication. Regardless of the nature of the person's disability, the core conditions of empathy, acceptance, honesty, genuineness, concreteness, and immediacy are necessary for the development of an effective helping relationship.

Overview of Responsive Listening Model

The responsive listening model is based on the work of Carkhuff (1983, 1986), Cormier (1998), Egan (1998), Gordon (1970), Ivey (1991), Ivey and Ivey

(1999), Kagan (1984), Okun (2002), and others who have developed systematic helper training systems derived from Rogerian client-centered theory. The communication skills presented in this chapter are based on the responsive listening format, which focuses on hearing verbal messages, perceiving nonverbal messages, and responding to these messages both verbally and nonverbally. The overall purpose of these communication skills is to build a helping relationship and to create an environment of support, trust, and open disclosure in order to uncover as much information and as many feelings as possible. This type of relationship highlights empathy, that is, understanding another person's emotions, feelings, and worldview from that person's frame of reference without judging or rejecting. An empathic relationship has been found to facilitate the clarification and exploration of apparent and underlying client concerns while simultaneously enhancing the client's self-concept and perceived abilities to take responsibility for making choices and determining life directions. This is critical for individuals with special needs who, as previously mentioned, may experience particular difficulties concerning self-concept and perceived abilities.

The major goals of responsive listening communication skills are (a) to reduce client defensiveness; (b) to create an empathic, supportive environment; (c) to facilitate the clarification and exploration of apparent and underlying issues; (d) to develop consistency and congruence between verbal and nonverbal messages; and (e) to respond to a message by clarifying the sender's underlying feelings and thoughts in such a way as to add to his or her self-understanding.

In this chapter, I focus on two units of communication: verbal messages and nonverbal messages. *Verbal messages* include the apparent and underlying cognitive and affective content of the communicator's statements. They are the words that tell what the person is thinking and feeling. *Nonverbal messages* refer to body language, vocal tone, facial expressions, and other gestures that accompany verbal messages. They indicate feelings and behaviors and are the cues that help the recipient to hear the message about the message (i.e., the metacommunication).

For example, if someone says, "I'm unable to get to that office in a wheelchair," the verbal message is clear that the individual cannot reach a particular destination. Depending on the nonverbal message, however, the demand or command message could be "I need your help to get there," "I have no interest in trying for a job that I'm going to have difficulty getting to," or "I need you to get them to meet me some other place." Because humans communicate both verbally and nonverbally, both types of messages are important to interpersonal relationships. Often it is the nonverbal part of the message that is unclear. Misunderstanding can result when communicators are unaware of the nonverbal commands they are giving, receiving, or obeying. In the above example, if the message sender was really asking for help and the communication recipient did not hear that message, the sender may feel resentful and hurt by the lack of response. The recipient may feel upset because he or she has no idea why the sender is acting hurt, as the recipient never received the intended command message. One of the strategies of effective communications is "checking out," whereby the hearer asks the sender to clarify the command message with a response such as, "I'm not sure if you want me to do something, and, if so, what that would be."

Effective responsive listening, then, means the capacity to listen, to pay attention, to perceive, and to respond verbally and nonverbally in such a way as to demonstrate that you have attended, listened, and accurately perceived. A helper can have all of the empathy and goodwill in the world, but if he or she cannot clearly communicate these qualities, they are ineffective. A client may possess all of the qualities and skills necessary for a particular job or training program, but if he or she is unable to communicate these attributes in an interview, a prospective employer is unlikely to know about them. These communication abilities can be learned by most people, regardless of their educational background or personality. These skills require continuous practice (as does any type of skill learning); however, time for this learning and practice must be built into the vocational planning process.

Positive and Negative Communication Behaviors

In the helping relationships individuals have judged to be most effective (Okun, 2002), helpers displayed listening and attending behaviors that communicated empathy, encouragement, support, honesty, caring, concern, respect, patience, sharing, affection, protection, potency, and nonjudgmental acceptance. These behaviors are considered helpful because the client felt worthwhile as a human being, was permitted to be his or her true self, and was able to have the freedom to explore true concerns. Nonhelpful communication behavior was noted as involving inattentiveness, imposition of the helper's values and beliefs on the client, judgment, and attitudes of "I know what's best for you" or "I'm better than you." These behaviors hindered the relationship because they put the clients on the defensive immediately and made them feel so worthless that they naturally chose avoidance rather than approach behaviors.

Much research has been conducted about the necessary characteristics of effective helpers (Carkhuff, 1983, 1986; Combs, 1989; Egan, 1998; Ivey & Ivey, 1999; Okun, 2002; Rogers, 1958). The major qualities appear to be the following:

1. *Self-awareness.* Individuals who continually develop their own self-understanding and self-awareness are more likely to be effective helpers than those who do not because they are able to separate their biases, needs, perceptions, and feelings from those

of their clients and are better able to use their self-awareness as a basis for helping others develop their own self-awareness. Individuals with self-awareness are more likely to differentiate communications, sending "I feel" messages as distinct from "You feel" messages.

2. *Gender and cultural awareness.* Helpers who are sensitive to the influence of gender and culture on their own perceptions, values, attitudes, and beliefs are likely to be open to the effects of these variables on others. They value rather than denigrate these differences and appreciate the deleterious effects of cultural discrimination and oppression on the day-to-day living of nondominant groups.

3. *Honesty.* One of the major variables in developing trust, honesty is a crucial ingredient for any effective interpersonal relationship. Helpers can communicate honesty by being open, by answering questions to the best of their ability, and by admitting mistakes or lack of knowledge. Honesty involves learning to give and receive positive and negative feedback in a helpful way.

4. *Congruence.* People who experience congruence between their own values and beliefs and their lifestyle communicate more credibility and exert more modeling potency than those whose energy is used to deny incongruence. Helpers can communicate congruence by sending out clear, consistent messages verbally and nonverbally.

5. *Knowledge.* Definite understanding and knowledge on the part of the helper is important for effective helping. To help students who have special needs with vocational planning, the helper must have a knowledge of the theories upon which effective helping is based, the ways in which individuals with disabling conditions approach vocational development, vocational assessment, work sites and the world of work, placement strategies, the role of the federal government, rights of those with disabilities, education and employment opportunities, health care, community resources, and so forth. As previously stated in this chapter, the helper must be able to communicate this knowledge in order for it to be effective.

6. *Communication.* In addition to communicating the previous five characteristics or qualities, the helper must communicate certain other qualities that have been found to be crucial to effective human relations. These characteristics are empathy (seeing a person's world from that person's perspective), positive regard and respect (accepting the helpee as a worthwhile person regardless of what the helpee says or does or whom he or she is), genuineness (being real, sincere, and honest), and concreteness (being specific, accurate, clear, and immediate).

Sometimes helpers may have subconscious and deeply rooted biases or prejudices that affect their communication behaviors with people with disabilities and can have a profound effect on the helping relationship. Nathanson (1979) suggested seven counseling "syndromes" that focus on some of the feelings, thoughts, and consequent verbal and nonverbal behavior of counselors working with clients with disabling conditions. I list these in the order that appears to me to be the most prevalent:

1. "Who's more anxious, you or me?" The client is the direct stimulus for the counselor's anxiety, which may be expressed by the counselor's tendency to speak more loudly, softly, slowly, quickly, or simply to clients with disabling conditions. This anxiety may come from inexperience, helplessness, an inability to understand what the client is saying, lack of ability to assist the client, or depression at the severity of the client's disabling condition.

2. "I'm amazed by your courage." The counselor overvalues actual achievements because such achievements are in marked contrast to the counselor's expectations for the client.

3. "I know what's best for you." The counselor typically reacts negatively to a client's aspirations and prejudges the client's potential for future success in a given endeavor accordingly. Actually, a counselor with this attitude probably does not listen at all to what the client is saying.

4. "All that matters is your label." Instead of perceiving the client as an individual with abilities, interests, or potentials, the client is perceived as "a cripple," an "epileptic," a "blind person," a "deaf person," and so on. The counselor makes assumptions about what the client can or cannot do and achieve. In other words, there is no regard for the individuality of the client.

5. "I feel sorry for you." The counselor's pity is shown through facial expressions or vocal tones. The helper focuses on the negative aspects of the client's life and potential, rather than on the positive.

6. "Don't worry, I'll save you." In addition to pity, the counselor views the client as incapable, dependent, inadequate, defenseless, and needy. The counselor plays the role of rescuer in finding a niche for the client.

7. "If I'm lucky, you will miss today's appointment." The counselor's revulsion and unconscious or conscious rejection of the client is expressed in avoidance and other distracting strategies.

Certainly these attitudes and communication behaviors do not reflect the facilitative conditions previously discussed. Instead, they create strain and defensiveness for both the counselor and the client, and they come across as patronizing, arbitrary, and ineffective. In addition to learning effective communication skills, helpers need to become fully aware of their own attitudes, thoughts, feelings, and beliefs about different types of clients and disabilities.

This awareness can help them to avoid imposing their biases on their clients and to open themselves up to learning from them.

Hearing Verbal Messages

It is much easier to hear the *cognitive content* (i.e., the actual facts and words) than the *affective content* (i.e., the feelings and attitudes) of a verbal message. Receiving verbal messages really involves hearing both cognitive and affective content and being able to discriminate between the two. The affective content sometimes differs from the cognitive content and is often less apparent.

Verbal Cognitive Messages

Cognitive messages concern things, people, and events and may involve one or several simple or complex themes. For many people, it is easier to talk about thoughts or behaviors than to feel them. Cognitive themes usually serve as the "topic" of discussion, and if helpers respond only to cognitive concerns, they might never discover the underlying feelings and concerns. Also, helpers might become so wrapped up in a particular topic that they miss the essence of a client's communication. The helper's response to a client's statement will depend on the helper's ability to hear what is being said and to uncover the underlying message. The helper's response will in turn influence the direction of the client's next statement. Thus, before helpers can learn to respond appropriately to clients' statements, they must learn to hear and discriminate between apparent and underlying cognitive messages.

For example, a client states, "I'm always having a lot of trouble with Mrs. Smith. She's always on my back, and whenever I hand in my homework, she makes some sarcastic comments, and then she gives me low marks no matter what. I can't do well in that course, and I'm very nervous about it. Math is important because I want to become an accountant." The presenting cognitive theme involves interpersonal difficulty between student and teacher. The helper could ask the student who said what, what happened next, and so forth, but the helper might end up with a detailed description of a particular incident that would not reveal much about the student's underlying concerns and feelings. In this case, it would be advisable for the helper to use this topic as an entrée into the student's vocational expectations, aspirations, and goals. Without other cues, it is difficult to prioritize different cognitive themes presented in the same message. Typically, one more often responds to the most recent theme rather than to the most important one. Helpers can use affective content as clues for establishing priorities and can train themselves to hear the whole message and to discriminate among themes.

EXERCISE 2.1

HEARING VERBAL COGNITIVE MESSAGES

To check how well you can hear verbal cognitive messages, choose the response to the following statements that best reflects the content of the student's statement. Remember that you are trying to paraphrase the main idea of the statement without changing it. This situation occurred in a high school guidance office with a student with special needs. Read the student's statements and select the proper counselor's response: a, b, or c.

1. STUDENT: "I'm not sure why I've been sent down here. I've been late a few times this week, and Mr. O'Brien is all upset about it."

    COUNSELOR: a. You think we're really uptight here.

    b. How do you feel things are going for you?

    c. You're concerned about your tardiness and your teachers' reactions to it.

2. STUDENT: "I know the stuff. I get mixed up on the tests, and I don't do well, but I know the stuff."

    COUNSELOR: a. You're frustrated because you feel you know the stuff, but you can't seem to get that across on your tests.

    b. You're trying to show your teachers that you know the material.

    c. You don't think you know how to study well enough to do well on the tests.

3. STUDENT: "The teachers don't really like me and they mark me down on tests just because I come late or talk."

    COUNSELOR: a. You think the teachers are treating you unfairly.

    b. You're using your absences and tardiness as excuses for not doing well on the tests.

    c. You really don't understand why you're having difficulty on the tests when you feel so sure about the material.

4. STUDENT: "I get bored here. None of the stuff is interesting, and the kids in my class are all dummies."

COUNSELOR: a. You think you know more than the other kids in the class.

                      b. Sounds like you would like to move back into the regular class.

                      c. You're not sure whether or not you're a "dummy."

5. STUDENT: "Those kids are going nowhere, I mean nowhere. I can't wait to get out of here because I know I can do something and be somebody."

COUNSELOR: a. You're eager to prove to yourself that you can really accomplish something.

                      b. You think you can do better than the other kids in your class.

                      c. You are determined to make it somehow.

This excerpt from an actual case indicates that you need to hear all of the cognitive themes, but if you focus strictly on the presenting theme, tardiness, you are likely to get sidetracked from the underlying cognitive theme that involves the student's self-concept. You will find answers on page 73 of this chapter.

To assess a client's ability to hear verbal cognitive themes, the helper periodically must ask for the client to say what he or she has heard the helper saying. Particularly in the area of vocational planning, which involves much cognitive information, the helper wants to be sure that his or her messages are being heard clearly and without distortion. If the helper discovers that a client has a weakness in this area, then the helper will need to focus more on developing the client's skill to hear all of the cognitive messages and to be able to discriminate between more important and less important themes.

Verbal Affective Messages

Although affective messages are communicated both verbally and nonverbally, this discussion focuses on verbal communication. Because people are much more aware of their thoughts than their feelings, they are often uncomfortable talking about their feelings. By hearing affective messages and in turn responding to them, the helper is communicating not only acceptance of these emotions but also permission for the client to experience and own these feelings.

Feelings usually occur in four major areas: anger, fear, sadness, and happiness. Many other feelings fall into one or more of these categories. For example, the frustration expressed nonverbally and verbally by the student in

Exercise 2.1 falls into the broader category of anger. Often one area covers up another (e.g., anger sometimes masks frustration, which in turn may mask fear).

Many different words can be used to identify feelings, but the helper should try to select vocabulary that is comfortable for the client. For example, if a teenager is using the current vernacular of his or her peer group, instead of using the word "angry" when identifying his or her feelings, the helper may say "pissed off" if he or she feels comfortable doing this and does not come across as a phony.

Identifying underlying feelings from verbal messages is difficult at first and is related to how comfortable and proficient the helper is in recognizing and expressing his or her own feelings. The helper must listen to the client's messages and identify his or her feelings rather than project those feelings onto the client.

One way for the helper and the client to develop their sensitivity to verbal affective messages is to brainstorm together all the words they can think of that express each of the four major emotions: anger, fear, sadness, and happiness. There are likely to be generational and cultural differences between the helper and the client, and this may be a fun way to bridge that gap and expand both participants' affective vocabulary. Next, the helper and the client can define as many verbal behaviors as possible that each uses when he or she feels each of the major emotions (e.g., when one is mad, he or she may swear; use short, clipped sentences or monosyllables; yell; whisper).

To help clients further develop their sensitivity to affective messages, ask them what they think other people are feeling in particular situations and whether they can identify the particular verbal message that supports their response. How does their mother verbally express anger, sadness, fear, or happiness? Their father? A particular teacher? A friend?

It is important to help clients differentiate between thoughts and feelings. If a client says, "I feel it's unfair when Mr. Nolan makes me stay and work late if I'm late in the morning," the helper thus can assist the client to learn that what was stated is a thought, not a feeling, but that the client probably feels angry about that thought. If helpers are able to differentiate among thoughts, behaviors, and feelings, they can more easily help others to do this and improve the clarity of their communications. By differentiating thoughts and feelings, helpers often learn that a client's problem is with his or her thinking and that through some education, the client can change both thought patterns and feelings. For example, if a client who has a disabling condition says, "Mr. Roberts feels I'm not going to be able to get into that training program," the helper can reframe that statement into the following: "Mr. Roberts does not think that a person with this disabling condition can function in that type of training program" and decide whether or not the client has information that will influence Mr. Roberts's thoughts, which will, in turn, influence his feelings.

In responsive listening, asking questions is more detracting than additive. Too many people have learned to hide behind questions, and they receive narrow answers that the respondents perceive as "the right answers." It is helpful to rephrase questions into more open-ended statements. For example, instead of using the question, "What did you do next?" the helper might employ a broader question: "Tell what happened then." Questions automatically produce heightened defensiveness, particularly after so many years of schooling where teachers asked questions that required the right answer.

 ## EXERCISE 2.2

IDENTIFYING VERBAL AFFECTIVE MESSAGES

See how well you can identify the verbal affective message. For each of the following statements, decide what you think the person is really feeling. Ask yourself, "What is the underlying feeling here?"

1. I can't do this. It's too hard.
2. Do you think that I can get into that program?
3. With braces, I can't climb all those stairs.
4. I know I'm slow and that I make mistakes. But I do get the work done.
5. Why are other people so insensitive to people who are different?
6. I hate those kids because they're always picking on us. You don't know what it's like on the school bus.
7. I know what I'm going to do when I get out of here, and I don't need any help from anyone.
8. What makes it easy for me is the way my friends help me out. They always hold the door and wait for me.
9. I didn't go on that interview because it was too far away and I couldn't get there.
10. I don't need to get a job. I want to stay in school for as long as I can.

There is no single answer for any of these statements. Hearing and discriminating between affective and cognitive verbal messages without body language cues is extremely difficult. Nevertheless, a feeling of some kind is associated with each cognitive message, and it is the helper's job to try and identify that feeling.

Due to cultural pressures, most people experience discomfort in accepting the presence and expression of anger and fear in themselves and in others. If the helper can empathically recognize and respond to the client's feelings of anger and fear when discussing sensitive issues, the client can learn to become more accepting of his or her painful feelings and, in turn, accept and express them more openly and constructively when dealing with others. If a person with a disabling condition senses that a friend is feeling some discomfort or fear about engaging in a particular activity with the person, the relationship between the two individuals is likely to be enhanced if the person with the disabling condition can say empathically to the friend something such as, "You seem to be feeling uptight about this with me."

EXERCISE 2.3

"YOU FEEL" STATEMENTS

Now that you have identified the underlying feeling in the above 10 statements, see how you can respond with a "You feel _____ when _____ because _____" statement. For example, with Statement 1, "I can't do this. It's too hard," you might respond, "You're feeling <u>angry when asked to do this</u> because <u>you're afraid you won't succeed</u>." Needless to say, an empathic, accepting tone and body language can mean the difference between this response being threatening or accepting. See if you can complete the blanks similarly for the other nine statements.

Perceiving Nonverbal Messages

Because perceiving nonverbal messages has not been emphasized in U.S. culture, doing so is often confusing and frustrating. A person can become aware of his or her dependence on nonverbal cues for understanding verbal messages by trying to block out nonverbal messages (e.g., by using the telephone or carrying on a dialogue for a few minutes while sitting back-to-back with the other person and then trying to identify the cognitive and affective messages).

Nonverbal perceptions provide clues, not conclusive proofs, of underlying feelings and often tend to be more reliable than verbal cues. People tend to deny verbally and even to themselves their negative feelings, even though their nonverbal behavior indicates the presence of negative feelings. Often when a helper suggests to clients that they are angry, they will deny feeling anger, even though their muscles are taut and their fists are clenched.

Helpers need to help clients become aware of their own nonverbal communications as well as those of others. Patterns of gestures, posture, facial expressions, spatial relations, personal appearance, and cultural characteristics can be used to develop a conscious awareness of nonverbal manifestations and their various meanings.

The helper and client can develop greater sensitivity to nonverbal messages by brainstorming together to list and define as many nonverbal behaviors as possible. For example, behaviors that represent anger include clenched fists; scowls; tightened lips; and erect, tense body posture. Behaviors that represent happiness are smiles, relaxed body postures, and flushed cheeks. Another way helpers can aid clients to become more aware of their nonverbal messages is to ask them to talk to themselves in front of a full-length mirror for a few minutes and to observe as many different nonverbal behaviors as possible. Also, the helper and the client can discuss those nonverbal behaviors that each observes in the other. After the helper and client have observed and identified each other's nonverbal behaviors, it is helpful to talk about the messages being communicated and to try to determine which behaviors are facilitative and which are not. In other words, the client may learn that certain nonverbal behaviors are distracting and do not enhance the messages intended for communication. After this assessment, helper and client can decide precisely which behaviors need to be modified.

Particular nonverbal behaviors may be associated with particular disabilities. Helpers need to assist clients to become aware of these patterns so they may highlight those that enhance communication and diminish those that are distracting or dysfunctional in some other way.

Likewise, helpers need to be aware of their own nonverbal behaviors and their potential effect on others. For example, if a helper walks into a room of students and proceeds to shake the hand of each student and then comes to a student who has, say, cerebral palsy or is missing a right arm, how can the helper communicate the same cordiality without causing discomfort to the client or to the helper?

 ## EXERCISE 2.4

NONVERBAL CUES

The following is a list of various nonverbal cues. What different kinds of messages are being communicated?

- *Body position:* tense, relaxed, leaning toward or away
- *Eyes:* teary, open, closed, excessive blinking, twitching
- *Eye contact:* steady, avoiding, shifty
- *Body movement:* knee jerks, taps, hand and leg gestures, fidgeting, head nodding, pointing fingers, dependence on arms and hands for expressing message, touching
- *Body posture:* stooped shoulders, slouching, legs crossed, rigid, relaxed

- *Mouth:* tight, loose, smiling, lip biting, licking lips, chewing gum
- *Facial expression:* animated, blank, distracting, frowning, puckered, grimacing
- *Skin:* blushing, rashes, perspiration, paleness
- *General appearance:* clean, neat, sloppy, well-groomed

Go over this list with clients to aid them in identifying the behaviors they need to improve in order to communicate clear, congruent messages.

Responding Verbally and Nonverbally

As mentioned previously, responsive listening is defined as responding verbally and nonverbally to both the apparent and underlying thoughts and feelings of the other person. Responsive listening also implies that a listener is able to communicate his or her genuine understanding (empathy), acceptance, and concern and, at the same time, add some understanding of the issue by clarifying the speaker's statement. The listener thus must be able to communicate to the speaker identification and understanding of the primary cognitive concern and the underlying feeling as well as the listener's own caring.

The following is an example of responsive listening:

CLIENT: I know I can't dance with my bum leg. That's why the kids never ask me to their parties.

HELPER: You really feel sad when you see everyone else having a good time, and you're hurt and angry that the kids don't include you even though you don't think you can dance.

What makes this brief dialogue an example of responsive listening is that it identifies an underlying feeling, relates it to the major cognitive concern, and adds clarity and understanding to the client's statement. Saying "Don't worry," or "It's not really important," is not helpful because those kinds of responses do not help clients increase their self-understanding or think about ways they can take responsibility for changing the situation.

Nonverbal Responding

Each helper needs to become aware of his or her own nonverbal behavioral patterns and decide which ones are helpful and which ones are not. Some questions for you, as a helper, to consider are as follows:

- How can you improve eye contact without making the other person uncomfortable or without staring?

- What is the comfortable physical distance for you and for your client?

- Should you sit side by side or across a desk?

- How comfortable are you with touching?

- Are you comfortable holding the client's hand or patting the shoulder or knee?

- What do these gestures communicate?

- How can you help your client to identify and select facilitative nonverbal behaviors?

- How can you help clients with special needs to focus on the most facilitative nonverbal behaviors and to diminish dysfunctional habits?

Desirable nonverbal behaviors for effective communication have proven to include occasional nodding (too much nodding may be distracting), smiling, appropriate touching (when the other person is judged to be at ease with touching), hand gestures, good eye contact, facial animation, leaning toward the other person, a moderate rate of speech, and a firm tone of voice. Use of videotape equipment is the best way for a helper and a client to study their own behaviors.

Verbal Responding

Through verbal responses, the listener attempts to communicate that he or she is really hearing and understanding the speaker's perspective; to communicate warmth, acceptance, and caring; to focus on major themes; to clarify inconsistencies; to reflect back the underlying feelings; and to synthesize the major apparent and underlying concerns. Ten major verbal responses are minimal verbal response, paraphrasing, probing, reflecting, clarifying, checking out, interpreting, confronting, informing, and summarizing. These are discussed in the following paragraphs.

Minimal verbal responses are the verbal counterpart of occasional head nodding. They are verbal cues, such as "mm-mm," "yes," "uh-huh," and "I see," indicating that the person is listening and following what the other is saying.

Paraphrasing is a verbal restatement by the listener that is interchangeable with what the speaker has said. The words the listener chooses may be synonyms rather than the actual words the speaker has used. The client should be asked to paraphrase what the helper has said to be sure that the client has heard correctly. It is helpful for clients to learn how to take the responsibility for clarifying what has been said if they are unsure or confused about the message.

Probing is an open-ended attempt to learn more about something and includes statements such as "Tell me more," "Let's talk about that," or "I'm wondering about . . . ." These statements tend to elicit more information than how, what, when, where, or who questions and are particularly effective in interview situations.

Reflecting refers to communicating an understanding of the speaker's stated or implied thoughts and feelings. Examples of reflecting are "You're feeling frustrated about not getting your work in on time," "Sounds as if you don't think you can work fast enough for this job," or "You're wondering how I would handle that situation."

Clarifying is an attempt to focus on or understand the basic nature of another's statement. Examples are "I'm confused about what you mean by that," "Could you go over that again, please?" or "I'm wondering if you mean that." Whenever a client is unsure or confused, he or she should take responsibility for requesting or attempting clarification.

Checking out occurs when a listener is genuinely confused about the apparent or underlying message or wants to test out a hunch about what is going on. The listener asks the other person to confirm or correct the hunch or thought. Rather than assume, for example, that a prospective employer does not think a client with a particular disability can handle a particular job, the client can check that out by saying something like, "It seems to me you don't think I can handle that. I wonder if my perception of what you're saying is right." Checking out is also important for individuals when they are unsure whether they are doing something correctly or perceiving something accurately; it involves taking responsibility for approaching the person involved and asking in a nonthreatening, nondefensive manner whether their perceptions or behaviors are correct. The nonverbal message to be communicated involves a willingness and readiness to learn and change if the perceptions and behaviors are deficient.

Interpretation involves adding something to what the other person has said and helping the other person to understand underlying feelings or how a particular feeling or thought relates to the present situation, as in the following example:

COMPANY INTERVIEWER:	We've never had someone in a wheelchair work here before.
APPLICANT:	You seem to be concerned that my difficulty is going to cause additional problems for you and that everyone will see them, you, and me as a big pain.

If the interpretation is correct, it will add to the original speaker's understanding. If it is not useful, he or she may say, "No, not that but . . . ."

Confrontation involves honest feedback about what a person thinks is really going on. The confrontation may focus on the discrepancies between the verbal and nonverbal messages or among thoughts, feelings, and behaviors. To be effective, confrontation must be positive and constructive as opposed to punitive and destructive. Helpers will not aid clients by clobbering them about the so-called "realities" of life. Many clients with special needs require gentle assistance in accepting their limitations and lowering their aspirations. Many others, however, need help in identifying their strengths and aiming higher. For example, some get into the habit of using whatever handicap they have as an excuse for not producing or working up to their capabilities. A skilled helper can get these clients in touch with whatever "game" pattern they have developed, such as "If only . . ." or "I'm helpless and you can't expect me to do that," as an excuse or avoidance of responsibility. This type of confrontation may include a focus on past successes and achievements and on strengths and assets as opposed to liabilities and weaknesses to aid clients in realistically assessing their options and opportunities.

Clients must learn how to handle confrontation from both the giving and receiving ends. Role playing and other simulations are important ways to teach clients how to deal with such confrontations. One particular verbal confrontation behavior is learning to send "I feel" messages as opposed to "You are" messages. For example, if a student with physical disabilities senses that a teacher is avoiding discussing the effect of these disabilities on classroom learning, the student can learn to confront the teacher by saying, "I feel you are uncomfortable with talking about how my particular disability interferes with what's going on here." This provides a facilitative context in which the teacher can relax and be more open about his or her reservations or feelings, whereas an aggressive statement, such as "You're uncomfortable with my handicap," or "You're avoiding talking about my handicap," may result in defensive denial or further avoidance and discomfort. A "you" message might be appropriate when an individual is sure that the problem belongs to the other person, but the message should be expressed tentatively, allowing for disagreement. For example, in the above situation, the student may say, "You seem to have reservations about my disability and what it means in this situation." As with the "I feel" message, this type of "you" message leaves room for the other person to reply, "No, that's not it, but . . . ," or "Yes, I'm wondering if . . . ." The goal is to facilitate the development of communications in a nonthreatening, nondefensive environment so that no doors are closed prematurely.

Informing is a particularly important skill in terms of vocational planning with clients with special needs. Helpers inform clients of employment possibilities, educational opportunities, legislative and regional resources, or any other realistic data. Clients need to inform their peers, family, and employers about their disabling condition, special issues, and considerations. It is important to distinguish between informing, when objective and factual information is shared, and advising, which has a subjective aura of suggestibility. Advising is acceptable as long as it is tentatively suggested with no strings attached and as long as it is labeled as advice, not as a demand.

Summarizing is a clarifying type of statement in which a person synthesizes what has been communicated and highlights the major affective and cognitive themes. It is helpful when both parties participate and agree with the summarizing message. Summarizing provides an opportunity for both people to share their feelings and thoughts about what has been accomplished. At the end of any interview or session, the client should summarize what he or she believes to have been communicated or decided upon; what the follow-up steps are to be; and who is to do what, when, and where. This prevents confusion and helps keep things moving. Helpers should encourage clients to take the initiative for summarizing different helping sessions.

The following are some general guidelines to follow when using these 10 major verbal responses:

- Phrase the response in the same type of vocabulary as the other person uses.

- Speak slowly enough so that the other person understands each word.

- Use concise rather than rambling statements.

- Pursue the topic introduced by the other person.

- Talk directly to the other person, not about him or her.

- Send "I" statements to state one's own feelings and perceptions and allow the other person to reject, accept, or modify these perceptions.

- Encourage the other person to talk about his or her feelings.

- Time responses to facilitate, not block, communications.

Preparing Clients for Interviews

Interview behavior depends on mastery of effective communication skills. Although the helper cannot ascertain what skills employment interviewers will use with a client, the helper can provide training and practice in the previously discussed skills as they apply to interview situations. Group or individual practice simulations and videotaped demonstrations and practice sessions are helpful in teaching clients to project positive images of themselves in interview situations. Optimally, this type of training and practice should be provided in the classroom for all students and should be a part of vocational planning in all settings. Obviously, the type and amount of training a helper can provide depends on the organizational setting and the age and type of clientele.

Framework for Positive Self-Esteem

As part of the preparation for an actual interview, it is important for you as a helper to aid clients in assessing and projecting their own strengths and assets.

 ## EXERCISE 2.5

IDENTIFYING AND PROJECTING STRENGTHS

Ask clients to tell you what it is they like about themselves, what they perceive as their greatest successes and strengths, and what their aspirations and goals are. (Goal identification and prioritizing are discussed further in Chapter 3.) This requires continued practice, as most people squirm and flush when asked to talk about themselves positively.

 ## EXERCISE 2.6

POSITIVE FEEDBACK

Ask your clients to write down three things they did well each day and three things they particularly like about themselves each day. On the following day, they are to take responsibility for verbally communicating one personal accomplishment and one thing they like about themselves to another person (e.g., a friend, teacher, counselor, or family member). After whatever amount of time seems reasonable to you, ask the client to give each day a positive feedback statement to a different person about him or her. This positive feedback statement must be direct and genuine. For example, a person might say to a friend, "I really like the way you asked Mr. Jones to clarify the homework assignment."

These exercises are important in developing a client's self-esteem, increasing positive attitudes, and overcoming shyness, in addition to providing practice of direct, clear verbal communicating. Modify these exercises according to the age and context of your clientele.

EXERCISE 2.7

PROJECTING POSITIVE SELF-IMAGE

Another way of developing these skills is to have your clients practice entering a room and making contact with you as if you were an interviewer. Remind them of the importance of eye contact, handshakes (where possible and appropriate), firm tone of voice, posture, gestures, and so on. Allow clients to practice projecting a positive self-image by asking them to tell you what their strengths and assets are and ease them into discussions of sensitive material so that they can become accustomed to speaking openly and assertively about their disability. Remind them to avoid interrupting, being excessively silent, or using distracting shrugs.

EXERCISE 2.8

ANSWERING SELF-STATEMENTS

Ask clients to complete the following sentences in a way that makes the statements true.

1. I feel pleased with myself when _____.
2. I cry when _____.
3. I am frightened when _____.
4. I laugh out loud when _____.
5. I get angry when _____.
6. I look forward to _____.
7. I get mad at myself when I _____.
8. I feel good on a job when _____.
9. The most satisfying project or piece of work that I ever did was _____.
10. When someone on the job criticizes me, I _____.
11. Really hard, sweaty work makes me feel _____.
12. When I have to go for a job interview, I feel _____.

Setting Up an Interview

Sometimes the client will arrange an interview. If this is done by telephone, specific communication skills should be used. First, a private telephone in a quiet place should be selected as opposed to a pay telephone in a noisy corridor. Second, the client should ask for a specific person or department and should clearly give his or her own name, for example, "I would like to speak to Mr. Peter Martinez in the art department. This is Paul White calling." When Mr. Martinez answers the telephone, the client can explain the purpose of the call, ask about a specific job, and mention where he or she heard of the job. If a secretary screens the call by asking, "Does he know you?" or "What are you calling in reference to?" the client can reply, "I would like to talk to him about the [specific] job that was advertised [or that Ms. Wang told me about]." It is important that clients learn to give short, clear answers to questions that are asked, providing important information about themselves that projects a positive attitude.

Interview Stages

The interview process can be subdivided into three phases: (a) initiation and entry, (b) clarification and exploration of issues, and (c) closure. Attentive responsive listening skills pertain to each of three phases or stages. In addition, clients need to learn to feel comfortable with each phase and to allow an interview to flow rather than push from one phase to another.

Initiation and Entry

The first phase involves getting acquainted and developing a relationship. The tone of an interview is actually set at the first moment of initial contact, and the client needs to be aware that self-esteem is communicated by both neat, appropriate dress and clear, attentive communication skills.

 EXERCISE 2.9

RECOGNIZING DEMONSTRATION OF SELF-ESTEEM

Ask clients to consider the following two applicants for an office clerk-typist position:

Tina, 17 years old, wore a freshly ironed cotton blouse and a corduroy skirt, projecting an overall neat appearance. She arrived on time, introduced herself by name, and shook the office manager's hand in a firm manner. She knew exactly for which position she was applying and when asked, "Tell me a little about yourself," gave several relative facts about her hobby and her difficulty in math but stressed her dependability and reliability.

Edith, 17 years old, was 10 minutes late for her interview and wore a T-shirt, jeans, and sneakers. She was chewing gum when she came into the office and was cooly polite to the office secretary when she rudely complained about her lateness. When asked, "Tell me a little about yourself," she described how she baby-sat last summer and how she got A grades when she was "turned on" to a subject or project.

Clients can be asked to consider whom they would hire if they were the employer, why they chose Tina or Edith, and what considerations were part of the decision-making process.

Clarification and Exploration of Issues

In the second phase, the interviewer and applicant get down to the purpose of the interview: giving and receiving information. This stage of the interview is actually a two-way process of communication. As the interviewer is trying to find out about the applicant and how the applicant may or may not fit into a particular job and organization, the applicant is also trying to find out about the job and organization so as to determine whether this would be an appropriate placement.

All 10 of the major verbal responses previously discussed apply during this phase of the interview. In particular, it is important for the applicant to probe, clarify, and check out; to raise issues and demonstrate concern; and, above all, to show the determination to find a job that will be satisfying and productive for the applicant as well as for the employer. The types of questions and the manner in which they are asked (and answered) will communicate the applicant's attitudes, values, and beliefs. Being open, honest, and realistic about a disability and its ramifications in a particular job situation can only help, rather than hinder, the applicant.

The helper thus should provide the applicant with practice interview simulations regarding the applicant's particular disability. The helper can initiate the following role plays:

1. Be a sensitive, empathic interviewer who gently asks the applicant about his or her disability and leads into a discussion about it.

2. Be an avoiding interviewer who deliberately refrains from noticing or discussing the applicant's disability, and teach the applicant to take the initiative. As you continue this simulation, continue to act uncomfortable and evasive about the applicant's disability.

3. Be an uninformed but well-meaning interviewer who makes prejudgments about the nature and ramifications of the applicant's disabling condition. Allow the applicant the opportunity to inform and clarify the nature of his or her disability.

The helper may want to review with the client the types of information about which to probe the potential employer regarding the job and worksite. Such information includes products or services; major operations and functions; physical features of the worksite (transportation, parking, access to and within buildings); types of employees; type of supervision; opportunities for socialization, for training, and for advancement; physical and psychological demands of the work; rewards; and so on. More information on job requirements, skills, and competencies are detailed in Chapter 9.

As the applicant assesses his or her disability in terms of this information, the helper assists the applicant in viewing his or her limitations as well as strengths. Helpers do clients with disabling conditions no favor by overprotecting them, doing the work for them, or giving them false reassurance or false encouragement. The literature is full of examples of people with disabling conditions who have been successful in finding fulfilling, productive jobs that mesh with their interests, aptitudes, and values, and helpers need to encourage clients to deal with frustration and disappointment and to continue to pursue an appropriate vocational choice.

One way that the helper can aid clients in preparing for this phase of the employment interview is to help them to research job requirements before the interview and to assess how they can make modifications or adaptations (e.g., to work flow (pace and quality), particular job elements, or work environment) to fulfill those requirements. Interviewers are often ignorant as to the actual competencies and skills required for a particular job and to the types of modifications or adaptations that can be easily achieved. After working with the client to identify these variables, the helper can then assist the client in initiating discussion of these variables with the potential employer and suggesting assertively how he or she can implement these suggestions.

For example, Jake, age 18, whose cognitive functioning falls in the mild range of mental retardation, applied for a job at a local full-service gasoline station. At first, the employer was reluctant to even talk to him, but after speaking with the rehabilitation counselor, he agreed to an interview.

EMPLOYER: We really need to have guys work here who are fast and can think on their feet.

JAKE: I took auto mechanics in school, and I can change the oil and oil filter, lubricate a car, pump gas, and change and plug up a flat tire.

It took several practice sessions with the rehabilitation counselor before Jake could respond in this fashion, focusing on the skills that he could demonstrate. He was then able to negotiate for a position without the term *special needs* being considered. Jake was well prepared in that he and his counselor had researched the job skill requirements and practiced direct, clear communications.

In some cases, the applicant may not be developmentally ready for this type of independent, assertive behavior. Although the helper does not want to encourage applicant dependency, he or she does need to recognize that depending on family situations and previous exposure and opportunities, clients are at different places developmentally, and some need more assistance and involvement from a helper than do others. Although all clients need communication training and interviewing practice, some need more intensive, lengthier practice. By the same token, the helper needs to accurately assess what levels of interviewee sophistication and independence an individual is likely to achieve and not expect the client to achieve what he or she is incapable of achieving. For example, some clients might require more direct assistance in placement until they have achieved some success in holding down a job and have proven to themselves that they are capable.

Closure

In this third phase, it is important for the applicant to participate in the summarizing, by sharing his or her perceptions of what has occurred and what is to be done after the interview. The applicant may ask whether the interviewer has any more questions or needs more information. Applicants must check out any reservations or "unfinished business" they feel remains.

The helper should remind clients how important it is to clarify as the interview ends when and by whom decisions will be made and how the applicant will be informed. It is also polite for the applicant to thank the interviewer and to shake the interviewer's hand or make some appropriate gesture to communicate respect and appreciation for the time spent on the interview.

 ## EXERCISE 2.10

MOCK INTERVIEW

Set up a mock interview with the client and ask the following types of questions during the interview. At the end of the mock interview, provide specific feedback about the client's verbal and nonverbal communication skills. You may want to tape this mock interview and have the client review the tape before discussing it with you.

1. What job are you applying for?
2. Do you have any experience in that area?
3. Can you tell me something about yourself?
4. Why did you leave your last job?
5. How does this job tie in with your long-range plans?
6. We have many people applying for this job. Why should we hire you?
7. If you were hired and couldn't make it to work for one day, what would you do?
8. Tell me about your last job and why you left. May I contact your last employer?
9. Have you had any courses in school related to this type of work?
10. If you were absent a couple of times, without a good reason such as illness, what would you expect me to do?
11. How have you come to think of a career in this field?
12. Do you think that your age, gender, or disabling condition might be a problem?

Begin discussing this mock interview by asking the applicant how he or she felt about it and what might have been done differently. Then share your reactions and perceptions, first as the "interviewer" and then as a teacher and helper. One way to get into this discussion is to ask your client to complete the following statements with the first response that comes to mind. There are no right answers, but these sentences may help you and your client to pinpoint underlying concerns and anxieties about interviewing and working that may be reflected in the actual interview.

1. When I think about walking into a business and applying for a job, I _____.
2. The worst thing that could happen to me during a job interview would be _____.
3. I think I would do the job if _____.
4. I might not do good work if _____.
5. If I apply for a job and get turned down, I'll _____.
6. What scares me about working is _____.
7. When the interviewer talks to me, I'm afraid he or she will think _____.
8. When I've been told that I have been hired for a job, I'll _____.

9. If I should apply for a dozen jobs and get turned down for every one, I'd _____.

10. When the interview is over and I'm ready to leave, I will

_____.

You may want to repeat the mock interview several times during the vocational planning process, varying it as you wish. Obviously, every interview does not lead to a job, but every interview is a learning situation that can be improved upon in the next one. To help clients learn to appraise interviews, ask them after each interview to:

1. Describe their feelings during the interview.

2. List the positive points of the interview.

3. Review replies to questions they could not answer during the interview.

4. List what they would do differently if they had to take the interview over.

5. Tell how they knew the interview was over.

6. Tell how and when they will hear about the results of the interview.

Throughout practice and discussion sessions, it is important for you to continue to model and teach effective communication skills and for you to assess continuously the development of your client's communication skills.

Written Communication Skills

Clients also must be prepared to fill out job applications and other forms. Careful attention to these skills prior to the scheduled interview can alleviate clients' anxieties about what to disclose and what not to disclose on employer forms. Some practice with the completion of such forms may be in order. The helper might have sample application forms available. If written communication is a problem for the client, the helper might assist the client (through role playing and coaching) to learn to ask the employer for the forms in advance so they can be completed more carefully and brought into the interview and/or permission to take the forms home to be completed and returned. At the very least, the helper should work with the client to prepare an up-to-date résumé, which can be attached to the application form and serve as a highlighter of the applicant's strengths and skills. Résumés can provide compelling information supplementary to that called for on a written form. It may also be appropriate and effective for the client to develop a portfolio to demonstrate his or her achievements and skills.

Conclusion

In this chapter, I have presented a model of responsive listening to facilitate the helping relationship between helpers and clients and to provide modeling and active teaching of effective communication skills to the client. I have highlighted some of the considerations necessary for clients with special needs and provided examples and exercises for enhancing helper skills and for teaching these same skills to clients for use in interpersonal relations and interview situations. I devoted part of the chapter to the application of effective communication skills to job interview situations. I presented specific questions that might be anticipated, guidelines for verbal and nonverbal behaviors on the part of the applicant, and other practical suggestions. The helper was encouraged to coach and prepare clients for interviews and to focus on communication skills that convey positive self-esteem and open discussion about an applicant's disabling condition and its ramifications on the job.

References

Anthony, W., & Carkhuff, R. (1977). The functional professional therapeutic agent. In A. Gurman & A. Razin (Eds.), *Effective psychotherapy* (pp. 103–119). Elmsford, NY: Pergamon Press.

Barrett-Lennard, G. (1962). Dimensions of therapist response as causal factors in therapeutic change. *Psychological Monographs*, 76(43, Whole No. 562).

Brammer, L., & McDonald, G. (1996). *The helping relationship: Process and skills* (6th ed.). Englewood Cliffs, NJ: Prentice Hall.

Carkhuff, R. (1983). *The art of helping* (5th ed.). Amherst, MA: Human Resource Development Press.

Answers to the exercise between student and counselor on pages 54 to 55: 1.c, 2.a, 3.c, 4.c, 5.a

Carkhuff, R. (1986). *Human processing and human productivity*. Amherst, MA: Human Resource Development Press.

Combs, A. (1989). *A theory of therapy: Guidelines for counseling practice*. Newbury Park, CA: Sage.

Condon, W. (1975). Multiple response to sound in dysfunctional children. *Journal of Autism and Childhood Schizophrenia, 5*, 37–56.

Corey, G. (2001). *Theory and practice of counseling and psychotherapy* (6th ed.). Pacific Grove, CA: Brooks/Cole.

Cormier, L. S. (1998). *Interviewing strategies for helpers: Fundamental skills and behavioral intervention* (4th ed.). Pacific Grove, CA: Brooks/Cole.

Egan, G. (1998). *The skilled helper* (6th ed.). Pacific Grove, CA: Brooks/Cole.

Ekman, P., Friesen, W., & Ellsworth, P. (1972). *Emotion in the human face*. Elmsford, NY: Pergamon Press.

Gerber, S., & Purkey, W. (1999). Responsive therapy: An invitational counseling model. In R. Corsini (Ed.), *Handbook of innovative psychotherapies* (pp. 342–354). New York: Wiley.

Gordon, T. (1970). *Parent effectiveness training*. New York: Wyden Press.

Humes, C. W., Szymanski, E. M., & Hohenshil, T. H. (1989). Roles of counseling in enabling people with disabilities. *Journal of Counseling and Development, 2*, 145–151.

Ivey, A. E. (1991). *Developmental strategies for helpers: Individual, family, and network interventions*. Pacific Grove, CA: Brooks/Cole.

Ivey, A. E., & Authier, J. (1978). *Microcounseling: Innovations in interviewing, counseling, psychotherapy, and psychoeducation*. Springfield, IL: Thomas.

Ivey, A. E., & Ivey, M. B. (1999). *Intentional interviewing and counseling: Facilitating client development in a multicultural society* (3rd ed.). Pacific Grove, CA: Brooks/Cole.

Kagan, N. (1984). Interpersonal process recall: Basic methods and recent research. In D. Larson (Ed.), *Teaching psychological skills: Models for giving psychology away* (pp. 229–243). Pacific Grove, CA: Brooks/Cole.

Labov, W., & Fanshel, D. (1971). *Therapeutic discourse*. New York: Academic Press.

Mayo, C., & LaFrance, M. (1973, November). *Gaze direction in interracial dyadic communication*. Paper presented at Eastern Psychological Association Conference, Washington, DC.

Merchant, D. J., & Gajar, A. (1998). A review of the literature on self advocacy components in transition programs for students with learning disabilities. *Journal of Vocational Rehabilitation, 8*, 223–231.

Nathanson, R. (1979). Counseling persons with disabilities: Are the feelings, thoughts and behaviors of helping professionals helpful? *Personnel & Guidance Journal, 58,* 233–238.

Okun, B. F. (2002). *Effective helping: Interviewing and counseling techniques* (6th ed.). Pacific Grove, CA: Brooks/Cole.

Okun, B. F., Fried, J., & Okun, M. L. (1999). *Understanding diversity: A learning-as-practice primer.* Pacific Grove, CA: Brooks/Cole.

Rogers, C. (1958). The characteristics of a helping relationship. *Personnel & Guidance Journal, 31,* 6–16.

Strupp, H. (1977). A reformulation of the dynamics of the therapist's contribution. In A. Gurman & A. Razin (Eds.), *Effective psychotherapy* (pp. 1–22). Elmsford, NY: Pergamon Press.

Sue, D. W., & Sue, D. (1999). *Counseling the culturally different: Theory and practice* (3rd ed.). New York: Wiley.

Toukmanian, S., & Rennie, D. (1975). Microcounseling versus human relations training: Relative effectiveness with undergraduate trainees. *Journal of Counseling Psychology, 22,* 345–352.

Truax, C., & Mitchell, K. (1971). Research in certain therapist skills in relation to process and outcome. In A. Bergin & S. Garfield (Eds.), *Handbook of therapy and behavior change* (pp. 240–267). New York: Wiley.

Vandergriff, A. F., & Hosie, T. W. (1979). PL 94–142: A role for counselors or just an extension of present role? *Journal of Counseling Services, 3*(1), 6–11.

C H A P T E R

Career Counseling Strategies

Thomas F. Harrington

Integral to career counseling are the communication and listening skills presented in the previous chapter. The development of the skill to facilitate client insight comes from a helper's willingness to practice reflecting, clarifying, and remaining silent. In everyday language, these skills promote drawing a person out and hearing the other person's views. A positive consequence to when someone feels listened to is that he or she usually feels good in a relationship.

Some novice helpers do not realize that the goal of counseling is to bring about behavioral change. Getting used to participating in the change process takes time for most people. Different methodologies or strategies exist for stimulating behavioral change: providing information; applying behavioral techniques, such as using positive reinforcement; creating structural changes; and developing insight. The first three methodologies listed rely primarily on an external agent to direct the change process, such as a teacher, a therapist, or an individual with the authority to order a structural change such as mandating that all clients will use a computer system to obtain occupational information and listing past company employers of graduates. The insight strategy, however, involves a helper facilitating individuals to explore their thoughts, feelings, or behaviors as to their intended or anticipated outcomes. The answers typically

Note. I am indebted to Robert W. Read, a colleague, for his patient reading and editing of this chapter and for the ideas integrated within it.

emerge from within the client, not from the helper. In the information, behavioral, and structural change methodologies, the change is usually cognitive and visual. In insight counseling, the change process may involve both cognitive and affective exploration, with results that are not immediately visible. The motivation for using the insight strategy may be the helper's belief that individuals have the capacity to control their own destiny as well as to assume responsibility for their actions.

One strategy is not better than another. There are times when the informational method is absolutely the proper strategy. It is not good practice, however, to suggest to a client immediately that an informational strategy is appropriate, such as matching one's interests with suitable jobs when the client has unclear career goals emanating from poor self-esteem issues. Subsequent sections reveal when behavioral techniques and use of structural techniques are not only appropriate but also when research has indicated that they are the most effective strategies.

Issues for Beginning Helpers

One more caution is in order before discussing career counseling strategies. Helpers-in-training often ask their clients one question after another. This is a natural tendency that needs to be broken because clients often adopt a passive role, only responding when a question is asked and developing an expectation that the role of the questioner is to provide the answers or solutions. Frequently when clients develop and create their own solutions, they assume ownership of the ideas, and implementation is the most effective. A questioning pattern also works against the helper's expectations that the client will expend an amount of time, investment, and work toward the resolution of the issue(s).

In Chapter 4, pervasive societal attitudes that embody negative attitudes toward individuals with special needs are presented. Helpers are no different from society members in general; thus, they may not like clients who express feelings of entitlement to benefits that they personally did not receive or clients who expect privileges, such as being given the same salary for a position if they do not have the qualifications as someone with the specified qualifications. The helper-in-training should expect to have some of his or her personal beliefs challenged during the learning process. For example, the helper will hear a client aspire to enter management who simultaneously describes being ill at ease with people, shy, and never involved in a leadership role. It is difficult to listen to someone's rationale when your immediate reaction is "No way!" Managers need to be good communicators and tend to be extroverted and decisive.

Career Counseling

As the authors of the cognitive information processing theory (Peterson, Sampson, Lenz, & Reardon, 2002) noted, career development theory is different from career counseling theory. This chapter therefore deals with issues and contextual factors that practitioners must consider.

Translating the vocational theories discussed in Chapter 1 into practice demands that the helper consider several contextual factors:

- Most people are confronted by the necessity of working under time pressures personally and professionally. Whether the focus of the theory's application is career development or career counseling, it is likely that the objective will take more time than what people expect; therefore, the amount of time required for a goal's attainment will need to be negotiated with both the individual and the setting if the practice occurs in an organization.

- Because the outcomes of career counseling appear quite clear and the means to the goals are seen as factual or informational, the expectation is that the process is easy, straightforward, and rapid. If, however, an individual is lacking in self-awareness, has not been accustomed to being self-initiating or self-directing, is unable to reach decisions independently with available information, or is lacking in self-efficacy and self-esteem, then an affective component, in addition to the cognitive dimension, becomes involved, making the process more complicated than initially perceived.

- Goal identification, which is often complicated by the fact that parents or others have imposed their own goals, creates uncertainty and risks for the client. To the degree that this is true, parents or guardians become a part of the career counseling process.

- This chapter has not used examples of people with disabling conditions who have low self-esteem, inappropriate goals, and so on, to avoid generalizations that these characteristics are more applicable to people with special needs than to all people. Also, disabling conditions are not always obvious or originally revealed by clients, which can eventually elongate a counseling process.

In summary, the real and imaginary reasons for a client to delay taking action on specific steps in pursuit of fulfilling a goal add unanticipated time to the career development process. To conceptualize how the career helper deals with these interacting complications, I propose the use of a dual-track counseling model.

A Dual-Track Counseling Model

Professional career counseling has dual purposes or goals and thus follows a dual-track model. In this model, the helper responds to the client's questions or concerns but at the same time relates to the issue according to the client's developmental stage. Like a railroad track, both sides are essential in order to be functional. Track 1 addresses the need for the helper to be responsive to or develop a plan for a specific or immediate client request, often involving information or advice on the steps to be taken. Track 2 ensures that helpers will use their training and education to evaluate each client's progress and commitment relevant to that client's personal readiness for the tasks of his or her career developmental stage. Specific content areas included in Track 2 are having the client review his or her different areas of mastery and coping style in age-appropriate situations, anticipating and planning for events that an individual will typically encounter, and verifying that some awareness and assessment of self-knowledge has occurred. This second track of an initial interview is very important, especially at the major transitional points in a client's development (e.g., going from middle school to senior high school). For example, if a person enters a new career developmental stage and has not yet mastered the tasks associated with the earlier stage, a more difficult period of adjustment can be predicted in the new stage.

The dual-track model is intended to communicate the total process to users. In some cases, what the public assumes vocational counseling to be — typically, providing career information or a more cognitive orientation as described here as Track 1 — is only one part of the process. As stated, the goals of Track 2 are essential because they involve integration of the information into self-awareness, which can relate to the affective domain of behavior. Information is only part of the equation for meaningful learning. (Some helpers may prefer not to implement some of the techniques described in this chapter for personal reasons or may lack the skills to deliver them effectively. Handling this helper decision is discussed later in the section titled "Working with Other Professionals.")

The objective of the dual-track model is to allow professionals to personalize the helping process. The goal is to show the helper how he or she can create a contract for specific services that may require an established time commitment with the client. An analogy is that an inventor must be capable of de-

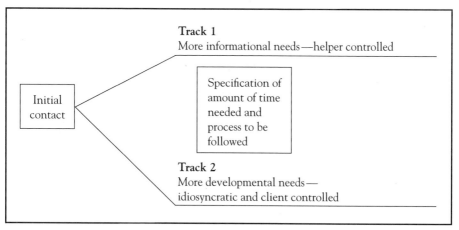

Figure 3.1. Illustration of the dual-track model.

scribing a final product before he or she begins building it. The technique thus calls for the helper and client to mutually envision what the client wants to be like or to be able to do at a specified point (e.g., at the end of this school year or at 14 years of age). The agenda for future sessions can either focus on one or more problematic issues or on the range of issues identified during goal identification and contracted for in future sessions. If any short-term goals are successfully resolved during Track 1, the accompanying positive reinforcement might increase an individual's motivation to deal with subsequent goals.

Figure 3.1 is an illustration of the dual-track model. The two tracks are detailed in the following text, using examples of issues illustrative of each track. Also presented are the amounts of time possibly needed for various phases. In the first meeting, the helper needs to be able to specify with the client the process to be used for each phase and the amount of time required.

Track 1

A. Helper responds to client informational needs:

   1. Provides specific description of a career's preemployment requirements and duties of work performance (career information).

   2. Seeks clarification of a career focus or abilities, which might come from a test or interest inventory (self-information).

   3. Provides help in how to interview (job-getting information).

   4. Explains how and where to find additional information and resources (job-finding information).

   5. Discusses how to get work experience (job-preparation information).

B. Helper specifies process and amount of time needed:

1. After a need is stated, makes available immediately the desired materials for client to read in the office or use at home.

2. If needed, schedules an intervention (e.g., taking an ability test or interest survey or visiting a person with a specific expertise) as a result of the initial contact. Estimates and communicates times required to clients.

3. Performs evaluation, no matter how brief, to determine whether the originally stated goal has been achieved and if it has been done satisfactorily; whether the goal was, in fact, the desired one; and whether any further steps are needed requiring an additional appointment.

Track 2

A. Helper responds to client's developmental needs and readiness:

1. Clarifies "I can't do that," "I don't know," "I wish," and similar statements.

2. Expands upon and understands "They won't let me," "I'm afraid to," "Everyone else [has money, is beautiful, can do what they want to, etc.]" and similar statements.

3. Elicits evaluative statements of accomplishments (the past is the best predictor of the future).

4. Has the client verbalize his or her self-assessment of abilities and experiences and how he or she reached the evaluative conclusions.

5. Has the client state his or her plans for next term, next year, after school, and so on.

B. Helper specifies amount of time needed with process indicated:

1. Allows sufficient time to listen and attend to each client as if he or she were a "customer."

2. Conducts a review of the client's progress in exploring self-knowledge, career awareness, career exploration, or career preparation.

3. Selects the appropriate developmental stage for the client as a frame of reference and reviews the client's awareness of the tasks to be encountered and assessment of his or her accomplishments.

Items 2 and 3 minimally require one session, which could be 20, 30, or 50 minutes.

Helper's Assessment Skills

Helpers use two activities before proceeding to exploring and pursuing another goal area. First, the helper evaluates the client's progress with the tasks undertaken; this process may determine further work that needs to occur with the client. Second, the helper makes the first of several self-assessments of his or her own skill levels. The helper can use the following list to simultaneously evaluate the client's progress and the helper's own adequacy in evaluating these developmental skills:

1. Did the client act independently in performing the given task?

2. Did the client demonstrate satisfactory use of the resources suggested?

3. Did the client use or collect the information correctly?

4. Did the client integrate the information adequately into his or her self-knowledge?

5. Could the client communicate adequately to the helper and appropriately to others the information explored and its value to him or her?

6. Did the client exhibit self-confidence in doing and reporting the activity?

7. Did the client speak in generalities or demonstrate specifics and use "I" statements about the task? For example, "I called for an interview, scheduled an appointment on [date], and spoke with [person's name]."

If the client's assessment reveals inadequacies, the helper must identify alternative ways to address the client's issue(s). If the helper feels inadequate in conducting this evaluation, he or she needs to devise creative ways to increase his or her own proficiency.

In summary, the content or work of Track 1 is for the helper to respond to client inquiries by providing career information, self-information, job-finding information, job-acquisition information, and job-preparation information. These are all very important goals, but they do not encompass the spectrum of goals specified in career development theory. Dimensions often not responded to by the Track 1 content are bringing unconscious material to the conscious level, integrating self-knowledge with career information to reflect a manifestation of self-concept, developing the readiness to make decisions, and using self-knowledge of personality type with corresponding knowledge about work environments.

For a holistic perspective of a person, cognitive informational-seeking behavior must be tied to or integrated with affective components of development, which involve coping, stress, and anxiety, much like a railroad track is held together by ties. As mentioned previously, the helper continually uses assessment skills during the implementation of the career planning process. A series of evaluations typically is made at the conclusion of any Track 1 goal(s). For example, considerations may include the following: Do situational blockages to goals exist? Are stated goals inappropriate? Is the client underaspiring and/ or is there a manifest pattern of underperformance? Is the use of nontraditional assessment methodology indicated? Although these issues, which are necessary to the effective delivery and implementation of Track 1 services, pertain to all individuals, they are of particular concern for those with disabling conditions.

A client's expectation is extremely important. If a client requests information, that is what the helper provides. The helper who uses interest inventories, however, is involved in more than merely providing information. According to the theory set forth by Holland (1997; described in Chapter 1), interest inventories are personality inventories. The helper thus is dealing with more complex issues than just information.

The two-track approach highlights when the helper is finishing one phase of the process with its prescribed roles for the client and helper and beginning a second phase in which the roles need to be defined a little differently. During the interpretation of an interest inventory, the helper needs to seek more client involvement in clarifying the client's self-perception (e.g., being more a doer than a thinker, enjoying working with people more than building things, etc.) and the implications for the client. The client should be alerted to the fact that a change is being made from one phase or track to another. The helper must spend time explaining to the client how he or she is to respond in the new role, and conceivably the client can say he or she does not wish to continue working on a specified goal at this time. Many individuals are not ready to pursue new goals at a specific time. Helpers must anticipate and respect clients' right to stop. (Cancelled appointments are a common way individuals communicate their intentions.) This practice conforms with ethical standards of informed consent and freedom of choice.

The First Meeting

The initial meeting with a client illustrates the dual-track model's application in the counseling process. At the first session, the helper should have six goals: establishing mutuality, identifying goals, setting goals, dealing with inappropriate goals, motivating the client, and closing. Issues of mutuality and motivation are not goals or tasks to be concluded; instead, they permeate all contacts. Every subsequent session also has a closing, which typically involves different strategies or techniques, as described later in the chapter.

Establishing Mutuality

Engaging in the type of communication and responsive listening described in Chapter 2 and in this chapter demands that a helper's initial goal be the development of mutual respect and appreciation. This is exemplified by how the helper opens the session. When dealing on a one-to-one basis, most helpers first greet a client with an opening such as, "Hi. My name is _____. How may I help you?" The objective is to allow the client to state his or her own needs and self-diagnosis, which will enable the helper to clarify the counseling process and determine whether any misconceptions are articulated. If the helper is already aware of the client's goal (e.g., a school career counselor knows the student is seeking career advice), the helper might say, "Hi. My name is _____. This morning I'd like to explore your thoughts about what you see yourself doing after high school."

Regardless of the opening statement, the key to establishing mutuality is for the helper to be a good listener. The helper focuses on hearing and responding to all of the client's verbal messages, including the affective and nonverbal messages. This is an especially difficult task with clients who are unskilled in communicating needs, particularly needs involving the affective domain. Good client–helper communication is critical for generating the content to which strategies, interventions, and techniques are applied, and it serves as the vehicle for developing a successful counseling relationship and rapport. The helper should not rush the process, because the helper and client may not identify the most appropriate goal(s) and achieve success.

Two techniques used for dealing with affect — reflection and clarification — are the easiest to present or demonstrate. In Chapter 2, Okun defined *reflecting* as communicating one's understanding of the stated or implied thoughts and feelings, and *clarifying* as adding something to what the other person has said and helping the other person to understand underlying feelings or how a particular feeling or thought relates to the present situation. Reflection of feeling can be mirroring back to a person what another expressed, restating the feeling that one has experienced, or possibly interpreting the feelings being expressed with a word that the person did not use (e.g., "You're angry," or "You're afraid"). Studies have shown that when the feeling is reflected, the individual will continue sharing and communicating. On occasion the helper perceives and reflects the feeling incorrectly; often, however, the client self-corrects with his or her own description and continues on, ignoring the fact that the helper was inaccurate because the client recognizes that the helper was listening intently.

Novice helpers typically experience difficulty dealing with affect. Novices are often hesitant to reflect or respond to affect. One reason is that they are afraid to give up a degree of control or power to the person with whom they are communicating. In addition, they are apprehensive that they will not know what will happen during the course of communication, which produces a risk for them. Dealing with affect often is a distraction to novice helpers who instead of concentrating on listening, are thinking of what to say next. Developing competence in dealing with affect requires time.

Clarification is a request for further elaboration or expansion (e.g., "Tell me more," or "I'm not quite sure what you're saying"). It is an attempt to focus on or understand the basic nature of another person's statement. Helpers need to recognize that in exploring affect they often encounter people's defenses, such as denial or rationalization. In dealing with affect, helpers must ask themselves why they are exploring certain areas. For example, the frequently encountered "I don't know" statement can be viewed simply as avoidant behavior, which helpers may or may not choose to ignore. "I'm not sure," on the other hand, can mask many alternative dynamics such as lack of confidence or trust, low self-efficacy, or insufficient information. Dealing with affect usually involves self-knowledge and self-expression, which are foundational components of career development.

Critical to the essential task of goal identification, which is discussed in the next section, is dealing with affect and scanning for other issues that have not yet surfaced. Failure to deal with affect and establish mutuality can result in important goals not emerging or being recognized or identified, which may negatively affect the attainment of stated goals.

Identifying Goals

Unfortunately, many practitioners' solution for identifying goals is to administer an interest inventory and/or ability measure. Presto! The results identify a person's goals and skills. A person has high scores, indicating an identification with clusters of careers or job titles. These practitioners have missed exploring some important areas: resolution of developmental tasks and potential faulty assumptions, beliefs, and implications; self-improvement goals; self-knowledge of what the client does well and what provides personal satisfaction; futuristic considerations of life roles and their compatibility; and goals or dreams of what "I want to be when I grow up."

Setting Goals

Goal setting is the logical sequel to identifying goals. Identifying goals requires the helper to use unique personal talents to cajole, nurture, and draw out clients' ideas and feelings. Goal setting requires organizational and planning skills to develop a plan of action. Typically the first step in goal setting is summation, in which the helper restates for the client the issues discussed as desired areas to be pursued and seeks verification of their accuracy from the client. After summation, the next step is prioritizing the agenda for further steps to be taken. The helper works from a motivational perspective, by first dealing with a client's expressed needs. This can be tricky. Goal setting is based on reinforcement theory and success is therefore the client's best motivator to continue. The helper thus orders the goals, with those that are easiest and require the least amount of time to achieve as the first objectives to pursue, followed by the more difficult ones that require prerequisite learnings or experiences. Goal setting establishes a structure for the helper–client relationship. The helper may need to suggest that the client undertake some experiences to increase the likelihood that a goal can be successfully achieved.

The process of career development is broken down into the subcomponents of self-awareness, career awareness, career exploration (of which goal identification is an important part), and career preparation. These subcomponents are sequential; thus, if a person begins with career preparation prior to having done an examination of self-knowledge, it is highly likely that his or her goals will not be adequately attained or that the process at least will be prolonged. The helper's knowledge can be beneficial in sequencing or structuring the order in which goals are addressed.

Because I am a visual person, I write down the goals for the client to see. I usually explain what I anticipate happening at each step, check this out as to whether the person agrees or desires clarification, and elaborate the reason for any additional steps. Some people like seeing the steps written out and, when asked if they agree or want further explanation, sense a greater involvement in the process. Some helpers would describe this process as contracting, that is, stating in writing what the helpers expect to do, what the client anticipates doing, how long each step might take, how behavioral outcomes will be used to evaluate the process, and how to secure an agreement to the process.

Dealing with Inappropriate Goals

Dealing with inappropriate goals is a Track 1 strategy in which the helper uses the techniques of reflection and clarification. This strategy often immediately follows the use of another strategy, such as administration of an interest survey.

In those cases where group interpretations of an interest survey are used (see the section "Group Techniques"), the helper should scan each individual's scores and results to identify whether a need exists for an individual meeting. Schools are notorious for underutilizing costly assessments, which can help to identify individuals at risk or in need. Criteria for closer individual attention are low or extremely high scores on most scales (this could be a noncaring test-taking attitude); reports based on incomplete test data; or any suspicion that a helper develops as a result of experience.

The helper can recognize unrealistic expectations or inappropriate goals because they are often incongruent or in disagreement with data from achievement, ability, personality, or interest domains. Experience suggests, however, that creative helpers can work with clients to make apparent mismatches actually work. For example, the introvert who wants to be a salesperson might master the computer to mount direct sales campaigns through the Internet, and the person with quadriplegia who wants to be a professional mountain climber might design a unique piece of equipment that wins the acclaim of climbers. If helpers respond to seemingly inappropriate goals without acknowledging the client's affective needs, outcomes may be jeopardized. Client verbalizations of a goal may reflect a desire for an affective need to triumph over reason.

Helpers face several options in working with inappropriate goals. One option is to tell a client he or she cannot reach the stated goal. Following this approach can be detrimental to a continuing relationship with the client. Another option is to suggest that the client read some information or speak with a knowledgeable resource and encourage the client to return to the helper to explore what he or she has learned. Some helpers have learned that when they say no, individuals later return to tell of their successes.

The helper's goals are to maintain a relationship and to participate in the individual's process of developing self-knowledge. The helper's projection of a negative attitude is not conducive to these goals. Helpers also need to remember that sometimes an original assessment that produces an inappropriate goal was based on faulty procedures and data. Although disabling conditions can be accommodated, the perception of a helper as negative can be lasting and could effectively eliminate a potential resource person for an individual.

Motivating the Client

A critical part of the first meeting is motivating the client to believe that it would be worthwhile to return to meet with the helper on another occasion. A key element in motivational theory is establishing a client's goals. Mechanically, goals are a means to an end, a motivational agent of the client. Goal identification thus can be viewed as developing the personal relevance of topics. Motivation, however, is an internal process that drives a person to act in a purposeful manner. Needs, drive, and action are parts of motives and the motivational process. Motives develop from needs, which are related to goals, which reflect what the individual wants. Goals can be articulated. Motives are inner drives that cannot be seen. Only inferences can be made about a person's motives; however, goal statements and actions that are movements toward a goal are observable and can serve as the means by which the strength and understanding of the drive and motive can be measured.

Motivation is the energy or the fuel that drives the career development process. Motivation is an internalization of a person's drive for goal attainment. Goal identification and goal attainment are parts of motivation, but the creation of excitement is also part of motivation. Dreaming or envisioning oneself in a certain career can be fun. As Drier (1995) noted, "An individual's future is limited only by the imagination of those involved in the planning." Although thinking about the future can be scary at times, anxiety is also the energy that drives a person to change and to learn.

Helpers' adoption of a positive psychology perspective helps: "Positive psychology is an attempt to urge psychologists to adopt a more open and appreciative perspective regarding human potentials, motives, and capacities" (Sheldon & King, 2001, p. 216). These authors pointed to the negative focus psychology has had, which limits its understanding of typical and successful functioning, such as "to view positivity with suspicion, as a product of wishful thinking, denial, or hucksterism" (p. 216).

Asking a client to describe or act out how he or she will perform in a job is a useful motivational technique. The client's self-description or acting out may indicate adequate or inadequate job knowledge. Whatever the case, a helper's accepting a statement of "I want to be a cook or restaurant manager" without encouraging an elaboration of a self-description is insufficient practice. A person's motivation is often embedded in his or her self-portrayal of actually doing the job.

Lock (1988) wrote, "The most common cause of failure in college is not lack of ability, it is the failure to establish a reason for being there" (p. 164). Without a reason, the person has no internal drive or motive to act, which could lead to failure. The task of the helper, therefore, is to work on setting goals, to observe actions, and to hypothesize by means of reflection and clarification with the individual about his or her motives. Examination of a client's goals is part of establishing motivation.

Another motivational approach involves aspiration and the capacity to work toward that aspiration. It is compatible with specifying goals and imparting a self-empowerment belief. Glasser (1965) theorized that people have a basic psychological need to feel worthwhile to themselves and to others. Movement toward satisfying this need is called *responsible behavior*. Acting responsibly is hypothesized as leading to the formation of a personality with a success identity. Responsible behavior is the ability to satisfy personal needs without interfering with other people's goals to meet their own needs. The helper, therefore, is encouraging and helping clients to accept responsibility for themselves and monitoring their behavior to check their movement toward their goals. Goal attainment stresses analyzing progress and learning and understanding the best choices for feeling worthwhile. Practice and perseverance are also stressed. (Later in this chapter I will explain Glasser's reality theory in greater detail.)

Closing

The important step of closing a session is often rushed. Therefore, adequate preparation time should be devoted to this step. The closing sequence often includes summarizing the session; establishing the content for the next session, if any; specifying any intermediate actions to be taken, such as "homework" for the client to do; obtaining the client's consensus on the process identified; and planning the time and place of the next session. Both summation and anticipation of the next steps require time for helpers to organize their thoughts. Frequently, during the summation statement clients realize that their full agenda, often not verbalized to this point, has not been addressed, and they bring up unresolved topics. Some helpers build sufficient time into the closing phase to minimally respond to added topics. Helpers often need to educate their clients, without scolding them, on the importance of making sure their agenda is known so that adequate time can be budgeted for full attention to their concerns.

A written description may convey an erroneous picture of the lockstep use of strategies and techniques compared with what occurs in reality. In reality, there are constant interactive effects among techniques and strategies as people grow to trust each other and rapport develops within a relationship. All goals do not surface in the first session, and a helper does not deal only with motivation in the initial sessions. Motivation is a constant issue to be maintained throughout contact with a client. Likewise, although dealing with affect may surface more on Track 2 issues, this does not mean the skills involved are not used in Track 1. My presentation of this process as a dual-track counseling model is for organizational purposes only.

Single-Session Brief Counseling

Given the time restraints of many counselors with large case loads, single-session counseling seems a natural alternative. Problem-focused therapy was originally set forth by Watzlawick, Weakland, and Fisch (1974). The process involved four steps: understand the client's concerns; explore solutions attempted by client; begin to work on a mutually defined specific, concrete goal; and assign a task for the client to do. In a study of single-session counseling by Littrell, Malia, and Vanderwood (1995), the authors noted that "High school students made significant changes from the second-week follow-up to the sixth-week follow-up in alleviating their concerns and increasing the percentage of goals achieved. Students dramatically decreased the intensity of undesired feelings from before the counseling session through the second follow-up" (p. 451). Advantages noted were that single-session counseling addressed the counselor's frustration at students not showing up for their second session and that about half of the students felt one session was sufficient, while the other half wanted more time, which obviously can be accommodated to meet their needs. The disadvantages were as follows: (a) focusing too quickly on the presenting problem and thus potentially cutting off the emergence of a more serious issue and (b) believing that because it is short, it is easy. In fact, setting small and meaningful goals requires considerable skill; brief counseling is not appropriate for all goals and issues.

Ethical Issues

When seeking professional service, all clients expect to be dealt with ethically. Not all service rendered in a career service office, however, is counseling. When the helper does engage in career counseling, an appropriate code of ethics is that of the American Counseling Association (ACA; 1995), whose code is included in Appendix E. In general, the code addresses several broad areas: the right of informed consent, confidentiality, assessment practices, and the appropriateness of existing theory for current multicultural practice. Responding to a few representative questions will assist the helper in preparing to address client queries that are based on ethical principles. The following questions are grouped by the eight sections making up the code. A good class activity is to listen to and discuss varied responses:

1. *The Counseling Relationship.* What does career counseling cost? (Although a site may not charge clients, consider salaries, overhead, and other expenses in your response.) What happens in career counseling? Does the delivery of career services at your setting accommodate different worldviews, cultures, and ethnicity?

2. *Confidentiality.* Do you disclose what is discussed in counseling and, if so, to whom? Do you keep records of career counseling sessions, and who has access to them?

3. *Professional Responsibility.* What are the credentials needed to do career counseling? What is your level of competence for doing career counseling?

4. *Relationship with Other Professionals.* Do career counselors work with other professionals such as psychiatrists, physicians, and others who are involved with special needs populations? How do they collaborate?

5. *Evaluation, Assessment, and Interpretation.* Do you have any special skills in the use of assessments, and do you provide complete evaluations and interpretations? If computerized assessments are used, will clients be able to comprehend and cope with their interpretations?

6. *Teaching, Training, and Supervision.* Were you supervised by a trained professional career counselor to prepare you for your work? Do you maintain your currency in the career counseling field and, if so, how?

7. *Research and Publication.* Do you participate in career research and, if so, do you keep participants' information confidential?

8. *Resolving Ethical Issues.* What is your responsibility for action if you believe you have reasonable cause that a career counselor is not acting in an ethical manner?

Working with Other Professionals

A common mistake novice helpers make is believing that they need to do everything themselves. This belief frequently overwhelms a helper. In order for the approach being set forth here to work, a helper must believe that he or she can provide a unique service or worthwhile contribution by helping clients know themselves better and by working with them to find a job or their niche in society. With that mind-set, the helper needs to consider whether identified goals might be better dealt with by different kinds of helpers with different skills in various settings. An added task for the new helper, therefore, is to identify resource people and/or agencies in the community and learn how to work with them. (Teamwork is discussed further in Chapter 14.)

The referral strategy in itself involves skills. The helper must be able to communicate to the client the reason for the referral, that is, that another professional possesses unique skills that will better serve the client's goal(s). The process of referral is also important. If minimal time lag and organizational interruption occur, the interconnectedness between the helper and other professionals is experienced as natural and normal. The helper often can facilitate the referral, with the client's consent, by initiating the contact with a telephone call. Communicating their intentions and telephoning for an appointment are not yet in some clients' skill repertoires. Finally, a referral is not completed until there is specific evidence that the client has established contact with the new agent. Follow-up on the referral is essential to the process.

Drier (1995) identified some collaborative areas among the features of a successful career planning program. The first column in the following list calls attention to the large number of individuals with whom the career counselor may be involved. The second and third columns list kinds of techniques, some of which are described in this chapter or in subsequent chapters of this text.

Parent participation	Goal setting	Group guidance
Employer participation	Goal implementation strategies	Educational plan
Mentors	Assessment	Career plan
Peer expectations	Career interest inventory	Work experience
Volunteers	Counseling	Employment portfolio
Staff involvement	Counselor use plan	Follow-up studies

In essence, this listing communicates the fact that career counseling does not occur strictly in a one-to-one relationship. It involves many outside agencies and uses many auxiliary vehicles.

Examples of collaboration are numerous. For instance, a helper may need to communicate one's expertise to a client who is deaf through a translator who uses sign language. Getting accustomed to this additional person's involvement and presence causes discomfort to some helpers. The helper may need to contact a physician to learn what, if any, limitations a client's disabling condition will have on work requirements. In this instance, there may be a role reversal in that the helper is supplying information about an individual to the physician. The helper often must seek resources that can specify the physical requirements of jobs to help identify potential work situations that do not exceed the person's adaptational capabilities. (This occupational information and its uses are detailed in Chapter 9.) In addition, because many individuals with disabling conditions take medicine as part of their treatment, the helper may need a psychiatrist or nurse practitioner to consider the effects of these medications in potential work situations.

Many different job titles, roles, and levels of expertise are involved in the career counseling field. Position titles include job developer, placement officer, careers teacher, career resource room technician, employment interviewer, guidance counselor, career counselor, college counselor, vocational assessor, and paraprofessional. The job titles suggest both the narrowness and the breadth of some helpers' roles. The level and amount of preemployment education for the above positions also varies. Some require on-the-job training, whereas others require a master's degree with specialization and the passing of a national credentialing examination. The dual-track model discussed previously takes into consideration the varied functions that different positions involve. According to the *Code of Ethics and Standards of Practice* of the American Counseling Association (1995), helpers must practice only within the boundaries of their competence, based on their education, training, supervised experience, and appropriate professional experience. They also must know and take into account the traditions and practices of other professional groups with which they work.

Interventions

Up to this point, the methodology or process has been general. The helper, always keeping in mind a motivational emphasis, listens, identifies a working agenda, prioritizes the agenda from the easiest topic to the hardest topic, and observes and responds to a client's feeling associated with those topics. The helper then presents specific strategies or interventions for dealing with some typical issues. The helper introduces each strategy, indicating the time involved and the methodologies and skills to be used.

Simply stated, an intervention is a strategy for working with a specific issue or subgoal. The value of interventions is that they reflect previously successful practices and frequently used strategies. They thus have a history and can be identified in the literature so helpers can learn more about their application to local situations. Interest inventories, described in Chapter 8, are perhaps the most frequently used career intervention.

Additional strategies are required to deal with the more affective and behavioral components of Track 2. Skill may be needed in dealing with defensive behavior encountered during the exploration of self-knowledge. Specifying a goal is the first step. If a person cannot negotiate its implementation, however, the consequence can be experienced as a failure and will possibly lower self-concept. Self-esteem is an integral part of career planning and implementation, as are risk taking and decision making. Interventions are offered here that are appropriate for dealing with self-esteem and indecisiveness related to career planning. Although many strategies exist, I will present a representative sampling to help define and demonstrate the complexity of career counseling.

Group Techniques

Helpers often employ groups in delivering services associated with Track 1 objectives. Most groups typically last 30 to 45 minutes. Interpretation of interest inventory results in groups, stimulates thinking as one individual probes the understanding of a score in a specific situation, which can trigger another group member to wonder about something that he or she had not previously considered. The group process clearly encourages people to seek out and make inquiries of others about questions or pose "what about" questions. The sharing and illustration of strategies that different people use to achieve desired outcomes are invaluable. This technique works well with younger individuals.

The following are some of the rationales for involving people in group work:

- To brainstorm ideas among group members and consequently empower them to be active thinkers and contributors

- To elicit perspectives that might emanate from different cultures and racial backgrounds

- To demonstrate that the helper is not the sole source of information

- To encourage manifestation of group members' expressive communication skills, which will be invaluable later in developing interviewing skills

- To develop interviewing skills (e.g., observing someone else role-play how to request a job application form can demystify the process and relieve anxiety for someone who has not previously done that task)

When doing group work, many leaders do not like a classroom setup (i.e., one row of chairs behind another row). Arranging chairs in a circle allows everyone to face each other and see each person who is speaking. The leader encourages members to speak spontaneously and communicate with each other; however, a rule needs to be set so that only one person talks at one time. The leader should avoid set speaking patterns, such as having each member in the circle speak as the person next to him or her finishes. This practice often contributes to the next "expected" speaker's not listening as he or she prepares what he or she will say next. The ideal is to have someone volunteer to speak next. An important goal to stress is that each member listen to the others. The leader easily assesses this goal by observing whether others hear accurately what was spoken as group communication continues.

The leader needs to work to avoid letting the group always return to the leader as the expert. The leader also needs to keep in mind that group involvement may be a new experience for some participants, and learning group skills and how to function in a group takes time. It helps to remember that some individuals have learned to speak only when asked; some teachers have shaped their students not to spontaneously express themselves; monopolizing all of the time is frowned upon by other group members; and the leader needs to convey that it is acceptable for a person to say, "I don't have anything to say right now." Group members need time to observe in order to understand how to function in a group. Finally, the skills of reflection, restatement, clarification, and summarization are also helpful in leading groups.

Skill Identification

Skill identification is applicable to Track 1 and can be an alternative to using tests to foster self-awareness. This intervention, which is an adaptation from Pearson (1981), works well with groups. Participants should be in the latter years of high school or older, so that they have had a sufficient range of exposure and experiences. The intervention involves a high level of participant involvement. Helpers assume a leadership role in this process which increases self-knowledge. The intervention follows Super's (1969) objective of helping individuals to develop and accept an integrated and adequate picture of themselves and their role in the world of work, to test this against reality, and to convert it into reality, thus bringing satisfaction to themselves and to society. The leader should allow at least one classroom period and a subsequent time block to follow up on results.

Step 1 is for the leader to tell members to recall five things they have done and enjoyed doing. After allowing time for the group to ponder, the leader says that these events, things, or experiences should be something one really enjoyed, felt one did well, and of which one is proud. People occasionally need prompting or to be provided with common examples, such as working at a job, playing a sport, being elected captain, making something, or doing something for someone. Each person writes down his or her selections. (During the next step, the helper may see people adding experiences to their lists, which is a natural process as an individual uses reflection.)

In Step 2, the helper asks people to describe in writing each experience listed. Before they begin, inform the group that each member will be sharing the first written description with another group member to practice how to do the task. This warning is to reduce any potential embarrassment as a result of self-disclosure. When everyone has finished describing one experience, the leader teams up two people. The leader tells the person on the right to share his or her description, and the partner, after listening, is asked to clarify anything not clear or to ask the person to expand on the description. The rationale is that many people are modest, have been conditioned not to boast, and frequently underreport their involvement. The person reporting is encouraged to write down any information he or she feels would add to the description. The partners then reverse their roles and repeat the process. Afterward, the leader asks people to complete the descriptions for their four other experiences.

Step 3 is identifying the transferable skills. Pearson (1981) developed a one-page Transkill Finder, which lists transkills in 22 categories, using words, numbers, artistic abilities, mechanical and technical abilities, the body, the senses, original thinking, intuitive thinking, gaining knowledge, thinking ahead, organizing, attending to detail, self-directing, persuading, performing for others, helping others, taking directions, instructing, leading, associating, competing, and being involved with the outdoors and nature. Transkills always use a verb to express action. For example, the transkills under the category of persuading are *influencing, selling, promoting, negotiating,* and *bargaining.* Using the written description of an activity, a person is directed to list the various transkills embedded in the description. The following is an example of an experience: "I explained to the person how to relax the body in order to float, showed how to move the hands and kick one's feet, and encouraged the person to learn how to swim." This example reveals three transkills: explaining, showing, and encouraging. Some helpers have people write the transkills for each experience on a large piece of newsprint and later involve the entire group in identifying people's best transkills when the newsprint is taped to the wall. The overall result of this activity is typically one of surprise at how many skills each person possesses.

Step 4 is organizing the transferable skills. A written form best helps in implementing this step. Across the single page form are five columns, one for each of the five experiences identified. On the side of the page, the 22 major transkill categories listed in Step 3 are written with three or four lines left blank under each category. The directions indicate that the person should decide into which category a transkill best fits and then write it down in its proper category. Each individual follows this procedure for his or her five experiences. It is hoped that a pattern will emerge among all five experiences (e.g., most of the transkills for the five experiences fall under the persuading and competing categories). Finally, individuals circle those skills that they enjoy and that are most meaningful to them.

This might be the point at which the group takes a break before the next session. The leader assigns "homework" for the next meeting, such as asking the group to observe a TV announcer, their teachers, or anyone else they meet to see what skills they possess.

Step 5 begins by soliciting the group's observations about the abilities that they have observed various workers using. The helper uses this information to highlight the purpose of this step, which is to assess the required transkills for a particular job. A translation process must occur prior to using occupational information because companies describe jobs in terms of tasks, which use abilities. The helper illustrates several sample tasks and demonstrates how abilities are involved in doing a task. At this point, people should be ready to use occupational information as described in Chapter 9 to match their abilities with specific jobs. As a result of this process, most people discover they possess some abilities for some tasks, but they also identify tasks that require future mastery.

The objectives of this intervention are to foster self-knowledge through a methodology other than tests and to use the information to integrate it with society's expectation that most people will work. When a person identifies abilities and, it is hoped, sees the same behaviors being repeated in different experiences, the task of communicating about himself or herself as required in an interview becomes easier.

Underperformance

This intervention, suitable for all ages, is appropriate to Track 1. The methodology is applicable for working with an individual or with a group of underperformers. Thirty to 40 minutes are set aside for this task, with additional time to be planned. The helper needs to clarify for the individuals that the focus is not on personal issues but rather on information regarding their performance to date and their articulated current or expected goals. Previous text sections about motivation, especially motives and inappropriate goals, may be applicable to this intervention.

This intervention could easily have been labeled "underachievement." Underachievement traditionally has been associated with tests; that is, a test predicts performance to be much higher than actual achievement or a person does not receive the same grades as he or she previously did. Lower than expected performance frequently leads parents, guardians, and teachers to share disappointment with individuals, who in turn are frustrated that they are not meeting someone's expectation of them. These attitudes are not conducive to fostering good interpersonal relationships.

The use of the term underperformance is an attempt to remove some of the focus on tests and suggests that everybody underperforms to some extent in some areas. The intent is to examine the topic of underperformance as a belief. As discussed in Chapter 1, according to Mitchell and Krumboltz (1990), beliefs can be generalized about the self or the world. Standards of acceptable performance — that is, thoughts about how good one needs to be in order to be successful — can be part of a world or a self-generalization. Distorted standards can result in low self-ratings of performance or ability. An example of a personal belief is, "I can be successful at anything, if I really try."

In this intervention, helpers focus on asking people to look at, clarify, and explain inconsistencies, and they exhort them to perceive something differently. Dealing with the anger, frustration, and other feelings of underperformers is embedded in this intervention. These feelings are not dealt with here; however, readers are referred back to the discussion of affect in the section "Establishing Mutuality."

Mitchell and Krumboltz (1990) suggested that a critical helper skill is determining how to better frame or state a generalization. For example, consider the statement "If you are good at something, you will be successful." A helper recognizes that what often makes parents angry is that their child never spends time studying or is always with a group of children who are not good role models. Restating the generalization as "Success depends on effort and practice" gives the helper more maneuverability by framing the belief to emphasize effort rather than being good at something.

Mitchell and Krumboltz (1990) offered practical applications for helpers to increase the chances of goal attainment, beginning with conveying that remedial solutions to a concern do exist; effort is needed to solve problems, and identification of appropriate alternatives increases the odds of satisfaction and success by reinforcing a person's belief in his or her capability to act. Helper techniques include examining and clarifying assumptions about a belief, pointing out inconsistencies between words and actions, identifying barriers to goals, and challenging the validity of a belief. Again, using the principle of assuming personal responsibility discussed in the section "Motivating the Client" is consistent with these steps.

A range of outcomes is possible. A person's initial expectation about his or her underperformance may prove to be inaccurate, but after this intervention, the person may better articulate a rationale for his or her behavior or motives. People learn more consciously about the power they possess (e.g., "You can lead a horse to water, but you can't make him drink"). If the helper accepts the belief that people do not deliberately desire to frustrate others or want poor interpersonal relations, then a goal in dealing with underperformance is to help an individual communicate his or her expectations with a rationale statement. With underperformance, there is a high probability that the individual's expectations might not satisfy others, but the primary issue is whether the individual can satisfy his or her own self-stated expectations.

Situational Blockages

Situational blockages is another intervention that is applicable to Track 1. Using a group setting, especially a small group, has been an effective method for exploring the implication of blockages. At a minimum, 20 to 30 minutes should be budgeted for this intervention. The amount of sharing of experiences may depend on the group members' level of trust. In the beginning, the group leader states that the session's goal — to explore whether there are any situations or personal reasons that may block or hinder achieving a group member's goal(s).

This intervention is based on an exercise that was developed by Stone and McCloskey (1993). Each person is given a list of specific illustrative blockages covering the areas of family, friends, and others, one's self, and "my situation." Each person is to check "yes" or "no" regarding whether a potential block exists. An example in the listing is "My family disapproves of my plans." Checklists are useful because they serve to generate thinking about other issues unique to an individual.

After people have completed the lists, the leader asks them to share any blockages that especially concern them. The group is encouraged to discuss why there is a concern and to devise possible strategies for dealing with it. It is especially helpful if the leader identifies someone else in the group with the same blockage, and in discussing this, it is revealed that the individuals did not use the same strategy. Group discussion can then focus on the pros and cons of different strategies. In conclusion, participants are asked to reflect on the suggested strategies, think about the reasons for their preferences, and prioritize them in writing. The leader again asks for volunteers to share their prioritized strategies and give their reasons, while emphasizing that there are no right or wrong strategies.

The leader's expected outcomes are to demonstrate that people can generate alternative solutions for themselves within an empowerment context, to illustrate how people make decisions from varied options, and to elicit a degree of personal comfort in implementing strategies to deal with specified blockages. Identifying a career goal and not exploring possible blockages is an incomplete process. Also, soliciting people's responses to their concerns about blockages introduces a degree of reality to the task.

Negotiating

The strategy of negotiating is applicable to Track 2. This technique can be used individually or in groups, where modeling is employed. At a minimum,

30 minutes are required. The process requires the helper to have a teaching orientation, to be able to deal with resistance, and to provide practice and support.

Negotiation is a lifelong skill that is not typically learned in a formal educational setting. Some people learn how to negotiate early, whereas others still have not mastered the skill as adults. This intervention is direct and active and is intended to replace earlier learned nondirect and passive approaches, such as manipulation. Good interpersonal relations are contradictory with manipulation. Many adults use earlier learned behaviors and continue to pout and act obnoxious to get their way, causing others to give in.

All people have experienced the importance of negotiating ability. Most individuals fulfill many roles — student, worker, son or daughter, spouse, and lover — and must negotiate the amount of time to spend in each role. Burn-out is a phenomenon people experience when they do not negotiate and keep assuming more roles or work while not giving up other responsibilities.

Negotiation involves goals, compromise, and direct communication. Because different strategies and styles can be used in negotiating, group demonstration is helpful. Clients can share how they negotiate and watch each other role-play or rehearse a strategy. Some preliminary reflection is important to learning to negotiate. Clients should consider questions such as, What do I hope to get out of this encounter? How much am I willing to give up? At what point will I no longer compromise?

To help clients practice negotiating skills, the helper creates some scenarios (e.g., one person wants to get out of the house to see a movie and the other wishes to stay home to watch a video because he or she is tired). The helper assigns roles to two people and allows them 4 minutes to negotiate a decision. A third person is given the role of observer to check whether the people used clear, declarative language; whether one person was willing to give in; and so on. After the role play, the helper opens the discussion to the group to hear the various strategies used. The helper can check out how the group felt about the strategies used and ask which strategy seemed most suitable. The helper summarizes these observations and solicits further feedback.

Another activity to practice negotiating skills involves having the clients watch a role play or videotape of a client being offered a job, where the conditions have not been previously negotiated (e.g., an employer calls and says, "Congratulations, you're our choice for the marketing manager's job. When can you start?"). The task is for the client to negotiate with the employer. The expected outcomes are to help people be aware of negotiating procedures, become more cognizant of their negotiating style, understand the importance of negotiating, practice negotiating skills, and understand that negotiation is an acceptable and necessary behavior.

Working with Indecisive Individuals

This intervention for working with indecisive individuals is appropriate in both Tracks 1 and 2. The indecisive individual is the most difficult of all career counseling clients. This person is perceived as one who has been provided all the information and simply will not decide; however, the undecided are not one homogeneous group. Some indecisive individuals are anxiety prone, whereas others are undecided because of situational factors (Krumboltz, 1992; Multon, Heppner, & Lapan, 1995).

Gati and Saka (2001) stated that the helper needed to differentiate the type of decision-making difficulties a person is experiencing in order to help. They identified three categories of characteristics: a personal lack of motivation to decide; lack of information about self or career options; and possession of inconsistent information, such as internal conflicts with external (e.g., parent's) expectations.

As soon as a helper can identify the type of undecided individual, both the helper and the client will benefit. From the helper's perspective, client indecisiveness leads to frustration at having spent more than the usual amount of time, at having followed good practice by being very responsive to the individual's requests, and at the client's lack of "movement" from the earliest contacts. Many helpers do not recognize early enough that a specific client rarely acts, do not note the indecision, and are unaware of the unique issues and processes involved in working with indecisive clients. From the client's perspective, he or she has spent considerable time on the process, may or may not have been actively involved doing activities, and has not been assessed in a way that will help identify his or her specific needs.

I provide two simple analogies to demonstrate indecisive individuals so helpers can differentiate Track 1 issues from Track 2 issues. Imagine a shoe clerk having shoe boxes on the floor representing 20 different types of shoes and having the customer say, "I can't make up my mind." (Track 1 issue) Envision the travel agent who has narrowed down and identified a person's dream vacation; worked to eliminate all the stated barriers, such as arranging for the care of the dogs and a sick mother-in-law; and trained the person to relax and reduce the fear of flying, only to hear, "I don't think I can go because it costs too much." The travel agent responds, "Didn't you say you had the money and you could spend it for this purpose?" (Track 2 issue)

The intervention for dealing with indecisiveness is built into the helper's typical method of working. The helper assesses a client's behavior periodically by considering the following questions:

1. Did I ask the client to do something, and he or she did it satisfactorily?

2. Did I ask the client to choose among several alternatives and the client did it convincingly?

3. Did the client demonstrate evasive language or avoidant behavior?

If the helper's strategies involve a cognitive basis and are not producing desired outcomes, it seems reasonable to consider changing to a behaviorally oriented approach.

Some people are undecided because of a lack of information. Others are having trouble deciding because they are still weighing the risks involved. For still others, information can be threatening, so there is a natural apprehension. These individuals are not indecisive. Indecisiveness is a condition in which a person repeatedly fails to act after informational deficits are ruled out; the person knows the consequences of each option, provision has been made for support, and reassurances have been made to reduce the threat of harmful effects. Indecisiveness is not a personality deficiency or pathology; however, dealing with indecisiveness requires a long-term effort. Reducing indecisive behavior may be best conceived as setting very short-term objectives and using a variety of strategies, recycling them if necessary. Career indecision has been viewed from a constructivist perspective, indicating a transformation in progress. Savickas (1995) described it as a hesitation in the transformational process of losing one's place and the making of a new place, both of which take time.

The helper needs to remember that making decisions is a learned process; that learning is motivated by reinforcement; and that, for some, the reinforcement occurs after brief involvements and with stronger levels of supportive behavior. One helper might try to attain client insight into his or her behavior, whereas another helper might focus on achieving specific goals. Regardless of the helper's efforts, some clients believe that keeping their appointments is all that is expected of them. The helper may have to change tactics if the client seems to believe that simply spending many hours seeking advice with a helper will produce a solution.

Improving Self-Esteem

Numerous studies have found that positive self-concept, perceptions of self-efficacy, and high self-esteem are the most powerful correlates with academic and vocational achievement (Lent, Brown, & Larkin, 1986; Lent & Hackett, 1987; Osipow & Fitzgerald, 1996). Glasser (1965) wrote that lack of self-esteem is the basis of nonachievement. Career development is seriously impaired when non-achievement and low self-esteem manifest themselves.

Good self-esteem is defined as having accepted one's self as one is. Towers (1991) wrote, "It means you are still working to improve yourself, and while the process is taking place, you have a healthy appreciation for yourself, your best qualities and your finest achievements" (p. 2). Answers to these four questions can assess a healthy self-esteem:

1. Do I accept myself for what I am?
2. Do I give myself credit for what I do?
3. Do I take time out to recognize my hard work?
4. Can I turn setbacks into victories? (Towers, 1991, pp. 3–4)

Multiple theoretical approaches have been used in working with self-esteem. I recommend Glasser's *Control Theory: A New Psychology of Personal Freedom* (1998) and *Every Student Can Succeed* (2000) because of the straightforward process presented for working with self-esteem. The principles in Glasser's theory are consistent with current thinking regarding disability, which does not place an emphasis on deficits. Glasser's emphasis is on the present and not the pathological past, on behavior as being responsible or nonresponsible, and on the abandonment of psychological labels. The goals of reality therapy are to assist people in meeting the basic needs that Glasser believes are encoded into human genes — the needs to survive and reproduce; to belong (to love, share, and cooperate); for power; for freedom; and for fun. Other people's rights to satisfy their own needs must be recognized, however. Empowerment is embodied in the belief that people are capable of assuming responsibility for themselves and their behavior. In working to satisfy the need for power, which provides control, an individual gains self-esteem. Human needs, or forces within individuals, affect behavior. Counseling or teaching enables people to take more effective control of their lives. In working with self-esteem issues, therefore, helping is a matter of fostering those responsible behaviors that satisfy the need to gain power and control over a person's life. Because we choose all we do, we either can choose to self-destruct or to act, feel, and think positively. This intervention's implementation may require the use of confrontational techniques.

Congruence is important in dealing with clients' self-esteem issues. When helpers are faced with clients who deny and rationalize, they need to help the clients become congruent with their own feelings, especially if not doing so may contribute to poorer performance on their part. *Denial* is regarded as one's making excuses, as not speaking what is on one's mind or acknowledging being afraid when facing uncertainty, even when observation suggests a degree of immobilization. *Rationalizing* is considered as one's having a sense of bravado that "I can do anything I want," whereas behavior suggests otherwise. Rationalizing is used as an avoidance strategy and contributes to not taking personal responsibility.

A common approach for dealing with denial and rationalization is the technique of confrontation. Okun (1997) defined confrontation as "A verbal technique whereby helpers present helpees with discrepancies between their verbal and nonverbal behaviors or between the helpee's and the helper's perceptions. Confrontation is often used to encourage approach, rather than avoidance, reactions" (p. 275). The focus is not on a person's denial of or rationalizing about his or her disabling condition but on mastering basic behaviors that can affect future behaviors. Timing can be an important consideration in the therapeutic process when a person is confronting a defense. The expected outcome of confrontation is to foster an honest relationship and, when appropriate, to remove blockages to communication to attain a quality of openness.

During Track 1 work, a job developer can observe the following instance of poor self-projection during the job-getting phase: The client has achieved well in school but in job interviews "comes across" horribly. Everybody can have a bad day, but this individual has failed to project himself or herself positively in several interviews. The helper is likely to first consider whether this is a skill question and whether the person has successfully attended role-playing sessions. The greater likelihood is that this individual may not credit himself or herself for his or her own talents, may fail to acknowledge the hard work he or she has done to get to his or her position, or simply may not like himself or herself. The helper recognizes the client's difficulty and arranges an interview with an employer friend who is sensitive to such issues.

Is this a good strategy? Instead of working with the client to gain self-esteem, the helper has accepted the client's low self-esteem and worked around it. Acquiring job-getting skills is much easier than developing job-keeping skills. As early as 1981, Shertzer, after researching the literature, wrote, "Studies of success and failure in work have shown that the lack of ability to do the job is the cause of only about 15 percent of all firings and dismissals" (p. 347). Most dismissals occur because of bad work habits (e.g., absenteeism, lateness, and loafing), including conflicts with fellow workers, which sometimes result from poor self-esteem. Although addressing self-esteem on a piecemeal basis is expedient, individuals with poor self-esteem do suffer because the issue is frequently not dealt with adequately.

One solution for a job developer who is able to identify people with self-esteem issues is to refer the individual to another professional. Another strategy is for the helper to ask the referral source to help him or her "practice" with people who have self-esteem issues. For example, if a client does not perform adequately in interviews, the helper rehearses with the client to improve interviewing skills and self-esteem. With patience, the individual gains confidence that he or she is capable and, given time, will perform in an acceptable way.

During Track 2 skill identification, a career counselor observes an individual with beliefs of inadequacy about his or her abilities. The concern can be framed by clients in numerous ways: "I'm dumb," "I can't do that," "Everybody else is smarter than I am." People's expressions of confidence in the individual are rebuffed by the person. The helper needs to generate hypotheses. As in most situations, single solutions do not exist because of various possible causes, and one solution can be more appropriate than another, depending on the etiology. For example, in listening to the person recant different versions of "People don't like me," the helper observes that scattered through the stories are references to parents and friends who want the client to have greater socialization. The helper may hypothesize that the client has a fear of failing, especially in someone else's eyes. Consequently, the helper sets up a schedule of reinforcing experiences to emulate successes in meeting people. Another hypothesis may be that the client approaches people impulsively, without using skill, and the helper focuses on practicing an appropriate strategy. Yet another hypothesis is that the client needs to feel free to live his or her own life independent of others' expectations, and the helper arranges reversals of situations to focus on achieving this latter need.

Conclusion

In this chapter I have presented a collection of strategies that helpers may find useful in their work with clients. Although the described interventions are not exhaustive, they illustrate the breadth of issues a helper doing career counseling might encounter. Each of the strategies fits well into the proposed dual-track counseling model.

In omitting within this chapter a section dealing with computer strategies and Internet applications, I was influenced by the conclusion of a study by Whiston, Sexton, and Lasoff (1998) that examined the effectiveness of 47 individual career intervention studies. The authors noted, "Individual career counseling was found to be the most effective and efficient treatment, whereas computer interventions were the most cost effective" (p. 150). Other chapters in this handbook will provide detailed illustrations of computer and Internet applications.

References

American Counseling Association. (1995). *Code of ethics and standards of practice.* Washington, DC: Author.

Drier, H. N. (1995). *Planning for life: A compendium of 1995 nationally recognized career planning programs.* Fort Knox, KY: U.S. Army Recruiting Command.

Gati, I., & Saka, N. (2001). High school students' career-related decision-making difficulties. *Journal of Counseling & Development, 79,* 331–340.

Glasser, W. (1965). *Reality therapy.* New York: Harper & Row.

Glasser, W. (1998). *Control theory: A new psychology of personal freedom.* New York: HarperCollins.

Glasser, W. (2000). *Every student can succeed.* Chatsworth, CA: William Glasser.

Holland, J. L. (1997). *Making vocational choices: A theory of vocational personalities and work environments* (3rd ed.). Odessa, FL: Psychological Assessment Resources.

Krumboltz, J. (1992). The wisdom of indecision. *Journal of Vocational Behavior, 41,* 239–244.

Lent, R. W., Brown, S. D., & Larkin, K. C. (1986). Self-efficacy in the prediction of academic performance and perceived career options. *Journal of Counseling Psychology, 33,* 265–299.

Lent, R. W., & Hackett, G. (1987). Career self-efficacy: Empirical status and future directions. *Journal of Vocational Behavior, 30,* 347–382.

Littrell, J. M., Malia, J. A., & Vanderwood, M. (1995). Single-session brief counseling in a high school. *Journal of Counseling & Development, 73,* 451–458.

Lock, R. D. (1988). *Taking charge of your career direction.* Pacific Grove, CA: Brooks/Cole.

Mitchell, L. K., & Krumboltz, J. D. (1990). Social learning approach to career decision making: Krumboltz's theory. In D. Brown, L. Brooks, & Associates (Eds.), *Career choice and development* (pp. 145–196). San Francisco: Jossey-Bass.

Multon, K., Heppner, M., & Lapan, R. (1995). An empirical derivation of career decision subtypes in a high school sample. *Journal of Vocational Behavior, 47,* 76–92.

Okun, B. F. (1997). *Effective helping: Interviewing and counseling techniques* (5th ed.). Monterey, CA: Brooks/Cole.

Osipow, S. H., & Fitzgerald, L. F. (1996). *Theories of career development* (4th ed.). Needham Heights, MA: Allyn & Bacon.

Pearson, H. G. (1981). *Your hidden skills: Clues to careers and future pursuits.* Wayland, MA: Mowry Press.

Peterson, G. W., Sampson, J. P., Jr., Lenz, J. G., & Reardon, R. C. (2002). A cognitive information processing approach to career problem solving and decision making. In D. Brown & Associates (Eds.). *Career choice and development* (4th ed., pp. 312–369). San Francisco: Jossey-Bass.

Savickas, M. (1995). Constructivist counseling for career indecision. *Career Development Quarterly, 43*, 363–373.

Sheldon, K. M., & King, L. (2001). Why positive psychology is necessary. *American Psychologist, 56*, 216–217.

Shertzer, B. (1981). *Career planning: Freedom to choose*. Boston: Houghton Mifflin.

Stone, W., & McCloskey, L. (1993). *Career exploration system*. Circle Pines, MN: American Guidance Services.

Super, D. E. (1969). Vocational development theory: Persons, positions, and processes. *The Counseling Psychologist, 1*(1), 2–9.

Towers, M. (1991). *Self-esteem: The power to be your best*. Shawnee Mission, KS: National Press.

Watzlawick, P., Weakland, J. H., & Fisch, R. (1974). *Change: Principles of problem formation and problem resolution*. New York: Norton.

Whiston, S. C., Sexton, T. L., & Lasoff, D. L. (1998). Career-intervention outcome: A replication and extension of Oliver and Spokane (1988). *Journal of Counseling Psychology, 45*, 150–165.

THE INDIVIDUAL
AND SOCIETY

DEVELOPMENT, INTERVENTION, AND CAREER PLANNING

Mary Reinke-Scorzelli and James F. Scorzelli

The possibilities for positive adjustment and successful rehabilitation of persons with disabilities have never been more hopeful than they are to-day. Moreover, with recent advances that have been made in all areas of technology, it appears that a disabling condition in itself (one present since birth or acquired later in life) places fewer restrictions on career planning and career choice than restrictions imposed by society or an individual's premorbid emotional and behavioral functioning (Goldberg, 1992; Rubin & Roessler, 1995). In other words, in career planning such variables as parental/family/ community support and acceptance, the opportunity for and availability of ed-ucation and training, intelligence, aptitudes, and personality characteristics and financial resources are of more importance than the severity of the dis-abling condition itself. We contend that children and adults with special needs often have negative life experiences and opportunities that present significant barriers to their career development and vocational choices. In this chapter, these barriers will be discussed in the context of developmental and social–emotional issues. We also describe recent advances in technology that we be-lieve will eliminate many of these barriers in the future. Finally, we will turn our attention to the major components of career planning with persons who have disabling conditions.

Developmental Issues

When discussing normal development at different ages, one must be aware that there are differences based on culture and environment in terms of behavioral expectations. Regardless of these differences, the onset of a chronic disease or disabling condition may result in what are called *developmental delays* that have similar consequences no matter where the person lives. In order to reach a clearer understanding of what these consequences are, in the following section we will use Piaget's model of development (Phillips, 1969; Piaget & Elkind, 1967) to highlight some of the effects of disability on the developing child. We will also discuss how recent technological advances may be useful in mitigating these effects.

Prenatal and Perinatal Periods of Development

Attention to developmental issues that affect career planning and vocational choice should ideally begin before the onset of pregnancy with prospective mothers and their physicians attending to any health issues that may cause negative outcomes. As pointed out by Allen and Jones (1986), one variable that inordinately contributes to the incidence of child disability is prematurity. Moreover, as medical technology has dramatically improved the survival rates for extremely premature infants, there has been a corresponding increase in the incidence of lesser morbidities (minimal cerebral dysfunction/learning disability, poor growth, postneonatal illnesses, rehospitalization), and in a small proportion of the survivors, severe ones (cerebral palsy, mental retardation, retrolenthal fibroplasia, severe chronic lung disease). Ironically, many of the causes of prematurity could be eliminated with careful attention to ongoing maternal health issues. For example, recent research has suggested that one of the primary causes of premature births is an infection—such as tooth decay—in the mother, which could be treated in advance. Nutritional adequacy is a crucial prenatal influence on brain development because of the growing brain's reliance on folic acid, iron, vitamins, and other nutrients (Morgan & Gibson, 1991). At this time, the woman should review her immunization history and get any vaccinations updated. Another maternal issue would be conducting a careful family health history and scheduling a meeting with a genetic counselor—if there are any causes for concern—to plan future strategies. During pregnancy, early and frequent obstetrical visits and careful monitoring of such important variables as diet and weight, smoking, alcohol consumption, and use of other substances will lead to treatment possibilities that may avert deleterious consequences. Medical technologies such as ultrasounds, amniocentesis, and intrauterine medical procedures offer the possibility of conducting a lot of interventions prior to birth. Finally, because health-care workers are a woman's primary contact during pregnancy, they should make her aware of published information, pregnancy support groups, and childbirth classes that may be useful.

Of course, perhaps the greatest barrier to implementation of these measures is economic hardship. In her review of research on socioeconomic disadvantage and child development, McLoyd (1998) noted that persistent poverty contributes to poorer birth outcomes, elevated exposure to acute and chronic stress (even prenatal), and greater rates of perinatal infections. Moreover, poverty limits opportunities to obtain useful information (for example, limiting access to technological advances such as the Internet) and can affect access to medical care, because of transportation difficulties. Another negative result of poverty is the frequent discrimination poor people experience from social institutions. It is probable that only through the development of programs that address prenatal and perinatal health issues, making them easily accessible to the economically disadvantaged in their own communities, will the barriers come down. Perhaps this can be accomplished by utilizing the institutions with which economically disadvantaged individuals frequently come into contact, such as churches, temples, schools, aid offices, or even through a home visiting program.

Sensorimotor Period (Birth to 2 Years)

Birth to 1 Month. Infants have sucking, grasping, startle, and foot and/or walking reflexes, which they exercise during this period. An infant this young has been shown to smile socially and can even stick out his or her tongue in imitation of the mother.

1 Month to 4 Months. Infants begin to interact with their environment and to note the effects their reflexes have on it. Reflexes now change, with certain ones dropping out. These reflexes, even sucking, are affected by learning. Infants repeat or practice things learned. They coo to voices, smile a lot, and if lying in a crib with a mobile, will learn that shaking their legs may cause the mobile to jump. These babies no longer hold their hands tightly closed and can hold a rattle placed in their hands. Some babies roll over from stomach to back.

4 to 8 Months. The infant is oriented to the world. He or she should sit up and exhibit some crawling behavior. Babies like to see the effects of their behavior on the environment; they can pick up objects and manipulate them. They show pleasure and sadness. At this age, babies should try to pull up to stand, hold more than two objects at a time, and exhibit stranger anxiety. They should become anticipatory and try to influence the future (e.g., they may recognize that when their mother puts on a hat, it means that she is going out, so they will fuss).

8 to 12 Months. The child begins to form words, pull up to a standing position, and play pat-a-cake.

12 to 18 Months. A child should walk. The child recognizes object permanence and cause-and-effect relationships. The child should walk up and down stairs with help. The child should also understand commands and follow directions.

18 to 24 Months. A child is now able to stand on one foot and walk up and down stairs, alternating feet in some instances. During this period, children learn to express affection, wash and dry their hands, feed themselves, ask for help, put on some clothes, help with simple in-house tasks, draw with large crayons (scribble), make a tower of nine cubes, combine words in sentences, point to one named body part, kick a ball, and walk backward. Children at this age begin to show foresight and the ability to plan.

Orthopedic, neurological, visual, auditory (deafness), and even social/emotional (autism) disabilities will cause developmental delays during the ages of 18 to 24 months. For instance, if a child has cerebral palsy, he or she will have difficulty sitting up, crawling, or manipulating objects. These delays may negatively affect the parents' interaction with their infant in that their protective responses may hamper the child's development by restricting his or her exploratory play. This overprotectiveness will result in the child's having fewer opportunities to become oriented toward his or her environment, and it will adversely affect the child's independent living skills and emotional development by fostering dependency.

Nonetheless, although the developmental impact of many disabling conditions begin to present themselves during this period, major educational, medical, and technological advances have made it possible to address them. In the educational arena, it has been shown that early interventions are more successful because they alter the experiences and behavior of individuals and their family members in a helpful direction. Ramey and Ramey (1998) summarized the history of these efforts and noted that although Pub. L. 105-17 (the 1997 amendments to the Individuals with Disabilities Education Act) mandated these services, they are complex and continue to evolve. Ramey and Ramey emphasized that only "intensive, high quality, ecologically pervasive interventions can and do succeed" (p. 109). They abstracted from the literature six psychosocial mechanisms repeatedly associated with positive cognitive, social, and emotional outcomes for children:

1. encouragement to explore the environment,
2. mentoring in basic cognitive and social skills,
3. celebrating new skills,
4. rehearsing and expanding new skills,

5. protection from inappropriate punishment or ridicule for developmental advances, and

6. stimulation in language and symbolic communication.

Because these priming mechanisms are hypothesized to be essential to normal development and must be present in children's everyday lives on a frequent and predictable basis, children with specific disabilities may require assistive technology to ensure they are. In support of this, Thompson and Nelson (2001), in their review of current research on developmental neuroscience as it pertains to early brain development, noted that "early experiences are crucial in shaping the cultivation and pruning of neural synapses that underlie the functional capabilities of the developing brain" (p. 6).

In the medical technology area, tremendous advances in orthopedic surgeries involving very young children have been made for physical disabilities that are correctable (e.g., limb abnormalities). For children with hearing impairments, cochlear implants are the most successful, and research on implant outcomes has suggested that this, along with early teaching of American Sign Language (ASL) and speech reading, has been particularly positive. Cranial facial surgeries are often undertaken at this time as well. All of these advances offer hope to many children with disabilities and their families.

In terms of computer technology, parents can access the Internet in order to search for information on recent treatment strategies and also check out chat rooms for parents of children with disabilities. For families already challenged by the emotional, social, and economic issues following a child's diagnosis, the latter offers interaction with others who have experience in dealing with children with disabilities. Beresford (1993); O'Brien (2001); Rogers and Blacher (1995); Luescher, Dede, Gitten, Fennell, and Maria (1999); Murphy (1997); and Stallard and Dickinson (1994) all wrote about the adjustment, stress, and burdens encountered by families and primary caretakers of newly diagnosed individuals; computer technology might be one means of addressing some of these concerns.

Preoperational Thought (2–7 Years)

Prior to the preoperational thought period, children know only by doing. When they reach the preoperational thought stage, they are able to learn by being told and by thinking about things internally. They do this using symbols and words. Children have the beginnings of a cognitive system that can transcend time, space, and reality. They can think of the past, present, and future; they can begin to share their thoughts with others and they can try out their social appropriateness. Children also have limitations, of course. They cannot argue different points of view effectively. They cannot assume other positions or ideas. Their egocentricity prevents them from feeling a need to defend their logic. At this age children also focus on the most compelling aspect of a situation, or they do what Piaget refers to as *centering*. They cannot review and integrate a variety of stimuli characteristics. For example, if a child is given two identical amounts of clay — one shaped in a mound and the other flat — he or she is likely to say that the mound has the most clay. The child centers on the height. A child's thought is also irreversible; he or she cannot move back and forth along a chain of thought elements without distorting them. Thus, the child in our clay example maintains that the clay is not the same because he or she cannot transform it back to a critical state. During this period, children also are unable to reason rationally. They are very rigid and think that they are always right.

At this age children should be able to dress themselves and to form friendships. They should be comfortable expressing themselves and be involved in group play situations. By 4 years of age, children should know their colors. By age 5, they should be able to stand on one foot and be able to feed themselves, dress, run, skip, and hop. By age 6, they should be able to catch a ball, define words, give personal information (such as name, address, and phone number), and demonstrate simple problem solving. Two of the most important clues to "normal" development at the lower range of this period are toileting by age 3½ years and speech by 2½ to 3 years.

During this 5-year period, the child's self-concept is being formed, which is greatly influenced by the child's ability to interact with the environment. A child with a disabling condition is often hindered by limited opportunities to do things that he or she observes others doing. The communication barriers for children who are deaf and the restrictions on mobility for children who are blind or have orthopedic problems can also cause difficulty in interacting with the environment. These children are made more aware of their differences in comparison to children who are physically able, and they can experience rejection and ridicule when they try to interact with their peers. When these children enter school, their self-concept is affected by their ability to learn and their peer interactions. Frequently, "invisible" disabling conditions, such as learning disabilities, are identified after the child's entry into school, and their impact on the child's self-concept can be detrimental when the child does not understand why his or her performance does not equal that of his or her peers.

Early intervention, preschool, sports, and activity (special art, music classes, etc.) programs that integrate children with disabilities into groups of children who are not disabled can be helpful in building a sense of belonging and identifying similarities even before a child enters school. The introduction of technology into the realm of play and education through the use of computer programs and games is also helpful for children who have the physical, auditory, and visual skills to use such games and other activities with their peers that are appealing to all. For children with mobility problems, tremendous advances in assistive technology have provided some robotics devices capable of substituting for a missing function. Others are being used with individuals with acquired motor disabilities to strengthen residual abilities. Some lightweight, commercially powered wheelchairs that can climb stairs and rough terrain are now available. Fioretti, Leo, and Longhi (2000) discussed the design of a navigational system and its integration into a commercially powered wheelchair. The design of the robotics device was adapted to assistive applications that are easy for the user. The authors noted that very young users preferred to directly control devices and that the system has satisfactorily offered this aspect of usability. It even allows for simple collision avoidance when an obstacle is detected without affecting security and response time. Such a device could significantly contribute to a child's positive self-concept by permitting independent movement within a school or other environment.

Developments in the area of computer-based technologies can now make a tremendous difference in the traditional educational environment by allowing even young children with special needs to participate. Hasselbring and Glaser (2000) presented an overview of the role computer technology can play in the classroom for word processing, communication, research, and multimedia projects that can help the estimated 3 million students with specific learning and emotional disorders keep up with their nondisabled peers. Hasselbring and Glaser also discussed more sophisticated devices that can assist the 2 million students with more severe disabilities in overcoming a wide range of speech and hearing impairments, blindness, and severe physical disabilities. Nonetheless, although these technologies can act as equalizers, many teachers aren't adequately trained to use them, and cost is also an obstacle.

A very special adaptive communication system has also been developed for individuals with mobility disorders who cannot use a keyboard effectively. This system uses a computer voice recognition system involving speech processing, speech recognition, and speech understanding called the Dragon Dictate (Dragon Systems, Inc., Newton, Massachusetts). Zimmer et al. (1991) noted that Dragon Dictate was the first large vocabulary speech recognition system that interactively learns a user's vocabulary and mode of speaking and responds to natural language rather than a limited number of words. Dragon Systems, Inc., has produced an updated version of the Dragon Dictate (1997) that recognizes continuous speech or fully connected speech. Although Dragon Systems, Inc., was sold in 2000 to a company called Lernout and Hauspie that has since filed for bankruptcy, Dragon Dictate is still being produced and is available at software outlets. At least one other voice synthesizing program is available. It is produced by IBM and called Via Voice. In company with Dragon Dictate, this program is likely to overcome another barrier between individuals with disabilities and general society (D. Tolkin, personal communication, October 26, 2001). Finally, Zuckerman (1984) discussed a system that allows people who are deaf-blind to work with microcomputers through the use of Morse code as a general communication medium. The individual "hears" Morse code via a vibrotactile device that allows him or her to "see" the computer's screen, receive immediate feedback from his or her typing, and scan the screen. Most comforting about this device is that the cost to equip a standard keyboard with the interface is negligible and it also can be adapted to the individual's particular tactile sensitivities. Although some of these technologies have yet to be used with the preschooler or early elementary child, adapting them for use with youngsters with disabilities will certainly empower them, screening them from the failure experiences that early on begin to impede their social, educational, and vocational achievements.

Concrete Operations (7–11 Years)

When children reach the period of concrete operations, they possess well-organized cognitive systems that help them deal more effectively with their environment. They can organize things in a hierarchy and see relationships by varying degrees and different levels. When shown the two pieces of clay described previously, they are certain that both balls of clay are the same quantity. Because of their increasingly sophisticated cognitive systems, children begin to fundamentally change their behavior and are able to actually deal logically with others. Children can formulate rules, and they like playing in groups and making up games. At this age, a child should be able to solve arithmetic word problems, comprehend social situations, and employ social intelligence (e.g., know what to do if a child younger and smaller than him or her starts a fight). In this period, children should read books, create new projects, and develop simple machines (e.g., using toy building sets). They should be empathic and sensitive to the feelings of others.

Except for the cognitive limitations of children with developmental disabilities, the major impact of disability in this period pertains to peer group acceptance and adjustment to new situations. Specifically, a lack of acceptance by the child's peer group may cause him or her to succumb to the limitations of the disability, adopting a "sick role" because he or she is "unlike" others or unable to function independently. A lot of the programmatic and technological advances in the treatment of very young children with disabilities should begin to "pay off" here — children in this age range should be more emotionally and socially healthy and have greater independence skills than in the past. In addition, in an effort to build on core value curriculums, many elementary school systems such as that in Newton, Massachusetts, have developed programs for this age group so they might learn about disabilities (Volunteers of Understanding Our Differences, 2001). The Newton program teaches children about different disabilities (learning disabilities, developmental disabilities/mental retardation, deafness/hard of hearing, blindness/visual impairment, physical disabilities) using activities that simulate their impact and how they can affect an individual's ability to function in the world. Programs like this one take a big step toward breaking down barriers to acceptance of children with disabilities as friends. Another helpful approach to self-esteem issues in this age group is counseling sessions, which can take place either individually or in groups and can also involve activities such as games or sports. Counseling might also be useful on a family basis because family support or denial is sometimes an issue as a child begins to grow and develop into an adult.

In terms of technology, continued use of computer activities and adaptive devices as well as access to Web sites for children with disabilities and their parents would be useful. There are also assistive technology adaptations that can be used with students with learning disabilities. Bryant and Bryant (1998) noted that although cooperative learning is a common instructional arrangement used by classroom teachers to foster academic achievement and social acceptance of students with and without learning disabilities, recent studies have suggested that these students may need adaptations to help them compensate for specific difficulties. Because these adaptations are technological, strategies are given for integrating them into instructional practices.

Formal Operations (11 Years and Older)

The formal operations period coincides with adolescence. Basically, children in this age group are capable of adult thought or higher reasoning ability. Not only can they use past information to solve new and different problems, but they can also create new information by synthesizing material from different sources. In this stage, thought begins with the hypothetical or theoretical rather than the real, which was the case at earlier stages. Thought at this stage can be characterized as propositional and hypothetical deductive, and plans are developed for problem solving, as in mathematics, which involves the use of formulas rather than trial and error.

During this stage the child's self-concept is formulated, and he or she now must deal with all of the problems that characterize adolescence, such as rebellion and sexuality. Behaviorally, the socioemotional realm becomes very important because it coincides with biological changes in the child. If there are any deep-seated psychological or personality problems in an individual (e.g., schizophrenia, obsessive-compulsive disorders, conduct disorders), they usually emerge during this period. The problem in detecting such problems is that adolescence is characterized by unusual behaviors, such as frequent baths and over-grooming, and it is hard sometimes to know where the extremes lie. Some of the most effective clues to abnormality are social isolation, either constant or newly arising (a symptom of depression and suicidal ideation); belligerence, constant or arising (drug and alcohol); bizarre eating patterns (anorexia, bulimia); and obsession with weight control and exercising. Dramatic changes in school performance also may indicate underlying emotional problems.

Cicchetti and Toth (1998) utilized a developmental psychopathology approach to elucidate the development of depressive disorders in children and adolescents. In their article, they reported on research suggesting that at some point in early to middle adolescence the overall prevalence of depressive symptoms increases significantly for both genders but even more so for girls. Using research results, they effectively argued that contributing factors are children who have depressed caregivers, who have high and perhaps unrealistic expectations for themselves, and who have had disadvantageous family and societal circumstances. These factors all detract from adolescents' ability to competently resolve developmental challenges. Because many of these risk factors are inherent in the backgrounds of adolescents with disabilities, it is critical that interventions occur early in life to promote child competence and to support adaptive family relationships.

Another issue, which is often overlooked, is the emerging sexuality of the adolescent with a disabling condition. Unfortunately, there are still societal misconceptions and myths about disability and sexuality, including such ideas as people with disabling conditions are uninterested, interested but incapable or frightened, and sexually interested and capable but behaviorally abnormal. As with negative attitudes, these misconceptions need to be addressed, and the adolescent with a disabling condition may require information regarding his or her own sexual potential, fertility, and contraception. If the disabling condition results in sexual limitations, the adolescent needs to accept these limitations and develop an expanding definition of sexuality beyond genital arousal and intercourse. Developing a positive body image — rather than comparing one's self to others or to one's self prior to the disability — helps. By providing information that addresses these issues, the helper has recognized that sexuality is integral to every person.

In terms of educational issues, career development and vocational planning should begin with vigor at this age. Vocational–technical or college planning with the student should be addressed, with particular attention to computer information and adaptive computer technologies as a necessity for involvement in future education, jobs, and community life (Fichten, Barile, Asuncion, & Fossey, 2000). Grossman (1997) noted that profound changes in the education of students with disabilities is producing a generation of undergraduate and graduate students who now are able to access academic departments and work-places. In order to accomplish this, institutions must work to provide access through measures as simple as lowering a laboratory bench or as advanced as making the Internet usable for persons who are blind or making a seminar class available to students who are deaf. Not all changes involve modification of the physical environment; some might involve programmatic modifications (i.e., changing the manner in which exams are given to address the auditory, visual, or physical limitations of a disability).

Socioemotional Issues

The discussion of the impact of disabling conditions on development clearly il-lustrates the importance of situational factors and that the social–emotional realm coincides with biological changes in the developing child.

Family Response

The significance of the social–emotional realm in child development has been illustrated by the impact of chronic disease or disability on the family, which has been equated to that of a crisis (Boyer, Knolls, Kaffalas, Tollen, & Swartz, 2000; Kosciulek, 1994; Martin, 1987; Perlesz, Kinsella, & Crowe, 1999). In a study of 49 families who had a member with multiple sclerosis, Powers (1985) found that all families experienced a crisis in accommodating the impact of illness; how-ever, Powers stated that 47% of these families were able to make an adaptive change to the onset of disability. Boyer et al. (2000) found that posttraumatic stress occurred in families with a child who had a spinal cord injury. Besides caus-ing marital discord and economic strain, the family's inability to cope with the onset of a chronic illness or disability can have devastating effects on the child with special needs (Boyer et al., 2000; Croake & Meyers, 1984; Sutton, 1985; Wright, 1983). The lack of family supports will affect the child's self-esteem and his or her interpersonal relationships, and it can cause the child to adopt a "sick role" within the family system. Adopting this role equates the disability with the person, and illness and helplessness replace normal development (Brett, 1988; Morris & Raphael, 1987; Radnitz, Bockian, & Moran, 2000; Ziegler & Holden, 1988). It is also common for the child to be subjected to unusual restrictions and demands that foster increased dependency (Bender, Vail, & Scott, 1995).

Although the impact of disability on a family can result in instability, Power (1985) and Kosciulek (1994) indicated that families are able to accommodate and provide the child with support and opportunities necessary for normal development. The accommodation can be facilitated by having the family obtain accurate information about the disabling condition (Harry, 1992; Leyser & Dekel, 1991; Patterson, 1991) and the supportive services of other parents and/or professionals (Kosciulek, 1994; Stallard & Dickinson, 1994). Eliminating architectural barriers and using adaptive equipment can also reduce the impact of disability on the family. In describing how families coped with a family member with a head injury, Kosciulek (1994) found that the families maintained a positive outlook and accepted the person as he or she is, rather than focusing on how the person was before the injury (positive appraisal). They were able to successfully manage family tensions by such activities as attending religious services and being able to express feelings and frustrations within the family system (family tension management). Even though some studies have indicated that there are some cultural-racial differences with respect to how a family copes with a disabling condition (Bruce & Schultz, 1994; Fatimilehin & Nadirshaw, 1994; Harry, 1992; Smart & Smart, 1991), the family's ability to accommodate a disabling condition will ensure that a child with special needs is involved in productive activities so as to maintain the customary social relationships that are essential for normal development (Fengler, 1984).

Attitudes

A major barrier to effective career planning for students with special needs are the negative attitudes held by society toward disability. This has been highlighted by studies indicating that persons with chronic illness or disabling conditions rate their lives as somewhat lower than those of people without disabilities (Adams, 1969; Koch, Rumrill, Roessler, & Fitzgerald, 2001; Nosek, Fuhrer, & Potter, 1995; Ryan, 1994; Schulz & Becker, 1985). However, these studies also suggested that the self-ratings that identified limitations in social-role performance were more related to the restrictions imposed on the individuals with disabilities by society than the limitations imposed by their disabling condition. These societal limitations pertain to both architectural barriers and negative attitudes. Although architectural barriers are being removed because of federal legislation and a better informed public, research has indicated that negative attitudes toward disability, which have existed since the beginning of civilization, still exist and present significant obstacles to societal integration (Altman, 1981; Arokisamy, Rubin, & Roessler, 1995; Hahn, 1982, 1983; Hernandez, Keys, & Balcazar, 2000). Arokisamy et al. described society's response to disability as being determined by the following factors: perceived cause, responsibility or threat of a disability, and the prevailing economic conditions and sociocultural milieu within a society. Briefly, attitudes toward a person with a disability are more negative if a person is viewed as being responsible for his or her disabling condition, or if the disability threatens one's personal safety or economic well-being. Arokisamy et al. described how the prevailing economic conditions and sociocultural values of and trends in a society can affect attitudes toward persons with disabling conditions. Similarly, Wright (1983) described the concept of expectation discrepancy in describing a person's (other or self) attitude or reaction to disability. Basically, the concept refers to the discrepancy between what a person expects and the actual behavior of a person with a disability. Wright indicated that this discrepancy is reconciled by an expectation revision, which usually results in a positive reaction to the disabling condition, whereas altering reality or anormalizing the person with the disability maintains the negative reaction toward it. For instance, many people without a disabling condition have a lower expectation of what people with disabilities can do, or they do not expect them to be able to function in a capable manner. When a person with a disabling condition is functioning in an effective or capable way, a reason must be provided in order to avoid dissonance. Frequently, the person with a disability is viewed as an exception, or some type of "supernatural" power is attributed to his or her accomplishment.

As can be seen from the previous discussion, the basis of attitudes toward disability are multidimensional and can relate to the specific condition, gender of the person, the social context, or cost-benefits of the condition (i.e., mainstreaming children with special needs) (Bell & Klein, 2001; Berry & Jones, 1991; Darrow & Johnson, 1994; Esten & Wilmott, 1993; Janney, Snell, Beers, & Raynes, 1995; Wiesel & Florian, 1990).

The research of attitudes of employers toward disability has been mixed, ranging from favorable to negative (Bell & Klein, 2001). Studies have indicated that employers expect to have more problems with workers who have disabling conditions, including such things as lower productivity, higher absenteeism, on-the-job injury, and an inability to perform a job to standards (Ellner & Bender, 1980). Even though these concerns are unfounded (DuPont Corporation, 1990), many employers continue to hold misconceptions about the worker with a disabling condition (Hernandez et al., 2000).

One way to counter negative attitudes is by increased contact or favorable exposure. Levy, Jessop, Rimmerman, Francis, and Levy (1993) found that employers who have had experience with workers with disabling conditions had more favorable perceptions toward persons with disabilities. Employer acceptance is essential and can be enhanced by providing employers with information about the needs of persons with disabilities and providing sensitivity training to the employers and employees of the company (Bell & Klein, 2001; Esposito, 1991; Lee-Tatie & Rodda, 1994). Berry and Meyer (1995) also discussed the importance of providing support services for workers with disabilities.

As indicated, misconceptions about the impact of disability contribute to the spread effect, or the tendency to equate the person with the disabling condition (i.e., because Jim cannot hear, he must also have limitations in all other aspects of his personality). Therefore, we believe that a negative attitude toward disability is a major obstacle that a student with special needs must overcome in order for him or her to reach an optimal level of social and vocational development.

Career Development Theory and Disability

Except for references to disability by Super (1957), there is a paucity of information concerning the application of theories of vocational development to persons with special needs (Conte, 1983; Goldberg, 1992; Szymanski & Parker, 1998). In discussing his theory of vocational development, Super made the distinction between the existence of a disabling condition since birth and one that is acquired later in life. With respect to the situation where a child is born with a disability, Super stated that because the person has always had the disabling condition, it has been incorporated into his or her self-concept; therefore, the disability will not disrupt a career, but because of the tendency to have a "dependency experience," it may affect the ability to plan for a career. This is because the individual may be afraid of failure or to compete with others. In contrast, a disability that is acquired later in life must be incorporated within a modified self-concept that will provide the person with the same fulfillment as existed prior to the onset of the disability. Super also briefly described the impact of both intrinsic and extrinsic attributes of a disability on an individual's career development. The intrinsic factors primarily pertain to the presence of the functional limitations of the disability, whereas the extrinsic factors are those environmental barriers, such as negative attitudes, that may affect one's vocational planning. As reflected in his theory, Super believed that the most important concept with respect to the vocational development and career planning of persons with disabilities was their ability to realistically incorporate the disability within their self-concept.

As long as it does not result in devaluation, the incorporation of a disability within one's self-concept is extremely important when adjustment to a disabling condition is discussed (Gibbons, 1985; Koch et al., 2001). Adjustment to disability, according to Wright (1983) and others (Koch et al., 2001; Mayer & Andrews, 1981; Schulz & Becker, 1985; Wood, Taylor, & Lichtman, 1985), will result in accepting one's condition, developing new interests, enlarging the scope of one's values — especially reducing the value placed on the body beautiful or in comparing one's self with certain internalized values rather than on what others can do, and viewing one's disabling condition as a facilitation for change or growth. These positive reactions are in contrast to the negative psychological reactions to disability, such as denial, overdependency, withdrawal, or aggression (Gordon, Bellile, Harasymiw, Lehman, & Sherman, 1982; Wright, 1983).

Legislative Mandates

Career planning with students who have special needs has been made less difficult by a number of federal mandates. The first federal mandate was the Rehabilitation Act of 1973. This action required private and nonprofit organizations that received one or more contracts of $2,500 or more to review and modify their programs and activities so that discrimination based on disability was eliminated (Section 504); described an affirmative action policy (Section 503); and formed an Architectural and Transportation Barriers Compliance Board so as to eliminate architectural and transportation barriers in organizations who own, lease, or use facilities constructed with federal financial support. In 1975, Congress passed the Education for All Handicapped Children Act, which mandated that children with special needs receive a free, public education in the "least restrictive setting appropriate to their needs." Amendments in 1983 added services for the transition of secondary students from school to work. In 1997, amendments to the Individuals with Disabilities Education Act provided a stronger role for parents in and greater access for children with disabilities to a general educational curriculum. Finally, in 1990, the landmark civil rights enactment of the Americans with Disabilities Act (ADA) was signed into law by the president. The provisions of ADA range from accommodating the physical needs of persons with disabilities (architectural, communication, and transportation accessibility) to ensuring equal treatment in the workplace. Even though Esposito (1991) indicated that the ADA applied to 43 million citizens, and most of the adults with disabling conditions indicated that they would like to work, only 34% of those of working age were employed full-time.

In order to increase the employment of persons with disabling conditions, especially those persons who have severe disabilities, the concept of supported employment was introduced by the 1986 amendments to the Rehabilitation Act (Wehman & Moon, 1988). Although the concept of supported employment is not new, especially in special education and psychiatric rehabilitation (transitional employment), its potential impact on career planning is enormous. According to the 1986 Rehabilitation Act amendments, supported employment was designated for individuals who appear to lack the potential for unassisted competitive employment and therefore will require the continuous provision of training, supervision, and support services in order to produce the same benefits that other people receive from work (i.e., income level, quality of working life, security, mobility, and advancement opportunities). To summarize, supported employment is identified with persons who have severe disabilities and involves competitive work in an integrated work setting with provision of ongoing support services. These support services are usually provided by rehabilitation or educational facilities that have contracts with their state's vocational rehabilitation agency and have developed an agreement with private employers to hire persons with severe disabling conditions. Even though the client populations in supported employment have traditionally focused on persons with developmental disabilities, psychiatric disorders, and brain injury, there have been reports of supported employment programs for persons with drug addiction, deafness, and visual disorders (Danek, Seay, & Collier, 1989; Griffin & Kendall, 1989).

In conjunction with the federal legislation, persons with disabilities have been more active in the educational and rehabilitation process, advocating for themselves and others. Within the last 10 years, consumerism has received considerable attention in rehabilitation. The use of the term *consumer* clearly implies that an individual with a disability has the ability to act on his or her behalf in the educational or rehabilitation system. In our opinion, consumerism enlarges the choices a person may have, as well as ensures his or her right to make informed choices (Nosek, 1993).

Career Planning

As indicated, career planning for students with special needs has been greatly facilitated because of federal mandates, supported employment, and the consumerism movement. Nevertheless, persons with disabling conditions have still been excluded from exercising options that most people without disabilities take for granted (Conte, 1983; Tsang, Lam, Ng, & Leung, 2000). Conte (1983) stated that a person's prior life experiences as they affect skill and the individual's self-concept require special consideration in counseling people with disabilities. The importance of environmental variables in affecting one's vocational behavior was illustrated by Goldberg (1992), who differentiated between the experiences of people with acquired disabilities and those with congenital disabilities. According to his findings, people with acquired disabling conditions (e.g., spinal cord injuries, heart disease, cancer) tended to choose postdisability vocational objectives that were consistent with previous occupations. This indicated that the person's predisability identity, as manifested by vocational plans, interests, and values, had a greater impact on the selection of a vocational goal than did the severity of the disability. With respect to persons with congenital disabilities, Goldberg stated that their vocational choices were consistent with parental aspirations and social class. Influences such as social discrimination or social stigma, and cognitive disorders, however, could impinge upon and impair a person's ability to make realistic choices. Although it is important to be realistic in making vocational choices, the helper must still be cautious not to overemphasize the physical limitations of his or her client. This is not to disregard the importance of physical attributes in the world of work or job match with accommodation (Siegel & Gaylord-Ross, 1991); for instance, a lack of vision would appear to restrict a person from entering a job that requires vision, such as driving a truck or bus. There are practicing physicians who are legally blind, however. The second author (J. Scorzelli), who is a counselor educator, recalls receiving a phone call from a person he could barely understand. The person inquired about one of the graduate programs in the department. As the author desperately tried to understand what the person was saying, asking again and again to repeat the statements, the individual's father got on the phone and explained his daughter's interest in the profession of counseling. Even though at first the author simply felt like saying that this profession would not be suitable due to the person's inability to communicate verbally, he hesitated in doing so and made an appointment with the young woman to explain the program and its requirements. Due to circumstances, the person never came for the appointment and the potential dilemma was avoided. But was it really a dilemma? One of the significant occupational characteristics of the job of a counselor is the ability to communicate. Although most communication is done verbally, this is not always the case. American Sign Language (ASL) is used by many people who are deaf, and communication boards and other forms of assisted technology provide alternate methods of communication. Because of the present technology and accommodations, we believe that a vocational choice can no longer be eliminated because of a person's physical limitations.

Vocational planning must always begin by determining the needs and job preferences of the client. Once this is accomplished, the helper must be able to indicate the requirements and skills of occupations in which the person is interested or be aware of the sources where this information can be obtained. One technique that we have found to be helpful has been simply to have students list the jobs in which they are interested, be they fantasies or realistic vocational options. After a thorough description of the requirements and skills necessary for these jobs, students are asked to indicate their strengths and work values and whether they possess the skills required for the jobs listed. Most people have a good grasp of their skills and abilities, and if they do not feel that they possess the required job skills or do not wish to obtain them, they usually will eliminate unsuitable job options. For students who have little vocational information, it may be necessary to provide them with this information before vocational planning can begin. Similarly, unrealistic job choices can be dealt with by presenting the student with objective information (e.g., educational requirements, aptitudes, traits), developing viable alternatives, or by simply allowing the student to try and fail. Regardless of the approach the helper uses, the importance of gaining as much information and evaluative data about the student as possible cannot be overstated.

Conclusion

We believe that career planning with students with special needs does not differ drastically from that used for students without disabilities. Nevertheless, the often restricted and limited opportunities that are available to many students with special needs are the result of faulty perceptions that our society still has concerning disability. These environmental barriers can be compounded by developmental problems related to parenting that can result in the lack of independence and vocational maturity. In order to overcome these obstacles, the helper must have adequate information about disability so that a student's condition will not become the major focus of the process of career planning. If this is done, the vocation chosen will be intrinsically rewarding.

References

Adams, D. L. (1969). Analysis of a life satisfaction index. *Journal of Gerontology, 24,* 470–474.

Allen, M. C., & Jones, M. P. (1986). Medical application of prematurity. *Obstetrics and Gynecology, 67,* 427–437.

Americans with Disabilities Act of 1990, 42 U.S.C. § 12101 *et seq.*

Arokisamy, C. M. V., Rubin, S. E., & Roessler, R. T. (1995). Sociological aspects of disability. In S. E. Rubin & R. T. Roessler (Eds.), *Foundations of the vocational rehabilitation process* (pp. 123–125). Austin, TX: PRO-ED.

Bell, B. S., & Klein, K. J. (2001). Effect of disability, gender and job ratings on job applicants. *Rehabilitation Psychology, 46,* 229–246.

Bender, W. N., Vail, C. O., & Scott, K. (1995). Teachers' attitudes toward increased mainstreaming: Implementing effective instruction for students with learning disabilities. *Journal of Learning Disability, 28*, 87–94.

Beresford, B. A. (1993). Easing the strain: Assessing the impact of a family fund grant on mothers caring for a severely disabled child. *Childcare, Health and Development, 19*, 369–378.

Berry, J. O., & Jones, W. H. (1991). Situational and dispositional components of reactions towards persons with disabilities. *Journal of Social Psychology, 13*, 673–689.

Berry, J. O., & Meyer, J. A. (1995). Employing people with disabilities: Impact of attitude and situation. *Rehabilitation Psychology, 40*, 211–222.

Boyer, B. A., Knolls, M. L., Kaffalas, C. M., Tollen, L. G., & Swartz, M. (2000). Prevalence and relationship of posttraumatic stress in families experiencing pediatric spinal cord injury. *Rehabilitation Psychology, 45*, 339–356.

Bruce, E. J., & Schultz, C. L. (1994). A cross-sectional study of parenting perceptions: Caring for children with intellectual disability. *Australian Journal of Marriage and Family, 15*, 56–65.

Bryant, D. P., & Bryant, B. R. (1998). Using assistive technology adaptations to include students with learning disabilities in cooperative learning activities. *Journal of Learning Disabilities, 31*, 41–54.

Cicchetti, D., & Toth, S. L. (1998). The development of depression in children and adolescents. *American Psychologist, 53*, 221–241.

Conte, L. (1983). Vocational development theories and the disabled person: Oversight or deliberated omission. *Rehabilitation Counseling Bulletin, 26*, 316–382.

Croake, J. W., & Meyers, K. M. (1984). Holistic medicine and chronic illness in children. *Individual Psychology Journal of Adlerian Theory, Research and Practice, 40*, 462–474.

Danek, M. M., Seay, P., & Collier, M. L. (1989). Supported employment for deaf people: Current practices and emerging issues. *Journal of Applied Rehabilitation Counseling, 20*(3), 34–43.

Darrow, A. A., & Johnson, C. M. (1994). Junior and senior high school music students' attitudes toward individuals with a disability. *Journal of Music Therapy, 31*, 266–277.

DuPont Corporation. (1990). *Equal to the task 11*. Wilmington, DE: author.

Education for All Handicapped Children Act of 1975, 20 U.S.C. § 1400 *et seq.*

Ellner, J. R., & Bender, H. E. (1980). *Hiring the handicapped: An AMA research study*. New York: American Medical Association Committee.

Esposito, M. D. (1991). Implementing the ADA: A guide to new employment regulations and how to comply. *Guide to Employment Law and Regulations, 33*, 3–64.

Esten, G., & Wilmott, L. (1993). Double blind messages: The effects of attitude toward disability on therapy. *Women and Therapy, 14*(3/4), 29–41.

Fatimilehin, I. A., & Nadirshaw, Z. (1994). A cross cultural study of parental attitudes and beliefs about learning disability (mental handicap). *Mental Handicap Research, 7*, 117–140.

Fengler, A. P. (1984). Life satisfaction of subpopulations of elderly. *Research in Aging, 6*, 189–212.

Ficten, C. S., Barile, M., Asuncion, J. V., & Fossey, M. E. (2000). What government agencies and organizations can do to improve access to computers for postsecondary students with disabilities: Recommendations based on Canadian empirical data. *International Journal of Rehabilitation Research, 23*, 191–199.

Fioretti, S., Leo, T., & Longhi, S. (2000). A navigational system for increasing the autonomy and the security of powered wheelchairs. *IEEE Transactions on Rehabilitation Engineering, 8*, 490–498.

Gibbons, F. X. (1985). A social-psychological perspective on developmental disability. *Journal of Social and Clinical Psychology, 3*, 391–404.

Goldberg, R. (1992). Toward a model of vocational development of people with disabilities. *Rehabilitation Counseling Bulletin, 35*, 161–173.

Gordon, W., Bellile, S., Harasymiw, S., Lehman, L., & Sherman, B. (1992). The relationship between pressure sores and psychosocial adjustment in persons with spinal cord injury. *Rehabilitation Psychology, 27*, 185–191.

Griffin, S. L., & Kendall, E. (1989). Supported employment for persons with visual impairment or blindness. *Journal of Applied Rehabilitation Counseling, 20*(3), 44–49.

Grossman, P. D. (1997). ADA in the academic workplace. *ACS National Meeting Book of Abstracts* (Vol. 213). Washington DC: American Chemical Society.

Hahn, H. (1982). Disability and rehabilitation policy: Is paternalistic neglect really benign? *Public Administration Review, 42*, 385–389.

Hahn, H. (1983). Paternalism and public policy. *Society, 20*(3), 36–46.

Harry, B. (1992). Making sense of disability: Low income, Puerto Rican parents' theories of the problem. *Exceptional Children, 59*, 27–40.

Hasselbring, R. S., & Glaser, C. H. (2000). Use of computer technology to help students with special needs. *Future of Children, 10*, 102–122.

Hernandez, B., Keys, C., & Balcazar, F. (2000). Employer attitude toward workers with disability and their ADA employment right: A literature review. *Journal of Rehabilitation, 66*(4), 4–16.

Janney, R. E., Snell, M. E., Beers, M. K., & Raynes, M. (1995). Integrating students with moderate and severe disabilities into general education classes. *Exceptional Children, 61*, 425–436.

Koch, L. C., Rumrill, P. D., Roessler, R. T., & Fitzgerald, S. (2001). Illness and demographic correlates of quality of life among people with multiple sclerosis. *Rehabilitation Psychology, 46,* 154–164.

Kosciulek, J. F. (1994). Relationship of family coping with head injury to family adaptations. *Rehabilitation Psychology, 39,* 215–230.

Lee-Tatie, M. C., & Rodda, M. (1994). Modification of attitudes toward people with disabilities. *Canadian Journal of Rehabilitation, 7,* 224–238.

Levy, J., Jessop, D., Rimmerman, A., Francis, F., & Levy, P. (1993). Determinants of attitudes of New York state employers towards the employment of persons with severe handicaps. *Journal of Rehabilitation, 59*(1), 49–54.

Leyser, Y., & Dekel, G. (1991). Perceived stress and adjustment in religious Jewish families with a child who is disabled. *Journal of Psychology, 125,* 427–438.

Luescher, J. L., Dede, D. E., Gitten, J. C., Fennell, E., & Maria, B. L. (1999). Parental burden, coping, and family functioning in primary caregivers of children with Joubert syndrome. *Journal of Child Neurology, 14,* 642–648.

Martin, D. A. (1987). Children and adolescents with traumatic brain injury: Impact on the family. *Family Therapy Networker, 11*(8), 16–23.

Mayer, T., & Andrews, H. (1981). Changes in self-concept following a spinal cord injury. *Journal of Applied Rehabilitation Counseling, 12,* 135–137.

McLoyd, V. (1998). Socio-economic disadvantage and child development. *American Psychologist, 53,* 185–204.

Morgan, B., & Gibson, K. R. C. (1991). Nutritional and environmental interactions in brain development. In K. R. C. Gibson & A. C. Peterson (Eds.), *Brain maturation and cognitive development* (pp. 91–106). New York: Aldine de Gruyter.

Morris, P. L., & Raphael, B. (1987). Depressive disorder associated with physical illness: The impact of stroke. *General Hospital Psychiatry, 9,* 324–330.

Murphy, K. E. (1997). Parenting a technology assisted infant: Coping with occupational stress. *Social Work in Health Care, 24,* 113–126.

Nosek, M. A. (1993). A response to Kenneth R. Thomas' commentary: Some observations on the use of the word "consumer." *Journal of Rehabilitation, 59*(2), 9–10.

Nosek, M. A., Fuhrer, M. J., & Potter, C. (1995). Life satisfaction of people with physical disabilities: Relationship to personal assistance, disability status and handicap. *Rehabilitation Psychology, 40,* 191–202.

O'Brien, M. E. (2001). Living in a house of cards: Family experiences with long term childhood technology dependence. *Journal of Pediatric Nursing, 16*(1), 13–22.

Patterson, J. M. (1991). A family systems perspective for working with youth with disabilities. *Pediatrician, 18,* 129–141.

Perlesz, A., Kinsella, G., & Crowe, S. (1999). Impact of traumatic brain injury in the family: A critical review. *Rehabilitation Psychology, 44,* 6–35.

Phillips, J. L. (1969). *The origins of intelligence: Piaget's theory.* San Francisco: Freeman.

Piaget, J., & Elkind, D. (Eds.). (1967). *Six psychological studies.* New York: Random House.

Power, P. W. (1985). Family coping behavior in chronic illness: A rehabilitation perspective. *Rehabilitation Literature, 46*(3/4), 78–83.

Radnitz, L. L., Bockian, N., & Moran, A. (2000). Assessment of psychopathology and personality impressions with physical disability. In M. G. Frank & T. R. Elliot (Eds.), *Handbook of rehabilitation psychology* (pp. 287–309). Washington DC: American Psychological Association.

Ramey, C. T. M., & Ramey, S. L. (1998). Early intervention and early experience. *American Psychologist, 53,* 109–120.

Rehabilitation Act of 1973, 29 U.S.C. § 701 *et seq.*

Rogers, D. J., & Blacher, J. (1995). African American families' religion and disability: A conceptual framework. *Mental Retardation, 33,* 226–238.

Rubin, S. E., & Roessler, R. T. (1995). *Foundations of the vocational rehabilitation process* (4th ed.). Austin, TX: PRO-ED.

Ryan, A. G. (1994). Life adjustment of college freshmen with and without learning disabilities. *Annals of Dyslexia, 44,* 227–249.

Schulz, R., & Becker, S. (1985). Long term adjustment to physical disability. *Journal of Personality and Social Psychology, 48,* 1162–1172.

Siegel, S., & Gaylord-Ross, L. (1991). Factors associated with employment success among youths with learning disabilities. *Journal of Learning Disabilities, 24,* 40–47.

Smart, J. F., & Smart, D. W. (1991). Acceptance of disability and the Mexican American culture. *Rehabilitation Counseling Bulletin, 34,* 357–367.

Stallard, P., & Dickinson, F. (1994). Groups for parents of preschool children with severe disabilities. *Child Care, Health, and Development, 20,* 197–207.

Super, D. E. (1957). *The psychology of careers.* New York: Harper & Row.

Sutton, J. (1985). The need for family involvement in client rehabilitation. *Journal of Applied Rehabilitation Counseling, 16*(1), 42–45.

Szymanski, E. M., & Parker, R. M. (Eds.). (1998). *Work and disability.* Austin, TX: PRO-ED.

Thompson, R. A., & Nelson, C. (2001). Developmental science and the media. *American Psychologist, 56*(1), 5–15.

Tsang, H., Lam, P., Ng, B., & Leung, O. (2000). Predictors of employment outcome for people with psychiatric disabilities: A review of the literature since the mid 80's. *Journal of Rehabilitation, 66*(2), 19–31.

Volunteers of Understanding our Differences, Inc. (2001). *Understanding our differences* (4th ed.). Newton, MA: Author.

Wehman, P., & Moon, M. S. (1988). *Vocational rehabilitation and supported employment.* Baltimore: Brookes.

Wiesel, A., & Florian, V. (1990). Same and cross gender attitudes toward persons with physical disabilities. *Rehabilitation Psychology, 35,* 229–238.

Wood, J. V., Taylor, S. E., & Lichtman, R. R. (1985). Social comparison in adjustment to breast cancer. *Journal of Personality and Social Psychology, 49,* 1169–1183.

Wright, B. (1983). *Physical disability: A psychosocial approach* (2nd ed.). New York: Harper & Row.

Ziegler, R., & Holden, L. (1988). Family therapy for learning disabled and attention deficit children. *American Journal of Orthopsychiatry, 58,* 196–210.

Zimmer, C. A., Devlin, P. M., Werner, J. L., Stamp, G. V., Bellian, K. T., Powell, D. M., et al. (1991). Adaptive communication systems for patients with mobility disorders. *Journal of Burn Care and Rehabilitation, 12,* 354–360.

Zuckerman, D. (1984). Use of personal computing technology by deaf-blind individuals. *Journal of Medical Systems, 8,* 431–436.

CHAPTER

5

ESTABLISHING CULTURALLY RELEVANT CONNECTIONS IN THE CAREER PLANNING PROCESS

William Sanchez and Dawna M. Thomas

There can be no doubt that the United States is a multicultural society. Baruth and Manning (1999) reflected briefly on our past and current cultural development:

> Through experiences commonly associated with daily living and working together, it was thought that this diverse range of people would acculturate or adopt "American" customs and values and, through a "melting pot," assimilate into mainstream America. For any number of reasons, however, many people opted to hold on to their cultural heritages, traditions, and customs; they wanted their cultural characteristics and values recognized as different, rather than as inferior or wrong. (p. 3)

The continuing increases in our multicultural populations was demonstrated in the 2000 U.S. Census. An overview of the current demographic context within which both clients and service providers will be situated is provided in Table 5.1.

As multicultural populations have continued to increase, a concomitant challenge for service providers has been working with increasing numbers of culturally diverse students with special needs, many of whom will require career planning assistance (Zunker, 1998). According to McNeil (2001, p. 1), "In

TABLE 5.1
United States Population Census 2000

Category	No. (in millions)	%
Total population	281,421,906	100.0
One race	274,595,678	97.6
Two or more races	6,826,228	2.4
White	211,460,626	75.1
Hispanic or Latino	35,305,818	12.5
Black/African American	34,658,190	12.3
American Indian, Alaska Native	398,835	0.1
Asian	10,242,998	3.6

Note. Adapted from Grieco, E. M., and Cassidy, R. C. (2001). Overview of race and Hispanic origin. *Census 2000 Brief,* Table 1.

1997, 52.6 million people (19.7% of the population) had some level of disability and 33.0 million (12.3% of the population) had a severe disability." The rate of disability was highest for Blacks at 21.3%, whereas the rate among Whites was 20.4%. The lowest rate of disability was among people of Hispanic origin, at 13.8%, and Asian Pacific islanders, at 13% (U.S. Census Bureau, 2001, Table 1). The disability rates from the 2000 Census in reference to Native Americans had not been released at press time; however, in 1994–1995, Native Americans had the highest rate of disability, at 23.9% (U.S. Census Bureau, n.d). As a result, traditional approaches to counseling, special education, and career planning will continue to be challenged by the country's growing pluralism (Aponte & Crouch, 2000; Baruth & Manning, 1999; Rounds, Weil, & Bishop, 1994; Smart & Smart, 1992; S. Sue, 1991).

Understanding and integrating important cultural variables will continue to be a basic professional and ethical requirement for professionals seeking to provide culturally relevant and empowering services to clients from diverse cultural communities (American Psychological Association, 1993; Aponte & Crouch, 2000; Helms & Cook, 1999; Ivey, Ivey, & Simek-Morgan, 1993). In this chapter, we examine important variables that need to be included in any career planning process that seeks to assist students with special needs from culturally diverse communities. Irrespective of the career planning orientation taken by the service provider, attempts to integrate these important variables are critical to the development of a culturally respectful dialogue between the career planner and the culturally diverse student with special needs. The career planning process presented here is within a format that seeks to affirm difference and enhance personal empowerment.

The student with special needs is embedded within multiple interacting systems, all having an impact upon the student and subsequently the career planning process. This embeddedness also signifies that the culturally diverse student with special needs also influences these systems as well. Therefore, the career planning process is also one of mutual change: It is about people with different cultural backgrounds learning about their unique integration within these complex coordinates. Clearly, in one chapter we cannot do justice to all of the vital elements that make up the cultural framework of students with special needs from culturally diverse settings (e.g., Latinos, Asian Americans, African Americans, Native Americans; as well as the other critical variables of class, gender, and sexual orientation); however, a general framework that is sensitive and applicable to the general issues of multiculturalism and difference within career planning is presented. In the following pages, we outline some of the major features that we have chosen as important in enacting a career planning process that is respectful of the social and cultural differences presented by students and families from culturally diverse settings.

A culturally relevant career planning process for service providers and vocational counselors working within diverse communities is needed in order to support the commitment to inclusion and diversity. There is a delicate balance, however, between acquiring general knowledge of cultures and working with specific populations (Okun, Fried, & Okun, 1999; Ridley, 1995; D. W. Sue & Sue, 1999). It involves empowering and affirming techniques that respect both the general cultural and individual differences exhibited by the client (Sanchez, 1999). Culture, history, and social context are critical components of a career planning process that seeks to understand the culturally diverse student in context (Helms & Cook, 1999). It is also a client-centered approach that helps guard against any generalizations that reinforce cultural caricatures (Barnes & Mercer, 2001; Okun et al., 1999; Ridley, 1995; Robinson & Howard-Hamilton, 2000; Sanchez, Thomas, & Lima, 2002). Service providers must be cautioned that there are no quick recipes or formulas to follow. Instead, individuals engaging in career planning with culturally different students with special needs must be aware that this type of planning is an evolving process of information gathering, community networking, and self-examination of cultural biases. It ultimately requires the provider to learn about different cultures and how his or her client is situated within that culture. It will also require the counselor to become aware of his or her own cultural background, expectations, and worldview (Helms & Cook, 1999). This chapter therefore outlines (a) broad-based concepts for developing a culturally relevant career planning process and (b) the influence of legislation, inclusion, and empowerment on this process.

Career Planning for Culturally Diverse Students

As previously stated, there are no easy formulas or quick ways for service providers to develop culturally relevant career planning. Integrating, affirming, and contextualizing diverse environments, histories, cultural perceptions, and one's own worldview into a collaborative career planning process is easier said than done. Service providers must be willing to go beyond the safe, secure, and at times detached, scientific structures to a more exploratory, dynamic, and open-ended process. Standardized test data may provide important "pieces" of information, but pieces is what they are and remain unless they are placed within the larger context composed of variables that influence the life of clients from culturally diverse backgrounds (Helms & Cook, 1999). This paradigm shift, and the process of letting go of traditional norms and practices, require risk taking and moving beyond one's fear of the unknown. The provider is challenged to accept a different role, not as the expert dictating rules, plans, and procedures, but as a collaborative worker with information to share and the willingness to learn from the client, families, and communities he or she serves (Sanchez & Thomas, 1997). The provider must build relationships and work in collaboration with clients, families, and the important social networks found in diverse communities.

What follows is a review of some of the components that we feel are critical to understanding the culturally diverse student with special needs and his or her sociocultural environment (see Figure 5.1). We want to reiterate that the provider must strike a balance between having a broad-based cultural awareness and respecting the individual's own particular integration of his or her culture. The service provider must be mindful of the client's level of cultural integration, acceptance, and/or practices (Helms & Cook, 1999). Each career planning endeavor will be a dynamic process of understanding the unique cultural and social context of the student with special needs and the meaning that he or she gives to it.

Integrating Family

Unlike traditional career planning models that focus predominately on the individual client, a culturally relevant process seeks to actively include the client's family. Understanding the importance of family in the life of the client is vital for a culturally aware practitioner (Ferguson, 2001; McGoldrick, Giordano, & Pearce, 1996; Paniagua, 1994; Sanchez & Thomas, 1998; D. W. Sue & Sue, 1999). Disability, the future, work, and life in the community have different meanings

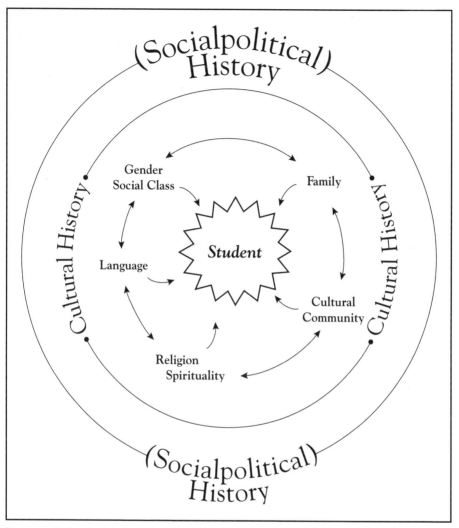

Figure 5.1. Culturally diverse student's worldview. Adapted from *Understanding Disability in the Capeverdean Community: An Analysis of Disability and Race in Massachusetts*, by D. M. Thomas, 2001, Doctoral Dissertation, Northeastern University, Boston. Adapted with permission.

within the cultural frameworks and belief structures of all families. An important concept in understanding clients from culturally diverse backgrounds is that of worldview (Sciarra, 1999). Sue, Ivey, and Pederson (1996, p. 7) offered the following definition:

> A *worldview* has been defined as "how a person perceives his/her relationship to the world ("nature, institutions, other people, etc.," "one's conceptual framework," "our philosophy of life," and "the way we make meaning in the world"). Worldviews are the reservoirs for our attitudes, values, opinions, and

concepts; they influence how we think, make decisions, behave, and define events.

A responsive provider who seeks to meet the challenges of integrating cultural beliefs and influences will strive to understand the family's cultural worldview and how it relates to expectations and goals for the student with special needs in work, life, relationships, recreation, and education.

A *family's level of integration* within the mainstream culture must be assessed (Sciarra, 1999). There are many different layers at which a culturally diverse family can be influenced by and situated within mainstream society. The young adult is affected not only by the family and its historical culture, but also by an outside culture that includes school and other important influencing systems related to youth in this society (Sanchez et al., 2002). The family's and student's cultures will overlap as well as have areas of separateness (Sciarra, 1999; Szapocznik & Kurtines, 1993; Szapocznik et al., 1997). This can be a source of conflict and tension in the planning process, particularly when dealing with different generations. A culturally sensitive service provider will seek to understand not only the individual client's cultural framework, but also how it may be similar and different from the family's cultural practices. This requires asking questions and engaging in a mutual learning process. Culturally diverse families, students, and providers may differ on what the career planning process should entail. For example, the provider's and/or the student's emphasis on personal achievement may clash with the family's perspective of a more collective decision-making approach that takes into account the needs, well-being, and wishes of all the family members (Okun et al., 1999; Paniagua, 1994; D.W. Sue & Sue, 1999). Differences in perception of the issue of independence, a traditional key concept in career planning, are common, with the family believing in more of an "interdependent" orientation (Axelson, 1999; Harry, 1992; Sanchez et al., 2002; Zea, Garcia, Belgrave, & Quezada, 1997). Related to this is questioning of authority and independent thinking versus exhibiting deference to persons in roles of authority (Harry, 1992; Helms & Cook, 1999; Sanchez, 1996). Career planning that stresses self-advocacy, which might include questioning those in authority, may conflict with the cultural orientation that stresses respect for persons in authority positions. Integrating both orientations — how to appropriately question and challenge, while also demonstrating respect, would be the goal for a career planner doing culturally sensitive work (Harry, 1992; Sanchez, 1996).

Gender roles and differences also need to be explored and contextualized (Zea et al., 1997). Across different cultures, the degrees of collaboration and the acceptance of various recommendations and expectations during the career planning process can be greatly affected by and dependent on the issues surrounding gender. Some Latino families, for example, may accept the plans of a young man with special needs to work and travel independently but express concerns and anxieties if the same plans are made for a young woman with special needs. An analysis of the differences between men and women of different cultures in their perception of work and career planning is an essential part of a culturally relevant career planning service. Of course, this does not preclude working toward gender equity; however, it must be done within a culturally respectful process that engages all the participants in a critical dialogue about gender issues within mainstream society and the specific cultural community of the client and family (Sanchez et al., 2002).

Traditional career planning approaches with some culturally diverse students address language in a formal manner, determining the clients' first language and their English literacy capabilities. Language also represents many cultural attributes, however. For example, the language of the family affects not only the concrete process of transmitting information but also the more complicated and subtle process of expressing affect or feelings and anchoring worldviews (De La Cancela, 1985; Gomez, Ruiz, & Rumbaut, 1985; Nuttall, Sanchez, Borras-Osorio, Nuttall, & Varvogli, 1996). It is also important to take into account how people communicate through direct language as well as indirect nonverbal means (Nuttall et al., 1996; D. W. Sue & Sue, 1999). Language is sometimes used to preserve culture and to make a political statement of resistance to mainstream structures (Sue et al., 1996). Service providers have to consider how language differences will be incorporated into the career planning process. Moreover, professionals who do not possess the language skills of the culturally diverse family must also examine their own views regarding language use (e.g., whether they advocate an English-only ideology and the problems involved in this current controversy; Padilla et al., 1991; D. W. Sue & Sue, 1999).

Social class is another variable that is rarely considered in the discussion of the culturally diverse client and family. Most analyses of U.S. social issues ignore class as a significant influence, sending the message that the U.S. is a classless society (Lott, 2002; Okun et al., 1999). All families are affected by class and economic structures that have a significant impact on their worldviews and future expectations, which in turn will affect their perception of career planning, their plans for the future, and their available options (Helms & Cook, 1999). Any cultural analysis of a family structure must also integrate culture within class structure in order to better contextualize and define issues related to empowerment (McGoldrick et al., 1996; Okun et al., 1999; Robinson & Howard-Hamilton, 2000).

Religious and spiritual beliefs are also rarely explored and integrated within the career planning process. Moreover, concerns regarding the separation of secular functions, such as career planning, from nonsecular activities, such as religious affiliation and spiritual beliefs, make many service providers unsure as to how to explore this very important element in the family life of many culturally diverse clients. It is an important area to explore in working with culturally different clients (Helms & Cook, 1999; Robinson & Howard-Hamilton, 2000). Although a family may or may not be connected to a specific institutional religion, understanding spiritual beliefs that are culturally specific provides a service provider with a broader understanding of the family's worldview and the ways in which the difference of disability and special needs are conceptualized within this spiritual framework. Some questions to explore include the following: What are the family's connections to organized religion? How do these connections provide support or create tension, both with respect to issues of cultural diversity and different understandings of disability? Is the family's participation within religious organizations consistent with their own spiritual belief system, or is it different, perhaps creating a source of tension? Spiritual beliefs need to be assessed for each family context and each individual client with special needs.

Integrating the Community

Any model or broad-based career planning process that seeks to embody a multicultural perspective must attempt to understand the community within which the student with special needs is situated (Rounds et al., 1994; Sanchez et al., 2002). Community is not simply geographic locale but the diverse, multicultural setting that is connected to the larger, mainstream society. Any model that seeks to empower the client with special needs from a diverse setting needs to examine potential resources and supports from the local church, culturally related social groups and organizations, after-school programs and activities, and grassroots political agencies involved in advocacy work within the community. All of these are systems in which the client may or may not be involved at the time, but which nevertheless exert influences on the family and client, have a presence within that community, and may potentially serve as important linkages. Evaluating the strengths and weaknesses, consistencies and inconsistencies, and possible resources of support enhances the service provider's attempt to provide meaningful, culturally relevant, and affirming connections for culturally diverse clients and their families.

The Importance of Cultural History

The ability to situate a client within cultural history allows for a clearer understanding of the present and a more empowered vision of the future (Sanchez & Garriga, 1995, 1996; Sanchez et al., 2002; D. W. Sue & Sue, 1999; Thomas, 2001). Unfortunately, service providers frequently ignore the sociocultural history of diverse groups, which perpetuates a decontextualized and culturally oppressive approach to providing services (Hare-Mustin & Marecek, 1997; Helms & Cook, 1999; Sanchez & Garriga, 1995; D. W. Sue & Sue, 1999). We are not referring to the history taught by mainstream culture, but to a history that speaks clearly and courageously about oppression and the movements people created to enhance social justice (Zinn, 1995). This is a history that for many culturally diverse communities speaks to issues of racism, class and gender discrimination, homophobia, and the exclusion of people with disabilities (Atkinson & Hackett, 1998; Helms & Cook, 1999; McGoldrick et al., 1996; Sanchez & Garriga, 1995; Russell, 1998; D. W. Sue & Sue, 1999; Young, 1990). Gaining insight into some of the history of the client's reference group is critical to understanding that individual and his or her place within that historical context (Harry, 1992; D. W. Sue & Sue, 1999). For example, while working with an adolescent from Cambodia, one of the authors of this chapter was required to learn more about Cambodia, the Vietnam War, and the history of Southeast Asia. Understanding the client's sociocultural history provided a foundation not only for understanding his childhood experiences but also for contextualizing his current functioning and life experiences. Having some insight into the general meaning and personal significance of this history that was so critical to the client helped clarify his reactions and behavioral issues as well as the family's expectations about what the career planning system had to offer. Understanding this history was also paramount in determining some of the service provider's reactions toward this young man. An attempt to understand the general cultural history of the culturally diverse client requires consulting with other providers, reading, examining the research, and giving the client the opportunity to educate the service provider as to how this history is or is not a part of his or her worldview.

Although the history of the cultural reference group may not be integrated as a critically conscious component of the client's worldview (Helms & Cook, 1999; Sanchez 1998b), the client may still be influenced by that history. The important issue is to move from the general level of information and understanding to the individual level; that is, to determine, within an individual's context, the significance of this history.

The Service Provider and Cultural Competency

Each service provider is influenced and shaped by his or her own personal framework of cultural diversity (Harry, 1992; Nuttall et al., 1996; Rounds et al.,

1994; D. W. Sue & Sue, 1999). In much of the career planning process, the effects of one's personal orientation and its relationship to the kinds of recommendations and goals presented by the service provider are rarely, if ever, elucidated. The ability to situate the service provider's cultural framework is critical in developing a flexible, open, and collaborative environment where a dialogue about differences can emerge (Harry, 1992; Helms & Cook, 1999). It is this dialogue that provides the potential for clarifying different points of view, establishing goals, and more important, providing an atmosphere of respect for the cultural and social differences of clients with special needs and their families.

Integrating Worldviews

One of the most difficult elements in establishing a level of cultural competency and attempting to understand difference is acquiring awareness of one's own cultural worldview (Helms, 1993; Ivey et al., 1993; Robinson & Howard-Hamilton, 2000; Rounds et al., 1994; Sue et al., 1996; D. W. Sue & Sue, 1999) and how it influences the career planning process. A provider's belief in scientific methods often dictates a notion of "objectivity" in looking at "data" that excludes the provider's worldview from the process. The scientific model, in which researchers, practitioners, and other providers are trained, struggles with concepts of the mysterious and the unknown (Porter, 1995)—concepts that many people from diverse settings and communities accept and integrate as part of their worldview. Emphasis on a linear, cause-and-effect model within scientific practice clashes with the holistic, circular understanding and definition of reality many groups from nondominant cultures possess (Brown, 2001; Cunningham, 1995; D. W. Sue & Sue, 1999).

Trying to integrate scientific models with real-life issues creates tension because the latter do not exist in a clean, linear environment. A person's need to categorize people (including one's self) and fit them into "little boxes" limits his or her ability to situate difference in a meaningful manner. These little boxes block the person's vision, both of himself or herself and of others with whom the individual attempts to work within a collective advocacy model. Thus, the way providers are taught and trained often equips them with "blinders" that need to be removed through a paradigm shift that focuses on understanding, respecting, and contextualizing themselves, their clients, and the families whom they are attempting to empower.

Service providers also carry their own cultural worldviews into their work. They are predisposed to their own upbringing, family of origin, religion, and belief structures (Baruth & Manning, 1999), and they bring these into their conceptualization of diversity and multiculturalism. Gaining insight into this critical element is essential to developing a reciprocal process of understanding cultural differences, both one's own and those of others. A service provider's culture, sociopolitical status, class, gender, religion, and spiritual views influence his or her perceptions of reality, which have a significant impact on how he or she interacts with clients who are different. For example, the first author of this chapter is male, Puerto Rican, bilingual, from a working class family, and now situated within a middle class professional environment. These are only some of the critical variables that would overlap, clash, complement, and interact with the worldviews of clients with special needs within a career planning process.

A service provider needs to think of the process of self-understanding as a continuous endeavor. It is contextually related to and dependent upon the particular client for whom he or she is advocating in the career planning process. It is always a process of renewal because the various combinations of differences between service provider and client are endless. When attempting to confront difference, many service providers have treated diversity as a liability rather than a strength (Kavanagh & Kennedy, 1992; McAdoo, 1993). Integrating the contradictions and differences is at the heart of the creative process, however, and these tensions can be viewed as assets.

This process becomes even more complex when the provider is attempting to creatively merge not only with the client's worldview, but also the worldviews of other professionals and service providers. Clashes between service providers' worldviews are based not only on disciplines, ideologies, and systems identities, but on sociocultural and sociopolitical issues as well. The provider committed to cultural competency must also be willing to become the "broker" for all of these differences. At times, these clashes in worldviews need to be openly and directly addressed so that they can be situated within the process of collaborative planning for the client with special needs. At other times, there will be no easy amalgamation. When this occurs, it should also be elucidated as part of the creative tension in the career planning process. In many ways, taking on the role of "cultural worker," as suggested by Giroux (1992), is critical to this awareness and integration process. It implies that the responsive service provider is committed to enhancing issues of difference and bringing to the center those elements that have often been marginalized or ignored by mainstream society and the professions that represent service provision systems.

Confronting Biases, Myths, and Stereotypes

Another crucial element to understanding one's own and others' worldviews is becoming aware of and clarifying the inconsistencies and negative elements about one's own beliefs, particularly as they relate to conceptualizing others from nondominant cultures (Baruth & Manning, 1999; Ramirez, 1999). "McAdoo (1993) noted, "All of us are biased; it is part of the human condition . . . . We are often unaware of these preconceptions, for they become part of our consciousness before we are even aware of them" (p. 333). Whether biases are expressed in overt or unintentional forms (Ponterotto & Pedersen, 1993; Ridley, 1995), it is necessary to question these beliefs and subsequent behavioral expressions. Ponterotto and Pedersen wrote, "Prejudice transcends all racial/ethnic groups in the United States and all nations of the world. For this reason, combating prejudice (and racism) is everyone's responsibility" (p. 13). This is baggage that will be light for some and extremely heavy for others; regardless, it is extremely important baggage. This baggage must be opened in each encounter, particularly if the provider is to understand the clashes, tensions, and blocking that can occur when attempting to work collaboratively with clients from culturally diverse settings. One's internalized social constructions must be critically examined because they structure reality, but they should not be confused with reality (Porter, 1995). Subtle, vague, and confused constructions about people who are culturally different are just as problematic as blatant and openly hostile views.

An aware, empowered professional can openly confront his or her views on race, culture, class, language use, gender, sexual orientation, religion, spiritual beliefs, and sociopolitical status, to name a few, always in relation to a particular client and community setting (Baruth & Manning, 1999; Helms & Cook, 1999; Rounds et al., 1994). Too often, the process of "working with diversity" has to do with questioning the other person's culture — both its strengths and weaknesses, including the client's own issues of prejudice. A provider engaged in career planning must also explore his or her own consistencies and inconsistencies, strengths and weaknesses, and how these are interdependent; that is, how they share cultural terrain with those individuals the provider is seeking to assist in the empowerment process.

The example of a counselor who was attempting to provide services for an adolescent who had emigrated from Colombia illustrates the complex nature of internal myths, biases, and stereotypes. Following the counselor's presentation of the student and family to the service team, team members noted that the counselor was particularly anxious and fearful, which she readily admitted. The counselor proceeded to say, "I don't know why, but this young man and his family just scare me." When asked what she knew about people from Colombia, she proceeded to present some of what she had heard in the media about the drug cartels and violence in that country. It was clear that this information was distorting her perceptions of the young man and his family, and her internal construction was also having a negative impact on her ability to see this student in a real cultural context. If this had not been brought to her awareness and analyzed, her negative perceptions and behaviors might have detrimentally affected the career planning process.

Understanding the Context of Power

Understanding and contextualizing the variable of power is a crucial element in developing cultural competency and a collaborative model (French & Swain, 2001; Sue et al., 1996; D. W. Sue & Sue, 1999). As Kavanagh and Kennedy (1992) noted, "Power is the crucial variable in minority-majority relations and affects the ability of individuals or groups to realize their goals and interests, even in the face of resistance to power" (p. 17). Society grants professionals and service settings a great deal of power (Albercht, 1992; Drake, 2001; French & Swain, 2001; Hare-Mustin & Marecek, 1997; Zola, 1987). Analysis of the use (and abuse) of power is vital to understanding and collaborating with clients and families from diverse multicultural settings. Power and the ability to influence can be used in a collaborative and nonhierarchical manner that seeks to affirm and empower different worldviews. Power can also be used to avoid recognizing and affirming cultural diversity and, more critically, to coerce the acceptance of a particular view of reality (Axelson, 1999; Kavanagh & Kennedy, 1992; Sanchez & Nuttall, 1995; D. W. Sue & Sue, 1999; Young, 1990). The use of power to avoid and coerce becomes detrimental to establishing an affirming, empowering, and respectful analysis of difference.

Developing a critical consciousness of one's cultural and professional worldviews must include an analysis and contextualization of the variable of power. As McAdoo (1993) noted, this is especially difficult for people who do have power:

> One of the requisites of being in a powerful and dominant group is that one is not even aware of being in that position. It comes with the territory. Until one has an itch, one does not scratch. Until one feels the pain of exclusion, one will not seek to overcome exclusionary tactics in others. (p. 333)

The ability to analyze and place in context the variable of power reflects back to a political framework. Empowerment and being enabled have to do not only with being allowed to "sit at the table," but also with being allowed to access the resources that are available, including culturally affirming career planning. A key component to a collaborative approach that is culturally competent is to confront the use of power and reconceptualize its use within the model (see Figure 5.2) so that it embodies a nonhierarchical, collaborative sharing of that power.

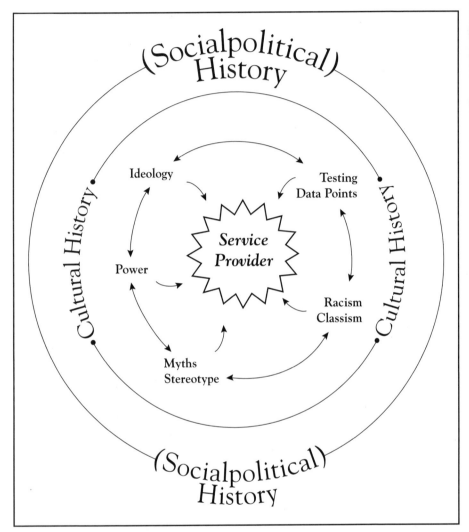

Figure 5.2. Service provider worldview. Adapted from *Understanding Disability in the Cape-verdean Community: An Analysis of Disability and Race in Massachusetts*, by D. M. Thomas, 2001, Doctoral Dissertation, Northeastern University, Boston. Adapted with permission.

Inclusion, Legislation, and Empowerment

The inclusion movement has emphasized the basic civil rights of people with disabilities to be educated, to work, to live, and to enjoy recreation within their own natural communities, schools, and employment settings that are not segregated and apart from mainstream society (Barton & Armstrong, 2001; Bickenbach, 2001; Hahn, 1996; National Council on Disability, 1996; Percy,

1989; Ravaud & Stiker, 2001; Sanchez & Thomas, 1998; Scotch, 1998). Legislative changes support and encourage the inclusion movement and the development of culturally relevant service delivery that ultimately empowers people with disabilities; however, it has added yet another level of complexity to career planning. Ideological and conceptual differences present challenges to service providers as to where and how the client is situated in the career planning process.

Ideological and conceptual differences suggest a paradigm shift with profound implications for career planning and service provision that previously routinely had been done within segregated and/or sheltered environments. The long-range goals of the National Institute on Disability and Rehabilitation Research (1998) suggest that "the new paradigm of disability is integrative and holistic and focuses on the whole person functioning in an environmental context" (p. 7). This new paradigm, and the momentum toward inclusion for people with disabilities, has been reflected in the most recent changes in disability law and policy objectives. The reauthorization of the Education for All Handicapped Children Act of 1975 (Pub. L. 94-142) to the Individuals with Disabilities Education Act of 1990 (IDEA; Pub. L. 101-476), the 1992 amendments to the Rehabilitation Act (Pub. L. 102-569), and the enactment of the Americans with Disabilities Act (ADA) of 1990 (Pub. L. 101-336) provide the most widespread and comprehensive policies regarding the participation of people with disabilities as full citizens in society (Wehman, 1993; West, 1991).

A major element of change brought about by IDEA and the Rehabilitation Act amendments has been the concept of *individualized* service provision and community integration (National Institute on Disability, 1998; Shreve, 1994; Thomas, 2001). In IDEA, the Individualized Educational Program (IEP) requires school districts to perform assessments and provide interventions based solely on a student's individual needs (Engel, 1991; Rothstein, 1998). The IEP mandates that every phase of the educational process be made to facilitate the student's success by including academic instruction, transportation, physical education, and extracurricular activities (Engel, 1991). The Rehabilitation Act of 1973 (Pub. L. 93-112) and its 1992 amendments focus on a client's need to be successful in the world. The amendments were designed to make service provision readily accessible through a shorter eligibility process, presumption of benefits, use of existing information, and provision of service to individuals who had not previously been served, such as persons with severe disabilities and persons from culturally diverse communities (Schriner, 1996; Whitney-Thomas, Timmons, Gilmore, & Thomas, 1999). Similar to the IEP within the school system, Vocational Rehabilitation's Individual Rehabilitation Work Plan (IRWP) focuses on individualized assessment and intervention provisions with the client, an active and empowered agent, as the critical component of the process (Engel, 1991). The ADA also brought about significant changes related to client/consumer empowerment by setting legal parameters for restructuring much of the physical environment that previously excluded people with disabling conditions from both public and private employment opportunities (West, 1991). Advances in technology, led by more powerful personal computers, have further enhanced the ability of people with disabling conditions to access the broader community. This too, however, is influenced by complex definitions as to what assistive technology is, who qualifies for it, who has access to it, and ultimately, who will pay for it (Litvak & Enders, 2001).

The paradigm shift has also brought about legislative mandates regarding reaching individuals who traditionally had been underserved (e.g., individuals from culturally diverse communities and individuals with severe disabilities). Policy makers, service providers, and researchers recognized that individuals from culturally diverse communities (e.g., African Americans, Asian Americans, Latinos, and Native Americans) were disproportionately underrepresented in most disability service systems (Feist-Price, 1995; Jenkins, Ayers, & Hunt, 1996; National Council on Disability, 1993; National Institute on Disability, 1998). Both IDEA and the Vocational Rehabilitation amendments mandated specific objectives for members of culturally diverse communities. In fact, multicultural outreach and infusion has become a priority within all aspects of the disability arena from policy, state planning, and direct service provision to culturally sensitive research approaches (Atkinson & Hackett, 1998; Jenkins et al., 1996; National Institute on Disability, 1998; Massachusetts Developmental Disabilities Council, 1996; Thomas, 2001). For example, the IRWP and the IEP must be written in the language of the client. Service agencies have implemented cultural diversity training and seminars, employed outreach strategies to connect with community networks, and made efforts to recruit and train individuals from the culturally diverse communities they would serve.

These advances and legislative initiatives have been a part of a growing political consciousness of people with disabilities that has been connected to a broader civil rights movement (Atkinson & Hackett, 1998; Barnartt, Schriner, & Scotch, 2001; Bickenbach, 2001; Hahn, 1988; Russell, 1998; Sanchez, 1998a; Shakespeare & Watson, 2001; Shapiro, 1993). This political consciousness has challenged service providers' notions of service strategies, including those within career planning. Now, in this redefined, politically empowered process, individuals with disabling conditions are conceptualized as the central and leading force.

Just as with other culturally different and nondominant groups within U.S. society (Feist-Price, 1995; Gill, 2001; hooks, 1989, 1990), the shift from voiceless object to subject with an empowered voice continues to be a struggle for many clients with disabling conditions (Gill, 2001; Sanchez, 1996; Wendell, 1996; Young, 1990). Although advances have made it possible for people with disabilities to be included on a physical level and develop an empowered voice

(Dybwad & Bersani, 1996), traditional frameworks still prevail throughout disability service-delivery systems. Those who do the planning and have power to decide the careers of people with disabling conditions still lag far behind in their commitment to this level of social change (Albercht, 1992; Atkinson & Hackett, 1998; French & Swain, 2001; National Council on Disability, 1996). Everyone involved in the process of collaboration, facilitation, and planning must continue to be aware of the conflict and ethics of the "empowered voice." This conflict and ethical dilemma involve the disempowering belief that individuals without disabilities have voice over and above individuals who are culturally different and have disabilities. This oppressive type of relationship must be countered by career planning strategies where the goals are to enable the clients to develop their own empowered voice (French & Swain, 2001; National Council on Disability, 1996).

Translating the Concept into Practice

How does a service provider proceed in integrating a collaborative career planning approach and demonstrating a willingness to take risks and act as a broker for cultural diversity? Unfortunately, there are no hard and fast formulas, no magic solutions or equations. There are, however, some basic concepts that, in our opinion, need to be integrated into any career planning process for clients with special needs from diverse cultural backgrounds. Table 5.2 lists some of the major concerns and guiding questions within a culturally sensitive career planning process. The service provider should keep in mind that these are viewed more as "process" questions, consistent with our presenting general concepts of integrating cultural diversity into the career planning process. It is hoped that the information in the table will lead the service provider to consider other clarifying and contextual questions and issues that are relevant to the individual client.

The questions and concerns presented in Table 5.2 can be situated within a process that affirms a person-centered orientation to planning. These person-centered planning approaches have been identified by a variety of different names, including whole-life planning (Butterworth et al., 1993), personal futures planning (Mount, 1991), and lifestyle planning (O'Brien, 1987), to name a few. Despite some variations in approach, they all share a common premise and some key principles that are consistent with using a collaborative career planning approach to understanding, integrating, and being responsive to clients with special needs and their families from diverse cultural backgrounds. The core basis of these planning processes is that individuals with disabling

TABLE 5.2
Summary of Concerns for a Culturally Relevant Career Planning Process
and Questions for Service Providers To Ask

Concern	Question
Need to take chances, exploring both client's and my own cultural history.	How are the behavior, needs, hopes, desires, and worldview that I am observing related to, influenced by, and centered within a particular cultural framework?
Need to go beyond traditional systems and ways of thinking about career planning.	How are my culture, social class, ideologies, and general worldview influencing my perceptions and analysis of the student with special needs, his or her family, and their embeddedness in diversity?
Need to ask very basic questions in a supportive and nonthreatening manner regarding: • Economics and poverty • Culture and history • Language and communication modes • Religion and spirituality • Political awareness regarding culture, race, and disability • Gender role issues • Class issues • Race issues	Am I looking at things in as open and flexible a manner as possible? Am I being pressured by systems issues? Do I understand the client's interests, hopes, dreams, and values about his or her future? Is this a collaborative, nonhierarchical relationship? Have I fully explored with the client and his or her family the full extent of their natural support systems to assist with both assessment and development of resources? Do I need a consultant? Am I at odds or in sync with the client and his or her worldview, and how does this affect our attempts at collaborative career planning?

conditions have a vision of what a desirable future will be for them and an idea of their own worldview, and these need to be the cornerstone and driving force of any planning.

Person-centered planning approaches respect the individual with a disability and provide an opportunity to gather and integrate information about the individual's vision for himself or herself within the context of the local community and life experiences, central elements of the contextualization process. Also central to this process is the ability to provide respect for and affirmation to the families and their contributions, as well as meaningful roles in the planning process for family members and significant others.

Although proponents of these person-centered planning approaches have not specifically articulated strategies for working with individuals from diverse cultural backgrounds, the individualized focus and inclusion of key people in the individual's family and community network seem compatible with integrating some of the ideas about understanding and integrating cultural influences. Service providers who are invested in this type of approach need to commit themselves to establishing relationships with grassroots community organizations. Direct observation and participation in activities that occur in the community further enhance the authentic involvement of the service provider with the client and his or her family. Exposure through relationship building thus presents the potential for a more conducive examination and incorporation of important information about different cultural values, norms, and expectations and for creating a more culturally responsive planning process.

Butterworth et al. (1993) described some of the key principles shared by these person-centered planning approaches. The client takes a lead role in directing the process, which focuses on his or her interests, talents, dreams, and vision for the future rather than on limitations and deficiencies. Family members and significant others (e.g., friends, neighbors, clergy, teachers) share ideas and information in the planning process, and personal social relationships are relied upon as primary sources of support. The approach requires developing an unrestricted vision of what the individual would like his or her future to be and then determining what goals are needed to achieve that vision. These elements are consistent with the goals of developing culturally relevant, respectful, and empowering career planning efforts for clients with special needs from diverse cultural backgrounds. The process of becoming an authentic service provider and advocate within culturally relevant career planning is enhanced by learning about the particular culture, exploring the client's worldview, and recognizing one's own worldview as a provider involved in the concrete actualities of the client's world and reality.

Conclusion

The career planning process is dedicated to the provision of ideas, options, and hope for clients with special needs from diverse multicultural settings. Developing respectful, empowering, and culturally relevant strategies for these individuals is a complicated, multidimensional process that requires the integration of critical features related to individuals with special needs, their families, and the providers. The service provider's understanding of his or her own worldview and its relationship and interconnections with the worldviews of the persons the service provider is seeking to empower is critical. Career planning must be able to articulate, contextualize, and appropriately situate cultural differences. The cornerstone of a culturally relevant planning process is the ability to understand these multiple variables within an ideological context that recognizes the individual with special needs as the best source of information regarding what his or her future should be. The ability to include the family, the community, and one's self as a service provider in that community establishes the ideological and—more important—the emotional and behavioral connections that will lead the service provider to a greater understanding of multicultural settings, the disability community, and ultimately himself or herself in this dynamic process. Understanding and accepting diversity and empowering those who have been marginalized because of difference to be able to move from the margins to the center of society remain great challenges to those seeking to embody a collaborative, person-centered, and career planning orientation. Hearing and affirming the voices of those who have been excluded is a crucial first step in any process seeking to help others.

References

Albercht, G. L. (1992). *The disability business: Rehabilitation in America.* Newbury Park, CA: Sage.

American Psychological Association. (1993). Guidelines for providers of psychological services to ethnic, linguistic, and culturally diverse populations. *American Psychologist, 48*(1), 45–48.

Americans with Disabilities Act of 1990, 42 U.S.C. § 12101 *et seq.*

Aponte, J. F., & Crouch, R. T. (2000). The changing ethnic profile of the United States in the twenty-first century. In J. F. Aponte & J. Wohl (Eds.), *Psychological intervention and cultural diversity* (2nd ed, pp. 1–17). Boston: Allyn & Bacon.

Atkinson, D. R., & Hackett, G. (Eds.). (1998). *Counseling diverse populations* (2nd ed.). New York: McGraw-Hill.

Axelson, J. A. (1999). *Counseling and development in a multicultural society* (3rd ed.). Pacific Grove, CA: Brooks/Cole.

Barnartt, S., Schriner, K., & Scotch, R. (2001). Advocacy and political action. In G. L. Albrecht, K. D. Seelman, & M. Bury (Eds.), *Handbook of disability studies* (pp. 430–449). Thousand Oaks, CA: Sage.

Barnes, C., & Mercer, G. (2001). Disability culture: Assimilation or inclusion? In G. L. Albrecht, K. D. Seelman, & M. Bury (Eds.), *Handbook of disability studies* (pp. 515–534). Thousand Oaks, CA: Sage.

Barton, L., & Armstrong, F. (2001). Disability, education, and inclusion: Cross-cultural issues and dilemmas. In G. L. Albrecht, K. D. Seelman, & M. Bury (Eds.), *Handbook of disability studies* (pp. 693–710). Thousand Oaks, CA: Sage.

Baruth, L. G., & Manning, M. L. (1999). *Multicultural counseling and psychotherapy: A lifespan perspective* (2nd ed.). Upper Saddle River, NJ: Prentice Hall.

Bickenbach, J. E. (2001). Disability human rights, law, and policy. In G. L. Albrecht, K. D. Seelman, & M. Bury (Eds.), *Handbook of disability studies* (pp. 565–584). Thousand Oaks, CA: Sage.

Brown, C. B. (2001). Methodological paradigms that shape disability research. In G. L. Albrecht, K. D. Seelman, & M. Bury (Eds.), *Handbook of disability studies* (pp. 145–170). Thousand Oaks, CA: Sage.

Butterworth, J., Hagner, D., Heikkinen, B., Faris, S., Demello, S., & McDonough, K. (1993). *Whole life planning: A guide for organizers and facilitators.* Boston: Institute for Community Inclusion.

Cunningham, L. M. (1995). Control theory, reality therapy and cultural bias. *Journal of Reality Therapy, 15*(1), 15–22.

De La Cancela, V. (1985). Towards a sociocultural psychotherapy for low-income ethnic minorities. *Psychotherapy, 22,* 427–435.

Drake, R. F. (2001). Welfare states and disabled people. In G. L. Albrecht, K. D. Seelman, & M. Bury (Eds.), *Handbook of disability studies* (pp. 412–429). Thousand Oaks, CA: Sage.

Dybwad, G., & Bersani, H. (Eds.). (1996). *New voices: Self-advocacy by people with disabilities.* Cambridge, MA: Brookline Books.

Education for All Handicapped Children Act of 1975, 20 U.S.C. § 1400 *et seq.*

Engel, D. M. (1991, Spring). Law, culture, and children with disabilities: Education rights and the construction of difference. *Duke Law Journal,* 141–150.

Feist-Price, S. (1995). African Americans with disabilities and equity in vocational rehabilitation services: One state's view. *Rehabilitation Bulletin, 39,* 119–129.

Ferguson, P. M. (2001). Mapping the family: Disability studies and the exploration of parental response to disability. In G. L. Albrecht, K. D. Seelman, & M. Bury (Eds.), *Handbook of disability studies* (pp. 373–395). Thousand Oaks, CA: Sage.

French, S., & Swain, J. (2001). The relationship between disabled people and health and welfare professionals. In G. L. Albrecht, K. D. Seelman, & M. Bury (Eds.), *Handbook of disability studies* (pp. 734–753). Thousand Oaks, CA: Sage.

Garcia, J. G., & Zea, M. C. (Eds.). (1997). *Psychological interventions and research with Latino populations.* Boston: Allyn & Bacon.

Gill, C. J. (2001). Divided understandings: The social experience of disability. In G. L. Albrecht, K. D. Seelman, & M. Bury (Eds.), *Handbook of disability studies* (pp. 351–372). Thousand Oaks, CA: Sage.

Gomez, R., Ruiz, P., & Rumbaut, R. D. (1985). Hispanic patients: A linguo-cultural minority. *Hispanic Journal of Behavioral Sciences, 7*(2), 177–186.

Grieco, E. M., & Cassidy, R. C. (2001, March). Overview of race and Hispanic origin. *Census 2000 Brief, U.S. Census Bureau.* Retrieved April 23, 2002, from http://www.census.gov/prod/2001pubs/c2kbr01-1.pdf

Hahn, H. (1988). The politics of physical differences: Disability and discrimination. *Journal of Social Issues, 44*(1), 39–47.

Hahn, H. (1996). Antidiscrimination laws and social research on disability: The minority group perspective. *Behavioral Sciences and the Law, 14*(1), 41–59.

Hare-Mustin, R. T., & Marecek, J. (1997). Abnormal and clinical psychology: The politics of madness. In D. Fox & I. Prilleltensky (Eds.), *Critical psychology: An introduction* (pp. 104–120). Thousand Oaks, CA: Sage.

Harry, B. (1992). Developing cultural self-awareness: The first step in values clarification for early interventionists. *Topics in Early Childhood Special Education, 12,* 333–350.

Helms, J. E. (Ed.). (1993). *Black and white racial identity: Theory, research and practice.* Westport, CT: Praeger.

Helms, J. E., & Cook, D. A. (1999). *Using race and culture in counseling and psychotherapy: Theory and process.* Boston: Allyn & Bacon.

hooks, b. (1989). *Talking back: Thinking feminist, thinking black.* Boston: South End.

hooks, b. (1990). *Yearning: Race, gender, and cultural politics.* Boston: South End.

Individuals with Disabilities Education Act of 1990, 20 U.S.C. § 1400 *et seq.*

Ivey, A. E., Ivey, M. B., & Simek-Morgan, L. (1993). *Counseling and psychotherapy: A multicultural perspective* (3rd ed.). Needham Heights, MA: Allyn & Bacon.

Jenkins, A. E., Ayers, G. E., & Hunt, B. (1996). Cultural diversity and rehabilitation: The road traveled. *Rehabilitation Education, 10*(2/3), 83–103.

Kavanagh, K. H., & Kennedy, P. H. (1992). *Promoting cultural diversity.* Newbury Park, CA: Sage.

Litvak, S., & Enders, A. (2001). Support systems: The interface between individuals and environments. In G. L. Albrecht, K. D. Seelman, & M. Bury (Eds.), *Handbook of disability studies* (pp. 711–733). Thousand Oaks, CA: Sage.

Lott, B. (2002). Cognitive and behavioral distancing from the poor. *American Psychologist, 57*(2), 100–110.

Massachusetts Developmental Disabilities Council. (1996). *Annual report.* Boston: Author.

McAdoo, H. P. (Ed.). (1993). *Family ethnicity: Strength in diversity.* Newbury Park, CA: Sage.

McGoldrick, M., Giordano, J., & Pearce, J. K. (1996). *Ethnicity and family therapy* (2nd ed.). New York: Guilford Press.

McNeil, J. (2001, February). *Americans with disabilities 1997: Household economic studies, current population reports, U.S. Census Bureau.* Retrieved November 27, 2002, from http://www.census.gov/prod/2001pubs/p70-73.pdf

Mount, B. (1991). *Dare to dream: An analysis of the conditions leading to personal change for people with disabilities.* Manchester, CT: Communities.

National Council on Disability. (1993). *Meeting the unique needs of minorities with disabilities: A report to the President and congress* [Monograph]. Washington, DC: Author.

National Council on Disability. (1996). *Achieving independence: The challenge for the 21st century: A decade of progress in disability policy setting an agenda for the future* [Monograph]. Washington, DC: Author.

National Institute on Disability and Rehabilitation Research. (1998). *Notice of proposed long-range plan for fiscal year 1999-2001* [Online]. Available http://ocfo.edgov/gophroot/4fedreg//grantannlgu981102698a.txt

Nuttall, E. V., Sanchez, W., Borras-Osorio, L., Nuttall, R. L., & Varvogli, L. (1996). Assessing the culturally and linguistically different child with emotional and behavioral problems. In M. J. Breen & C. R. Fiedler (Eds.), *Behavioral approach to assessment of youth with emotional/behavioral disorders: A handbook for school-based practitioners* (pp. 451–501). Austin, TX: PRO-ED.

O'Brien, J. (1987). A guide to life-style planning: Using The Activities Catalog to integrate services and natural support systems. In B. Wilcox & G. T. Bellamy (Eds.), *A comprehensive guide to The Activities Catalog: An alternative curriculum for youth and adults with severe disabilities* (pp. 175–189). Baltimore: Brookes.

Okun, B. F., Fried, J., & Okun, M. L. (1999). *Understanding diversity: A learning-as-practice primer.* Pacific Grove, CA: Brooks/Cole.

Padilla, A. M., Lindholm, K. J., Chen, A., Duran, R., Hakuta, K., Lambert, W., et al. (1991). The English-only movement: Myths, reality, and implications for psychology. *American Psychologist, 46,* 120–130.

Paniagua, F. A. (1994). *Assessing and treating culturally diverse clients: A practical guide.* Thousand Oaks, CA: Sage.

Percy, S. L. (1989). *Disability, civil rights, and public policy: The politics of implementation.* Tuscaloosa: University of Alabama Press.

Ponterotto, J. G., & Pedersen, P. B. (1993). *Preventing prejudice: A guide for counselors and educators.* Newbury Park, CA: Sage.

Porter, G. (1995). Exploring the meaning of spirituality and its implications for counselors. *Counseling and Values, 40*(1), 69–79.

Ramirez, M. (1999). *Multicultural psychotherapy* (2nd ed.). Boston: Allyn & Bacon.

Ravaud, J. F., & Stiker, H. J. (2001). Inclusion/exclusion: An analysis of historical and cultural meanings. In G. L. Albrecht, K. D. Seelman, & M. Bury (Eds.), *Handbook of disability studies* (pp. 490–512). Thousand Oaks, CA: Sage.

Rehabilitation Act of 1973, 29 U.S.C. § 702 *et seq.*

Rehabilitation Act Amendments of 1992, 29 U.S.C. § 701 *et seq.*

Ridley, C. R. (1995). *Overcoming unintentional racism in counseling and therapy: A practitioner's guide to intentional intervention.* Thousand Oaks, CA: Sage.

Robinson, T. L., & Howard-Hamilton, M. F. (2000). *The convergence of race, ethnicity, and gender: Multiple identities in counseling.* Upper Saddle River, NJ: Prentice Hall.

Rothstein, L. F. (1998). *Disability law: Cases, materials, problems* (2nd ed.). New York: Lexis Law.

Rounds, K. A., Weil, M., & Bishop, K. K. (1994, January). Practice with culturally diverse families of young children with disabilities. *Families in Society: The Journal of Contemporary Human Services, 3–15.*

Russell, M. (1998). *Beyond ramps: Disability at the end of the social contract.* Monroe, ME: Common Courage Press.

Sanchez, W. (1996). Special education advocacy and Latinos: Empowerment and becoming a good consumer. *Special Services in the Schools, 12*(1/2), 87–107.

Sanchez, W. (1998a). The critical link between disability and culture: The political. *Connections, 4*(7), 7, 11.

Sanchez, W. (1998b). Quality world and culture. *International Journal of Reality Therapy, 17*(2), 12–16.

Sanchez, W. (1999). Reality therapy, choice theory, multiculturalism and special needs students: Practical guidelines. In L. Litwack & R. Renna (Eds.), *Special education and quality inclusion: A choice theory approach* (pp. 145–156). Denton, TX: RonJon Publishing.

Sanchez, W., & Garriga, O. (1995). The helping professions, training and Puerto Ricans: The colonialist syndrome revisited. *Latino Studies Journal, 6*(3), 63–97.

Sanchez, W., & Garriga, O. (1996). Psychotherapy, Puerto Ricans and Colonialism: The issue of awareness. *Latino Studies Journal, 7*(2), 29–50.

Sanchez, W., & Nuttall, E. V. (1995). It's about time! *Ethics and Behavior, 5,* 355–357.

Sanchez, W., & Thomas, D. (1997). Disability and health care in the Capeverdean community: Some preliminary findings. *Cimboa: A Journal of Letters, Arts and Studies, 2*(4), 43–47.

Sanchez, W., & Thomas, D. (1998). The Americans with Disabilities Act: Meeting basic needs and quality world enhancement for people with disabilities. *International Journal of Reality Therapy, 18*(1), 12–17.

Sanchez, W., Thomas, D., & Lima, A. (2002). Special services and Capeverdean children: Establishing culturally relevant connections. *Special Services in the Schools, 18*(1/2), 23–42.

Schriner, K. (1996, Spring). The Rehabilitation Act amendments of 1992: Initiatives and issues. *Journal of Applied Rehabilitation Counseling, 27*(1), 37–41.

Sciarra, D. T. (1999). *Multiculturalism in counseling.* Itasca, IL: Peacock.

Scotch, R. K. (1998). Disability as the basis for a social movement: Advocacy and the politics of definition. *Journal of Social Issues, 44*(1), 159–172.

Shakespeare, T., & Watson, N. (2001). Making the difference: Disability, politics, and recognition. In G. L. Albrecht, K. D. Seelman, & M. Bury (Eds.), *Handbook of disability studies* (pp. 546–564). Thousand Oaks, CA: Sage.

Shreve, M. (1994). The greater vision: An advocate's reflections on the Rehabilitation Act Amendments of 1992. *American Rehabilitation, 20*(1), 8–3.

Smart, J. F., & Smart, D. W. (1992). Curriculum changes in multicultural rehabilitation. *Rehabilitation Education, 6,* 105–122.

Sue, D. W., Ivey, A. E., & Pederson, P. B. (1996). *A theory of multicultural counseling and therapy.* Pacific Grove, CA: Brooks/Cole.

Sue, D. W., & Sue, D. (1999). *Counseling the culturally different: Theory and practice* (3rd ed.). New York: Wiley & Sons.

Sue, S. (1991). Ethnicity and culture in psychological research and practice. In J. D. Goodchilds (Ed.), *Psychological perspectives on human diversity in America* (pp. 51–85). Washington, DC: American Psychological Association.

Szapocznik, J., & Kurtines, W. (1993). Family psychology and cultural diversity. *American Psychologist, 48,* 400–407.

Szapocznik, J., Kurtines, W., Santiesteban, D. A., Pantin, H., Scopetta, M., Maancilla, Y., et al. (1997). The evolution of a structural ecosystemic theory for working with Latino families. In J. G. Garcia & M. C. Zea (Eds.), *Psychological interventions and research with Latino populations* (pp. 217–234). Boston: Allyn & Bacon.

Thomas, D. M. (2001). *Understanding disability in the Capeverdean community: An analysis of disability and race in Massachusetts.* Unpublished doctoral dissertation, Northeastern University, Boston.

U.S. Census Bureau. (2001, March). *Americans with disabilities: 1997–Table 1.* Retrieved November 27, 2002, from http://www.census.gov/hhes/www/disable/sipp/disab97/ds97t1.html

U.S. Census Bureau. (n.d.). *Americans with disabilities: 1994–1995, Table 1.* Retrieved November 27, 2002, from http://www.census.gov/hhes/www/disable/sipp/disable9495.html

Wehman, P. (Ed.). (1993). *The ADA mandate for social change.* Grand Rapids, MI: Brookes.

Wendell, S. (1996). *The rejected body: Feminist philosophical reflections on disability.* New York: Routledge.

West, J. (Ed.). (1991). The Americans with Disabilities Act: From policy to practice [Special issue]. *The Milbank Quarterly, 69*(1/2).

Whitney-Thomas, J., Timmons, J. C., Gilmore, D. S., & Thomas, D. M. (1999). Expanding access: Changes in vocational rehabilitation practices since the 1992 Rehabilitation Act Amendments. *Rehabilitation Counseling Bulletin, 43*(1), 30–40.

Young, I. M. (1990). *Justice and the politics of difference.* Princeton, NJ: Princeton University Press.

Zea, M. C., Garcia, J. G., Belgrave, F. Z., & Quezada, T. (1997). Socioeconomic and cultural factors in rehabilitation of Latinos with disabilities. In J. G. Garcia & M. C. Zea (Eds.), *Psychological interventions and research with Latino populations* (pp. 217–234). Boston: Allyn & Bacon.

Zinn, H. (1995). *A people's history of the United States: 1492–present* (Rev./updated ed.). New York: HarperCollins.

Zunker, V. G. (1998). *Career counseling: Applied concepts of life planning* (5th ed.). Pacific Grove, CA: Brooks/Cole.

A TREATMENT PLANNING MODEL AND IMPACT OF CONTEMPORARY ISSUES

C H A P T E R

ADOLESCENTS WITH EMOTIONAL
AND BEHAVIORAL DISORDERS

*Shirley K. Chandler, Kim E. Simmons,
and David K. Hollingsworth*

More than 7.5 million children in the United States have been diagnosed with mental illnesses and emotional and behavioral disorders (EBD), with this number continuing to grow annually. Figures from the National Alliance for the Mentally Ill place the number of young people with anxiety disorders at 13% and the number of adolescents with depression at 5% to 8%, with depression rates higher in adolescence than in childhood (Cole et al., 2002). In a longitudinal study, Cole and colleagues found that the rate of emergence of depressive symptoms increased during early adolescence, particularly between the sixth and seventh grades. This study showed a more rapid rate of increase for girls than boys, and cited possible factors such as early puberty, changes in androgen and estrogen levels, body dissatisfaction, and rape and sexual abuse. Although not all young people experience increased stress and difficulties during adolescence, factors such as mood changes and problematic family or social lives lead to increased rates of high-risk behaviors, difficulty with educational transitions, poor school attendance, deficient interpersonal and social skills, substance abuse, and self-esteem issues for many adolescents.

In 1996, Carson, Butcher, and Mineka described the field of child and adolescent abnormal behavior as lagging behind the current understandings of adult psychopathology. They identified the importance of developmental processes in any consideration of child and adolescent psychopathology. The

163

term *developmental psychopathology* became synonymous with the term *child and adolescent abnormal behavior*. In his review of the literature on psychological development and functioning during adolescence, Steinberg (2001) pointed to (a) the focus of recent research on behavioral problems, puberty, parent–adolescent relationships, and the development of self- and peer relationships and (b) the lack of research on the psychological development of the individual adolescent. Such a foundation, he stated, would provide a comprehensive theory for both normal and atypical adolescent development.

Carson et al. (1996) reported multicultural estimates of childhood maladaptive emotional and behavior rates ranging from 17% to 22%, with boys being diagnosed at a rate of two to one for girls. Husted (1997) reported that the diagnosis and treatment of adolescents with serious mental health issues seriously lagged behind that of adults. She cited professional reluctance to place a diagnostic label on a child that might "stigmatize" a child throughout his or her academic career, the difficulty in diagnosing mental illness from the developmental difficulties of adolescence, as well as the possibilities of misdiagnosis due to the side effects of medications for childhood disorders such as attention-deficit/hyperactivity disorder (ADHD). This data regarding the paucity of services for children was further supported by Davis and Stoep (1997), who estimated that only 6% to 20% of adolescents needing mental health services receive them.

Multiple changes occur during the teenage years. Adolescent behavioral problems were once considered a typical developmental occurrence (Conger, 1991), with adolescence traditionally being viewed as a stage marked by escalating periods of intense emotions, depression, and anxiety. Most adolescents resolve these issues and forge a sense of themselves, a positive self-concept, and solid family ties, and they complete the transition into early adulthood without significant emotional or behavioral difficulties (Powers, Hauser, & Kilner, 1989; Steinberg, 1999). Unfortunately, a significant number of youth do experience strong psychological difficulties during this transition that if left untreated become the roots of later adult problems (Rutter, Graham, Chadwick, & Yule, 1976). These youth tend to be undereducated and underemployed; have limited social supports; and are subject to homelessness, criminal activity, and drug use (Davis & Stoep, 1997).

Abnormal development and adolescent issues present exacerbated levels of behavioral problems that further test adult acceptance. Adolescence is an identity formation period, with adolescents striving for a balance between their personal needs and desires and the rules set forth by society. This is a time when they must differentiate themselves from their parents in both complex and subtle ways and become autonomous (Davis & Stoep, 1997). However, adolescents with serious EBD often have delayed cognitive development, lower IQ scores, and a higher rate of learning disabilities. These developmental and cognitive delays may contribute to the development of conduct disorders and impede educational, vocational, and social outcomes. Many of these youth are sexually active and are prone to sexually transmitted diseases due to poor impulse control, have problems with the legal system, are frequently expelled or suspended from school, and often run away and/or drop out of school. Davis and Stoep found that caregivers of adolescents with EBD were themselves faced with mental illness, substance abuse, and poverty. They pointed out that adolescents with EBD are more likely than their nondisabled peers to experience multiple separations from family members due to divorce, death, incarceration, or institutionalization.

Mental health problems for adolescents include all diagnosable mental, emotional, and behavioral disorders. Undiagnosed or untreated, these disorders can lead to violent or suicidal behavior in adolescents. The National Youth Violence Prevention Resource Center (2001) statistics indicated that between 70% and 80% of children with diagnosable mental disorders receive services through the school or juvenile justice systems, which are generally ill-equipped to recognize or address mental disorders.

Children who are depressed do not behave like adults who are depressed, (Weiner, 1980). According to the classification criteria found in the *Diagnostic and Statistical Manual of Mental Disorders–Fourth Edition–Text Revision* (DSM–IV–TR; American Psychiatric Association, 2000), the behavioral component of an adult with depression more likely contains depressed behavior and demonstrates depressed affect. In adolescents, the behavioral component could be substance abuse, aggression, antisocial acts, or social withdrawal from adults (Balk, 1995). Weiner (1980) suggested that these behaviors result from the tendency of adolescents *to do* things rather than *to think* about their lives. Their behavior becomes an attempt to resolve feelings or thoughts that are unwanted or intolerable. Perhaps the period of adolescence also poses such serious challenges to their self-esteem that adolescents who are depressed tend to disguise their feelings to protect themselves. This type of adolescent, faced with feelings of incompetence, would feel great distress centered on an increased self-consciousness and doubts about his or her self-worth, which are critical during this time when the individual is fighting for independence and a separate identity.

Anger and strong feelings of resistance to dependency upon adults lead to a variety of acting-out behaviors (Petti & Larson, 1987). Restlessness, anxiety, and alienation are typical symptoms for adolescents who are depressed. As they fight these feelings, they may engage in several types of behavior — temper tantrums, oppositional behaviors, and delinquent acts (Weiner, 1980; White, 1989)— as signals for help. These become elaborate, well-established patterns of behaviors, trapping both adults and adolescents in repetitive spirals of negative behaviors and consequences.

Furthermore, other disorders show a common comorbidity with depression. The comorbidity of depression and anxiety was found by Kovacs (1990) to run between 30% and 70% among all adolescents. Some authors (Kashani, Reid, & Rosenberg, 1989; Kovacs, Paulaskas, Gastonis, & Richards, 1988) found that depression is present in 10% to 35% of conduct disorders. Eating disorders and substance abuse also are common companions of depression (Attie & Brooks-Gunn, 1990).

Depression appears to be correlated with a broad spectrum of other disorders and behavioral problems in adolescence, such as conduct disorders and ongoing anxiety-related disorders. Although such depression may have direct etiological links, it may be masked by more overt behaviors and not readily identified. This masking can lead to confusion of reports by various observers of that behavior (e.g., the adolescent, parents, teachers, and mental health professionals). In that treatment plans are based on self-reports and other reported data, treatment would then be poorly focused and ineffective. Husted (1997) pointed out that most teachers, school counselors, and even pediatricians do not recognize the symptoms of DSM–IV–TR diagnoses. According to the National Institute of Mental Health (NIMH, 2001), there is a "heated debate" in our society regarding the issue of medication and psychotherapies for children. Children who go untreated cannot learn, do not form healthy relationships, and are often placed on the road to jail, rather than college, at an early age.

Takanishi (1993) wrote that complicating the issue was a major shift that is occurring in the way adolescence is conceptualized in U.S. society. She suggested that society is beginning to view adolescents as more positive, less alienated from adults, and growing through a period of greater social and personal opportunity. To assist this transition, this focus on the individual adolescent must shift toward the critical nature of the social institutions and processes — including family and schools — that shaped him or her. They must collaborate strongly together to produce solid developmental outcomes that encourage the adolescent's adaptability. Unfortunately, such collaboration rarely occurs. This is especially true for the adolescent with emotional and behavioral issues, whether he or she is considered at risk or has been diagnosed as having a disorder.

The original and subsequent edition of this chapter pointed to adolescence as the "ideal and only realistic period to initiate vocational interventions" with children and adolescents who have EBD (Hollingsworth, 1982, p. 186). The logic for this was, and remains, valid in that adolescence is when an individual begins to actually try out various vocational roles; however, for that very reason, it was also a faulty assumption. Due to the behavioral and emotional difficulties that exist at this period, it seems more appropriate to begin to assist children in developing solid self-esteem and a conceptual basis of self at an earlier age. Hartoonian and Van Scotter (1996) summarized one method for accomplishing these tasks in a model for learning a living. They suggested that children and adolescents must be exposed at an early age in the educational process to the requisites of citizenship: (a) fairness, (b) cooperation, (c) integrity, (d) responsibility, and (e) performance of quality work. These building blocks of success in U.S. society are the ingredients least likely to be found in children and adolescents with EBD.

Who are the adolescents with EBD, and how do they develop these disorders? Certain facts are understood. For example, children who are experiencing emotional and behavioral difficulties are at a higher risk of experiencing those same difficulties during adolescence than children who are physically, cognitively, or sensory challenged. Their behavior poses a greater risk, and the environmental responses only amplify the normal developmental stressors of growing up. Children who are diagnosed as schizophrenic or who suffer from an acute mood disorder often regress so badly under the stress of adolescence that they are under constant supervised care or therapy. The etiological link between childhood adolescent disorders and young adult psychiatric disorders has been established (American Psychiatric Association, 2000; Carson et al., 1996; Cobb, 1995; NIMH, 2000; Steinberg, 2001).

The DSM–IV–TR lists 10 diagnostic categories in the section that addresses disorders first diagnosed in infancy, childhood, and adolescence (see Table 6.1).

In this chapter, we focus on attention-deficit disorder (ADD); disruptive behavior disorders; and other disorders of infancy, childhood, and adolescence. These categories capture the majority of the disruptive emotional and behavioral responses that children and adolescents display or present.

TABLE 6.1
General Categories of Mental Disorders
of Children from the DSM–IV–TR

Mental retardation

Learning disorders

Motor skills disorders

Communication disorders

Pervasive developmental disorders

Attention-deficit and disruptive behavior disorders

Feeding and eating disorders of infancy or early childhood

Tic disorders

Elimination disorders

Other disorders of infancy, childhood, or adolescence

The Adolescent with EBD:
A Conceptual Definition

The contiguous nature of the development of childhood to adolescent to young adult EBD is illustrated in the DSM–IV. The DSM–IV–TR recognizes the age of onset as an important feature in determining the course and prognosis of any disorder. Disorders usually first diagnosed in infancy, childhood, or adolescence make up a separate section of the DSM–IV–TR from those that typically appear in adulthood. Ten major groups are presented in the infancy, childhood, or adolescence section, each determined by a specific disturbance in intellectual, behavioral, emotional, or physical development.

Behavioral Disorders

Behavioral disorders include both attention-deficit and conduct disorders. Attention-deficit disorders (ADD) are those in which the clinical signs are "developmentally inappropriate" inattention and impulsivity. This disorder has three variants: predominantly hyperactive-impulsive type, predominantly inattentive type, and a combined type. Conduct disorders can be mild, moderate, or severe in intensity and have two variants: childhood onset and adolescent onset.

Hyperactive-impulsive type is evidenced by an inability to stay with tasks, problems with task-attack strategies, and difficulties in completing tasks. Work is often done sloppily and in an impulsive manner. School activities presented in a group format are particularly difficult and tend to exaggerate the difficulties of a young person with this disorder because sustained attention is required. In other words, this type of ADD is manifested by exaggerated gross-motor activity. In adolescence, such activity takes the form of restlessness and fidgeting. Haphazard efforts, poor organization, and lack of goal orientation distinguish this disorder from overactivity. The features of the predominantly inattentive type are similar to those of the predominantly hyperactive-impulsive type, but they are milder, with fewer hyperactive behaviors and shorter duration. This type is primarily manifested by an inability to focus attention and to complete tasks, as well as in impulsive task-attack strategies.

Conduct disorders in adolescence have a repetitive and persistent pattern of conduct that violates either the rights of others or socially normative behavior. The two categories of this disorder, childhood onset and adolescent onset, are based on whether the disordered behavior was established before or after 10 years of age. The earlier the onset, the more likely it is that the individual will demonstrate a preceding oppositional-defiant disorder and a following antisocial personality disorder as an adult. Individuals with the childhood-onset type usually are male; however, the male-to-female ratio is much smaller with adolescent-onset type. The general etiology suggests that severe or acute forms of this disorder tend to become lifelong personality features, whereas milder forms tend to improve slightly toward the acceptable norm. Furthermore, both subtypes lack a competent self-view; have poor frustration tolerance; are prone to hyperirritability and temper outbursts; and tend toward highly provocative, reckless behaviors. Academic performance is often lower than expected for age and intelligence levels. In short, these are adolescents who are vested in their toughness and lack the more normative appropriate skills for success in life.

With the prevalence of juvenile-related violence, such as shootings not only in the United States but elsewhere in the world, we would be remiss not to discuss the problems of school violence and gang-related behaviors. Delinquency, substance abuse, conduct-disordered behavior, school failure, and adolescent violence are all dynamically linked (Adams, Gullotta, & Markstrom-Adams, 1994; Henggler, 1989; Kazdin, 1987; NIMH, 2000, 2001; Schenicke, 1991). Gaskins (2001) cited teen violence statistics that showed that 17% of students in Grades 9 through 12 carried a gun, knife, or other weapon to school in 1999; firearm-related homicides are the second leading cause of death among teens 15 to 19 years of age; and 3 out of 10 students in high school reported that they had committed a violent act such as armed robbery or aggravated assault the previous year. The National Center of Juvenile Justice's 1999 figures cited 103,900 arrests for violent crimes committed by people younger than 18. These figures included 1,400 arrests for murder and 69,600 arrests for aggravated assault. An average of six to seven youths are murdered each day in this country (NIMH, 2000). Wheeler and Baron (1994) summarized the issue of violence by simply stating that in 1991, 1.9 million violent victimizations occurred among the 18.1 million U.S. teenagers. They suggested that adolescents ages 12 to 15 are twice as likely as older adolescents to be victimized at school. Perhaps more sobering is that 282,000 students are physically attacked in secondary-level schools *each month of the school year.* Gang-related violence prevention is beyond the scope of this chapter; however, because millions of adolescents attend school each day in a state of fear, it is conceivable that this fear will have a negative affect on the child who is vulnerable. Children who have behavioral difficulties do tend to get caught up in this cycle more easily than those without such difficulties. As a result, they are less likely to be in school, with peers, and at home.

Emotional Disorders

Emotional disorders include mood, anxiety-oriented, and other adjustment-related disorders. The DSM–IV–TR also lists separation anxiety and reactive attachment disorders of infancy and childhood. Although separation anxiety disorder is far from uncommon, with a 4% prevalence estimate, reactive attachment disorder is relatively uncommon. The overanxious disorder of childhood and adolescence is now included under the adult generalized anxiety disorder. The avoidant disorder of adolescence is not in the DSM–IV, but the developmental pathway to the DSM–IV–TR diagnosis of avoidant personality disorder is made much clearer in the introductory material to that diagnosis. The increasingly shy and avoidant adolescent, who clearly has problems establishing and maintaining social relationships, is at risk for clinically avoidant behaviors.

In adolescents who are clinically avoidant, the practitioner will find far more avoidance and overanxiousness. Avoidance-prone adolescents show a persistent and excessive shyness, and they shrink away from strangers with sufficient severity as to interfere with normal social activities (i.e., relationships with family members, peers, and others). If sufficiently developed, this adolescent behavioral disorder will become the avoidant personality disorder in adulthood.

Overanxious adolescents are fearful and worry excessively. Their behavior is not focused on any single situation or object (phobic responses) and is not a response to a specific event or traumatic experience. These adolescents tend to be hypermature, obsessive, and perfectionistic. They tend toward excessive conformity, yet are extremely tense and unable to relax, and they express fears regarding competency, embarrassment, and success.

These adolescent behaviors are often overlooked because they are not affrontive or confrontive to adults. However, students exhibiting these behaviors can benefit from vocational counseling interventions. These behaviors (inability to attach themselves to others in relationships, fear of failure and success, obsessive-compulsiveness, and insistent worrying) are now recognized as indicators in the developmental course of adult diagnoses, such as generalized anxiety disorder, obsessive-compulsive disorder, schizoaffective disorder, and schizophreniform disorder. These behaviors are also linked to adolescent depression (Hollingsworth, 1995; NIMH, 2000). In short, the behaviors become chronic as they develop, thus further inhibiting the individual from obtaining a normal, satisfying life. The link between the unimpeded development of adolescent abnormal behaviors and adult abnormal behaviors makes it crucial to detect and treat adolescents with EBD. Unfortunately, they may be best recognized as having disorders after they become adults.

In discussing this group of adolescents, it is very important to avoid stereotyping or labeling. The EBD categories contain many of the observable characteristics used to define the troubled adolescent: attentional deficits, distractibility, impulsivity, hyperactivity, conduct disruptions, argumentativeness, provocative behavior, severe immaturity, severe depressions, and substance abuse. This listing, which essentially describes students with emotional and behavioral troubles, is composed of observable behaviors that result in adult predispositions, rather than labels that may serve to create prejudicial judgments.

The use of such observable behaviors aids practitioners in forming a consistent clinical picture of an adolescent's needs. This practice is consistent and corresponds with the appropriate diagnostic strategies in the DSM–IV–TR and other relevant research literature (Hollingsworth, 1991, 1995; Ollendick & Hersen, 1993; Reynolds, 1992; Satcher, 2000).

The adolescent with emotional and behavioral difficulties focused on in this chapter is a child whose adaptive strategies have failed in normal developmental tasks. As a result, that person manifests varying degrees of emotional and behavioral difficulties, which are primarily an attempt to make sense out of what to that person is a terribly indifferent or inconsistent world. Adolescents with overt psychiatric impairments (anxiety, avoidance, reactive attachment, overanxiety, schizoaffective, elective autism, and identity disorders) are excluded from this chapter because they are considered a specific subgroup whose behaviors tend to be more extreme, isolating them from any contact with that world they find so abhorrent. Without attempting to link childhood and adolescent psychiatric disorders to the definition of adolescents with EBD, we can say that psychiatric impairment *does* seem to become the ultimate failure of the child's ability to adapt successfully to his or her world (Hollingsworth, 1995; Reynolds, 1992; Wallbrown, Fremont, Nelson, Wilson, & Fischer, 1979). Thus, the adolescent with a psychiatric impairment is not ready to benefit from the efforts of vocational planning. When he or she approaches lower incidences of behaviors that incurred the diagnosis, then the initial steps of vocational planning may commence.

Understanding Adolescent Behavior: A Clinical Perspective

Even with the aid of the DSM–III, and its subsequent revisions, it was not until the 1980s that the field of childhood mental health began to change. These changes happened, in part, because of tougher reimbursement and practice guidelines (Lonigan, Elbert, & Johnson, 1998). Most disorders are diagnosed by their symptoms as well as by a functional impairment. A diagnosis is made when these symptoms and signs meet the DSM–IV–TR criteria for a disorder. Diagnosing childhood mental disorders is much more difficult, however, in that many of the symptoms such as fearfulness, food fads, habitual behaviors, episodes of aggression, or difficulty paying attention may occur normally throughout childhood. Clinicians thus may overdiagnose normal behavior or miss a diagnosis by failing to recognize abnormal behavior (Satcher, 2000).

Current treatments are more apt to use a multimodal approach and may include pharmacological and psychosocial therapies. This type of approach has been especially beneficial in working with adolescents with ADHD, anxiety, and depression (Kearney & Silverman, 1998; Satcher, 2000). Major forms of psychotherapy for children include supportive psychodynamic, cognitive–behavioral, interpersonal, and family counseling. These types of therapies are especially important for adolescents who cannot take — or whose parents do not want them to take — medications. The multimodal type of intervention also helps to relieve parental and sibling stress, and it provides parents and teachers with methods for managing symptoms.

Pharmacological therapies for adolescents with mental disorders have dramatically increased over the past 10 years, but research in this area has lagged behind. Only a few studies have focused on the safety and efficacy of medications utilized for mental and somatic disorders. This is even more problematic when medications developed for adults are prescribed for adolescents. Multimodal treatments have the potential to reduce the amount of psychotropic medication considered necessary, thereby improving parental and patient compliance. The combined effectiveness of pharmacological and psychosocial treatments is seldom studied, however (Satcher, 2000).

Depression

Depression is the most frequently diagnosed mood disorder in adolescents, and it is associated with an increased risk for suicidal behaviors. According to NIMH (2001), the suicide rate among adolescents and young adults has doubled since 1964 and is now the third leading cause of death among 15- to 24-year-olds and the fourth leading cause among 10- to 14-year-olds. Children who are depressed are sad; lose interest in activities; criticize themselves; and feel unloved, pessimistic, and hopeless about the future. They are often irritable, and this irritability may lead to aggressive behaviors (DSM–IV–TR). For adolescents with bipolar disorder, the initial symptoms may start with depression and alternate with episodes of mania. According to Anderson and McGee (1994), approximately two thirds of adolescents with a major depressive disorder have another mental illness. Treatment includes both antidepressant medications and cognitive–behavioral therapy.

Anxiety Disorders

Anxiety disorders are the most common mental health problems for adolescents (Costello et al., 1996). According to a study of 9- to 17-year-olds, the prevalence is 13%. For a diagnosis in this area, the anxiety or fear must cause distress or affect academic, social, or vocational functioning. Symptoms may include excessive worry, redoing of tasks, the need for constant reassurance, social phobias, extreme fear, intrusive thoughts/memories, and separation anxiety. Individual disorders in this area include panic, posttraumatic stress, obsessive compulsive and generalized anxiety. Cognitive–behavioral therapy and psychodynamic treatment, along with serotonin reuptake inhibitors, have been found to be useful.

Attention Deficit/Hyperactivity Disorder

ADHD is the most commonly diagnosed psychiatric disorder of childhood and is characterized by both inattention and hyperactivity-impulsivity. Three to 5% of school-age children are estimated to have ADHD, and research has shown that ADHD tends to run in families (Shaffer et al., 1996). Children with ADHD have difficulty with multiple settings and peer relationships, are easily distracted, and do not appear to listen when spoken to. ADHD has been shown to have long-term effects on academic and vocational functioning. Two major interventions, the use of psychostimulants and behavioral modification, have been the mainstay of treatment for ADHD. Other treatments in this area include biofeedback, special diets, allergy treatment, megavitamins, chiropractic adjustment, and specially colored glasses. None of these treatments, however, have been proven scientifically to work.

Understanding Adolescent Behavior: A Theoretical Perspective

Many models have been proposed to aid the helper in understanding adolescent behavior (Conger, 1991; Hollingsworth, 1995; Jones, 1980; Takanishi, 1993). One commonality exists: Adolescent needs are very similar to adult needs. Adolescents need to know they are liked, appreciated, respected, and valued. They need control over their environment and to feel a part of that environment. The adolescent has a need to experience a sense of personal significance, a sense of personal competency, and a sense of personal potency. The practioner plays a critical role by establishing opportunities for such experiences to occur. To accomplish this through a vocationally oriented intervention, the helper must focus on the positive elements of the adolescent's behavior and feelings. Many behaviors are very normal responses by the adolescent to what he or she may perceive as an abnormal world — one in which he or she does not feel a part. It is especially important that adults who are helpers keep this firmly in mind.

Adolescents with troubled behavior and emotional problems have difficulties at school or home in one or more of three areas, involving feelings of significance, power, and competency. For example, the DSM–IV–TR describes adolescents with conduct disorders as those who have chosen abnormal methods to meet their needs for power and competency through very poor relationship patterns and aggressiveness. Adolescents with attentional deficits and affective disorders have these same three needs but have developed behaviors that even further frustrate their ability to satisfy them (i.e., extreme impulsivity, worry, heightened levels of fear, and avoidance of contact with others). If adolescents cannot meet these needs in a socially acceptable manner, they turn to unacceptable behaviors. For example, an adolescent's disruptive behavior is most often used as a means to gain support or approval from his or her peers. This provides the adolescent with a sense of significance and acceptance while confirming his or her control over the environment by giving the adolescent the knowledge that he or she can successfully frustrate adults. In this way, such behavior becomes valued and necessary because it earns the adolescent the needed elements of self-esteem — that is, opportunities to gain recognition, control of the environment, and the ability to achieve in a meaningful way. Disruptive and antisocial behaviors thus are often developmentally "normative" for these individuals.

Adolescence is a time when young people are seeking to establish their self-concepts, build personal relationships, and clarify their responsibilities. It is a time when it is normal to actively and intensely confront and question the world. Although adults tend to view the adolescent's activity as unproductive or annoying, many times an adolescent's acting-out behavior is merely a natural part of normal developmental growth.

As adolescent developmental psychology literature clearly suggests, developing a personal identity and gaining independence from parents and other adults are major tasks (Conger, 1991; Santrock, 1993; Steinberg, 1999). During this time, both the adult and adolescent experience some confusion and ambiguity concerning the outcomes of these tasks. It is difficult for parents and other adults in the growing adolescent's world to adjust to these role changes and to allow the adolescent to make his or her own decisions and cope with the natural consequences or outcomes of those choices. Adults also find it hard to accept the fact that the adolescent's confrontive nature is much less of a response to adult behavior than to his or her own need to identify and experience his or her limitations and inabilities. Adults often fail to recognize that their role is not to control adolescent behavior but to facilitate more productive ways of expressing needs and desires.

Adolescents often cite their peer relationships within and outside the school setting as the single most interesting aspect of their life. This is amplified for those who are behaviorally and emotionally troubled. Because these adolescents are more likely to have experienced failure both at home and at school, it is only natural that they turn toward peer relationships as a more satisfying aspect of their life. Peer interaction and relationships are, therefore, more likely to replace failure in other areas of their lives and to accord them some sense of worth and opportunity to experience success.

The adolescent has the need to form a self-identity but is constantly faced by the pressures of peers, family, and school to conform to what the norm might be at the time. In addition, although adolescents have a need for independence, in order to feel safe, to feel a part of their daily life, they have to assume a certain amount of dependency. Adolescents have a need to express their thoughts and their feelings, but society, especially the school environment, always presents them with evidence of their skill deficits. Societal norms often discourage or punish personal expressions. The bottom line for adolescents, as for children and for many adults, is that self-gratification and the attempts to fulfill that drive are punished. It is difficult for adolescents to learn to put off the need for immediate gratification in return for rather doubtful long-range benefits. In short, it is very difficult for adolescents to adapt to this complex and often inconsistent, inconsiderate society. Adolescents find themselves inundated with a large amount of value-laden information and find themselves overloaded daily by new ideas, new feelings, and new choices. This creates confusion and anxiety, and the adolescent naturally experiences a sense of impotence and frustration.

If adolescents are experiencing difficulties in forming their sense of personal significance, personal competency, or personal potency, additional frustration from day-to-day life compounds problems in these areas. Adolescents often are granted personal freedoms for which they are unprepared, and they do not know how to act. They may lack the skills and attitudes necessary to function effectively in an environment that emphasizes personal freedom and self-motivation. In any environment or program that emphasizes these skills, deficiencies will doom the adolescent to failure.

The DSM–IV–TR recognizes many such developmental etiologies. Underachievement and alienation in childhood and adolescence may become Schizoid Personality Disorders; avoidant behaviors become Avoidant Personality

Disorders; oppositional behavior becomes Conduct-Disordered Behavior, which becomes an Antisocial Personality Disorder; and identification issues become Borderline Personality Disorders. In each case, the lack of a therapeutic environment — an environment with a clear and adequately defined set of rules — will lead to the exacerbation of the adolescent problematic behavior and its transformation into the corresponding adult behavior disorder (Halleck, 1978; Kazdin, 1996).

It is not uncommon to describe adolescents who have behavioral problems or who are experiencing difficulties in school as being devoid of any preparation for responsible, self-initiated behaviors. Like any manual skill, responsibility takes practice and is usually acquired gradually. Responsibility therefore should be given gradually and accompanied, as with any kind of skill training, by continual feedback and guidance. Adolescents should be expected to make mistakes to acquire the skills of self-direction, self-motivation, and responsibility. Adults must be willing to commit the time and energy to assist adolescents in developing these skills.

An additional area of difficulty for the developing adolescent is ineffective or faulty adult role modeling. Adolescents draw their important role models from a variety of sources, such as popular friends and successful musicians, sports figures, and media personalities. Unfortunately, most troubled adolescents have rarely been exposed to adults who modeled the important values that lead to success. These values include warmth, excitement about life, interpersonal competency, and basic human concern. Longitudinal studies have shown that higher levels of parental supervision during childhood correlate with less antisocial behavior. On the more troubling side of role modeling, researchers have found that parents often do not define antisocial behavior, such as bullying or hitting other children or engaging in delinquent acts such as shoplifting, as something that should be discouraged (NIMH, 2000).

Research has shown that troubled adolescents are more likely than their peers to have poor relationships (Hollingsworth, 1991; Jorne, 1978; Lytell, 1978). More specifically, family relationships are dominated by parental rejection or indifference and a reciprocal hostility. Role models who tangibly interact with the adolescent are more likely to directly influence behavior. Vicarious models also influence the adolescent's behavior, but with much less force. If an adolescent is presented with adults who are overtly judgmental and fail to show warmth and support, he or she probably will not develop a strong sense of personal significance. Furthermore, if this adolescent is labeled deviant, either behaviorally or emotionally, he or she probably will resort to increased or continued levels of antisocial behavior. In sum, the label becomes a self-fulfilling prophecy.

Understanding Adolescent Behavior: A Career Development Perspective

During the 1998–1999 school year, 463,172 children and youth with serious emotional disabilities were served in the public schools (*Twenty-Second Annual Report to Congress*, U.S. Department of Education, 2000). The National Longitudinal Transition Study completed in 1992 identified being classified as emotionally disturbed as negatively associated with school performance and completion (Benz, Lindstrom, & Yovanoff, 2000; DeStefano & Wagner, 1991). The educational implications for students with serious behavioral disorders encompass the mastering of academic skills; the development of social skills; and self-awareness, self-esteem, and self-control (Chandler & Pankaskie, 1997, 2002). Career education, both in vocational and academic programs, is a major part of secondary education for all students, including those with EBD.

Wehman (1992) suggested that EBD could be summarized as (a) an inability to learn that is not based on physiological factors, (b) poor relationship skills, (c) ongoing unhappiness or depression, and (d) inappropriate feelings and behaviors in normal situations. There are millions of adolescents with these disorders, perhaps as high as 12% of all children and adolescents in the United States. Nationally, the high school dropout rates average approximately 12% (Scanlon & Mallard, 2002). The 1998 U.S. Department of Education statistics indicated that only 30% of high school students with disabilities graduate with a high school diploma (Benz et al., 2000). However, the dropout rate for students with EBD has been estimated to be as high as 64% (Scanlon & Mallard 2002), twice the dropout rate of children with disabilities. In addition, Wehman (1992) reported that only 40% to 50% of individuals with EBD are employed and only 17% go on to postsecondary school programs. These rates are less than half of the general population rates. Common factors cited by students with EBD for dropping out of school included lack of interest and poor attendance. Consequently, young adults with EBD generally have lower self-efficacy and low self-esteem, with little confidence in their work skills or an ability to take control of their lives (Chandler & Pankaskie 1997, 2002; Scanlon & Mallard, 2002). They are less prepared to participate in educational programs after leaving high school and less likely to successfully take on adult roles that lead to self-sufficiency.

A career development perspective for this group of adolescents centers on the need to define career exploration, education, and preparation for entry into the world of work. Phelps and Lutz (1997) suggested a need to assess each adolescent's developmental ability and current achievement levels. Wehman (1992) stated that "students with behavior disorders are spending too much time in the classroom, too little time in community-based training and virtually no time in paid work experience" (p. 361). They virtually have no experience and little appropriate knowledge about the world of work. These adolescents need vocational training and placement activities that are built on integrated situations in well-supported transition plans.

Four factors are significant in considering career development for adolescents with behavioral and emotional difficulties (Tolbert, 1980). The *reality factor* refers to the environmental pressures involved in making vocational decisions. In adolescence, reality factors, that is, those aspects of the adolescent's life that can facilitate decision making and those that will inhibit such decision making, are acutely important. Wehman (1992) noted that this factor is crucial when considering career development planning for this population. As a system, education has not focused on jobs, paid work experiences, and unpaid work experiences as part of school activity. Students such as those described in this chapter are impulsive and act out, often unnecessarily, which can serve to keep them from successful work. They have little or no real-life, appropriate experience and thus rely on old behaviors.

The second significant factor is the *influence of the educational process*. Successful educational experiences facilitate flexibility in the individual's ability to make vocational choices. This is a challenge that schools have not been successful at addressing (Wehman, 1992). The adolescent with EBD requires an individualized curriculum to meet his or her unique and specific educational and psychological needs. Wehman stated that this can be addressed through concrete instruction in real settings. The troubled adolescent's difficulties in establishing a sense of personal significance often preclude success within the school environment; therefore, as Wehman suggested, "Less time should be spent trying to solve the student's underlying problems and more time should be used developing an array of competent vocational and community skills" (p. 362). Unfortunately, the school setting often reinforces a person's previous or current difficulties.

The third factor is the *emotional factor*. Adolescence is an extremely troubled time even for nondisabled adolescents, but for the adolescent who is mentally troubled, it is horrendous. The turmoil, upheavals, and instability are all very real for the adolescent. The greater the emotional unrest, the less likely the adolescent will be ready or willing to make vocational decisions.

Finally, individual values are very significant in making vocational choices. To make decisions about different careers, adolescents must have a *life perspective*. Individuals must have a sense of what they want from life. Adolescents who are troubled do not usually have a long-term perspective of life.

The school-to-work transition movement, which has evolved since the first edition of this book, began to address adolescents with EBD in the late 1980s.

The approach taken by this movement seems to be most associated with functionalism and lacks a theoretical framework. Although traditional vocational development models were not intended for the complexity of today's youth, one must have a starting point for conceptualizing the process. The most parsimonious view of vocational development that would be useful in this discussion is Ginzberg's (1971) approach, which utilizes three chronological periods in vocational development: *fantasy, tentative,* and *realistic.* The adolescents that this chapter addresses have unique issues in each period that serve to exacerbate vocational immaturity and indecision. The focus of this discussion is on the tentative and realistic periods; however, most adolescents with behavioral and emotional impairments are fixated in the fantasy period of vocational development. Because they lack concrete experience in the world and strong role models, they never acquire the values, behaviors, or abilities required for vocational success. This problem will haunt them throughout their development.

The tentative period is composed of interests, capacity, value, and transition stages, and it runs from about age 12 through age 18. It is called *tentative* because reality factors are neither adequately developed nor included in the choices and activities. Career options at each stage for this group are severely limited. The adolescents lack solid role models and prior experiences to build on. Their peers probably are similar and have not been overly successful in school. As a group, adolescents who are troubled are usually prone to frustration and easily upset by dependency on another person, especially if he or she is a caretaker or parent. These adolescents approach the last stage of this period, the transitional stage, with a poorly developed sense of responsibility, no sense of directedness, and little insight into their abilities and skills. They have had little success in school or at home in pursuing their own ends. Instead, they have had years of exhibiting behaviors that are not conducive to encouraging adults to grant them further independence. Whether this is a by-product of adult frustration with the adolescent's behavior or of more benign efforts to protect him or her, the outcome is the same. The adolescent is not prepared for self-directed, responsible ventures into the world of work.

The realistic period consists of the exploration and crystallization stages. This period presents the adolescent with the need to make actual choices about vocations, education, and almost all aspects of adult life. At this period, in terms of development, adolescents are expected to begin their final exploration of their vocational options. Unfortunately, adolescents who are troubled are very poorly prepared for activity in the realistic period. They have poor decision-making skills, lack work experience and knowledge, and generally have poor relationship skills. In sum, they are in need of remediation provided by adequate vocational counseling and planning.

The Helper as a Factor in the Developmental Process

Perhaps the most difficult thing for a helper to realize in dealing with adolescents who are troubled is that adults' biggest problem can often be themselves. Most adults have a problem with the acting-out behavior of adolescents. The adolescent often comes to the helper with a variety of labels, including learning disabled, hyperactive, delinquent, behaviorally disordered, and emotionally disturbed. The individual has a long history of behavioral manifestations that have earned him or her the given label. The labeling process is known to be detrimental and harmful because it comes with a set of negative expectations. The adolescent also knows that he or she is different, is considered "dumb," and is a problem to adults. The helper's major goal is to avoid the labeling process and begin with the positive behavioral elements that the adolescent offers.

The helper's primary goal is to facilitate the adolescent's social competencies through developing a belief in themselves, a sense of personal significance or positive self-concept, and planning. A secondary goal is to establish effective problem-solving strategies and decision-making skills for these adolescents. Although the assumption still exists that therapeutic interventions are handled by therapists and counselors and vocational planning is a separate issue, both are intertwined inexplicably but as separate tasks. The final task is to assist the adolescent in finding a productive vocational pursuit and surviving that transition.

Acceptance in the Here-and-Now

Although the adolescent with EBD learns little in the traditional educational process, any intervention should be geared at reducing skill deficits. First, however, the helper must forge a relationship with the adolescent. Relationships must be based on a collaborative approach that builds upon the existing situation for the adolescent. Often these adolescents are poor decision makers and have weak or poor relationship-building and maintenance skills. They also have little to no occupational knowledge. The helper must constantly guard against overwhelming the adolescent with performance demands for which he or she does not have the skills. The helper instead should present the adolescent with responsibilities and opportunities commensurate with what can be realistically expected. To accomplish this, the helper must provide the adolescent with opportunities to practice responsible behaviors. Youth with EBD do try to prove to helpers and themselves that they can be successful at a behavioral goal. Adult acceptance of their behavior and feedback about its impact facilitates trust and communication. Adolescents often respond with surprising maturity to adult trust and, conversely, with anger and resentment to adults who lack trust in them.

Developing Readiness

Many adolescents who are troubled have poor adult role models who demonstrate inadequate parenting or inappropriate adult concerns rather than consistent concern, competency, and warmth. Adolescents need consistent structure and discipline. They expect rules and boundaries, and low expectations and lack of discipline indicate to them a lack of concern and respect. Any helper working with this population therefore must help adolescents to feel that their struggles to define themselves and their roles are meaningful and worthy. To accomplish this, the helper must devise activities in response to a variety of needs the struggling adolescent has, both internal (e.g., access to adequate career information, consistent decision-making strategies, relationship building and maintenance skills) and external (e.g., barriers presented by others' response to the behavior, such as acting out and other provocative behaviors). These activities are designed to move the adolescent to a state of readiness for career and vocational counseling. The more deeply troubled the adolescent is, the less likely he or she will be ready for or able to handle a vocational intervention. Interventions aimed at facilitating productive vocational behaviors require a helper who can communicate effectively with these adolescents, one who can provide an open and honest relationship.

The increase in the amount of quality contact with open, caring adults tends to reduce the adolescent's ever-present fear and anxiety. The perception of comfort increases as the adult's behavior becomes more understood by and predictable to the adolescent. There are two caveats: Not all adolescents want to be open and will suspect the adult's behavior, and when an adult displays a need for acceptance, there is a natural tendency for adolescents to abuse it and take advantage of the looseness and lack of structure. Any lack of expectations becomes a void that the adolescent must attempt to fill. As in the case of too much structure, the adolescent will resort to more available behaviors to fill that perceived void. The adolescent with EBD resorts to acting out or other disruptive behaviors. The helper's primary goal thus is to begin with structure, yet to have a genuine interest and concern for the adolescent.

The helper must focus on responding in a genuine and straightforward manner to any situation that evolves. Each adolescent is unique and able to accept varying degrees of both openness and genuineness from adults. Focusing on the behavior of the moment accomplishes two things in the growing relationship. First, it provides consistent feedback for the adolescent, who often has not been given that courtesy in his or her relationships with adults. This minimizes chances for misunderstanding and provides opportunities for modeling appropriate relationship-maintenance skills for the adolescent. Second, if problems do arise, as often is the case, this method encourages their resolution. While this is a trial-and-error learning method for the practitioner and takes time to perfect, the benefits far outweigh the effort spent. It will take time for any adolescent client to reciprocate, but once begun, this signals a readiness to proceed.

Developing Effective Behavioral Change Programs

The goal of any program or intervention with adolescents who are behaviorally or emotionally troubled is to enhance their basic self-concept while increasing their sense of personal self-control and, ultimately, their sense of significance. The process involves defining their responsibilities and encouraging their growth. The behavioral approach has as its ultimate goal the changing of the client's behavior by using a behavioral counseling approach that maximizes the adolescent's interaction with the practitioner.

Behavioral counseling involves the use of contracts, that is, long- and short-term goal specification. This is especially relevant when working with adolescents. By collaboratively defining goals, the helper and adolescent establish expectations and present them in a concrete manner. This focus tends to subvert the typical defense mechanisms of adolescents with EBD and serves to increase the opportunities for growth and self-understanding. Volatile adolescents often find it difficult to focus on their problem behavior, however. Although behavioral counseling is often best handled by mental health professionals, vocational counselors need to be aware of techniques that encourage and facilitate interaction between the helper and adolescent. The use of contracts maximizes this facilitative relationship. The specificity of goals, the long- or short-term nature of the goals, and the intensity (magnitude) of any expectations have to be defined on an individual basis.

Practitioners must be aware of the importance of the therapeutic nature of any relationship with an adolescent with EBD. These adolescents have long histories of poor relationships, with the majority of them coming from environments that are devoid of security, love, and respect. Instability, indifference, and overly strict and harsh parenting patterns are the norm. School has often further confounded their ability to experience success, support, and warmth in their relationships with adults. They tend to have very poor self-concepts and experience difficulty in approaching new relationships, especially meaningful and satisfying interpersonal relationships.

Any therapeutic relationship must have as necessary ingredients warmth, genuineness of concern, empathy, understanding, and, in particular, realistic expectations. The adolescent needs to experience a relationship with clearly articulated and realistic limits. In addition, growth should be enhanced by allowing these limits to change as the adolescent changes. Most of all, the practitioner should understand that failures will occur. Helpers have to deal positively with their own limitations and shortcomings in order to facilitate adolescents' looking at their own. Helpers' failure to model that behavior in a most positive and realistic manner will result in the adolescent's refusing to take a risk. For instance, the adolescent's acting-out behaviors must be reframed. Many of these behaviors have been deemed abnormal, but in reality are the adolescent's attempt to respond to the environment with a limited skill set and understanding of the environment. These behaviors thus are normative and adaptive from that adolescent's perspective. The adult's behavior becomes suspect in the adolescent's eyes.

In developing programs to change the means or methods used by the adolescent, the helper must be acutely aware of several factors. The behavioral focus should be on the positive, not the negative. Focusing on the things done well rewards positive behavior by the adolescent. By requiring that positive behavior be substituted for negative behavior, the helper encourages the adolescent to demonstrate control over the environment. The skill focus allows the adolescent to see clearly and concretely what is required for evaluation and mastery, thus developing the independence that is needed for adequate vocational planning.

Developing a Sense of Competency

Practitioner expectations are self-fulfilling prophecies. If the adolescent is expected to be a pain in the neck and the helper's behavior relays that to the adolescent, the helper will not be disappointed. If the goal is to develop positive performance and a sense of personal competency, then positive expectations must be developed on both the helper's and the adolescent's parts. Although this is not a complex process, it will take a substantial amount of time.

A helper must work to develop an open, trusting relationship with the adolescent. The ability to feel accepted and respected, no matter what the behavior, is at the root of growth. Adolescents with psychiatric diagnoses or behavioral disorders are somewhat excluded from this statement because their behavior is often bizarre or hurtful, and it lacks any referent. Nevertheless, acceptance of individuals rather than their behaviors is a crucial aspect in the maintenance of the therapeutic relationship. In this way, a practitioner's expectations do not become mechanisms for failure but a means of motivating the adolescent to develop even more skills and successes. In the same light, failure does not equate to lack of success but to learning what will and will not work and in what situations. It provides an opportunity to develop better strategies, skills, and abilities. Failure should become a stepping stone that defines a skill deficit that can be corrected through further development. Practitioners need to minimize the negative aspects of their client's failure to complete a task or activity and at the same time maximize the gains that occurred through performance. This is accomplished by highlighting performance rather than lack of performance.

Developing a Sense of Personal Potency

Independence is the strongest need an adolescent has. Although feeling a sense of independence does not mean that adolescents need to make all their own decisions, it does mean that they must participate in the decisions that affect them, which can be accomplished only in a constructive structure. Methods that increase adolescents' sense of control involve increasing their role in decision making and their participation in the helping process. A constructive environment includes a specific amount of structure and discipline, such as explicit rewards and punishments for various behaviors and actions. The structure changes as an adolescent develops increasing self-discipline. Increased participation requires the practitioner to be sensitive to each adolescent's needs and existing abilities.

Practitioners should model behaviors that adolescents need in order to experience a positive sense of power and control over their environment. Helpers should solicit feedback; however, common sense dictates that just as it is unlikely that adolescents would survive and prosper when immediately dropped into an environment with total lack of control, it is unlikely that they can be expected to give and take feedback without practice. Rules and processes for feedback need to be developed, and the environment should be primed to facilitate and support the give-and-take of feedback.

Criteria for the giving and soliciting of feedback (e.g., active listening, paraphrasing, and other attending or influencing skills) have been suggested in a previous chapter. Feedback should be descriptive, specific, behaviorally oriented, and timely, and it should include both positive and negative behaviors. Practice is required for the acquisition of feedback skills. Jones (1980) described a very clear and simple procedure and provided the most appropriate criteria:

1. Feedback should be descriptive rather than evaluative. It is the most helpful when people tell someone how his or her behavior made them feel.

2. Feedback is most useful when it is specific rather than general. People need to tell the person specific, observable behaviors to which they can respond positively or negatively.

3. Feedback should focus on the behaviors the receiver can change. For example, it is useful to inform a person that he or she lectures too much, but it is not useful to inform him or her that his or her age makes it impossible to communicate with him or her.

4. Feedback is most helpful when it is given at the earliest convenient opportunity.

5. Positive feedback is as helpful as negative feedback. Although it helps to know what people do that bothers others, it is also nice to know what they do that pleases others.

The helpers should provide opportunities for feedback as well as devise concrete methods that adolescents can use to solicit feedback. This may involve the formation of specific contracts that have feedback loops involved or scheduled client–practitioner conferences. As an example, adolescents could be asked to identify, monitor, and analyze behaviors they feel are nonproductive for them. They would then be taught self-monitoring skills and be reinforced for seeking feedback from the persons who are affected by the targeted behavior.

To be more specific, an adolescent may have difficulty with speaking to adults in authority, such as the teacher, and thus may be unable to solicit help. The frustration of wanting to succeed in school and being unable to solicit the needed assistance would tend to feed that adolescent's negative perceptions of the activity. This soon generalizes or spreads to the teacher, who sees only the adolescent's negative responses, not the original desire for help. The program for this individual would involve self-monitoring of both the specifics of the feelings that are generated *and* the triggering mechanisms. It would also involve increasing student–teacher contact and instructing the teacher in methods to assist acquisition of the needed student skills. The end product is an adolescent with an increased sense of personal growth.

Developing a Sense of Personal Value

A sense of personal significance is an absolute necessity for adolescents to be able to involve themselves in activities around them (personal investment).

Personal investment tends to facilitate an adolescent's ownership or feeling of being the architect of outcomes. In a similar way, such ownership develops a sense of belonging. Without this personal investment, it is very difficult for someone to envision an environment in a positive manner. This is especially true for adolescents with EBD whose home lives have not encouraged developing a sense of belonging or a sense of personal value. There are two skills adolescents need in order to acquire a sense of personal value or worth. The first concerns relationship skills and has been discussed at length. The second concerns appropriate self-expectations of their behavior. These self-expectations facilitate feelings of success or at least an ability to predict the effect their behavior will have on others.

Appropriate self-expectations probably vary as widely as do each adolescent's needs. A practitioner can do several things to facilitate the development of appropriate self-expectations. First, the helper needs to conduct an accurate "soft" assessment of the adolescent's skills that will provide the helper with a basic understanding of the individual's level of communication, ability to tolerate ambiguity, and ability to accept constructive feedback. Such assessment gives the helper an understanding of where to begin the relationship. Second, the helper needs to assess the individual's listening skills. An adolescent who has behavioral or emotional difficulties will have several different, often conflicting, responses to the helper's efforts. The practitioner needs to be able to separate those behaviors that are actual responses to him or her from those behaviors that are due to other aspects of the adolescent's life. Finally, the helper must recognize the adolescent's accomplishments in school and nonschool settings in order to promote the student's sense of personal value. This also sends the message that the helper values and respects the adolescent. This recognition, even in small amounts, is critical to successful career planning for adolescents.

The Ideal Vocational Planning Model

Vocational planning is indeed demanding for adolescents with EBD. The negative behaviors exhibited by these individuals often limit their chances of participating in regular vocational programs. They are not viewed in the same manner as their peers with other disabilities. Their negative or aberrant behaviors often alienate them from their peers, their teachers, and most others in their community. Their emotional and behavioral volatility has disrupted their lives. They become easily frustrated, resent or ignore discipline efforts, and often view the school as the major source of their problems and failures. This view has been reinforced by the fact that few opportunities for either success or

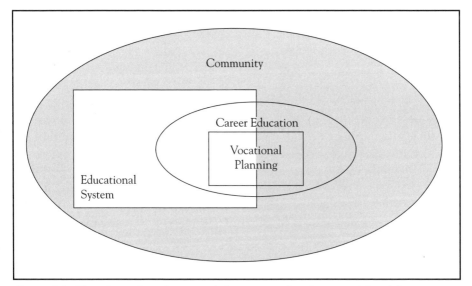

Figure 6.1. The relationship of vocational planning to other elements of the adolescent's life.

participation in vocational activities have been offered to these students because of their negative behaviors (Wehman, 1992). Students with EBD are less prepared to participate in educational programs after leaving high school and less likely to successfully take on adult roles that lead to self-sufficiency. Two years after leaving high school, less than one third of these students are in postsecondary education or are working (Wehman, 1992). For these young people to be successful, they need to be allowed to participate in vocational placements and training in the community.

As depicted in Figure 6.1, vocational planning is embedded within the school and the community. Actually, vocational planning is the very core of career education. Major aspects of vocational planning models should be found in the community and must include the school system and home.

Transition Services

The 1992 amendments to the Individuals with Disabilities Education Act (IDEA) defined transition as a coordinated set of activities that will lead to improved postschool outcomes in the areas of job training, employment in an integrated environment, integration into the community, continuing educational opportunities, and independent living. Transition is an integral part of a student's Individualized Education Program (IEP), first addressed at age 14, with adult service agencies brought into the process by age 16. Transition services are to be highly individualized, based upon the student's preferences, interests, abilities, and capabilities. Vocational decision making is an integral component of the career development process (Chandler & Czerlinsky, 1994). Each adolescent must express his or her career and vocational interests, and these interests should be used in the vocational planning stage. Wehman (1992) pointed out that failure to do this will almost certainly lead to an exacerbation of the adolescent's problems. Students identified as having EBD have performed poorly on almost every transition outcome when compared not only with their nondisabled peers but also with peers with other types of disabilities (Bullis & Cheney, 1999). This poor performance has generated many studies regarding which transition practices hold the most promise for this population. Chapter 12 deals with transition planning extensively.

Person-Centered Planning

All students are unique, as are their home and family situations. For vocational planning to be successful, this uniqueness must be taken into consideration. A person-centered approach (Menchetti & Bombay, 1994; Menchetti & Sweeney, 1994) will ensure that each student's strengths and interests are emphasized. This type of planning includes a long-term vision for vocational success, has a plan of action with specific activities, and empowers the student and his or her family.

Depending on the level of functioning of each student, a variety of person-centered strategies can be used. Options include MAPS (which asks the helper, "What is your dream for this student?"); Group Action Planning (which asks participants to share expectations and asks "What if?" and "Why not?"); and/or self-directed IEPs and Individualized Transition Plans (ITPs), which teach students to direct the development of their own educational, vocational, and career planning (Forest & Snow, 1990).

Wraparound Planning

Wraparound planning takes this one step further by using a system-of-care approach to providing transition services in the natural environment in which the need for the services is evidenced. The goal of wraparound planning is to allow the student to be successful in the least restrictive environment, both at school (i.e., being taught in an inclusion classroom with supports vs. being removed to a self-contained EBD environment) and at home (i.e., avoiding out-of-home or inpatient psychiatric placement). Although this approach is particularly applicable to the most intensive level of intervention, it has also shown promise as an early intervention for students at risk for EBD. In wraparound planning, services are tailored to the student's needs rather than being provided from a standard range of what a particular eligibility program normally has to offer. If the services do not produce the desired effect, the student is not "dropped" from that particular program; instead, the services are modified until the desired results are obtained. Areas of the student's life that are assessed and addressed include educational and vocational goals, residential and independent living goals, social interaction, emotional and psychological treatment needs, safety and legal considerations, medical and spiritual needs, behavioral issues, and family support. Key stakeholders in the wraparound team include the student, his or her family and teacher, and representatives from community service providers and agencies. All members work cooperatively under the lead of a head facilitator familiar with the strengths of the student and his or her family. Such intensive multiagency coordination requires the participating agencies to be flexible in their own service-delivery approaches and to consider the impact of the other agencies when coordinating services (Eber, Nelson, & Miles, 1997). Data from studies of the wraparound planning process revealed that students with EBD who have been served in this manner have improved school attendance and performance, more stable living arrangements, improved behavior ratings, and increased parental satisfaction with services (Eber et al., 1997).

Implicit in the process of wraparound planning is the expectation that school staff members will have a high level of close involvement with the student with EBD. Common beneficial aspects not available in a traditional classroom include intensive individualized academic instruction, consistent support from staff, staff persistence (although not always welcome at the time support was given, but reported as significantly more important by youth with EBD or considered to be at risk), opportunities to explore careers, and learning how to set goals. Students felt that this led to increased self-efficacy and self-confidence because their strengths were identified and their unique self-identified goals were supported (Benz et al., 2000).

The successful intervention program involves community, home, school, and vocational training programs. Each program element must be aimed at erasing or easing a vocationally oriented skill deficit for the adolescent. Community programs included in these wraparound services or in other types of programing may include supported employment with job-coach supervision, apprenticeships, work and community-based learning programs, vocational or technical preparation programs, and volunteer placement. These cooperative approaches may amplify, augment, or supplant the vocational training.

Vocational Assessment

A cardinal rule is for interventions to maximize the ability of the adolescent with EBD to cope on his or her own. Vocational assessments should be used to focus on strengths and interests and to determine work behaviors. Specific attention must be paid to defining any verbal, cognitive, or performance areas that will need remediation or support services.

Some adolescents with EBD also have other disabilities that either compound, or may be one of the major reasons behind, the negative behaviors. Many students also have learning disabilities (Chalfant & King, 1976; Wehman, 1992). Vocational assessments enable the helper to determine what support and learning modalities will most benefit the person with these additional difficulties.

Situational Assessments

Situational assessments are conducted in actual work environments and allow helpers to focus on each adolescent's strengths and interests. This type of assessment enables adolescents who are too easily frustrated or who refuse to participate in the traditional assessment methods to try a number of community work options prior to being placed in a setting that may not be to their liking or that best utilizes their strengths. Wehman (1992) stated that standardized vocational testing does not yield the behavioral data needed to predict work performance of students with behavioral disorders. In addition, the involvement of the student in the situational assessment process provides the helper with information that is useful for both relationship building and long-term vocational planning.

Functional Programming Examples

This section describes a range of programming options appropriate for career planning for adolescents with EBD.

Work Experience and On-the-Job Training

Negotiating the labor market is difficult for many youth today, especially those who do not pursue a college degree (Glover & Marshall, 1993). It is especially difficult for adolescents with EBD who are unable to benefit from regular or adapted vocational education programs because of their academic demands. These individuals may benefit, however, from actual work experience in the community (Wehman, 1992) or from apprenticeships and internships in general industrial training programs. Participation in a work-study program may be used as preparation for transition to full-time employment or postsecondary training after the individual completes high school.

Supported Employment

As of 1991, 75% of individuals with severe mental illness were unemployed. Sheltered or transitional employment rarely leads to competitive employment for this population, although most individuals with mental illness state that they want to work in regular (i.e., competitive) employment settings. Supported employment allows individuals with severe behavioral and emotional problems to be placed in paid jobs in the community that offer training on the job, with support provided by a job coach or employment specialist (Chandler, 1995; Latimer, 2001). This type of placement allows individuals who may not have had prior opportunities to work because of their "aberrant" behaviors to be placed in competitive jobs in the community. This unique approach involves recruiting area businesses, educating them as to how supported employment can meet their personnel needs, identifying existing supports on the worksite, providing job analyses to ensure that the employee is capable of performing the major functions of the job, and building natural supports via a worksite mentor/buddy (Wehman, 1992, West, Targett, Steininger, & Anglin, 2001). Placement in a job in the community often decreases or eliminates behaviors that were problematic in other settings, and studies have shown that students with EBD who are employed through supported employment programs have higher competitive employment rates than those who have completed pre-vocational training and have been placed in employment without long-term supports (Latimer, 2001).

Apprenticeships

Glover and Marshall (1993) pointed out that apprenticeships provide an opportunity for individuals to "earn while they learn." In apprenticeships, individuals learn job skills in real job settings with direct contact with employers and coworkers. Studies in this area have shown that individuals trained in apprentice programs learn new skills faster and earn more than their peers who are trained by other methods (Glover & Marshall, 1993). With the emphasis on "high-tech" jobs, this option will allow individuals with EBD to compete in an ever-changing work environment.

Vocational Education

Vocational education and/or technical preparation programs provide specific skill training in a variety of skill areas (e.g., aviation design, automobile mechanics, carpentry, childcare, computer software development, robotics, agriculture, business and office occupations, health occupations). Unlike apprenticeships, vocational education programs are typically based in schools; however, many school districts have developed classrooms in the community in conjunction with business and industry. Completion of a vocational education program typically leads to postsecondary advanced training, an entry-level job, or an apprenticeship. Many students with EBD are capable of participating in and benefiting from regular vocational education. These students range from those needing no support services to those who need minimal support services (note taking, counseling, special materials, etc.) to those who need more specific adaptions to the programs, such as curriculum modifications; different instructional modalities; or special textbooks, materials, and/or multiple exit points to allow for entry into the whole spectrum of jobs in that field (e.g., from tire changer to oil and lube changer to mechanic to service manager).

Postsecondary Vocational Training

The vocational options found in most school districts frequently provide enough training and experience for individuals to enter into an entry-level, competitive job. For those desiring or requiring additional training or experience, a range of postsecondary vocational options exists that is similar to that found in school districts. Vocational technical schools and community colleges provide in-depth skills training in a number of occupational areas for those capable of fairly stringent academic work.

Responsibility for instruction and training in these vocational options varies from city to city and state to state. Exceptional education teachers generally assume the overall responsibility for monitoring each student's vocational development while the students are in school. They may also assume responsibility for a portion of the actual training. School guidance counselors, vocational education teachers, community business persons, and vocational rehabilitation specialists also may be involved in the vocational preparation process. Vocational rehabilitation agencies usually assume responsibility for the vocational preparation of postschool students with disabilities, either by providing the services themselves or by contracting with other social service agencies or private business.

Conclusion

When developing vocational plans for adolescents with EBD, the practitioner must remember that the school and specialized public agencies typically have an entirely different orientation from business and labor. A successful vocational program for youth with EBD must be multidisciplinary and must meet the needs of a number of individuals and community partners. Given the increased dropout rates and decreased employment rates for students with EBD, it is imperative that studies continue to focus on alternative strategies of service delivery that show promise in promoting successful transition outcomes for this population. Career planning for these students draws heavily from transitional counseling and consultation. Practitioners must provide constant, visible environmental support for these clients. This translates into a need for constant program monitoring. Success will require that agencies and schools forge strong relationships, with common goals, absence of "turf guarding," and flexibility in service delivery in order to improve the future for this population.

References

Adams, G. R., Gullotta, T. P., & Markstrom-Adams, C. (1994). *Adolescent life experiences*. Pacific Grove, CA: Brooks/Cole.

American Psychiatric Association. (2000). *Diagnostic and statistical manual of mental disorders* (4th ed., text rev.). Washington, DC: American Psychiatric Association.

Anderson, J. C., & McGee, R. (1994). Comorbidity of depression in children and adolescents. In W. M. Reynolds & H. F. Johnson (Eds.), *Handbook of depression in children and adolescents* (pp. 581–601). New York: Plenum Press.

Attie, I., & Brooks-Gunn, J. (1990). Developmental issues in the study of eating problems and disorders. In J. H. Crowther, D. L. Tennebaum, S. E. Hofboli, & M. A. P. Stephens (Eds.), *The etiology of bulimia nervosa: The individual and familial context* (pp. 38–58). Washington, DC: Hemisphere.

Balk, D. E. (1995). *Adolescent development: Early through late adolescence*. Pacific Grove, CA: Brooks/Cole.

Benz, M. R., Lindstrom, L., & Yovanoff, P. (2000). Improving graduation and employment outcomes of students with disabilities: Predictive factors and student perspectives. *Exceptional Children, 66,* 509–529.

Bullis, M., & Cheney, D. (1999). Vocational and transition interventions for adolescents and young adults with emotional or behavioral disorders. *Focus on Exceptional Children, 31*(7), 1–24.

Carson, R. C., Butcher, J. N., & Mineka, S. (1996). *Abnormal psychology and modern life* (10th ed.). New York: HarperCollins.

Chalfant, J., & King, F. (1976). An approach to operationalizing the definition of learning disabilities. *Journal of Learning Disabilities, 9,* 228–243.

Chandler, S. K. (1995). *The supported employment model of competitive employment: A training manual.* Tallahassee: Florida State University, Center for Policy Studies in Education.

Chandler, S. K., & Czerlinsky, T. (1994). Vocational Decision-Making Interview – Revised: Assessing the vocational decision-making of individuals with disabilities. *Assessment in Rehabilitation and Exceptionality, 2,* 111–124.

Chandler, S. K., & Pankaskie, S. C. (1997). Socialization, peer-relationships and self-esteem. In P. Wehman & J. Kregel (Eds.), *Functional curriculum for elementary, middle, and secondary age students with special needs* (pp. 123–154). Austin, TX: PRO-ED.

Chandler, S. K., & Pankaskie, S. C. (2002). Socialization, peer-relationships and self-esteem. In P. Wehman & J. Kregel (Eds.), *Functional curriculum for elementary, middle, and secondary age students with special needs* (2nd ed.). Austin, TX: PRO-ED.

Cobb, N. J. (1995). *Adolescence: Continuity, change, and diversity.* Mountain View, CA: Mayfield.

Cole, D. A., Tram, J. M., Martin, J. M., Hoffman, K. B., Ruiz, M. D., Jacquez, F. M., et al. (2002). Individual differences in the emergence of depressive symptoms in children and adolescents: A longitudinal investigation of parent and child reports. *Journal of Abnormal Psychology, 111,* 156–165.

Conger, J. J. (1991). *Adolescence and youth: Psychological development in a changing world* (4th ed.). New York: HarperCollins.

Costello, E. J., Angold, A., Burns, B. J., Stangl, D. K., Tweed, D. L., Erkanli, A., et al. (1996). The Great Smoky Mountains study of youth. Goals, design, methods, and the prevalence of DSM-III-R disorders. *Archives of General Psychiatry, 53,* 1129–1136.

Davis, M., & Stoep, A. V. (1997). The transition to adulthood for youth who have serious emotional disturbance: Developmental transition and young adult outcomes. *Journal of Mental Health Administration, 24,* 400–427.

DeStefano, L., & Wagner, M. (1991). *Outcome assessment in special education: Lessons learned.* Menlo Park, CA: SRI International. (ERIC Document Reproduction Service No. ED 327 565)

Eber, L., Nelson, C., & Miles, P. (1997). School-based wraparound for students with emotional and behavioral challenges. *Exceptional Children, 63,* 539–555.

Forest, M., & Snow, J. (1990). *The MAPS process.* Toronto, Canada; Frontier College.

Gaskins, P. (2001). Teen violence. *Scholastic Choices, 17*(2), 8–9.

Ginzberg, E. (1971). *Career guidance.* New York: McGraw-Hill.

Glover, R. W., & Marshall, R. (1993). Improving the school-to-work transition of American adolescents. In R. Takanishi (Ed.), *Adolescence in the 1990s* (pp. 130–152). New York: Columbia University, Teachers College.

Halleck, S. L. (1978). *The treatment of emotional disorders*. New York: Jason Aronson.

Hartoonian, M., & Van Scotter, R. (1996). School-to-work: A model for learning a living. *Phi Delta Kappan, 77*, 555–560.

Henggler, S. W. (1989). *Delinquency in adolescence*. Newbury Park, CA: Sage.

Hollingsworth, D. K. (1982). The mentally troubled. In T. F. Harrington (Ed.), *Handbook of career planning for special needs students* (pp. 187–211). Austin, TX: PRO-ED.

Hollingsworth, D. K. (1991). Youth at-risk: An analysis from a counselor's perspective. *Louisiana Journal of Counseling and Development, 11*(2), 21–31.

Hollingsworth, D. K. (1995). The convergence of cross-informant perspectives for adolescents with behavior disorders. *Dissertation Abstracts International, 56*, 3838 A.

Husted, J. R. (1997, June). *Mental illness in children and adolescents* [Newsletter]. Long Beach, CA: Alliance for the Mentally Ill.

Jones, V. (1980). *Adolescence with behavioral problems*. Boston: Allyn & Bacon.

Jorne, P. (1978). The acquisition of career planning and career decision-making skill to raise self-concept in emotionally disturbed adolescent males. *Dissertation Abstracts International, 38*, 6537.

Kashani, J. H., Reid, J., & Rosenberg, T. (1989). Levels of hopelessness in children and adolescents: A developmental perspective. *Journal of Consulting and Clinical Psychology, 57*, 496–499.

Kazdin, A. E. (1987). *Conduct disorders in childhood and adolescence*. Newbury Park, CA: Sage.

Kazdin, A. E. (1996). Developing effective treatments for children and adolescents. In E. Hobbs & P. Jensen (Eds.), *Psychosocial treatments for child and adolescents disorders* (pp. 7–18). Washington, DC: American Psychological Association.

Kearney, C. A., & Silverman, W. K. (1998). A critical review of pharmacotherapy for youth with anxiety disorders: Things are not as they seem. *Journal of Anxiety Disorders, 12*, 83–102.

Kovacs, M. (1990). Comorbid anxiety disorders in childhood-onset depressions. In J. D. Maser & C. R. Cloniger (Eds.), *Comorbidity of mood and anxiety disorders* (pp. 272–281). Washington, DC: American Psychiatric Association.

Kovacs, M., Paulaskas, S., Gastonis, C., & Richards, C. (1988). Depressive disorders in childhood: A longitudinal study of comorbidity with adolescents at-risk for conduct disorders. *Journal of Affective Disorders, 15*, 205–217.

Latimer, E. (2001). Economic impacts of supported employment for persons with severe mental illness. *Canadian Journal of Psychiatry, 46*, 496–506.

Lonigan, C. J., Elbert, J. C., & Johnson, S. B. (1998). Empirically supported psychosocial interventions for children: An overview. *Journal of Clinical Child Psychology, 27*, 138–145.

Lytell, R. (1978). Aptitudes and self-perceptions relating to the employability of the emotionally disabled. *Journal of Employment Counseling, 15*, 134–142.

Menchetti, B., & Bombay, H. (1994). Facilitating community inclusion with vocational assessment portfolios. *Assessment in Rehabilitation and Exceptionality, 1*, 213–222.

Menchetti, B., & Sweeney, M. (1994). *Person-centered planning* (Technical Assistance Packet No. 5). Gainesville: University of Florida.

National Institute of Mental Health. (2000). *Child and adolescent violence research* [Fact sheet]. Washington, DC: Author.

National Institute of Mental Health. (2001). *Youth in a difficult world* [Fact sheet]. Washington, DC: Author.

National Youth Violence Prevention Resource Center. (2001). *Child and adolescent mental health* [Fact sheet]. Rockville, MD: Author.

Ollendick, T. H., & Hersen, M. (1993). *Handbook of child and adolescent assessment.* Needham Heights, MA: Allyn & Bacon.

Petti, T. A., & Larson, C. N. (1987). Depression and suicide. In V. B. Von Hasselt & M. Hersen (Eds.), *Handbook of adolescent psychology* (pp. 288–312). New York: Pergamon Press.

Phelps, L., & Lutz, R. (1997). *Career exploration and preparation for the special needs learner.* Boston: Allyn & Bacon.

Powers, S. I., Hauser, S. T., & Kilner, L. A. (1989). Adolescent mental health. *American Psychologist, 44*, 200–208.

Reynolds, W. M. (1992). *Internalizing disorders in children and adolescents.* New York: Wiley.

Rutter, M., Graham, P., Chadwick, O. P. D., & Yule, W. (1976). Adolescent turmoil: Fact or fiction? *Journal of Child Psychology and Psychiatry, 17*, 35–56.

Santrock, J. W. (1993). *Adolescence: An introduction* (4th ed.). Madison, WI: Brown & Benchmark.

Satcher, D. (2000). *Mental health: Report of the Surgeon General — Chapter 3: Children and mental health.* Washington, DC: U.S. Government Printing Office.

Scanlon, D., & Mallard, D. (2002). Academic and participation profiles of school-age dropouts with and without disabilities. *Council for Exceptional Children, 68*, 239–258.

Schenicke, S. P. (1991). *Substance abuse in children and adolescents: Evaluation and intervention.* Newbury Park, CA: Sage.

Shaffer, D., Gould, M. S., Fisher, P., Trautmen, P., Moreau, D., Kleinman, M., et al. (1996). Psychiatric diagnosis in child and adolescent suicide. *Archives of General Psychiatry, 53*, 339–348.

Steinberg, L. (1999). *Adolescence* (5th ed.). New York: McGraw-Hill.

Steinberg, L. (2001). Adolescent development. *Annual Review of Psychology, 52,* 83–110.

Takanishi, R. (1993). *Adolescence in the 1990s.* New York: Columbia University, Teachers College.

Tolbert, E. L. (1980). *Counseling for career development* (2nd ed.). Boston: Houghton-Mifflin.

U.S. Department of Education. (2000). *Twenty-second annual report to Congress.* Washington, DC: U.S. Government Printing Office.

Wallbrown, F. H., Fremont, T. S., Nelson, E., Wilson, J., & Fischer, J. (1979). Emotional disturbance or social misperception? An important classroom management question. *Journal of Learning Disabilities, 12*(10), 11–14.

Wehman, P. (1992). Applications for youth with behavior disorders. In P. Wehman (Ed.), *Life beyond the classroom: Transition strategies for young people with disabilities* (pp. 357–372). Baltimore: Brookes.

Weiner, I. B. (1980). Psychopathology in adolescence. In J. Adelson (Ed.), *Handbook of adolescent psychology* (pp. 288–312). New York: Pergamon Press.

West, M., Targett, P., Steininger, G., & Anglin, N. (2001). Project Corport Supports (CORPS): A model demonstration project on workplace supports. *Journal of Vocational Rehabilitation, 16*(2), 111–118.

Wheeler, E. D., & Baron, S. A. (1994). *Violence in our schools, hospitals, and public places: A preventative and management guide.* Ventura, CA: Pathfinder Publishing of California.

White, J. L. (1989). *The troubled adolescent.* New York: Pergamon Press.

C H A P T E R

CONTEMPORARY ISSUES CHANGING THE CAREER PLANNING CONTEXT
Richard W. Feller and Timothy Gray Davies

All students face formidable decisions as they plan for careers and a lifetime of transitions. Students with disabilities may face unique challenges within a context of accelerating change, expanding choices, and increasing uncertainty in all facets of work, family, and community life. Advanced technology, global competition, economic malaise, and increased academic and behavioral expectations affect helpers as they seek opportunities to honor student strengths while helping them transition toward career and technical education (CTE) and postsecondary education success.

Career planning greatly affects the quality of a student's life roles, learning options, and work experiences within the workplace, classroom, and society. Within a knowledge-based economy, individuals with postsecondary skills have prospered, leaving behind persons with high school educations or less. Earning a postsecondary credential and obtaining technical skills are closely related to earning a livable income. This premium on higher education and training is expected to increase over time. As Carnevale and Fry (2001) noted, access to postsecondary education and training has become the threshold for experiencing economic success in the new economy.

This chapter identifies contemporary issues influencing students' career choices. Continually seeking self-knowledge, exploring life roles, and learning to navigate the education and employment system are key success factors in a world filled with complexity and opportunity. Recording how the workplace is changing and examining current career planning issues, interventions, and innovations within the context of CTE and increased postsecondary enrollments by students with disabilities is instructive. Examining barriers confronting students and an examination of promising programs can enhance transition support services. As helpers gain and provide better information about the forces changing the world of work (DeBell, 2001), and career planning interventions become more efficient, student potential to become self-sufficient, self-advocating and enrolled in CTE and postsecondary education should grow.

Aiming at a Moving Target

Change within learner and worker demographics (DeBell, 2001) and the impact of the "office economy" (Carnevale & Rose, 1998) are quite easy to identify. Trying to reconcile conflicts between standards-based education and individualized education, in which equity and diversity concerns are of great importance, is harder to describe (Hanley-Maxwell, Phelps, Braden, & Warren, 2002). Changing career and technical education's conceptual framework (Castellano, Stringfield, & Stone, 2001; Rojewski, 2002) while simultaneously assisting low-performing students to raise achievement levels to meet state standards continues to be the vision of educators (Bottoms, 2002). Such commitments, combined with innovative career planning interventions and transition services, suggest interesting and challenging times for professionals who are assisting students with disabilities.

As students and employees increasingly self-advocate for control over their personal and vocational futures, interest in career development grows stronger. Understanding the impact of change and making accommodations so that career planning and transition services reach all students, however, demands leadership, creativity, and new directions in career planning (Adelman & Taylor, 2002; Collet-Klingenberg, Hanley-Maxwell, & Stuart, 2002; Kummerow, 2000).

One of education's greatest challenges is to assess the needs of this moving target. In the 1990s, as the economy boomed, attention to human resource development grew, welfare-to-work policy transformed social services, school-to-work legislation elevated career development within educational settings, and individual career transitions increased dramatically (Feller & Davies, 1999). While labor shortages created competitive advantages for students of all skill levels, the aftermath of the terrorist attacks of September 11, 2001, accentuated a reversal of good fortune, and "jobless growth" became a popular scenario. With the "new economy" still being defined or debated, educators currently see that jobs are no longer being created at the pre–September 11 rate. In the early years of the 2000 decade, employers' search for skilled talent continued, but most students found a workplace with fewer available opportunities.

As education and workforce development tried to provide a stable environment critical to students' developmental needs, the workplace became defined by its inability to provide stability, offer security, or instill confidence. Pink's (2001) "free agentry" was not well understood or welcomed by workers or helpers providing career planning to students.

Preparing students to design their careers on the run, while understanding that learning has become a job requirement, is a significant challenge for any helper. Motivating learners and employees to remain flexible, mobile, and able to live with less security is an even more daunting task. Today's fast-changing workplace requires skills and competencies necessary to ensure future employability without consistent employer support. Being able to manage new work and life realities, find a work–life balance, and feel a sense of control over one's economic life within a less stable labor market has become a common necessity for all workers. Such a context creates challenges to even those most sensitive and committed to serving students with disabilities.

The Changing Workplace in a New Economy

Increasingly the "new workplace" is more dynamic, entrepreneurial, and less patient with workers unable to add value quickly. The responsibility for obtaining basic skills, training, and postsecondary education needed for job longevity has gradually shifted to the employee. Agility, innovation, and a willingness to redefine one's job description is as close to "employment security" as the "new workplace" offers. More competitive, global, and technical advances challenge employees' tenure and vertical mobility. More and more, the primary labor market's less skilled and inexperienced workers are expected to be more competent in communication, math, computer skills, self-management, and decision-making skills as the economy centers on information flow and knowledge creation.

Workers formerly tied to jobs matching "wages with ages," or highly educated and traditionally credentialed employees, have learned that merged and evaporated companies — and stockholder decisions — have little interest in yesterday's contributions. Workers at all levels have become "transitional casualties" within command economies where entrepreneurs see the entire world as one market. Persons with disabilities have been subjected to the same consequences and have been negatively and disproportionately affected by general employment trend changes.

Yesterday's Career Rules Are Not as Effective

Many workers had come to believe that employers could guarantee lifetime employment. High school diplomas were the minimal requirement for livable wage jobs, and postsecondary education was either absent from job descriptions or seen as necessary only for professional or managerial jobs. In return for loyalty, endurance, and hard work, employers were expected to provide a paycheck and upward mobility tied to personal networking and one's ability and willingness to follow orders.

Large and established employers were seen as havens for continuous employment; however, transportation, satellite transmission, and Internet connectivity soon reduced the importance of a company's name or geographic location. The current world labor force offers abundant and cheap labor, not job security, permanent positions, or stepladder career paths. In the past, traditional workplaces honored the top 15% to 25% of workers as the professional managerial class who made the decisions and exerted control. The 85% known as the "blue collar" workers took direction, did what they were told, and were rewarded for leaving their brains, heart, and soul at the door. By fulfilling very narrow job descriptions with stable skill requirements, there were ample entry points for students leaving high school. Beginning and low-skilled workers were welcomed and used as human assembly-line robots in manufacturing lines and clerical office pools.

Work designed for rote learners performing a small number of routine operations didn't demand many thinking or teamwork skills. Self-management and self-directed learning were seen as having limited value, and self-advocacy was often interpreted as resistance. With less interest and few expectations about what non – college-bound students knew or thought, the majority of employers prized a worker's ability to conform, tolerate repetition, and respond to hierarchical supervision. North America dominated the world economy, and its competitive advantages created jobs for low-skilled, but middle-wage, workers who saw little value in postsecondary education. Through seniority, collective bargaining, and continuous economic growth, workers could obtain more than average wages in the traditional triangle-shaped workplace (Feller, 1995).

As the workplace became more global, characterized by unprecedented technological change and the mobility of people and money, competition crossed borders. Management's many layers became cost-prohibitive, thus making way for the computer and the Internet to disseminate information in "real time." As a result, assumptions about traditional jobs, workplaces, school-to-work programs, career transitions, and student career options were transformed (Feller, 1996; Feller & Splete, 1996; Feller & Walz, 1996). Increasingly the workplace became home to fewer living-wage jobs for unskilled and low-skilled workers. More work followed workers rather than workers having followed work to specific locations. Employment opportunities noticeably shifted from larger to smaller organizations where work required more cross-training.

In an emerging diamond-shape model (Feller, 1996), the workplace rewarded different skills, broader responsibilities, and more flexible workers. Far fewer supervisors increasingly "coached" more broadly skilled workers seeking to be aligned with the organization's most profitable and core competency units. Rewarded more by "adding value" to a company's core mission than through an accumulation of degrees and titles, workers began seeing the value of developing core competencies through learning on their own, taking risks, and seeking opportunities within new projects and technical postsecondary education options.

Where it existed, job security became much more vulnerable as more workplaces demanded constant learning as a job requirement for those seeking livable wages. Workers are now measured against traits of globally competitive, high-performance organizations such as sustained market success or, in the public sector, achievement of and accountability for organizational objectives; a focus on customers and continuous improvement; a focus on the workplace as a source of added value; innovation in quality and customer satisfaction; and, in the private sector, product or service differentiation; use of self-managed work teams; clear links between training and development and organizational objectives; and support for organizational and individual learning.

Continuous improvement, international quality standards, self-management, teamwork, and transferable skill expectations have become the norm. Intense global competition, time-compressed distribution and product development, and process innovation have transformed work roles, job titles, and organizational structures. In terms of job options, the emerging diamond-shaped workplace requires fewer managers or supervisors. Fewer primary, entry-level, livable-wage jobs are available to students or new workers who lack basic skills, the ability to access and gain occupational proficiencies, the ability to access current information through technology, or motivation and self-direction.

Economic fluctuations influence employment as well as support for learning and development options. Skills and competencies tied to adding value increasingly determine the quality of jobs, length of employment, and future opportunities to learn and develop on the job. As the workplace becomes more service based, changes in consumer spending can quickly affect job growth, job security, and paid employment options.

A National Look at Mainstream
Career Planning

Because the context of the workplace has changed, it seems imperative to ascertain how career planning itself is developing. Annual career development
research reviews published within the *Career Development Quarterly* offer significant guidance, but little else is available for tracking trends. The National
Career Development Association (NCDA, 1999) assessed information about
emerging career planning trends aligned with new rules of a changing workplace. The survey sample consisted of 1,003 adults 18 years of age and older,
who represented a total population of 185 million adults. Many of the findings are useful when considering the context within which career planning is
conducted.

The survey findings identified "a career information digital divide" (p. 3),
noting that people without computer skills and Internet access face a disadvantage in pursuing job and career opportunities. Individuals with limited incomes and lower education levels, and some minority groups, have less access
to job and career information. This past year, 1 working adult in 10 reported
that they needed to make career plans or select, change, or get a job. Seven
in 10 adults reported that if they were starting over, they would obtain more
information about job and career options as compared to their first employment
experience. Individuals with less than a 4-year college degree were more likely
than college graduates to say they would try to get more information.

Similar to many previous studies, 42% of the sample indicated that friends
and relatives were the primary source of help in locating employment. Thirty-
nine percent would go to some type of career counselor. Forty-four percent indicated that the available career information was adequate, whereas 47% said it
should be improved. One in 5 adults reported visiting a counselor or career specialist to learn about possible career choices, and the majority said it was helpful. Forty-one percent indicated that they started in a job through a conscious
choice and plan. College-educated respondents used a deliberate plan more frequently than did respondents with less education. Seven in 10 employed adults
reported receiving some career assistance from their employers, and 53% said
they would need more training or education to maintain or increase their earning power.

Thirty-two percent reported getting training to improve job skills, and one
in four respondents received yearly evaluations or training that helped them
advance. More than half of surveyed adults said they would need education or
training to maintain or increase their earning power. Eighteen to 25-year-old
adults said they would get the training from 4-year colleges. One in five would

get additional training through courses or programs provided by their employer. Close to an equal number said they would take courses at a community college, business and technical school, or trade school.

Globalization has become a major issue and continues to gain attention as a factor shaping career planning. Within the NCDA study, 38% of the adults reported that globalization would affect their job, 18% said it would cause them to learn new skills, 18% said it would result in fewer jobs in the United States, and 7% said it would cause them to need retraining.

Content and Sequence of Career Interventions

In identifying common career development interventions utilized in secondary schools, Dykeman et al. (2001) created a taxonomy to help practitioners evaluate and improve the effectiveness of career planning activities. They standardized career planning language in terms of content and structure, provided a framework for identifying program gaps, and made it possible to compare the impact of specific interventions. After consulting with career guidance specialists and researchers and conducting an extensive review of the literature, they identified a comprehensive list of 44 interventions, categorized into the four areas.

Work-Based Interventions

These are defined as interventions designed to promote student knowledge and motivation through sustained and meaningful interactions with work sites in the community. They are cooperative education, internship, job shadowing, job coaching, job placement, mentorship programs, service learning/volunteer programs, work-based learning project, work study, and youth apprenticeships.

Advising Interventions

This group of interventions is designed to provide direction, resolve impediments, and sustain career planning for future goals by students. They are academic planning counseling, career-focused parent/student conference, career peer advising/tutoring, career map, career maturity assessment, career counseling, career interests assessment, career library/career resource center, career cluster/pathway/major, career passport/skill certificate, college admissions testing, computer-assisted career guidance, cooperative/dual enrollment, information interviewing, job-hunting preparation, personal/social counseling, portfolio/individual career plan, recruiting, referral to external training programs, and referral to external counseling/assessment.

Introductory Interventions

This class of interventions is designed to awaken the interest of students in their own personal and professional growth. They include career day/career fair, career field trip, career aptitude assessment, community members teaching in the classroom, guidance lessons on personal/social development, guidance lessons in career development, and guidance lessons on academic planning.

Curriculum-Based Interventions

Interventions such as these are designed to promote core student knowledge and skills through means and content relevant to the world of work. These include career information infused into the curriculum, career/technical education course, career skills infused into the curriculum, career academy/career magnet school, school-based enterprise, student clubs/activities, and tech prep 2 + 2 curriculum.

Educational and Occupational Information as Empowerment

Accessing usable career information is vital to successful career decision making (Patton & McCrindle, 2001). Information regarding education plans, and school-to-work or postsecondary education transition options are fundamental if students with disabilities are to gain self-sufficiency. As the workplace changes and postsecondary options develop, accurate information is needed throughout one's life. As individuals self-advocate, they need to ask a series of complex questions: Who am I? What should I explore next? How can I prepare for my next transition? Recent trends have illustrated the importance of career information within the career development of students with disabilities (O'Reilly,

2001; Sommers, 2000). Kennedy, Christian, and Bell (1999) concluded that adolescents have unrealistic expectations and inconsistencies in their views for their future. Roney (1999) found that adolescents overaspire in career expectations because they make inaccurate judgments about the ease of attaining high-status jobs.

Canada's *Blueprint for Life* (2001) outlines competencies related to career information for students from kindergarten to adulthood, with examples of what individuals should know and be able to do in regard to career information at each level. Because the best career planning integrates strong self-knowledge with accurate career information, it leads to more satisfying education and employment decisions. The following competencies offer strategies to empower students in this way.

Elementary Education: Understand and Use Career Information

- Explore the work of family and community members
- Identify occupations by people, data, things
- Discover how interests, knowledge, skills, beliefs, and attitudes relate to work roles
- Learn how parents, friends, and relatives can provide career information
- Explore work roles and settings of interest
- Explore the concept of work information and how parents, relatives, adult friends, and neighbors can provide this information

Middle School: Locate, Understand, and Use Career Information

- Identify ways occupations are classified
- Identify occupational groups for exploration
- Use school and community resources to identify occupational groups and work roles
- Discover how skills, knowledge, and attitudes can be transferable from one work role to another
- Identify community employment sources

Secondary Education: Locate, Evaluate, and Interpret Career Information

- Explore the educational and training requirements of various work roles

- Acquire knowledge of classification systems and career ladders

- Discover how key personnel in selected work roles could become information resources and/or role models; explore how trends and work opportunities in various economic/work sectors affect the nature and structure of work roles

- Understand how a variety of factors (e.g., supply and demand for workers, demographic changes, environmental conditions, geographic location) affect work opportunities

- Understand how labor market information (profiles, statistics, etc.) should be used when making life and work decisions

- Explore a variety of work alternatives

Postsecondary/Adult Education: Locate, Evaluate, and Interpret Career Information

- Identify and use career information resources (computer and Internet-based career information delivery systems, print, media, mentors)

- Identify available work opportunities with respect to one's set of work skills, knowledge, and attitudes

- Understand how to assess the reliability of career information

- Explore opportunities for self-employment

- Assess information and evaluate its impact on one's life/work decisions

See Appendixes A through D for a full set of student and adult competencies and indicators.

Students have taken notice that education offers a significant premium in the new workplace, and they see the value of making better use of career information. Students with special needs in secondary CTE programs are less likely to drop out and more likely to be employed, to have paid competitive jobs, and to work full time after high school (Cobb, Halloran, Simon, Norman, & Bourexis, 1999; Colley & Jamison, 1998). High school students with disabilities who completed paid or unpaid work experience had better employment outcomes, higher wages, more hours worked, and more continuous employment; therefore, it can be expected that students will increasingly enroll in career and technical education.

As postsecondary education enrollment continues to increase, career interventions help students access opportunities to improve skills that constantly require updating within a changing workplace. As Grubb and Associates (1999) pointed out, the expansion of postsecondary education, including the growth of open-access community colleges, has provided opportunities for some students with disabilities where none existed before.

Increased Enrollments for Students with Disabilities

Students with disabilities are protected under Section 504 of the Rehabilitation Act of 1973, the Individuals with Disabilities Education Act (IDEA) of 1975, and the Americans with Disabilities Act of 1990; therefore, it is unlawful for postsecondary institutions to deny these students admission based on their disabilities. In addition, all postsecondary institutions must make reasonable modifications in course and program requirements when necessary to provide complete educational opportunities. In the late 1980s, 7% of all incoming freshmen in postsecondary schools had a disability (West et al., 1993). In the early 1990s, the number of incoming students with a disability entering postsecondary institutions had risen to 9% (Yost, Shaw, Cullen, & Bigaj, 1994), but only half requested assistance from disability support services (Barnett & Li, 1997).

Although there is every indication that the enrollment of students with disabilities continues to rise, they still represent a small percentage of students across all postsecondary sectors. Community colleges enroll 53% of public postsecondary students and 71% of all students with disabilities enrolled in public postsecondary institutions (Pacifici & McKinney, 1997). An American Association of Community College (AACC) survey of 672 community colleges found the three most prevalent categories of student disabilities were learning disabilities, orthopedic and mobility disabilities, and chronic illness or other disabilities (Barnett & Li, 1997; Treloar, 1999). Unfortunately, only 12% of those students with disabilities who do enroll in community colleges actually complete their planned program (Edgar & Polloway, 1994; Fairweather & Shaver, 1991).

This is particularly disconcerting, given the open-door philosophy of the U.S. community college. The Illinois Community College Board stated that philosophy most eloquently in its 1992 goals and objectives document: "No individual is inherently more important than another, and each must be provided an equal opportunity to achieve success, regardless of heritage or environmental condition (Illinois Community College Board, 1992). Community colleges especially, but indeed all postsecondary institutions, have an obligation to students with disabilities beyond simply admitting them. There is a professional and ethical responsibility to assist them in career planning and in developing their own self-sufficiency so that they may achieve their individual independence. This self-sufficiency will not be won until these students have increased their knowledge and skills in interviewing for a job; have become more assertive in self-advocating for needed accommodations both in school and in the workplace; and have achieved self-knowledge, exploration, and career planning behaviors necessary for job retention. Postsecondary institutions need to accept the responsibility for helping students with disabilities self-advocate on campus and in their transition to the workplace (Norton & Field, 1998).

What are the reasons more students with disabilities currently are entering postsecondary institutions? Although there are probably as many reasons as there are individuals matriculating, several categorical explanations have been identified in the literature. First, federal mandates requiring transition services for students from high school to postsecondary institutions have made the potential of college as a post–high school outcome seem more realistic to students with disabilities (Dukes & Shaw, 1998). Fairweather and Shaver (1990) suggested that these students are turning more frequently to postsecondary education and training institutions in part because there is easier transition and access than in the past. Two recent changes seem to account for this easier access: (a) the increased participation of students with disabilities in high school college preparatory and vocational educational programs and (b) improved collaborations and partnerships between secondary and postsecondary institutions.

Pacifici and McKinney (1997) pointed out that increased mainstreaming of students with disabilities in the high schools has opened the college preparatory and vocational educational program doors to these students. Their success at this level (in addition to the federal mandates) has spurred efforts by postsecondary institutions to increase both facility and program accessibility to students with disabilities. In addition to access becoming easier for students with disabilities, they also seem to be encouraged by the success their peers who preceded them are experiencing (Fairweather & Shaver, 1990).

Second, the growth of students with disabilities in the postsecondary population has been fueled by an increase of students with learning disabilities. Henderson (1992) identified that approximately 25% of all first-time, full-time freshmen reported having a disability; students with learning disabilities made up approximately 2.2% of the total freshman class. Wagner et al. (1991) pointed out that persons with learning disabilities attended 2-year colleges more frequently than 4-year colleges or universities. This was further substantiated by Henderson, who reported that 59% of students with learning disabilities attended community colleges, 40% attended 4-year colleges or universities, and 1% attended historically black colleges and universities. In community colleges, students with learning disabilities constituted the largest single category of disability served by their disability services offices (Barnett, 1993).

Third, community college, college, and university faculty and staff found that students with disabilities seek postsecondary educational experiences for the same reasons as their nondisabled peers: to expand their formal education beyond high school, to increase their employment opportunities, and to fulfill their personal goals and quality of life (Butler-Nalin & Associates, 1989; Pacifici & McKinney, 1997). Fourth, earning comparisons between students with disabilities and their nondisabled peers demonstrated that the students in both groups who successfully completed a college degree would receive comparable incomes. In addition, students with disabilities who graduate from college earn more in today's workforce than their peers who did not attend college (Task Force on Postsecondary Education and Disabilities, 2000). The New York State Task Force Committee exploring the state's strategies to increase higher education access and opportunity for individuals with disabilities pointed out that the more education individuals with disabilities acquired, the higher their employment and earning levels would be (Pacifici & McKinney, 1997).

A fifth reason for the increase relates to the fact that three quarters of all jobs currently in the labor force require some postsecondary education. Nothing on the employment horizons suggests that new employment opportunities will require less formal postsecondary education and training. Students with disabilities cannot expect to be exempted from these educational requirements if they wish to garner their share of these job opportunities (Weiss & Repetto, 1997).

Although ease of access and increases in collaborative partnerships have increased the number of students with disabilities entering postsecondary institutions, the reasons for their attendance are as pragmatic as those of their nondisabled peers. The realization that it will take more than a high school education to earn a family wage is not lost on these students simply because of their disability. If anything, their need to develop self-sufficiency and independence makes attending postsecondary institutions for additional education and training even more important for them. They simply do not have as many options from which to select. Their path from high school to an independent, self-sufficient life best runs through a postsecondary institution (Bigaj, Shaw, Cullen, McGuire, & Yost, 1995; Trach & Harney, 1998). That being said, it must be noted that the barriers they encounter are sometimes daunting.

Barriers Affecting Students with Disabilities

Despite the increase of students with disabilities in postsecondary classrooms, their overall success rate remains far less than would be hoped (HEATH, 1999). As mentioned earlier, only 12% of those students with disabilities entering community colleges actually leave as certificate or degree completers (Edgar & Polloway, 1994). National research has continued to suggest that barriers to student success are complex and involve students, parents, educators, institutions, and postsecondary support personnel.

In Lancaster, Mellard, and Hoffman's (2001b) study of selected community and technical colleges in three states, students with disabilities were surveyed. The completed questionnaire results showed that these students' greatest difficulties were with concentration, distraction, frustration, test anxiety, memorization, and mathematics. The most frequent accommodations and services requested were note takers, extended testing time, quiet testing rooms, and tutors. These students then identified several issues that were important to them in selecting and using accommodations: the amount of training they would need to effectively use the accommodation, task appropriateness, personal cost, availability, and the amount of independence they would have in using the accommodation.

Increased numbers of students with disabilities also means a greater diversity of disabilities needing to be accommodated by postsecondary institutions' faculty and staff. This diversity has increased the complexity of issues and responsibilities for disability service providers (Heyward, 1998). Increased numbers and more diverse students create greater need for faculty and staff who are knowledgeable about laws, disability issues, reasonable accommodations, and resources (Dukes & Shaw, 1998). However, current research regarding how faculty members view students with disabilities and their own roles and responsibilities has confirmed a lack of understanding relative to the basic disability issues (Hill, 1996).

Examination accommodations are the most frequently requested modifications. Although some faculty members were willing to grant extended time on course tests (Hauck, Assoline, Troutman, & Arrington, 1992), many others believed that granting extended time was unfair to their nondisabled students (Runyon & Smith, 1991). Although many faculty were willing to extend time on exams, only half would permit an alternative form of testing (Nelson, Dodd, & Smith, 1991). Still other studies spoke to faculty members' lack of knowledge about students with disabilities in that they held low expectations regarding their potential (Minner & Prater, 1984; Vanderputten, 1993). In what seems to be a reasonable expectation, McWhirter and McWhirter (1990) found that faculty members depended on students with learning disabilities to be able to explain their disability and how it would impact their classroom performance. This ability to self-advocate had not been acquired by all students with learning disabilities entering the postsecondary classroom; yet, when students were not able to meet this expectation, faculty members were less willing to cooperate and to make appropriate accommodations.

Furthermore, disability resources staff generally are not formally trained for their profession due to the limited availability of such training (Dukes & Shaw, 1998). This lack of general knowledge becomes apparent in the generic and seemingly disorganized ways student services are provided to students with disabilities (Finn, 1999).

Using interviews and panel discussions with community and technical college administrators, faculty, staff, and students in three different states, Lancaster, Mellard, and Hoffman (2001a) found that the recruitment of students with disabilities was inconsistent across these colleges. In addition, once enrolled, students found the lack of accessible housing and transportation major stumbling blocks to successfully reaching their goals. Within the colleges, this study found that even well-developed support service programs became underused if communication about them was ineffective in reaching the target population. Lancaster et al. recommended that what was needed was an intervention to assist faculty members and staff outside the support service area in detecting and assisting students with disabilities. This intervention would have to address the negative attitudes and behaviors toward students with disabilities.

In another study, which examined learning disability service delivery practices, staff in more than 500 two- and four-year postsecondary institutions were surveyed. Forty-three percent of those responding worked in 2-year institutions, and the respondents represented 48 states. Although the study showed that community college students with learning disabilities had a higher rate of participation in their programs and services, it also found that both 2- and 4-year institutions had similar services for these students, with the major difference being that more remedial services were provided at the community colleges (Bigaj et al., 1995).

The study reported some encouraging findings in the programs and services preparing students with learning disabilities to become successful in the classroom and the workplace. The results showed that learning disabilities service providers were teaching skills that promoted student development in functioning on their own in postsecondary settings. Program staff taught organizational skills, time-management skills, test-taking skills, memory strategies, listening skills, and communication skills. Some areas that were identified were less encouraging. Some essential skills and practices, such as metacognitive strategy training and social interpersonal skill training, needed to be taught and developed more effectively among students with learning disabilities in both 2- and

4-year schools. But it is these skills that are needed to function successfully in the workplace—metacognition, self-advocacy skills, and social interpersonal skills (Carnevale, Gainer, Metzer, & Holland, 1988). Both 2- and 4-year providers needed to help students learn how they learn and how to monitor their own learning in postsecondary environments and in the workplace.

Bigaj et al. (1995) recommended that community colleges would be an appropriate starting place for students with learning disabilities who lacked the basic knowledge essential for advancing in one's educational career and in employment. They cautioned that effective transition plans must be in place to assist students from high school to the community college and then to either the workforce or to a 4-year college or university environment.

Lehmann, Davies, and Lauren (2000) formed a collaboration between a community college and a university school of education to identify and systematically eliminate barriers to postsecondary education and improve students' potential for having successful postsecondary experiences. In their study, which used focus groups, four dominant themes emerged.

Theme 1: Students felt a lack of understanding and acceptance concerning their disabilities on the part of fellow students, staff, and faculty members. They expressed their frustration with instructors who were not knowledgeable or experienced in modifying classroom environments, instructional strategies, or grading methods. As one student said in a reporting session, "Some teachers and some teaching assistants don't have an understanding of student needs. They cause damage to students with disabilities through their lack of understanding. It makes me think sometimes, so who has the real problem? Me or them?" (Lehman et al., 2000, p. 62.) This theme was also identified by Yocom and Coll (1995), who found that community college counselors working with students with disabilities had very little coursework or supervised training experiences to assist them.

Theme 2: Students identified inadequate services for assisting them in tackling academic and nonacademic responsibilities. Almost to a person, they found themselves in academic support laboratories in math, writing, reading, and computer literacy with nondisabled students. The staff and tutors assigned to these laboratories knew little about the students and their disabilities and could not assist them effectively. In many cases, the students with disabilities needed services that went beyond the scope of these support laboratories, but those additional and much needed services were not available. Their nonacademic needs included reliable transportation to campus as well as on the campus. They were in need of networking with community employers for part-time work to help defray the expense of college as well as a systematic career services network to assist them in obtaining full-time employment.

Theme 3: Students felt they lacked sufficient financial resources and the knowledge of how to acquire these resources in order to be self-sufficient. Self-sufficiency was a major concern and goal for the majority of these students. They needed to develop a reliable stream of income so that they could move out on their own and become self-sufficient and independent. In regards to part-time campus employment to help with expenses, they observed that there were fewer opportunities for them than for nondisabled students. They also realized that they did not have as much time available to them for work because they had additional hours they needed to spend in support laboratories and with their tutors.

Theme 4: Students acknowledged their lack of self-advocacy skills and training for living independently. This theme ran across all the barriers that were identified by the students. The students needed to gain the respect of both the campus and the work community, and they had to learn to advocate for themselves. They felt they had to become more assertive in gaining more knowledge concerning their own disability. Upon reflection, they felt they needed to deepen their own understanding, self-esteem, and self-worth. As one student quipped, "This part has to be an inside job."

In considering the above comments, remember that only half of eligible students with disabilities requested assistance for disability support services (Barnett & Li, 1997). Not all students with disability conditions think the same. The literature also pointed to inadequate funding as a major institutional barrier: inadequate funding for physical plant accommodations; for keeping current in upgrading adaptive technology, especially in some of the vocational, technical, and allied health programs; and for faculty and staff development to help them better understand and appreciate both the disabilities and the students who had them (Pacifici & McKinney, 1997). To be sure, some institutions and their leadership have become concerned and have been working to address these barriers. Their efforts have been assisting students with disabilities in successfully completing their postsecondary career and have provided career planning and transitional services to help them succeed in the contemporary workforce. It is to a sample of these programs that we now turn.

Promising Programs Assisting Students with Disabilities

Assisting students with disabilities in making the transition from postsecondary institutions to the working world has become an important part of many vocational, technical, and allied health programs, whether at the community college, 4-year college, or university level. Collaborative efforts among the disability student services center, the various instructional programs, existing service agencies in the community, and willing employers help transition students with disabilities into the workforce. Programs can creatively help develop workplace support services, counseling, and work site mentors to help the new employee adjust to the work environment. The addition of a community/ business/college advisory group to monitor the progress once students have been hired, to identify new internships, and to identify new positions for students with disabilities is a common thread throughout many successful partnerships between postsecondary institutions and their local work world.

There is little that is new or innovative in the concept of connecting work and school from the early apprenticeship experiences to the most recent school-to-work legislation. For students with disabilities, this connectivity may be more necessary than it is for their nondisabled peers. Combining the academic classroom with the world of work helps students make connections between the skills and concepts they learn and their actual application in the field. This reinforcement of classroom learning helps students with disabilities make the direct connection. They are assisted in determining realistic career options through seeing a career firsthand, in developing job-acquisition skills, and in gaining a better understanding of the world of work. Being on the job as an intern or in a cooperative education program, or completing clinical requirements allows the student with disabilities to experience personal growth in self-confidence, increased self-awareness, improved communication skills, accepted interpersonal skills, and clarification of personal values. These benefits would accrue to all students but most especially for students whose path from high school to adult life is best traveled through a community college or a postsecondary institution that will assist them in acquiring vocational preparation.

In its survey of 672 community colleges, the American Association of Community Colleges found that 80% had established a disability support service center (DSS) on their campuses (Barnett, 1993). Similar indications of support have been found in other postsecondary institutions as well (Pacifici & McKinney, 1997). Generally, these centers provide registration assistance, counseling, alternative exam formats or times, note takers, and readers, and they increasingly house much of the adaptive equipment and technology that is not specific to a program. Some programs have accepted the responsibility for the retention of students with disabilities: They work to ensure that these students receive accurate information in preparation to transfer to a 4-year college or university and accept the responsibility to place and transition students from the institution to the workplace (Pacifici & McKinney, 1997).

Four main factors contribute to the success of these DSS centers:

1. There is administrative commitment at each point in the institution to deliver the services that research and practice have shown are successful with these students.

2. Community linkages are formed so that there is genuine concern and assistance on the part of community agencies and the business community.

3. The centers concentrate on hiring and training staff members who have the expertise to help make students with disabilities successful in the classroom and in the workplace.

4. These institutions with successful centers have involved and educated faculty to be supportive of these students and to be creative and flexible in their teaching styles and in their evaluation and assessment techniques.

Additional factors that were found through the survey were stable funding through priority setting; a student-oriented approach throughout the center; and a flexible and creative approach to service delivery, adaptive technology, and transition and placement services to the workplace (Barnett, 1993).

A Florida study describing the types of educational services, programs, and equipment provided by 42 area postsecondary vocational technical centers (AVTCS) and 28 community college districts (CCS) to meet the needs of students with disabilities was completed by Weiss and Repetto (1997). They described seven areas of service. In summarizing their results, they found that both the CCS and the AVTCS provided flexibility in their course and program offerings. They both had physical plants that were accessible and reflected a genuine interest in welcoming and serving students with disabilities. The CCS (68%) and the AVTCS (46%) both had developmental laboratories for both individualized learning and support for job-seeking and job-keeping skills. The CCS provided for meeting more individualized needs in specific classes, such as reader services, interpreters, and test modifications, whereas the AVTCS provided more comprehensive services in job-placement supports and assessments and coordinated with other service agencies to provide additional services to students with disabilities. Very few CCS offered similar support.

A West Coast community college helps students with disabilities make the transition to the workforce through two courses developed to prepare students for the work world and to provide support to the students as they adjust to work. The college provides counseling services, assessment services, and placement services. It has developed an active advisory board for student placement and a transition committee involving representatives from the college and community agencies (Palomar College, 1992).

A southeastern community college developed a microcomputer program to prepare students with disabilities for careers as business applications software specialists. As the microcomputer industry changes and evolves, the advisory committee, which represents more than 100 cooperating businesses, and the college adjust the curriculum to keep it current. The program focuses on job readiness and placement. The program goals are to provide technical skills training, provide job-skills development, and develop students' interpersonal skills. The program is intensive, running 9 months with 40-hour weeks, followed by a 3-month internship in one of the cooperating businesses. Over a 10-year period, the program has achieved an 80% placement rate for its students in competitive employment opportunities. In most cases, no special accommodations are required to hire these graduates with disabilities (King, 1994).

A midwestern university developed a 3-year federally supported project to enhance the career potential of students with disabilities. The university provided such career services as workshops, conference presentations, disability networking events, and job fairs. Employers were assisted through employer forums on hiring and supervising people with disabilities and job fairs that focused on hiring a diverse workforce. The major successes were increased interagency communication among the university, the community agencies, and the businesses; changes in accessibility practices and policies for people with disabilities; and successful employment for 88% of the graduates with disabilities (Aune, 1995).

A northeastern community Board of Cooperative Educational Services (BOCES) serves students with disabilities by preparing them for the workplace. This program serves students with and without disabilities but focuses on students with disabilities. Students are enrolled in academic courses and spend half their day there and the other half in the vocational transition program. The program serves students ages 13 to 21 but divides the students into a prevocational training program (ages 13–15) and an on-site vocational training program (ages 16–21). The vocational placement is based on the student's interests and strengths and on the availability of specific jobs. The vocational placement also has an ongoing evaluation that can lead to a variety of job experiences. This transitional services program has reduced the dropout rate of at-risk students by increasing their awareness of job opportunities available to them with training and a diploma (Onondaga-Dortland-Madison Board of Cooperative Educational Services, 1998).

A northeastern technical community college has designed and prepared a manual for its graduates both with and without disabilities to assist them in conducting a successful job search. The manual lists the entire preemployment process, from résumé to interview, as well as how to accept and reject offers. More important, it strongly advises its graduates to disclose only those disability accommodations that are needed for the interview itself. During the hiring interview, the student is to state clearly the workplace accommodations that will be needed on the job (Kerner & Kucinski, 1998).

It is important to point out that no matter the barrier students face, the amount of support or career planning an institution provides, the state of the new economy, or how plentiful or lacking current jobs are within the new workplace, what matters most is how self-reflective helpers are in examining biases related to persons with disabilities. When we choose to serve as helpers, we accept the responsibility of preparing ourselves to deal with each and every person who enters our classroom, career planning workshop, or support office. It is incumbent upon each of us to identify our beliefs about individual learning styles, strengths, and potential. Treloar (1999) closed her article with the following statement:

> Disability, hidden or obvious, changes the packaging of our bodies. People with disabilities are the same, but different from nondisabled persons. Educators who build community in their classrooms begin with a view of each student as a person having value and worth. Effective teachers don't assume they understand disability: They ask the other person to describe his or her world. Disability challenges all of us to capitalize on the differences of each student, and to anticipate success in learning. These actions by faculty and staff are necessary to ensure that all students have equal opportunity to participate. (p. 39)

Improving student access and the effectiveness of career planning and transition support can lead to a more prepared workforce able to adjust to constant change and complexity. Career planning first and foremost is about promoting individual growth and aspirations, however. Transition support is about making connections — calling upon and utilizing others to create opportunities and maximize potential. As Pennington (2001) says in *Connecting the Dots: The Leadership Imperative for the New Century*: "The United States is fundamentally a society based on the promise of opportunity, and a basic part of the contract for a healthy democracy is that people feel they have a meaningful way to move forward toward better opportunity in their lives" (p. 1).

Conclusion

Any university or community college, degree, technical certificate, or CTE program or apprenticeship competencies can enhance the income and self-sufficiency of students, regardless of special need or disability. Continuous change within a turbulent workplace confronts all students with new rules about how to learn, work, and develop their careers. As career specialists and helpers gain insight regarding new career interventions and promising practices, student opportunities and access should improve.

Although academic and technical skills are clearly needed to gain an employer's attention, career planning facilitates life skills, which determine success, achievement, and satisfaction. Providing students with life-planning skills to balance work and family, demonstrate resiliency, and master metacognition learning skills prepares them for the transitions that will occur throughout life. Helping students identify aspirations, realize their full potential, and use their strengths to search for self-sufficiency is most attainable when students and helpers better understand the changing workplace and the context within which career planning takes place.

References

Adelman, H. A., & Taylor, L. (2002). School counselors and school reform: New directions. *Professional School Counseling, 5*, 235–248.

Barnett, L. (1993). *Services for students with disabilities in community colleges* (Final report). Washington, DC: American Association of Community Colleges. (ERIC Document Reproduction Service No. ED364308)

Barnett, L., & Li, Y. (1997). *Disability support services in community colleges.* Washington, DC: American Association of Community Colleges. (ERIC Document Reproduction Service No. ED422044)

Bigaj, S. J., Shaw, S. F., Cullen, J. P., McGuire, J. M., & Yost, D. S. (1995). Services for students with learning disabilities at two and four year institutions: Are they different? *Community College Review, 23*(2), 17–36.

Blueprint for Life/Work Designs. (2001). Ottawa, Ontario, Canada: National Life-Work Centre.

Bottoms, G. (2002). *Raising the achievement of low-performing students: What high schools can do.* Washington, DC: U.S. Department of Education.

Carnevale, A. P., & Fry, R. (2001). *The economic and demographic roots of education and training.* Washington, DC: The Manufacturing Institute, Center for Workforce Success.

Carnevale, A. P., Gainer, L. J., Metzer, A., & Holland, S. (1988). Workplace basics: The skills employers want. *Training and Development Journal, 42*, 22–30.

Carnevale, A. P., & Rose, S. J. (1998). *Education for what? The New Office Economy.* Princeton, NJ: Educational Testing Service.

Castellano, M., Stringfield, S., & Stone, J. R. (2001). *Career and technical education reforms and comprehensive school reforms in high schools and community colleges: Their impact on educational outcomes for at-risk youth.* Columbus, OH: Ohio State University, National Dissemination Center for Career and Technical Education.

Cobb, B., Halloran, W., Simon, M., Norman, M., & Bourexis, P. (1999). *Meeting the needs of youth with disabilities: Handbook for implementing community-based vocational education programs according to the Fair Labor Standards Act* (2nd ed.). Minneapolis: University of Minnesota, Institute on Community Integration, National Transition Network.

Collet-Klingenberg, L., Hanley-Maxwell, C., & Stuart, S. (2002). *The relationship of an ecological model of career development of authentic learning.* Madison: University of Wisconsin, Research Institute on Secondary Education Reform.

Colley, D. A., & Jamison, D. (1998). Post school results for youth with disabilities: Key indicators and policy implications. *Career Development for Exceptional Individuals, 21,* 145–160.

DeBell, C. (2001). Ninety years in the world of work in America. *Career Development Quarterly, 50,* 77–88.

Dukes, L. L., & Shaw, S. F. (1998). Not just CHILDREN any more: Personnel preparation regarding postsecondary education for adults with disabilities. *Teacher Education and Special Education, 21*(3), 205–213.

Dykeman, C., Herr, E. L., Ingram, M., Wood, C., Charles, S., & Pehrsson, D. (2001). *The taxonomy of career development interventions that occur in America's secondary schools* [Electronic version]. Minneapolis: University of Minnesota, National Dissemination Center for Career and Technical Education.

Edgar, E., & Polloway, E. A. (1994). Education for adolescents with disabilities: Curriculum and placement issues. *The Journal of Special Education, 27,* 438–452.

Fairweather, J. S., & Shaver, D. M. (1990). A troubled future? Participation in postsecondary education by youths with disabilities. *Journal of Higher Education, 61,* 332–348.

Fairweather, J. S., & Shaver, D. M. (1991). Making the transition to postsecondary education and training. *Exceptional Children, 57,* 264–267.

Feller, R. (1995). Action planning for personal competitiveness in the "broken workplace." *Journal of Employment Counseling, 32,* 154–163.

Feller, R. (1996). Redefining "career" in the work revolution. In R. Feller & G. Walz (Eds.), *Career transitions in turbulent times: Exploring work, learning and careers* (pp. 143–154). Greensboro, NC: ERIC/Counseling and Student Services and National Career Development Association.

Feller, R., & Davies, T. (1999). Elevating career development in counselor education's pecking order. *Career Planning and Adult Development Journal*, 15(2), 43–52.

Feller, R., & Splete, H. (1996). Career transitions to adulthood. In J. Rotter & W. Bailey (Eds.), *Transitions: Education and employment* (pp. 151–176). Dubuque, IA: Kendall Hunt.

Feller, R., & Walz, G. (1996). *Career transitions in turbulent times: Exploring work, learning and careers*. Greensboro, NC: ERIC/Counseling and Student Services and National Career Development Association.

Finn, L. L. (1999). Learning disabilities programs at community colleges and four year colleges and universities. *Community College Journal of Research and Practice*, 23, 629–639.

Grubb, W. N., and Associates (1999). *Honored but invisible: An inside look at teaching in community colleges*. New York and London: Routledge.

Hanley-Maxwell, C., Phelps, A., Braden, J., & Warren, V. (2002). *Schools of authentic and inclusive learning*. Madison: University of Wisconsin, Research Institute on Secondary Education Reform.

Hauck, C., Assoline, S., Troutman, G., & Arrington, J. (1992). Students with learning disabilities in the university environment: A study of faculty and student perceptions. *Journal of Learning Disabilities*, 25, 678–684.

HEATH. (1999). *Update on college freshmen with disabilities*. Washington, DC: American Council on Education, HEATH Resource Center.

Henderson, C. (1992). *College freshmen with disabilities: A statistical profile*. Washington, DC: Higher Education and Adult Training for People with Handicaps (HEATH).

Heyward, S. (1998). *Disability and higher education: Guidance for Section 504 and ADA Compliance*. (ERIC Document Reproduction Service No. ED441315)

Hill, J. L. (1996). Speaking out: Perceptions of students with disabilities regarding adequacy of services and willingness of faculty to make accommodations. *Journal of Postsecondary Education and Disabilities*, 12, 22–43.

Illinois Community College Board. (1992). *Goals and objectives, fiscal year 1992: Final report*. Springfield, IL: Author.

Kennedy, R., Christian, L. G., & Bell, D. (1999, November). *Adolescent identity development: Views of the future*. Paper presented at the annual conference of the Mid-South Educational Research Association, Point Clear, AL.

Kerner, T., & Kucinski, C. (1998). *Quick results in your job search: A job search manual for prospective and recent graduates with and without disabilities*. Springfield, MA: Springfield Technical Community College, Office of Disability Services. (ERIC Document Reproduction Service No. ED432112)

Kummerow, J. (2000). *New directions in career planning and the workplace.* Palo Alto, CA: Davis-Black.

Lancaster, S., Mellard, D., & Hoffman, L. (2001a). *Current status on accommodating students with disabilities in selected community and technical colleges. The individual accommodations model: Accommodating students with disabilities in postsecondary settings.* Lawrence: University of Kansas, Center for Research on Learning. (ERIC Document Reproduction Service No. ED452618)

Lancaster, S., Mellard, D., & Hoffman, L. (2001b). *Experiences of students with disabilities in selected community and technical colleges.* Lawrence: University of Kansas, Center for Research on Learning. (ERIC Document Reproduction Service No. ED452617)

Lehmann, J. P., Davies, T. G., & Laurin, K. M. (2000). Listening to student voices about postsecondary education. *Teaching Exceptional Children, 32,* 60–65.

McWhirter, O., & McWhirter, J. (1990). University survival strategies and the LD student. *Academic Therapy, 25,* 345–356.

Minner, S., & Prater, G. (1984). College teachers' expectations of LD students. *Academic Therapy, 20,* 225–229.

National Career Development Association. (1999). *Career counseling in a changing context: A summary of the key findings of the 1999 National Survey of Working America.* Tulsa, OK: Author.

Nelson, J., Dodd, J., & Smith, D. (1991). Faculty willingness to accommodate students with learning disabilities: A comparison among academic divisions. *Journal of Learning Disabilities, 23,* 185–189.

Norton, S. C., & Field, K. F. (1998). Career placement project: A career readiness program for community college students with disabilities. *Journal of Employment Counseling, 35*(1), 40–44.

Onondaga-Dortland-Madison Board of Cooperative Educational Services. (1998). *Transition services: School-to-work outreach project.* Minneapolis: University of Minnesota, Institute on Community Integration. (ERIC Document Reproduction Service No. ED420801)

O'Reilly, E. (2001). *Making career sense of labour market information* (2nd ed.). Ottawa, Ontario, Canada: Canadian Career Development Foundation.

Pacifici, T., & McKinney, K. (1997). *Disability support services for community college students.* (ERIC Document Reproduction Service No. ED409972)

Palomar College. (1992). *Partnerships for employing students with disabilities.* San Marcos, CA: Office of Disabled Students. (ERIC Document Reproduction Service No. ED371817)

Patton, W., & McCrindle, A. (2001). Senior students' views on career information. *Australian Journal of Career Development, 10*(1), 32–36.

Pennington, H. (2001, October 11). *Connecting the dots: The leadership imperative for the new century.* Retrieved December, 1, 2001, from http://www.jff.org/jff/PDFDocuments/ConnectingtheDots.pdf

Pink, D. (2001). *Free agent nation: How America's new independent workers are transforming the way we live.* New York: Warner Books.

Rojewski, J. W. (2002). *Preparing the workforce of tomorrow: A conceptual framework for career and technical education.* Columbus: Ohio State University, National Dissemination Center for Career and Technical Education.

Runyon, M., & Smith, J. (1991). Identifying and accommodating LD law students. *Journal of Legal Education, 41,* 317–349.

Sommers, D. (2000). *Work force information and career-technical education. In brief: Fast facts for policy and practice no. 10.* Columbus: Ohio State University, National Dissemination Center for Career and Technical Education.

Task Force on Postsecondary Education and Disabilities. (2000). *Postsecondary education and individuals with disabilities: Recommendations to New York State for strategies to increase access and opportunity.* New York: Author. Retrieved March 15, 2000, from http://www.sysadm.suny.edu/tfpsed/

Trach, J. S., & Harney, J. Y. (1998). Impact of cooperative education on career development for community college students with and without disabilities. *Journal of Vocational Education Research, 23,* 147–158.

Treloar, L. L. (1999). Lessons on disability and the rights of students. *Community College Review, 27*(1), 30–40.

Vanderputten, J. (1993). Residence hall students' attributes toward resident assistants with learning disabilities. *Journal of Postsecondary Education and Disability, 10*(2), 21–26.

Wagner, M., Newman, L., D'Amico, R., Jay, E. D., Butler-Nalin, P., Marder, C., et al. (1991). *Youth with disabilities: How are they doing? The first comprehensive report from the National Longitudinal Study of special education students.* Menlo Park, CA: SRI International.

Weiss, K. E., & Repetto, J. B. (1997). Support services for students with disabilities. *Community College Journal of Research and Practice, 21,* 709–720.

West, M., Kregel, J., Getzel, E. E., Zhu, M., Ipsen, S. M., & Martin, E. D. (1993). Beyond Section 504: Satisfaction and empowerment of students with disabilities in higher education. *Exceptional Children, 59,* 456–467.

Yocom, D. J., & Coll, K. M. (1995). Community college students with learning disabilities: A national survey of perceptions and procedures. *Community College Journal of Research and Practice, 19,* 571–581.

Yost, D. S., Shaw, S. F., Cullen, J. P., & Bigaj, S. J. (1994). Practices and attitudes of postsecondary LD service providers in North America. *Journal of Learning Disabilities, 27,* 631–640.

S E C T I O N

IV

VOCATIONAL PLANNING, CAREER ASSESSMENT, AND INFORMATIONAL RESOURCES

C H A P T E R

CAREER ASSESSMENT AND DEVELOPING A VOCATIONAL PLAN

Thomas F. Harrington

In his book *If You Don't Know Where You're Going, You'll Probably End Up Somewhere Else*, David Campbell (1974) identified the establishment of a career goal as a major task in career planning, and he made several points about the formulation of career goals. Identification of a career choice must be preceded by sufficient experience and opportunities to explore a wide range of occupational options. In fact, Super (1994) believed that most people in their early 20s have insufficient experience to make a career commitment. Super also portrayed jobs as vehicles for individuals to express their talents and manifest their values. He presented work and self-concept as related and emphasized the individual's responsibility to play an active role in his or her career determination and selection. For the client with special needs, Super, as early as 1957, suggested that the disabling condition be ignored initially, to allow for an unbiased exploration of careers.

Many career assessment tools are available. Most instruments focus on an individual domain, such as ability or interests, but few deal with all of the major areas deemed necessary for an integrated comprehensive evaluation. The instrument used in this chapter to demonstrate career assessment is *The Harrington–O'Shea Career Decision-Making System–Revised* (CDM-R; Harrington &

Note. Many of the materials for this chapter were drawn from publications of *The Harrington–O'Shea Career Decision-Making System*. I therefore wish to acknowledge the contributions of my coauthor, Arthur O'Shea.

229

O'Shea, 2000). The CDM-R was recognized by the Association of Assessment in Counseling (AAC), which gave it the 2002 Exemplary Practices Award. AAC is a division of the American Counseling Association. The CDM-R is an evaluative tool that not only is comprehensive in scope but also has programmatic schema to facilitate career planning. Freeman (1996) reported that the CDM-R was rated the most effective career assessment tool of those evaluated by a national sampling of high school counselors who were members of the American School Counselors Association. Droege (1988) wrote that "the CDM is an excellent sample of a systems approach to career decision making . . . . The CDM was a good example of a new generation of instruments for use in career exploration and guidance" (p. 87). Vansickle (1994) wrote that the CDM-R "would be a good choice for those practitioners wishing to provide clients with a positive, active, and helpful career exploration experience" (p. 177).

In this chapter, I present (a) the CDM-R as a career planning tool to help formulate a vocational plan; (b) rationale statements and research support for the components of the CDM-R system; (c) a description of a program for use with the CDM-R whose purpose is to investigate people's vocational abilities, values, and interests; apply this information to career goals; and develop decision-making skills; and (d) a career planning aid that can be used by people without extensive professional assistance. I then describe computer software and information systems that assist independent and self-directing individuals in pursuing systematic career planning and accurate, up-to-date information with minimal professional involvement. In addition, I discuss the *Ability Explorer* (Harrington & Harrington, 1996) to illustrate (a) an assessment tool that measures many more abilities than typical aptitude tests permit, (b) a process by which people can develop and optimize their abilities, (c) a procedure that delivers jobs related to their strongest abilities, and (d) information that reflects a person's self-esteem and self-efficacy in regard to one's abilities. Finally, I describe several models of career portfolios.

The Harrington–O'Shea Career Decision-Making System–Revised

The CDM-R is a systematic career decision-making approach that assesses three major dimensions of the career choice process — abilities, values, and interests — and relates them to occupational information. The system's overall framework and six interest scales are both theoretically based. The system follows the definition of career awareness as the interaction between knowledge, values, preferences, and self-concept as originally set forth by the National

Institute of Education (Wise, Charner, & Randour, 1976). *Knowledge* involves the question, "What do I know?" *Values* involve the question, "What is important to me?" *Preferences* involve the question, "What do I like?" *Self-concept* involves the question, "What do I do well?" The interest scales relate to Holland's (1997) vocational development theory.

The CDM-R is a simulation of a career counseling situation. The instrument can be self-administered, self-scored, and self-interpreted, offering the advantage of immediate results and feedback; can be machine scored, which is a time-saver; and also is available on the computer. There are English and Spanish versions, each with two levels, offering varying degrees of complexity. The levels do not include the same components. The CDM-R can be administered to individuals or groups. Some helpers administer it individually to clients with special needs, such as those with physical handicaps or learning disabilities, and the helpers fill in the clients' responses. An audiocassette presentation is also available for poor readers.

Level 1 is designed for younger students, such as those in middle or junior high school, and people of all ages with limited learning and reading ability. Ninety-six interest survey items are written at the fourth-grade reading level; are gender neutral; and use words that are simple, active, and descriptive. The survey and interpretive sections are combined into one easy-to-use, self-contained booklet. Administration takes approximately 20 minutes. Interpretation requires additional time and culminates in the user's developing a personalized profile related to the two highest interest areas for future planning purposes.

Level 2 is for students with stronger reading skills and is, overall, written at a seventh-grade level. Level 2 uses a self-report methodology that provides, in addition to an interest inventory (containing 120 current and gender-neutral activities), a profile of a person's self-stated job choices, best-liked school subjects, future plans, preferred values, and strongest abilities. The entire assessment takes about 40 minutes to complete and score. Interpretation requires additional time. A separate interpretive folder, which includes a guide to college majors and training programs related to interests, is used for educational and career planning. Personality characteristics related to the major interest areas also are described. Level 2 provides more precision than Level 1 in that the occupations reported for consideration offer 3 or 4 out of 18 career clusters of jobs related to one's inventoried interests.

Rationale and Research Support for CDM-R Components

The Congruence Model

The CDM-R provides the helper with a global perspective of individuals' vocational self-concepts by including, within the same instrument, self-reported occupational preferences, school subject preferences, future plans, job values, and abilities, in addition to measured interests. The helper should look for the degree of congruence among an individual's self-descriptions and compare the stated occupational preferences of career clusters with the career clusters derived from the person's interest inventory scores. Do they match? Are the abilities selected by the individual those required by occupations in the clusters suggested for exploration? A person's self-confidence is often enhanced when he or she experiences congruence.

Stated Occupational Preferences

The research literature on occupational choice clearly supports the predictive power of stated job choices. Studies have suggested that expressed interests have greater predictive validity than measured interests (Bartling & Hood, 1981; Slaney, 1988). When stated and measured interests are in agreement, predictive ability is even higher. Based on the research literature, helpers must give considerable attention to stated choice. Where there is disagreement, the helper must closely work to explore career clusters derived from both stated and measured interests. Where there is agreement and measured interests confirm expressed choice, the literature has suggested that people will have greater confidence in their career focus. However, in a 20-year follow-up study, Harrington (2002) found that interest inventory results were a better predictor than stated choices.

The user of Level 2 is asked to read the definitions of the 18 Career Clusters of Jobs listed below and then to select the first and second choices that he or she would like to pursue.

Manual	Customer Service
Skilled Crafts	Personal Service
Technical	Social Service
Math-Science	Education
Medical-Dental	Sales
Literary	Management
Art	Legal
Music	Clerical
Entertainment	Data Analysis

Subject Preferences

Inspections of job descriptions show that many jobs require proficiency in designated school-subject areas. For example, managers need financial skills, and engineers require a knowledge of physics. Competency need not always be developed in school, as has been shown in the case of artistic talent or skills gained through on-the-job experience. Subject preferences also can indicate potential areas of interest. For example, it is not uncommon for a girl to indicate she likes a scientific school subject, but neither her stated nor measured interests match this statement. The helper must be sensitive to the possibility that gender-role stereotyping has negatively influenced a girl's perceptions about women working as engineers or scientists. Likewise, sometimes a person indicates that he or she desires to be a physician, but the preferred subject areas do not correspond to the subject-matter proficiency required of physicians. The listing of school subjects that are related to jobs in the Career Clusters Charts can be helpful in dealing with this latter instance.

The user of CDM-R Level 2 is asked to read each of the 15 groupings of school subjects and then to select the four he or she likes the most. Level 1 includes the listing of subjects but does not ask the user to rank his or her choices. The following subjects are listed:

Agriculture	Management
Art	Math
Clerical Studies	Music
English	Science
Family/Consumer Science	Shop
Finance	Social Science
Health	Technology
Languages	

Job Values

In career planning, people must ask themselves what they need for job satisfaction. The answer to this question is highly personal, because the same job may satisfy different values in different people. Despite this fact, certain values are commonly associated with particular career clusters. This was exemplified by a study of workers in 53 different occupations, in which job values were indicated in the logical direction: Editors expressed a preference for creativity, managers valued leadership, nurses selected working with people, and computer programmers preferred working with their minds. Many workers in different jobs, however, chose the same values, such as independence, a good salary, and high achievement (Harrington & O'Shea, 2000).

The purpose of the CDM-R is to introduce the concept of job values into the career planning process so that helpers can expand on this topic. Values are viewed as cognitive representations of personal needs, are considered basic to a person's belief system, and are thought to be fairly resistant to change. People learn values from their parents, significant others, and daily living experiences. The purpose of the values clarification process is to help individuals identify personal values and study their relative importance. According to Simon (1974), for a belief to be considered a value, all seven of the following standards must be met: It must be chosen freely, chosen from alternatives, chosen after due reflection, prized and cherished, publicly affirmed, acted upon, and be part of a pattern that is a repeated action.

The Level 2 user is asked to read the following 14 values with their definitions and then to select the 4 values believed to be the most important to him or her. Level 1 includes the listing of values but does not ask a person to select the top 4 preferred.

Creativity	Physical Activity
Good Salary	Prestige
High Achievement	Risk
Independence	Variety
Job Security	Work with Hands
Leadership	Work with Mind
Outdoor Work	Work with People

Abilities

Abilities are those talents judged important in career choice. Abilities have long been considered a primary factor in job performance. Frequently, ability has been assessed through the use of testing, but many ability tests have been considered unsuitable and/or invalid for individuals with particular disabilities or special needs. Individuals using the CDM-R choose abilities through self-ratings or estimates of their greatest strengths. A considerable body of research has suggested that self-estimates of ability are efficient predictors of achievement and are often more efficient than standardized tests. For example, Baird (1969), an early proponent of self-rated abilities and a research psychologist at the Educational Testing Service, the developers of the College Board Entrance Examination, reported that self-estimates of scholastic ability were the best predictors of grade point average. Test scores added little to the multiple regression equation in the study of 5,129 college freshmen at 29 colleges.

Self-estimates of ability are an expression of a person's self-perception, and people tend to behave in a manner consistent with their image of themselves. The use of self-estimates permits helpers to focus on this important piece of information in career planning. Many times a person's abilities have been insufficiently discussed with him or her because assessment information on all the abilities relevant to work has not been available.

The CDM-R authors noted that educators are often too concerned that young people will overestimate their abilities. The implication is that more objective data are needed to verify a person's ability. Work study and cooperative education programs have some potential for evaluating ability.

The Level 2 user is asked to read the 14 abilities with their definitions and then to select 4 abilities believed to be his or her best. Level 1 includes the listing of abilities but does not ask a person to select the 4 best. The 14 abilities are

Artistic	Mechanical
Clerical	Musical
Computational	Persuasive
Language	Scientific
Leadership	Social
Manual	Spatial
Mathematical	Teaching

Future Plans

Developing appropriate training plans is an essential part of career decision making. Many individuals naively believe that without any additional skills, they will get a job that in fact involves many specialized skills they do not possess. One requirement of career planning is learning what skills are required to perform a job, where to obtain these skills, and how much the necessary training or education will cost. Of course, if job training is viewed as an investment, a prudent person will consider the number of jobs available once he or she is trained. This information is indicated by the employment forecasts provided in the CDM-R Career Clusters Charts.

The Level 2 user is asked to read the nine choices below and select the one that reflects current plans.

4-year college or university

Graduate or professional school (such as law or medical school)

High school diploma

Hospital nursing program

Military service

On-the-job training or apprenticeship

1-year business school

Community/junior college

Vocational, trade, or technical school

No additional training or education (I already have what is needed for the career I want to pursue)

Interests

CDM-R users are asked to respond to each interest statement by writing a "2" if he or she likes the activity, a "1" if he or she cannot decide, and a "0" if he or she dislikes the activity. For example, one user may put down 2 for "Solve crimes," 1 for "Design clothes," and 0 for "Sell computers."

Interests express the direction of a person's preferences and also indicate work areas that a person dislikes. In general, the higher a person's interest score on a particular scale, the more likely he or she will find the activities of that scale enjoyable, satisfying, and rewarding. The six CDM-R interest scales correspond to the personality types described in Holland's (1997) theory in Chapter 1; however, the CDM-R scales have been retitled using more occupationally relevant terms (Holland's terminology is in parentheses following the CDM-R scale name): Crafts (Realistic), Scientific (Investigative), The Arts (Artistic), Social (Social), Business (Enterprising), and Office Operations (Conventional).

The highest two interest scores identify clusters of jobs that are related to the individual's unique constellation of interests. According to Holland's belief that interests measure personality, a high score on the Crafts scale could also be interpreted to mean that the individual is a doer rather than an abstract thinker; is pragmatic; prefers precise, concrete tasks to undefined tasks; prefers to build things rather than relate to people; enjoys physical movement; and does not mind getting his or her hands dirty. High scores on the Scientific scale could mean a person is curious, creative, and studious; likes to work with theories or unproven ideas; prefers to work alone; and highly values math and science. A person who scores high on the Arts scale prizes independence; enjoys creative activities such as music, writing, entertainment, and art; appreciates the artistic work of others in museums, theaters, and books; and seeks opportunities for self-expression. The Social scale often indicates a person who cares about the well-being of others; gets along well with people; has strong verbal skills; and likes to provide services for others. Business people usually see themselves as skilled with words, seek careers where they can lead others, enjoy convincing others to think the way they do, and can persuade others to buy their products. A high score on Office Operations indicates a person prefers jobs with clearly defined duties, likes to work with words and numbers, is orderly and systematic, and values financial success and status. It is understood, however, that a person does not have just one of these personality types but a combination of several of them.

Vocational Self-Concepts

A professional reviewer commented on the CDM as following a systems approach to career planning and decision making. Review the components just set forth — are they also not asking a person to state and clarify six different aspects of his or her self-concepts in a vocational application? Those aspects are as follows:

1. What type of work would you like to do?
2. What school subjects, and thus competency areas, are your best?
3. What values are most important to you in your work life?
4. What are your best talents and your strongest abilities?
5. How much of an investment do you wish to put into your future development? Doesn't a person who selects to attend college possibly think differently about himself or herself initially than someone who goes to work immediately after high school?
6. What type of person are you? Will one career area better fit your personality than another?

The purpose of the Career Clusters Charts discussed in the next section is to interpret the information discussed previously while asking the person to integrate them with occupational information.

Career Clusters Charts

Users of Levels 1 and 2 receive the same information about the most common jobs in the United States. In Level 1, which is a single booklet, the occupational information is chunked into six Career Charts shown on 12 pages, with larger print, simpler directions, and a lower reading level than the material presented in Level 2. Level 2 consists of a survey booklet and a 4-page Interpretive Folder. Figure 8.1 displays pages 2 and 3 of the Level 2 Interpretive Folder and presents the same career information as Level 1 in a large chart. The Career Clusters Charts feature a step-by-step explanation of how to relate jobs to the components assessed in the system. Individuals are told to circle on the Career

(text continues on p. 250)

CRAFTS

TYPICAL JOBS

Manual

Construction
Construction Laborer 2-G
Drywall Worker 2-E
Roofer 2-E

Forestry/Mining/Oil
Logger 1-P
Miner 2-P
Roustabout 2-P

Industrial Production
Fork Lift Operator 1-G
Machine Operator 2-F
Material Handler 1-G
Packager 1-G
Product Assembler 1/2-F
Sewing Machine Operator 1-P
Textile Machine Operator 2-P

Material Control
Shipping/Receiving Clerk 1-F
Stock Clerk/Order Filler 1-F

Plants/Animals/Fish
Animal Caretaker 1-G
Farmworker 1-E
Fisher 1-P

Landscape/Groundskeeping/Nursery Worker 1-E

Transportation
Deckhand/Sailor 1/2-P
Locomotive Engineer 2-P
Truck Driver 1/2-G

Other
Cleaner/Janitor 1-G
Dry Cleaner 1-NA
Firefighter 2-P
Highway Maintenance Worker 1-F
Hotel/Hospital Housekeeper 1-G
Private Household Worker 1-G
Short Order Cook 1-G

Skilled Crafts

Construction/Maintenance
Bricklayer/Stonemason 3-E
Carpenter/Cabinetmaker 3-E/G
Carpet Installer 3-G
Cement Mason 3-E
Construction Equipment Operator 3-G
Glazier 3-E
Insulation Worker 3-E
Painter/Paperhanger 3-G
Plasterer 3-G
Plumber/Pipefitter 3-E
Tilesetter 3-G

Electrical/Electronics
Appliance Repairer 3-F
Broadcast Technician 3-F

Mechanical
Air Conditioning/Heating Mechanic 3-E
Aircraft Mechanic 3-G
Auto Technician/Mechanic 3-E
Boilermaker 3-F
Building Maintenance Repairer 3-G
Diesel Technician/Mechanic 3-G
Elevator Installer/Repairer 3-F
Farm Equipment Mechanic 3-G
Heavy Mobile Equipment Mechanic 3-G
Industrial Machine Repairer 3-G
Millwright 3-G
Motorcycle/Boat Mechanic 3-F
Musical Instrument Repairer 3-G
Office Machine Servicer 3-G

Food Preparation
Baker 3-G
Cook 3-E
Meat Cutter 3-F

Commercial/Industrial Electronic Equipment Repairer 3-G
Computer Service Technician 3-E
Electric Power & Telephone/TV Cable Line Installer/Repairer 3-G/F
Electrician 3-E
Electronics Assembler 2-F
Home Entertainment Equipment Repairer 3-P
Telecommunications Equipment Mechanic 3-P

Medical Manufacturing
Dental Lab Technician 3-G
Manufacturing Optician 2-F

Metal Work/Machining
Auto Body Repairer 3-G
Machinist 3-E
Sheet Metal Worker 3-E
Structural Steel Worker 3-G
Tool and Die Maker 3-E
Welder 2/3-E

Printing
Bindery Worker 2-F
Desktop Publishing Specialist 3/4-E
Prepress Technician 3-P
Printing Press Operator 3-P

Systems Operation
Power Plant Operator 3-F
Stationary Engineer 3-F
Waste Treatment Plant Operator 3-G
Water Treatment Plant Operator 3-G

Other
Blue Collar Worker Supervisor 3-G
Factory Inspector 2/3-F
Farmer 3-P
Jeweler 3-E
Livestock Rancher 3-P
Military Service 2-G
Photo Process Worker 2-P
Precision Woodworker 3-P
Shoe and Leather Worker/Repairer 3-P
Tailor 3-P
Upholsterer 3-G

Technical

Computer/Engineering Technology
Computer Network Control Operator 4-E
Computer Technical Support Specialist 4-E
Cost Estimator 3/4/5-G
Drafter 4-G

Electronic Semiconductor Processor 4-G
Engineering Technician 4-G
Surveyor 4-G
Technical Illustrator 4-P
Tool Programmer 3-E

Medical/Laboratory Technology
Biological Technician 4-G
Chemical Lab Technician 4-G
EEG/EKG Technician 2-P
Environmental Science/Protection Technician 4-NA
Food Science Technician 4-G

Medical Lab Technician 4-G
Medical Sonographer 3-G
Nuclear Medicine Technologist 4-G
Quality Control Technician 3-F

Plants and Animals
Forestry Technician 4-G
Veterinary Technologist E

Transportation
Air Traffic Controller 3-P
Airline Pilot 4-P
Flight Engineer 4-P
Ship's Captain 3/4-P

(continues)

COLLEGE MAJORS & TRAINING PROGRAMS

SCHOOL SUBJECTS	WORK VALUES	ABILITIES
Manual		
Agriculture	Outdoor Work	Manual
Family/Consumer Science	Physical Activity	Mechanical
Shop	Risk	Spatial
	Work with Hands	
Skilled Crafts		
Agriculture	Good Salary	Artistic
Family/Consumer Science	Independence	Computational
Health	Outdoor Work	Manual
Math	Physical Activity	Mathematical
Science	Risk	Mechanical
Shop	Work with Hands	Scientific
Technology		Spatial
Technical		
Agriculture	Good Salary	Artistic	Scientific
Art	Job Security	Computational	Spatial
Math	Outdoor Work	Leadership
Science	Physical Activity	Manual
Shop	Risk	Mathematical
Technology	Work with Hands	Mechanical
	Work with Mind	

College Majors & Training Programs

Construction Trades
- Cabinetmaking
- Carpentry
- Construction Technology
- Electrical Studies
- Heavy Equipment Operation
- Masonry/Bricklaying
- Plumbing
- Sheet Metal Technology
- Tile Setting

Craft Technologies
- Building Maintenance
- Computer Technology
- Desktop Publishing
- Drafting (CAD-CAM) Technology
- Electronics
- Furniture Upholstering
- Mining Technology
- Surveying
- Watch/Jewelry Repair
- Woodworking

Education
- Industrial Arts Education
- Vocational Education

Food Preparation
- Baking
- Culinary Arts

Health Technologies
- Dental Lab Technology
- EEG/EKG Technology
- Optical and Laser Technology

Home and Office Equipment Repair
- Appliance Repair
- Computer Repair
- Office Machine Repair
- TV/Radio/Stereo Repair

Installation
- Heating/Air Conditioning/Refrigeration
- Telephone and Cable Installation/Repair

Mechanical Repair
- Aircraft Mechanics
- Auto Repair/Technology
- Diesel Repair
- Farm Equipment Repair
- Heavy Equipment Repair
- Small Engine Repair

Plants/Animals/Fish
- Agriculture
- Animal Care
- Farm/Ranch Management
- Fish/Game Management
- Forest Harvesting
- Horticulture
- Landscape Architecture

Production
- Machine Shop
- Printing Technology
- Quality Control Technology
- Textile Technology
- Tool and Die Technology
- Welding

Security Services
- Fire Protection Technology
- Military Science

Systems Operation
- Energy/Power Technology
- Power Plant Operation
- Stationary Engineering
- Water/Wastewater Technology

Transportation
- Aircraft Piloting/Navigation
- Air Traffic Control
- Merchant Marine Training
- Truck Driving

(continues)

Figure 8.1. Continued.

SCIENTIFIC

TYPICAL JOBS

Math–Science

Computers
Computer Programmer 4/5-G
Computer Scientist 5-E
Computer Security Specialist 4/5-E
Database Administrator 4/5-E
Network Administrator 4/5-G
Network Analyst 4/5-E
Software Engineer 5-E
Systems Analyst 4/5-E
Web Site Developer 4-E
Webmaster 4-E

Design
Architect 5-F
Landscape Architect 5-G

Engineering
Aerospace Engineer 5-G
Chemical Engineer 5-F
Civil Engineer 5-G
Computer Engineer 5-G
Electrical and Electronics Engineer 5-G
Mechanical Engineer 5-G

Metallurgical, Ceramic, and Materials Engineer 5-F
Mining Engineer 5-P
Nuclear Engineer 5-G
Petroleum Engineer 5-G
Laboratory Technology
Medical Lab Technologist 5-G
Pharmacist 5-E
Life Sciences
Agricultural Scientist 5-F
Biologist 5-G

Environmental Scientist 5-G
Forester 5-F
Pharmacologist 5-NA
Soil Conservationist 5-F
Mathematics
Actuary 5-F
Mathematician 5-F
Statistician 5-G
Physical Sciences
Chemist 5-G
Geologist 5-F

Meteorologist 5-F
Oceanographer 5-G
Physicist/Astronomer 5-G
Other
Economist 5-G
Engineering/Science & Computer Systems Manager 5-F/E
Experimental Psychologist 5-G
Market Research Analyst 5-G
Math–Science Teacher 5-E
Operations Research Analyst 5-G
Urban and Regional Planner 5-G

Medical–Dental

Dentistry
Dentist 5-G
Orthodontist 5-G
Health Specialties
Audiologist 5-E

Chiropractor 5-G
Dietian/Nutritionist 5-G
Optometrist 5-G
Physical Therapist 5-G
Speech Pathologist 5-E

Medicine
Anesthesiologist 5-G
Cardiologist 5-G
General Practitioner 5-G
Neurologist 5-G

Obstetrician 5-G
Orthopedist 5-G
Pathologist 5-G
Pediatrician 5-G
Podiatrist 5-G

Psychiatrist 5-G
Radiologist 5-G
Surgeon 5-G
Veterinary Medicine
Veterinarian 5-G

(continues)

Figure 8.1. Continued.

COLLEGE MAJORS & TRAINING PROGRAMS

Math–Science

SCHOOL SUBJECTS	WORK VALUES	ABILITIES	COLLEGE MAJORS & TRAINING PROGRAMS
Agriculture	Creativity	Artistic	**Architecture**
Art	Good Salary	Computational	Architecture
English	High Achievement	Language	Landscape Architecture
Finance	Independence	Leadership	**Engineering**
Math	Job Security	Manual	Aerospace
Science	Leadership	Mathematical	Chemical
Technology	Outdoor Work	Mechanical	Civil
	Prestige	Scientific	Computer
	Variety	Spatial	Electrical and Electronics
	Work with Hands	Teaching	Mechanical
	Work with Mind		Mining/Petroleum
			Nuclear
			Health Sciences
			Audiology/Speech Pathology
			Chiropractic/Osteopathy
			Dentistry/Pre-Dentistry
			Food Science/Nutrition
			Medicine/Pre-Medicine
			Optometry
			Pharmacy/Pharmacology
			Physical Therapy
			Podiatry
			Public Health
			Veterinary Medicine
			Information Sciences/Systems
			Computer Programming
			Computer Science
			Network/Database Admin.
			Systems Analysis
			Life Sciences
			Agronomy
			Animal/Dairy Science
			Biochemistry
			Biological Sciences
			Environmental Science
			Forestry/Horticulture
			Marine Biology
			Natural Resources Mgmt.
			Mathematics
			Actuarial Science
			Mathematics/Statistics
			Physical Sciences
			Chemistry
			Geography/Oceanography
			Geology
			Metallurgy
			Meteorology
			Physics/Astronomy
			Scientific Technologies
			Engineering Technology
			Medical Lab Technology
			Social Science
			Archaeology
			Economics
			Experimental Psychology
			Urban & Regional Planning

Medical–Dental

SCHOOL SUBJECTS	WORK VALUES	ABILITIES
Agriculture	Creativity	Language
English	Good Salary	Leadership
Math	High Achievement	Manual
Science	Independence	Mathematical
	Job Security	Mechanical
	Leadership	Scientific
	Prestige	Social
	Variety	Spatial
	Work with Mind	
	Work with People	

(continues)

Figure 8.1. *Continued.*

THE ARTS
TYPICAL JOBS

Literary

College is listed as usual minimum training for all Literary jobs. However, very talented persons may achieve success in creative writing without completing a college education.

Communications
Columnist/Commentator 5-P
Newswriter 5-P
Reporter 5-P
Technical Writer 5-G

Creative Writing
Copywriter 5-F
Novelist 5-F
Playwright 5-F
Poet 5-F
Script Writer 5-F

Editing
Editorial Assistant 5-F
Film Editor 5-F
Print Editor 5-F

Translating
Interpreter 5-G
Translator 5-G

Art

Commercial Art
Animator 3-P
Camera Operator 3-P
Cartoonist 3-P
Commercial Designer 4-P
Display Worker 2-P
Fashion Designer 4-P
Floral Designer 2-G
Graphic Designer 4-P
Illustrator 3-P

Industrial Designer 5-P
Interior Designer 5-P
Photographer 3/4-P
Photojournalist 5-P
Printmaker 3-P
Set Designer 5-P

Studio Art
Painter (Artist) 3-P
Sculptor 3-P

Other
Art Teacher 5-G
Curator 5-P

Music

Very talented persons may achieve success in music or dance without completing a college degree. However, a degree may be helpful, and years of training and practice are necessary.

Dance
Choreographer P
Dancer P
Dancing Instructor NA

Music
Choral Director P
Composer P
Conductor P
Music Arranger P
Music Teacher NA

Musician P
Singer P

Entertainment

Announcing
Disc Jockey 3-P
Radio/TV Announcer 3-P

Directing
Radio/TV Production Assistant 5-F
Radio/TV Program Director 3-P
Radio/TV/Movie Producer 3-P
Stage Director 3-P

Modeling
Model 1-P

Performing
Actor/Actress 3-P
Comedian 3-NA
Stunt Performer 3-NA

Promotion
Advertising Manager 5-P
Public Relations Specialist 5-P

Teaching
Drama Teacher 3-NA

(continues)

Figure 8.1. *Continued.*

COLLEGE MAJORS & TRAINING PROGRAMS

SCHOOL SUBJECTS	WORK VALUES	ABILITIES	COLLEGE MAJORS & TRAINING PROGRAMS
Literary			
English Languages Social Science	Creativity Good Salary High Achievement Independence Leadership Prestige Variety Work with Mind Work with People	Language Leadership Persuasive Social	**Communications** Advertising Broadcasting Communications Journalism Public Relations Technical Writing **Language Study** Classics Creative Writing English Linguistics World Languages **Performing Arts** Dance Dramatic Arts Modeling Music Music Education Music History **Philosophy** Philosophy
Art			**Visual Arts** Art Education Art History Commercial Art Fashion Design Film Studies/ Cinematography/ Animation Floral Design Graphic Design Illustration Industrial Design Interior Design Photography Set Design Studio Art
Art English Family/Consumer Science	Creativity High Achievement Independence Prestige Variety Work with Hands Work with Mind Work with People	Artistic Language Manual Spatial For Art Teachers: Social, Teaching	
Music			
English Music	Creativity High Achievement Independence Prestige Variety Work with Hands Work with Mind Work with People	Language Leadership Manual Musical For Music Teachers: Social, Teaching	
Entertainment			
Art English Management Music Social Science	Creativity Good Salary High Achievement Independence Prestige Risk Variety Work with Mind Work with People	Artistic Language Leadership Musical Persuasive For Drama Teachers: Social, Teaching	

(continues)

Figure 8.1. Continued.

SOCIAL

TYPICAL JOBS

Customer Service

Barber/Beauty Services
Barber 3-P
Cosmetologist/Hair Stylist 3-G
Manicurist 2

Hotel/Restaurant Services
Bellhop 1-G
Food Counter Worker 1-E
Food Preparation Worker 1-E
Restaurant Host/Hostess 1-E
Vending Machine Attendant 2-G
Waiter/Waitress 1-E

Passenger Services
Ambulance Driver 2-G
Baggage Porter 1-G
Bus Driver 1-G
Flight Attendant 2-G
Taxi/Limo Driver 1-NA

Protective Services
Corrections Officer 2-E
Fish and Game Warden 2-P
Park Ranger 2-NA
Police Officer 2-F
Security Guard 1-E

Other Services
Gas Station Attendant 1-P
Merchandise Deliverer 1-P
Parking Lot Attendant 1-G

Personal Service

Child/Adult Care
Child Care Worker 1-G
Emergency Medical Technician 3-G
Home Health Aide 1/2-E
Homemaker 1-E

Nursing Aide 1/2-E
Occupational Therapy Aide 2-E
Physical Therapy Aide 2-E
Psychiatric Aide 1/2-E
Social/Human Service Assistant 2-E

Instruction
Adult Education Teacher 3/5-E
Farm and Home Management
 Advisor 5-F
Physical Education Teacher 5-G

Recreation Leader 3/5-P
Tour and Travel Guide 2-G
Vocational Instructor 3/5-E

Sports
Athlete 2-P
Coach/Sports Instructor 2-G

Social Service

Counseling/Social Work
Clinical/Counseling Psychologist 5-G
Counselor 5-G
Probation Officer 5-G
Recreational Therapist 5-F
Social Worker 5-F

Patient Care/Therapy
Dental Assistant 2-G
Dental Hygienist 4-E
Licensed Practical Nurse 4-G
Medical Assistant 3/4-E

Occupational Therapist 5-G
Pharmacy Technician 2-G
Physician Assistant 4-G
Radiologic (X-Ray) Technologist 4-G
Registered Nurse 4-E
Respiratory Therapist 4-G
Surgical Technician 4-G

Religious Work
Clergy, Catholic 5-E
Clergy, Jewish 5-G
Clergy, Protestant 5-F

Social Research
Anthropologist 5-F
Historian 5-F
Political Scientist 5-F
Sociologist 5-F

Education

College Student Personnel Work
Dean of Students 5-G
Director of Admissions 5-E
Director of Career Services 5-G
Director of Student Affairs 5-E
Financial Aid Officer 5-G

Administration
College Administrator 5-G
School Administrator 5-E

Library Services
Archivist 5-P

Librarian 5-F
Library Technician 3-G

Teaching
College Professor 5-F
Elementary School Teacher 5-G

Preschool Teacher 3/4-E
Secondary School Teacher 5-E
Special Needs Teacher 5-E
Teacher Aide 3-G

Note: See other clusters for
secondary school teachers of specific
subject areas. For example, you will
find Math–Science teacher in the
Math–Science cluster.

(continues)

Figure 8.1. Continued.

COLLEGE MAJORS & TRAINING PROGRAMS

SCHOOL SUBJECTS	WORK VALUES	ABILITIES
Customer Service		
Family/Consumer Science Math Shop	Outdoor Work Physical Activity Risk Work with Hands Work with People	Artistic Social Clerical Spatial Computational Language Manual
Personal Service		
Agriculture Math Health Science Social Science Shop Family/Consumer Science	Outdoor Work Physical Activity Risk Variety Work with Hands Work with People	Computational Social Language Spatial Manual Teaching Mechanical Scientific
Social Service		

English
Languages
Math
Science
Social Science
	Creativity Job Security Leadership Prestige
	Good Salary Variety
	High Achievement
	Independence
	  Work with Mind
	  Work with People
		Language
		Leadership
		Mathematical
		Persuasive
		Scientific
		Social
		Teaching

Education		

Administrators: Finance,
Management
Librarians: Clerical Studies,
English, Languages
Teachers/Professors:
Depends on Subject Taught
	Creativity Leadership Prestige Variety
	Good Salary
	High Achievement
	Job Security
	  Work with Mind
	  Work with People
		Clerical
		Language
		Leadership
		Persuasive
		Social
		Teaching

Education
Athletic Training
Early Childhood Education
Educational Administration
Elementary Education
Health Education
Home Economics
Instructional Design
Library Science
Physical Education
Secondary Education
Special Education
Teaching English as a
  Second Language

Health Care
Dental Assisting
Emergency Medical Assisting
Medical Assisting
Occupational Therapy Assisting
Physical Therapy Assisting
Practical Nursing
Radiologic Technology

Nursing and Therapy
Dental Hygiene
Nursing
Occupational Therapy
Physician Assisting
Recreational Therapy
Respiratory Therapy

Personal Service
Barbering/Hair Styling
Cosmetology/Beauty Culture
Flight Attendant Training

Social Service
Child Care and Development
Counseling
Human Services
School Psychology
Social Work

Social Studies
Anthropology
Clinical/Counseling Psychology
Criminal Justice
Criminology
Ethnic Studies
Family Studies
Gerontology
History
International Relations
Political Science/ Government
Psychology
Religious Studies
Sociology
Theology
Women's Studies

(continues)

Figure 8.1. Continued.

BUSINESS

TYPICAL JOBS

Sales

Purchasing
Buyer 3-P
Purchasing Agent 3-G

Sales
Automobile Sales 2-G
Counter/Rental Clerk 1-G
Dispensing Optician 3-G
Employment Interviewer 2-F
Financial Planner 5-G
Fund Raiser NA
Insurance Sales 3-G
Manufacturer's Representative 3-F
Parts Sales 2-P
Real Estate Sales 3-G
Retail Sales Worker 1-G
Route Sales Driver 2-G
Stock and Bond Sales 5-G
Telemarketer 1-G
Travel Agent 2-F
Wholesale Sales Representative 3-F

Technical Sales
Computer and Business Services Sales Representative 3-G
Sales Engineer 5-G

Note: There are sales agents for many other goods and services

Management

Administration
Administrative Services Manager 3-F
Bank Manager 5-F
Business Executive 5-P
Government Administrator 5-P
Human Resources Manager 5-P
Legislative Assistant NA
Office Manager 3-P
Sales/Marketing Manager 3-F

Management
Auto Service Station Manager 3-F
Chef 3-E
Construction Superintendent 3-E
Farm Manager 3-F
Food Service Manager 3-G
Funeral Director 3-G
Health Services Manager 5-G
Hotel/Motel Manager 3-F
Production Manager 5-F
Property/Real Estate Manager 5-G
Restaurant Manager 3-G
Sales Worker Supervisor 3-F

Planning
Contractor 3-E
Industrial Engineer 5-F
Management Consultant 5-P

Legal

Contracts and Claims
Claims Adjuster 3-G
Title Examiner 2-F

Law
Judge 5-F
Law Clerk 5-G
Lawyer 5-P
Paralegal Assistant 3/4-P

Safety/Law Enforcement
Building Inspector 3-G
Customs Inspector 3-P
FBI Agent 5-P
Fire Chief 3-P
Food and Drug Inspector NA
Occupational Health & Safety Specialist 5-G
Police Chief 3-P
Private Detective 3-P
Special Agent 3/5-P

(continues)

Figure 8.1. *Continued.*

COLLEGE MAJORS & TRAINING PROGRAMS

SCHOOL SUBJECTS	WORK VALUES	ABILITIES	COLLEGE MAJORS & TRAINING PROGRAMS
Sales			

English
Management
Math
For Sales Engineers:
Science
Technology
Finance
	Creativity
	Good Salary
	High Achievement
	Independence
	Leadership
	Outdoor Work
	Variety
	Work with Mind
	Work with People
		Clerical
		Computational
		Language
		Leadership
		Mathematical
		Persuasive
		Scientific
		Social
			Financial
			Banking and Finance
			Business Economics
			Financial Planning
			Insurance
			Investment and Securities
			
			Legal
			Claims Adjusting
			Criminal Justice/ Corrections
			Labor/Industrial Relations
			Law Enforcement
			Law/Pre-Law
			Legal Assisting
			Paralegal Studies
			
			Management
			Agribusiness Management
			Aviation Administration
			Business Administration
			Culinary Arts
			Food Production
			  Management
			Food Service Management
			Health Care Management
			Hospital Administration
			Hotel Management
			Human Resource
			  Management
			Industrial Engineering
			International Business
			Management Science
			Medical Records
			  Administration
			Mortuary Science/Funeral
			  Service
			Park and Recreation
			  Management
			Production Management
			Public Administration
			Restaurant Management
			Retail Management
			Small Business Management
			Transportation Management
			
			Sales/Marketing
			Advertising
			Fashion Merchandising
			Marketing
			Ophthalmic Dispensing
			Real Estate
			Retail Merchandising
			Tourism/Travel

Management			
Agriculture Finance Management Science Social Science	English Languages Math	Creativity Good Salary High Achievement Independence Leadership Outdoor Work	Prestige Variety Work with Mind Work with People
Legal			
English Management Math Science Social Science Finance	Creativity Good Salary High Achievement Independence Job Security Leadership	Prestige Risk Variety Work with Mind Work with People	Computational Language Leadership Persuasive Scientific Social

Figure 8.1. *Continued.*

OFFICE OPERATIONS

TYPICAL JOBS

Clerical

Keyboard Operation	Cashier 1-G	Human Resources Assistant 2-G	**Scheduling/Registration**	**Secretarial Services**
Data Entry Keyer 2-P	Post Office Clerk 2-P	Library Assistant 1-G	Dispatcher 2-G	Administrative Assistant 4-G
Medical Transcriptionist 2-G	**Records Processing**	Mail Carrier 1-P	Hospital Admitting Interviewer 2-G	Secretary 4-F
Typist/Word Processor 2-P	Court Reporter 3-G	Mailroom Clerk 1-G	Hotel/Motel Clerk 2-G	**Switchboard Services**
Paying and Receiving	Customer Service Representative 2-G	Medical Record Technician 3-E	Production Clerk 2-G	Switchboard Operator 1-P
Bank Teller 2-F	File Clerk 1-G	Messenger/Courier 1-P	Receptionist 1-G	Telephone Operator 1-P
Bill Collector 2-G	General Office Clerk 1-G	Office Machine Operator 1-P	Ticket/Reservation Agent 2-P	
		Order Clerk 2-F		

Data Analysis

Bookkeeping/Computation	Credit Authorizer 3-F	**Computer Operation**	Auditor 5-G	Real Estate Appraiser 2-G
Accounting Clerk 3/4-G	Insurance Clerk 2-P	Computer Operator 2-P	Budget Analyst 5-P	Tax Accountant 5-G
Billing Clerk 2-F	Payroll Clerk 2-F	**Finance/Accounting**	Insurance Underwriter 5-F	Tax Examiner 5-F
Bookkeeper 3/4-G	Statistical Clerk 2-F	Accountant 5-G	Investment Analyst 5-P	Treasurer/Controller 5-G
Brokerage Clerk 5-P			Loan Officer 5-G	

(continues)

Figure 8.1. *Continued.*

SCHOOL SUBJECTS | WORK VALUES | ABILITIES | COLLEGE MAJORS & TRAINING PROGRAMS

Clerical

SCHOOL SUBJECTS	WORK VALUES	ABILITIES	COLLEGE MAJORS & TRAINING PROGRAMS
Clerical Studies	Job Security	Clerical	**Clerical Support** — Administrative Assisting, Library Assisting, Office Management
English	Outdoor Work	Computational	**Data Analysis** — Accounting, Bookkeeping, Insurance Underwriting, Real Estate Appraisal, Taxation
Finance	Physical Activity	Language	**Education** — Business Education
Management	Work with Hands	Manual	**Information Processing** — Computer Equipment Operation, Data Processing, Typing/Keyboarding, Word Processing
Math	Work with Mind	Social	**Record Keeping** — Court Reporting, Medical Record Technology
	Work with People		**Secretarial** — Legal Secretarial, Medical Secretarial, Secretarial Studies

Data Analysis

SCHOOL SUBJECTS	WORK VALUES	ABILITIES
Clerical Studies	Good Salary	Clerical
English	High Achievement	Computational
Finance	Job Security	Language
Management	Leadership	Leadership
Math	Prestige	Mathematical
	Work with Hands	
	Work with Mind	

Figure 8.1. *Continued.*

Clusters Chart those subjects, values, and abilities that match their selections. In a very concrete way, circling highlights the degree of congruence in a person's career thinking. It also provides the helper with an opportunity to discuss the ways that subjects, values, and abilities relate to successful job performance and work satisfaction. The interpretive materials confront naiveté and provide answers to questions such as, "Why do I have to take an English course to be a social worker?" or "Of what use are science courses when I want to work with computers?"

Considerable amounts of specific occupational information are given for jobs that employ the majority of people in the United States. For each job, the Career Clusters Charts provide a U.S. Department of Labor employment outlook forecast ranging from excellent to poor. Interpretive materials that are part of both CDM-R Levels 1 and 2 are updated every 2 years to coincide with the most recent U.S. job projections. Minimum educational and training requirements are listed first, using the following codes:

1. **Entry-level skills** learned on the job by training for a few days up to 2 months with an experienced worker

2. **On-the-job training** for 2 to 6 months with an experienced worker

3. **Apprenticeship or intensive on-the-job training** for 6 months to 5 years with an experienced worker

4. **Technical/vocational program** completed in a high school community college, technical college, or business college

5. **College degree** or, in some cases, a professional or graduate degree

Inspection of Figure 8.1 reveals a large number of jobs that require only an apprenticeship or on-the-job training.

Because many CDM users are involved in a transitional process, the college majors and training programs related to each cluster are listed on page 3 of Level 2. These listings are broken up into subcategories to facilitate a search; for example, the Scientific area includes Architecture, Engineering, Health Sciences, Information Sciences/Systems, Life Sciences, Mathematics, Physical Sciences, Scientific Technologies, and Social Science. The purpose of this information, close to related job titles, school subjects, and required abilities, is to help people identify college and university major areas of study associated with their interests, as well as vocational–technical programs, which have shorter completion times.

The critical message on page 4 of the Level 2 Interpretive Folder exhorts people to continue their career exploration by accessing the U.S. Department of Labor's O*NET occupational information database on CareerZone. Users can learn more about the jobs they indicated on the Career Charts by going to the Web site (www.cdmcareerzone.com).

An experience I had while conducting a workshop brings out an important point: People must believe that they have real choices before proceeding with the career decision-making process. Because the workshop was held in a community that was rural, remote, and economically depressed, people felt lucky to have jobs. Workshop participants said they did not believe the people within their region had career choices because they were forced to take whatever work was available. The participants believed that their capacity to choose reflected that of the residents overall in the region. Many people said that they had few choices in their own lives due to the community's remote location and poor economy. In this situation, my objective changed from teaching career decision making to helping people identify the decisions they made in their everyday lives and examine their risk-taking tendencies in making these decisions. The outcome revealed that many people did indeed feel that they had choices. This experience reminded me that the helper constantly needs to evaluate the developmental stage of the person(s) with whom he or she is working before proceeding to a higher level developmental task.

CDM-R Computer Software

The computer version was designed with flexibility in mind. The software has three main applications:

1. in conjunction with a scanning scoring machine, the capability to score large-group administrations using specially designed machine-scorable answer sheets;

2. capability for the examiner to enter an individual's assessment responses on the computer to generate a report; and

3. a stand-alone, self-administered personal computer (PC) option.

The only difference between the computer-based CDM-R version and the paper-and-pencil version of the self-assessment portion, other than the fact that the computer scores the instrument, is that the computer allows for an intermediate step, which reflects people's thinking process. Whereas the user of the pencil-and-paper version selects only four for each category — best abilities, preferred values, and best school subjects — the computer version requires the user to prioritize his or her choices. Kapes and Vansickle (1992) reported that the computer-based CDM-R version is more reliable than the paper-and-pencil version.

The advantages to scoring the machine-scored answer sheets with the software are as follows: scoring costs are lower because local equipment is used, and the amount of time between testing and having the results returned to the client is potentially lessened. The main advantages of the personal computer option are as follows: Paper-and-pencil assessments have a built-in time lag while individuals proceed to look up specific information, whereas the computer permits instantaneous searching of the designated career cluster's occupational information related to a person's results, with specific job titles provided if Internet access is available. More important, the computer highlights the degree of agreement between self-assessed school-subject preferences, job values, and abilities with actual job requirements. The computer version highlights this CDM-R feature more than the paper-and-pencil version. The hand-entered score option can be valuable for some students with special needs who can have someone else administer the survey because they do not totally comprehend questions either due to reading difficulties or to trouble in seeing or writing. A computer-generated report thus still can be completed. In all three computer applications, local agencies determine the type of report they wish to receive: a single-page personal profile — sometimes referred to as an individualized career plan —for insertion into a person's record folder or career portfolio (see later section); an approximately 8-page self-interpreting personalized report that a client immediately can take with him or her; or a counselor's report.

The stand-alone computer version has considerable versatility. Absenteeism is a major issue in school districts, and many schools require every student to have a career plan available. The absentee can take the instrument on a computer and get a personalized interpretation, thus saving time for the administrator. Continuous availability to any client through a computer offers a career planning service that most experts have judged as being needed. Within a client session, the counselor can determine the need for a career or educational plan and can use the computer as a personal assistant. In addition, many clients have expressed a preference for using a computer database rather than interaction with a counselor. If an Internet connection is available, the CDM-R computer version can instantaneously move an individual from a career assessment to the career exploration process in CareerZone.

Interpretation Aids

In a visual age, videos make a greater impact and are more exciting than many presenters who explain score results. The video series Tour of Your Tomorrow (Feller & Vasos, 2001) gives an overview of occupations in the six CDM-R career options, helps people to understand differences between each area, and addresses how to use the information. Interviews with real workers show the breadth and diversity of each career area. Viewers see and hear what people in more than 60 different jobs do, as well as explanations of why individuals chose their jobs, the abilities and skills they use in their work, the education and training they obtained, and the values that they receive from doing the work. The video gives greater meaning to the terms that clients discover on their CDM-R profiles.

Also available are two workbooks that use CDM-R information in greater depth: *The Career Exploration System* (Stone & McCloskey, 1993b) and *Beginning Career Exploration System* (Stone & McCloskey, 1993a) for middle or junior high school students contain a series of career planning activities. The goals of the activities, which are facilitated by a Leader's Guide, are to develop self-knowledge, career awareness, and career exploration and preparation skills, which include interviewing skills and résumé writing. These worktexts are suitable for use in a career program or as a basis of a curriculum for a career guidance class.

A Career Exploration and Career Decision-Making Program

The CDM-R materials state that choosing a job requires time and hard work. In this section, I suggest five sessions (45 to 60 minutes each) for leading a career exploration program. The length of time can be shortened or lengthened as the size of the group dictates. Although the program format will tend to remain constant, people will respond to its content differently, depending on their life experiences and career maturity levels.

Session 1

Each person is told the program objectives: to discover his or her interests and identify related jobs; to learn the major components of career decision making; to identify specific job titles for further study; to assist in his or her selection of a course of study, if appropriate; and to use available occupational information to narrow the choices. The helper then should administer the CDM-R. Session 2 should follow as soon as possible to take advantage of the natural curiosity created by the self-scoring and immediate feedback feature of the CDM-R. For example, in Level 1, Session 2, which deals with interpretation, could easily become integrated with Session 1 or at least partially begun.

Session 2

The helper should prepare beforehand any career information materials to be used as added resources for job exploration purposes, any information from the state Department of Employment and Training about employment availability, and job projections for the immediate geographic region available from the state Department of Labor. The interpretive Career Clusters Chart offers step-by-step directions for organizing and using the survey results and occupational information. The amount of assistance that the helper provides is dependent on the group's ability to independently comprehend the tasks. The significance of the previously mentioned congruence model becomes apparent after individuals have circled their preferred school subjects, values, and abilities and matched them with those printed on the CDM-R Career Clusters Chart. People will be curious about the meaning of specific disagreements. The helper should provide information about the types of training and skills needed for various jobs to clarify misconceptions about job qualifications. Helpers should also teach people how to use resource materials such as career briefs or, if available, a computer information system. A lack of congruence among self-perceived abilities, values, and interests is best examined in individual sessions with helpers to clarify these issues.

In preparation for Session 5, the helper should have each person select a job for intensive research and assist people in preparing for this project by outlining available sources of printed information; suggesting people to interview, such as relatives, neighbors, and friends; and possibly arranging for visits to worksites. The helper should provide an outline of information to be gained from this job search, such as job title, job descriptions, interests, tasks, skills, knowledge, education, school programs, wages, job outlook, similar jobs, sources of additional information, result of job site visit or interview, and personal attitude toward the job before and after the research. This information is available on the Internet (www.cdmcareerzone.com) or in the local library in the U.S. Department of Labor's very popular *Occupational Outlook Handbook*. The video series Tour of Your Tomorrow is a good resource for Session 2.

Session 3

The CDM-R highlights the need for further examination and clarification of values by teaching people how important personal goals are reflected in work. For the helper, three additional steps are recommended: identifying other values, examining goal-setting behaviors, and evaluating risk-taking behaviors. These additional steps are implemented through a values clarification process that typically involves exercises or games. The exercises are usually done in small groups, and public sharing of views is encouraged. As a result of this process, an individual often gains a greater awareness of the diversity of values held by others and learns to express his or her own commitments.

Identification of additional values is very important because the CDM-R list is not all-inclusive. In one gaming approach, people are told that they have more than enough money, time to do anything they want, and a powerful job position that allows them to order other people to do their bidding. The helper then asks each group member to write down what he or she personally would do in each of the above three situations. The purpose is twofold: The task teaches people to recognize the effects of certain values, such as money, personal freedom, and power, and it enables individuals to prioritize values.

Goal-setting behaviors can be related to values. In one approach, the helper tells people to choose between two jobs — one that pays well but is boring and another that is exciting but provides minimal pay. People then write each option — salary and exciting work — on separate pieces of paper and place the two in order, indicating their first and second choices. The helper tells people that a third exciting and good-paying job might make demands on family relationships. He or she then asks people to write time for family on a third piece of paper, consider this new option along with the previous two, and prioritize the three choices. The helper repeats this process until all the following values have been considered: good health, geographic location, use of an individual's talents, recognition for contributions, time to relate to children, seeing the results of work, inclusion in decision making that affects other individuals' work, and working in a friendly environment. People then share the rationale statements behind their choices with the rest of the group.

Risk taking is part of everyday life. Some people choose to avoid risk; they carefully weigh the consequences and select the "safe" choice or outcome. Others are dreamers whose choices express the most desirable option but disregard the possibility that the option will be achievable. Still other people use a combination strategy and select the alternative that has medium desirability and probability. Risk taking has an impact on decision making. Often, individuals know exactly what they want and how to implement their goal, but are hesitant to decide because they are unsure of the outcome. This very common phenomenon provides the rationale for the inclusion of risk taking in the career planning process so as to offer suggestions to enhance an individual's decision-making abilities. Making a decision involves taking risks. The helper assists people by examining the probabilities of outcomes for various options and by determining the level of risk they would accept. The work books *The Career Exploration System* and *Beginning Career Exploration System* are good resources for Sessions 3 and 4.

Session 4

In Session 4, people identify their abilities, skills, and talents. Although this topic is appropriate for everyone, it is especially critical for individuals with special needs. The following is a listing of views often associated with the assessment of abilities, each with a definite implication:

- People should be realistic in their knowledge of what they can do.

- Tests cannot accurately portray abilities.

- If people never have had the chance to do a task, they do not know whether they can do it.

- A person's "true" ability may be unknown due to a history of failure and poor self-esteem.

In my experience, all people, from the brightest to those with less cognitive proficiency, must be coaxed to provide information about their accomplishments. Because most people have been conditioned not to boast, the helper must work to identify the individual's skills and undeveloped talents. This process will take time. (Strategies for doing this are included in Chapter 3.)

As a professor at Northeastern University, which operates the world's largest cooperative education program with thousands of students each year involved in work-study and practice-oriented education, my observation is that learning is not achieved simply by doing a job. People need to communicate their experience to be aware of what they are doing. Sharing enhances the learning experience. Getting students to describe their experiences and talk about the skills and values involved will heighten awareness of their assets. What better way is there to prepare a person for a job interview?

Optional Session for Parents' and Guardians' Night

Parents and guardians often exert a very strong influence on their children's career choices. Many parents and guardians expect children to make career commitments before they are ready or have sufficient information. Parents often project their own desires and fears on the child's career selection. In doing so, parents and guardians are denying the reality of learning for one's self because they have observed others use the benefit of experience to alter their educational direction or change a job in the pursuit of work satisfaction.

For parental or guardian influence to be based on factual information, the helper should invite the adults to an evening program and have them bring the child's CDM-R Career Clusters Chart. The helper should explain the materials, such as CareerZone, to the parents and guardians, discuss the concept of career exploration, and show them the local supplementary materials provided to the child. The helper should also emphasize the value of workplace visits, shadowing experiences, and volunteer exploratory opportunities. He or she should recruit the parents' and guardians' assistance in this latter project.

Session 5

At the end of Session 2, each person identified a particular job to research through career information material, discussion with an employed worker, and/or a site visit. The purpose of Session 5, which may need to be scheduled for more than one day, is for each person to report the results of his or her research. It is valuable for people who have researched the same job to detect discrepancies, because the same job titles can be experienced differently in various work settings. The helper should have individuals emphasize any changes in their perception of the job that occurred as a result of this project. In an individual's explanation of the reasons for his or her changed view about a job, myths, stereotypes, and misinformation frequently emerge.

Ability Explorer

The career development theorists discussed in Chapter 1 emphasize the importance of self-awareness of abilities in vocational planning. The *Ability Explorer* (AE; Harrington & Harrington, 1996, 2003) is an instrument designed to help people complete a self-exploration of their abilities and relate this information to career and/or educational planning. In fact, the *Ability Explorer* implements seven of Super's theoretical propositions that relate to self-concepts of ability (Harrington & Harrington, 2002).

The AE recognizes 14 major work-related abilities: Artistic, Clerical, Interpersonal, Language, Leadership, Manual, Musical/Dramatic, Numerical/Mathematical, Organizational, Persuasive, Scientific, Social, Spatial, and Technical/Mechanical. The micro-ability statements surveyed in the instrument emanate from the U.S. Department of Labor job analysts' findings gathered through worker performance observations. Two hand-scored levels of the AE are available, each of which takes about 45 to 50 minutes to administer.

Level 1 is designed primarily for use with students in middle or junior high school and people of all ages with limited learning and reading ability. Its purpose is to help people explore their abilities and related careers and to plan courses for high school or continuing education. Level 1 consists of work-related skill statements for each ability area and behavioral reinforcements consisting of activities, experiences, and school subjects related to each ability.

There are three sections to the *Ability Explorer*. Sample items from Level 1 are as follows:

1. *Abilities Section*—Users rate how good they are at doing an activity (e.g., measuring amounts, remembering lines for a school play, deciding who will do what job, taking care of young people) according to the following categories: very good, good, little above average, little below average, poor, or very poor.

2. *Activities Section* (behavioral reinforcers)—Users state whether they have done an activity (e.g., drew cartoons, taught someone to swim, put a toy together, cooked or baked) and how well, according to the following categories: very well, well, not well, or never tried.

3. *School Subjects Section* (behavioral reinforcers)—Users state the grade (A or B, C, D, F, or Not Taken) for courses they may have taken in school (e.g., Art, Shop, Language Arts, Computers, Mathematics).

Level 2 is used with students in high school as well as with adults. Its purpose is to help individuals continue learning about their abilities, prepare to make the transition from school to work, and develop plans for postsecondary education and training. Level 2 items reflect more advanced skills and experiential opportunities related to each ability area (e.g., "communicating well with people with different backgrounds" [an ability item] and "prepared tax returns" [an activity item]). Both Levels 1 and 2 are written at a Grade 5 or lower reading level.

Two major outcomes of the *Ability Explorer* are (a) a profile of the self-perceived strengths and weaknesses of one's 14 abilities and (b) job options related to the ability areas. This information can be surprising because most people realize their greatest strength but are not always aware of their secondary abilities. Knowing all of one's abilities is important because most jobs require multiple abilities. Also, after completing the *Ability Explorer*, because its related jobs are the occupational titles used in CareerZone, the Department of Labor's extensive occupational information system, users can proceed at no cost to the Internet site at www.nycareerzone.org. This next step permits a person to continue a more comprehensive career exploration process. CareerZone is a user-friendly version of O*NET described in detail in Chapter 9.

Jobs with similar ability requirements are reported in groupings. Providing a grouping of occupations as opposed to a single occupational title is especially valuable in working with people with disabling conditions. Also, exploration of each occupation is essential to consider unique requirements relevant to the individual. For example, the grouping for Manual Ability includes "roofer," which involves climbing ladders, lifting heavy materials, bending and balancing while on roofs, and working outside, often in the extreme cold and heat; "assembler," which involves little lifting of heavy objects but may require standing for long periods; "construction laborer," which requires strength, mobility, skills to manipulate controls and mechanical equipment, and full use of fingers, hands, and feet; "cook," which requires a person to work quickly, understand directions often received under rushed and noisy circumstances, and perform under pressure; and "nursery worker," which may require a person to work independently and to have a driver's license to get to different locations. Changing the situation (e.g., working as a gardener for a hotel), however, may alter the work functions and requirements, which, in the gardener example, would eliminate the ability to drive and the need to get to different locations. "Rancher" is another occupation listed in the Manual Ability grouping. However, examining the occupational information in CareerZone will reveal that this occupation requires more education and training than the previously listed jobs. This information illustrates the multiple considerations involved in career planning and identifying appropriate work for people with special needs.

Each ability is accompanied by two behavioral reinforcer ratings (activities and school subjects), which may identify people whose lack of experience has given them few opportunities to develop specific abilities. The helper can optimize these individuals' potential by suggesting related activities to perform. Behavioral reinforcers thus can be used to learn how to improve an ability. The first step is for the helper to believe and convey that abilities can be improved, and the second step is to identify opportunities. The following are examples of abilities with activities or experiences that might help develop specific abilities:

- *Numerical*— created a budget, balanced a checkbook, understood the financial pages of a newspaper, kept scores for sports event

- *Scientific*— used first aid; grew plants, flowers, or vegetables; took part in an environmental group; did science projects on a computer

- *Technical/Mechanical*— maintained a computer, helped someone repair a car, showed someone how a machine works, fixed a broken bicycle

Another AE goal is illustrated by the following example. Once I was trying to understand a person's low numerical ability score. The 24-year-old reported, "It's always been like that. My third-grade teacher told me that I would never be able to do math." There was a concrete level of thinking exhibited in the remark. Although I doubted the accuracy of the statement, I realized that changing this individual's self-belief would take a great deal of effort. Interpretation of scores can indicate how some individuals' self-appraisals develop and possibly identify ways for the helper to attack this observation. The reader may wish to refer to Krumboltz's social learning theory, described in Chapter 1, which deals with self-observation generalizations and faulty beliefs, or social cognitive career theory, which deals with self-efficacy.

AE results also can be used to examine whether the individual has performed well scholastically and in activities that offer support for the high ability self-rating. Assessment can help determine how realistic the self-evaluation is. For example, based on the following Activities Section self-ratings for a 15-year-old, an inquiry into the basis of the person's self-rating of artistic for the highest ability area seems appropriate if the person has not tried many activities and only rated one as being done well, as the report indicates:

- *Well*—Recognized famous paintings at an art display

- *Never tried*— Carved designs in wood or clay; made posters; made jewelry; did arts and crafts; created a new hair style

The intent is not to deflate the person's ego but to let the person communicate a rationale for the rating. The person's assessment may be very accurate. The best message the report should send to the helper is that the individual may have had limited exposure to activities and needs to explore all the many skills that comprise an ability area, such as fine-motor coordination, spatial, and color blending, for example.

Another use of the reported information is to explore why a person receives high grades but acknowledges only average ratings in ability and performance of related activities. Do other people see greater self-efficacy than the individual does? Is this an ability in which an individual has little interest and thus high self-esteem in this area is not deemed important?

Career Portfolio

A career portfolio, sometimes referred to as a demonstration instrument, is a structured tool designed to allow students the opportunity to collect a great deal of information about themselves (McDivitt, 1994). It is used to integrate career development into a curriculum and help students understand the link between school and work. In the School-To-Work Opportunities Act of 1994, which was updated in 2001, programs are required to integrate work-based and school-based learning and provide all students with the opportunity to complete a career major. Lambert (1994) described these two types of learning, whose outcomes are collected in an individualized career plan within a career portfolio. The school-based component includes the following:

- career exploration and counseling,
- identification of a career major,
- a study program that meets requirements needed to earn a skill certificate, and
- regularly scheduled student evaluations.

The work-based component requires the following:

- a planned job training and work experience program,
- paid work experience,
- workplace mentoring,
- instruction in workplace competencies, and
- instruction in a variety of industry elements.

The CDM-R and AE provide a core for some of the above school-based components. During interpretation of these instruments, a plan and information will emerge that fit, for example, the contents of a *Career Options Portfolio* developed by the University of Wisconsin Board of Regents/Wisconsin Career Information System/Center on Education and Work (1993). This portfolio includes statements of interests, skills (abilities), values, achievement test scores, study skills, career clusters, work preferences (tasks, environments, and accommodations needed), occupational (job) preferences, educational courses needed, career goals, junior and senior high school plans, and personal development activities. Portfolios expand these topics, enriching the presentation and showing a record of accomplishment and achievement. Portfolios may be a folder, journal, notebook, diary, computer disc, or any medium, such as the Internet, that enables students to present information about themselves.

Another portfolio model is the *Life Work Portfolio* (National Occupational Information Coordinating Committee, 1995), which includes the following topical contents:

- *Who I Am:* Personal Data, What I Stand For, How I Operate, My Interests, My Personal Management Styles, My Wellness Strategies, Life Roles, Thinking About Roles, What I Have To Offer, My Work Experience, What I Can Do, My Personal Qualities, Challenges and Realities, How I Can Grow From Here

- *Exploring:* My Ideal Job, Career Exploration Activities, Networking, Exploring Training Options, Working for Myself

- *Deciding:* A Model for Career Decision Making, Decide to Decide, Gather Information About Yourself, Explore What's Out There, Generate Options and Consequences, Career Options Grid

- *Planning and Acting:* Put Together a Plan, Job Seeking Checklist, Job Application Fact Sheet, Resume Worksheet, Cover Letter Outline, Interview Questions, First Week on the Job, Growing on the Job, Training on the Job, Evaluate Your Progress, Planning and Acting Checklist, Your Plan

With the acceptance of portfolios by the professional community, a shift has occurred away from their production to an expansion of their use. Consequently, their content and organization have been adapted to purposes such as tools to organize educational and career searches, enhance job interviews, and support annual performance reviews. The portfolios of the 2000s increasingly will be electronic portfolios and will be driven by the ability of teachers to obtain the training to implement them, decisions as to whether or not to use digital cameras and scanners for portfolios, and costs of implementing available commercial products. Portfolios have been adopted to create literacy profiles for first- and third-grade students, to monitor the progress of individuals studying English as a second language, to be used as computerized report cards for providing glimpses of student progress three times a year, and as presentations and working portfolios for counselors themselves (Hackbarth & Greenwalt, 2001). There are some concerns regarding portfolios: They require a lot of time to maintain, and online availability raises security and confidentiality issues.

The goal of the portfolio is to collect documentation of successful mastery of competencies and empower individuals by conveying the control one has over what is and is not included in their self-descriptions. It is a process whereby students learn to self-assess. Feedback from sharing this information can be a valuable experience, especially using the Internet's flexibility with family members. Paulson, Paulson, and Meyer (1991) cited the following portfolio features: (a) the student can monitor self-progress over time, (b) the selection of work to be included reflects what the student values regarding his or her work, and (c) a variety of work can document multifaceted evidence of competence.

The implicit use of a portfolio is for decision making. Consider the personal message that a person gains from having assessed the following questions: How well do you know yourself? How much effort have you put into exploring future options? What is your decision-making strategy — intuitive, systematic, fatalistic and so on? How much planning do you do? Strategies can lead the person to making a decision, as exemplified in the *Activity Guide: Becoming the Architect of Your Career* (Schutt, 2002). Schutt listed several items: "Identify your decision points. Identify the last three career-related decisions that you have made. What played into these decisions? Family considerations? Financial? Values? What is the next career decision you anticipate you will make?" (p. 10).

Some concerns about the use of portfolios were summarized by McDivitt (1994) as follows:

1. Some educators fear that portfolios will be used instead of standardized testing and consequently will not prepare students for the realities of college and employment testing.

2. Comparability of assessed examples of a work's quality may be dependent on a teacher's learning objective, which might be unidimensional and not assessed according to state-specified performance standards.

3. Some educators may have very limited knowledge of workplace competencies; thus an evaluation may not be compatible with industry standards.

Regarding performance assessments, Messick (1995) wrote that the traditional principles of validity apply: "For example, student portfolios are often the sources of inferences — not just about the quality of the included products but also about the knowledge, skills, or other attributes of the student — and such inferences about quality and constructs need to meet standards of validity" (p. 741).

Yet to be resolved, if portfolios are to be used for assessment purposes, is the agreed-upon set of principles capable of application on a unified basis. The criteria for evaluation need to be specified. For example, for content knowledge, are workplace competencies used? For behaviors, what is the focus: higher-thinking processes, problem solving, or teamwork? For personal characteristics, is the focus on effort, work habits, or attitudes? Are the ratings verifiable? Regardless of the criteria, portfolios have definite benefits for career assessment and development.

Conclusion

In this chapter, I have described processes for collecting information needed for a vocational plan. The procedures detailed involve clients in self-assessment and career exploration. The expected outcome of the process is the identification of a vocational goal (either a specific job title or a cluster of occupations); an awareness of the relationships among work, interests, abilities, and values; a knowledge of the training requirements needed to achieve a specific goal; and recognition of any issues that may deter the achievement of a goal. Collected information was not set forth in a specified vocational plan because no universally accepted format exists, and procedures vary depending upon institutional policies and practices.

Career planning is not a choice made once in a lifetime. Career exploration and development of a vocational goal require time and considerable effort on the client's part. The process is developmental, cyclical, and continuous. A theoretical framework that ensures that all four dimensions — abilities, values, interests, and information — are used in the formulation of a career plan will maximize a person's opportunity to be independent, self-directing, and actualized in his or her work life.

References

Baird, L. L. (1969). The prediction of accomplishment in college: An exploration of the process of achievement. *Journal of Counseling Psychology, 16,* 246–254.

Bartling, H. C., & Hood, A. B. (1981). An 11-year follow-up of measured interests and vocational choice. *Journal of Counseling Psychology, 28*(1), 27–35.

Campbell, D. P. (1974). *If you don't know where you're going, you'll probably end up somewhere else.* Niles, IL: Argus Communications.

Droege, R. C. (1988). Review of the Harrington-O'Shea Career Decision-Making System. In J. T. Kapes & M. M. Mastie (Eds.), *A counselor's guide to career assessment instruments* (2nd ed., pp. 86–90). Alexandria, VA: National Career Development Association.

Feller, R., & Vasos, J. (2001). *Tour of your tomorrow.* Circle Pines, MN: American Guidance Service.

Freeman, B. (1996). The use and perceived effectiveness of career assessment tools: A survey of high school counselors. *Journal of Career Development, 22,* 185–196.

Hackbarth, J. S., & Greenwalt, B. (2001). Documenting success and achievement: Presentation and working portfolios for counselors. *Journal of Counseling & Development, 79,* 161–165.

Harrington, T. F. (2002, January). *A 20-year predictive validity study of The Harrington–O'Shea Career Decision-Making System.* Paper presented at the University of Wisconsin-Madison's Center on Education and Work Career Conference.

Harrington, T. F., & Harrington, J. C. (2002). The integration of Super's ability-related theoretical propositions into a psychometric assessment: The ability explorer. *Career Development Quarterly, 50*(4), 350–358.

Harrington, T. F., & Harrington, J. C. (2003). *Ability explorer.* Austin, TX: PRO-ED.

Harrington, T. F., & O'Shea, A. J. (2000). *The Harrington–O'Shea career decision-making system manual* (Rev. ed.). Circle Pines, MN: American Guidance Service.

Holland, J. L. (1997). *Making vocational choices: A theory of vocational personalities and work environments.* Odessa, FL: Psychological Assessment Resources.

Kapes, J. T., & Vansickle, T. R. (1992). Comparing paper-pencil and computer-based versions of the Harrington-O'Shea Career Decision-Making System. *Measurement and Evaluation in Counseling and Development, 25*(1), 5–13.

Lambert, R. (1994, January). *Tech prep and youth apprenticeship: What every counselor needs to know.* Paper presented at the National Career Development Association National Conference, Albuquerque, NM.

McDivitt, P. J. (1994). Using portfolios for career assessment. In J. T. Kapes, M. M. Mastie, & E. A. Whitfield (Eds.), *A counselor's guide to career assessment instruments* (3rd ed., pp. 361–371). Alexandria, VA: National Career Development Association.

Messick, S. (1995). Validity of psychological assessment. *American Psychologist, 50,* 741–749.

National Occupational Information Coordinating Committee, the Maine Occupational Information Coordinating Committee, and the Career Development Training Institute at Oakland University. (1995). *Life work portfolio.* Washington, DC: National Occupational Information Coordinating Committee.

Paulson, F. L., Paulson, P. R., & Meyer, C. A. (1991). What makes a portfolio a portfolio. *Educational Leadership, 48*(5), 60–63.

School-To-Work Opportunities Act of 1994, 20 U.S.C. § 6101 (2001).

Schutt, D. (2002). *Activity guide: Becoming the architect of your career.* Madison: University of Wisconsin, Office of Human Resource Development.

Simon, S. B. (1974). *Meeting yourself halfway.* Niles, IL: Argus Communications.

Slaney, R. B. (1988). The assessment of career decision making. In W. B. Walsh & S. H. Osipow (Eds.), *Career decision making* (pp. 33–76). Hillsdale, NJ: Erlbaum.

Stone, W., & McCloskey, L. (1993a). *Beginning career exploration system.* Circle Pines, MN: American Guidance Service.

Stone, W., & McCloskey, L. (1993b). *Career exploration system.* Circle Pines, MN: American Guidance Service.

Super, D. E. (1957). *The psychology of careers.* New York: Harper & Row.

Super, D. E. (1994). A life span, life space perspective on convergence. In M. L. Savickas & R. W. Lent (Eds.), *Convergence in career development theories: Implications for science and practice* (pp. 63–74). Palo Alto, CA: CPP Books.

University of Wisconsin Board of Regents/Wisconsin Career Information System/ Center on Education and Work. (1993). *Career options portfolio*. Madison, WI: Author.

Vansickle, T. R. (1994). Review of the Harrington-O'Shea Career Decision-Making System-Revised (CDM-R). In J. T. Kapes, M. M. Mastie, & E. A. Whitfield (Eds.), *A counselor's guide to career assessment instruments* (3rd ed., pp. 172–177). Alexandria, VA: National Career Development Association.

Wise, R., Charner, I., & Randour, M. L. (1976). A conceptual framework for career awareness in career decision-making. *The Counseling Psychologist, 6*(3), 47–53.

OCCUPATIONAL INFORMATION: LINKING SYSTEMS, SOURCES, AND SITES TO JOB SEARCH

Thomas F. Harrington and Richard W. Feller

Occupational information is essential to researchers, labor market specialists, and career specialists in documenting opportunities and suggesting options to clients, educational planners, and job developers. Attaining self-knowledge, exploration, and career planning competencies depends on the integration of information so that individuals can take action. Systems, sources, and Web sites can create dependency on professional helpers, however, when materials lack ease of use and friendliness, offer limited motivational appeal, are beyond the user's reading comprehension, or fail to enhance self-directed exploration and job search. Since publication of the *Handbook's* second edition, much has changed in the world of occupational information and its ability to empower individuals in the career planning process.

Technology's availability, speed, and appeal have influenced occupational information's potential to enhance career development competency attainment. The Internet has made searching for information about careers, employers, and jobs easier by expanding access to Web sites in real time. Enhanced formats using imagery and interactive video have added to motivational power and user friendliness, and in making messages more cogent. In some cases, it overcomes language and reading deficiencies to reach previously underserved populations. The ease of updating information and databases promotes greater

267

accuracy and reliability. Connecting multiple sources creates greater efficiency and integration of exploration, planning, and advocacy.

Of equal importance is the helper's awareness of expanded options for individuals within the changing workplace. Guiding learners and clients to be self-directed in career exploration and skilled in interviewing and the job search has become a priority as institutions meet accountability standards. This is an important message for young people from different cultures to comprehend. Parents accustomed to their own experiences may not understand or appreciate how their children will compete for employment in the United States. As job content and context have changed, the job-interview process has been transformed within many organizations. Employers seek greater evidence of specific performance skills and behavioral competencies. Helping candidates translate past behavior and performance into added value language is a critical link to successful interview and job-search experiences. As a result, interview methods are changing the way candidates should prepare, and employers are conducting in-person and online job searches.

Historically, career information was transferred from friends and family. Observing workers through direct experience within a local community presented vocational role models. Government print documents became an additional source and companion to professional helpers assisting with career planning. Today, technology has increasingly shaped the collection, presentation, and utilization of occupational information, just as it has changed most forms of social interaction and communication. As a result, we argue that professional helpers can increase effectiveness by understanding and utilizing four types of occupational information: traditional print, technology-enhanced, Web site–based, and behavior-based.

Five prominent occupational information systems and two allied sources are reviewed in this chapter. The Internet and its impact are addressed, and a representative sample of popular career Web sites is provided. An introduction to the use of behavior-based interviewing is offered as a method of gaining occupational information from past experience. Finally, making a link from occupational information to job search is suggested.

The well-known U. S. Department of Labor's *Dictionary of Occupational Titles* (DOT; 1991), *Occupational Outlook Handbook* (OOH; 2002b), and *Selected Characteristics of Occupations Defined in the Dictionary of Occupational Titles* (1993) provide valuable information for career planning, as does the *Guide for Occupational Exploration–Third Edition* (GOE; Farr, Ludden, & Shatkin, 2001). The *Occupational Information Network–O*NET* (U.S. Department of Labor, 2002a), a comprehensive database of worker attitudes and job characteristics that is still in development, offers a unique and instructive way to understand and view information critical to building relationships between individuals' assets and job options. Professional helpers' work is greatly enhanced when they can proficiently navigate these materials.

Web site resources, an additional set of powerful online tools, are changing the way career planning is conducted. The underpinnings of behavioral interviewing included within this chapter suggest a new way to help learners explore, evaluate, and validate specific occupational information gathered from past experience. This method of collecting occupational information is often overlooked and underutilized, yet it is an indispensable source. It can turn occupational information into career knowledge and help learners imagine what their career can become. Through the use of these occupational information tools, individuals can become intentional and self-directed about exploration and job-search endeavors. In doing so, they acquire valuable lessons they will use throughout their lifetime of career transitions.

Understanding Occupational Information

To suggest that occupational information has become increasingly more available as a result of technology is not surprising. Reflecting on how it has been transformed from a predominantly print- and experience-based system to a multisourced access system is useful. To suggest that a vast amount of new and quality information is available because of technology is debatable, however. Change in the demand for occupational information has not been shaped by significantly improved quality. The most noticeable changes have occurred as a result of the increased number of venues and access points from which individuals can explore, evaluate, and integrate occupational information. New ways of organizing, presenting, and creating occupational information offer significant opportunities for helpers in guiding individual progress.

Traditional Print Occupational Information

From the earliest days of vocational guidance and "true reasoning" suggested by the first career theory of counseling, information was written down to help add quality, increase access, and improve the efficiency of matching individuals with job requirements and environments. This process was how the qualities of a person and the requirements of the job were matched. The DOT and the OOH are the most well-known examples of using print media to provide occupational information. The *Selected Characteristics of Occupations Defined in the*

Dictionary of Occupational Titles and the GOE are lesser known, but complementary, resources.

Technology-Enhanced Occupational Information

Based on the success of the DOT and OOH, computer versions have been developed to provide similar information with graphic, visual, video, and CD-ROM enhancements. Popular examples include DISCOVER (http://www.act.org/discover), Sigi (http://www.ets.org/sigi/index.html) and Choices (http://www.careerware.com/products/us/choices.htm). A most recent development is the U.S. Department of Labor's O*NET, which combines a series of databases and enhancements delivered online. Its content, flexibility, and variety of elements are discussed in this chapter.

Web Site–Based Occupational Information

Although the computer has revolutionized how work is done, it can be argued that the Internet has changed where one goes to work as well. The Internet's ability to open a helper's door to untold numbers of Web sites creates tremendous opportunities for individual employment as well as for a helper's resources. The Internet's speed and potential for making information inexpensive, attractive, and universally available have made acquisition of Web literacy skills a requirement for both helper and the person being helped. Diligence in ensuring that this new technology is used with integrity is essential as well. An overwhelming number of career Web sites have surfaced, and a representative sample of sites from which readers can find, evaluate, and integrate occupational information is presented in this chapter.

Behavior-Based Occupational Information

Dissatisfaction with traditional job interviews has led employers to increasingly use behavior- or performance-based assessments during interviews. We suggest that the assumptions behind behavior assessment can lead to a tremendous wealth of personal occupational information. Many employers are moving away from a résumé-driven style of interviewing to a very probing type of interview based on the assumption that "past behavior is the best prediction of future behavior." As candidates learn to identify and evaluate what they have done in the past, they gain tremendous insight into occupational information and its importance in adding value in the future. Success in behavioral interviewing requires that individuals know and be able to explain their very personal occupational information in ways that can convince employers that they hold the competencies that match the employer's need. Principles and techniques that are useful in creating personal occupational information and a comparison of traditional and behavior-assessment interviews are provided here.

Occupational Information and Its Use

Helpers must be knowledgeable about occupational informational resources to successfully assist individuals in gathering, evaluating, and then arriving at realistic vocational decisions (Cohen, 1997). Regardless of the approach, helpers increase their impact by moving beyond traditional print information to include technology-enhanced, Web site–based, and behavioral-assessment information sources. The U.S. Department of Labor supports such development, as witnessed by the development of the O*NET. The O*NET database has taken the place of the DOT as the nation's primary source of occupational information. Its databases and related products are intended to help millions of employers, workers, educators, and students make informed decisions about education, training, career choices, and work through its online system and accompanying print documents. O*NET is administered and sponsored by the U.S. Department of Labor's Employment and Training Administration and will serve as the predominant occupational system for some time to come.

Although the O*NET was intended to replace the DOT, the latter will remain in use for a time and thus remains in this chapter. Why is this the case? It is because most existing career practitioners were trained in this material. The Rehabilitation Services Administration requires the use of a DOT number. Supportive government documents such as the *Selected Characteristics of Occupations Defined in the DOT* are companions to a professional helper's work, especially for people with disabling conditions. The DOT maintains its value because it is a well-researched printed source.

Dictionary of Occupational Titles

The DOT is a widely known U.S. occupational classification system that provides a definition of a job and lists the various activities involved in performing the work. The current revised fourth edition includes 12,741 occupations. The following is an example of a DOT entry:

238.367-038 HOTEL CLERK (hotel & rest.) alternate titles: motel clerk; motor-lodge clerk Performs any combination of following duties for guests of hotel or motel: Greets, registers, and assigns rooms to guests. Issues room key and escort instructions to BELLHOP (hotel & rest.) 324.677-010. Date stamps, sorts, and racks incoming mail and messages. Transmits and receives messages, using telephone or telephone switchboard. Answers inquiries pertaining to hotel services; registration of guests; and shopping, dining, entertainment, and travel directions. Keeps records of room availability and guests' accounts, manually or using computer. Computes bill, collects payment, and makes change for guests [CASHIER (clerical) 211.362-010]. Makes and confirms reservations. May post charges, such as room, food, liquor, or telephone, to ledger, manually or using computer [BOOKKEEPER (clerical) 210.382-014]. May make restaurant, transportation, or entertainment reservation, and arrange for tours. May deposit guests' valuables in hotel safe or safe-deposit box. May order complimentary flowers or champagne for guests. May rent dock space at marina-hotel. May work on one floor and be designated Floor Clerk (hotel & rest.). May be known as Key Clerk (hotel & rest.); Reservation Clerk (hotel & rest.); Room Clerk (hotel & rest.) or according to specific area in which employed as Front Desk Clerk (hotel & rest.).

GOE: 07.04.03 STRENGTH: L GED: R3 M3 L3 SVP: 4 DLU: 81

The first item in a DOT occupational definition is the nine-digit occupational code (in the preceding example, 238.367-038). In the DOT occupational classification system, each set of three digits in the nine-digit code number has a specific purpose or meaning. Together, they provide a unique identification code for a particular occupation, which differentiates it from all others.

The first three digits identify a particular occupational group. All occupations are clustered into one of nine broad categories (first digit), such as professional, technical and managerial, or clerical and sales occupations. These categories break down into 83 occupationally specific divisions (the first two digits), such as occupations in architecture and engineering within the professional category, or stenography, typing, and related occupations in the clerical and sales category. Divisions, in turn, are divided into 564 small, homogeneous groups (the first three digits). The nine primary occupational categories are listed below:

0/1   Professional, Technical, and Managerial Occupations

2   Clerical and Sales Occupations

3   Service Occupations

4   Agricultural, Fishery, Forestry, and Related Occupations

5   Processing Occupations

6   Machine Trades Occupations

7   Benchwork Occupations

8   Structural Work Occupations

9   Miscellaneous Occupations

In the example, the first digit (2) indicates that this particular occupation is found in the category of Clerical and Sales Occupations. The second digit refers to a division within the category. The divisions within the Clerical and Sales Occupations category are as follows:

20   Stenography, Typing, Filing, and Related Occupations

21   Computing and Account-Recording Occupations

22   Production and Stock Clerks and Related Occupations

23   Information and Message Distribution Occupations

24   Miscellaneous Clerical Occupations

25   Sales Occupations, Services

26   Sales Occupations, Consumable Commodities

27   Sales Occupations, Commodities, N.E.C.

29   Miscellaneous Sales Occupations

Some divisions or groups end in the designation "N.E.C." (not elsewhere classified). This indicates that the occupations do not logically fit into precisely defined divisions or groups, or that they could fit into two or more of them equally well.

In the example, the second digit (3) locates the occupation in the Information and Message Distribution Occupations division.

The third digit defines the occupational groups within the division. The groups within the Information and Message Distribution Occupations division are as follows:

230   Hand Delivery and Distribution Occupations

235   Telephone Operators

236   Telegraph Operators

237   Information and Reception Clerks

238   Accommodation Clerks and Gate and Ticket Agents

239   Information and Message Distribution Occupations, N.E.C.

In the example above, the third digit (8) locates the occupation in the Accommodations Clerks and Gate and Ticket Agents group.

The middle three digits of the DOT occupational code are the Worker Functions ratings of the tasks performed in the occupation. Every job requires a worker to function to some degree in relation to data, people, and things. A separate digit expresses the worker's relationship to each of these three groups:

DATA (4th Digit)	PEOPLE (5th Digit)	THINGS (6th Digit)
0 Synthesizing	0 Mentoring	0 Setting Up
1 Coordinating	1 Negotiating	1 Precision Working
2 Analyzing	2 Instructing	2 Operating– Controlling
3 Compiling	3 Supervising	3 Driving–Operating
4 Computing	4 Diverting	4 Manipulating
5 Copying	5 Persuading	5 Tending
6 Comparing	6 Speaking– Signaling	6 Feeding– Offbearing
	7 Serving	7 Handling
	8 Taking Instructions– Helping	

Data

The worker whose function involves data works with information, knowledge, and conceptions related to data, people, or things that are obtained by observation, investigation, interpretation, visualization, and mental creation. Data are intangible and include numbers, words, symbols, ideas, concepts, and oral verbalization. The nature of that work is described by the fourth digit of the occupational code:

0   **Synthesizing:** Integrating analyses of data to discover facts and/or develop knowledge concepts or interpretations.

1   **Coordinating:** Determining time, place, and sequence of operations or action to be taken on the basis of analysis of data; executing determination and/or reporting on events.

2   **Analyzing:** Examining and evaluating data. Presenting alternative actions in relation to the evaluation is frequently involved.

3   **Compiling:** Gathering, collating, or classifying information about data, people, or things. Reporting and/or carrying out a prescribed action in relation to the information is frequently involved.

4   **Computing:** Performing arithmetic operations and reporting on and/or carrying out a prescribed action in relation to them. Does not include counting.

5   **Copying:** Transcribing, entering, or posting data.

6   **Comparing:** Judging the readily observable functional, structural, or compositional characteristics (whether similar to or divergent from obvious standards) of data, people, or things.

People

The worker whose function involves people works with human beings (or animals dealt with on an individual basis as if they were human). The fifth digit of the occupational code describes the nature of that work:

0   **Mentoring:** Dealing with individuals in terms of their total personality in order to advise, counsel, and/or guide them with regard to problems that may be resolved by legal, scientific, clinical, spiritual, and/or other professional principles.

1   **Negotiating:** Exchanging ideas, information, and opinions with others to formulate policies and programs and/or arrive jointly at decisions, conclusions, or solutions.

2   **Instructing:** Teaching subject matter to others, or training others (including animals) through explanation, demonstration, and supervised practice; or making recommendations on the basis of technical disciplines.

3   **Supervising:** Determining or interpreting work procedures for a group of workers, assigning specific duties to them, and promoting efficiency. A variety of responsibilities is involved in this function.

4   **Diverting:** Amusing others (usually accomplished through the medium of stage, screen, television, or radio).

5   **Persuading:** Influencing others in favor of a product, service, or point of view.

6   **Speaking–Signaling:** Talking with and/or signaling people to convey or exchange information. Includes giving assignments and/or directions to helpers or assistants.

7   **Serving:** Attending to the needs or requests of people or animals or the expressed or implicit wishes of people. Immediate response is involved.

8   **Taking Instructions–Helping:** Attending to the work assignment instructions or orders of supervisor. (No immediate response required

unless clarification of instructions or orders is needed.) Helping applies to "nonlearning" helpers.

Things

The worker whose function involves things works with substances or materials, machines, tools, equipment, and products. A thing is tangible and has shape, form, and other physical characteristics. The sixth digit of the occupational code describes the nature of that work:

0   **Setting up:** Adjusting machines or equipment by replacing or altering tools, jigs, fixtures, and attachments to prepare them to perform their functions, change their performance, or restore their proper functioning if they break down. Workers who set up one or a number of machines for other workers or who set up and personally operate a variety of machines are included here.

1   **Precision Working:** Using body members and/or tools or work aids to work, move, guide, or place objects or materials in situations where ultimate responsibility for the attainment of standards occurs and selection of appropriate tools, objects, or materials, and the adjustment of the tool to the task require exercise of considerable judgment.

2   **Operating–Controlling:** Starting, stopping, controlling, and adjusting the progress of machines or equipment. Operating machines involves setting up and adjusting the machine or material(s) as the work progresses. Controlling involves observing gauges, dials, and so on, and turning valves and other devices to regulate factors such as temperature, pressure, flow of liquids, speed of pumps, and reactions of materials.

3   **Driving–Operating:** Starting, stopping, and controlling the actions of machines or equipment for which a course must be steered, or which must be guided, in order to fabricate, process, and/or move things or people. Involves such activities as observing gauges and dials, estimating distances, and determining speed and direction of other objects; turning cranks and wheels; pushing or pulling gear lifts or levers. Includes such machines as cranes, conveyor systems, tractors, furnace charging machines, paving machines, and hoisting machines. Excludes manually powered machines, such as hand trucks and dollies, and power-assisted machines, such as electric wheelbarrows and hand trucks.

4   **Manipulating:** Using body members, tools, and/or special devices to work, move, guide, or place objects or materials. Involves some latitude

for judgment with regard to precision attained and selecting the appropriate tool, object, or materials, although this is readily manifest.

5 **Tending:** Starting, stopping, and observing the functions of machines and equipment. Involves adjusting materials or controls of the machine, such as changing guides, adjusting timers, and temperature gauges; turning valves to allow flow of materials; and flipping switches in response to lights. Little judgment is involved in making these adjustments.

6 **Feeding–Offbearing:** Inserting, throwing, dumping, or placing special materials in or removing them from machines or equipment that are automatic or tended or operated by other workers.

7 **Handling:** Using body members, hand tools, and/or special devices to work, move, or carry objects or materials. Involves little or no latitude for judgment with regard to attainment of standards or in selecting appropriate tool, object, or material.

Once helpers have an in-depth understanding of the functions that must be performed in an occupation and are aware of the client's specific disability, the helper and client can begin to plan accommodating the job to the client. For example, the helper may be dealing with a client with a cognitive impairment who can compare, copy, and compute but cannot compile or synthesize data. Clients with learning disabilities may be able to perform precision work, providing they are not given written instructions, but would probably find it difficult to supervise or instruct others because of the need to read training manuals.

The fourth, fifth, and sixth digits of the DOT code designate exactly what tasks the person will be performing relative to data, people, and things. Thus, if the first six digits of an occupational code are 238.367, the helper would know the following information regarding the occupation:

2 Clerical and Sales Occupations
3 Information and Message Distribution Occupations
8 Accommodation Clerks and Gate and Ticket Agents
3 Compiling
6 Speaking–Signaling
7 Handling

If the occupational code for Hotel Clerk is 238.367-038, the digits 038, the last three digits in the nine-digit code, distinguish this job from another 238.367 occupation. For instance, 238.367-030, Travel Clerk, with the alternative title of Transportation Clerk, is different from 238.367-034 Scheduler, with the alternative title Educational Department Registrar or Museum Service Scheduler.

The trailer (the coding at the end of the occupational definition) following the. previously given example for Hotel Clerk was *GOE: 07.04.03 STRENGTH: L GED: R3 M3 L3 SVP: 4 DLU: 81*. This trailer provides the following information:

GOE — This reference is explained in detail later in the chapter under the separate heading of "The Guide for Occupational Exploration."

Strength — This factor is defined by one of five levels: Sedentary (S), Light (L), Medium (M), Heavy (H), and Very Heavy (V). For more in-depth information concerning specific strength factors, refer to Appendix 9.A, Physical Demands, Factor 1, Strength, at the end of this chapter.

GED (General Educational Development)—Jobs require various levels of reasoning, language, and mathematical development. These areas of knowledge embrace skills acquired through formal and informal education and are augmented by experience and self-study. Teachers generally know the level of their students' basic skills. The grade the student obtained in school may not be an accurate measure of educational competencies. (For example, some high school graduates have been found to be functional illiterates.) Condensed definitions of the six reasoning, mathematical, and language levels are provided in Appendix 9.B, Scale of General Education Development, at the end of this chapter.

SVP (Specific Vocational Preparation)— All jobs involve some aspect of training. The training can consist of simple directions, short on-the-job training, or longer and more formal learning (see Table 9.1).

Among many factors to consider in selecting an occupation is the motivation of an individual to undergo training. The specific vocational preparation represents the amount of time required to learn the techniques, acquire the information, and develop the facility needed for average performance in a specific work situation. The training may be acquired in a school, work, military, institutional, or vocational environment. According to the DOT, specific vocational training includes training given in any of the following circumstances:

a. Vocational education (such as high school business or shop training, technical school, art school, and that part of college training that is organized around a specific vocational objective)

b. Apprentice training (for apprenticeable jobs only)

c. In-plant training (given by an employer in the form of organized classroom study)

TABLE 9.1
Levels of Specific Vocational Preparation

Level	Time
1	Short demonstration only
2	Anything beyond short demonstration up to and including 1 month
3	More than 1 month, up to and including 3 months
4	More than 3 months, up to and including 6 months
5	More than 6 months, up to and including 1 year
6	More than 1 year, up to and including 2 years
7	More than 2 years, up to and including 4 years
8	More than 4 years, up to and including 10 years
9	More than 10 years

Note. The levels of this scale are mutually exclusive and do not overlap. Adapted from *Selected Characteristics of Occupations Defined in the Revised Dictionary of Occupational Titles* by U.S. Department of Labor, Employment and Training Administration (1993), p. B-1.

d. On-the-job training (serving as learner or trainee of the job under the instruction of a qualified worker)

e. Essential experience in other jobs (serving in less responsible jobs that lead to the higher grade job or serving in other jobs that qualify)

The information contained in the trailer for the example DOT code 238.367-038 (Hotel Clerk) is as follows:

• GOE-07.04.03. This code indicates that the job is one of a subgroup of additional Registration jobs, within the workgroup Oral Communications.
• Strength — Light. This code indicates that the worker should be able to lift up to 20 pounds of force occasionally, or up to 10 pounds of force frequently, or a negligible amount of force constantly to move objects.
• GED — Reasoning Development (R) 3 means that the worker must apply commonsense understanding to carry out instructions in written, oral, or diagrammatic form, and deal with problems concerning several concrete variables in or from standardized situations. Mathematics Development (M) 3 means that the worker can compute discount, interest, profit, and loss; commission, markup, and selling price; ratio and proportion; and percentage. He or she can calculate surfaces, volumes, weights, and measures.

In addition, the worker must be able to calculate variables and formulas, monomials and polynomials, ratio and proportion variables, and square roots and radicals. He or she must be able to calculate plane and solid figures, circumference, area, and volume. The worker should understand kinds of angles and properties of pairs of angles. Language Development (L) 3 specifies how the worker is expected to perform in skills related to reading (read a variety of novels, magazines, atlases, and encyclopedias; read safety rules and instruction in the use and maintenance of shop tools and equipment; and read methods and procedures in mechanical drawing and layout work); skills related to writing (write reports and essays with proper format, punctuation, spelling, and grammar, using all parts of speech); and skills related to speaking (speak before an audience with poise, voice control, and confidence using correct English and well-modulated voice).

- SVP: Code 4 means that the work requires more than 3 months, up to and including 6 months of specific vocational preparation.
- DLU: 1981. The job was last studied in 1981.

Selected Characteristics of Occupations Defined in the Dictionary of Occupational Titles

The *Selected Characteristics of Occupations Defined in the Dictionary of Occupational Titles*, published in 1993 by the U.S. Department of Labor, Employment and Training Administration, provides more detailed occupational data than that found in the DOT. It presents occupational information in terms of physical demands required of the job, the environmental conditions in which one must work, and specific vocational time required to prepare for the job. All are very important and dependent on the unique needs of an individual.

Physical Demands

The data, people, and things concept explains the functional tasks a worker has to perform on the job. The level of physical demands refers to the specific physical activities involved, such as climbing, reaching, kneeling, crouching, stooping, fingering, and feeling. After a client has tentatively identified a job as a vocational goal, a comparison of the client's capabilities and the job's physical requirements will identify potential obstacles to performing the occupation. Definitions of physical demands are presented in Appendix 9.A.

Environmental Conditions

The work setting can be a critical factor in an individual's successful employment. Not only can workers' health be affected, but some people may be unable to work under certain conditions, such as heat, cold, inside, outside, humidity, and around toxins. Definitions of environmental conditions are provided in Appendix 9.C.

Specific Vocational Preparation

The Specific Vocational Preparation (SVP) was previously explained in the section on the DOT.

An Example

To illustrate how the book is used, Hotel Clerk (238.367-038) is presented as an example.

- Specific Vocational Preparation 4
- Physical Demands R/O, H/O, F/F, T/F, H/F, N/F
- Environmental Conditions N/3

These codes are specific to the hotel clerks job. The explanation of the codes follows. The Specific Vocational Preparation indicates the work would need from 3 months up to and including 6 months to learn to perform this job. The Physical Demands require the motions of (R) reaching and (H) handling occasionally, that is, up to one third of the time. The motion of (F) fingering occurs frequently, that is, from one third to two thirds of the time. The worker will be (T) talking, (H) hearing, and (N) needing clarity of vision at 20 inches or less frequently, that is, from one third to two thirds of the time. The Environmental Condition (N/3) involves a moderate level of noise intensity that is consistent with a business office where typewriters and computers are used or a department or grocery store; light traffic; or a fast-food restaurant at off hours.

The Guide for Occupational Exploration

The third edition of the GOE clusters nearly 1,000 related jobs into 14 interest areas and 158 work groups. Using new information, the GOE integrates data from the O*NET, which is discussed in the next section. Each work group describes the kind of work one does in this area, gives clues as to whether one would like to perform jobs in this area, lists the skills and knowledge required, and provides information on how to prepare for entering the field. The listing of related jobs is valuable. Other useful GOE features are the crosswalks that connect individual values, leisure activities, favorite school subjects, preferred work settings, skills, abilities, and knowledges to related work groups. The information in the *Selected Characteristics of Occupations Defined in the Dictionary of Occupational Titles* requires the use of the second edition of the GOE.

O*NET

The format of the O*NET description given here follows a practitioner's perspective. It describes some of the content that users see, with examples cited on the use of the information, followed by the model on which the O*NET is based.

Each occupation's information is organized into six interrelated areas:

1. **Experience Requirements** — describes the education, training, skills, licensing, and experience required for entry and advancement.

2. **Occupation Requirements** — outlines the typical tasks associated with each occupation or group of occupations, including specific physical, social, or structural demands on workers.

3. **Worker Requirements** — includes individual performance factors, such as basic skills and knowledge, including basic skills and cross-functional skills.

4. **Worker Characteristics** — represents the work styles, interests, and abilities that are important to job seekers evaluating potential career opportunities.

5. **Occupation Characteristics** — includes links to current labor market information on occupations, including wages, employment outlook, and industry size.

6. **Occupation-Specific Information** — provides comprehensive details for a single occupation or narrowly-defined job family.

The above information can be accessed in three ways — searching for one specific occupational title, searching for job families, or browsing an alphabetical listing of more than 974 occupations included in the O*NET. Users must know their client's learning style, however. For some people, more information is provided than they need, and the system can be overwhelming. For example, all that one client wants are the educational requirements for an occupation, whereas for another client, the focus is on the occupation's specific physical, social, and structural demands. The user also must keep in mind that the reading level of the information is at Grade 12, which is high. For these reasons, a more user-friendly version, CareerZone (www.nycareerzone.org), is described in Figure 9.1 and shows the comprehensiveness of an occupational brief. The New York State Department of Labor developed CareerZone as an interactive, online system powered by the O*NET database for students, youth, and job seekers. Individuals can easily use CareerZone without the assistance of helpers. It also permits users to build résumés, generate cover letters, fill out job applications, learn more about entry-level jobs, and explore career opportunities. O*NET can be used differently by clients and practitioners.

The O*NET System's Flexibility

An objective of most helpers is to target information to a client's unique needs. "I'm interested in working in social services, but I don't want to go to school. Can you help me find a job?" Answering this question suggests that some clients will not be able to or will find it difficult to work independently on the computer. For example, this question asks for a search for jobs that a person liked *and* the amount of training needed for entry into the occupations. Therefore, a preliminary step before an occupational search is to establish two criteria: a person's interests, described in Holland's RIASEC model in Chapter 1 (Holland, 1997) and the preparation needed (this is job zone information, which is described below). The process described here can narrow down a career search to fit personal specifications. Another example is to use three criteria — such as interests, preparation needed, and one's most important work value — to provide for a more specific search. For example, criteria might include one's need or desire for achievement but not independence, recognition, relationships, support, or particular working conditions.

Each job in O*NET is grouped into one of five job zones, defined by the preparation needed for job entry. A job zone represents a group of occupations that are similar in terms of how most people get into the job, how much overall experience people need to do the job, how much education people need to do the job, and how much on-the-job training people need to do the job. Job zones are similar to the measures of specific vocational preparation used in the DOT.

(*text continues on p. 286*)

JOB DESCRIPTION

Accommodate hotel, motel, and resort patrons by registering and assigning rooms to guests, issuing room keys, transmitting and receiving messages, keeping records of occupied rooms and guests' accounts, making and confirming reservations, and presenting statements to and collecting payments from departing guests.

INTERESTS

Conventional–Conventional occupations frequently involve following set procedures and routines. These occupations can include working with data and details more than with ideas. Usually there is a clear line of authority to follow.

TASKS

1. Greets, registers, and assigns rooms to guests of hotel or motel.
2. Date-stamps, sorts, and racks incoming mail and messages.
3. Deposits guests' valuables in hotel safe or safe-deposit box.
4. Answers inquiries pertaining to hotel services
5. Issues room key and escort instructions to bellhop.
6. Computes bill, collects payment, and makes change for guests.
7. Makes and confirms reservations.
8. Transmits and receives messages, using telephone or telephone switchboard.
9. Posts charges, such as room, food, liquor, or telephone, to ledger, manually or using computer.
10. Keeps records of room availability and guests' accounts, manually or using computer.

SKILLS

Service Orientation–Actively looking for ways to help people

Speaking–Talking to others to effectively convey information

Active Listening–Listening to what other people are saying and asking questions as appropriate

Mathematics–Using mathematics to solve problems

Coordination–Adjusting actions in relation to others' actions

Writing–Communicating effectively with others in writing as indicated by the needs of the audience

Social Perceptiveness–Being aware of others' reactions and understanding why they react the way they do

(continues)

Figure 9.1. A CareerZone occupational brief for hotel desk clerks. From CareerZone 2003, Albany: New York State Department of Labor, Research and Statistics Division. Available at www.nycareerzone.org

KNOWLEDGE

Customer and Personal Service–Knowledge of principles and processes for providing customer and personal services, including needs assessment techniques, quality service standards, alternative delivery systems, and customer satisfaction evaluation techniques

Clerical–Knowledge of administrative and clerical procedures and systems such as word processing systems, filing and records management systems, stenography and transcription, forms design principles, and other office procedures and terminology

Computers and Electronics–Knowledge of electric circuit boards, processors, chips, and computer hardware and software, including applications and programming

Mathematics–Knowledge of numbers, their operations, and interrelationships, including arithmetic, algebra, geometry, calculus, statistics, and their applications

English Language–Knowledge of the structure and content of the English language, including the meaning and spelling of words, rules of composition, and grammar

Economics and Accounting–Knowledge of economic and accounting principles and practices, the financial markets, banking, and the analysis and reporting of financial data

Telecommunications–Knowledge of transmission, broadcasting, switching, control, and operation of telecommunications systems

EDUCATION

Job Zone Two: Some Preparation Needed

Education: These occupations usually require a high school diploma and may require some vocational training or job-related course work. In some cases, an associate's or bachelor's degree could be needed.

Training: Employees in these occupations need anywhere from a few months to one year of working with experienced employees.

SCHOOL PROGRAMS

Hospitality and Recreation Marketing Operations, General: An instructional program that generally prepares individuals to perform marketing tasks applicable to a wide variety of hospitality and leisure industry settings.

Hotel/Motel Services Marketing Operations: An instructional program that prepares individuals to perform marketing tasks specifically applicable to hotels and motels.

WAGES

In 2002, the New York annual wage range was between $15,142.40, and $25,313.60.

(continues)

Figure 9.1. *Continued.*

JOB OUTLOOK

- In 1997, employment for Hotel, Motel, and Resort Desk Clerks was: 6,424.
- It is anticipated that in the year 2007, employment in this area will number 8,262. There will be an increase of 184 new positions annually (2.86%). In addition, 2,709 jobs per year (42.16%) will become available due to employee turnover.

SIMILAR JOBS

Central Office Operators–Operate telephone switchboard to establish or assist customers in establishing local or long-distance telephone connections.

Counter Attendants, Cafeteria, Food Concession, and Coffee Shop–Serve food to diners at counter or from a steam table. Exclude counter attendants who also wait tables.

Counter and Rental Clerks–Receive orders for repairs, rentals, and services. May describe available options, compute cost, and accept payment.

Food Servers, Nonrestaurant–Serve food to patrons outside of a restaurant environment, such as in hotels, hospital rooms, or cars.

License Clerks–Issue licenses or permits to qualified applicants. Obtain necessary information; record data; advise applicants on requirements; collect fees; and issue licenses. May conduct oral, written, visual, or performance testing.

Receptionists and Information Clerks–Answer inquiries and obtain information for general public, customers, visitors, and other interested parties. Provide information regarding activities conducted at establishment, location of departments, offices, and employees within organization.

Travel Clerks–Provide tourists with travel information, such as points of interest, restaurants, rates, and emergency service. Duties include answering inquiries, offering suggestions, and providing literature pertaining to trips, excursions, sporting events, concerts and plays. May make reservations, deliver tickets, arrange for visas, or contact individuals and groups to inform them of package tours.

Ushers, Lobby Attendants, and Ticket Takers–Assist patrons at entertainment events by performing duties, such as collecting admission tickets and passes from patrons, assisting in finding seats, searching for lost articles, and locating such facilities as rest rooms and telephones.

Figure 9.1. *Continued.*

The five job zones are as follows:

Job Zone 1 — occupations that need little or no preparation

Job Zone 2 — occupations that need some preparation

Job Zone 3 — occupations that need medium preparation

Job Zone 4 — occupations that need considerable preparation

Job Zone 5 — occupations that need extensive preparation

A community-based work development/training site asked the authors for help in getting employment for their "graduates" who are hands-on learners and social individuals with limited educations. In an O*NET search, this information would mean we would identify Job Zone 1 occupations for people with realistic (hands-on)- and social (people)-oriented interests. A resulting search would produce two listings of occupations to allow a job developer to investigate whether there are any employers for the identified occupations in the community. (This information also is available through the Internet by zip code at America's Job Bank [www.ajb.dni.us].) Experience has shown that this population often depends on public transportation to get to work; therefore, subsequent questions arise: Do these persons have the skills to use public transportation? Can they interview appropriately? Do they know how to contact an identified employer for an interview? The use of the O*NET information database fits into providing a more comprehensive counseling or job placement service.

Searches

Different career planning questions demand specific information. A frequent client question is "What jobs am I qualified for with my skills?" Through Skills Search, O*NET lets candidates assess their skills and preferences against the requirements of more than 900 current occupations.

Skills Search helps a person create a list of skills and identify occupations where those skills are needed. The results of a Skills Search tell the person if there are any skills needed that the person has *not* put into his or her list. A helper then can identify local resources to get the needed skills or training. For example, a client with limited educational success is seen as being social, being good at convincing others, and enjoying helping people, and he or she would like to use these skills in a job. The skills that would be entered into Skills Search are *active listening, speaking, persuasion,* and *service orientation.* The search listed 10 out of 71 occupations that use all four skills. By examining the 61 jobs that had less than the four matches, the person also could see what skills he or she would need to develop for employment in a specific occupation.

A helpful feature at the end of Skills Search is Job Accommodation Network (JAN). By clicking ENTER, a person would be able to peruse an array of information options. The Web site By Specific Disability also may prove helpful. Some areas included are Addictions, Cognitive and Developmental, including Attention Deficit Disorder and Learning Disability—all of which provide additional exhaustive Web sites. Another feature at the end of Skills Search is SOAR (Searchable Online Accommodation Resource). SOAR is a job accommodation network designed to let users explore various accommodation options for people with disabilities in work and educational settings.

Having the skills to do the job is an important first step for good job performance and personal satisfaction. For an employer, a skills-based search can help create job descriptions and locate workers whose skills are transferable. Such a search is also recommended for workers seeking to use their current skills in new careers. This is the type of information included in a behavioral interview, which is discussed later in this chapter.

Skills are grouped into six broad areas that are then broken down into more specific categories. Those six areas are the following:

1. **Basic Skills** — developed capacities that facilitate learning or the more rapid acquisition of knowledge.

2. **Social Skills** — working with people to achieve goals.

3. **Complex Problem-Solving Skills** — solving problems in real-world settings.

4. **Technical Skills** — designing, setting up, operating, and correcting malfunctions involving machines and technological systems.

5. **System Skills** — understanding, monitoring, and improving organizations and systems.

6. **Resource Management Skills** — allocating resources efficiently, including finances, materials, human resources, and time.

Report Options

For each occupation there are three report options: Summary, Details, and Custom. Although most people will only use the Summary Report, the two other reports provide comprehensive information, possibly too much for an individual to comprehend. The information in the report is organized as follows: Task, Knowledge, Skills, Abilities, Work Activities, Work Context, Job Zone, Interests, Work Values, Related Occupations, and Wages and Employment. The Summary Report highlights the most important of the aforementioned descriptors, that is, Tasks, Knowledge, and Skills. The Details Report provides the importance level ratings for each of the descriptors, and the Custom Report lets a person select whatever importance and skills level he or she desires for designated descriptors. The Details and Custom reports should be very valuable in matching a person's skill level with specific job requirements and then developing an educational and training plan.

O*NET Content Model

This sections allows the reader to fully appreciate the comprehensiveness of the components of the O*NET database and to identify other uses. The rationale for the O*NET began with the fact that the DOT is limited in that it cannot provide a common framework for describing occupations. The DOT represents an occupation-specific descriptive system where each occupation is dealt with as a unique, qualitatively different entity. This focus makes it difficult to conduct cross-occupation comparisons and formulate general classifications of occupations. In today's economy, information must be collected to allow occupations to be described in terms of more general, cross-job descriptors to promote person-job matching, training, and counseling. As Mumford and Peterson (1995) noted,

> These applications require two different kinds of cross-occupation descriptors. First, descriptors detailing the kind of work being done and the conditions under which this work is being performed are needed to describe the nature of requisite work activities. Second, it is necessary to consider the requirements these activities impose on the people doing the work. Thus a complex, multivariate, descriptive system is required that considers a variety of attributes of both the occupation and the worker. (1–6)

The content described here provides the framework for the development of the O*NET. It should also be considered to be subject to revision and refinement as O*NET's development continues.

Figure 9.2 is the O*NET content model. The description of the content that users can access within O*NET is set forth in a logical sequence, beginning with worker characteristics, followed by worker requirements, experience requirements, occupational requirements, occupation-specific requirements, and occupation characteristics. More detailed descriptions have been given by Mumford and Peterson (1999).

Worker Characteristics

Worker characteristics include abilities, occupational values and interests, and work styles.

- **Abilities.** Abilities relate to a person's cognitive, psychomotor, physical, and sensory capacities or enduring attributes. Revised instrumentation (Hubbard et al., 2000) allows for the evaluation of performance requirements in occupations of 52 abilities.

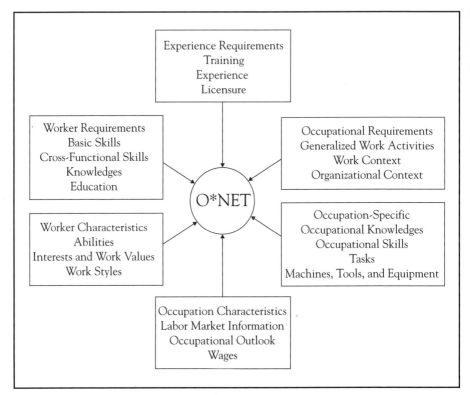

Figure 9.2. O*NET content model. From Occupational Information Network (O*NET), by U.S. Department of Labor, 2002. Available at http://online.onetcenter.org/content_model

- **Occupational values and interests.** Abilities address the following question: Can the individual do the work? They do not address whether the individual is willing to do the work. Values can be described as reinforcers. Preference for certain kinds of work can be ascertained by the importance that a person attaches to doing an activity. Occupational Values are assessed by the *Work Importance Locator* (U.S. Department of Labor, Employment, and Training Administration, 2000b). Interests are commonly associated with either liking an activity or not liking it. Interests can also be associated with describing one's personality patterns. Interests are measured by the *Interest Profiler* (U. S. Department of Labor, Employment, and Training Administration, 2000a).

- **Work Styles.** Work styles are motivational influencers of task performance. The current 15 work styles (Hubbard et al., 2000) are achievement/effort, persistence, initiative, leadership, concern for others, social orientation, self-control, stress tolerance, adaptability/flexibility, dependability, attention to detail, integrity, independence, innovation, and analytical thinking.

Worker Requirements

Worker requirements include basic skills, cross-functional skills, knowledges, and education.

- **Basic Skills.** *Basic skills* refer to procedures such as reading that facilitate the acquisition of new knowledge.

- **Cross-functional skills.** *Cross-functional skills* refer to procedures that are extended across general domains of work activities, such as problem solving and social skills.

- **Knowledges.** *Knowledges* are the organized sets of facts and principles unique to an educational field. The current 33 Knowledges (Hubbard et al., 2000) are administration and management; clerical; economics and accounting; sales and marketing; customer and personal service; personnel and human resources; production and processing; food production; computers and electronics; engineering and technology; design; building and construction; mathematics; physics; chemistry; biology; psychology; sociology and anthropology; geography; medicine and dentistry; therapy and counseling; education and training; English language; foreign language; fine arts; history and archeology; philosophy and theology; public safety and security; law, government, and jurisprudence; telecommunications; communications and media; transportation; and mechanical.

- **Education.** Years of schooling or grade level finished are common ways that people determine the amount of general knowledge or basic skills that a person has attained. The data collected for occupations in O*NET were for 15 subject area education levels (Anderson, 1999). Levels are assessed on a 5-point scale (0 = *subject not required*, 4 = *graduate school or other postbaccalaureate education*). The subject areas are technical–vocational, business vocational, English/language arts, oral communication, languages, basic math, advanced math, physical sciences, computer sciences, biological sciences, applied sciences, social sciences, arts, humanities, and physical education.

Experience Requirements

Experience requirements include training/experience and licensure. The goal of education is to provide general knowledge and skills; training, experience, and licensure are linked to specific kinds of work activity.

- **Training/experience.** *Training/experience* ascertains for each occupation whether any of four types of training/experience is needed and the amount required for job entry. The four types are related work experience, on-site training, on-the-job training, and apprenticeship. The level is assessed from 0 (*not applicable*) to 10 (*more than 10 years of experience needed*).

- **Licensure/certification.** *Licensure/certification* determines for an occupation the name of the license required; requirements needed to get a license (postsecondary degree, graduate degree, on-the-job training, examination, character references, and coursework); and who requires the license (law, employer, union, or association).

Occupational Requirements

Occupational requirements include generalized work activities, work context, and organizational context. The type of information included here shifts away from the personal descriptors in the previous content sections to definitions of the tasks performed in the occupation.

- **Generalized work activities.** Generalized work activities summarize the specific kinds of tasks occurring in multiple occupations. Revised instrumentation (Hubbard et al., 2000) assesses 41 Generalized Work Activities for each occupation. Examples include using information to determine compliance with laws, regulations, or standards; working with computers; selling or convincing others.

- **Work context.** Work context describes the conditions under which job activities are carried out for each occupation. The descriptors include physical and social–psychological conditions. The current instructions assess 57 descriptors (Hubbard et al., 2000). Sample questions include the following: How often does your job require face-to-face discussions with individuals and within teams? How frequently does your job require telephone conversation? How often are conflict situations a part of your regular job?

- **Organizational context.** Organizational context describes the characteristics of organizations in which people work. The authors of these components were especially interested in high-performance workplaces.

Occupation-Specific Requirements

Occupation-specific requirements include occupational knowledges/skills, tasks, duties, and machines, tools, and equipment.

- **Occupational knowledges/skills.** Occupational knowledges/skills are common ways used to describe jobs to show a person's expertise. The technique has been used with computer jobs and medicine to identify specific required skills or licensing requirements.

- **Tasks.** Tasks are usually identified by a job analysis that is based on observations or interviews with people performing the job. A task is an activity that occurs in order to produce some product or outcome required on the job. Tasks are job specific.

- **Duties.** Employers can group tasks into duties to be performed. According to Mumford and Peterson (1999), "This duty-based description of job activities often provides a basis for the development of performance appraisal instruments" (p. 29).

- **Machines, tools, and equipment.** Some jobs are simply the function of a person being capable of operating a machine, tool, or piece of equipment.

Occupational Characteristics

Occupational characteristics include labor market information, occupational outlook, and wages. These invaluable resources to career planning and job searches are not direct parts of O*NET; however, O*NET is designed to connect with these databases.

O*NET is a very powerful, comprehensive, and technology-enhanced resource.

Occupational Outlook Handbook

The OOH is published biennially (most recently in 2002) by the U.S. Department of Labor, Bureau of Labor Statistics, to provide information on the projections of the availability of future employment opportunities on a nationwide basis. The *Occupational Outlook Quarterly*, another Bureau of Labor Statistics publication, keeps the OOH current as an interim document and provides very timely career counseling articles. The main body of the OOH groups occupations into 10 clusters of related jobs: Management and Business and Financial Operations; Professional and Related Occupations; Service; Sales and Related Occupations; Office and Administrative Support; Farming, Fishing, and Forestry; Construction Trades; Installation, Maintenance, and Repair; Production; and Transportation and Material Moving. A separate section discusses jobs in the armed forces.

Overall, the OOH describes in detail more than several hundred occupations covering about 128 million jobs, or 88% of all jobs in the nation; it also provides summary information on about 7% more occupations. For each of the occupations detailed (see Figure 9.3 for an example of Hotel, Motel, and Resort Desk Clerks), the OOH presents the following information in a nontechnical narrative format: nature of work, working conditions, employment, training/ other qualifications and advancement, job outlook, earnings, related occupations, and sources of additional information. Earnings, sources of additional information, and employment outlook deserve further discussion because these are unique to this resource and are not covered in the other publications previously described. Figure 9.3, for example, includes information on Hotel/Motel Clerks, stating that there are plentiful opportunities for part-time work because front desks are generally staffed 24 hours a day, 7 days a week. This alerts people that they might work late evenings or early morning shifts or weekends and cautions that employment can be seasonal. Trade association information offers in-depth coverage of the industry in which the job falls.

For each industry, the OOH presents the hourly and beginning wage rates, as well as the expected wages after a few years on the job. The OOH contains information on various ways in which to obtain more information about the industry. It lists names and addresses of related organizations, such as professional organizations, unions, business firms, and community colleges. The OOH

NATURE OF THE WORK

Hotel, motel, and resort desk clerks perform a variety of services for guests of hotels, motels, and other lodging establishments. Regardless of the type of accommodation, most desk clerks have similar responsibilities. Primarily, they register arriving guests, assign rooms, and check out guests at the end of their stay. They also keep records of room assignments and other registration information on computers. When guests check out, they prepare and explain the charges, as well as process payments.

Front desk clerks always are in the public eye and, through their attitude and behavior, greatly influence the public's impressions of the establishment. When answering questions about services, check-out times, the local community, or other matters of public interest, clerks must be courteous and helpful. Should guests report problems with their rooms, clerks contact members of the housekeeping or maintenance staff to correct them.

In some smaller hotels and motels, clerks may have a variety of additional responsibilities usually performed by specialized employees in larger establishments. In these

(continues)

Figure 9.3. Hotel, motel, and resort desk clerks. From *Occupational Outlook Handbook, 2002–2003 Edition,* by U.S. Department of Labor, Bureau of Labor Statistics, 2002, Washington, DC: U.S. Government Printing Office.

places, the desk clerk often is responsible for all front office operations, information, and services. These clerks, for example, may perform the work of a bookkeeper, advance reservation agent, cashier, laundry attendant, and telephone switchboard operator.

EMPLOYMENT

Hotel, motel, and resort desk clerks held about 177,000 jobs in 2000. This occupation is well-suited to flexible work schedules, as about 3 in 10 hotel clerks work part time. Because hotels and motels need to be staffed 24 hours a day, evening and weekend work is common.

JOB OUTLOOK

Employment of hotel, motel, and resort desk clerks is expected to grow faster than the average for all occupations through 2010, as more hotels, motels, and other lodging establishments are built and occupancy rates rise. Job opportunities for hotel and motel desk clerks also will result from a need to replace workers, as thousands of workers transfer to other occupations that offer better pay and advancement opportunities or simply leave the work force altogether. Opportunities for part-time work should continue to be plentiful, as front desks often are staffed 24 hours a day, 7 days a week.

Employment of hotel and motel desk clerks should be affected by an increase in business and leisure travel. Shifts in travel preference away from long vacations and toward long weekends and other, more frequent, shorter trips also should increase demand as this trend increases the total number of nights spent in hotels. The expansion of budget and extended-stay hotels relative to larger, luxury establishments reflects a change in the composition of the hotel and motel industry. As employment shifts from luxury hotels to these extended-stay establishments offering larger rooms with kitchenettes and laundry services, the proportion of hotel desk clerks should increase in relation to staff such as waiters and waitresses and recreation workers. Desk clerks are able to handle more of the guest's needs in these establishments, answering the main switchboard, providing business services, and coordinating services like dry cleaning or grocery shopping.

New technologies automating check-in and check-out procedures now allow some guests to bypass the front desk in many larger establishments, reducing staffing needs. As some of the more traditional duties are automated, however, many desk clerks are assuming a wider range of responsibilities.

Employment of desk clerks is sensitive to cyclical swings in the economy. During recessions, vacation and business travel declines, and hotels and motels need fewer clerks. Similarly, desk clerk employment is affected by seasonal fluctuations in travel during high and low tourist seasons.

SOURCES OF ADDITIONAL INFORMATION

Information on careers in the lodging industry, as well as information about professional development and training programs, may be obtained from: Educational Institute of the American Hotel and Lodging Association, 800 N. Magnolia Ave., Suite 1800, Orlando, FL 32803. Internet: http://www.ei-ahma.org

(See introductory statement on information and record clerks for information on working conditions, training requirements, and earnings.)

Figure 9.3. *Continued.*

remains one of the most user-friendly and popular career information tools available in print as well as through technologically enhanced adaptations.

Web Site–Based Sources

Used intelligently, the Internet can be a great link to quick, easy-to-access, and comprehensive occupational information. It can be a place to work on one's career development competencies, locate job leads, and enhance job-search skills. The Internet has become a local library for many people. It has grown from a home for academics and researchers to a global marketplace for employers and consumers. It has also become a personal assistant for career planners and job seekers that demands the attention of all effective helpers.

The Internet continues to mushroom as a powerful source of information on career assessment, career information, and job search (Bowlsbey, Dickel, & Sampson, 1998). Bolles (1996) confirmed that there are hundreds, if not thousands, of Web sites that post job vacancies.

One of the most well-known sources promoting the use of the Internet for career planning, the *Riley Guide* (www.rileyguide.com/jobsrch.html), offers five reasons for using the Internet in a job search:

1. You can access current information at all hours of the day or night.

2. You can reach deeper into your local area and search far beyond local sources.

3. Your use of the Internet in your search demonstrates technical literacy skills.

4. The Internet lets you meet new people and initiate new relationships with others in your profession or region.

5. The Internet can help you explore career alternatives and options that perhaps you hadn't considered.

Examples of Web Sites

Whether you are an at-risk student seeking occupational information or job forecasts, a first-time job seeker searching for employer information, or an adult with a disability learning about self-employment, Web sites are available to meet your need. The following five Web sites illustrate the range of available opportunities.

An exceptional source of nontraditional labor market information is **Associations Unlimited** at (http://galenet.gale.com). This Web site includes 460,000 groups representing almost every line of work available. An individual can identify groups directly related to his or her career planning need or job-search interest with the click of a button. **America's Career InfoNet** (www.acinet.org) is a joint venture between the U.S. Department of Labor and a marketing data company, InfoUSA. The Web site offers wage and employment trends, occupational requirements, state-by-state labor market conditions, millions of employer contacts nationwide, and a very extensive online career resource library. **JobSmart** (www.jobstar.org/tools/salary/index.htm) provides links to and descriptions of more than 300 salary surveys or summaries. **Disability.gov** (www.disability.gov) is a resource where employers can go to help them find workers with disabilities. **Career builder** (www.careerbuilder .com), a comprehensive site, includes options ranging from leads to 300,000 jobs to modules such as "Getting Hired" and "Surviving a Layoff."

Specific Web Sites as Resources

The authors of *The Internet: A Tool for Career Planning* suggest that Web sites can assist individuals with career planning in the following four ways:

1. Self-assessment instruments can provide information about individual traits.

2. Web sites offer database searches to help individuals identify occupations for exploration.

3. Web sites provide linkages to government agencies, professional associations, and newspapers and trade journals.

4. Web sites offer opportunities for networking, acquiring mailing lists, joining chat rooms and support groups, posting résumés for job placement, and connecting with national professional organizations.

The Web site of the National Association of Colleges and Employers (www.jobweb.com) is an outstanding site for career management content, ranging from an online "Career Fair" to an "Internship Search." The Job Hunter's Bible site (www.jobhuntersbible.com) provides Richard Bolles's insights to using the Web as a job search tool.

298 ◇ T. F. Harrington and Feller

Crispin and Mehler (2002) wrote what they claimed to be the leading directory to job, résumé, and career management sites on the Web, with 2,100 job and résumé sites listed. Their *CareerXRoads: The Directory to Job, Resume and Career Management Sites on the Web* also includes reviews of their best 500 sites. Table 9.2 provides a representative sample of popular career sites.

Although career Web sites clearly are an essential tool in providing occupational information, helpers still must evaluate them so that their content can be integrated into a career plan and job search. As Bob Nelson (2001) noted in *Please Don't Just Do What I Tell You!*, adding value to the employer is essential. He suggested that job searchers do this by mapping out a specific strategy for fulfilling what he called "the ultimate expectation." Nelson argued that at every workplace, people use their best judgment to figure out what needs to be done and then do it without having to be told. Having the opportunity to meet "the ultimate expectation" first requires a person to have the information employers need to successfully evaluate his or her competencies prior to completing the job interview. As occupational information tools have changed, so has the technology of job interviewing. We argue that behavioral assessment of one's experience is critical to success during behavioral job interviews. Such "inside-out" occupational information is an excellent and very personal resource.

Behavior-Based Occupational Information

Most forms of education provide feedback in terms of course grades. While useful for many purposes, little information about competency attainment is suggested or can be generalized. Competency-based career guidance has attempted to reform institutional career development efforts by focusing on self-knowledge, educational and occupational exploration, and career planning competencies. Most individuals have limited knowledge of and language to express their strengths, assets, or added value experiences, however, and they are challenged by having to articulate competencies they can apply in the workplace. Extensive portfolios, internships, or work-based learning opportunities offer some experience validation.

Most individuals approach interviews with standardized test scores, transcripts, or recommendations in hand. In contrast, employers seek candidates who can apply what has been learned in schools or in past employment to solving current problems. Validating outcomes with a portfolio by providing concrete examples from past experience and showing projects that can add value to employers is a key to successful job interviewing and securing a job.

TABLE 9.2
Sample of Popular Career Web Sites

Site	Description
www.monster.com Monster	Posts more than 25,000 openings and more than 300,000 résumés
http://careerplanning.about.com About.com's Career Planning Center	Unique and comprehensive site led by a professional guide
www.theodora.com/dot_index .html The DOT on-line	*The Dictionary of Occupational Titles* on-line
www.bls.gov/oco/home.htm The OOH on-line	The 2002–2003 edition of the *Occupational Outlook* on-line
www.ajb.dni.us America's Job Bank	State agencies post an average of 5,000 new openings per day, and companies contribute more than 3,000 per day
www.cando.com Can Do.com	Founded in 1999 to create an on-line community of people with disabilities
www.4work.com 4Work	E-mail listings that match one's skill sets by specific state
www.careers.wsj.com Career Journal	Free career service updates daily offering articles from the *Wall Street Journal* and the *National Business Employment Weekly*
www.nationjob.com Nation Job	More than 15,000 jobs nationwide
http://jobcorps.doleta.gov Job Corp	The nation's largest and most comprehensive residential education and training program for at-risk youth ages 16–24
www.militarycareers.com *Military Career Guide* on-line	*Military Career Guide* on-line
www.hoovers.com Hoovers on-line	An on-line version of the business almanac subtitled "The Ultimate Source for Company Information"
www.doleta.gov/atels_bat/ Bureau of Apprenticeship and Training	The Bureau of Apprenticeship and Training for U.S. Department of Labor
http://safetynet.doleta.gov/netsourc.htm Using Internet Resources to Plan Your Future	Includes the *Riley Guide* and a host of items related to job search and general career related items
www.myfuture.com My Future	Geared to high school graduates
www.newwork.com New Work News	Analysis of news about life and work in the new economy, with attention to business, education, and career issues

An increasing number of employers are using behavior-based assessment methods to screen applicants. Helpers who are aware of the shift from traditional to behavioral interviewing may see this as an advantage to clients who can interpret and present occupational information from a behavioral performance perspective. By evaluating past experiences for competencies, and presenting them as evidence, candidates gain in five ways:

1. It allows them to honor and confirm the value of past experience.

2. It helps them respond to any question in terms of what they did in a real situation rather than speculate about what they might do hypothetically.

3. It helps them think in terms of specific benefits and added value from the employer's point of view.

4. It allows them to "authentically" tell a true story while projecting confidence, positive affect, and excitement.

5. Employers not trained in behavior-based methods will be impressed by individuals who talk in specific terms about past experiences that demonstrate competencies.

With its O*NET database, CareerZone (see Figure 9.1 and the earlier discussion) is behavior-based occupational information. Helpers can use this rich resource in preparing a person for a behavioral interview for a specific occupation. Both CareerZone and O*NET can be viewed as comprehensive curriculum guides that describe the work activities, tasks performed, skills, abilities, and knowledges required for every job.

Behavioral interviewing is touted as generating more objective occupational information and facts from which to make employment decisions than traditional interviewing methods. Traditional interviews predominantly focus on what candidates have: the right coursework or degree, specific experience or references, and so forth. They are often conducted without a common structure for all candidates, lack adequate probing, and can be heavily influenced by first impressions of preconceived characteristics. Behavior-based interviewing focuses on core competencies considered to be essential for success. Examples of behavioral approaches include Green's (1996) suggestion that candidates prepare skill-benefit statements such as I can _____ (add a skill) so I will be able to _____ (add a benefit to the employer). Hansen suggests that candidates follow the STAR method: They should look into their past and describe a situation (S) or task (T), explain the specific action (A) taken to have an effect on the situation, and describe the positive result (R) or outcome (www.QuintCareers.com).

Stimac (1997) went further in developing *The Ultimate Job Search Kit*, which provides a "Position Analyzer" and 280 question cards asking for behavioral evidence of 22 job competencies ranging from assertiveness to goal setting to time management. Each card provides probing follow-up questions that help the person to further explore his or her personal occupational information and gain insight into the objectives behind each question. Practicing this kind of occupational information search helps candidates respond to such questions as the following: "Tell me about a time you . . . ." "Give me an example when you. . . ." "Describe a specific situation where you . . . ." In each case, behavior assessment requires individuals to explore their rich and personal experience source for occupational information from the "inside out."

Linking Systems, Sources, and Sites to the Job Search

Regardless of the present or future, individuals with special needs are challenged to find and maintain employment in a dynamic marketplace. The dramatic change in the way work is organized suggests employment arrangements are more vulnerable, more temporary, and less stable. Compensation has shifted to reward risk taking and a sense of "free agency." Continued learning has become a requirement to acquire a livable wage. Technology and globalization seem inseparable, and most information-based work can be completed from anywhere at anytime at wages determined by a worldwide labor pool. Clearly, career planning has become more important and challenging as barriers to finding satisfying and rewarding jobs confront all workers at some point in their careers.

In this chapter we have argued that traditional print, technology-enhanced, Web site–based, and behavior-based occupational information all play a key part in career planning. Quality information that enhances one's self-knowledge, exploration, and career planning is invaluable, regardless of its form. As career transitions occur, individuals are best prepared if they know what activities give them meaning, define their purpose, and help them make a contribution. Utilizing information systems, sources, and sites is essential to self-directing the career planning process.

Attaining career planning competencies and translating strengths, assets, and experiences into action while mastering behavior-based assessment can lead to a successful job search. All of these career planning components are possible through access to good occupational information and commitments on the parts of the helper and the job seeker to maximize their use. As occupational information becomes increasingly more accurate, easy to access, and motivational, linking to systems, sources, and sites holds great promise for making career planning successful for all individuals.

Appendix 9.A
Physical Demands

The physical demands listed in this appendix serve as a means of describing the physical activities that an occupation requires of a worker. This allows the helper to match the physical requirements of the job with the physical capabilities of the client.

The Factors

1. Strength: This factor is expressed in terms of Sedentary, Light, Medium, Heavy, and Very Heavy. It is measured by involvement of the worker with one or more of the following activities:

   a. Body Position

      - *Standing:* Remaining on one's feet in an upright position at a workstation without moving about.

      - *Walking:* Moving about on foot.

      - *Sitting:* Remaining in a normal seated position.

   b. Weight/Force

      - *Lifting:* Raising or lowering an object from one level to another (includes upward pulling).

      - *Carrying:* Transporting an object, usually holding it in the hands or arms or on the shoulder.

      - *Pushing:* Exerting force upon an object so that the object moves away from the force (includes slapping, striking, kicking, and treadle actions).

      - *Pulling:* Exerting force upon an object so that the object moves toward the force (includes jerking).

The five degrees of Physical Demands Factor 1 (strength) are as follows:

Sedentary Work — Involves exerting up to 10 pounds of force occasionally, or a negligible amount of force frequently, to lift, carry, push, pull, or otherwise move objects, including the human body. Sedentary work involves sitting most of the time, but may involve walking or standing for brief periods of time. Jobs may be defined as Sedentary when walking or standing are required only occasionally and all other Sedentary criteria are met.

Light Work—Involves exerting up to 20 pounds of force occasionally, up to 10 pounds of force frequently, or a negligible amount of force constantly to move objects. Physical demand requirements are in excess of those for Sedentary Work. Even though the weight lifted may be only a negligible amount, a job/occupation is rated Light Work when it requires: (1) walking or standing to a significant degree; (2) sitting most of the time while pushing or pulling leg controls; or (3) working at a production rate pace while constantly pushing or pulling materials, even though the weight of the materials is negligible. (The constant stress and strain of maintaining a production rate pace, especially in an industrial setting, can be and is physically demanding of a worker, even though the amount of force exerted is negligible.)

Medium Work—Involves exerting 20 to 50 pounds of force occasionally, 10 to 25 pounds of force frequently, or an amount greater than negligible and up to 10 pounds constantly to move objects. Physical demand requirements are in excess of those for Light Work.

Heavy Work—Involves exerting 50 to 100 pounds of force occasionally, 25 to 50 pounds of force frequently, or 10 to 20 pounds of force constantly to move objects. Physical demand requirements are in excess of those for Medium Work.

Very Heavy Work—Involves exerting in excess of 100 pounds of force occasionally, in excess of 50 pounds of force frequently, or in excess of 20 pounds of force constantly to move objects. Physical demand requirements are in excess of those for Heavy Work.

Absence or Presence of Other Physical Demand Components

The following codes indicate the absence or presence (and when present, the frequency of occurrence) of the other 19 Physical Demand Components.

N (Not Present) Activity or condition does not exist.

O (Occasionally) Activity or condition exists up to one third of the time.

| F | (Frequently) | Activity or condition exists from one third to two thirds of the time. |
| C | (Constantly) | Activity or condition exists two thirds or more of the time. |

2. *Climbing (Cl)* — Ascending or descending ladders, stairs, scaffolding, ramps, poles, ropes, and the like using the feet and legs and/or hands and arms.

3. *Balancing (Ba)* — Maintaining body equilibrium to prevent falling when walking, standing, crouching, or running on narrow, slippery, or erratically moving surfaces, or maintaining body equilibrium when performing gymnastic feats.

4. *Stooping (St)* — Bending the body downward and forward by bending spine at the waist, requiring full use of the lower extremities and back muscles.

5. *Kneeling (Kn)* — Bending the legs at the knees to come to rest on knee or knees.

6. *Crouching (Co)* — Bending the body downward and forward by bending legs and spine.

7. *Crawling (Cw)* — Moving about on the hands and knees and feet.

8. *Reaching (Re)* — Extending the hands and arms in any direction.

9. *Handling (Ha)* — Seizing, holding, grasping, turning, or otherwise working with the hand or hands. Fingers are involved only to the extent they are an extension of the hand, such as to turn a switch or shift automobile gears.

10. *Fingering (Fi)* — Picking, pinching, or otherwise working with the fingers rather than with the whole hand or arm, as in handling.

11. *Feeling (Fe)* — Perceiving attributes of objects and materials as size, shape, temperature, or texture, by touching with skin, particularly that of fingertips.

12. *Talking (Ta)* — Expressing or exchanging ideas by means of the spoken word to impart oral information to clients, or to the public, and to convey detailed spoken instructions to other workers accurately, loudly, and quickly.

13. *Hearing (He)* — Perceiving the nature of sounds by ear.

14. *Tasting/Smelling (TS)* — Distinguishing, with a degree of accuracy, differences or similarities in intensity or quality of flavors or odors, or recognizing particular flavors or odors using tongue or nose.

15. *Near Acuity (NA)* — Clarity of vision at 20 inches or less.

16. *Far Acuity (FA)* — Clarity of vision at 20 feet or more.

17. *Depth Perception (DP)* — Three-dimensional vision. Ability to judge distances and spatial relationships so as to see objects where and as they actually are.

18. *Accommodation (Ac)* — Adjustment of lens or eye to bring an object into sharp focus.

19. *Color Vision (CV)* — Ability to identify and distinguish colors.

20. *Field of Vision (FV)* — Observing an area that can be seen up or down or to right or left while eyes are fixed on a given point.

Note. From *Selected Characteristics of Occupations Defined in the Dictionary of Occupational Titles* (Appendix C-1), by U.S. Department of Labor, 1993, Washington, DC: U.S. Government Printing Office.

Appendix 9.B
Scale of General Education
Development (GED)

General Education Development encompasses those aspects of education (formal and informal) that are required of the worker for satisfactory job performance. This education is of a general nature that does not have a recognized, fairly specific occupational objective. The following table shows the requirements and scale levels applicable to each.

Level	Reasoning Development	Mathematical Development	Language Development
6	Apply principles of logical or scientific thinking to a wide range of intellectual and practical problems. Deal with nonverbal symbolism (formulas, scientific equations, graphs, musical notes, etc.) in its most difficult phases. Deal with a variety of abstract and concrete variables. Apprehend the most abstruse classes of concepts.	*Advanced Calculus:* Work with limits, continuity, real number systems, mean value theorems, and implicit functions theorems. *Modern Algebra:* Apply fundamental concepts of theories of groups, rings, and fields. Work with differential equations, linear algebra, infinite series, advanced operations methods, and functions of real and complex variables. *Statistics:* Work with mathematical mathematical statistics, probability and applications, experimental design, statistical inference and econometrics.	*Reading:* Read literature, book and play reviews, scientific and technical journals, abstracts, financial reports, and legal documents. *Writing:* Write novels, plays, editorials, journals, speeches, manuals, critiques, poetry, and songs. *Speaking:* Conversant in the theory, principles, and methods of effective and persuasive speaking, voice and diction, phonetics, and discussion and debate.
5	Apply principles of logical or scientific thinking to define problems, collect data, establish facts, and draw valid conclusions. Interpret an extensive variety of technical instructions in mathematical or diagrammatic form.	*Algebra:* Work with exponents and logarithms, linear equations, quadratic equations, mathematical induction and binomial theorem, and permutations. *Calculus:* Apply concepts of analytic geometry, differentiations, and integration of algebraic functions with applications.	Same as Level 6

(continues)

Level	Reasoning Development	Mathematical Development	Language Development
	Deal with several abstract and concrete variables.	*Statistics:* Apply mathematical operations to frequency distributions, reliability and validity of tests, normal curve, analysis of variance, correlation techniques, chi-square application and sampling theory, and factor analysis.	
4	Apply principles of rational systems to solve practical problems and deal with a variety of concrete variables in situations where only limited standardization exists. Interpret a variety of instructions furnished in written, oral, diagrammatic, or schedule form.	*Algebra:* Deal with system of real numbers; linear, quadratic rational, exponential, logarithmic, angle, circular, and inverse functions; related algebraic solution of equations and inequalities; limits and continuity; and probability and statistical inference. *Geometry:* Deductive axiomatic geometry, plane and solid; and rectangular coordinates. *Shop Math:* Practical application of fractions, percentages, ratio and proportion, mensuration, logarithms, slide rule, practical algebra, geometric construction, and essentials of trigonometry.	*Reading:* Read novels, poems, newspapers, periodicals, journals, manuals, dictionaries, thesauruses, and encyclopedias. *Writing:* Prepare business letters, expositions, summaries, and reports using prescribed format and conforming to all rules of punctuation, grammar, diction, and style. *Speaking:* Participate in panel discussions, dramatizations, and debates. Speak extemporaneously on a variety of subjects.
3	Apply commonsense understanding to carry out instructions furnished in written, oral, or diagrammatic form. Deal with problems involving several concrete variables in or from standardized situations.	Compute discount, interest, profit, and loss; commission, mark-up, and selling price; ratio and proportion; and percentage. Calculate surfaces, volumes, weights, and measures. *Algebra:* Calculate variables and formulas, monomials and polynomials, ratio and proportion variables, and square roots and radicals. *Geometry:* Calculate plane and solid figures; circumference, area, and	*Reading:* Read a variety of novels, magazines, atlases, and encyclopedias. Read safety rules, instruction in the use and maintenance of shop tools and equipment, and methods and procedures in mechanical drawing and layout work. *Writing:* Write reports and essays with proper format, punctuation,

(continues)

Level	Reasoning Development	Mathematical Development	Language Development
		volume. Understand kinds of angles and properties of pairs of angles.	spelling, and grammar, using all parts of speech. *Speaking:* Speak before an audience with poise, voice control, and confidence, using correct English and well-modulated voice.
2	Apply commonsense understanding to carry out detailed but uninvolved written or oral instructions. Deal with problems involving a few concrete variables in or from standardized situations.	Add, subtract, multiply, and divide all units of measure. Perform the four operations with like common and decimal fractions. Compute ratio, rate, and percentage. Draw and interpret bar graphs. Perform arithmetic operations involving all U.S. monetary units.	*Reading:* Passive vocabulary of 5,000– 6,000 words. Read at rate of 190–215 words per minute Read adventure stories and comic books, looking up unfamiliar words in dictionary for meaning, spelling, and pronunciation. Read instructions for assembling model cars and airplanes. *Writing:* Write compound and complex sentences using cursive style and proper end punctuation, and employing adjectives and adverbs. *Speaking:* Speak clearly and distinctly with appropriate pauses and emphasis, correct pronunciation, and variations in word order, using present, perfect, and future tenses.
1	Apply commonsense understanding to carry out simple one- or two-step instructions. Deal with standardized situations with occasional or no variables in or from these	Add and subtract two-digit numbers. Multiply and divide 10s and 100s by 2, 3, 4, 5. Perform the four basic arithmetic operations with coins as part of a dollar.	*Reading:* Recognize meaning of 2,500 (two- or three-syllable) words. Read at rate of 95–120 words per minute. Compare similarities and differences between

(continues)

Level	Reasoning Development	Mathematical Development	Language Development
	situations encountered on the job.	Perform operations with units such as cup, pint, and quart; inch, foot, and yard; and ounce and pound.	words and between series of numbers. *Writing:* Print simple sentences containing subject, verb, and object, and series of numbers, names, and addresses. *Speaking:* Speak simple sentences, using normal word order, and present and past tenses.

Note. From *Dictionary of Occupational Titles* (4th ed., Rev., Vol. 11, App. C-111), by U.S. Department of Labor, 1991, Washington, DC: U.S. Government Printing Office.

Appendix 9.C
Environmental Conditions

Environmental Conditions are the physical surroundings of a worker in a specific job.

Environmental Condition Factors and Definitions

1. *Exposure to Weather (We)* — Exposure to outside atmospheric conditions.

2. *Extreme Cold (Co)* — Exposure to nonweather-related cold temperatures.

3. *Extreme Heat (Ho)* — Exposure to nonweather-related hot temperatures.

4. *Wet and/or Humid (Hu)* — Contact with water or other liquids or exposure to nonweather-related humid conditions.

5. *Noise Intensity Level (No)* — The noise intensity level to which the worker is exposed in the job environment. This factor is expressed by one of five levels.

Code	Level	Illustrative Examples
1	Very Quiet	Isolation booth for hearing test, deep sea diving, forest trail
2	Quiet	Library, many private offices, funeral reception, golf course, art museum
3	Moderate	Business office where typewriters are used, department store, grocery store, light traffic, fast-food restaurant at off-hours
4	Loud	Can manufacturing department, large earth-moving equipment, heavy traffic
5	Very Loud	Rock concert – front row, jack hammer in operation, rocket engine test area during test

6. *Vibration (Vi)* — Exposure to a shaking object or surface.

7. *Atmospheric Conditions (Ac)* — Exposure to such conditions as fumes, noxious odors, dust, mists, gases, and poor ventilation that affect the respiratory system, eyes, or the skin.

8. *Proximity to Moving Mechanical Parts (MP)* — Exposure to possible bodily injury from moving mechanical parts of equipment, tools, or machinery.

9. *Exposure to Electrical Shock (ES)* — Exposure to possible injury from electrical shock.

10. *Working in High, Exposed Places (HE)* — Exposure to possible bodily injury from falling.

11. *Exposure to Radiation (Ra)* —Exposure to possible bodily injury from radiation.

12. *Working with Explosives (Ex)* —Exposure to possible injury from explosions.

13. *Exposure to Toxic, Caustic Chemicals (TC)* — Exposure to possible bodily injury from toxic or caustic chemicals.

14. *Other Environmental Conditions (Ot)* — Other environmental conditions not defined above. These may include, but are not limited to, such settings as demolishing parts of buildings to reach and combat fires and rescue persons endangered by fire and smoke; mining ore or coal underground; patroling assigned beat to prevent crime or disturbance of peace and being subjected to bodily injury or death from law violators; diving in ocean and being subjected to bends or other conditions associated with high water pressure and oxygen deprivation; patroling ski slopes prior to allowing public use and being exposed to danger of avalanches.

Note. From *Selected Characteristics of Occupations Defined in the Dictionary of Occupational Titles* (Appendix D-1), by U.S. Department of Labor, 1993, Washington, DC: U.S. Government Printing Office.

References

Bolles, R. (1996). *Job-hunting on the Internet*. Berkeley, CA: Ten Speed Press.

Bowlsbey, J., Dickel, M., & Sampson, J. (1998). *The Internet: A tool for career planning*. Columbus, OH: National Career Development Association.

Cohen, P. (1997). The employability plan/individual service strategy and occupational information resources. In T. Harrington (Ed.), *Handbook of career planning for special needs students* (pp. 235–265). Austin, TX: PRO-ED.

Crispin, G., & Mehler, M. (2002) *CareerXRoads: The directory to job, resume and career management sites on the Web*. Kendall Park, NJ: MMC Group.

Farr, J. M., Ludden, L. L., & Shatkin, L. (2001). *Guide for occupational exploration* (3rd ed.). Indianapolis, IN: JIST Works.

Green, P. (1996). *Getting hired: Winning strategies to ace the interview*. Austin, TX: Bard Press.

Holland, J. L. (1997). *Making vocational choices: A theory of vocational personalities and work environments*. Odessa, FL: Psychological Assessment Resources.

Hubbard, M., McCloy, R., Campbell, J., Nottingham, J., Lewis, P., Rivkin, D., et al. (2000). *Revision of O*NET data collection instruments*. Raleigh, NC: National O*NET Consortium.

Mumford, M. D., & Peterson, N. G. (1995). Introduction. In N. G. Peterson, M. D. Mumford, W. C. Borman, P. R. Jeanneret, & E. A. Fleishman (Eds.), *Development of prototype occupational information system network (O*NET) content model* (Vol. 1, 1–16). Salt Lake City: Utah Department of Employment Security.

Mumford, M. D., & Peterson, N. G. (1999). The O*NET content model: Structural considerations in describing jobs. In N. G. Peterson, M. D. Mumford, W. C. Borman, P. R. Jeanneret, & E. A. Fleishman (Eds.), *An occupational information system for the 21st century: The development of O*NET* (pp. 21–30). Washington, DC: American Psychological Association.

Nelson, B. (2001). *Please don't just do what I tell you!* New York: Hyperion.

Stimac, J. (1997). *The ultimate job search kit*. Lawrence, KS: Seaton.

U.S. Department of Labor. (1991). *Dictionary of occupational titles* (Rev. 4th ed.). Washington, DC: U.S. Government Printing Office.

U.S. Department of Labor. (1993). *Selected characteristic of occupations defined in the Dictionary of Occupational Titles*. Washington, DC: U.S. Government Printing Office.

U.S. Department of Labor. (2002a) *Occupational information network*. Washington, DC: Author. (Available at http://www.doleta.gov/programs/one)

U.S. Department of Labor. (2002b). *Occupational outlook handbook*. Washington, DC: U.S. Government Printing Office.

U. S. Department of Labor, Employment, and Training Administration. (2000a). *Interest profiler*. Washington, DC: U.S. Government Printing Office.

U.S. Department of Labor, Employment, and Training Administration. (2000b). *Work importance locator*. Washington, DC: U.S. Government Printing Office.

DISABILITY AND THE LABOR MARKET

Neeta P. Fogg and Paul E. Harrington

An essential step in providing services designed to bolster the employment and earnings experiences of persons with disabilities is an understanding of the labor market environment of the nation and how persons with disabilities fit into the structure of employment. Like every other
group in the U.S. labor market, persons with disabilities are unique with respect
to both their characteristics and behaviors. This chapter is designed to provide
the reader with an overview of the characteristics and behaviors of the population of persons with disabilities and how those characteristics and behaviors
influence their basic interactions with the job market and their likely position
in the dynamic and ever-changing labor market of the future.

The chapter begins with a discussion of the measure of disability. Disability,
like many other concepts employed by economists and social sciences, is simply
a convenient construct or definition that is used to learn about the magnitude
and characteristics of a population subgroup. Unfortunately, there is no single
definition of what exactly constitutes a disability and certainly none that could
be used effectively in a large-scale survey of households that is designed to
measure the size, characteristics, and behaviors of the population with disabilities in the United States. Consequently, proxy measures of disability are employed that are utilized in different contexts to estimate the desired data
(Burkhauser & Haveman, 1982). One consequence of this is that as the context, goals, and objectives of data collection efforts differ, the definitions, and
hence the findings, of the individual surveys will differ as well. The introductory
section of this chapter describes three alternative measures of the population of

316 ◇ Fogg and P. E. Harrington

persons with disabilities in the United States. In it we examine alternative estimates of the size and characteristics of this population. The discussion about the measure of disability is followed by an analysis of the labor market activities of persons with disabilities, including their labor force attachment and an assessment of the nature and determinants of their job access. This discussion is followed by a brief review of the growth path of the U.S. economy and its likely meaning for efforts to provide improved employment and earnings opportunities for persons with disabilities.

Three Alternative Measures

Estimates of the size and characteristics of the number of persons with disabilities in the United States are derived from three major sources: the *Current Population Survey* (CPS), the *National Health Interview Survey* (NHIS), and the *Survey of Income and Program Participation* (SIPP). These surveys are similar in that they are based on information collected from a random sample of households across the nation. A key feature of household surveys is that essentially all the information provided about characteristics of members of a household is self-identified. In other words, the race or ethnicity, or the disability status, of the respondents is self-determined. In the case of race and ethnicity, respondents are asked to categorize themselves into one of a number of groups included on the survey questionnaire. Each respondent's self-identified race and ethnic category is taken as a given, and no efforts are made to verify this response or to have a second-party determination of the race or ethnicity of the respondents (Skerry, 2000). The three surveys also rely on self-identification to determine the disability status of respondents. However, the disability concepts and definitions do differ in terms of scope across all three surveys.

The CPS is a monthly survey conducted by the U.S. Bureau of the Census that captures a variety of information about the characteristics of the U.S. population. It is perhaps best known as the source of information for the nation's monthly unemployment rate. Each month, the CPS survey has a supplementary questionnaire that is used to gather data on specific subjects. In 2001, the February supplement to the CPS was used to gather data on the disability status of the population of the nation. The CPS asks respondents if they have a work disability that limits the kind or the amount of work that they could perform. The CPS questionnaire also asks questions to make a determination of the degree of disability. The CPS categorizes persons as severely disabled if they meet the following criteria:

- Had a *long-term* physical or mental condition that prevented them from working during the reference week of the survey.

- Did not work at all in the previous year because of the illness or disability.

- Were under the age of 65 and covered by Medicare.

- Were under the age of 65 and received Supplemental Security Income payments in the survey month (Yelin & Katz, 1994).

In February of 2001, the CPS survey estimated that about 17.6 million persons between the ages of 16 and 64 reported that they had a disability. This group represented about 9.5% of the 16- to 64-year-old population in the nation. Among those who said that they had a disability, 11.6 million, or 68%, said that they met at least one of the four criteria for a severe disability. The CPS thus suggests that 1 of 10 nonelderly adults were disabled and that more than two thirds of this population had a severe disability (U.S. Bureau of the Census, 2002).

The NHIS survey assesses the disability status of the population between the ages of 18 and 69 by asking them if they have a limitation in their "major activity" due to a chronic health condition (Centers for Disease Control, 2002). Respondents in the NHIS are asked if they are unable to work or are limited in their work as a result of a chronic health condition. In 1997, the NHIS survey found that 16.7 million persons, or about 9.8% of all persons between the ages of 18 and 69, classified themselves as having a work limitation associated with a chronic health condition. Of this group, about 9.9 million, or nearly 60% said they were unable to work at all because of their condition.

The SIPP is an annual, longitudinal study conducted by the U.S. Bureau of the Census. The SIPP survey has a set of questions to derive the disability status of respondents. These questions employ a much broader definition of disability than either the CPS or the NHIS surveys. The SIPP survey classified disability into four conceptual areas:

- a specific health condition that interferes with normal daily activities;

- an impairment that involves losses that occur after a health condition is controlled or eliminated or losses in physical or mental abilities not associated with any specific condition;

- a functional limitation in everyday activities such as seeing, hearing, and walking; and

- an inability to perform a social role such as work or school-related activities.

The broader concept of disability employed by the SIPP survey yields a much larger estimate of the size of the U.S. population with disabilities. The SIPP survey estimated that 29.9 million persons had some type of disabling condition at the time of the survey. Unlike the CPS and the NHIS, which both estimated that less than 10% of the nation's nonelderly adult population was disabled, the SIPP found that 19.5% of all persons between the ages of 20 and 64 had some type of disability. Like the other two survey programs, the SIPP also distinguished between disability and severe disability in its estimates. According to the SIPP survey, in 1994 there were 14.3 million persons, or about 48% of all persons with a disability, who had a severe disability.

The data in Table 10.1 summarize information regarding populations with disabilities from all three surveys. Although each of the three survey programs has its advantages in examining the characteristics of the population with disabilities, the remainder of this chapter will utilize findings from the SIPP survey for October 1994 and January 1995. We chose the SIPP because it provides a far more detailed depiction of the disabled population than the other two surveys and thus offers richer insights into the employment and earnings experiences of persons with a disability (Kruse, 1998).

TABLE 10.1
Alternative Estimates of the Size of Population
with Disabilities in the United States, Various Years

Population	No.	%
CPS 2001		
Total population ages 16–64	161,135,000	100.0
Total population with disabilities	17,067,000	10.6
Population with severe disabilities	11,646,000	68.2
NHIS 1997		
Total population ages 18–69	172,861,000	100.0
Total population with disabilities	16,647,000	9.6
Population with severe disabilities	9,865,000	5.7
SIPP 1994		
Total population ages 20–64	152,961,000	100.0
Total population with disabilities	29,919,000	19.6
Population with severe disabilities	14,350,000	48.0

Note. CPS = Current Population Survey (U.S. Bureau of the Census, 2001); NHIS = National Health Interview Survey (U.S. Bureau of the Census, 1997); SIPP = Survey of Income and Program Participation (U.S. Bureau of the Census, 1994).

Demographic Characteristics

The characteristics of the disabled population in the United States differ from the general population in a number of important ways. Moreover, the characteristics of individuals with a moderate disability differ considerably from those of individuals who have a severe disability. The findings provided in Table 10.2 examine the gender and the race/ethnic characteristics of the disabled population in the nation at the time of the SIPP survey. These data reveal that persons with disabilities are more likely to be female and a member of a racial or ethnic minority group. Women were disproportionately represented among individuals with severe disabilities, accounting for 55.9% of all persons with a severe disability — about 10% more than would be expected on the basis of their share of the overall nonelderly adult population. African Americans were much more likely to be severely disabled than were members of other racial or ethnic groups. African Americans made up 18% of the disabled population — a share that was nearly 50% higher than their proportion of the nondisabled population

TABLE 10.2
Gender and Race/Ethnic Composition of the Population
with Disabilities in the United States

Characteristic	Nondisabled	Nonsevere Disability	Severe Disability
Total number	138,142,000	16,497,000	14,552,000
Gender	%	%	%
Female	50.5	47.0	55.9
Male	49.5	53.0	44.1
Race/Ethnic Origin			
White	83.6	87.7	78.7
African American	12.1	9.5	18.0
American Indian	0.7	1.1	1.0
Asian and Pacific Island	3.7	1.8	2.4
Hispanic	10.1	7.7	10.8
Non-Hispanic	89.9	92.3	89.2
Age (yrs.)			
15–24	23.8	14.6	7.5
25–34	26.5	18.5	16.4
35–44	24.7	25.0	20.7
45–54	15.8	23.4	23.3
55–64	9.3	18.5	32.1

Note. Data from "People with Disabilities: Demographic, Income, and Health Care Characteristics," 1993, by D. L. Kruse, April 1998, *Monthly Labor Review*, pp. 13–22.

in the nation. Asians and Pacific Islanders were less likely to be classified as severely disabled. Only 2.4% of all nonelderly members of this group were severely disabled, whereas they accounted for 3.7% of the nondisabled population.

Unsurprisingly, age appears to be an important determinant of the likelihood that a person will have a disability. Young adults ages 15 to 24 accounted for 23.8% of the nondisabled population but only 7.5% of persons with severe disabilities and 14.6% of persons with moderate disabilities. The data reveal that as the population ages, the proportion of persons with disabilities will shift radically. Persons ages 45 to 54 accounted for about 15.8% of the nondisabled population but 23% for each of the moderately disabled and severely disabled groups. Thus, persons in the middle-age groups are about 50% more likely to be disabled than would be expected relative to their share of the population. Persons in their preretirement years accounted for nearly one in three persons with a disability, although they represented only 9.3% of the nonelderly population.

The likelihood that a nonelderly adult will have a disability is closely related to his or her level of educational attainment. Among those persons with a severe disability, 38% had not graduated from high school, whereas only 12% of the nondisabled population failed to graduate from high school. This means that individuals who dropped out were more than three times as likely to be severely disabled relative to their proportion of the population. In contrast, 27% of the nondisabled population were college graduates, but only 8.5% of individuals with a severe disability were college graduates. Part of this result is associated with the disproportionately low levels of educational attainment of older persons with disabilities.

These findings also suggest that increasing one's level of educational attainment helps that person avoid disabilities through differing lifestyle choices and differing occupational access. Among persons with a moderate disability, the relationship between educational attainment and disability status was not as strong as that for the severely disabled population. Persons with moderate disabilities were only about half as likely as persons with severe disabilities to be high school dropouts and were more than twice as likely to hold a college degree (see Figure 10.1).

Labor Market Activities of the Disabled Population

The labor market activity of the disabled population differs sharply from that of the nondisabled population; however, these differences cannot be attributed

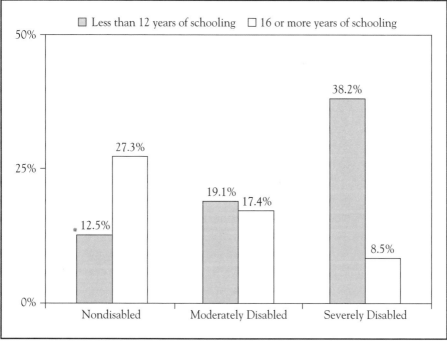

Figure 10.1. Disability status and educational attainment. Data from "People with Disabilities: Demographic, Income, and Health Care Characteristics," 1993, by D. L. Kruse, September 1998, *Monthly Labor Review*, pp. 13–22. Tabulations and figure created by authors.

solely to disability status. Indeed, educational attainment, age, and gender (and to a lesser extent, race/ethnicity) play important roles in influencing the willingness and ability of different population groups to actively participate in the job market. As was noted previously, the population with severe disabilities is much more likely to be female and older, and to have fewer years of schooling — three factors that (aside from disability status) contribute to reduced labor market activity.

Perhaps the most fundamental measure of labor market activity employed by economists is the labor force participation rate. The nation's labor force is composed of the total number of persons who are employed in a specified time period, plus all those who are jobless but actively seeking a job and available for work during a time period. The labor force participation rate is calculated by dividing the number of persons in the labor force by the total number of persons over 16 years old in a given population group. It provides a measure of the degree to which a given population group is actively engaged in the job market, either through employment or active job search.

TABLE 10.3

Labor Force Participation Rates of the 20- to 64-Year-Old
Population by Disability Status, Gender, Age, and Level
of Educational Attainment

Characteristic	No Disability (%)	Moderate Disability (%)	Severe Disability (%)
All	84.5	81.6	29.5
Gender			
Female	76.7	73.0	27.7
Male	92.4	89.9	31.8
Age (yrs.)			
20–24	76.8	79.6	37.2
25–44	87.6	84.2	36.4
45–54	89.4	87.6	31.6
55–64	68.4	68.2	18.0
Educational attainment			
Less than 12 years	75.2	74.4	17.3
12 years only	84.7	81.2	31.2
13–15 years	87.3	85.7	39.1
College graduate	90.0	86.4	52.4

Note. Data from "Persons with Disability: Labor Market Activity, 1994," by T. W. Hale, H. V. Hayghe, & J. M. McNeil, September 1998, *Monthly Labor Review*, pp. 3–12.

Table 10.3 provides information on the labor force participation rates of persons in various gender, age, and educational attainment groups by their disability status. These data reveal that only 29.5% of persons with a severe disability were active participants in the labor market at the time of the survey. This means, of course, that almost 70% of the individuals with severe disabilities were not engaged in the job market at all. During the same time period, almost 85% of the nondisabled population — and a surprisingly high 81% of the moderately disabled population — were active in the nation's job market.

The data reveal fairly large differences between the labor force attachment of men and that of women. More than 92% of nondisabled men were in the job market at the time of the study, whereas about 77% of women were active participants. The size of the gender gap was similarly large for the moderately disabled group but much smaller for the group with severe disabilities. Men and women who were severely disabled were almost equally unlikely to be active in the labor market, with only modest differences in participation rates between them. Job market attachment among persons without a severe disability rises

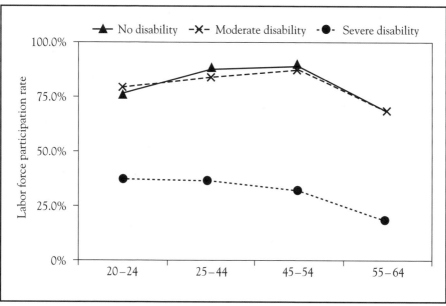

Figure 10.2. Labor force attachment of the 20- to 64-year-old population by disability status and age. Data from "People with Disabilities: Labor Market Activitiy, 1994," by T. Hale, H. Hayghe, & J. McNeil, September 1998, *Monthly Labor Review*, pp. 3–12. Tabulations and figure created by authors.

each year between initial entry into the labor market until the preretirement years, beginning around age 55, when it begins to decline. The participation rate for the severely disabled group has a markedly different pattern relative to age. The job market attachment of this is highest when they are young and first entering the jobs market; however, it declines steadily with age (see Figure 10.2).

Educational attainment and labor force attachment are strongly linked, according to the findings in Table 10.3, especially among persons with a severe disability. The data reveal that among the nondisabled population, the labor force participation rate for dropouts was 75.2%, rising to 90.0% for college graduates — a 15% difference, but a 20% difference in the probability of participating in the job market between the two groups. The labor force attachment of the moderately disabled population was similar to that of the nondisabled population, with a relative difference of 16% in job market attachment. Among the severely disabled population, a much stronger relationship existed between educational attainment and labor force participation. Individuals who dropped out of high school and had a severe disability had a participation rate of just 17.3%, whereas the labor force participation rate of high school graduates was 31.2%, a difference of about 14 percentage points, but it represents an 80%

difference in the probability of participation in the labor market. The job market attachment of persons with a college degree who had a severe disability was quite high — 52.4% — a level of participation that was 67% greater than that of similar high school graduates and more than 200% greater than that of the group of high school dropouts with severe disabilities.

The findings on educational attainment suggest that additional years of schooling for those with the most severe disabilities have a strong pay-off in the labor market. Persons with higher levels of educational attainment have greater access to employment and earnings opportunities than do persons with fewer years of schooling. The SIPP survey also revealed similar relationships between educational attainment and income for persons with disabilities. High school graduates with a severe disability had a monthly income that was 21% higher than the income of the high school dropout with a severe disability. College graduates with severe disabilities had monthly income levels more than double those of their high school graduate counterparts. Although education alone cannot eliminate the employment and income gaps that exist between the severely disabled and nondisabled populations, it can contribute substantially to reducing the size of these differences.

Employment and Disability

Although the labor force participation of the population with severe disabilities is well below that of the nondisabled population and those with moderate disabilities, they are employed in a wide array of industries and occupations in the U.S. economy. The data provided in Table 10.4 reveal that when people with severe disabilities are employed, they work across the whole array of industries in the nation in roughly the same proportion as the nondisabled and the group with moderate disabilities. Like most employed individuals, most persons with severe disabilities work in nonagricultural jobs. About 73% work in wage and salary jobs collecting a check from an employer — a proportion almost identical to that for nondisabled individuals. Similarly, approximately 10% of employed persons with severe disabilities are self-employed, operating their own businesses, and approximately 15% work for federal, state, or local government agencies, again in the same proportions as for the group with moderate disabilities and the nondisabled group.

Within the private (nongovernmental) sector of the economy, persons with a severe disability are somewhat more likely to be employed in the services

TABLE 10.4

Distribution of Employed Persons by Disability Status
and Major Industry Sector

Characteristic	No Disability (%)	Moderate Disability (%)	Severe Disability (%)
Total	100	100	100
Agriculture (wage and salary and self-employed)	1.2	1.3	1.6
Nonagricultural wage	98.8	98.7	98.4
Private wage and salary	73.0	70.8	72.4
Mining	6.0	0.7	0.5
Construction	4.3	4.4	2.4
Manufacturing	17.3	17.5	16.2
Transportation and utilities	5.1	5.0	3.5
Wholesale trade	3.7	3.5	2.8
Retail trade	13.7	14.3	16.8
Finance, insurance, and real estate	6.0	3.8	4.5
Service	22.3	21.7	25.8
Government	15.5	14.9	15.5
Self-employed	10.3	13.0	10.4

Note. Data from "Persons with Disability: Labor Market Activity, 1994," by T. W. Hale, H. V. Hayghe, & J. M. McNeil, September 1998, *Monthly Labor Review*, pp. 3–12.

industry. Private-sector job access to the broad range of industries in the U.S. economy appears similar across all three groups, however.

Although individuals with severe disabilities have similar access to employment in a wide range of industries in the U.S. economy as the nondisabled and the group of persons with moderate disabilities, their access to employment across occupations is somewhat diminished. They have less access to high-skill jobs in the economy. Lower levels of education and inadequate skills development limit the occupational access of these persons with the most severe disabilities. The findings in Table 10.5 reveal that the moderately disabled group and especially the severely disabled group are substantially less likely to be employed in a managerial professional or technical occupation. Both groups are only about two thirds as likely to hold an executive or managerial position as the nondisabled group. Within the professional fields, the gap is even larger. Persons without a disability were 1.75 times more likely to hold a professional position than were persons with severe disabilities, and only 1.36 times more likely to hold such a job relative to persons with moderate disabilities.

TABLE 10.5
Distribution of Employed Persons by Disability Status
and Major Occupational Category

Characteristic	No Disability (%)	Moderate Disability (%)	Severe Disability (%)
Total	100	100	100
Executive, administrative, and managerial	12.7	8.9	8.3
Professional specialty	15.1	11.1	8.6
Technicians and related support	4.4	4.4	2.2
Sales workers	10.4	10.1	9.5
Administrative support, including clerical	17.3	15.7	17.0
Service occupations	12.4	15.7	21.6
Precision production, craft, and repair	10.7	12.2	8.8
Operators, fabricators, and laborers	15.8	20.0	21.2
Farming, forestry, and fishing	1.3	1.9	2.7

Note. Data from "Persons with Disability: Labor Market Activity, 1994," by T. W. Hale, H. V. Hayghe, & J. M. McNeil, September 1998, *Monthly Labor Review*, pp. 3–12.

Employed persons with severe disabilities were much more likely to be employed in service occupations and in operative and fabricator positions. More than 21% of all workers with severe disabilities were employed in service occupations, which generally require fewer skills. Examples include parking lot attendant, maid, and security guard. Because these jobs have lower skill content, they provide little opportunity for training or advancement. Frequently, these jobs are part-time and/or part-year. This combination implies that workers in service occupations have earnings that are well below the average of most U.S. workers.

Operative and fabricator jobs are largely semiskilled and unskilled blue-collar positions with low literacy skill demands. Workers in these jobs learn their specific occupational skills largely through short on-the-job training. Persons with moderate and severe abilities are also overrepresented in operative and fabricator positions. The data reveal that like the service occupations, about 21% of those with a severe disability were employed in semiskilled or unskilled blue-collar jobs, with 20% of the employed individuals with moderate disabilities working in these occupations.

Educational attainment is a key determinate of labor market success. The heavy concentration of persons with severe disabilities in service occupations and lower-skilled blue-collar jobs, and their underrepresentation in professional, managerial, and technical jobs, is largely a reflection of their lower levels of educational attainment. Access to employment in professional, technical, and managerial occupations is largely via the attainment of a college or university degree. The nation's service industries have become the major source of new job creation as manufacturing employment has continued to decline. Many counselors and placement professionals often think of service industries as providing low-quality job opportunities. Although it is true that many service occupations are indeed low level in terms of skills and pay, the service industries employ the majority of professional workers in the labor market. Service industries in the United States are dominated by the delivery of professional services such as health, legal, social, and business services. Firms in these industries in turn demand professional workers with high levels of educational attainment, strong basic skills, and occupational proficiencies. As service industry employment has increased, the demand for individuals with a postsecondary degree has increased, while persons with fewer years of schooling have found themselves increasingly at a disadvantage in the labor market.

Changing Job Content of the U.S. Economy

The job content of the U.S. economy has changed sharply over the past two decades. Most of the job growth has occurred in the service-producing sector of the economy while jobs in the goods-producing sector have been shrinking. A large portion of the goods-producing sector consists of the manufacturing industry — an industry that historically has employed large proportions of blue-collar workers. In 2000, nearly 6 out of 10 manufacturing workers were employed in blue-collar occupations (see Figure 10.3), most often in semiskilled and unskilled machine operative, fabricator, and laborer positions. As noted previously, these jobs do not require high levels of formal educational attainment. Although the production process in manufacturing has become much more sophisticated in recent years, it still continues to be an important source of employment for persons who do not possess high levels of formal education.

The service-producing sector consists of industries with very different occupational staffing patterns from those in the manufacturing sector. The occupational staffing patterns in these industries are dominated by college labor market occupations, which consist of four major occupational groups: professional, technical, managerial and high-level sales jobs (e.g., insurance sales, real estate sales, security and financial services sales). These occupations require

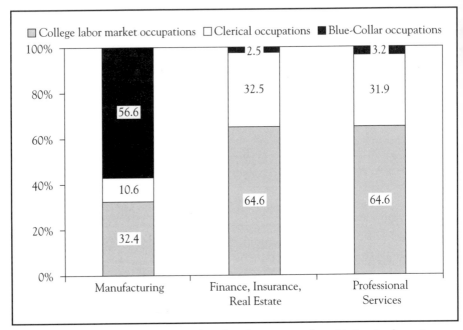

Figure 10.3. Percentage distribution of employed persons in selected industries, by major occupational area, United States, 2000. Data from Center for Labor Market Studies, Northeastern University and U.S. Bureau of the Census CPS Micro Data Files, various years. Tabulations by the authors.

high levels of literacy proficiencies, which are acquired through formal education. The professional services industry makes up a sizable portion of the services industry. Nearly 65% of all jobs in this industry are college labor market occupations. About one third of the jobs are in clerical and administrative support occupations, with only 3% of all jobs in this industry being blue-collar positions. With an occupational staffing pattern that is similar to the one in the professional services industry, the finance, insurance, and real estate industries also are disproportionate employers of college graduates (see Figure 10.3).

Employment developments over the 1990s accelerated the trends that began in the 1980s: the creation of new jobs occurred largely in the services industries, with little net job creation in manufacturing. During that decade, the U.S. economy added 21.9 million nonagricultural wage and salary jobs, a very strong 20% increase in employment. With the exception of the manufacturing sector, jobs in every industrial sector grew, albeit at varying rates. The services industry added 12 million jobs, a 44% increase in employment over the 10 years. The construction industry, which accounts for only 5% of all nonagricultural wage and salary jobs, added 1.5 million jobs, expanding employment levels by

TABLE 10.6
Trends in the Nonagricultural Wage and Salary Employment
in the United States by Major Industry, 1990–2000 (in Thousands)

Major Industry	1990	2000	Absolute Change	Relative Change (%)	Share of Change (%)
Nonagricultural wage and salary	108,760	130,639	21,879	20.1	100.0
Construction	5,120	6,698	1,578	30.8	7.2
Manufacturing	19,077	18,469	−608	−3.2	na
Transportation and utilities	5,776	7,019	1,243	21.5	5.7
Wholesale trade	6,173	7,024	851	13.8	3.9
Retail trade	19,601	23,307	3,706	18.9	16.9
Finance, insurance, and real estate	6,700	7,560	860	12.8	3.9
Service	27,291	39,340	12,049	44.2	55.1
Government	18,304	20,680	2,376	13.0	10.9
Other	718	542	−176	−24.5	na

Note. Data from "Industry Output and Employment Projections to 2010," by J. M. Berman, November 2001, *Monthly Labor Review*, pp. 39–56.

31%. Employment in the retail trade sector was nearly one fifth higher in 2000 compared to 1990 (see Table 10.6). The only industry to see a decline in employment was manufacturing, which lost 608,000 jobs, 3.2% of the total 1990 employment in this industry.

The services industry dominated the nation's employment growth over the 1990s. Figure 10.3 reveals that the service industry's share of change was 55%. This means that of the 21.9 million new jobs created in the nation during the 1990s (see the absolute change column), firms in the service industry created more than 12 million, or about 55 of 100, net new nonagricultural wage and salary positions. The share of new jobs in the retail trade sector was 17% and the public sector added 11% of all net new jobs. The addition of new jobs in the construction, transportation, wholesale trade, and finance/insurance/real estate sectors accounted for between 7% and 4% of the net new jobs added in the nation's economy between 1990 and 2000. The industry employment changes in the nation's economy over the 1990s continued the past trend of the service industry's increasing dominance.

TABLE 10.7
Employment by Major Industry Sector in the United States,
2000 and Projected 2010 (in Thousands)

Major Industry	2000	Projected 2010	Absolute Change	Relative Change (%)
Nonagricultural wage and salary	130,639	152,447	21,808	16.7
Mining	543	488	−55	−10.1
Construction	6,698	7,522	824	12.3
Manufacturing	18,469	19,047	578	3.1
Transportation and utilities	7,019	8,274	1,255	17.9
Wholesale trade	7,024	7,800	776	11.0
Retail trade	23,307	26,400	3,093	13.3
Finance, insurance, and real estate	7,560	8,247	687	9.1
Service	39,340	52,233	12,893	32.8
Government	20,680	22,436	1,756	8.5

Note. Data from "Industry Output and Employment Projections to 2010," by J. M. Berman, November 2001, Monthly Labor Review, pp. 39–56.

Industry Employment Projections, 2000–2010

The long-term shift of employment toward the nation's service sector is expected to continue and perhaps accelerate over the next decade. National projections of employment trends during the 2000 to 2010 period suggest a slowdown in the rate of new job creation in the nation, but continued strong growth in the demand for workers in the services industries. The industry forecasts of employment provided in Table 10.7 indicate that the U.S. economy is expected to add 21.8 million new employment opportunities. Although these forecasts suggest that a large number of new jobs will be created in the future, they also suggest a slowdown in the rate of new job creation relative to the 1990s. Over the forecast period, employment is expected to increase by 16.7%, a considerably slower rate than that achieved during the 1990s. The trend of increasing service sector employment is projected to continue through the year 2010.

The service industry sector is projected to add 12.9 million jobs between 2000 and 2010 (see Table 10.7), but the rate of job growth in this sector is projected to slow relative to its rate in the 1990s. Jobs in the service industry are pro-jected to grow by one third between 2000 and 2010, down from a job growth rate of 44% between 1990 and 2000. The retail trade sector is expected to create an additional 3.1 million jobs over the next decade. Together, services and retail trade are expected to generate nearly three quarters of all the new jobs created in the nation over the next decade. Few new jobs are expected to be created in the nation's goods-producing sector, which obviously means fewer employment op-portunities for blue-collar workers — an area in which workers with disabilities are disproportionately employed. Indeed, the entire nation's manufacturing sec-tor is expected to add less than 600,000 jobs. Labor-saving technologies and the continued move of manufacturing jobs to other countries means that at best, the nation's manufacturing sector will grow only very slowly during the decade. The two factors heavily influencing the expected slow growth in manufacturing employment also alter manufacturing staffing patterns. Technological change and "off shoring" have the largest impact on lower-skill blue-collar occupations. Technological change tends to eliminate low-skill jobs while actually increasing the demand for workers in the college labor market. The off shoring of manufac-turing is very heavily concentrated in low-skill occupations because plenty of low-skill, low-wage workers are available overseas.

Changes in Occupational Employment

Trends in the industry sources of job growth have a powerful impact on the job growth in different occupations and the changes that occur in the nation's la-bor markets. The data on industry staffing patterns provided in Figure 10.3 re-veal sharply different staffing structures across major sectors of the U.S. econ-omy. Moreover, changes in employment levels within an industry sector affect the level of demand for workers in occupations that dominate that industry's staffing patterns. For example, the decline in manufacturing employment that occurred during the 1990s would be expected to result in a reduction in demand for blue-collar workers in the nation. Similarly, rapid expansion in service-sector employment would be expected to result in strong growth in that nation's college labor market occupations. Changes in the industrial structure of em-ployment is not the only major factor that will influence the demand for work-ers over time. Changes in the staffing structure of industries largely associated with technological change and firm reorganization also influence the level of demand for workers across occupations.

   Sharp changes in industry source of job growth, in combination with the forces of technology and innovations, have resulted in powerful changes in the

TABLE 10.8

Change in the Number of 22- to 64-Year-Old Employed Persons
by Major Occupations, United States, 1983–2001

Major Occupation	1983	2001	Absolute Change	Relative Change (%)	Share of Total Change (%)
All occupations	84,522,251	119,284,529	+34,762,277	+41	100
Professional, technical, managerial, and high-level sales (college labor market occupations)	30,839,987	51,833,412	+20,993,426	+68	60
Low-level sales, services, and clerical occupations	27,487,442	34,403,522	+6,916,079	+25	20
Blue-collar occupation	23,736,571	28,756,084	+5,019,513	+21	14
Proportion employed in professional, technical, managerial, and high-level sales occupations	36%	43%	+7%	+19	na

Note. Data from Center for Labor Market Studies, Northeastern University and U.S. Bureau of the Census CPS Micro Data Files, various years. Tabulations by the authors.

occupational composition of the nation as a whole. The findings provided in Table 10.8 display trends in employment across broad occupational groups over the past two decades as the forces of international competition and technology fundamentally altered the occupational structure of labor demand in the nation (see Note at bottom of page).

The data provided in the table reveal that the biggest single increase in employment that occurred across all the different occupational groups was in the college labor market occupations of professional, technical, managerial, and high-level sales jobs. The number of persons employed in these occupations increased by 21 million, or 68%, over the 18-year period. Growth in college labor market occupations accounted for 60% of the total increase in employment among adults in the nation's economy over the past two decades. This dramatic shift in the demand for professional, technical, managerial, and high-level sales

Note. Table 10.8 begins with 1983 because the occupational coding system employed in the CPS survey was changed at that time, breaking the time series and the ability to compare occupational data collected prior to 1983 to data collected after that date.

workers has resulted in a sharp rise in the demand for workers with postsecondary degrees. The dominance of growth in the demand for workers with a college degree has resulted in diminished job access for persons with disabilities — especially those individuals with severe disabilities. Our earlier analysis of data on the educational attainment of persons with disabilities revealed that individuals with severe disabilities were much less likely to have graduated from college and much more likely to have failed to complete high school than either their nondisabled or moderately disabled counterparts. As the demand for labor has shifted sharply toward college graduates over the past two decades, it has had a disproportionately adverse impact on the population with severe disabilities because they are much less likely to have earned a college degree than other employed adults. The shift of employment into services and retail trade has also increased the demand for lower level sales, service, and clerical occupations over the past two decades, although the pace of growth in these fields has been much slower than that observed in the college labor market.

Employment in low-level sales, service, and clerical occupations increased by 6.9 million persons, or 25%, since 1983, accounting for about 20% of the total increase in the number of employed adults since that time. As noted previously, persons with severe disabilities are much more likely to be relegated to employment in these jobs because of their low average levels of educational attainment. Unfortunately, these jobs are frequently characterized by low-skill, poorly paying, and unstable employment.

The number of blue-collar jobs also increased over the past two decades. Unfortunately, most of that increase did not occur within operative and fabricator jobs — areas of the heaviest employment concentration for those employed persons with a severe disability. Much of blue-collar employment gains were actually derived from employment growth in the construction trades and in selected blue-collar jobs distributed in the service industry. The total increase in blue-collar employment accounted for about one in six new jobs over the past two decades.

The disproportionate change in employment across different occupations is evident in the share of these occupational groups in the total employment growth. Six out of 10 new (additional) employees between 1983 and 2001 were employed in college labor market jobs. One out of 5 additional employees were employed in clerical or administrative support occupations. Only 14% worked in blue-collar occupations. Clearly, the importance of blue-collar occupations in the nation's total employment declined sharply over time at the same time as the importance of college labor market jobs increased. The college labor market occupations' share of total employment increased from 36% in 1983 to 43% in 2001.

Occupational Employment Projections 2000–2010

The most recent round of employment projections by occupation revealed that the demand for labor with higher levels of educational attainment will likely grow most rapidly between 2000 and 2010. Continuing the long-term shift in occupational demand toward college labor market fields, the projections revealed that employment in the professions will increase by more than one quarter, growing more rapidly than any other major occupational group, and accounting for nearly one in three new jobs in the nation.

Computer science and mathematics will lead the growth in demand for professional and related workers. These fields alone are expected to generate nearly 2 million of the projected 6.9 million new jobs in the professions by 2010. The teaching fields are also expected to grow at an above-average pace, with employment expected to increase by nearly 1.6 million workers through 2010, accounting for 22% of the total professional occupations increase. Health-care fields employment levels are also expected to expand rapidly between 2000 and 2010. Employment in health-related professional fields is expected to increase by 1.6 million workers, or about 25% over the decade. The number of registered nurses is expected to increase by more than 560,000 workers by 2010. Rapid rates of new job creation are also expected in therapy fields such as physical therapy, respiratory therapy, occupational therapy and speech–language pathology.

The high demand in the professional fields, including computer and math, education, and health, all require high levels of educational attainment, very often at the bachelor's and master's degree levels. Moreover, access to employment in these fields usually requires a degree in highly specialized fields of study — often with field or clinical experience required.

Employment in managerial, business, and financial positions is expected to grow more slowly than overall employment in the economy and well below the projected rate of growth in the professions (see Table 10.9). However, much of this slow rate of growth is a result of projected reductions in the number of workers engaged in various farm-related and agricultural management–related activities. Demand for computer and management information managers is expected to rise by nearly 50% over the next decade, creating 150,000 additional jobs. Employment in advertising, marketing, and sales management is also expected to grow rapidly over the next decade, adding 229,000 jobs and rising by about one third. Business and financial occupations, particularly accountants and management analysts, are expected to be strong in the coming years as well.

Together, the business, management, and professional fields are expected to create a total of more than 9 million net new employment opportunities in the

TABLE 10.9
Employment by Major Industry Sector in the United States,
2000 and Projected 2010 (in Thousands)

Occupation	2000	2010	Absolute Change	Relative Change (%)	Share of Total Change (%)
Managerial, business and financial	15,519	17,635	2,116	13.6	9.5
Professional	26,758	33,709	6,951	26.0	31.4
Service	26,075	31,163	5,088	19.5	23.0
Sales	15,513	17,365	1,852	11.9	8.4
Clerical and office support	23,882	26,053	2,171	9.1	9.8
Construction occupations	7,451	8,439	988	13.3	4.5
Installation, repair and maintenance	5,820	6,482	662	11.4	3.0
Production	13,060	13,811	751	5.8	3.4
Transportation and material moving	10,088	11,618	1,530	15.2	6.9
Total	145,594	167,754	22,160	15.2	100.0

Note. Data from "Occupational Employment Projections to 2010," by D. E. Hecker, November 2001,
Monthly Labor Review, pp. 57–84.

U.S. economy (see Table 10.9). These major occupational groups accounted for 30% of employment in the nation in 2000, but they will account for more than 40% of the new jobs created in the country over the next decade.

The growth in high-end professional and managerial labor will be accompanied by an expansion of employment opportunities in low-level service occupations. Between 2000 and 2010, employment in service occupations is expected to increase by nearly 5.1 million jobs, second only to professional services in the absolute number of new jobs (see Table 10.9). Food preparation workers — particularly food and beverage servers — will lead the growth in service occupation employment, with nearly 1.6 million jobs over the forecast period. Health-support occupations, led by home health aides, nursing aides, and orderlies, will add more than 1 million jobs between 2000 and 2010. Protective service workers, led by security guards and corrections officers, will increase by more than 800,000 jobs over the period. Personal-care workers, led by personal and home care aides and childcare workers, will grow by more than 850,000, increasing employment levels by 21%. Finally, employment in buildings and grounds maintenance jobs, including landscaping occupations, will rise by an expected 780,000 by 2010.

Employment in semiskilled and unskilled blue-collar production jobs is expected to grow very slowly over the next decade. Total production employment is expected to increase by only 750,000 jobs, or less than 6% (see Table 10.9). Growth in production jobs will be concentrated in assembly and fabrication, which are expected to add about 170,000 workers over the decade, while the number of jobs in welding and brazing is forecast to rise by about 97,000. Machine operative employment is expected to perform poorly in the next decade, with losses among shoe machine and sewing machine operatives.

These projections paint a picture of a future labor market that will provide relatively plentiful employment opportunities for persons with skills and educational levels that can provide access to employment in professional and managerial/business occupations. Within those fields, persons with educational backgrounds in specific fields, such as computer science and information technology, health, and education, can expect a strong job outlook. Unfortunately, the expected strong growth in the college labor market will provide much greater opportunity for individuals without a severe disability. The previously mentioned low average educational levels of persons with a severe disability will result in diminished access to employment. Further compounding this poor outlook will be the slow growth in the demand for semiskilled and unskilled blue-collar workers. As noted earlier, the disproportionate representation of persons with severe disabilities in these comparatively low-skilled production jobs is largely the product of their low education levels. The projections seem to suggest that although they have the access to blue-collar production jobs, relatively few employment opportunities will occur over the next 10 years, and considerable dislocation is likely in a number of the machine-operative fields.

These occupational projections suggest that the single largest major occupational source of new job creation for persons with severe disabilities will be in the service sector. Personal services, janitorial and cleaning services, low-end food services, and protective services jobs are expected to grow at an above-average rate over the next decade. Given the overrepresentation of persons with severe disabilities in these fields, they may well prove to be the largest source of new job access.

The future employment success of individuals with severe disabilities will become increasingly tied to their ability to gain access to more education, to obtain stronger basic skills, and to acquire more substantive and relevant occupational proficiencies. Access to employment in the high-growth, high-paying professional and business-related occupations requires high levels of educational attainment. Persons with or without disabilities who have fewer years of schooling will have a great deal of difficulty in finding employment. The basic pathway to access into careers in these fields is through the nation's colleges and universities. Unless strategies can be put in place to sharply increase the number of persons with severe disabilities who earn a postsecondary degree, it is quite likely that they will be relegated to service jobs. Ultimately, the gap between the socioeconomic status of individuals with severe disabilities and nondisabled workers will continue to grow.

Compared to the population with severe disabilities, persons with moderate disabilities will have far better employment prospects in the coming years. Their higher levels of educational attainment and stronger skills base will provide a much greater likelihood of employment in the nation's rapidly expanding college labor market. As the job content of the economy continues to give the advantage to individuals with more years of schooling, persons with moderate disabilities will be able to take advantage of the growing number of available opportunities.

References

Berman, J. M. (2001, November). Industry output and employment projections to 2010. *Monthly Labor Review*, pp. 39–56.

Burkhauser, R., & Haveman, R. (1982). *Disability and work: The economics of American policy*. Baltimore: Johns Hopkins University Press.

Centers for Disease Control. (2002). *Work limitations status of working-age people, 18 to 64*. Washington, DC: Centers for Disease Control, National Center for Health Statistics.

Hale, T. W., Hayghe, H. V., & McNeil, J. M. (1998, September). Persons with disability: Labor market activity, 1994. *Monthly Labor Review*, pp. 3–12.

Hecker, D. E. (2001, November). Occupational employment projections to 2010. *Monthly Labor Review*, pp. 57–84.

Kruse, D. L. (1998, September). Persons with disabilities: Demographic, income and health care characteristics, 1993. *Monthly Labor Review*, pp. 13–22.

Skerry, P. (2000). *Counting on the Census*. Washington, DC: The Brookings Institution.

U.S. Bureau of the Census. (2002). Disability labor force status of civilians 16 to 74 years old by educational attainment and sex. Retrieved April 2002 from www.census.gov/hhes/www/disable

Yelin, E. H., & Katz, P. P. (1994, October). Labor force trends of persons with and without disabilities. *Monthly Labor Review*, pp. 36–42.

SECTION

DELIVERY OF SERVICES

C H A P T E R

11

PURSUING POSTSECONDARY EDUCATION OR TRAINING

Ruth Torkelson Lynch and Ross K. Lynch

Postsecondary education and training is a major link to the workplace, to social networks, to personal fulfillment, and to financial stability. Postsecondary education takes place in a range of settings and time frames, from institutions that provide short-term vocational training (less than 2 years) to 4-year colleges and universities that offer bachelor and graduate degree programs. Legislative mandates for access to postsecondary education, such as the Rehabilitation Act of 1973 and the Americans with Disabilities Act of 1990 (ADA), have greatly expanded access to postsecondary education and training for students with disabling conditions. Postsecondary education is a key for quality employment, better careers, and better futures for individuals with disabilities (Price-Ellingstad & Berry, 2000; Stodden & Dowrick, 2000). For this progression to occur successfully, however, several critical steps are necessary: effective preparation in secondary education, effective transition services from secondary to postsecondary settings, effective services for access and reasonable accommodations within the postsecondary setting, and effective transition from postsecondary education to the workforce.

Congressional legislation is not the only variable that has affected the increase in the numbers of students with disabilities participating in higher education. Students with disabilities have been included in general education programs during grade school and high school. Those same students have higher expectations for participation in postsecondary education and more varied career expectations than those held by students with disabilities in the past.

Students with learning disabilities, for example, have been diagnosed and helped earlier in life through resources that resulted from the Individuals with Disabilities Education Act of 1975, which in turn has led to more college enrollment (Hebel, 2001a). In 1995–1996, about 6% of all undergraduates reported that they had a disability. Twenty-nine percent of those students indicated they had a learning disability, 23% noted an orthopedic impairment, 16% listed a noncorrectable vision impairment, 16% noted a hearing impairment, 3% a speech impairment (U.S. Department of Education, National Center for Education Statistics, 2000). The composition of freshman classes tends to indicate future trends. Figures for 1996 for freshmen indicated a greater percentage of them reporting a disability (9% of incoming freshmen as compared to 6% of total undergraduates) and an increasing percentage of students with learning disabilities (35% of freshmen reporting a disability; HEATH Resource Center, 1998).

Support services for students with disabilities in postsecondary education institutions have also expanded dramatically. In surveys during the 1996–1997 and 1997–1998 school years, approximately 75% of 2- and 4-year postsecondary education institutions in the United States enrolled students with disabilities, and nearly all (98%) of these institutions provided at least one support service or accommodation for these students. The most frequently selected service or accommodation was alternative exam formats or more test-taking time, followed by tutors to assist with ongoing coursework; readers, notetakers, or scribes; registration assistance or priority registration; adaptive equipment/ technology; and textbooks on tape (U.S. Department of Education, 2000).

By themselves, legislative mandates and support service availability are not necessarily sufficient for successful integration into and completion of postsecondary education and training. First, students with disabilities need to complete high school successfully, acquiring the basic academic skills necessary to compete for admission and to be able to do college-level work. Once a student with disabilities does complete high school and enters postsecondary education, research has indicated that a number of variables contribute to a successful postsecondary experience. The most critical variables include a positive connection between student and teacher; faculty awareness of accommodation options; inclusion of students with disabilities in various university-wide programs, services, and activities to meet social as well as academic goals; intensive transition planning and preparation; utilization of learning and writing centers for workshops and tutoring on time management, study skills, and writing improvement; and participation in orientation and precollege summer orientations (Brinckerhoff, McGuire, & Shaw, 2002; Harris & Robertson, 2001; Paul, 2000). Because more students with disabilities are participating in and completing postsecondary education, more individuals with disabilities are applying to enter the workforce. Job-application and job-maintenance skills are therefore essential to making an effective transition from postsecondary training to the workplace. Innovative co-op and internship programs such as Entry Point! (an internship program of the American Association for the Advancement of Science) can provide valuable work experience for students with disabilities prior to postsecondary graduation (for more information on Entry Point! see www.aaas.org).

This chapter will describe the legislative mandates affecting postsecondary education for students with disabilities; discuss the rights and responsibilities of institutions and students; and provide recommendations for facilitating and enhancing postsecondary education, training opportunities, and career planning for individuals with disabling conditions. Discussion of several new trends, such as on-line learning, distance education, and universal instructional design, will be incorporated. In Appendix 11.A, we provide a list of resources that may help the student with a disabling condition who wishes to pursue postsecondary education.

Legislative Mandates

Civil rights legislation has resulted in a pronounced increase in postsecondary educational opportunities for individuals with disabling conditions. Essentially, all postsecondary institutions are subject to both the ADA and Section 504 of the Rehabilitation Act of 1973.

Section 504

The passage of Section 504 was a noteworthy breakthrough because the act is a nondiscrimination statute affecting all areas of life, including postsecondary education. Section 504 states, "No otherwise qualified handicapped individual in the United States shall, solely by reason of his handicap, be excluded from the participation in, be denied the benefits of, or be subjected to discrimination under any program or activity receiving Federal financial assistance." Although it is one brief sentence, this statute has had more widespread effect on the successful integration of persons with disabilities into the mainstream of U.S. life than any other single factor.

For the purposes of this statute, a *handicapped person* is defined as "any person who (1) has a physical or mental impairment which substantially limits one or more of such person's major life activities, (2) has a record of such an impairment, or (3) is regarded as having such an impairment" (41 C.F.R., § 60,741.2

(1977)). Second, a definition of *qualified* is needed. For the purposes of enrollment at a postsecondary institution, persons with disabilities are qualified if they "meet the academic and technical standards requisite to admission or participation in the [institution's] education program or activity" (45 C.F.R. § 84.3 (k)(3) (1977)). Furthermore, "The term 'technical standards' refers to all nonacademic admission criteria that are essential to participation in the program in question" (45 C.F.R. Part 80, Appendix A, Paragraph 5 (1977)). Finally, regarding the institutions that are required to abide by Section 504, the law states that every institution that receives federal financial assistance is required to accommodate students with disabling conditions. The term *federal financial assistance* is broadly defined as "any grant, loan, contract (other than a procurement contract of insurance or guaranty) or any other arrangement by which the Department provides or otherwise makes available assistance in the form of (1) Funds; (2) Services of Federal personnel; or (3) Real and personal property or any interest in or use of such property" (45 C.F.R. § 84.3 (h) (1977)). This definition includes federal monies provided to the school or awarded directly to the students; therefore, the law has widespread applicability in that almost every postsecondary institution receives some form of federal assistance.

Subpart E of Section 504 addresses the rights of people with disabilities in federally funded institutions of postsecondary education, including both public and private institutions whose students received guaranteed student loans or other federal assistance. Although Section 504 does not provide the same level of substantive programming that is required by laws targeting children with disabilities, it does require reasonable accommodations, including auxiliary aids and services and program modification (Rothstein, 1998). The following requirements regarding postsecondary institutions and students with disabilities were mandated by Section 504: (a) access to facilities and activities, (b) admission policies and practices that do not discriminate on the basis of disability, (c) testing procedures with appropriate accommodations, and (d) provision of auxiliary aids and services (e.g., large print, sign language interpreters, and adaptive equipment; Jarrow, 1993).

The Americans with Disabilities Act

The ADA extends the mandate for nondiscrimination on the basis of disability to the nonfederal public sector (i.e., state and local educational institutions; Title 11: Public Services) and to private institutions (i.e., private undergraduate or postgraduate schools; Title 111: Public Accommodations and Services Operated by Private Entities). Although Section 504 is a short statute, the ADA is lengthy and much more detailed. The ADA definition of a person with a disability refers to someone with a physical or mental impairment that sub-stantially limits one or more major life activities, whether he or she has the dis-ability, has a record of the disability, or is regarded as having the disability. The ADA definition eliminated protection for current illegal drug users. Not every impairment qualifies as a disability protected by the ADA, because not every impairment is substantially limiting. Determination of disability must be on an individualized, case-by-case basis, and a finding of disability cannot be based solely on the name or diagnosis. Instead, it must be based on the effect of that impairment on a major life activity (e.g., stage of the disease or disorder, presence of other impairments, duration, permanency of limitations; Heyward, 1998).

Protection against discrimination under the ADA is directed to "qualified individuals with a disability who, with or without reasonable modifications to rules, policies, or practices, the removal of architectural, communication, or transportation barriers, or the provision of auxiliary aids and services, meet the essential eligibility requirements for the receipt of services or the participation in programs or activities provided by a public entity" (ADA, Title II, Subtitle A, § 201 (2)). Discrimination includes (a) the imposition or application of eli-gibility criteria that screen out or tend to screen out individuals with disa-bilities; (b) failure to make reasonable modifications in policies, practices, or procedures; (c) failure to take such steps as may be necessary to ensure that no individual with a disability is excluded, denied services, segregated, or oth-erwise treated differently than other individuals because of the absence of auxiliary aids and services; and (d) failure to remove from existing facilities ar-chitectural barriers and communication barriers that are structural in nature (ADA, Title III, § 302 (2)(A)).

Rights and Responsibilities

It is important to clarify that the ADA and Section 504 are not affirmative-action laws — they are nondiscrimination laws. Standards are not lowered for academic performance, nor is there a requirement for considering disability fac-tors as a priority for admission. Some of the changes on campuses brought about by the ADA and Section 504 have been physical changes to buildings, includ-ing the addition of elevators and signs, replacement of steps with ramps, and enhancement of sound and lighting systems. Other changes have had an im-pact on how instruction and evaluation of learning take place. Implementation of the ADA and Section 504 requirements involves a series of competing rights and responsibilities on the part of students with disabilities and the post-secondary institutions (R. T. Lynch & Gussel, 1996). Attitudes and personal perspectives also greatly influence the actual integration and ultimate success of students with disabling conditions in postsecondary endeavors.

Postsecondary School Rights, Responsibilities, and Challenges

The postsecondary institution has essentially two categories of responsibility: physical access and reasonable accommodations. Public colleges and state vocational rehabilitation agencies often struggle over who should pay for costly services for students with disabilities. Colleges typically agree to pay for academic-specific accommodations such as removing architectural barriers from classrooms and providing computer software (Hebel, 2001b). Rehabilitation agencies typically pick up the tab for tuition and other expenses that may help the individual to be successful in obtaining employment (e.g., computers). Each side may argue that the other is primarily responsible for the most expensive and disputed services, such as sign language interpreters, classroom note takers, and real-time closed captioning in classrooms. Shared expense agreements have been attempted in several states, with varying success.

Physical Access

Postsecondary institutions have a responsibility to make the campus and programs accessible, so architectural access is usually handled on a university-wide basis. Occasionally, even when general accessibility standards have been followed, a particular student still may have difficulty accessing a particular instructional or other campus space due to specific functional limitations (e.g., limited hand function to push a lever door knob). In such situations, that individual student must identify the specific access difficulty.

Reasonable Accommodations

The postsecondary institution is required to provide students who have disabling conditions with access to the services, benefits, and programs that it offers and to ensure that it does not discriminate against qualified individuals with disabling conditions. Furthermore, under Title II of the ADA, public entities are required to provide notice to persons with disabling conditions regarding their rights and responsibilities under the ADA, with clearly stated policies and procedures for accommodation requests and appeals available to students, staff, faculty, and the public. The institution is not required, however, to provide an accommodation until a student notifies the institution of his or her disability and needs, makes a request for accommodation, and provides documentation supporting the request (Heyward, 1993). Although reasonable accommodations are expected, postsecondary institutions are not required to take actions that can be characterized as affirmative action, that make fundamental alterations in the nature of their programs, or that result in undue financial and administrative burdens (Heyward, 1993). In that postsecondary institutions have a responsibility to maintain the academic integrity of their programs, it is advisable for institutions to distinguish between poor learning strategies, limitations due to accessibility, and lack of academic preparedness (R. T. Lynch & Gussel, 1996). Support and curriculum modifications cannot compensate for lower cognitive functioning or insufficient academic preparation. Students who are academically marginal will have difficulty with postsecondary education and training, irrespective of course modifications. Reasonable accommodation implies equal access to learning rather than lenient or relaxed admission and academic policies. Basic academic competencies and cognitive skills are essential for all postsecondary students, including students with disabilities.

Student Rights, Responsibilities, and Challenges

At this juncture in career planning, individuals must undergo a critical self-evaluation (R. K. Lynch & McSweeney, 1982). Section 504 and the ADA ensure certain rights, but responsibilities accompany those rights. By applying to postsecondary institutions, individuals with disabilities vouch that they are capable of meeting the standards and required tasks and are able to compete academically with the rest of the student body. If they fail to meet these prerequisites, individuals should reappraise their career plans. If, however, individuals feel confident that these prerequisites can be met, they should continue with their postsecondary education plans.

Requests for Reasonable Accommodations

Although students have the right to nondiscrimination, meaningful access, individualized assessments, effective academic adjustments and aids, and confidentiality (Heyward, 1993), the critical feature in postsecondary education is that students themselves have the responsibility to request reasonable modifications, to meet eligibility standards for qualified status, and to provide documentation and other necessary information. In elementary and secondary education, the institution has the obligation to identify and provide services to students with special needs, and parents tend to advocate for their children. Access to accommodation services in postsecondary education is dependent on student disclosure of disability-related needs, which sometimes requires acquisition of decision-making, self-advocacy, and negotiation skills (R. T. Lynch & Gussel,

1996). Self-determination, which is key, emphasizes knowing one's self, making choices, taking control, believing in one's self, and taking actions to reach one's goals (Field, 2002). To the degree possible, students must take control of the environment and adapt it to their needs. Students have the responsibility for making their needs known, for coordinating necessary services, and for approaching professors about needed accommodations, because such accommodations need to be individualized. Effective interactions between students with disabilities and their professors can be facilitated through recognition of the thoughts and feelings that tend to promote or hamper effective interaction and accommodation (Fichten, Goodrick, Tagalakis, Amsel, & Libman, 1990). It is also important to remember that if no accommodations are needed or a decision has been made to personally accommodate for potential needs (e.g., tutoring, spelling and grammar checks within word processing programs, personally arranged note taking), there is no need to disclose a disability to the postsecondary institution, particularly if the disability is not visible (e.g., HIV/AIDS, learning disability, emotional disability).

Effective Disclosure and Self-Advocacy

For effective disclosure, students first must establish themselves as otherwise qualified and competent, rather than focusing on deficits and problems. Self-advocacy for college students requires recognition of one's own specific needs without compromising the dignity of one's self or others (Brinckerhoff, 1993). It is particularly helpful if a student can state and specify, as early in the semester as possible, the exact nature of services that are needed. For example, a student with a slight hearing impairment may simply alert the professor so that the professor will face the class at all times and the student can read lips. Another student may need an interpreter for the class and therefore must alert the institution so the necessary arrangements can be made (R. K. Lynch & McSweeney, 1982).

Self-advocacy is often challenging, may not be a comfortable or desired role, or may be done ineffectively. The environmental support received in previous educational settings (e.g., parental advocacy, Individualized Education Programs, team staffings) is not present in postsecondary settings (R. T. Lynch & Gussel, 1996). The striving (and sometimes struggling) for independence that often occurs in young college students may affect self-advocacy if the student with a disabling condition rejects outside assistance in an effort to exhibit personal autonomy and independence. Also, unless accompanied by potential solutions (e.g., alternative methods, aids, assistive devices), disclosure and self-advocacy efforts can unintentionally reinforce beliefs that a disability precludes successful performance in class (Kubaiko, 1984) or lead to exemption from certain learning activities that later limits job-relevant skills. If, for example, a student who is a quadriplegic requests that a science requirement be waived on the basis that he or she cannot manipulate the test tubes and other equipment in the laboratory component of the course, it could not only be an unreasonable accommodation but could also limit the individual's experiences in terms of later coursework and employment. A more equitable solution would be to provide an aide who could do the physical manipulations as the student with a disabling condition told him or her what to do. The point is that when the student's needs are made known, an equitable solution, based on mutual, conciliatory actions, can usually be obtained (R. K. Lynch & McSweeney, 1982). Students may benefit from skill-acquisition training regarding effective methods for obtaining assistance (Balcazar, Fawcett, & Seekins, 1991), and this training is appropriately initiated as a component of transition from secondary to postsecondary education (Ness, 1989).

In an effort to build self-advocacy skills for college students with disabilities in requesting classroom accommodations, Palmer and Roessler (2000) developed an 8-hour training program in self-advocacy and conflict resolution/negotiation skills. Using an experimental design, these authors demonstrated that the group who participated in Self-Advocacy and Conflict Resolution Training (SACR) exceeded a control group in acquired levels of self-advocacy and conflict resolution behaviors, in knowledge about academic accommodations, and in self-efficacy and social competence. The SACR training program included information about academic barriers, reasonable accommodations, and civil rights laws; training in social competence skills such as self-assertion and self-advocacy; and practice in situational conflict resolution strategies. To be an effective self-advocate, students may need opportunities to develop and practice skills prior to actual implementation in the classroom.

Challenges

Academic Readiness. Many students with disabling conditions who seek higher education are not prepared for the academic rigor that such an endeavor requires. For students with disabling conditions, this is more likely if they were involved in special education programs that taught only basic, essential academics, or if they were mainstreamed but "protected" from certain courses. This is particularly true in the areas of mathematics and science. Much of the students' lack of preparation may stem from beliefs that students with disabling conditions cannot succeed in these areas, and therefore they are not encouraged, and perhaps are even prevented, from becoming well-versed academically. This problem is being slowly remedied by including students in general education early in elementary and secondary school; however, it is still the students' responsibility to obtain whatever aids are needed to academically prepare for postsecondary education. For example, tutorial and other types of assistance may be secured and paid for through the public vocational rehabilitation agency. Other aids and devices are often available through an office of the college or university that serves students with disabilities.

Recognition of Needs. When a disability (e.g., traumatic brain injury, spinal cord injury) is acquired in late childhood or as an adult, there is often a period of adjustment, including realistically assessing the full impact of abilities and limitations. A student who is unable to acknowledge that a problem exists is unlikely to accept problem-solving assistance, accommodations, or other services (Nordlund, 1994). Sometimes, taking a "right to fail" approach leads the student to the realization that help is needed or allows him or her the chance to personally develop accommodations that are comfortable and personally workable.

Maturity and Emotional Readiness. During postsecondary education, students mature a great deal in the areas of personal growth and independence. Many students take control of their lives for the first time and learn how to take care of themselves, both physically and emotionally. During this time, students need the freedom to grow and to become assertive about their needs, but they also must be able to negotiate solutions and become independent. In some cases, this need may be even greater for students with disabling conditions because they may have been overprotected in the past. Numerous support services are available to assist students with disabilities in maximizing independence, but it is incumbent upon them to seek out those services they wish to use. It is also important to promote career maturity, interpersonal relationship skills, and positive career attitudes as components of the maturation experience of postsecondary education because these have been documented as developmental skill needs of college students with disabilities (Benshoff, Fried, & Roberto, 1990; Benshoff, Kroeger, & Scalia, 1990).

Attitudes. Besides the students' own attitudes about learning to negotiate the environment, an additional consideration is the attitudes of those around them; for example, secondary school personnel perceptions regarding potential for college-level work (Dickey & Satcher, 1994; Prater & Minner, 1986) and the perceptions of postsecondary personnel (e.g., professors, administrators) and other students. Programs for persons with disabling conditions can be legislated, but attitudes must be nurtured. Consequently, attitudinal barriers are often the most difficult obstacle to overcome and may be the result of personal fears and anxieties due to lack of exposure or experience. These attitudes are formulated in advance of sufficient evidence and result in prejudgment of individuals in terms of group or categorical membership. Examples of such prejudices include the belief that all persons with epilepsy have uncontrolled grand mal seizures or that all persons with disabling conditions have psychological problems. In the academic environment, attitudinal barriers may take the form of lowered expectations, stereotyping, reluctance to ask and seek answers to questions, assumptions of inferiority, the idea that teaching persons with disabling conditions takes a great deal of time and effort, and the belief that persons with disabilities want special concessions made for them. In other cases, students with disabling conditions may be perceived as having stereotypical strengths and limitations. For example, Kelly, Sedlacek, and Scales (1994) found that college students without disabilities rated students with disabilities as more conscientious, responsible, and practical but less popular, talkative, and relaxed.

Students with disabling conditions need to be aware that these attitudes and stereotypes exist and that they must be addressed realistically. The key element for eroding these barriers is increased exposure. Public awareness of disabling conditions is gradually being improved by mainstreaming individuals with disabling conditions from very early ages on, but a great deal remains to be done in this area. Students therefore must take on the added responsibility of educating others about disability or at least about their own particular functional abilities.

Resolution of Disputes

The postsecondary institution must establish grievance procedures that provide due process for equitable resolution of any discriminatory complaints within the institution. When disputes do arise, students are encouraged to resolve their difficulties internally before contacting the federal regulatory office. When difficulties persist, the student should contact the institution's 504/ADA grievance committee. This committee usually is composed of the campus 504/ADA coordinator, faculty members, administrators, and students. In a typical procedure, students are encouraged to speak to the people in the unit (e.g., a department from which the grievance is originating) regarding resolution of the complaint, with the coordinator acting as facilitator, if necessary. If the situation is not resolved at this stage, the student submits a written complaint to the coordinator, who reviews it and presents it to the committee as a whole. The committee then makes a decision and communicates it to the student.

Postsecondary Process and Procedures

Postsecondary institutions are responsible for determining what the term *otherwise qualified student* means (Scott, 1990). As stated previously, the law protects students against possible discrimination and helps them attain an otherwise difficult acceptance into a college or university. As a result, certain considerations need to be taken into account by the university to more effectively integrate qualified individuals with disabilities into the mainstream of university life.

College Entrance Examinations

The following principles guide the American College Testing (ACT) service in responding to requests from examinees for testing accommodations: (a) requirements and procedures must ensure fairness for all candidates, whether seeking accommodations or not; (b) accommodations must be consistent with ADA requirements and appropriate and reasonable for the documented disability; (c) accommodations must not result in undue burden or fundamentally alter that which the test is designed to measure; and (d) documentation of the disability must meet guidelines that are considered appropriate by qualified professionals and must provide evidence that the disability substantially limits one or more major life activities; applicants must also provide information about prior accommodations made in a similar setting, such as academic classes and test taking (American College Testing, 2002). Requests for accommodations are initially reviewed by trained ACT staff or expert reviewers. Specific diagnostic documentation materials are provided by ACT for learning disabilities, attention-deficit/hyperactivity disorder, visual impairment, hearing impairment, and other physical disorders. The diagnostic reports must include specific recommendations for accommodations as well as an explanation of why each accommodation is recommended and how it alleviates the impact of the impairment when taking a standardized test. A prior history of accommodation does not, in and of itself, and without supporting documentation of a current need, warrant the provision of a similar accommodation (American College Testing, 2002).

When accommodations are provided on standardized entrance examinations, the scores from entrance examinations are less valid predictors of postsecondary education grade point average (GPA) for students with learning disabilities (Zurcher & Bryant, 2001). These authors noted that when students with learning disabilities are provided with accommodations, however, their scores as a group are similar to those of examinees without learning disabilities who took the test under standard administration. Testing modifications had assisted the students with disabilities in achieving scores comparable to those of individuals without disabilities. How and when accommodations in testing are appropriate and what modified tests end up predicting continues to generate controversy.

Flagging of test scores (i.e., a notation on an examinee's score report to show that the test was administered in a nonstandard fashion) has also been a controversial topic without universal consensus. As a result of a 1999 lawsuit in federal court that challenged flagging practices by testing organizations, however, Educational Testing Service agreed to stop flagging for accommodation of extended time on the *Graduate Record Examination* (GRE), the *Graduate Management Admission Test* (GMAT), the *Test of English as a Foreign Language* (TOEFL), *Praxis,* and many other standardized admission tests that it administers as of October 1, 2001 (Educational Testing Service, 2001). In 2002, the College Board followed up with a review of practices for the tests they are responsible for administering, including the *Scholastic Achievement Test* (SAT). As evidence that this issue is not without controversy, the expert panel recommended, on a vote of four to two, that the College Board discontinue flagging score reports. The College Board agreed to discontinue the practice of identifying score reports taken by students who require extended test-taking time due to documented disabilities as of October 1, 2003 (College Board, 2002). To help ensure that accommodations are given only to test takers whose disabilities require their use, the College Board will continue its process of routine documentation reviews, which are meant to ensure that the eligibility requirements are being consistently and fairly applied to all students.

Preadmission Policies of Postsecondary Institutions

All recruitment activities run by institutions and states must be accessible to persons with disabling conditions. The institution has the responsibility to provide services, such as interpreters, at all recruitment activities or to make sure that those individuals who conduct recruitment activities have made arrangements to provide such services for students who request them. Institutions are not allowed to make any preadmission inquiry as to whether an applicant for admission has a disability, and if the disability becomes known during recruitment, no written record may be made for the admissions office. The only exception to this preadmission inquiry rule is when the institution is taking remedial action to correct the effects of past discrimination or when the institution is taking voluntary action to overcome the effects of conditions that resulted in limited participation. The institution may invite applicants to indicate whether and to what extent they have a disabling condition, provided that the institution clearly states that the information requested is voluntary and is intended solely for use in connection with its obligations for remedial action or its voluntary efforts (R. K. Lynch & McSweeney, 1982). The institution must state clearly that it will not subject the applicant to any adverse treatment (Section 504, 45 C.F.R., § 84.42 (c) (1977)).

Section 504 does not require that postsecondary institutions lower their admissions standards for students with disabling conditions, nor does it require any affirmative action program for admissions. It merely requires nondiscrimination. In this respect, all applications should be processed in exactly the same manner. The institutions are forbidden from setting limits on the number of students with disabling conditions they will admit. The institutions also cannot subject applicants with disabling conditions to more stringent requirements than other applicants. For instance, students with physical limitations cannot be asked how they will live independently or meet course requirements.

Language used on applications also may have discriminatory implications. Phrases such as "We ask you to state any physical disabilities" or "Please specify any physical handicaps" that are incorporated into a university's application are viewed as discriminatory by Section 504. To circumvent legal tangles, universities may only request such information, not require it. The application may have a phrase such as "The University invites applicants to supply a brief description of their functional limitations in order to better meet their individual needs." This information is requested so that the university can make the necessary modifications and marshal the available resources well in advance of the beginning of classes (R. K. Lynch & McSweeney, 1982). Such advance preparation will ease the transition and lessen the probability of unforeseen obstacles.

A preadmission campus visit may be especially helpful, although such visits cannot be required by the institution. Through university visits, students can determine how geographically accessible the campus is for their particular needs and what can be done to improve the situation. For example, a student with mobility limitations may determine that he or she would be more mobile in a motorized wheelchair on a particular campus because of the terrain. Such preadmission visits also allow students to make any preparations they think would be helpful before beginning classes. It is possible that students may decide not to attend the university due to personal accessibility issues or for a myriad of other reasons. For example, an individual with a great deal of upper body strength may not mind a campus that is hilly, even if he or she is in a wheelchair, whereas an individual who is not as strong may decide such terrain is too formidable.

Once the student has decided to enroll, the institution, usually through the intermediary of its office that provides services to students with disabilities, relies on the person who is the expert on the subject — the student. The only way the institution can make proper accommodations is to find out directly from him or her what is needed. An accommodation that is appropriate for one student may be entirely inappropriate for a second student with a similar disability. For this reason, the institution must inquire about the student's functional limitations and seek the student's involvement in any modifications that are made.

Admission Policies

Fair admissions in terms of students with disabling conditions means that they are to be judged on their abilities, not their disabilities. Discriminatory criteria are prohibited by the law, and subtle barriers in the admissions procedures must also be removed. To aid in this process, institutions have been urged to form an admissions/recruitment advisory committee that represents students, faculty, and staff, and includes one or more persons with disabling conditions. This committee can try to anticipate problems and think of ways to ensure equal access for all individuals. In a comprehensive survey of postsecondary institutions, it was noted that admission procedures and/or standards were not changed for applicants who disclosed that they had a learning disability in almost half (45%) of the institutions (Vogel et al., 1998). These authors noted that 26% of the schools added review of the admissions folder by a knowledgeable faculty or staff member to the regular admissions procedures and 21% of the schools chose to review and modify admission standards (i.e., make them less stringent for students who disclosed disabilities).

We have stated repeatedly that institutions may not discriminate against qualified individuals with disabilities, but how do they determine who is qualified and who is not? Currently, many universities use standardized tests for evaluation. The debate over whether or not these instruments are a fair measure for predicting success for any student continues today. It is argued that if the validity of standardized tests for all students is in question, their lack of validity must be amplified in the case of students with disabling conditions. Strictly speaking, the regulations state that no admissions tests or criteria that have an adverse effect on individuals with disabling conditions can be used unless they can be validated "as a predictor of success in the education program or activity in question" and unless better criteria are unavailable (45 C.F.R., § 84.42 (b)(2) (1977)). If standardized admissions tests are employed, and the student with a disabling condition feels that his or her disability prevents optimal performance, he or she should request evidence of the test's validity and/or alternate admissions procedures.

In admissions decisions, problems often develop in determining what technical standards are essential to the program and what technical standards can be modified. This issue is particularly pertinent to graduate schools or programs in which a practicum element is involved, such as nursing. The question of "essential technical standards" has been brought all the way to the U.S. Supreme Court, in the case of *Southwestern Community College v. Davis* (1979). In this precedent-setting case, the court ruled that the college could refuse to admit an applicant with a hearing disability to its registered nursing program on the opinion that patient safety might be jeopardized. The college maintained that to ensure the patients' safety while Davis was participating in the clinical component of the program, she would need close individual attention. This close individual attention, which was not needed by the other students, was construed to be a "device or service of a personal nature" and was therefore excluded from the types of auxiliary aids the institution was required to provide. The court further ruled that the college was not required to alter the basic nature of the program by waiving the clinical training requirement. It should be pointed out that because the ruling is based on one particular set of facts, the court's decision may not be broadly applicable (R. K. Lynch & McSweeney, 1982).

Universities still have an obligation to make reasonable accommodations to enable students with disabling conditions to participate to the greatest extent possible. If program requirements limit involvement by students with disabling conditions, the postsecondary institution must demonstrate that such requirements are essential to the overall program.

An open admissions policy may also pose problems for students with disabling conditions. When an institution enrolls students by open admissions, the time span between the student's admission and the beginning of classes may be quite short. Such short notice may cause problems in acquiring the necessary support services. Resultant inconveniences may cause students to develop negative attitudes toward the institution and may also put such students behind academically. For instance, in the case where a student in a wheelchair registers one day and shows up for class the next day, only to discover that the class is located in an inaccessible building, the inconvenience, aggravation, and hurried changes could have been easily avoided with advance planning. To guard against this type of situation, institutions should develop a system of support services that can respond promptly to the students' needs. Rather than relying on such systems, however, students are encouraged to contact the institution before arriving for open admissions to talk to the coordinator of services for students with disabilities or the dean of students to arrange for necessary services. In addition to inquiring about admission programs, students should determine whether the school offers a special orientation program that deals with matters of particular concern to students with disabling conditions, such as mobility, access to facilities, and sources for support services. Advance planning will reduce the possibility of problems and ease the transition into the university environment.

Financial Aid

Once an individual has been accepted for postsecondary education and has decided to attend, the issue of financing becomes paramount. Financial aid must be awarded on a nondiscriminatory basis, and students with disabilities are entitled to the same scholarships, awards, and financial aid as their nondisabled counterparts. In fact, students with disabilities may have far greater educationally related expenses and may be entitled to more financial aid. Because determining financial need is an individualized process, both the campus office financial aid and the office for services to students with disabilities can assist the student with university financial aid policies and procedures. Students with disabling conditions may obtain aid from additional sources. For instance, the state/federal Vocational Rehabilitation Program may cover expenses if the rehabilitation counselor determines that the education is specifically career related and can justify its cost in the individual's rehabilitation plan. Financial assistance may also be available from the Veterans Administration, Worker's Compensation Insurance carriers, the Social Security Administration, and other federal sources. Information on these and other sources can be obtained from the coordinator for services for students with disabilities. An excellent resource, *Creating Options: A Resource on Financial Aid for Students with Disabilities* is available from the HEATH Resource Center (2001).

University Resources — Disabled Student Services Office

As a result of Section 504 and ADA, institutions that previously had only a moral obligation to provide for students with disabling conditions now have a legal one. Universities were mandated to have a campus 504/ADA coordinator, and through this person, universities began instituting various services to aid students (and staff) with disabling conditions. A focal point was needed, however, to ensure the provision of services in an integrated and timely fashion. This need usually resulted in the formation of a Disabled Student Services (DSS) Office. This office's duties basically are coordinating services, acting as liaison between students and faculty, developing and implementing public awareness activities for the faculty and student body, and providing counseling services. The office usually is set up for two purposes: assisting the university in meeting 504 and ADA requirements and assisting students with disabling conditions. The latter can receive a variety of services from the DSS office, including information and assistance with academic adjustments; vocational planning and placement; accessible housing and transportation; financial aid; recruitment of auxiliary aids such as readers, interpreters, and personal attendants;

adapted educational materials; and loan or repair of equipment (e.g., wheelchairs; R. K. Lynch & McSweeney, 1982). The DSS office will also coordinate services, become involved in arbitration if necessary, help plan campus accessibility modifications, promote awareness activities, and act as an information clearinghouse. This office helps tailor the other student services to the needs of students with disabling conditions and assists with unique problems that may not be faced by the majority of students. The basic philosophy of the DSS office is not to do things for the students but rather to help individuals learn how to help themselves. The DSS office publicizes the services that it offers and makes these services available upon request. Students have the option of using these services as they see fit. The services are available not to give students with disabling conditions an advantage over other students but merely to assist them in eliminating some of the disadvantages that may preclude them from full participation.

Counseling

Most campuses provide various types of counseling for their students. Students with disabling conditions can benefit from counseling provided through either the DSS office or the campus counseling center. Counseling may take many forms, such as developing a positive self-image, promoting appropriate coping skills, assisting with academic and career decisions, enhancing adjustment to the disability, overcoming a variety of barriers, or reducing the effects of overprotectiveness by parents. One form of counseling that is often quite helpful on both formal and informal bases is peer counseling, in which students with disabilities counsel other students with disabilities. This type of arrangement often provides insights and assistance that may not be readily available in other counseling contexts. Peer counseling can usually be arranged through the DSS office or the campus counseling center. Similar to the benefits of peer counseling, students interested in a particular occupational field should find out if there are professional contacts with disabilities who are willing to function as mentors.

Academic Requirements and Adjustments

Section 504 regulations state that institutions must make whatever adjustments are necessary to enable a student with a disabling condition to participate in an academic program. Modifications may include changing the way a course is taught or allowing a student to make substitutions for certain requirements. Many times it is necessary to provide alternative methods for taking examinations. Examples of such adjustments might be using Braille, large print, or dictation for a blind student; allowing a student with manual limitations to take examinations that are untimed or to take them orally; permitting lectures to be recorded; providing sign language interpreters; lengthening time restrictions on degree programs; or adjusting course loads. There are some exceptions to the academic modifications legally required by Section 504. If curriculum requirements can be demonstrated to be essential to the program of instruction and directly related to licensing requirements, they are not regarded as discriminatory and therefore need not be modified.

Academic adjustments are usually done on a case-by-case basis, and students are encouraged to make their arrangements directly with faculty members. The coordinator of DSS, dean of students, or other staff member responsible for 504/ADA implementation may provide support by facilitating the interaction or participating in discussions between the student and the professor. The coordinator may act as an arbitrator and negotiate terms that are acceptable to both parties. The DSS office does not have any administrative authority in and of itself to ensure the enforcement of 504, however, but must rely on university-wide policies adopted and enforced by top administrators. As mentioned earlier, the faculty member often has little or no knowledge of reasonable accommodations. In such cases, the coordinator and the student can help him or her understand what is needed and how to provide it. For example, professors can accommodate a blind student by reading what they write on the blackboard. Other modifications may be more complex, such as making laboratory experiences fully accessible by altering the height of equipment and controls, adequately labeling chemicals and other equipment, and taking the necessary precautions to ensure safety. In the case of student teaching, necessary arrangements must be made to place a student with a disabling condition in a fully accessible school. Ideas for modifications should be critically examined and fairly negotiated to allow all students to pursue the training they desire. Scott (1994) wrote a potentially valuable resource for ideas and guidelines regarding reasonable academic adjustments specific to college students with learning disabilities. Roth (1991) provided some potentially valuable suggestions for accommodating students with both learning disabilities and hearing impairment.

Universal Design for Learning

A relatively new paradigm for teaching, learning, assessment, and curriculum development is Universal Design for Learning (UDL), which draws upon and extends the principles of universal design used in architecture and product design (National Center for Accessing the General Curriculum, 2002). The principle behind universal design is that designing for divergent needs of special populations increases usability and learning for everyone. Just as making curb cuts eases travel for persons pushing baby carriages as much as it helps individuals in wheelchairs, curriculum design that is flexible for different learning styles will benefit all students. New digital multimedia learning tools, new networking technologies, and presentation of material in a variety of formats are examples of universal design for learning applications.

Distance and On-line Education Considerations

Most postsecondary institutions have added classes taught either partially or solely over the Internet in order to reach students who are unable to attend a traditional course, to provide alternative learning methods, and to facilitate time and space utilization. In contrast to classroom instruction, where accommodations can be worked out individually and in person with the instructor, on-line and distance courses pose new challenges for both instruction-learning, and self-advocacy. The overall design of Web sites can have a great impact on their accessibility to persons with disabilities. The Web is predominantly a visual medium, which therefore poses great challenges to individuals with visual impairments (Wilson, 2000). The majority of students with disabilities use computers and the Internet, but some may need some type of adaptation to use computers effectively. Developers of instructional materials and technologies, professors, and curriculum planners are urged to consider access to educational and instructional computer technologies (Fichten, Asuncion, Barile, Fossey, & deSimone, 2000). Reasonable accommodations and accessibility have entered a new realm — cyberspace — with resultant challenges for access to Web pages, streaming media, bulky PDF files, color contrast concerns, and issues of time (e.g., live interactions, bulletin boards, chatrooms).

Architectural Considerations

In spite of great strides in recent years, the typical environment is composed of narrow doorways, steep steps, high curbs, piercing sirens, clanging bells, and blinking signs. These architectural characteristics not only limit access but also pose safety concerns.

Classroom Accessibility

Campuses are certainly more accessible today than ever before, with all new construction meeting ADA accessibility guidelines and older buildings gradually being made accessible. A challenge in accessibility is to meet the needs of persons with visual and auditory limitations.

The Section 504 phrase "when viewed in its entirety" (45 C.F.R., Appendix A, Subpart C, Paragraph 20 (1977)) is important to note, because the law does not require campuses to make every existing facility or every part of a facility accessible. It may very well require modifications to existing facilities so that students with disabling conditions have equal opportunity for full participation in all programs and activities, but the university is not required to make structural changes if other methods are effective in achieving program accessibility. The point of the regulation is not to ensure that a student in a wheelchair can enter every classroom on the campus. Although this would be an ideal situation, most campuses simply cannot afford to do a complete renovation, and realistically it is not necessary for every student to enter every classroom. Consequently, the purpose of the regulation is to make *every program accessible* to every student. If this can be done satisfactorily and more efficiently by simply moving the program, then that is what should be done. Facilities therefore need not be physically renovated when any of the following actions (or similar types of actions) are successful in ensuring full participation in programs and activities: redesign of equipment, reassignment of classes or other services to accessible buildings, assignment of aides to persons with disabilities, home visits, or delivery of services at an alternate accessible site (R. K. Lynch & McSweeney, 1982).

The regulations are flexible and permit institutions to determine their needs and the ways to meet these needs. When pursuing options, however, the institution is required to offer programs and activities to persons with disabling conditions "in the most integrated setting appropriate" (45 C.F.R., § 84.43 (d) (1977)). In other words, institutions are not permitted to make one corner of the campus accessible and segregate all students with disabling conditions to that area (R. K. Lynch & McSweeney, 1982).

Housing Accessibility

Students with disabling conditions are entitled to accessible housing that is comparable to university housing for nondisabled students in terms of convenience, variety, and cost. It is not necessary that all dormitory rooms be accessible; however, the ones that are must be in the "most integrated setting appropriate" (45 C.F.R., § 84.43 (d) (1977)).

Making housing accessible may include modifying curbs, entrances, ramps, doors, stairs, elevators, corridors, and walkways. In addition, furnishings, floor materials, and walls need to be considered to achieve full accessibility. For example, to help make a wheelchair roll easily, a commercial-grade carpet without a pad and glued to prevent rippling might be installed. Walls could be covered with heavy-duty vinyl and extra padding to help withstand bumps from the wheelchair. Shelves, cabinets, and storage units can be lowered and secured so they can be pulled on for support. Accessible furniture, such as a platform bed with the base recessed and a dining room table high enough for a wheelchair to fit underneath it comfortably, can be purchased. With thoughtful planning, only minor changes in design are necessary to make housing accessible and decorative. A visit by the student to the housing unit prior to admission is critical to determining the total accessibility of the living environment (R. K. Lynch & McSweeney, 1982).

Accessibility to Transportation

Because mobility limitations may make it difficult for some students to fully participate in academic courses, recreational activities, social events, and other campus activities, accessible transportation must be available. If transportation services are already available on campus, then these services must be made accessible with equipment such as lifts. During months when snow and ice hamper mobility even further, specially equipped buses may literally become life-savers. If transportation is not available for the student body as a whole, it is the university's responsibility to seek funds from local, state, and federal sources for vehicles and staff for a specialized system.

Aside from an accessible transportation system, parking spaces must be made available for persons with disabilities. These spaces should be clearly marked, be placed close to the buildings, and be a minimum of 12 feet wide to allow ease of access for adaptive equipment. In addition, routes into buildings should be as flat and as barrier-free as possible.

Accessibility to Social, Recreational, and Cultural Activities

Most student groups, whether social (e.g., fraternities, sororities) or recreational, receive some form of support from the institution. Any group that receives significant assistance must comply with university regulations of nondiscrimination. Significant assistance refers to assistance without which the group could no longer exist. This includes free campus facilities, financial support, assistance in communication to members, and assistance in planning activities. It must be publicized that such groups will provide means of access (including interpreters) if such services are requested. Furthermore, policies for recruiting members must be nondiscriminatory.

Many schools have a campus organization specifically for students with disabling conditions. Such organizations have a wide range of functions, with the coordinator of DSS usually acting as the group adviser. In addition, other special activities may include wheelchair basketball teams and mime theater groups for deaf students. These types of activities help to increase awareness and acceptance.

On an individual basis, recreational activities may be as varied as the individuals themselves. Physical education staff must make activities available and should be open-minded in allowing students with disabling conditions the use of facilities. As for safety precautions, persons with physical limitations can be subjected to the same safety screening criteria as other individuals and should avail themselves of the safety and procedural instruction offered to everyone.

Auxiliary Aids

The regulations state that institutions that are recipients of federal financial assistance must "ensure" that handicapped students are not discriminated against because of lack of "educational auxiliary aids" (45 C.F.R., § 84.44 (d) (1977)). The regulations also state that this can usually be done by helping students use "existing resources . . . such as state vocational rehabilitation agencies and private charitable organizations" (45 C.F.R., § 84, Appendix A, Subpart D (1977)). Traditionally, vocational rehabilitation agencies have been a valuable resource for auxiliary aids such as readers or interpreters.

When auxiliary aids are necessary for a student's personal needs, it is primarily the student's responsibility to pay for these. Personal aids would include an attendant needed due to the individual's medical condition or an item kept by an individual such as a wheelchair, cane, mobility aid, or guide dog. The state division of vocational rehabilitation and other sources can often assist with the purchase of these aids.

In terms of financial responsibility, access to optional cultural events is in the questionable category. Because these events are open to all students, they should be accessible. Institutions have the responsibility to publicize the fact that interpreters will be provided if requested. Persons with hearing impairments are encouraged to submit their requests for interpreters as early as possible due to the difficulties sometimes encountered in securing an interpreter.

Career Considerations

Career counseling should play a vital role in the university's overall program. Helping students take direction of their lives before and after graduation is a developmental process that should be actively addressed from the beginning to the end of their college careers.

Career planning may carry greater importance for students with disabling conditions. In many cases, these students have had limited exposure to the working world, and they are facing added obstacles such as accessibility, transportation, negative attitudes, communication barriers, and other functional limitations. Students often are unaware of career and job-search options that apply to them. Thompson and Dickey (1994) found that college students with disabling conditions were unclear as to how the ADA protects them in their career search and were not confident in their ability to disclose their disability to an employer. Self-perceptions of job-search skills were most positive in individuals who were satisfied with their college major, knew what kind of job to look for upon graduation, had paid work experience, and had an acquired disability (Thompson & Dickey, 1994). Understanding these variables could become valuable for building student confidence and easing the transition from college to the workforce. Lack of career readiness among graduating college students with disabilities can be related to a number of variables, including minimal recognition that difficulties encountered in college may reappear in the workplace (e.g., problems with processing and remembering information will interfere with getting assigned work done on time; Hitchings et al., 2001). As jobs become more complex, individuals are required to organize many tasks, take initiative, work independently, and demonstrate flexibility. These demands can pose substantial problems for individuals with learning challenges who have not effectively planned for self-advocacy and personally managed accommodations they can use in the workplace

Internships and cooperative education experiences during postsecondary training can play a significant part in preparing for careers beyond graduation. Job-related work experience is deemed as very valuable by employers when considering graduates for positions. Because college students with disabilities may have little or no relevant work experience prior to or during college, internship experience can provide an opportunity to develop an employment history and to assess current and future support needs for the transition from postsecondary education to work. Briel and Getzel (2001) provided a description of an internship program, the Virginia Commonwealth University Career Connections Program, along with a number of suggestions for effective implementation (e.g., assist student to break tasks into smaller components rather than assigning one large project, extend learning time for initial skill acquisition, identify stress management strategies and encourage use at the worksite, provide coaching, link with community resources).

The importance of sound career planning for students with disabling conditions who are considering postsecondary education cannot be overstated. All students should take advantage of the counseling services available from the career center as early in their academic career as possible. With the assistance of a trained counselor, students should take a realistic, investigative look at their capabilities, skills, and interests. They must evaluate themselves with respect to the knowledge, skills, and abilities required by various occupations. With accurate information about themselves, the environment, and occupations, much more realistic career plans can be formulated.

In addition to career counseling, college and university career centers usually offer seminars on employability skills. Students with disabling conditions should take advantage of these seminars to learn how to best market themselves in today's competitive labor market. Workshops might deal with topics such as the rights of persons with disabilities to employment, job modifications, special equipment, employer attitudes, demands of specific careers, or how to deal with rejection. In addition to the normal anxiety associated with employment interviews, interviewees with disabling conditions are particularly concerned with how to maximize recognition of their assets and strengths for the essential functions of the job. Seminars offered by the career center may provide students with the practice necessary to succeed in the competitive job market. In the case of students with severe disabilities, if the college counselor is unaware of resources to facilitate employment access, then consultation with rehabilitation specialists (e.g., rehabilitation counselors, rehabilitation engineers) is advisable.

Conclusion

The Rehabilitation Act of 1973 and the ADA have opened many doors for individuals with disabling conditions, including improved access to postsecondary education. Many changes have been and are continuing to be made on campuses across the nation. Institutions now have the responsibility to comply with the federal guidelines on accessibility and make all of their programs fully accessible. Students with disabling conditions themselves also have a responsibility to take control of their educational programming — to prepare effectively for college, to self-advocate during college, and to gain career experience to prepare effectively for work life after college. They must first have academic readiness and self-discipline and determination to succeed in postsecondary education. Although many supportive services are available that the students can use in order to successfully manage the academic environment, it is important to be aware of rights, responsibilities, and possible obstacles. The laws do not provide special favors for students with disabilities but intend to offer them a chance equal to that of their counterparts without disabling conditions.

Appendix 11.A
Publications and Other Resources

The following is a list of publications that should be helpful for the student with a disabling condition who is interested in pursuing a postsecondary education.

College Testing and Admissions Process

ACT policy for documentation to support requests for testing accommodations on the ACT assessment is available at www.act.org/aap/disab/policy.html.

Guides to Postsecondary Education Opportunities and Access

The following is a sampling of resource papers available from the Higher Education and Adult Training for People with Disabilities (HEATH) Resource Center: 800/544-3284 or 202/939-9320; fax 202/833-5696 (e-mail: heath@ace .hche.edu). Some of these resources are also available on the Internet at www .heath-resource-center.org.

- *Make the Most of Your Opportunities*
- *College Freshmen with Disabilities: A Statistical Profile*
- *How To Choose a College: Guide for the Student with a Disability*
- *Career Planning and Placement Strategies for Postsecondary Students with Disabilities*
- *The HEATH National Resource Directory on Postsecondary Education and Disability*

Directory of College Facilities and Services for People with Disabilities (4th ed.), by Carol Thomas, James Thomas, and Rhona Hartman (Eds.), 1995, available from Modoc Press, Santa Monica, California. Includes more than 1500 institutions of higher learning in the United States, Puerto Rico, and Canada, with a profile of each institution and lists of services provided.

Peterson's Colleges with Programs for Students with Learning Disabilities or Attention Deficit Disorders (6th Rev. ed., 2000), edited by Stephen Strichart and Charles Mangrum, available from Peterson's Guides, Stamford, Connecticut. Available at www.petersons.com.

The K&W Guide to Colleges: For Students with Learning Disabilities or Attention Deficit Disorder (6th ed., 2001), by Marybeth Kravets and Imy Wax; available from Princeton Review, New York.

Guides to Laws Affecting Postsecondary Education Access and Participation

Accommodations in Higher Education under the Americans with Disabilities Act (1998), edited by Michael Gordon and Shelby Keiser; available from Guilford Press, New York.

Books with Tips and Strategies for Success in Postsecondary Education

ADD and the College Student: A Guide for High School and College Students with Attention Deficit Disorder (2001), edited by Patricia O. Quinn; available from Magination Press, Washington, D.C. (e-mail contact: magination@apa.org) or 800-374-2721.

Survival Guide for College Students with ADD or LD (1994), edited by Kathleen Nadeau; available from Magination Press, Washington, D.C. (e-mail contact: magination@apa.org) or 800-374-2721.

College and Career Success for Students with Learning Disabilities (1996), by Roslyn Dolber; available from McGraw Hill, New York (e-mail contact: www.books.mcgraw-hill.com).

Learning Outside the Lines: Two Ivy League Students with Learning Disabilities and ADHD Give You the Tools for Academic Success and Educational Revolution (2000), by Jonathon Mooney and David Cole; available from Simon and Schuster, New York at www.simonsays.com.

Organizations and Research Centers

The following organizations and research centers may be able to provide some useful information for the college student with a disability.

Association on Higher Education and Disability (AHEAD)

University of Massachusetts
100 Morrissey Boulevard
Boston, MA 02125-3393
Phone: (617) 287-3880
Fax: (617) 287-3881
Web site: www.ahead.org

HEATH Resource Center

George Washington University
National Clearinghouse on Postsecondary Education for Individuals with Disabilities
2121 K Street NW, Suite 220
Washington, DC 20037
Voice/TTY: (202) 973-0904 or (800) 544-3284
Fax: (202) 973-0908
E-mail: askheath@heath.gwu.edu
Web site: www.heath.gwu.edu

Project PACE (Postsecondary Academic and Curriculum Excellence)

University of Arkansas at Little Rock
2801 S. University
Stabler Hall, Suite 104
Little Rock, AR 72204
Phone: (501) 569-8410
Fax: (501) 569-8240
Project PACE is a demonstration project for faculty and staff development to ensure students with disabilities receive a quality higher education.

National Center for the Study of Postsecondary Educational Supports (NCSPES)

University of Hawaii at Manoa
1779 University Avenue, UA 4/6
Honolulu, HI 96822
Phone: (808) 956-9199
Fax: (808) 956-5713
Web site: www.rrtc.hawaii.edu

Center on Postsecondary Education and Disability
University of Connecticut at Storrs
Department of Educational Psychology
Neag School of Education
362 Fairfield Road, Unit 2064
Storrs, CT 06269-2064
Fax: (860) 486-5799
Web site: vm.uconn.edu/~wwwcped/

Creating and Implementing a Summer College Preparation Experience for Students with Disabilities
University of Wisconsin–Madison
Center on Education and Work, School of Education
964 Educational Sciences Building
1025 West Johnson Street
Madison, WI 53706-1796
Phone: (800) 446-0399
Fax: (608) 262-3050
Web site: www.cew.wisc.edu/disted/

References

American College Testing. (2002). *ACT policy for documentation to support requests for testing accommodations on the ACT assessment.* Retrieved April 26, 2002, from http://www.act.org/aap/disab/policy.html

Americans with Disabilities Act of 1990, 42 U.S.C. § 12101 *et seq.*

Balcazar, E. E., Fawcett, S. B., & Seekins, T. (1991). Teaching people with disabilities to recruit help to attain personal goals. *Rehabilitation Psychology, 35*(1), 31–42.

Benshoff, J. J., Fried, J. H., & Roberto, K. A. (1990). Developmental skill attainment among college students with disabilities. *Rehabilitation Counseling Bulletin, 34,* 44–52.

Benshoff, J. J., Kroeger, S. A., & Scalia, V. A. (1990). Career maturity and academic achievement in college students with disabilities. *Journal of Rehabilitation, 56*(2), 40–44.

Briel, L., & Getzel, E. (2001). *Internships in higher education: A pivotal point in the career path for students with disabilities.* Retrieved April 26, 2002, from http://www.rrtc.hawaii.edu/products/published/MS009-H01.htm

Brinckerhoff, L. C. (1993). Self-advocacy: A critical skill for college students with learning disabilities. *Family* and *Community Health, 16*(3), 23–33.

Brinckerhoff, L. C., McGuire, J. M., & Shaw, S. F. (2002). *Postsecondary education and transition for students with learning disabilities* (2nd ed.). Austin, TX: PRO-ED.

College Board. (2002, July 17). *The College Board and Disabilities Rights Advocates announce agreement to drop flagging from standardized tests.* Retrieved November 12, 2002, from http://www.collegeboard.com/press/article/0,1443,11360.00.html

Dickey, K. D., & Satcher, J. (1994). The selection of postsecondary placement options by school counselors for students with learning disabilities. *The School Counselor, 41,* 347–351.

Educational Testing Service. (2001, February 7). *ETS agrees with disability groups to stop "flagging" on graduate admissions tests.* Retrieved November 11, 2002, from http://www.ets.org/news/01020701.html

Fichten, C. S., Asuncion, J. B., Barile, M., Fossey, M., & deSimone, C. (2000). Access to educational and instructional computer technologies for post-secondary students with disabilities: Lessons from three empirical studies. *Journal of Educational Media, 25,* 179–201.

Fichten, C. S., Goodrick, G., Tagalakis, V., Amsel, R., & Libman, E. (1990). Getting along in college: Recommendations for college students with disabilities and their professors. *Rehabilitation Counseling Bulletin, 34,* 103–125.

Field, S. (2002). Self-determination: Assuming control of your plans for postsecondary education. *Information from HEATH* (April, 2002). Retrieved from http://www.heath.gwu.edu/Templates/Newsletter/issue2/Self-determinationpaper.htm

Harris, R., & Robertson, J. (2001). Successful strategies for college-bound students with learning disabilities. *Preventing School Failure, 45*(3), 125–132.

HEATH Resource Center. (1998). *Profile of 1996 college freshmen with disabilities.* Washington, DC: Author.

HEATH Resource Center. (2001). *Creating options: A resource on financial aid for students with disabilities–2001 edition.* Washington, DC: Author.

Hebel, S. (2001a). How a landmark anti-bias law changed life for disabled students. *Chronicle of Higher Education, 47*(20), p. A23.

Hebel, S. (2001b, July 6). Who pays the costs to help students with disabilities: Colleges and state agencies struggle to divide up their responsibilities. *Chronicle of Higher Education, 47*(20), p. A19.

Heyward, S. M. (1993). Students' rights and responsibilities. *New Directions for College Student Services, 64,* 17–29.

Heyward, S. M. (1998). *Disability and higher education: Guidance for Section 504 and ADA compliance.* Horsham, PA: LRP Publications.

Hitchings, W. E., Luzzo, D. A., Ristow, R., Horvath, M., Retish, P., & Tanners, A. (2001). The career development needs of college students with learning disabilities: In their own words. *Learning Disabilities Research and Practice, 16*(1), 8–17.

Jarrow, J. (1993). Beyond ramps: New ways of viewing access. *New Directions for Student Services, 64,* 5–16.

Kelly, A. E., Sedlacek, W. E., & Scales, W. R. (1994). How college students with and without disabilities perceive themselves and each other. *Journal of Counseling* and *Development, 73,* 178–182.

Kubaiko, J. (1984). Why are you taking this class? In J. M. Graner, P. K. Kile, K. Lesh, & J. E. Jarrow (Eds.), *Proceedings of the 1985 AHSSPPE Conference: Association of Handicapped Student Service Programs in Post-secondary Education* (pp. 56–58). Kansas City, MO: Association of Handicapped Student Service Programs in Post-secondary Education.

Lynch, R. K., & McSweeney, K. (1982). Issues in pursuing a postsecondary education. In T. Harrington (Ed.), The *handbook of career planning for special needs students* (pp. 267–287). Austin, TX: PRO-ED.

Lynch, R. T., & Gussel, L. (1996). Disclosure and self-advocacy regarding disability-related needs: Strategies to maximize integration in postsecondary education. *Journal of Counseling* and *Development, 74,* 352–357.

National Center for Accessing the General Curriculum. (2002). *Summary of universal design for learning concepts.* Retrieved April 18, 2002, from http://www.cast. org/udl/

Ness, J. E. (1989). The high jump: Transition issues of learning disabled students and their parents. *Academic Therapy, 25*(1), 32–40.

Nordlund, M. R. (1994). Transition to postsecondary education. In R. C. Savage & G. E. Wolcott (Eds.), *Educational dimensions of acquired brain injury* (pp. 507–518). Austin, TX: PRO-ED.

Palmer, C., & Roessler, R. (2000). Requesting classroom accommodations: Self-advocacy and conflict resolution training for college students with disabilities. *Journal of Rehabilitation, 66*(3), 38–43.

Paul, S. (2000). Students with disabilities in higher education: A review of the literature. *College Student Journal, 34*(2), 200–211.

Prater, G., & Minner, S. (1986). Factors inhibiting the performance of learning-disabled students in postsecondary settings. *Reading, Writing, and Learning Disabilities, 2,* 273–277.

Price-Ellingstad, D., & Berry, H. G. (2000). Postsecondary education, vocational rehabilitation, and students with disabilities: Gaining access to promising futures. *American Rehabilitation,* Winter 1999–2000, 2–10.

Rehabilitation Act of 1973, 29 U.S.C. § 701 *et seq.*

Roth, V. (1991). Students with learning disabilities and hearing impairment: Issues for the secondary and postsecondary teacher. *Journal of Learning Disabilities, 24,* 391–397.

Rothstein, L. F. (1998). The Americans with Disabilities Act, Section 504, and adults with learning disabilities in adult education and transition to employment. In S. A. Vogel & S. Reder (Eds.), *Learning disabilities, literacy, and adult education* (pp. 29–42). Baltimore: Brookes.

Scott, S. S. (1990). Coming to terms with the "otherwise qualified" student with a learning disability. *Journal of Learning Disabilities, 23,* 398–405.

Scott, S. S. (1994). Determining reasonable academic adjustments for college students with learning disabilities. *Journal of Learning Disabilities, 27,* 403–412.

Southwestern Community College v. Davis, 442 U.S. 397 (1979).

Stodden, R. A., & Dowrick, P. W. (2000). Postsecondary education and employment of adults with disabilities. *American Rehabilitation,* Winter 1999–2000, 19–23.

Thompson, A. R., & Dickey, K. D. (1994). Self-perceived job search skills of college students with disabilities. *Rehabilitation Counseling Bulletin, 37,* 358–370.

U.S. Department of Education, National Center for Education Statistics. (2000). *The condition of education 2000* (NCES 2000-062). Washington, DC: U.S. Government Printing Office.

Vogel, S. A., Leonard, F., Scales, W., Hayeslip, P., Hermansen, J., & Donnells, L. (1998). The national learning disabilities postsecondary data bank: An overview. *Journal of Learning Disabilities, 31,* 234–247.

Wilson, T. (2000). *Distance learning over the Internet: Access for the disabled.* Retrieved April 18, 2002, from http://www.appassionato.org/NACUA/distance_learning.htm

Zurcher, R., & Bryant, D. P. (2001). The validity and comparability of entrance examination scores after accommodations are made for students with LD. *Journal of Learning Disabilities, 34,* 462–471.

C H A P T E R

TRANSITION PLANNING
Mary E. Cronin, James R. Patton, and Robin H. Lock

lanning for the future has long been recognized as a good idea. Unfortunately, little attention, relative to what is needed, has been given to the systematic planning for adult life for students with special needs. Although many students have access to quality career counseling programs, others do not. For the most part, when efforts to plan for a student's future have been made, they have traditionally focused on further education or employment, ignoring other key areas in which competence will be needed (e.g., daily and community living skills; Sitlington, 1996). We believe that if students have the knowledge, skills, services, and/or supports to deal effectively with the various demands of adulthood, their lives probably will be more enriched and satisfying.

Students acquire knowledge and skills and access services and supports that are required to meet everyday challenges in a number of different ways. Although families often are the source of much of the information young adults will need to know and the skills they will need to employ, students on their own also pick up useful information and learn needed skills through incidental, nonprogrammed events. As a support to the family, schools should also be addressing the important demands of adulthood through as many options as possible. Unfortunately, these sources, singly or in combination, are not preparing youth as comprehensively as is needed to deal competently with the demands faced by adults.

Note. Parts of the beginning section of this chapter have been adapted from "Transition and Students with Learning Disabilities: Creating Sound Futures," by G. Blalock and J. R. Patton, 1996, *Journal of Learning Disabilities, 29*, pp. 7–16. Copyright 1996 by PRO-ED, Inc. Adapted with permission.

In many schools, activities and services designed to help prepare students with special needs for adult life have been operative for quite some time, although they may not have been labeled as transition activities. For example, many work-study programs for students with mental retardation that were common in the 1960s focused specifically on training and employment issues that were linked to postsecondary outcomes. With this in mind, it is important to acknowledge that many special education teachers, guidance counselors, and other school-related personnel are very much in the business of preparing students and their families for the realities of life after high school. These professionals have been practicing long before the current emphasis on transition commenced. In addition, many families, to whom much of the planning for the future has fallen, have also done a splendid job of getting their adolescents ready for adulthood.

The formal transition movement in special education, which began in the mid-1980s, was precipitated by realities that were coming to light about the bleak adult outcomes of many students who had been in special education for significant parts of their school careers. Various follow-up studies (Affleck, Edgar, Levine, & Kottering, 1990; Hasazi, Gordon, & Roe, 1985; Mithaug, Horiuchi, & Fanning, 1985; Sitlington, Frank, & Carson, 1992; Wagner et al., 1991) painted a picture of unemployment, long-term underemployment for those with jobs, minimal participation in postsecondary education, inability to live independently, limited social experiences, restricted participation in community activities, and inordinately high arrest rates. In the mid-1980s, comprehensive transition services were proposed, and planning for such services was mandated by the Individuals with Disabilities Education Act of 1990 (IDEA; P.L. 101-476). Unfortunately, what is mandated is not always implemented; evidence continues to mount indicating that students' total transitional needs are not being met at the time they leave school (Benz & Halpern, 1993). Wehman (1993) offered one reasonable explanation for this phenomenon: "Clearly, no law can 'make' service providers, school districts, and state agencies enact policies and procedures that they do not want to enact" (p. 181). Nonetheless, the need to provide comprehensive transition planning for students with special needs is warranted, even with certain barriers.

Concept of Transition

In this section we examine the many transitions that people make in their lives. The evolution of the concept of transition used in this chapter, which focuses on the movement from school to adult life, is chronicled.

Transitions Along and Across the Life Span

Important transitions occur regularly during everyone's life. Some are normative and predictable; others are specific to a time or situation and may not be experienced by everyone. Polloway, Patton, Smith, and Roderique (1991) referred to the former as vertical transitions and to the latter as horizontal transitions. Vertical transitions are associated with major developmental life events, such as beginning school, leaving school, and turning 50 years old. Coordinated planning for some of these events can minimize the trauma and anxiety that may arise. Little comprehensive planning for key transitions occurs in the lives of most individuals. Planning for individuals with disabilities is mandated by IDEA for certain specific transitions: the transition from early intervention programs to early childhood special education or other preschool settings; the transition from early childhood special education programs to kindergarten, special education, or another formal school setting; and the transition from high school to young adulthood. Some type of formalized transition planning process is required for all of these situations.

Horizontal transitions involve movement from one situation or setting to another. These may occur at any given time in one's life. One of the most important and frequently discussed horizontal transitions is the movement from separate special settings to less restrictive, more inclusive ones. This type of transition is not age-specific, because such movement may occur at any number of occasions during the lives of persons with disabling conditions.

Even though most of the vertical and some of the horizontal transitions are worthy of study, this chapter focuses on the transition from the school environment to any one of a number of postschool settings. The next section highlights how the professional conceptualizations of transition have evolved.

Evolution of the Concept of Transition

In 1984, a policy on transition was promoted by the Office of Special Education and Rehabilitative Services (OSERS) within the U.S. Department of Education. At that time transition was defined as "an outcome-oriented process encompassing a broad array of services and experiences that lead to employment" (Will, 1984, p. 1). This "bridge-from-school-to-working-life" model of transition, as depicted in Figure 12.1, emphasized employment as the primary outcome on which training and services — whether time-limited or ongoing — should be based. This model had a clearly singular focus on employment, regarding nonvocational aspects of adult adjustment as "significant and important only insofar as they contribute to the ultimate goal of employment" (Halpern, 1985, p. 480).

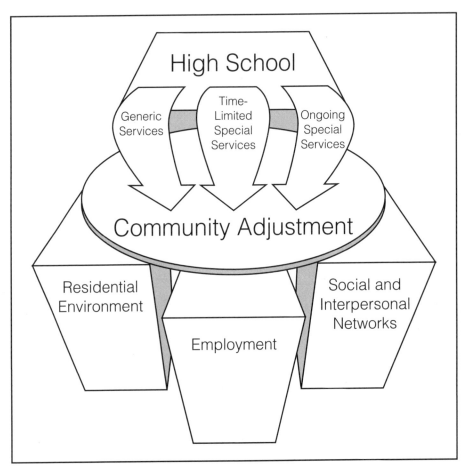

Figure 12.1. Model of transition promoted by the Office of Special Education and Rehabilitative Services (1984).

Recognizing the limited scope of the OSERS model of transition, Halpern (1985) presented an alternative perspective to Will (1984) on transition. His model suggested that two other dimensions — the quality of one's residential environment and the adequacy of one's social and interpersonal networks — are as important to successful adjustment as employment is. Halpern's revisionist thinking reflected the opinion of other professionals working in the area of transition at the time, who also felt that additional dimensions must be considered if comprehensive transition planning and preparation were to be accomplished.

As the work from various federally funded transition projects of the mid-1980s was disseminated, it became clear that many transition areas were being identified as critical to transition planning. The 1990 amendments to the Education for All Handicapped Children Act of 1975, which changed the name of the law to the Individuals with Disabilities Education Act, had a significant effect on transition services. IDEA now mandated that one of the purposes of the annual Individualized Education Program (IEP) meeting for students with disabilities, upon reaching 16 years of age, would be to plan for necessary transition services. The law defined these services as follows:

> A coordinated set of activities for a student, designed within an outcome oriented process, which promotes movement from school to post-school activities, including post-secondary education, vocational training, integrated employment (including supported employment), continuing and adult education, adult services, independent living or community participation.
>
> The coordinated set of activities shall be based upon the individual student's needs, taking into account student preferences and interests and shall include instruction, community experiences, and the development of employment and other post-school objectives, and if appropriate, acquisition of daily living skills and functional vocational evaluation. [§ 300.18]

Individual planning for transition services, as prescribed in the legislation and accompanying regulations, includes three important components: assessment, family participation, and specific procedures to be followed in the development of the IEP. Since these requirements have gone into effect, states and school districts have developed a variety of ways to address them, ranging from comprehensive planning to minimal compliance.

In 1994, the Division on Career Development and Transition (DCDT) of the Council for Exceptional Children adopted a new definition of transition that arguably best reflects contemporary thinking on this concept. It relates easily to the concept of career development and is in line with recent efforts to require that transition planning be in place at an earlier age. Moreover, the definition promotes two extremely important concepts: transition education should begin in the early grades, and the transition planning process should be student driven. The DCDT definition reads as follows:

> Transition refers to a change in status from behaving primarily as a student to assuming emergent adult roles in the community. These roles include employment, participating in post-secondary education, maintaining a home, becoming appropriately involved in the community, and experiencing satisfactory personal and social relationships. The process of enhancing transition involves the participation and coordination of school programs, adult agency services, and natural supports within the community. The foundations for transition should be laid during the elementary and middle school years, guided by the broad concept of career development. Transition planning should begin no later than age 14, and students should be encouraged, to the

full extent of their capabilities, to assume a minimum amount of responsibility for such planning. (Halpern, 1994, p. 117)

When examined closely, the transition planning process is found to be a multifaceted series of events. Ultimately, all transitions, if approached systematically, are composed of three key parts: assessment, planning, and follow-through. Although these elements are discussed in detail in subsequent sections of this chapter, it is important to accentuate them here.

Model of Successful Adult Functioning

The model depicted in Figure 12.2 is an attempt to conceptualize the relationship of transition to successful adult adjustment. The model suggests that being reasonably successful in meeting the challenges of everyday living (i.e., demands of adulthood), whether at work, at home, in school, or in the community, contributes to one's personal fulfillment — an idea that relates closely to the concept of quality of life as discussed by Halpern (1993). To be successful

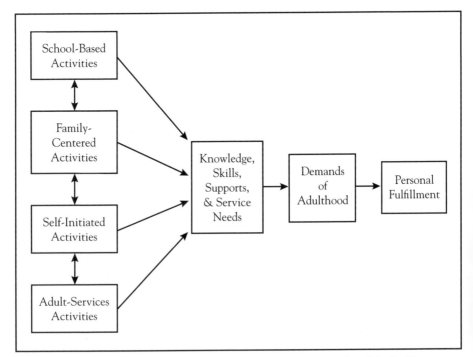

Figure 12.2. Key elements of the transition process. From *Transition from School to Young Adulthood: Basic Concepts and Recommended Practices* (p. 5), by J. R. Patton & C. Dunn, 1998, Austin, TX: PRO-ED. Reprinted with permission.

with such demands requires that an individual possess the critical elements of everyday functioning: certain levels of knowledge, ability to apply specific skills to everyday problems and challenges, and a variety of supports and/or services to call upon when needed. If these elements are in place, the chances of handling the complexities of everyday life are enhanced. The best way to get these elements in place is through comprehensive transition planning. The model suggests that the primary responsibility for addressing these critical elements should be shared by the student, his or her parents or guardians, and the school; however, initially the school is charged with taking the lead in ensuring that transition planning occurs. Subsequently, students and their parents or guardians are to assume full responsibility.

Transition Services and Students with Special Needs

As Dunn (1996) pointed out, much of the early emphasis in transition activities was directed toward individuals with more extensive needs. The common assumptions were that students with mild disabilities (e.g., learning disabilities) were able to make the transition to adult life without too much difficulty and that emphasis should be placed on academic-related topics. In Chapter 10 of this book, Fogg and Harrington offer futuristic educational and occupational directions to remedy past nonproductive work histories for individuals with disabling conditions. The fact that many students with learning disabilities are in diploma-track programs with a mainly academic orientation contributes to the dilemma of transition to postsecondary situations.

A number of authors have suggested that the transitional needs of students with mild disabling conditions are not entirely being met (Benz & Halpern, 1993; Karge, Patton, & de la Garza, 1992). Transition planning for such students must be comprehensive in nature and, as defined by IDEA, address all the major areas of adult functioning: employment, continuing education, daily living, health, leisure, communication, interpersonal skills, self-determination, and community participation.

Two important issues have been raised regarding transition efforts and students with different types of special needs. First, given that a limited number of individuals with mild disabilities are entering postsecondary education (Wagner, Blackorby, Cameto, Hebbeler, & Newman, 1993), transition efforts must better address employment needs, particularly in times when the nature of the workplace is changing. Second, other nonemployment areas critical for successful adult functioning, such as daily living skills, cannot be taken for granted; transitional needs in these areas have to be identified, planned for, and acted on (see Sitlington, 1996).

A General Timeline for the Transition Process

School districts throughout the United States are working hard to develop and refine their transition services programs and to meet the mandate set forth in IDEA. In most cases, the development of a timeline for these services has been a helpful framework to guide practitioners and researchers. The timeliness of various services (assessment, planning, and instruction) is the main component in the career development theories (i.e., those aimed at the general population) of Donald Super, John Holland, and others (see Chapter 1). Specifically, opportunities for career awareness activities at the elementary level, career exploration at the middle school or junior high level, and career education at the high school and postsecondary levels are important for all students. They are particularly critical for students with special needs, who can benefit from exposure to transition education at young ages. With this in mind, comprehensive, focused instruction in various life skills areas is recommended for most of these students to enable them to reach their educational and vocational goals. A schemata for considering this ongoing transition process is presented in Table 12.1.

Guiding Principles

Certain themes are extremely important in meeting the transition needs of students with special needs. The following principles pervade the entire transition planning process and are considered minimal guidelines for professionals.

1. Student participation is crucial. As Karge et al. (1992) noted, "It is an inherent right to be involved in one's own life planning" (p. 65). To do this effectively, students must be more than observers at their IEP meetings; they need to be given the tools to be effective participants. At the very least, a student's interests and preferences should be determined. It is more desirable, however, to have the student actively contribute to the development of his or her transition plan. This movement to an assumption of responsibility by the individual and the need for greater independence is clearly made evident in Chapter 11 in the expectations for postsecondary school and college students.

2. Efforts should be made to get families involved in the transition process. School-based personnel need to be sensitive to family values, needs, and situations, and families should be encouraged to participate to whatever degree possible in identifying transition needs, determining transition goals, and acting directly or indirectly on achieving those goals.

TABLE 12.1
Timelines for Transition Planning and Services
for Students with Learning Disabilities

Preschool	Elementary	Mid-school	High School	Postsecondary
Developmental assessment	Academic, developmental, and informal interest surveys	Academic, adaptive, and interest assessments	9th — vocational interest aptitude, and values; 11–12th — update same; ongoing academic assessment	Formal vocational and academic
Individualized Family Services Plan (IFSP)	Individualized Education Program (IEP)	IEP, 4-year plan for high school	Individualized Transition Planning (ITP) as part of IEP	IEP/ITP and possible Indiv. Written Rehabilitation Plan (IWRP) or other individual plans
Developmental and other curricula	Basic skills; Work-related behaviors[a]; Self-determination; Instruction; Career awareness	Basic skills; Work-related behaviors[a]; Self-determination; Career exploration	Basic skills (within functional context and/or college prep); Self-determination; Career education	Specific academic and vocational curricula
Chores at home	Chores, hobbies at home and in school	Rotated, varied small job try-outs, supervised experiences	Paid jobs (varied) with supervision gradually faded	Career entry placements

Note. From "Transition and Students with Learning Disabilities: Creating Sound Futures," by G. Blalock and J. R. Patton, 1996, *Journal of Learning Disabilities, 29*(1), p. 13. Copyright 1996 by PRO-ED, Inc. Reproduced with permission.

[a]Work-related behaviors include social skills, work ethic, reasoning/problem-solving skills, punctuality, dependability, following through on tasks, following directions, and so forth.

3. Transition efforts should start early. Various aspects of the transition process can easily begin at the elementary level. *Transition education* (i.e., content related to ultimate transition areas) can be initiated through the teaching of life skills and career education. Families can be introduced to the major areas of transition planning when their children are young so that they become aware of areas that will be very important for their children in the future.

4. Transition planning must be sensitive to cultural factors. Professionals involved in transition planning need to be aware of various cultural factors that can affect the

nature of student and family participation in the transition planning process. The way families participate may differ from what school-based personnel desire; for example, involvement with the schools may not be a priority. As a result, getting families involved with transition planning will be difficult. Furthermore, cultural factors may very well influence the priority of transition needs, again in potential contrast to what school-based individuals think is important. The goal of transition planning is to act on areas of student need. Agreeing on what the most important areas of need are sometimes requires mediation and collaboration among all individuals involved.

5. Transition planning must be comprehensive. As important as employment is as an outcome, it is only one of many areas for which transition needs should be evaluated. Edgar (1988), in summarizing his thoughts (shared by others), cautioned, "In our society, employment, and the money earned from employment, plays a critical role in everyone's quality of life — hence the focus on employment. But we must remain aware that employment and jobs do not guarantee quality of life" (p. 5). The important point is that we need to reach a workable balance across all of the transition areas.

6. Transition planning must be based on both a student's strengths and his or her areas of need. Building on a student's strengths and interests, rather than solely on his or her deficits, contributes to successful transition planning efforts. Every student will have some strengths, and identifying them provides the basis for effective outcome-oriented planning.

7. Differences of opinion must be addressed. Differing wishes among any of the key players (student, family, school) in the transition planning process will need to be resolved, compromised on, or even mediated, but the requests of any party must be respectfully considered. Quality transition needs assessment is likely to lead to differences of opinion. Most of the time, resolution of different perceptions is easily obtained; however, some situations will require skillful negotiation.

8. Someone in the school needs to take primary responsibility for coordinating the transition planning process. Even though Figure 12.2 suggests that the transition process is a shared responsibility, it is essential that some school-based person coordinate the transition process. Without such leadership, the chances are too great that the transition process will be ineffective.

Current Forces Influencing Transition Programs

Bassett and Smith (1996) discussed the influence that educational reform has had (or may have) on transition efforts in the United States. The inclusion movement, teacher preparation reform, special education reform, and standards-based education serve as both threats to and strategies for provision of transition services. More than nondisabled students, students with special needs are in a position to benefit from these reforms — as well as to lose certain options — due to the nature of their disabling conditions. Careful collaborative planning, as mentioned previously, should ensure that a student's transition needs receive the attention required for successfully moving from school life to adult life. Collaboration is addressed specifically in Chapter 14.

A more recent educational initiative promises a much stronger imperative for transition planning for students with special needs because it mandates school-to-work transition education for all students in the educational system. The School-to-Work Opportunity Act of 1994 (P.L. 103-239), coupled with the Goals 2000: Educate America Act of 1994 (P.L. 103-227), prompts school-based education that is tied to employment and other adult outcomes (as in a career education model) and work-based education that provides the rationale for learning applied academic skills and information. As long as students with special needs are not excluded from these general curricular options, these legislative additions offer many more opportunities for meaningful transition education than any singular special education or rehabilitation act has been able to deliver.

Transition Planning Process

Planning for transition is critical. This preparation sets the stage for everything else to happen in a timely manner. This is an exciting time for the students, their families, and the professionals who work with them. Visions are played out, options are discussed, activities are scheduled, and contacts are made. Most of all, the future is becoming reality and, if done correctly, with the assurance of success for the student. Planning done during this time will open the doors of the future for the student. Case management facilitates successful outcomes.

In this section we discuss several important components of the transition planning process. First, we identify the domains that are addressed in the transition process. Next, we describe the components necessary to carry out transition: assessment of student needs, the Individual Transition Plan (ITP), instructional considerations in the classroom and in the community, linkage considerations to adult service providers, and the student transition packet.

Transition Domains

A structure is needed to organize the areas of transition to be addressed when assessing student needs, planning the student's transition program, and organizing instructional situations. Domains critical to planning for transition are interpreted differently from state to state. Table 12.2 is an overview by Clark and Patton (1997) of the variety of domains identified by 11 selected states as planning areas important to the transition process. Although 20 areas have

TABLE 12.2
Transition Planning Areas

Major Domains	States																
	AL	AR	CA	CO	CT	FL	HI	ID	IL	IA	KS	KY	LA	MN	NJ	TX	UT
Adult Services				×	×	×		×				×			×		
Advocacy/Legal	×						×						×				
Assistive Technology												×					
Career Planning Options							×										
Communication												×					×
Community Participation	×		×	×	×	×	×	×			×	×	×	×	×		×
Daily Living (including domestic areas)		×	×	×		×	×			×	×	×	×		×		×
Employment (including workplace readiness and specific job skills)	×	×	×	×	×	×		×	×	×	×	×	×		×	×	×
Financial/Income/Money Management	×		×		×		×	×		×	×	×	×				
Functional Academics															×		
Health (including medical services)	×			×	×		×	×		×	×	×	×		×		×
Independent Living (including living arrangements)	×	×	×		×	×		×	×		×	×	×	×	×	×	×
Insurance							×				×						
Leisure/Recreation		×	×	×	×		×	×		×	×	×	×	×	×	×	×
Lifelong Learning										×							
Personal Management	×																
Postsecondary Education		×	×	×	×	×	×	×	×		×	×	×	×	×	×	×
Relationships/Social Skills			×	×	×			×		×	×	×	×				×

(continues)

TABLE 12.2 Continued.

Major Domains	AL	AR	CA	CO	CT	FL	HI	ID	IL	IA	KS	KY	LA	MN	NJ	TX	UT
States																	
Self-Determination/Self-Advocacy				×			×			×	×	×		×			×
Transportation/Mobility	×	×	×	×		×	×			×	×	×	×	×			
Vocational Evaluation	×																
Vocational Training			×	×	×	×	×	×						×	×	×	×

Note. From *Transition Planning Inventory* (p. 4), by G. M. Clark & J. R. Patton, 1997, Austin, TX: PRO-ED. Copyright 1997 by PRO-ED, Inc. Reproduced with permission.

been collectively identified, no one state utilizes all areas. Some states use as many as 14 planning areas, and others as few as 5 or 6 areas. Regardless of the number of planning areas used, the important factor is that each of these states employs a structure by which planning for transition to postsecondary situations can be launched.

Components of the Transition Planning Process

The challenge of planning a transition program for a student includes many components that are important to the successful implementation of the transition process. The essential components include assessment of student needs, the ITP, instructional considerations in the classroom and the community, linkage considerations to adult service providers, and a student transition portfolio.

Assessment of Student Needs

Before any planning for a student's future begins, an assessment of his or her current skills and situation must be completed. In addition, the impact of the student's ability to demonstrate said skills in future subsequent environments must be determined. This factor cannot be stressed enough. The transition service provisions in IDEA clearly state that individual planning must be the driving force in the development of programs and services necessary for successful transition to postsecondary situations and/or adult life (Clark, 1996). Not all students perform tasks at the same level or are attracted to the same type of job or recreation activity. Each transition plan therefore must reflect the abilities and stated needs and preferences of a particular student and not what someone else thinks the person should do or what the school's limited options offer. There is a strong movement emphasizing the need for students and parents to actively participate in the transition planning process, with the student not only attending the meeting but, when appropriate, running his or her own IEP/ITP meeting (Clark, 1996; Field, 1996; Halpern et al., 1997; Martin & Huber Marshall, 1997). A variety of assessment options exist to assist in determining a student's present level of functioning in a variety of transition-related skills. Clark (1996) summarized the current published standardized and nonstandardized transition instruments (see Table 12.3, which identifies the focus group and some of the features of each transition referenced instrument).

Clark (1996) also suggested that in developing an ITP, the development of "a transition assessment approach that is not only culture/language fair, but also culture/language enhanced" (p. 89) is imperative. There is a great risk of cultural bias in assessing preferences, interests, and nonacademic knowledge and skills without careful consideration of language level and cultural appropriateness to the individuals being tested.

The Transition Planning Document

The IEP is the primary planning document in special education designed to individualize goals and instruction and coordinate services needed to complete those goals for students with special needs at all age levels. The mandated statement of transition by IDEA needs to be included in the IEPs of all students ages 16 and over (age 14 when appropriate). Individual states have complied with this mandate in various ways. Some have incorporated a place for the statement of transition, with the transition-related goals and objectives, into the IEP document itself. Others have developed a separate document, referred to as the ITP, which is appended to the IEP. ITP documents appear in varying formats from state to state and differ in how they communicate a student's current level of functioning and need in the various transition domains outlined in Table 12.2. Some states use checklists, whereas others have individual sections addressing each of the identified domains of that state. Regardless of the format used, the ITP document represents a more detailed description of the current level of functioning, the needs, and the preferences of individual students in the targeted transition domains. Most important in the long run is to have a functional transition planning format to assist in the planning process.

(text continues on p. 392)

TABLE 12.3
Summary of Current Examples of Transition-Referenced Assessment Instruments

Instrument/Procedure Name	Target Group	Features
Social and Prevocational Information Battery–Revised (Halpern, Irvin, & Munkres, 1986)	Adolescents and adults with mild mental retardation or low-functioning students with learning disabilities.	1. Subscales including Banking, Budgeting and Purchasing Skills Job Skills and Job-Related Behavior, Home Management, Health Care, Hygiene and Grooming, and Ability to Read Functional Words. 2. Orally administered except for items on functional signs. 3. Designed especially for secondary school students 4. True–false item format. 5. 277 items in the battery. 6. 20–30 minutes administration time.
Tests for Everyday Living (Halpern, Irvin, & Landman, 1979)	All junior high students and average- to low-functioning senior high school students in remedial programs, including those labeled as having learning disabilities or learning handicaps.	1. Subtests include Purchasing Habits, Banking, Budgeting, Health Care, Home Management, Job Search Skills, and Job-Related Behavior. 2. Orally administered except where reading skills are critical to an item. 3. 245 items across seven subtests. 4. Diagnostic at the subtest level. 5. 20–30 minutes estimated administration time per subtest.

(continues)

TABLE 12.3 *Continued.*

Instrument/Procedure Name	Target Group	Features
Transition Behavior Scale (McCarney, 1989)	Any disability group; mild to severe levels of disability.	1. Subscales include Work-Related Behaviors, Interpersonal Relations, Social/Community Expectations.
		2. Ratings are completed by at least three persons.
		3. Items are rated on a 3-point scale.
		4. Estimated completion time is 15 minutes.
		5. Scores in percentile ranks are based on national standardization sample.
LCCE Knowledge Battery (Brolin, 1992)	Mild cognitive disabilities; moderate to severe learning disabilities; mild to moderate behavioral disorders; Grades 7–12.	1. Curriculum-based assessment related to LCCE Curriculum.
		2. 200 multiple-choice items covering 20 of 22 LCCE competency areas.
		3. Standardized on a national sample.
Quality of Life Questionnaire (Schalock & Keith, 1993)	Mild to severe cognitive disabilities; ages 18 and older.	1. Subscales include Satisfaction, Competence/Productivity, Empowerment/Independence, and Social Belonging/Community Integration
		2. Administered in interview format for most persons; alternative format is possible by obtaining two independent ratings and averaging.
		3. Items are rated on a 3-point scale.
		4. Administration time is estimated at 20 minutes.

(continues)

TABLE 12.3 *Continued.*

Instrument/Procedure Name	Target Group	Features
		5. Scores in percentile ranks are based on standardization sample.
Quality of Student Life Questionnaire (Keith & Schalock, 1993)	All disability populations, ages 14–25; mild through severe levels of disability.	1. Subscales include Satisfaction, Well-Being, Social Belonging, and Empowerment/Control.
		2. Administered in interview format for most persons; alternative formats include a written format or obtaining two independent ratings and averaging.
		3. Items are rated on a 3-point scale.
		4. Administration time is estimated at 15 minutes.
		5. Scores in percentile ranks are based on secondary and postsecondary standardization samples.
Transition Planning Inventory (Clark & Patton, 1997)	All disability populations, ages 14–25; mild through severe levels of disability.	1. Areas covered in the inventory include Employment, Further Education/Training, Daily Living, Living Arrangements, Leisure Activities, Community Participation, Health, Self-Determination, Communication, and Personal Relationships.
		2. 0–5 rating scale completed independently by student, parent/guardian, and a school representative.

(*continues*)

TABLE 12.3 *Continued.*

Instrument/Procedure Name	Target Group	Features
		3. Administration may be self-administration, guided administration, or oral administration.
		4. 56 inventory items plus open-ended items on the student form (optional on parent form) related to preferences and interests.
		5. A profile sheet permits visual comparisons of the respondents' responses to each item.
		6. Planning notes form encourages transformation of relevant assessment data into IEP goals, objectives, and interagency linkages.
Enderle-Severson Transition Rating Scale (Enderle & Severson, 1991)	Any disability group; mild to severe levels of disability; ages 14–21.	1. The scale is an informal, criterion-referenced instrument.
		2. Subscales include Jobs and Job Training, Recreation and Leisure, Home Living, and Post-Secondary Training and Learning Opportunities
		3. Scale is completed by the student's teacher and a parent or primary caregiver. Framework for transition planning.
LCCE Performance Battery (Brolin, 1992)	Mild cognitive disabilities; moderate to severe learning disabilities; mild to moderate behavioral disorders; Grades 7–12.	1. The battery is a nonstandardized, criterion-referenced instrument providing skill rather than knowledge assessment of critical life skills.
		2. Items are based on skills related to LCCE Curriculum.

(continues)

TABLE 12.3 *Continued.*

Instrument/Procedure Name	Target Group	Features
		3. Estimated time for administration is 3–4 hours.
Life Skills Inventory (Brigance, 1995)	All disability populations, high school ages and adults; mild cognitive disabilities, with Reading Grade Levels 2–8.	1. Subscales including Speaking and Listening, Functional Writing, Words on Common Signs and Warning Labels, Telephone Skills, Money and Finance, Food, Clothing, Health, Travel, and and Transportation.
		2. Administered individually or in groups; administration may be oral or written.
		3. Criterion-referenced assessment, providing specific knowledge and skill assessments for life skill items paired with instructional objectives.
		4. Learner Record Book provided to show color-coded record of performance and instructional objectives generated from the results.
		5. Optional Program Record Book is available to track progress of a group or class; optional Rating Scales are available to evaluate behavior, attitudes, and other traits related to life skills and employability.

Note. From "Transition Planning Assessment for Secondary-Level Students with Learning Disabilities," by G. M. Clark, 1996, *Journal of Learning Disabilities, 29*(1), pp. 86–87. Copyright 1996 by PRO-ED, Inc. Reprinted with permission.

Figure 12.3 provides a comprehensive case study on Chris. This case study shows the necessary components of the transition planning process for designing an appropriate plan of action. The case includes the following five elements:

(*text continues on p. 401*)

PART 1: BACKGROUND INFORMATION

Chris is a 17-year-old who has been diagnosed with attention-deficit/hyperactivity disorder (ADHD) and Tourette syndrome (TS). He is highly artistic and has been involved in several commercial art projects. He is a staff member of the school newspaper and the yearbook. He usually gets along well with peers and takes pride in seeing his work in school publications. Peer and teacher conflicts with Chris often involve inappropriate comments he makes impulsively. He occasionally misses social cues, and his peers sometimes find him annoying.

Chris has difficulty controlling his impulsiveness and often acts before thinking, which results in poor decisions and sometimes painful consequences. As a result of TS, Chris has several facial tics. If Chris's stress level is high, his facial tics tend to be more exaggerated and more frequent. He dislikes public speaking and other scenarios in which he is expected to perform in front of others. He is currently taking prescription medication to control the symptoms of TS, but this drug has the side effect of making Chris feel tired and drowsy. Chris has difficulty staying awake in classes that involve sitting at a desk for the entire period, but he is unwilling to go off of the medication because he feels self-conscious about the facial tics.

Academically, Chris's grades range between Bs and Ds. His parents report that he frequently misjudges his progress in school and believes he is doing higher quality work than his actual grades reflect. He strongly dislikes English, and he rarely completes reading assignments for any class. His major complaint is that reading is boring and he doesn't get much out of it anyway. During silent reading time in class, Chris is highly distracted by auditory stimuli. Chris is sometimes fidgety and often gets up from his desk and moves around the classroom. He has tried Ritalin and other medications commonly used to treat ADHD, but each exacerbated his TS and made him lose weight. He and his parents have told teachers that Chris prefers to deal with his ADHD without medication.

Chris's written assignments are very short and simplistic. He has great difficulty organizing details in essays, and his topic sentences lack sufficient support. Although Chris generally does poorly on essay tests, he performs very well on objective tests. His academic strengths are math and science; he enjoys hands-on projects. He has a keen ability to note and remember detail, which is most remarkable in his artistic creations. His future plans include pursuing an art career, but Chris does not elaborate on any specific art careers he finds interesting. He is ambivalent about going to college, as he intensely dislikes traditional learning exercises. He is aware of his academic strengths and needs, but he lacks an understanding of how these will affect future options for education and employment.

(*continues*)

Figure 12.3. Case study scenario for Chris. *Note.* From *Case Studies In Transition*, by A. Trainor, J. R. Patton, and G. M. Clark, in press, Austin, TX: PRO-ED. Copyright 2003 by PRO-ED, Inc. Reprinted with permission.

PART 2: TRANSITION PLANNING INVENTORY PROFILE

TPI	Section I. Student Information
Transition Planning Inventory Profile and Further Assessment Recommendation Form	**Student's Name:** Chris Tyler **Birth Date:** 8/23/1985 **Age:** 17 Years, 0 Months, 1 Days **School:** Pro-Ed High School **Grade:** 11 **Projected Graduation Date:** 6/18/2003 **IEP/ITP Conference Date:** 5/6/2002

Section II. Results of Other Assessments

Employability/Vocational Aptitude: Chris has been an asset to the yearbook. He will be a great graphic artist.
Life Skills:
Social/Emotional/Behavioral: Sometimes Chris lacks self-confidence and he is impulsive. He needs help in these areas.
Academic Achievement: Chris's achievement is below expected.
Other:

Section III. Student's Preferences and Interests

Section IV. Likely Postschool Setting(s)

Employment/Further Education or Training
- Home Form: work/full-time vocational training
- Student Form: work/full-time
- School Form: vocational training work/part-time

Living Arrangement
- Home Form: live by himself/herself live with others who are not related to him/her (without adult supervision)
- Student Form: live by himself/herself live with others who are not related to him/her (without adult supervision)
- School Form: live with parents or other relatives; live with others who are not related to him/her (without adult supervision)

Section V. Planning Area Inventory

	Home Rating	Student Rating	School Rating	Average Rating
Item#: 1 Planning Area: Employment Statement: knows job requirements and demands	3	4	3	3.33
Item#: 2 Planning Area: Employment Statement: makes informed choices	3	4	3	3.33

(continues)

Figure 12.3. *Continued.*

	Home Rating	Student Rating	School Rating	Average Rating
PART 2, Section V. *Continued.*				

	Home Rating	Student Rating	School Rating	Average Rating
Item#: 3 Planning Area: Employment Statement: knows how to get a job	2	3	2	2.33
Item#: 4 Planning Area: Employment Statement: demonstrates general job skills and work attitude	3	3	3	3
Item#: 5 Planning Area: Employment Statement: has specific job skills	4	4	4	4
Item#: 6 Planning Area: Further Education Statement: knows how to gain entry into community employment training	3	2	2	2.33
Item#: 7 Planning Area: Further Education Statement: knows how to gain entry into GED program	NA	NA	NA	NA
Item#: 8 Planning Area: Further Education Statement: knows how to gain entry into vocational/technical school	2	3	2	2.33
Item#: 9 Planning Area: Further Education Statement: knows how to gain entry into college or university	2	3	1	2
Item#: 10 Planning Area: Further Education Statement: can succeed in a postsecondary program	DK	4	2	More Information Needed
Item#: 11 Planning Area: Daily Living Statement: maintains personal grooming and hygiene	5	5	5	5
Item#: 12 Planning Area: Daily Living Statement: knows how to locate place to live	3	4	2	3
Item#: 13 Planning Area: Daily Living Statement: knows how to set up living arrangement	3	4	3	3.33
Item#: 14 Planning Area: Daily Living Statement: performs everyday household tasks	4	4	3	3.67
Item#: 15 Planning Area: Daily Living Statement: manages own money	3	5	3	3.67
Item#: 16 Planning Area: Daily Living Statement: uses local transportation systems	5	5	5	5
				(continues)

Figure 12.3. *Continued.*

PART 2, Section V. *Continued.*				
	Home Rating	Student Rating	School Rating	Average Rating
Item#: 17 Planning Area: Leisure Activities Statement: performs indoor activities	5	5	5	5
Item#: 18 Planning Area: Leisure Activities Statement: performs outdoor activities	5	5	4	4.67
Item#: 19 Planning Area: Leisure Activities Statement: uses settings that offer entertainment	5	5	5	5
Item#: 20 Planning Area: Community Participation Statement: knows basic legal rights	3	4	2	3
Item#: 21 Planning Area: Community Participation Statement: participates as an active citizen	3	3	2	2.67
Item#: 22 Planning Area: Community Participation Statement: makes legal decisions	3	4	2	3
Item#: 23 Planning Area: Community Participation Statement: locates community services and resources	2	3	2	2.33
Item#: 24 Planning Area: Community Participation Statement: uses services and resources successfully	2	3	1	2
Item#: 25 Planning Area: Community Participation Statement: knows how to obtain financial assistance	1	1	1	1
Item#: 26 Planning Area: Health Statement: maintains good physical health	3	4	4	3.67
Item#: 27 Planning Area: Health Statement: addresses physical problems	2	3	4	3
Item#: 28 Planning Area: Health Statement: maintains good mental health	2	3	3	2.67
Item#: 29 Planning Area: Health Statement: addresses mental health problems	1	3	2	2
Item#: 30 Planning Area: Health Statement: knows about reproduction	5	5	4	4.67
Item#: 31 Planning Area: Health Statement: makes informed choices regarding sexual behavior	3	5	3	3.67
				(continues)

Figure 12.3. *Continued.*

PART 2, Section V. *Continued.*				
	Home Rating	Student Rating	School Rating	Average Rating
Item#: 32 Planning Area: Self-Determination Statement: recognizes and accepts own strengths and limitations	3	3	2	2.67
Item#: 33 Planning Area: Self-Determination Statement: expresses feelings and ideas appropriately	2	2	1	1.67
Item#: 34 Planning Area: Self-Determination Statement: expresses feelings and ideas confidently	2	3	1	2
Item#: 35 Planning Area: Self-Determination Statement: sets personal goals	3	4	3	3.33
Item#: 36 Planning Area: Self-Determination Statement: makes personal decisions	4	5	3	4
Item#: 37 Planning Area: Communication Statement: has needed speaking skills	3	3	3	3
Item#: 38 Planning Area: Communication Statement: has needed listening skills	2	4	2	2.67
Item#: 39 Planning Area: Communication Statement: has needed reading skills	1	0	2	1
Item#: 40 Planning Area: Communication Statement: has needed writing skills	2	3	2	2.33
Item#: 41 Planning Area: Interpersonal Relationships Statement: gets along with family members	3	4	3	3.33
Item#: 42 Planning Area: Interpersonal Relationships Statement: demonstrates knowledge and skills of parenting	NA	NA	NA	NA
Item#: 43 Planning Area: Interpersonal Relationships Statement: establishes and maintains friendships	3	4	3	3.33
Item#: 44 Planning Area: Interpersonal Relationships Statement: displays appropriate social behavior in variety of settings	2	3	3	2.67
Item#: 45 Planning Area: Interpersonal Relationships Statement: demonstrates skills for getting along with coworkers	2	3	2	2.33
Item#: 46 Planning Area: Interpersonal Relationships Statement: demonstrates skills for getting along with supervisors	3	3	2	2.67
				(continues)

Figure 12.3. *Continued.*

PART 3: FURTHER ASSESSMENT RECOMMENDATIONS

Section A. TPI — Levels 2 and 3

Transition Domain	Items for Level 2 Analysis (circle selected items)	Level 3 Instruments (indicate reference)
Employment	1 2 3 4 5	
		Study Skills Inventory
Further Education	6 7 8 9 ⑩	
Daily Living	11 12 13 14 15 16	
Leisure Activities	17 18 19	
Community Participation	20 21 22 23 24 25	
Health	26 27 28 29 30 31	
Self-Determination	32 33 34 35 36	
Communication	37 38 39 40	
Interpersonal Relationships	41 42 43 44 45 46	
Other _____		

Section B. Other Assessments

TPI Item Number	Instrument/Technique (observations, interviews, checklists/rating scales, curriculum-based measures, teacher-constructed devices, assistive technology evaluation, formal tests/inventories)
_____	_____
_____	_____
_____	_____

Section C. Special Evaluation(s):

Area	Contact
• Functional Behavioral Assessment	_____
• Speech/Language Evaluation	_____
• Vision Evaluation	_____
• Hearing Evaluation	_____
• Medical Examination	_____
• Physical Therapy Evaluation	_____
• Occupational Therapy Evaluation	_____
• Functional Vocational Evaluation	_____

Goals/ Objectives Needed	Further Assessment Needed	Transition Knowledge and Skill Statements	Notes
☐	☐	10. Can succeed in an appropriate postsecondary program.	_____ _____
☐	☒	Can use the academic support skills (e.g., organizational skills, time management, and other study skills) necessary to succeed in a given postsecondary setting.	_____ _____ _____ _____ _____
☐	☐	Can perform reading skills required in the program.	
			(continues)

Figure 12.3. *Continued.*

Goals/ Objectives Needed	Further Assessment Needed	Transition Knowledge and Skill Statements	Notes
		PART 3, Section C. *Continued.*	
☐	☐	Can perform writing skills required in the program.	———— ————
☐	☐	Can perform math skills required in the program.	————
☐	☐	Can analyze information and draw conclusions.	————
☐	☒	Can manage finances.	————
☒	☒	Knows how to balance priorities among classes, work, home duties, and leisure time.	———— ————
☒	☐	Knows how to use disability support services.	————
☒	☐	Knows how to develop a social support system.	————
☒	☐	Knows how to assess (with others) what types of support/modifications are needed.	———— ————
☐	☐	Knows how to appropriately meet with instructor (or professor) to discuss and advocate for reasonable accommodations (e.g., manner of presentation, timeliness, knowledge of necessary reasonable accommodations).	———— ———— ———— ———— ————
☐	☒	Knows how to develop and implement a plan and a time line for completion of postsecondary training program.	———— ———— ————

PART 4: PLANNING NOTES FORM

Student: Chris   Date: May 4, 2001

Likely Postschool Settings:

Employment/Further Education: Community college or training program
Living Arrangement: Independent with friends

Directions: List the important strengths and suggested transition needs on this page that you conclude from your analysis of the TPI Profile. Under the needs section, add any **new** transition needs **after** further assessment on TPI items showing discrepancies, "Don't Know" responses, or the need for more specification.

If desired, each need can be coded as an instructional need (**I**), a linkage need (**L**), or both (**I/L**).

Relative Strengths		Transition Needs	
		Initial Analysis	After Further Assessment
E	• Work completion on deadline schedule • Unpaid work experience • Creativity	• Career goal • Connection between artistic talent and career options	*(continues)*

Figure 12.3. *Continued.*

PART 4. *Continued.*

	Relative Strengths	Transition Needs	
		Initial Analysis	After Further Assessment
FE	• Math and science • Project work • Objective test-taking skills	• Organizational study skills • Reading • Note taking • Organizational/ writing	3/30/01 • Strategies for comprehension of information presented auditorally • Concentration on auditory stimuli
DL	*NA*	*NA*	*NA*
L	*NA*	*NA*	*NA*
CP	• Church volunteer	• Decision-making strategies • Impulsivity control • Awareness of responsibility	
H		• Sleep regulation • Alternatives to medication for attention deficits	
S-D	• Knowledge of personal strengths and weaknesses	• Self-assessment skills • Goal setting	
C	• One-on-one communication skills	• Communicating in groups • Interpreting nonverbal communication cues	
IR	• Personal friendships • Working relationship with yearbook staff	• Impulsivity control in social settings	

Additional Comments:

_____

_____

_____

Figure 12.3. *Continued.*

PART 5: PRESENT LEVELS OF PERFORMANCE AND GOAL STATEMENTS

Employment	PLOP: Chris is able to complete work on a deadline schedule. He has identified a career area of interest, but he has not made specific postsecondary plans.	
	Instructional Goal: Chris will be able to locate and describe requirements and benefits of three art-related careers.	Linkage Goal: Chris will participate in shadowing an art student from a local community college to learn more about the demands of college.
Postsecondary Education/ Training	PLOP: Chris excels in math and science. He is highly distracted during silent reading assignments, and he dislikes written work. He needs study skills to help him organize his thoughts in writing.	
	Instructional Goal: Chris will utilize prewriting activities or graphic organizers as a preliminary step in completing written work or note taking.	Linkage Goal:
Community Participation	PLOP: Chris participates in volunteer programs. He sometimes disregards rules as a result of making decisions impulsively.	
	Instructional Goal: Chris will demonstrate his ability to utilize three strategies for impulse control.	Linkage Goal:
Health	PLOP: Chris maintains his current medicine schedule for his TS. He continues to have difficulty maintaining a sleep schedule that accommodates his school life.	
	Instructional Goal: Chris will learn how his sleep deficits affect his academic performance and maintain a daily routine that accommodates his sleep pattern.	Linkage Goal: Chris will meet with his psychologist and discuss alternative strategies to medicine for reducing his impulsivity.

(continues) |

Figure 12.3. *Continued.*

PART 5. *Continued.*		
Self-Determination	PLOP: Chris knows his own strengths and weaknesses. He has difficulty assessing his academic progress and clearly defining his goals.	
	Instructional Goal: Chris will demonstrate his ability to maintain a progress sheet for each of his classes, recording assignment lists and grades.	Linkage Goal: Chris will meet with the school guidance counselor to determine two postsecondary programs to which he will apply.
Communication	PLOP: Chris's one-on-one communication skills are sufficient. Speaking in front of large groups and using written communication pose difficulties for him.	
	Instructional Goal: Chris will develop and utilize three strategies that facilitate his communication skills during group activities.	Linkage Goal:
Interpersonal Relationships	PLOP: Chris has many friends and works well collaboratively. He lacks strategies to control his impulsivity, resulting in strained social and work relationships.	
	Instructional Goal: Chris will demonstrate his ability to reflect on social interactions by maintaining a self-reflective journal.	Linkage Goal: Chris will participate in peer support group for teens in his church community.

Figure 12.3. *Continued.*

a brief background sketch of Chris; a profile generated from the administration of the *Transition Planning Inventory* (higher scores indicate perceived strength and lower scores indicate perceived need); further assessment activities; a planning notes form that summarizes strengths and needs; and selected present levels of performance and goal statements that should be part of Chris's IEP and/or transition plan. Chris's situation shows the complexity and thoroughness that is required in this planning process.

No matter what format is used, several aspects of transition planning must be addressed during the planning stage. Wehman (1995) suggested developing a plan that has the following characteristics:

- Involves choice and participation by the student
- Involves choice and participation by the family
- Involves options in postsecondary education, employment, community living, and other post–age-21 choices
- Involves individualized annual goals with steps planned to reach each goal, including skills for employment and community living
- Identifies individual(s) responsible for each aspect of the plan
- Plans 5 to 7 years prior to exiting
- Becomes part of the IEP and eventually part of the individual rehabilitation plan or service plan of the major adult service provider
- Encourages the coordinated efforts of all appropriate agencies, including local education agencies (LEAs); vocational education, rehabilitation, and adult service providers; and related services, to name a few (students and parents need to recognize that adult agencies, such as state labor departments, use different types of plans to reflect the goals of individual agencies)
- Develops a plan that is easy for students and parents to understand and use

Instructional Considerations

The instructional component of the transition process is the nuts and bolts of daily life in the student's school experience. What is taught and how it is taught can make the difference in the level of accomplishment a student will achieve in a transition program — and eventually in adjustment to adulthood (Cronin & Patton, 1993; Sitlington, 1996; Wehman, 1992). School-based personnel must take into consideration not only what is taught but where the instruction takes place, the method or technique used, and materials used during the instructional process (Cronin & Patton, 1993). In this section we provide an overview of the two instructional situations advocated by numerous professionals (Cronin & Patton, 1993; Evers, 1996; Falvey, 1996; Sitlington, 1996; Wehman, 1992; Woolcock & Domaracki, 1995) in preparing students for transition to the next subsequent environment: classroom-based and community-based instruction.

Classroom instruction is important in preparing students to apply basic academic skills to real-life situations in natural environments (Cronin & Patton, 1993). Classroom instruction gives students the opportunity to be introduced to, and practice, skills prior to encountering them in the natural environment. Examples include money identification; how to make change; use of calculators; vocabulary development; how to fill out various types of applications for employment, credit, and housing; and so on. The classroom can also be the place where people from the natural environment are introduced prior to actual on-site visits by the students. These resource people are valuable to teachers and schools who are preparing for community instruction or have experienced barriers to instruction taking place in the community. They can introduce concepts, describe their job tasks and the types of jobs associated with their business, outline the training needed to perform those jobs, and so forth.

Traditionally, instruction in schools has taken place in individual classrooms, and topics found naturally outside the classroom have rarely ventured past the front door of the school building. The few exceptions to this are science classes (studying plant life, water habitats such as ponds and creeks), physical education classes (practicing outdoor sports), and driver's education. The trend in recent times has been to explore the value of going into the natural environment to apply the basic skills of reading, writing, speaking, listening, mathematics, and thinking skills to real-life situations. Examples of community-based activities include the following:

- Comparison shopping for everything from food to clothes to cars

- Depositing weekend babysitting or lawn-mowing money in a savings account in a bank

- Preparing lunch for the class within a budget, reflecting nutritional guidelines and taking into consideration the group's likes and dislikes

- Learning how to ride public transportation using transfers to and from school, work, shopping areas, and so on

- Exploring the recreational activities available in the community that meet interests and economic resources (e.g., free concerts, high school or university sporting events, movies, eating out, car shows)

- Exploring volunteer options in the community to gain experiences and exposure to a variety of jobs and working situations (e.g., hospitals, day-care centers, camps, libraries, city or county agencies, fire or police departments, plant nurseries, recycling centers)

When instruction takes place in the community, students must be adequately prepared prior to leaving campus (e.g., permissions are sought, safety instruction given, adequate insurance coverage obtained). Community sites also need to be prepared for instruction to take place at their location (e.g., notification of visit sent to site manager, with an explanation of the purpose of the visit; ensurance of adequate supervision of the students at the site). In addition, an evaluation of each student's performance of tasks in the community is essential.

Transition Linkage Considerations

As a student enters the final year or two of formal schooling, the process of identifying the adult agencies and resources necessary to coordinate the transition to the student's next subsequent environment becomes imperative. This concept is by no means a new one, as noted earlier in this chapter. High school students, their parents, and guidance counselors have been using a process to link high school juniors and seniors with potential colleges and universities through holding high school college nights, preparing students for college entrance tests, sharing college and university admission contacts with students and parents, and setting meetings with college recruiters and potential students. In formalizing transition planning for students with special needs, this process has extended to additional adult service providers other than institutions of higher education.

Employment

Employment is one of the most frequently chosen postsecondary options for students when exiting a high school. This is the obvious option when a student has to work for economic reasons, is not considering further education, or chooses not to continue school at this point. For many persons, once employment starts, it continues until retirement. In the current business environment, however, which is characterized by company downsizing, merging, and restructuring, people need to be prepared for the possibility of multiple jobs before retirement. To best prepare students for employment under any circumstances, instruction in general job skills that gives the student the background for finding a job (e.g., the type of job that best suits the individual's interests and abilities, places to look for a job, application and interviewing skills) as well as keeping and maintaining the job he or she eventually gets (e.g., the interpersonal/social skills needed on the job, financial skills to manage money earned) becomes a necessity.

The transition coordinator often needs to make contacts in the community to find situations for students who need additional support on the job in the initial stages of learning job tasks or who will need ongoing support. The transition coordinator needs to determine which employers would be willing to employ students of varying abilities. Some students will need little, if any, assistance in acquiring and mastering job tasks, whereas others will need help initially for a few weeks up to several months, and still others will need ongoing workplace support from a job coach throughout their employment. In this latter situation, the student and school need to arrange for transition services with the state vocational rehabilitation agency or other designated service provider.

Additional Education / Training

The additional education and training option will be as varied as the students using it. An important factor to consider with this option is the availability of postsecondary educational experiences in the student's immediate community and in surrounding or nearby communities. Postsecondary experiences are defined as those experiences open to any adult in the community who wants to further his or her knowledge. These options may include the following:

- Noncredit classes at local colleges, universities, local school systems, YMCA/YWCA, recreational centers, adult education centers, hospitals, car dealerships, and so forth

- Credit classes at colleges and universities

- Vocational/technical institutes and colleges

- Military training/service

Living Arrangements

When students exit high school, many anticipate leaving their parents' home and seeking their own housing. Options include a dormitory room; an apartment by themselves; or a house or apartment shared with roommates, siblings, or other relative(s). Whatever the chosen option, many basic life skills (i.e., cooking, cleaning, banking, shopping) need to be mastered in preparation for the experience. Independent living centers are resource centers that provide a variety of courses and instructional opportunities for individuals who are interested in acquiring different life skills. These centers are located in each state.

Community/Daily Living Skills

In order to prepare young people for life after high school, community or daily living skills instruction must begin early in their school careers. In preschool and kindergarten, children learn the importance of dressing one's self, cleaning up one's mess, sharing a toy, "cooking" in class, having the responsibility of a "job" in class, going on field trips, and so on, and the life skill is introduced or taught within an academic situation. Unfortunately, after kindergarten the application to daily life of what one learns in an academic situation is rarely emphasized. This approach is discontinued, lost, or thought not to be important until high school graduation. Each person observes the day-to-day experiences of life during elementary and secondary years. Some life skills are taught directly, whereas others are imitated and learned, but many are taken for granted because someone else takes the responsibility for doing the task. We advocate the teaching of life skills throughout the student's school experience, regardless of the student's age or grade.

Student Transition Portfolios

Each student should leave school with documentation of experiences he or she had up to that point. Transcripts offer information only on the academic experiences of an individual. Especially for individuals with disabilities, whose records do not provide a clear picture of their accomplishments, portfolios are essential. Additional documentation could be assembled in a resume, portfolio, packet, dossier, file, or scrapbook to reflect the student's nonacademic experiences. These could include activities that took place during their school years, such as work experiences (both paid and volunteer); travel, both independent and with others; special training; special competitions; performances; and so on. Documentation could be in the form of letters of recommendation, evaluations, photographs, awards, videos, journals, permanent products, newspaper clippings, and so forth. The format and extent of such a collection of documents can be as different as the individuals whose life experiences are reflected in them. The permanent documentation of activities for future reference is the important factor for a student when he or she is preparing for transition to postsecondary settings.

Issues Related to Transition Planning

Transition planning for students with disabilities encompasses a number of components, including the instructional considerations and linkages that must be addressed for the students to be successful after leaving the formal school situation. Within the transition planning process, however, additional related issues should be considered. These issues include family involvement; social skills development; student choice and consumer-directed activities; collaboration between and within the school, the district, and other agencies; and the need for follow-up or follow-along studies during the transition process.

Family Involvement

Family involvement in the transition planning process would seem to be a natural outgrowth of the mandate for parental involvement delineated in IDEA. Although IDEA did not specifically change the parental role in the transition planning process, parents, guardians, and advocates for students can make critical contributions and add perspectives regarding the students' observed preferences, interests, and abilities (Clark, 1996). Parents and guardians also play a key role in the coordination of transition services after their child formally exits the school system. Parents and guardians must be aware of the overall direction the student's transition plan is taking as they perform their role as service coordinators. Parents are the indirect consumers of transition services, often coordinating not only those services but also the adjustments in daily living that must take place in order for the student to successfully participate.

The involvement of parents and guardians in the transition planning process empowers them to serve as both advocates and service coordinators for their adolescent with special needs (Patton & Browder, 1988). Through the ITP process, parents, the student, school officials, and the adult service providers can come to an agreement regarding the direction the transition plan will take. All parties involved in the process must clearly identify their goals and values with respect to the student's future. This helps to clarify differences in goals early in the planning process and allows for resolution of those differences. School officials must also recognize the importance of active and equal participation in the ITP decision-making process by parents and students (Blalock & Patton, 1996).

In addition to identifying goals and values, educators and adult agency providers also need to coordinate the ITP to accommodate the student's cultural values and traditions. "Successful comprehensive service planning will need to acknowledge values, value conflicts, and their possible consequences for the youth in transition" (Patton & Browder, 1988). The transition plan must match the needs and values of the student and his or her family to ensure the success of the actual transition.

Social Skills Training

Persons with disabilities are often unemployed or underemployed (Elksnin & Elksnin, 1995). Although the lack of basic academic skill development or appropriate vocational training might seem to be the cause of under- or unemployment, social skills deficits are the primary reason (Okolo & Sitlington, 1986). In a survey of employers, Elksnin and Elksnin reported that the most common reason for the rejection of a job applicant is interpersonal skills deficits. An inability to communicate, immaturity, a lack of appropriate manners, and affected mannerisms were often cited as the primary causes for rejection of an applicant.

Although employers value social skills development as a positive indicator of future job success, most are unwilling to provide time or opportunities for job applicants to learn these skills on the job (Schloss & Schloss, 1984). The transition process therefore must address social skills development prior to completion of the student's school experience. A review of social skills curricula made it apparent that many traditional programs do not address specific job-related social skills (Elksnin & Elksnin, 1995). Within the transition planning process, both assessment and planning for social skills training must take place.

Elksnin and Elksnin (1995) reviewed studies of necessary social skills for job readiness as identified by employers, vocational educators, and vocational counselors. Examples of social skills thought to be essential on the job include abilities to work effectively with and without supervision, to take criticism constructively, and to give instructions to another employee. Many commercially available social skills curricula do not address such skills. The ITP committee must assess the level of the student's social skills ability and address any specific social skills needed with respect to those identified by employers for job success and those required of particular jobs.

Student Choice and Consumer-Directed Activities

The transition planning process, as outlined in IDEA, stipulates that not only should the student be present at the ITP meeting but that his or her preferences and interests are to be taken into account when writing the ITP. Without careful decision-making training and opportunities to participate in decision-making activities prior to the transition planning process, students with disabilities may not be able to participate fully and effectively. There is increasing evidence that students who are actively involved in the decision making, planning, and implementing of their own ITPs perform better than students who simply attend the ITP meeting (Wehmeyer, 1992).

Self-determination, or the ability to make decisions about one's future, is a key element in achieving success for the student with a disabling condition (Field, 1996). Not only is self-determination necessary for consumer-directed participation in the transition planning process, but self-determination skills play a large part in the success of the student in the workplace or postsecondary educational experience. In studying the literature on self-determination and success in the workplace, Deci, Connell, and Ryan (1989) concluded that self-determination not only is related to more effective employee performance but is positively associated with employee satisfaction, quality of life, and organizational effectiveness.

To participate in self-determination, a student must understand his or her strengths and weaknesses and accept those as part of himself or herself (Field & Hoffman, 1994). Through this understanding and acceptance, the student is then able to more effectively learn to plan, initiate a behavior, and respond effectively to the changing needs of his or her environment (Field, 1996). Self-determination is not a skill that is developed overnight. Ideally, it is part of the overall experience for the student with disabilities, beginning early in the educational process; however, it is necessary for the overall success of both the transition plan and its outcome to address student choice and consumer-directed activities early in the transition process. See Table 12.4 for a discussion of types of meetings that can be held to encourage self-determination.

Collaboration

Collaboration among the school, the local education agency, and adult service providers frequently has been discussed as necessary to promote effective transition planning (Patton & Browder, 1988). Although interagency collaboration is identified as one of the three most important aspects in successful transitions, it is often ill defined and not in place (Kohler, 1993). Parents and guardians find that as the student leaves the educational system, the support provided by the system for years disappears and they are left to figure out by themselves how to maintain the collaboration among various agencies.

This lack of collaborative effort among agencies serving young adults with disabling conditions indicates the need for a more formalized collaborative structure. Patton and Browder (1988) delineated four steps that facilitate inter-agency cooperation:

1. The development of interagency agreements that formalize the collaborative process would enable the parents and student to coordinate services effectively.

2. The loosening of organizational and procedural constraints would facilitate the provision of necessary services from different agencies.

3. Interagency meetings to negotiate the scope, parameters, responsibilities, and funding configurations for persons with disabilities would provide more effective service delivery.

TABLE 12.4
Types of Meetings to Encourage Self-Determination

Characteristic	Student-Led Conferences	Student-Centered Planning	Student-Directed Meeting
Purpose	Student shares academic and classroom work with family and teacher(s); normally uses portfolio or some other information-gathering system	Student is at the center of planning for school, community, and future	Student leads or is active facilitator in IEP or transition planning
Grade level	Elementary grades through graduation	Elementary grades through graduation and beyond	Middle grades through graduation and beyond
Who is involved?	Student, family members, teacher(s)	Student, family members, friends, relevant professionals	Student, family members, relevant professionals
How often does the meeting occur?	Each time a school-based conference is held (e.g., every quarter, every semester, annually)	Depends, could be once, annually, or multiple times	Annually or upon need of student, family, or school personnel
Average length of meeting	30 minutes–1 hour	1–3 hours	1–3 hours
Outcomes of the meeting	Student learns to assess value of work, selects appropriate artifacts, articulates progress and needs for improvement	Student is central to capacity-based discussion on strengths and needs, vision for the future, and development of an action plan to achieve goals	Student provides self-assessment, current and future goals, and ways to achieve them

Note. From *Student-Focused Conferencing and Planning* (p. 11), by D. S. Bassett & J. Lehmann, 2002, Austin, TX: PRO-ED. Copyright 2002 by PRO-ED, Inc. Reproduced with permission.

4. An agreement on the method for implementing collaborative agreements would put the needs of the client, rather than the needs of the agencies, at the forefront.

As parents and guardians grapple with the enormous job of coordinating services for adult children with disabilities, it becomes apparent that they need a transition specialist to help them in this process (Patton & Browder,

1988). Transition specialists could serve as liaisons between the parents and the schools and other agencies to coordinate adult programs and services, assist in the establishment and accomplishment of goals, and support the individuals with disabilities and their families. The use of informal strategies for collaboration to assist individuals with disabilities and their families continues to be the most prominent method for enabling students to effectively use the transition planning period to make a successful entry into the adult community, however.

Follow-Up/Follow-Along

The final related issue to transition planning has to do with follow-up/follow-along studies of individuals with disabilities. Sitlington (1996) addressed the need to document the preparation of young adults with disabilities for life in the community. She identified several key issues that should be studied to determine how to most effectively serve these students as they enter the community. The issues can be divided into two areas: the identification of skills and abilities necessary for successful life in the community and the determination of the programs and planning processes used to successfully integrate individuals with disabilities into the adult community.

To determine those skills and abilities necessary for successful adult transitions, Sitlington (1996) called for the development of competencies that focus not only on employment skills but also on the skills necessary to maintain a home; to have appropriate involvement in the community, including recreation and leisure activities; and to develop satisfying personal and social relationships. Programs to enhance and develop these skills should be available not only to students with disabilities in special education settings but also to students in general education settings. In addition, Sitlington advocated for these skills being integrated into the current curriculum rather than simply added on as experiences reserved for students with more severe disabilities.

Sitlington (1996) also stated that follow-up/follow-along studies must look beyond employment outcomes to adjustment to life in the adult community. Studying the experiences the student encounters, the instruction given both in and out of the classroom, and the planning done for the student's move into the adult community will give a clearer picture of the most effective transition practices. Through this examination process, educators and other professionals can begin to formulate more effective strategies for enabling students with disabilities to become successful adults.

Conclusion

In this chapter, we have reviewed the importance and stages of the transition planning process for special populations. We firmly believe that these concepts are important for all students, not only those with special needs. All professionals who work with students with special needs must constantly remind themselves of their roles as advocates for these students' futures.

References

Affleck, J. Q., Edgar, E., Levine, P., & Kottering, L. (1990). Postschool status of students classified as mildly retarded, learning disabled, or nonhandicapped: Does it get better with time? *Education and Training in Mental Retardation, 25*, 315–324.

Bassett, D., & Smith, T. E. C. (1996). Transition in an era of reform. *Journal of Learning Disabilities, 29*, 161–166.

Bassett, D. S., & Lehmann, J. (2002). *Student-focused conferencing and planning.* Austin, TX: PRO-ED.

Benz, M., & Halpern, A. S. (1993). Vocational and transition services needed and received by students with disabilities during their last year of high school. *Career Development for Exceptional Individuals, 16*, 197–211.

Blalock, G., & Patton, J. R. (1996). Transition and students with learning disabilities: Creating sound futures. *Journal of Learning Disabilities, 29*, 7–16.

Brigance, A. H. (1995). *Life skills inventory.* North Billerica, MA: Curriculum Associates.

Brolin, D. E. (1992). *Life-centered career education (LCCE) knowledge and performance batteries.* Reston, VA: The Council for Exceptional Children.

Clark, G. M. (1996). Transition planning assessment for secondary-level students with learning disabilities. *Journal of Learning Disabilities, 29*, 79–92.

Clark, G. M., & Patton, J. R. (1997). *Transition planning inventory.* Austin, TX: PRO-ED.

Cronin, M. E., & Patton, J. R. (1993). *Life skills instruction for students with special needs: A practical guide for integrating real-life content into the curriculum.* Austin, TX: PRO-ED.

Deci, E. L., Connell, J. P., & Ryan, R. M. (1989). Self-determination in a work organization. *Journal of Applied Psychology, 74*, 580–590.

Dunn, C. (1996). A status report on transition planning for individuals with learning disabilities. *Journal of Learning Disabilities*, *29*, 17–30.

Edgar, E. (1988). Employment as an outcome for mildly handicapped students: Current status and future directions. *Focus on Exceptional Children*, *21*(1), 1–8.

Education for All Handicapped Children Act of 1975, 20 U.S.C. § 1400 *et seq.*

Elksnin, L., & Elksnin, N. (1995). *Assessment and instruction of social skills.* San Diego, CA: Singular.

Enderle, J., & Severson, S. (1997). *Enderle-Severson transition rating scale–revised.* Moorehead, MN: Practical Press.

Evers, R. B. (1996). The positive force of vocational education: Transition outcomes for students with learning disabilities. *Journal of Learning Disabilities*, *29*, 69–78.

Falvey, M. A. (1996). *Community-based curriculum.* Baltimore: Brookes.

Field, S. (1996). Self-determination instructional strategies for youth with learning disabilities. *Journal of Learning Disabilities*, *29*, 40–52.

Field, S., & Hoffman, A. (1994). Development of a model of self-determination. *Career Development for Exceptional Individuals*, *17*, 159–169.

Goals 2000: Educate America Act of 1994, 20 U.S.C. § 5801 *et seq.*

Halpern, A. S. (1985). Transition: A look at the foundations. *Exceptional Children*, *51*, 479–486.

Halpern, A. S. (1993). Quality of life as a conceptual framework for evaluating transition outcomes. *Exceptional Children*, *59*, 486–498.

Halpern, A. S. (1994). The transition of youth with disabilities to adult life: A position statement of the Division on Career Development and Transition, The Council for Exceptional Children. *Career Development for Exceptional Individuals*, *17*, 115–124.

Halpern, A. S., Herr, C., Wolf, N., Doren, B., Johnson, M. D., & Lawson, J. D. (1997). *NEXT S.T.E.P.: Students' transition and educational planning.* Austin, TX: PRO-ED.

Halpern, A. S., Irvin, L., & Landman, J. J. (1979). *Tests for everyday living.* Monterey, CA: CTB/McGraw-Hill.

Halpern, A. S., Irvin, L., & Munkres, J. (1986). *Social and prevocational information battery–Revised.* Monterey, CA: CTB/McGraw-Hill.

Hasazi, S. B., Gordon, L. B., & Roe, C. A. (1985). Factors associated with the employment status of handicapped youth exiting from high school from 1979 to 1983. *Exceptional Children*, *51*, 455–469.

Individuals with Disabilities Education Act of 1990, 20 U.S.C. § 1400 *et seq.*

Karge, B. D., Patton, P. L., & de la Garza, B. (1992). Transition services for youth with mild disabilities: Do they exist, are they needed? *Career Development for Exceptional Individuals*, *15*, 47–68.

Keith, K. D., & Schalock, R. L. (1995). *Quality of student life questionnaire.* Worthington, OH: IDS.

Kohler, P. (1993). Best practices in transition: Substantiated or implied? *Career Development for Exceptional Individuals, 16,* 107–121.

Martin, J. E., & Huber Marshall, L. H. (1997). *Choicemaker: Self-determination for transition.* Longmont, CO: Sopris West.

McCarney, S. B. (1989). *Transition behavior scale* (2nd ed.). Columbia, MO: Hawthorne Educational Service.

Mithaug, D. E., Horiuchi, C. N., & Fanning, P. N. (1985). A report on the Colorado statewide follow-up survey of special education students. *Exceptional Children, 51,* 397–404.

Okolo, C., & Sitlington, P. A. (1986). The role of special education in LD adolescents' transition from school to work. *Learning Disability Quarterly, 9,* 292–306.

Patton, J. R., & Browder, P. M. (1988). Transitions into the future. In B. L. Ludlow, A. P. Turnbull, & R. Luckasson (Eds.), *Transitions to adult life for people with mental retardation: Principles and practices* (pp. 293–312). Baltimore: Brookes.

Patton, J. R., & Dunn, C. (1998). *Transition from school to young adulthood: Basic concepts and recommended practices.* Austin, TX: PRO-ED.

Polloway, E. A., Patton, J. R., Smith, J. D., & Roderique, T. W. (1991). Issues in program design for elementary students with mild retardation: Emphasis on curriculum development. *Education and Training in Mental Retardation, 26,* 142–150.

Schalock, R. L., & Keith, K. D. (1993). *Quality of life questionnaire.* Worthington, OH: IDS.

Schloss, C. N., & Schloss, P. J. (1984). Evaluation of table game designed to promote the acquisition of vocationally oriented social skills with mildly and moderately retarded adults. *Journal of Industrial Teacher Education, 21*(2), 12–25.

School to Work Opportunity Act of 1994, 20 U.S.C. § 6101 *et seq.*

Sitlington, P. A. (1996). Transition to living: The neglected component of transition programming for individuals with learning disabilities. *Journal of Learning Disabilities, 29,* 31–39.

Sitlington, P. A., Frank, A., & Carson, R. (1992). Adult adjustment among graduates with mild disabilities. *Exceptional Children, 51,* 221–233.

Wagner, M., Blackorby, J., Cameto, R., Hebbeler, K., & Newman, L. (1993). *The transition experiences of young people with disabilities: A summary of findings from the National Longitudinal Transition Study for Special Education Students.* Menlo Park, CA: SRI International.

Wagner, M., Newman, L., D'Amico, R., Jay, E. A., Butler-Nalin, P., Marder, C., et al. (1991). *Youth with disabilities: How are they doing? The first comprehensive report from the National Longitudinal Transition Study for Special Education Students*. Menlo Park, CA: SRI International.

Wehman, P. (1992). *Life beyond the classroom: Transition strategies for young people with disabilities*. Baltimore: Brookes.

Wehman, P. (1993). Transition from school to adulthood for young people with disabilities: Critical issues and policies. In R. C. Eaves & P. J. McLaughlin (Eds.), *Recent advances in special education and rehabilitation* (pp. 178–192). Boston: Andover Medical.

Wehman, P. (1995). *Individual transition plans: The teacher's curriculum guide for helping youth with special needs*. Austin, TX: PRO-ED.

Wehmeyer, M. (1992). Self-determination and the education of students with mental retardation. *Education and Training in Mental Retardation, 27*, 302–314.

Will, M. (1984). *OSERS programming for the transition of youth with disabilities: Bridges from school to working life*. Washington, DC: Office of Special Education and Rehabilitative Services.

Woolcock, W. W., & Domaracki, J. W. (1995). *Instructional strategies in the community: A resource guide for community instruction for persons with disabilities*. Austin, TX: PRO-ED.

WORKING WITH FAMILIES THROUGH
INTENTIONAL FAMILY INTERVIEWING

*Salvatore J. Rizzo, Pamela H. Varrin,
and Andrea G. Gurney*

amilies of individuals with disabling conditions are much like other families. They come in a variety of sizes, shapes, and compositions, each providing a unique learning environment for the developmental emergence
of family members. They change in response to predictable developmental
events or unpredictable life crises but bring a continuity of style to their attempts
to master life tasks. Like all families, they must adjust over time to the discrepancies between their ideal and real family lives, and they must manage transitions in a way that balances the needs of the whole family with those of each
member.

A main difference in families that have a member with a disability is that
problems associated with life transitions are often intensified (Mitchell &
Rizzo, 1985; Rolland, 1993). Negotiation of changes throughout the family life
cycle tends to occur with heightened emotions and in a wider social context.
The family whose child has a developmental disability meets the demands of
family life with concerns that are amplified but not necessarily different from
any family (Featherstone, 1980; Seligman, 1991). For helpers, the nature and
scope of challenges in a family with a child with a disabling condition may seem
foreign and overwhelming compared to other family experiences in their professional or personal lives.

One critical transition in the family life cycle is the launching of its dependent members toward autonomous functioning outside the family (Walsh, 1993).

Among other things in our society, this typically means occupational self-sufficiency. Launching is not a discrete event. It involves an extended educational process, usually culminating in an entry-level position in a crowded job market. The prospect of a child's becoming occupationally self-sufficient arouses much anxiety in any family (Gerson, 1995). For the family of a child with special needs, issues of occupational independence have likely stirred intense concern since the moment of the child's diagnosis. Often the family members shoulder added stress and responsibility throughout their child's development, as individuals with learning difficulty typically have limited awareness of the impact of their disability on their goals and tend to be less active participants in their own process of career development (Hitchings & Retish, 2000). Occupational concerns intensify for the family as young adulthood approaches.

Our purpose in this chapter is to assist the practitioner in working with families on problems of vocational transitioning as part of the launching of a young adult with special needs. We offer a systems perspective for understanding families, with consideration of the unique issues regarding vocational development that face families of children with disabling conditions. The focus is on assisting the helper in developing practical strategies to promote vocational solutions through use of systems interviewing techniques with families and individuals. The chapter describes Intentional Family Interviewing, a competency-based method of training helpers to refine their skills in structuring systems-oriented interventions with individuals and families. The case illustrations consider various types of disabilities in a representative, rather than exhaustive, fashion.

Choosing the Family Unit

A helper working from a systems framework is much like a photographer using a camera equipped with a zoom lens. The helper can vary perspectives by positioning the lens of assessment and intervention at graduated points on a range from environmental to individual levels. The most fundamental task of the helping professional is to select the social unit on which to focus energies as a means of solving the presenting problem (Haley, 1987) while still keeping the large picture in mind.

When the problem concerns the launching of a young adult with special needs into the workforce, the helper faces a complicated and sometimes overwhelming array of choices. Typically, families of children with special needs have had to manage relationships with multiple caregiving systems since the onset of the disability. In addition to issues that arise regarding vocational transitions at the individual and family levels, each caregiving system may exert a powerful effect on the course of vocational decision making. The helping professional needs to widen the lens of observation to take into account the role of each system in the vocational transition. He or she must then decide at which level to focus an intervention that can effectively advance the next step in a solution sequence. For example, the helper might choose to work at any point in time with the individual, members of the family unit, one or both parents, parts of the extended family, the school system, hospital or health systems, community or government agencies, or some combination of these systems. The choice is a judgment that the helper makes based on (a) an assessment of what is prompting the impasse in development and (b) a determination of the system that can most readily mobilize resources toward the resolution of the presenting problem.

Traditionally helpers have chosen to focus on the individual with special needs as the primary social unit, either by intentional selection or more probably due to routine practice. Most helpers receive training primarily in providing direct experiential services to the person defined as having the problem. In counseling for career development, the individual has historically held the central focus (Osipow & Fitzgerald, 1996). Consider the wealth of available aids for career planning, such as occupational information, interest inventories, and sophisticated decision-making systems. As common sense might dictate, these materials address the individual as the primary unit of assessment and intervention. Although the usefulness of these materials to individuals with special needs may vary, by their structure they have established a norm that the major work of vocational problem solving must logically be accomplished with the individual.

At the other end of the spectrum, some helpers focus on the wider social realities that impinge on the occupational opportunities available to individuals with special needs (Edmister, 1996; Gill, 1994; Singer & Powers, 1993). In a landmark study of children with disabilities, *The Unexpected Minority,* which is still relevant today, Gliedman and Roth (1980) made a strong case for the confining influence that societal factors play in the construction of most disabilities. They noted, "Perhaps 10 percent of all handicapped children possess a disability so limiting mentally or emotionally that they would not be able to lead normal lives even if prejudice against them melted away" (p. 4).

Recognizing that societal responses to disability may provide more daunting obstacles to employment than the disability itself, helping professionals may choose to focus their efforts on advocating for social change. For example, helpers may engage in political activism to equalize access to training and jobs through increasing public awareness and supporting legislation prohibiting discrimination in employment. Environmental interventions can focus on community, state, or federal levels. The current movement for inclusion of individuals with disabling conditions in all aspects of community life provides many opportunities for advocacy at a local level for equal participation in schools, recreational programs, and community activities.

For the helping practitioner, the family system offers an efficient social unit for understanding and organizing vocational problem solving for young adults with special needs. In whatever form a family is constructed, it is an essential social unit that bridges the gap between individual and environmental levels of social organization. Across the range of types and degrees of disability, the family operates as the mediating unit between the individual and society (Doherty & Campbell, 1988; Rolland, 1994). The family is the primary unit of socialization, the means through which social expectations are translated and transmitted to the individual. Family influences exert a powerful force on the development of career attitudes and options of persons with disabling conditions (Szymanski, 1994; Wehman, 1992). Reciprocally, the challenges of launching the young adult with special needs into the work world involves a significant developmental process that can reshape the family dramatically. The family can also act as a conduit to the larger society, conveying messages about how to change institutions to accommodate the needs of individual family members. Families can be both a potent source of change for the individual with a disabling condition and a potent resource for advocacy to larger social institutions.

When the helper determines that the family unit represents a crucial context for aiding the career development of a given individual, he or she needs to involve family members in a central way in the process of vocational problem solving. The importance of family members in this process cannot be emphasized enough. To engage the family or any part of it as primary rather than peripheral may demand a shift in theoretical orientation as well as an expansion of knowledge and skills. The experience of working collaboratively with the family system can also provide the practitioner with a model for working more effectively with other parts of the often complicated helping system.

Youth with Special Needs in Family Context

Any helper wishing to assist in the career development of a young adult with a disabling condition must possess an ecological awareness, recognizing that the development of this particular individual occurs in the interactive contexts of the family and larger social systems. From the moment of diagnosis, health professionals, school personnel, government agencies, and other players in this larger system have joined the family in determining expectations and deciding how best to support development. The extent to which the relationships between the family and parts of the larger system have been contentious or collaborative, mutual or disempowering, plays an important role in the family's expectations and resources when they arrive at the developmental task of launching the child into the workforce.

When the helper chooses to work with any part of the family unit in the career development of the young adult with a disabling condition, it reflects both an inclination toward systems thinking and a decision to focus the zoom lens on a specific scene in the social landscape. The systems orientation is a basic frame of reference for helping, a manifestation of a worldview that transfers attention beyond the individual to the social network. In the general systems theoretical approach, any unit of social organization takes on the characteristics of a living and self-regulating organism that is capable of initiating autonomous action as well as responding to outside stimulation (Bertalanffy, 1968). Concentration is on the interconnectedness of parts or elements of the system that are evident through observable sequences of information exchange. Social context is far more critical than is any individual element in isolation.

At the family level, this translates to an emphasis on patterns of interaction and organization among members rather than on the actions or feelings of an individual member. When career development of the individual with a disabling condition is at issue, the family systems approach regards the family's management of the problem as a mirror of the family organization. The family response is one illustration of standard sequences of problem solving in the family that probably applies to other problem issues as well. It is also a reflection of the family's historical experience in collaborating with the various parts of the larger helping network.

A major strategy for working effectively with family systems is to concentrate deliberately and exclusively on the solution of the presenting problem (Cummings, 1990; de Shazer, 1991; Haley, 1990). All families organize and mobilize around identified problems in a way that yields an immediate indication of typical family process. The presenting problem in a family can afford the helper with an energized access route to change repetitive family patterns while also solving the problem. A critical aspect of a problem-solving approach is to respect the presenting concern as real, not illusory. The problem and the family response to it are crucial features of the way the family functions. There is no need for the helper to regard the presenting problem as a distraction intended to divert attention from more basic family issues. Likewise, the helper need not impose speculative interpretations that connect the problem to fundamental difficulties within the individual or family unit that are somehow bubbling beneath the surface of the expressed concern. By simply seeking resolution of the presenting difficulty, the helper gains an opportunity to change the family organization concurrently. Haley (1987) stated, "With this approach the focus is on respecting and utilizing what the family considers important, the presenting problem, and what the therapist thinks is important, an organizational change" (p. 85).

Consider the case of Anita, a 17-year-old high school student with a developmental disability. Anita had been enrolled for the past year in a general course of study at the regional vocational technical school. The combination of Anita's enthusiasm and dedication, with the academic supports available in this program, had resulted in a more successful year than anyone had imagined when her mother had requested her inclusion in the program. Midway into Anita's second year of the program, her academic performance began to decline. Her teachers, thinking the academic material might be getting too challenging for her, responded by increasing the time she spent in one-on-one academic support outside the classroom. After several months of increased services, her academic performance had not improved, and more troubling, her enthusiasm had given way to almost complete social withdrawal. School personnel were beginning to consider a transfer back to a substantially separate special needs program when the school counselor was asked to call Anita's parents for a conference. Through the use of a family systems approach, the school counselor hoped to mobilize the family toward a more effective organization in the process of resolving the identified problem with Anita.

The first task for the counselor was to decide whom to invite to the session. The family constellation included Anita, her mother, a recently included stepfather, and an older sister. Anita's parents had divorced when Anita was a toddler. Her father remarried several years later and presently lived out of state with his new family. Anita visited her father and his family often, and he and Anita's mother enjoyed a relatively cooperative co-parenting relationship. Anita's mother had remarried within the past year, and relations between father and new stepfather were also cordial. Anita's older sister commuted from home to a private college in a neighboring city where she was enjoying a successful freshman year. The counselor decided to engage the new parental subsystem in this phase of problem solving, and invited Anita's mother and stepfather to join Anita in the first meeting.

It was strikingly evident to the counselor early in the first meeting that this was a family in transition. Since the time of her divorce, Anita's mother had been accustomed to making decisions regarding Anita's care essentially by herself, with long-distance support and input from Anita's father. In this structure she carried the major responsibility for vigilance concerning Anita's welfare. With her remarriage, another interested and concerned adult entered the system, but he did not have a clearly defined role with regard to Anita. In the course of the session dialogue, the counselor observed that Anita's mother wished to share parenting responsibility with her new husband, but she seemed to feel both unsure of his capabilities and wary of overburdening him with challenging tasks. For his part, the new husband appeared eager to share parenting but seemed hesitant to take initiative out of respect for his wife's experience with her daughter and because of uncertainty regarding his own skills.

The counselor became increasingly aware of a level of tension in the marital relationship when they discussed issues relating to Anita's care. With further inquiry and observation of related sequences, the counselor noticed that Anita's escalating problems seemed to have the paradoxical effect of reducing the level of tension in the relationship. Once a problem escalated in intensity above a certain threshold, Anita's mother would turn to her new husband for support, while Anita would sit passively looking confused and somewhat upset. By giving the stepfather a framework in which to respond in a parenting role, Anita's mother had begun to break the impasse about what roles they could each play in the new parenting relationship; however, nobody seemed clear or comfortable with the process or outcome. The parents remained blocked in translating these exchanges into deliberate decisions about how to handle shared parenting.

The helper's observation and testing of patterns in the session led to a tentative working hypothesis that marital tension regarding Anita apparently began shortly after the stepfather entered the family. The tension seemed related to an organizational pattern in which the mother was quite vigilant about Anita's well-being while the stepfather remained excluded but interested in Anita's day-to-day problems. Anita's regression at school seemed to serve the functions of reducing marital discord and keeping the newly blended family system intact by focusing the couple's energies on her. With access to such data, the temptation for a helper is to tread fearlessly into an open explanation of the observed difficulties in family adjustment or to explicitly label the problem as the pathological reaction of one of the members (probably Anita or the mother). Instead, the counselor remained centered on the problem in hopes of directing the family toward a solution that would give the stepfather a clearer role within the family without displacing the mother from her important position.

As a first step, the counselor directed the stepfather to speak with school personnel to better understand the problems and explore available options. The stepfather would then present this information to his wife, who would add her experience and expertise to the mix. Together they would decide on a course of action to be carried out with the school. A follow-up meeting with the family one month later revealed more joint participation in Anita's activities. Through their teamwork in gathering information and negotiating with school personnel, the parents were instrumental in focusing attention on the need for curriculum-based modifications within the classroom rather than out-of-class tutoring. With the appropriate supports in school and in the family, Anita's functioning had begun to improve on both academic and social dimensions.

A family systems approach that is focused concurrently on problem resolution and organizational change can be helpful in prompting career development of a young adult with a developmental disability, even when that is not the primary issue in counseling. Let us speculate that Anita's family had made its request for help to a mental health facility with a presenting problem of marital discord or even the stepfather's depression. It would be similarly important for the helper to respect that problem while simultaneously moving toward family restructuring. Here the counselor might promote the stepfather's inclusion in family activities through assigning tasks aimed at increasing marital partnership or alleviating his depression. Such tasks could even include greater participation in Anita's school activities. In this approach it is only by explicit agreement with the family that the helper in either the school or mental health setting would focus on solution of a presenting problem different from the one negotiated at the onset of the helping contract. As family organization changes toward the solution of the primary problem, however other problems frequently are spontaneously resolved.

A solution-centered strategy within the family systems perspective is well tailored for professional settings that address vocational development of youth with special needs. It is a flexible and short-term method that is consistent with the time-limited helping contacts that most agencies and school settings demand of their staff. The emphasis on positive resource mobilization over pathology identification is congruent with the functional, developmental, and humanistic frameworks that should be present in educational and rehabilitation facilities. As an active, strength-based approach that respects the statement of the problem offered by the family, the method tends also to elicit the cooperation of important family members.

Successful use of systems strategies depends largely on the helper's skill in reconceptualizing the problem in system terms. To help families reorganize around the career decision making of a member with special needs necessitates that the helper formulate a systems redefinition of the presenting problem. This involves expanding the lens of observation and assessment to a macro systems level and refocusing down to family system or subsystem themes, patterns, and sequences. The helper's capacity to do so is based in part on openness to clinical intuition and on nurturance of that instinct with a solid knowledge base. At minimum, the helper needs to have familiarity with (a) the basic concepts and language of family systems thinking, (b) the unique issues facing families of children with developmental disabilities, and (c) an ecological framework for understanding the career life cycle in families with a child who has a disability.

Applied System Concepts

Within the expanding field of family systems therapy, there are a number of core concepts, including the ideas of homeostasis, stuck communication sequences, boundaries, hierarchy, and family life cycle. These concepts form the theoretical foundation of helper behaviors in performing a family evaluation and in conducting interventions with the family system.

Helpers must understand that all members of the family need not be present to accomplish a family assessment or intervention. The systems-oriented counselor can explore and assess patterns related to these core concepts with as few as one family member present. Skilled helpers use the gathered information to actively promote change in problem patterns on a step-by-step basis, something that can be done quite effectively with any number of family members in the room (Allen, 1994). The role of the systems-oriented counselor is much like a consultant to the family system. The counselor collaborates with the family member(s) present to gain an understanding of patterns associated with the problems and solutions. The helper is mentally quite active (and sometimes also very active verbally) in trying to gain information about how patterns and sequences fit together to help make sense of the problem. The core concepts described in the following paragraphs help the counselor organize the data into a conceptual scheme that promotes the co-generation of ideas about what steps might be taken next to solve the presenting problem.

Homeostasis refers to the tendency of the family organism to resist change in order to maintain a comfortable status quo. It is a dynamic equilibrium, a delicate set of balances that allows constant fluctuation but only within established limits. Even when the family is faced with potential upheaval from internal or external stresses, homeostatic mechanisms in the family exert a stabilizing influence on family exchanges. Homeostasis becomes manifest in the recurrent roles that members occupy, in rules that govern distance and closeness among family members, and in the intensity with which the family shields itself from events or information that might disturb the current family configuration. By virtue of homeostatic principles, all behavior in family systems becomes functional either in maintaining or transforming the complex set of balances in the family (Rolland, 1994). Even behavior that appears dysfunctional at first glance becomes sensible and purposeful when viewed within the perspective of family homeostasis.

For example, parental expectations about a child's vocational potential are a frequent source of discussion and difference in vocational problem solving with helpers across school or agency settings. From a nonsystems perspective, the helper may judge the parental expectations as too high or too low and may consider the parents and their attitudes to be an obstacle to the child's progress. From the wider vantage point of family homeostasis, parental expectations of vocational success or failure for their child take on a balancing or unbalancing function within the family. Like all behavior of family members, parental expectations come to serve a purpose within the family system. Rigid expectations for success or failure can maintain family equilibrium by blocking developmental changes in the family. The expectations may encourage prolonged schooling for the young adult that allows the family to remain stalled at the more familiar prelaunching phase of family development. Strong expectations in any direction can ultimately unbalance the family toward transformation and change. Any member of the family, including the young person with special needs, can learn to oppose such expectations and enter into family alliances that foster reconsideration of the expectations and the emergence of all family members as more autonomous individuals.

Homeostatic processes are acted out in families via repetitive sequences of communication exchanges among members. Content of the messages is far less important than the patterns of transactions that recycle in predictable ways. Accurate charting of *stuck communication sequences* requires that the helper attend to manageable components of family communication (Haley, 1987). It is important to differentiate between report and command aspects of communication, that is, information in message (the report) versus relationship implication of messages (the command). Typically, systems helpers concentrate more on the command aspects of family transactions, observing or discussing stuck family communication in patterns involving three or more people.

Accumulated information on communication sequences can be summarized efficiently as structural characteristics of the family. The most critical concept of structural family assessment is that of *boundaries*. Minuchin (1974), a pioneer in structural family therapy, defined boundaries as "the rules defining who participates, and how" (p. 53) in the activities of a given system. Boundaries cordon off various subsystems within the family, each as a functional unit composed of one or more members. Each subsystem has its own set of rules for communicative and homeostatic processes within the unit as well as for interfacing with other units inside and outside the family. According to Minuchin, boundaries vary on a continuum from enmeshed to clear to disengaged. *Enmeshed boundaries* are diffuse and porous barriers that do not effectively differentiate participation among subsystems. *Clear boundaries* are defined, flexible barriers that allow undistorted information flow and effective problem resolution between interdependent subsystems. *Disengaged boundaries* are impermeable and rigid barriers that prevent useful exchanges of information for problem solving among subsystems. Family subsystems are organized in hierarchy. They stand in vertical relation to one another. At any given point in time, one sub-system has an executive status and functions to regulate family processes.

Returning for a moment to the case of Anita, the counselor noted stuck communication patterns among the threesome, with the mother speaking to and for the daughter and the stepfather interjecting his opinions only when requested to do so by the counselor or when the mother became exasperated. Structurally this translates to enmeshed boundaries in the mother–daughter subsystem, with disengaged boundaries to the stepfather subsystem. The split within the couple subsystem diminishes its ability to adequately carry out its executive function in parenting Anita. In the absence of clear parental hierarchy, Anita's school problems escalated and Anita, through her problems, became a controlling influence in the family configuration.

Systemic formulations do not place blame for the problem on any individual or subsystem. In more traditional orientations, the helper might attribute the cause of the problems in Anita's family to the mother's "overinvolvement," the stepfather's "passivity," Anita's "immaturity," or the parents' recent marriage. Systems thinking regards the attempt to assess blame as an indicator of reliance on a linear model of problem formulation. Systems theory dismisses linear cause and effect as an artificial and incomplete punctuation of extremely complex patterns of interaction (Minuchin, Rosman, & Baker, 1978). The linear model's narrow framing of causal chains is arbitrary and largely for the conceptual convenience of the family members and the helper. In family systems thinking, as in modern physics, the principles of uncertainty and reciprocity of influences prevail; no single event, historical or current, can account for behavior in systems (Bertalanffy, 1968). Systemic formulations emphasize the patterned and interdependent configuration of the family in the immediacy of the current moment, as well as the functions that even deviant behaviors serve in maintaining or transforming the balances of that configuration. As Barragan (1976) stated, "No symptom, structure or system can survive without a function" (p. 238). From a systems perspective, Anita's problems serve a stabilizing or destabilizing purpose in the family.

The family life cycle challenges the family unit to continuously transform itself to adapt to developmental transitions and nondevelopmental crises. A common conceptualization of the developmental life cycle of the family involves an eight-stage sequence, with each stage making specific demands on the family unit for negotiated organizational change before transition into the next stage. These stages are the *beginning family, infant family, preschool family, school-age family, adolescent family, launching family, post-parental family,* and *aging family* (Duvall, 1971). Another popular formulation has reduced to six the number of stages in the life cycle of the intact U.S. family and makes note of the implications of divorce, single parenting, remarriage, and cultural diversity (Carter &

McGoldrick, 1999). The core stages in this model are *single young adults, the new couple, families with young children, families with adolescents, launching children,* and *families in later life.* In both conceptualizations, each transition represents a crisis to the family that has the potential to disrupt the equilibrium of the present stage. The crisis is magnified to the degree that old problem-solving mechanisms no longer fit the tasks of the new stage. Families often retain awkward solutions to new developmental problems as a way of struggling to maintain their system's status quo.

For the family with a child who has a disabling condition, vocational decision making presents a developmental crisis over a number of stages of the family life cycle. The crisis is usually most pressing in the adolescent and launching phases of the cycle. Parents become increasingly aware that their child with a disability lags behind others in virtually every area of economic advancement (Ettinger, 1996). Depending on how the family manages occupational self-sufficiency of its members, the crisis can persist or even magnify in later stages of the family life cycle.

One example of an awkward solution at the launching stage is the case of Mark, an 18-year-old with cerebral palsy who had been accepted to college in a neighboring state. The family had great difficulty incorporating a new image of Mark as a young man capable of attempting more independence. The parents insisted that he continue to live at home and enroll at a local community college even though the curriculum and supportive services were not consistent with Mark's needs. Rather than transform old rules and configurations within the family to adapt to the emerging occupational potential of the son, the family seemed to cling to comfortable patterns that restrained the advancement of the family and its members into the next developmental stage of more autonomous functioning. Although averting the immediate family dilemma, the delayed launching prolonged family patterns that were probably more useful in prior stages and may have laid the groundwork for confusion in solving independence themes in subsequent stages.

Within the family life cycle, change is also stimulated by nondevelopmental crises, that is, unpredictable and often traumatic events that are not a part of an expected developmental progression (Carter & McGoldrick, 1999; Harway, 1996; Seligman & Darling, 1989). The work of Okun and Rappaport (1980) advanced a practical framework for understanding nondevelopmental crises through classification of such crises as *involuntary* (externally imposed) or *voluntary* (participatory). Virtually all disabling conditions initially represent an involuntary nondevelopmental crisis. They are events outside of the direct control of the family that have a resounding impact on family equilibrium. A few disabling conditions are more accurately considered voluntary nondevelopmental crises; these are crises precipitated by family members with a rather clear function in stabilizing or disturbing the family system.

We provide here a few examples to illustrate the difference between involuntary and voluntary nondevelopmental crises. The following is an example of an involuntary crisis: Robert, a 19-year-old college sophomore living on the college campus, sustained a spinal cord injury in an automobile accident. Even after Robert passed beyond the acute stages of his recovery, family balance and development were upset as he and his family faced decisions about new living arrangements and occupational preparation. The following describes a crisis that is more voluntary or participatory: Joyce, a 17-year-old high school junior in a business curriculum, has a severe but treatable diabetic condition, but she has not recently complied with her medical regimen. Joyce is the youngest of five daughters in a family with an alcoholic father. Her symptoms simultaneously impede successful job placement and provide the family system with an available caretaker for the troubled parental dyad.

For the practitioner working with families of youth with special needs, it is useful to formulate occupational dilemmas from the blended perspective of developmental and nondevelopmental family crises. Especially for families that have experienced the disability over an extended period of time, developmental and unpredictable crises seem to fuse together. Concerns often persist in a way that complicates smooth transitions throughout the family life cycle, including the present developmental crisis related to the child's vocational functioning.

Once the helper has formulated the problem in systems terms, the task is to creatively devise ways to nudge the system to surrender the status quo in favor of proceeding toward organizational change and problem resolution. An awareness of the unique issues facing families with a child with a disabling condition can suggest to the helper where and how to nudge.

Unique Issues in Families of Children with Disabling Conditions

It is no more possible to construct a generalized profile of the organization of families with children with developmental disabilities than it is to identify a universal personality structure for the individual with a disability. In reality, many factors influence the manner in which the family interweaves the disabling condition of the child into the fabric of family life. Important objective variables include the severity and visibility of the disability, age of onset, prospect for remediation, and degree of impairment across physical, cognitive, and social/emotional dimensions of functioning (Marshak & Seligman, 1993; Power, Dell Orto, & Gibbons, 1988). Important considerations in the family context include the meaning attributed to the disability in the family constellation, the degree of felt responsibility for the condition, and the intensity with which the disability interferes with the family's capacity to accomplish the tasks of its developmental life cycle (Edmister, 1996; Harway, 1996; Rolland, 1993).

One place for the helper to seek guidance is the literature on characteristics of families that adapt well to the disability of a family member. By comparing the organization and relationship patterns of a given family with this hypothetical reference group, the helper gains a sense of the effectiveness with which the family is managing the disability and some direction for changes that would promote career development of the child. Unfortunately, the characteristics described in the literature tend to be vague and to reflect the value orientation of the various authors (Elman, 1991; Mitchell & Rizzo, 1985; Olkin, 1994).

In the absence of definitive research on resiliency in families with children with developmental disabilities, we have attempted to isolate several factors that seem to promote healthy functioning. Correlates of physical and emotional health in families include openness to new information, flexibility in response to new situational demands, capacity for affective statement, and member autonomy to pursue outside interests (Beavers, Hampson, Hulgus, & Beavers, 1986; Kirshbaum, 1994). Similarly, other authors (Singer & Powers, 1993; Strozier, 1996) have emphasized the need for role flexibility among members, clear and direct communication, clear boundaries among generations, and tolerance for member individuation (i.e., development of a firm sense of self that is distinct from the emotional life of the family system). Marital satisfaction, a family's capacity to enforce disciplinary restrictions on members, accurate perception of the problem, democratic environment, nonmaterialistic orientation, and involvement of the mother outside the home are additional characteristics of families that successfully adjust to disability, as mentioned in the literature (Harway, 1996; Seligman & Darling, 1989). In systems terms, these characteristics denote as the ideal an open family system with intact generational hierarchies and a strong encouragement of self-differentiation of members. It is important to highlight that single-parent and nontraditional families can also be high-functioning family units that successfully manage the tasks of raising a child with special needs (Shank & Turnbull, 1993; Strozier, 1996).

Beyond these broad themes, little is known about families and disabilities that can be of much use to the helper during a consultation. Gliedman and Roth (1980) playfully stated, "Anyone with some familiarity with the general literature on families and a good imagination can construct almost any kind of theory he wishes about the interaction of a particular handicap with family life" (p. 61). Featherstone (1980), educator and parent of a son with multiple disabilities, wrote in her classic work on this issue, "One important conclusion is that families are too intricately complex to generalize about: it all depends"

(p. 165). Given the lack of consistent data about families of children with disabilities, it seems naive and perhaps unfair for helpers to impose on families common stereotypes such as family discord, unrelenting sadness, and enduring stress (Campbell, 1995; Elman, 1991; Jordan, Kraus, & Ware, 1993). It is also inaccurate for helpers to believe that all families with a child with a disabling condition require counseling interventions to facilitate the occupational success of their child. A useful summary statement is Featherstone's concept that family life with a child with a disability "rarely follows anticipated patterns" (p. 27).

For the family whose child has a disabling condition, daily and developmental activities are generally accomplished in a more emotionally charged climate than in many other families. The discrepancies between ideal and real regarding the child and the totality of family life are experienced more suddenly, discontinuously, and often earlier in the family life cycle. This requires the family to begin the process of reconciling expectation and reality sooner and in a more concentrated way than other families. The family whose child has special needs has likely been involved with a variety of caregiving systems from the time the disability was first suspected. These systems, and the individuals who work in them, experience their own struggles to reconcile images of the real and ideal child with a disabling condition, as well as the real and ideal family. The awareness and outcome of this struggle shape the institutional images of what can be expected or hoped for in the future for the child. Involvement with caregiving systems complicates family development in that it requires the family whose child has a disabling condition to function comfortably with caregiving systems as a kind of extended family. Adults outside the nuclear family are empowered to give opinions and contribute to decision making about the child's development and future. At the same time, extra demands are put on family members, by virtue of their involvement with caregiving systems, to set appropriate boundaries in relation to the outside world. Effective boundaries enable the family to function autonomously and discharge the universal family obligation to protect its members. Marking boundaries does, however, exact a toll in time, energy, and often uncertainty.

Families raising children with developmental disabilities do so in a culture that, although changing, displays prejudicial and devaluing attitudes toward individuals with disabilities (Gill, 1994). This adds intensity to the family's job of processing and reality-testing the judgment of the environment regarding the competency and worth of the child. It can add the crucial and consuming role of advocate to the role descriptions of family members. This becomes more difficult when one considers that unlike other minority groups, the family is not a member of the same minority as the child (Gill, 1994; Gliedman & Roth, 1980; Kirshbaum, 1994).

Career Life Cycle Applied

Planning for the career development of youth with special needs involves a complex interaction of a number of social systems, as well as a shattering of confining myths about the incompatibility of disability with adult competence. Issues regarding career decision making are multisystemic and ecological in nature. They can involve various levels of social organization, including the individual, family subsystems and unit, educational and medical helping systems, vocational rehabilitation systems, and local job market factors. In addition, the United States' evolving diversity of familial, cultural, and societal heritages make demands on the effective helper for respectful sensitivity to differences at each level of an ecological formulation.

Although a career counselor's ultimate focus is on the workplace, Salomone (1996) noted the importance of considering the reciprocal influences of three ecological factors:

1. the family (i.e., family expectations, conflicts that can impede work attendance, and practical considerations such as child care arrangements and transportation);

2. cultural attitudes that may clash with work attitudes and behaviors of the majority culture (i.e., less concern with work punctuality and deadlines, unique attire or headwear, and use of a native language other than English); and

3. societal attitudes and behavior that isolate a minority of people (i.e., biases and prejudices toward people with disabilities that impede and affect individuals' attainment of their goals and aspirations.

A number of theorists have proposed frameworks for understanding life-cycle factors in occupational and career progression (Osipow & Fitzgerald, 1996; Super 1990). (Chapter 1 details Super's self-concept developmental model). An enduring and useful model of career development over the life span has been developed by Schein (1978) with variations by Okun (1984) and Schlossberg and Robinson (1996). Schein examined three interlocking cycles: the biosocial cycle, the work career cycle, and the family cycle. With minor adaptations, the model applies well to vocational problem solving from a systems perspective for individuals who have developmental disabilities. The *biosocial cycle* centers on individual maturation as shaped by specific functional limitations and social expectations. The *work career cycle* involves the process of building a model career and the multiple constraints that interfere with that ideal. The *family cycle* considers the influence of family environment on career development of the member who has special needs and, reciprocally, the manner in which that member affects the career progression of other members over the stages of the family's development. Schein hypothesized that the more cycles that are involved in a given career problem, the more difficult effective coping becomes.

In the biosocial cycle for the individual with a disability, biological factors intrude on career development to varying degrees, depending on the type and severity of the disability. More important in most situations is the interaction of biology with environmental pressures that yields the social and vocational disadvantage. Every disability denotes a loss of some aspect of functioning. Society has traditionally defined disability with an emphasis on what the individual cannot do. The assumption has been that if any area of functioning is limited, then all functioning is limited. All individuals experience areas of greater and lesser competence in their own functioning. Although the areas of limitation may be more obvious or more severe in individuals with disabling conditions, limitation in functioning in one area does not automatically define the level of functioning in other areas. Just as individuals without identified disabilities use their areas of strength to compensate for their weaknesses, so do individuals with special needs. A helper therefore has to use the model as the basis of a developmental assessment checklist. Frequently, the evaluation reveals that the developmental disability in and of itself does not interfere with developmental tasks of the specific life stage. Present definitions of disability place emphasis on what individuals with developmental disabilities are able to do and how supports can improve functioning in areas of limitation (Hagner & DiLeo, 1993). In other words, these are strength-based models as opposed to deficit models.

Prevalent myths, expectations, and practices regarding vocational handicaps tend to accentuate rather than accommodate individual discontinuities. For example, helpers and parents may impose on youth with special needs the myth of a one-career decision. By placing so much emphasis on occupational preparation and placement, they often neglect to consider the need for preparation in lifelong career decision making (Biller, 1988; Szymanski, 1994). It is as if parents and counselors are so relieved that the individual has overcome the barriers to becoming employable that they participate in a subtle expectation that the person will remain vocationally satisfied and static. Traditionally, only a narrow range of stereotypically low-status jobs have been open for persons with disabilities (Hagner & DiLeo, 1993), making the issue of full career development for such individuals more of an abstraction than a reality. The guidelines of the Americans with Disabilities Act of 1990 (ADA), which was signed into federal law in 1990, may begin to challenge the assumptions and pragmatics of such socially constructed limitations. The ADA mandates that individuals with special needs should have equal opportunity and access to all areas of U.S. life, including employment.

Currently the work–career cycle for many individuals with disabilities tends barely to reach the stage of full career membership, with no opportunity to progress to more advanced stages of career development. Typically, preparation for incomplete participation in the work–career cycle begins early in the first stage of the cycle (fantasy and exploration). Throughout the cycle, the combined constraints of the disabling condition and social expectations leave youth with special needs with restricted opportunities to acquire skills and negotiate tasks of career awareness and career exploration. Career development programs and counseling for youth with developmental disabilities tend not to encourage the most fundamental attribute of career development: the construction of a vision of occupational progression (Wehman, 1992).

According to Gysbers, Heppner, and Johnston (1998), people with disabilities face specific difficulties in career planning: limited social and vocational experiences in their early development, lack of opportunities to participate in decision making to help develop their skills, and a "negative worker self-concept resulting from certification processes" (p. 111). A major need in career development for youth with special needs is to prepare each person for an individualized but systematic progression through the work–career cycle. Over the span of their work life, these youth require training to assist them in developing a more internal locus of control, as well as advocacy and support to assist them in circumventing realistic obstacles to occupational successes. Such efforts are at once remedial and preventive. Resources like *Everyday Life Skills* (American Guidance Service, 2001) ease the training process by providing a curriculum with multiple lessons in transitional skills that are adaptable to most disabilities. The program includes skill modules on a healthy lifestyle, household smarts, a safe lifestyle, nutrition and fitness, emotional health and self-advocacy, financial responsibilities, use of computer technology, social awareness, the ability to express one's self, career planning, the employment setting, and the educational setting.

The family is the primary organizational context for the career development of the individual with a disabling condition and a necessary ally of the professional helper in activating the individual's career progression. Recognizing this, many experts advocate family involvement in the career development of youth with special needs as a regular part of education or rehabilitation programs (Singer & Powers, 1993; Szymanski, 1994). Often the recommendation is for family members to participate in a peripheral way as an occasional contextual consultant to the individual's progress or lack of it. Awareness of the family cycle as a principal force in career development demands more active participation of family members in each step of a youth's educational and career path. It also compels a more knowledgeable consideration of the reciprocal influences that family members exert on each other's career progression over the life cycle.

Intentional Family Interviewing

Fortified by a sound knowledge base and a systemic attitude, a helper may still not feel adequately skilled to do effective family interventions. Skills in family interviewing and consultation are critical factors in working successfully with families. At the most fundamental level, a skilled helper finds ways to connect with the family. There is recognition that establishing a rapport and a relationship with the family is the foundation for any further work. As Hirshberg (1996) stated,

> With all the things to consider in the interview process — the technical procedures and paperwork, the diagnostic and developmental considerations and complications, and the frantic scheduling and juggling of time and needs — it is easy to lose sight of this simple basic fact. The professional should not lose sight of it. The most essential job of the person conducting the clinical interview . . . is to be able to hold . . . the family in his or her mind as fully and completely as possible. (p. 86)

For a helper without a strong sense of how to conduct a family session or consultation with a family member, family members' emotionality and resistance to change can immobilize the helper's well-intentioned efforts to assess and reorganize the family. In attempting to assist the family to manage the career development problem of the young adult with a disability, the helper can become easily sidetracked and thoroughly confused when inducted into the family's patterns and organization. Families who seek assistance are typically in organizational crises. A family in crisis is usually anxious to appoint the helper as a new and honorary member of the family in hopes of returning the system to a balanced state. To be effective, the helper must function both as an involved member and a detached bystander. Possession of a flexible framework and a repertoire of executive skills enable the helper to perform this dual role in family sessions or consultations in a purposeful and nonreactive way.

Intentional Family Interviewing is a skill-based approach for training helpers to formulate and perform interventions in family systems. It offers the helper guidelines for managing a family session or consultation, identifying the basic stages of the systems-oriented interview, and developing the skills needed to accomplish the objectives of each stage. The idea is to demystify family intervention or consultation. By clarifying what the skilled family helper does and how specific activities work to restructure the family, Intentional Family Interviewing allows a helper to make more informed decisions concerning how to proceed through a given session toward the desired family outcome. The approach is labeled "intentional" based on the belief that at any moment in a session,

skilled helpers know what they are attempting to accomplish and have a repertoire of skills to begin accomplishing it. When flexibly applied, the model assists the helper to become a part of the family system while maintaining an outsider's sense of direction and purpose that reduces the possibility of becoming
incapacitated by the system. In most settings, a helper has only limited
opportunities to work with a family, and it is essential to use the time in an
efficient and targeted way.

In its complete format, Intentional Family Interviewing trains helpers
through the use of video models and feedback. The procedure provides a separate video training package for each cluster of family skills identified in the
model. Concentration is on refining a helper's skills in assessment of and intervention for family patterns. Training occurs through a modified Microtraining
procedure that builds on the basic skills of attending and influencing used in
individual counseling (Ivey & Ivey, 1999).

The core components of Intentional Family Interviewing are summarized
in Table 13.1. The interview is divided into four stages: *entering*, *defining* (composed of two phases — problem explanation and system observation/descrip-
tion), *changing*, and *consolidating*. For each stage of the session, there are explicit
objectives as well as possible tactics and specific counseling skills to aid in accomplishing the objectives. The stages apply to the initial session or subsequent
sessions. The helper is free to determine how much energy to invest in each
stage. In most sessions there is a continuous shifting from one stage to another
in varying orders. The primary function of the helper is to negotiate transitions
between stages. Sometimes the helper intentionally arranges transitions to a
designated stage; sometimes family members maneuver the session into a different stage from the one intended by the helper.

The major helping skill in the session application of the model is Directives
for Communication Flow (DCF), a series of helper activities that set and enforce communication rules throughout the interview. The helper intentionally
blocks, channels, and refocuses family communication to accomplish the designated objectives of each stage. The emphasis on intentionality and directives
in this model does not mean that the helper constantly imposes a choice of
stage on the family. It does confer on the helper an obligation to know what
stage the session is in and to make continuous decisions as to whether to stay at
that stage or progress to some other stage. The model works most fluidly when
at least three family members are present, but it can be used with any configuration of the family system from individual to full nuclear family and beyond.
When the helper is working with only one family member in the room, DCF
skills change slightly to become DDCF (Directives for Description of Communication Flow). Here the helper advances through the same stages but asks the
family member to describe rather than demonstrate patterns, reactions, and
possibilities as they relate to the presenting problem.

TABLE 13.1

A Model for Structuring an Intentional Family Interview

Stage	Major Objectives	Some Tactics	Major Skills
(Presession)	Establish arrangements and initial relationship with family representative	Dialogue with family representative regarding goals and expectations of family intervention	Individual helping skills: 1-2-3 Sequence (Listen, Influence, Check-out)
1. Entering	Enter the system		
	Reduce resistance to helper's entry Make family comfortable in the setting	Attend to each member No discussion of problems yet	Attending skills with each member — e.g. open questioning, reflection of content/feeling
2. Defining	Frame the problems and assets in the system		
a. Problem Explanation	Define specific problem for the session Gain individual perceptions of problem Establish therapeutic control	Attend to each member Help each member state problem and goal for session, uninterrupted by others	Directives For Communication Flow — rule setting and rule enforcing — blocking and channeling
b. System Observation	Identify organization of family by promoting exchanges among members on the problem issues chosen for session	Have members discuss disagreements Be prepared to introduce a third member into two-way conversations	Directives For Communication Flow — rule setting and rule enforcing — blocking and channeling
3. Changing	Change the system within interview through active interventions		
	Promote functional communication ("I" statements, in here and now, with affect, to each other)	Teach functional communication Translate "talk about" into action	Directives For Communication Flow — coaching for functional communication

(continues)

TABLE 13.1 Continued.

Stage	Major Objectives	Some Tactics	Major Skills
	Reconstruct generational boundaries		Directives For Immediate Reenactment
	Relabel problem in systems terms	Detriangulate system	Directive For Detriangulation
		Express assessment of system in terms system can manage	Sequence For Reframing
4. Consolidating	Support changes of the system between interviews		Sequence For Conflict Negotiation
	Take next step in solving problem and attaining goal	Set goals, usually with member consensus	Sequence For Conflict Negotiation
		Assign simple tasks involving all members	Directives For Task Assignment —straight directives —paradoxical directives

Note. From "A Model for Structuring an Intentional Family Interview," by S. J. Rizzo, 1999, Canton, MA: Author. Copyright 1999 by Salvatore J. Rizzo. Reprinted with permission.

To apply the model to problems of career decision making of young adults with special needs and their families, the helper need only center the content of the session on the stated problem. The process of the session remains focused on three-way transactions. Interactions in emotional organizations such as families tend to occur in triangular patterns involving three members. Family triangles are three-way communication circuits that are central to Intentional Family Interviewing. The helper can structure the entire session by simply arranging various configurations of three participants at any given point in the session. By design, the helper participates in some of the arranged threesomes and observes others. For consultations with an individual family member, the counselor simply requests descriptions of triangular sequences in which the member participates actively or as a bystander.

The triangle, according to Bowen (1976), is the "smallest stable relationship system"; it is "the molecule or basic building block" (p. 76) of the family emotional system. Family members behave as if they are emotionally and almost physically connected to one another in consistent configurations of threes. In recurrent, reciprocal, and reflexive patterns, the movement in one position of the triangle prompts movement in the other positions to stabilize the system. When the emotional distance in a two-person system becomes more intense or separate than permitted by current relationship rules, the third position is introduced to change the distances back to acceptable levels. The third position of a triangle may be a topic or a person. A topical triangle exists when two people regulate the intensity of their relationship by talking about some topic or person outside of their current relationship. To get a sense of how common topical triangles are in daily life, examine how many two-person relationships seem to survive on impersonal dialogue or on gossip about others. A personal triangle occurs when three persons agree, usually covertly, to assist each other in the regulation of a two-person relationship in times of stress. Consider the police officer who referees two motorists at the scene of an accident or a child who stabilizes the relationship of two upset parents by playfully distracting them during a minor disagreement.

With repetition over time, triangular circuits become imprinted in families, and major triangular structures emerge with members in highly predictable patterns of interaction with one another. Simply stated, triangles are stuck threesomes. However, triangles may not function indefinitely. Stresses in family relationships may deplete a triangle's resources to regulate distances and solve problems effectively. In triangles with spent resources, the participants look to other persons or subsystems to thrust new energy and stability into the triangle. When families are under intense or enduring stress, complex patterns of interlocking or overlapping triangles form in an effort to reestablish equilibrium in the family (Bowen, 1978). To get a glimpse of the complexity and intrigue of interlocking triangles, think for a moment of the multitudes of people involved in a multiproblem family situation that is familiar to you in a real-life or television drama.

In family interviews and consultation, triangles are usually more manageable to the extent that the helper is able to keep focused on the presenting issue and move the session or consultation along in a purposeful and intentional manner. The remainder of this section offers brief excerpts and commentary from the aforementioned interview with Anita's family. The purpose of the illustration is threefold: it demonstrates the helper's deliberate use of triangular patterns to move through the stages of the Intentional Family Interview, it indicates how to use triangles to understand and change the family structure toward the solution of the presenting problem, and it introduces the skill sequence of Directives for Detriangulation. Used in the changing stage, this sequence is an active strategy to systematically apply DCF to dissect the major family triangle into its component dyads with the goal of reestablishing clear generational boundaries. Because family interviewing is a directive process, the excerpts highlight the helper's role in prompting stage transitions and family reorganization.

Following each excerpt from the interview is an explanation of the events from the perspective of the Intentional Family Interviewing model, with special attention given to the use of DCF skills for setting and enforcing the rules of stage transitions.

> HELPER: Thank you for coming. I'm John Matthews, the counselor for Anita's program here at school. I know something of the problem that brought you here from our discussion on the phone. Before we talk about Anita's difficulties in her program, I want to take some time to meet with each of you. Mrs. G, can you introduce your family to me and then tell me something about you as a person? (The helper makes short personal contact with each of the three members present.)

This is an example of the helper's initial rule setting for the entering stage. The directives establish a focus on the problem but deter discussion of it to emphasize the importance of people over problems. By speaking comfortably and separately with each member, the helper reduces anxiety and breaks the family system into more manageable units. These tactics reduce resistance to the helper's entry into the family system. Helper dialogue with each member sets up nonthreatening triangles (helper–member–comfortable topic).

Occasionally the helper may need to preserve these triangles through the use of DCF to stop discussion of patterns or to block interruptions from overinvolved members. In subsequent sessions, the helper is likely to spend less time in this stage.

HELPER: Okay, let's speak for a while about the specific difficulty that brought you here. Anita, you haven't been doing as well as you used to do in the program, and everyone is afraid that if things don't improve you may have to switch out of this program. Let's take a moment to get an idea of everyone's understanding of Anita's problem. Mr. G, from your perspective, how do you see Anita's problem?
(The helper takes a short statement of the problem from each member, attempting to elicit personal impressions and attitudes.)

This excerpt illustrates the helper's rule setting that affords a transition into the problem explanation phase of the defining stage. During this segment of the interview, the helper establishes triangles that are more emotional than before (helper–member–daughter's problem). These triangles are more like those that occur in the home in that the member with the presenting problem gets talked about. The helper can heighten the anxiety level by use of terms such as "Anita's problem." It is often a useful tactic to plan for the problem member to give the last problem statement (Haley, 1987). This increases emotionality so that the problem person is quite willing to talk when requested. With the emotional intensity that is characteristic of this phase of the interview, the helper commonly relies on DCF skills to block and channel members who interrupt or those who solicit help from the family authority.

It is sometimes draining to keep members focused on discussing the problem directly with the helper during this phase; consequently, the helper may choose to allow people to interact rather than enforce the communication rules of the phase. The helper should recognize, however, that the choice to allow family discussion brings the session into the system observation phase of the defining stage.

HELPER: Anita, so you're telling me the problem is that you're not sure you want to stay in the program. For a couple of moments let's have a family discussion about this. I'll just move my chair back for a while so you can all talk freely. Anita, you start. Tell your mother and stepfather some of your reasons.
(From an observer's position, the helper promotes dialogue among all family members.)

This helper statement represents the rule setting for intentional transition into the system observation phase of the defining stage. In this segment, the family demonstrates the structural organization that gives the stated problem a function. The helper's job is simply to sit back and observe patterns of triangulation in the family, watching for the emergence of a major and repetitive triangle.

As tensions often escalate during this phase, a member will attempt to engage the helper into the discussion, usually by asking advice or by questioning the relevance of what is happening in the session.

MRS. G (TO HELPER):   I don't understand where this kind of discussion is going to get us. We've talked about her reasons a million times at home. We're here for you to help us get answers.

HELPER (TO MRS. G AND FAMILY):   Try to discover a new reason or arrive at some agreement about the most valid reasons Anita has for not doing as well as she did before in her program. (Gesturing to family to speak with one another.)

In the Intentional Family Interviewing model, Mrs. G's attempt to include the helper in the family discussion is regarded as an effort to recycle the session to the problem explanation phase. The challenge to the helper is to decide whether to use DCF skills to continue in the system observation phase or to allow Mrs. G and other members an opportunity for fuller problem explanation before making another effort at formal observation of the system's triangles. In the preceding example, the helper chose to respectfully block the mother and channel further family transactions in the system observation phase.

(After observing a number of cycles of the triangular pattern in which Mrs. G spoke to Anita and then Anita to Mr. G, the helper decided to disturb the configuration as a test of the system's openness to change.)

HELPER (MOVING CHAIR AND BODY TOWARD FAMILY AND SPEAKING INITIALLY TO THE MOTHER):   Mrs. G, I'd like you to observe Mr. G offer some suggestions to Anita on what she can do to like the program better. (Then to the stepfather) Mr. G, you're new to the family. Sometimes an outsider can have good ideas, sometimes not. Would you offer some suggestions to Anita, and the two of you talk about them together. Later you'll have a chance to ask your wife how good your suggestions were for this situation in this family. Okay, go ahead.

With information on the explained problem and direct experience of the structural problem from prior stages, the helper moved into the changing stage with the goal of detriangulation. He used the skills of Directives for Detriangulation to sequentially dissect the triangle into its three component dyads (mother–father, mother–Anita, father–Anita). Observation had indicated that the mother–Anita dyad was active but that the father–Anita dyad and the mother–father dyad needed activation. The helper chose to address the father–Anita dyad first, carefully disengaging the mother in the process.

The session progresses with the helper alternating between the changing stage and the system observation phase of the defining stage. The helper uses judgment on how actively to use DCF skills to promote the prescribed communication patterns of each segment of the session. When active, the helper is in the changing stage; when observing for lengthy periods, the session has recycled back to the system observation phase to further refine definition of the family's organizational problem. Toward the end of the session, and as possible courses of action emerge, the helper moves into the consolidating stage. The main objective of this stage is to build upon the work accomplished in the session by coming to some consensus on what members will do next to solve the identified problem. The helper uses the skills of Directives for Task Assignment to collaborate with members on manageable tasks, such as those outlined earlier in the Anita case, that can be a reasonable next step in problem resolution.

Conclusion

The real world of working with families bears only an approximate resemblance to this idealized and incomplete account of a family intervention. In reality, even a magnificent interview or consultation does not guarantee resolutions to problems. Vocational solutions for families with youth with special needs occur over time as an intricate and stepwise process. It is often the sessions that the helper assesses as failures that in fact precipitate systems change.

References

Allen, D. M. (1994). *A family systems approach to individual psychotherapy*. Northvale, NJ: Jason Aronson.

American Guidance Service. (2001). *Everyday life skills*. Circle Pines, MN: Author.

Americans with Disabilities Act of 1990, 42 U.S.C. § 1400 *et seq*.

Barragan, M. (1976). The child-centered family. In P. J. Guerin (Ed.), *Family therapy: Theory and practice* (pp. 234–248). New York: Gardner Press.

Beavers, J., Hampson, R., Hulgus, Y., & Beavers, W. (1986). Coping in families with a retarded child. *Family Process, 25,* 365–378.

Bertalanffy, L. V. (1968). *General systems theory*. New York: George Braziller.

Biller, E. F. (1988). *Understanding adolescents and young adults with learning disabilities: A focus on employability and career placement.* Springfield, IL: Thomas.

Bowen, M. (1976). Theory in the practice of psychotherapy. In P. J. Guerin (Ed.), *Family therapy: Theory and practice* (pp. 42–90). New York: Gardner Press.

Bowen, M. (1978). *Family therapy in clinical practice.* Northvale, NJ: Jason Aronson.

Campbell, T. L. (1995). Families and chronic illness reconsidered. *Family Systems Medicine,* 13(1), 109–117.

Carter, B., & McGoldrick, M. (Eds.). (1999). *The expanded family life cycle: Individual, family, and social perspectives* (3rd ed.). Boston: Allyn & Bacon.

Cummings, N. (1990). Brief intermittent psychotherapy throughout the life cycle. In J. K. Zeig & S. G. Gilligan (Eds.), *Brief therapy: Myths, methods and metaphors* (pp. 169–184). New York: Brunner/Mazel.

de Shazer, S. (1991). *Putting difference to work.* New York: Norton.

Doherty, W. J., & Campbell, T. L. (1988). *Families and health.* Newbury Park, CA: Sage.

Duvall, E. M. (1971). *Family development.* Philadelphia: Lippincott.

Edmister, P. (1996). Mental health approaches to working with families with disabled children. In M. Harway (Ed.), *Treating the changing family: Handling normative and unusual events* (pp. 219–245). New York: Wiley.

Elman, N. S. (1991). Family therapy. In M. Seligman (Ed.), *The family with a handicapped child* (2nd ed., pp. 369–406). Needham Heights, MA: Allyn & Bacon.

Ettinger, J. M. (1996). Meeting the career development needs of individuals with disabilities. In R. Feller & G. Walz (Eds.), *Career transitions in turbulent times* (pp. 239–244). Greensboro, NC: ERIC Counseling and Student Services Clearinghouse.

Featherstone, H. (1980). *A difference in the family: Life with a disabled child.* New York: Basic Books.

Gerson, R. (1995). The family life cycle: Phases, stages, and crises. *Psychotherapy Bulletin,* 30(3), 43–46.

Gill, C. (1994). A bicultural framework for understanding disability. *The Family Psychologist,* 10(4), 13–16.

Gliedman, J., & Roth, W. (1980). *The unexpected minority: Handicapped children in America.* New York: Harcourt Brace Jovanovich.

Gysbers, N., Heppner, M., & Johnston, J. (1998). *Career counseling.* Needham Heights, MA: Allyn & Bacon.

Hagner, D., & DiLeo, D. (1993). *Working together: Workplace culture, supported employment, and people with disabilities.* Cambridge, MA: Brookline Books.

Haley, J. (1987). *Problem solving therapy* (2nd ed.). San Francisco: Jossey-Bass.

Haley, J. (1990). *Strategies of psychotherapy* (2nd ed.). Rockville, MD: Triangle Press.

Harway, M. (Ed.). (1996). *Treating the changing family: Handling normative and unusual events*. New York: Wiley.

Hirshberg, L. M. (1996). History-making, not history-taking: Clinical interviews with infants and their families. In S. J. Meisels & E. Fenichel (Eds.), *New visions for the developmental assessment of infants and young children* (pp. 85–124). Washington, DC: Zero to Three/National Center for Infants, Toddlers, and Families.

Hitchings, W. E., & Retish, E. (2000). Career development needs of students with learning disabilities. In D. A. Luzzo (Ed.), *Career counseling of college students* (pp. 217–231). Washington, DC: American Psychological Association.

Ivey, A. E., & Ivey, M. B. (1999). *Intentional interviewing and counseling: Facilitating client development in a multicultural society* (3rd ed.). Pacific Grove, CA: Brooks/Cole.

Jordan, J., Kraus, D., & Ware, E. (1993). Observations on loss and family development. *Family Process, 32*, 425–440.

Kirshbaum, M. (1994). Family context and disability culture reframing: Through the looking glass. *The Family Psychologist, 10*(4), 8–12.

Marshak, L. E., & Seligman, M. (1993). *Counseling persons with physical disabilities: Theoretical and clinical perspectives*. Austin, TX: PRO-ED.

Minuchin, S. (1974). *Families and family therapy*. Cambridge, MA: Harvard University Press.

Minuchin, S., Rosman, B. L., & Baker, L. (1978). *Psychosomatic families: Anorexia nervosa in context*. Cambridge, MA: Harvard University Press.

Mitchell, W., & Rizzo, S. J. (1985). The adolescent with special needs. In M. Pravder & S. Koman (Eds.), *Adolescents and family therapy* (pp. 329–342). New York: Gardner Press.

Okun, B. F. (1984). *Working with adults: Individual, family, and career development*. Monterey, CA: Brooks/Cole.

Okun, B. F., & Rappaport, L. J. (1980). *Working with families: An introduction to family therapy*. North Scituate, MA: Duxbury Press.

Olkin, R. (1994). Introduction to the special issue on physical and sensory disabilities. *The Family Psychologist, 10*(4), 6–7.

Osipow, S. H., & Fitzgerald, L. F. (1996). *Theories of career development* (4th ed.). Needham Heights, MA: Allyn & Bacon.

Power, P. W., Dell Orto, A. E., & Gibbons, M. B. (1988). *Family interventions throughout chronic illness and disability*. New York: Springer.

Rizzo, S. J. (1999). *A model for structuring an intentional family interview*. Canton, MA: Author.

Rolland, J. S. (1993). Mastering family challenges in serious illness and disability. In F. Walsh (Ed.), *Normal family processes* (2nd ed., pp. 444–473). New York: Guilford Press.

Rolland, J. S. (1994). *Families, illness and disability: An integrative treatment model.* New York: Basic Books.

Salomone, P. (1996). Career counseling and job placement: Theory and practice. In E. M. Szymanski & R. M. Parker (Eds.), *Work and disability* (pp. 365–420). Austin, TX: PRO-ED.

Schein, E. H. (1978). *Career dynamics: Matching individual and organizational needs.* Reading, MA: Addison-Wesley.

Schlossberg, N. K., & Robinson, S. P. (1996). *Going to plan b: How you can cope, regroup, and start your life on a new path.* New York: Simon and Schuster.

Seligman, M. (1991). Family systems and beyond: Conceptual issues. In M. Seligman (Ed.), *The family with a handicapped child* (2nd ed., pp. 27–53). Needham Heights, MA: Allyn & Bacon.

Seligman, M., & Darling, R. B. (1989). *Ordinary families, special children: A systems approach to childhood disability.* New York: Guilford Press.

Shank, M. S., & Turnbull, A. P. (1993). Cooperative family problem solving: An intervention for single-parent families of children with disabilities. In G. H. S. Singer & L. E. Powers (Eds.), *Families, disability and empowerment: Active coping skills and strategies for family interventions* (pp. 231–254). Baltimore: Brookes.

Singer, G. H. S., & Powers, L. E. (1993). *Families, disability and empowerment: Active coping skills and strategies for family interventions.* Baltimore: Brookes.

Strozier, A. M., Jr. (1996). Families with chronic illness and disability. In M. Harway (Ed.), *Treating the changing family: Handling normative and unusual events* (pp. 246–270). New York: Wiley.

Super, D. E. (1990). A life-span, life-space approach to career development. In D. Brown, L. Brooks, & Associates (Eds.), *Career choice and development: Applying contemporary theories to practice* (2nd ed., pp. 197–261). San Francisco: Jossey-Bass.

Szymanski, E. M. (1994). Transition: Life-span and life-space considerations for empowerment. *Exceptional Children, 60,* 402–410.

Walsh, F. (Ed.). (1993). *Normal family processes.* New York: Guilford Press.

Wehman, P. (1992). *Life beyond the classroom: Transition strategies for young people with disabilities.* Baltimore: Brookes.

A TEAM APPROACH TO PLANNING
AND EVALUATING CAREER
DEVELOPMENT PROGRAMS

Louis J. Kruger and David Shriberg

A systematic approach to planning based on a sound conceptual foundation is necessary for effective delivery of career development services. Although most planning occurs as if planning participants are going to be paddling a canoe through a peaceful river, the reality of most organizations more closely resembles a state of permanent white water (Vaill, 1989). Systems constantly fluctuate, and calmness is rarely the context for making decisions (Shriberg, Lloyd, Shriberg, & Williamson, 1997). This type of rapidly changing environment, including local and national job markets, trends in educational reform, and funding levels and staff commitment to career planning, is the context within which career development planning takes place. A systematic approach can prevent wrong turns in implementing a complex array of services, thereby conserving the valuable time of helpers. A systematic approach also illuminates how to avoid possible obstacles that might otherwise block the provision of services to clients.

Teams have many advantages in planning complex tasks, such as career development services. Teams can facilitate a division of labor and the sharing of multiple perspectives. Whereas planning might be a daunting and time-consuming job for one individual, it can be a job-enriching learning experience when several people tackle the process. A team approach can also capitalize on the unique strengths of different individuals. Thus, a person who has strong

447

interpersonal skills might be given the responsibility of interviewing potential clients relative to their career development needs, another team member with good writing skills can document the program's services, a third person with excellent coordination skills might schedule meetings and deadlines, and so forth.

In consideration of these emphases, this chapter presents a sequential, five-phase approach to planning programs:

1. Building the planning team
2. Identifying the clients' career development needs
3. Designing the career development program
4. Implementing the program
5. Evaluating implementation and outcomes

These phases are adapted from descriptions of problem-solving processes (e.g., Maher & Bennett, 1984). Although each phase is discussed separately, in actuality, the phases overlap and are continually revisited while planning career development services. Moreover, phases often do not occur in a specific order. For instance, after identifying a client's career development needs, a team may decide to enhance its expertise by adding another member who has knowledge pertaining to a previously unanticipated client need.

Planning and teamwork are embedded in a larger system of interdependent elements that can either impede or support the planning of career development services. An example might help elucidate this point. The replacement of an administrator who is supportive of the systematic planning of career development services with one who is ambivalent about the process might result in important resources being siphoned away from the planning team; therefore, before initiating the systematic planning of services, the team needs to ascertain the larger organization's support for the planning. In particular, sufficient release time *must* be provided for members of the planning team. Without this time, the quality of the planning will be compromised and team members are likely to experience subsequent frustration. A systems perspective also suggests that the planning team should work closely with the relevant stakeholders (i.e., those individuals who have an investment in the success of the program). Stakeholders might include, but are not limited to, clients, parents or guardians, helpers, and administrators. For example, the team might want to obtain feedback from key administrators prior to having staff take a needs assessment questionnaire. This feedback might help conserve the team's time and avoid possible conflicts between administration and the team. A participatory approach allows helpers and others to have a voice in program planning. Although it is time-consuming, this approach can increase the likelihood that the helpers and other stakeholders will be unified in their commitment to the program's purpose and goals, a necessary ingredient in the planning and implementation process.

Building the Planning Team

Forming the Planning Team

The initial tasks in building a team are selecting the individuals who will conduct the planning and forming them into an effective team. If a team already exists, then attention should be devoted to improving the team's effectiveness. The characteristics of the team members and their relationships to one another are important factors in determining the success of the planning. Indeed, because the team members are the most important resources, several factors are noteworthy in regard to selecting team members.

Consideration should be given to the competencies needed on the team. Three important competencies are general teamwork skills, problem-solving skills, and content knowledge (Cannon-Bowers, Tannenbaum, Salas, & Volpe, 1995). Two types of general teamwork skills are task and interpersonal facilitation skills (Bales, 1958). Successful teams are able to make progress with the task at hand while also addressing the interpersonal climate. Indeed, a single-minded preoccupation with the task can lead to neglect of social and emotional issues, which at a later date can interfere with task accomplishment. For example, if a team member believes that his or her contributions to the planning process are unappreciated, then he or she might be less invested in the process. A team thus needs at least one member who is able to keep the team focused on the task and one member who is able to help people feel that they are making important contributions to the team. Problem-solving skills also are important. Members should understand the overarching planning process, including the planning phases. Specific problem-solving skills, such as how to collect and summarize data, are needed as well. With respect to content knowledge, the team should have one or more members who are familiar with the scope of career planning services that have been and can be offered, important theoretical models of career development, and relevant professional standards. The team that possesses these diverse talents is more likely to develop a successful program.

A second consideration in selecting the team members concerns the idea of "chemistry." A team can possess all the aforementioned skills and yet perform poorly because of problems associated with team composition. Shriberg,

Shriberg, and Lloyd (2001) described several common barriers to effective team functioning related to group chemistry. Among these are "groupthink," which occurs when group members dismiss information that undermines their position, shun dissidents, and ultimately lead the large group to unify around a decision that may be unfounded (Janis, 1982). Another potential problem with teams occurs when a few team members do all of the work and the remaining team members engage in what is known as "social loafing"— the tendency for individuals to lower their level of effort when it is believed that the results of their efforts will not be directly attributed to them but will instead be shared by the team as a whole. In essence, people tend to hide in groups when they either do not have power or they think they won't be noticed. Awareness of these and other possible barriers can help teams prevent them from interfering with planning. For example, a team might be able to prevent the negative effects of groupthink by developing a decision-making procedure that includes the reexamination of initially preferred alternatives for nonobvious risks.

Effective teams have members who gravitate toward roles that complement rather than conflict with one another. For example, if two members both want to lead the team and neither wants to share that responsibility, then the team might be saddled with a protracted power struggle. Some teams have a member who does not believe in the team concept and repetitively puts his or her personal goals above the team goals. Both difficulties can cripple a team's morale and ability to attain its goals. The optimal solution to these potential difficulties is preventative: Compose the team in such a manner that these problems are unlikely to occur. This entails an assessment of how each member fits into the overall mission and the interpersonal fabric of the team.

Team members also should be representative of the stakeholders of the career development program. Such representativeness is likely to increase the perceived legitimacy of the team and its recommendations. Quotas often are set for the total number of team members, as well as the number from each representative constituency (e.g., helpers). Quotas can prevent groups from being under- or overrepresented on the planning team. Sometimes, in the interest of being inclusive, too many individuals are given places on the planning team. Indeed, having more than 10 members on a planning team can either make members feel as if they are not making worthwhile contributions or slow team progress to a crawl.

Despite this caution, some teams might find it advantageous to include a representative from the local educational service agency (ESA) or at the least designate a team member as the liaison with the ESA. ESAs (also known as educational collaboratives in some states, such as Massachusetts) have assumed an increasingly important role in the planning of career development services. They often are financially supported by local school systems and are intended to supplement the current educational services offered by these systems. The growth of ESAs has been fueled by the realization that school systems can provide better services to students who have low-incident needs when the systems pool their resources. Although it might be highly inefficient to create a career development program for only a few students who have the same needs, it becomes more feasible to design such services for a larger group. ESAs that draw students from multiple school systems can use their larger student base to efficiently create programs that might be prohibitively expensive for any single school system to develop. For example, if one school system typically prepares its students to attend community colleges and universities, it might not be able to plan career services for students who want to enter the U.S. military services. Whereas only a handful of these students might attend a small- to medium-sized school system, there might be many of these students across multiple systems within the same geographic region. An ESA can capitalize on the economy of scale by providing career services for these students. Most states have formally recognized and provided support for ESAs. (More information about ESAs can be obtained from the Association of Educational Service Agencies, http://www.aaesa.org/).

Another consideration in forming the team is the method of selecting team members, which can affect the perceived legitimacy of the planning team and its effectiveness. Although a democratic process, such as an election or request for volunteers, might enhance the perceived legitimacy of a team, these processes might not produce a team that has the desired skills, chemistry, or diversity. Some administrators therefore prefer to appoint members to a planning team; however, this approach increases the risk that non–team members will perceive the planning process and outcomes as unfair and biased. For instance, staff members might suspect that the administration is "hand picking" team participants to further some type of covert agenda. In an attempt to balance these risks, some administrators use a combined strategy of appointments and volunteers (or election) in composing the team.

Improving the Planning Team

The mere formation of a team does not ensure that it will do a good job. Systematic and ongoing efforts must be directed toward helping the team improve. Actions to improve the team should be based on a comprehensive assessment of the team's functioning (Kruger & Kaplan, 1994). Although the team facilitator or leader might initiate the assessment, the commitment to improving the team's performance will be greater if all team members are involved in routinely assessing the team's functioning. Team planning is a complex endeavor, and without a comprehensive assessment viewed from multiple perspectives, it is easy for team members to overlook areas of weakness that might impede their

TABLE 14.1
PERFORMS: Team Assessment Framework

All successful teams have a common core of characteristics. These characteristics can be
identified by the acronym, PERFORMS. In this regard, successful teams have . . .

Purpose	a clear and important team purpose and goals that are consistent with the purpose;
Empowerment	a leader who empowers team members to take a leadership role when they have skills important to task accomplishment;
Relationships (Internal)	relationships among team members that are characterized by collaboration, trust, mutual respect, and frequent communication;
Feedback	members who routinely monitor progress, obtain feedback on group process, goal attainment, and consumer reactions;
Organization	an appropriate organizational structure that includes roles, a problem-solving process, regular meeting times, time lines for completing tasks, and methods for measuring and documenting progress;
Relationships (External)	support from the larger organization, and continually scan the external environment for threats and opportunities;
Motivation	members who are motivated to attain team goals and complete tasks;
Skills	team members have skills and knowledge relevant to team tasks.

progress. There are seven areas of functioning that might affect a team's success.
These areas are delineated in Table 14.1 by the acronym PERFORMS. The assessment of each area can be used to target specific areas for improvement. For instance, if team members determine that they want, but are not receiving, frequent feedback (the F of PERFORMS) from clients' parents or guardians, they can develop a procedure for soliciting oral or written feedback. A routine assessment might serve a preventative function for the team, alerting its members to incipient problems. Parents or guardians, for instance, might inform helpers that they do not understand the goals of specific career planning activities. This knowledge might lead to (a) better communication between parents or guardians and helpers and (b) an examination of the activities in regard to program goals.

Maintaining Team Effectiveness

Many recent advances hold promise for improving the planning process, but none holds as much potential as the use of computers. Particularly intriguing is the use of a computer to facilitate communication among the planning team members and relevant stakeholders. Indeed, communication is a key element in maintaining the ongoing effectiveness of the planning team. In contrast to face-to-face meetings, computer-mediated communication can allow people to exchange ideas without needing to be in the same location at the same time. Indeed, the scheduling of meetings can be one of the principal obstacles in implementing a team approach to planning. Kruger, Cohen, Marca, and Matthews (1996) described how they helped a planning team develop a needs assessment questionnaire by means of both e-mail communication and face-to-face meetings. Consultation was provided by means of a "linch-pin expert" model, whereby an entire team of consultants was able to assist the planning team in a time-efficient manner by using one of the consultants as a communication bridge between the other consultants and the planning team. Members of the planning team used an e-mail group to communicate with one another as well as with the external consultant. When a message was sent to the e-mail group's address, all members of the project could read and respond to the message. The e-mail group facilitated communication at times when members could not meet face to face. This type of communication model could be easily adapted for coordinating the efforts of a planning team with the staff from an ESA, whereby one member of the planning team might assume the responsibility for using e-mail to correspond with the ESA's staff. These types of e-mail groups are relatively easy to develop. In fact, many school systems have the technology and expertise to establish such e-mail groups. In addition, some Web sites, such as Yahoo! (http://groups.yahoo.com), provide free e-mail group services for those willing to tolerate advertisements on their e-mails.

Despite the potential of e-mail for facilitating communication among planning team members, it also can be misused. For example, research has suggested that e-mail may be ill-suited for making complex decisions (see, e.g., Kiesler & Sproull, 1992). Based on research, expert opinion, and extensive experience, the Global School Psychology Network (www.schoolpsychology.us) developed a set of guidelines for the appropriate use of e-mail (see Table 14.2).

The Consultant and the Planning Team

Often, a decision is made to engage the services of a consultant who is not a member of the agency or school. This decision might be prompted by perceived gaps in the team's expertise; however, consultants also are hired to bring a "fresh" or objective viewpoint to the planning process. Regardless of the reason, a contract between the consultant and the organization is highly desirable and should clarify the obligations of each party, the role of the consultant with

TABLE 14.2
Guidelines for Computer-Mediated Teamwork

Leave important decisions to face-to-face meetings. Use e-mail for generating possible alternatives.

Remember that many social cues are absent when using e-mail; therefore, don't use phrases that might be misconstrued as being critical, insulting, or dismissive. When you are unsure of the intent or meaning of a message, ask the sender to clarify the point.

Sometimes it is easier to clarify an issue with a brief telephone conversation or an in-person meeting than through e-mail. Use e-mail, telephone, and in-person meetings as needed.

If the matter is urgent and you are unsure of when the person will read your e-mail message, don't hesitate to use the telephone.

Do not use information that will lead to the possible identification of a student, parent, or colleague. For example, use a pseudonym in place of the actual name. Be careful to protect the identity of others.

Use only high security e-mail systems to discuss sensitive issues. If you are in doubt about the security of your system, consult with your computer administrator.

If you use a computer that is accessible to other individuals, do not leave your user ID and password on the computer. If you do, other people can log on to your account.

If you download files or messages to your computer, make sure that other people will not have access to those files.

Identify the context of your message and to what you are responding. This will help orient the reader. If warranted, include the part of the previous message to which you are replying in your message.

Try to keep your message relatively brief, no more than several sentences. It sometimes is difficult for people to spend long periods of time reading messages. Also, it is time-consuming to write and read long messages.

Indicate when you want the person to respond to you. If your need is urgent, clearly communicate the urgency.

End your message with a clear direction of what will happen next. Indicate what you would like from the other participants in their next messages to you.

Respond promptly to messages. A rapid response indicates that you care about what the person is saying and also encourages the other person to respond promptly to your messages. In contrast, it is a "bummer" to send a message and to get no response or a late response.

Try to build e-mail into your daily schedule. Develop a regular schedule of reading e-mail and share it with your on-line colleagues. This will allow you to use your time efficiently.

If you can't be on-line for an extended period of time (e.g., vacation), inform people of your timetable so that they won't waste their time waiting for your responses to messages.

Note. Adapted with permission from the Global School Psychology Network (www.schoolpsychology.us).

respect to the planning team, and relevant timelines. Moreover, the consultant should be informed if any constraints might be imposed on his or her actions that might hinder the planning process or compromise its objectivity. Clarifying these issues prior to beginning the consultative relationship can help determine if there is a good match between the consultant's planning philosophy and what the agency or school needs. In addition, such clarification can help prevent potential misunderstandings and conflicts between the consultant and the organization.

Although a consultant can offer much-needed technical expertise to the planning process, organizations should guard against becoming overly dependent on an outside consultant to drive the process. Indeed, a summarization of research (McLaughlin, 1989) has indicated that (a) meaningful and enduring change is created and sustained by the local stakeholders and (b) these people should be supported and not supplanted by consultants. Despite this caveat, not only can consultants be useful in providing initial assistance, but they can also be used periodically over time as a type of "booster shot" to ensure that the team does not drift from its intended process or goals. When members leave the team, for example, a consultant might be used to provide training in teamwork skills for the new members. The team approach can also help ensure that the consultant is used appropriately. A team characterized by a breadth of perspectives is more likely than one individual to comprehensively describe the clients' needs, thereby facilitating the match between the consultant's skills and the planning tasks. In addition, if the team is composed of skilled individuals, it is improbable that people will perceive the consultant as the only person who has the expertise to lead the planning process. The consultant should work with the group as a facilitator and collaborator, frequently involving the local people in the planning and evaluation process because only they can determine their own needs.

Identifying the Client's Career Development Needs

Team members work together to identify the career development needs of the clients. The program's content and goals should in large part be derived from the assessment of needs. Research and professional literature on common developmental competencies for clients of different ages or disabilities are sources of data that can aid in the identification of needs and provide theoretical models for program development.

The Research and Professional Literature

In general, career development models are comprehensive and require adaptation and integration into the organizational routine. Teams can facilitate integration of both the content and the processes. Content consists of four areas: self-knowledge, educational experiences, vocational experiences, and career planning and exploration. The goals inherent in the content develop across the life span. Preparation for various life roles, such as worker, retiree, and parent, is influenced by gender, ethnic origin, and race. Processes include classroom instruction, counseling, assessment, career information, placement, consultation, and referral.

The National Occupational Information Coordinating Committee (NOICC) has provided a comprehensive set of competencies and indicators of accomplishment for three of the general content areas indicated above. All of these competencies and indicators of accomplishments are now part of the *National Career Development Guidelines K–Adult Handbook* (Kobylarz, 2001), which contains guidelines for elementary, middle, and high schools, as well as for community and business organizations. These guidelines have been endorsed by eight national professional associations, including the American Counseling Association, and are relevant to the settings where they would be implemented. The competencies for the elementary-school level are broad (see Appendix A at the end of this book), whereas the competencies for the middle/junior-high school level are more specific and build on the foundation laid in the earlier grades (see Appendix B). For example, for elementary students the emphasis is on knowledge of the importance of a positive self-concept, whereas middle-school students are expected to be able to examine the specific effects of a positive self-concept. At all age levels, indicators of competencies are specific manifestations of basic skills and attitudes. At the elementary-school level, for instance, one of the multiple ways students demonstrate competency relative to a positive self-concept is to verbalize positive and negative feelings. In contrast, at the middle-school level, students are expected to be able to specifically pinpoint personal likes and dislikes. The competencies at high school are to bring students to preemployment levels and to readiness for further postsecondary education (see Appendix C), whereas the competencies for adults address adapting, coping with stress, and assuming additional life roles (see Appendix D).

Planning teams can adapt these competencies for the purposes of providing a direction for a needs assessment and setting goals for their local programs. Nonetheless, these competencies should be used in a judicious and selective manner. Needs, resources, constraints, and values might differ in small but important ways among communities, thus making a list of national competencies only a good starting place for thinking about a local needs assessment and a program's goals. Taking advantage of leverage funding to support the development and improvement of comprehensive career development during the early 1990s, 40 states used these guidelines as the foundation of their career development efforts. Although different state and local career development programs have different needs, the key is to develop goals that are age-appropriate and that systematically build upon competencies attained during earlier grades.

Although the National Career Development guidelines remain quite influential in the goals of career development programs at national, state, and local levels, the passage of the School to Work Opportunities Act (SWOA) in 1994 has also played a significant role in the way that career development programs are commonly conceptualized and implemented. A variety of factors, such as a stagnant economy, concern about international competition, and general dissatisfaction with the ability of public schools to prepare students for a competitive workforce led to the passage of SWOA, and since 1994, the federal government has allocated $1.6 billion to states and local partnerships to develop effective school-to-work (now more commonly termed "school-to-career") programs (Kazis & Pennington, 1999). As with the National Career Development guidelines, a broad national template has been created that provides an overarching conceptual foundation for school-to-career programs, with individual states and local programs typically adapting this template to meet their goals. Sample items from this template are presented in Figure 14.1. One of the unique features of this template is that it provides a framework for teams to evaluate their progress with respect to building the capacity for comprehensive career development programs. To learn more about the overarching school-to-work template and to find links to individual states' school-to-work initiatives, readers are encouraged to visit the U.S. Department of Education's Office of Vocational and Adult Education Web site (www.ed.gov/offices/OVAE/).

SWOA ended in 2001, and the beginning of the 21st century has been marked by the continued emergence of standards-based school reform. As of the fall of 2001, a passing grade on a state-mandated achievement test was a graduation requirement in 23 states — a number that is expected to rise to 29 by 2003 (Heubert, 2001). In addition, 13 states (almost twice as many as the year previous) now require students to achieve a passing score on a specific test in order to be promoted from grade to grade (Heubert, 2001). As Dorn (1998) commented, "The short-term question about high-stakes testing is not whether it shall prevail but who shall control it" (p. 1).

Although the standards movement did not emanate from career development practitioners, there can be no disputing the impact of a public movement toward making a single test the sole criterion on which educational success is measured. Such a movement provides several challenges for career development

	Stage of System Building			
	Vision	Planning	Early Implementation	Maintaining the System
School-Based Components				
Restructure school schedules				
Develop and integrate curricula				
Build in collaboration time for teachers				
Provide professional development				
Use authentic assessment				
Work-Based Components				
Recruit employers				
Recruit unions				
Adopt work-based learning curricula				
Review health, safety, and legal issues				
Establish occupational skill standards				
Connecting Activities				
Generate strategies to connect school-based and work-based learning				
Develop collaborative agreements between schools and employers				
Establish governance, leadership, and coordination at all levels				
Conduct labor market research and analysis				
Leverage resources to institutionalize system				

Figure 14.1. Sample components of a school-to-career template. *Note.* Creating a template that addresses critical school and work-based components and connecting activities can be a very helpful tool in assessing the status of a school-to-career program. This sample was adapted from a national template developed by the U.S. Department of Education. To view the full template from which this sample was derived, please go to www.literacynet.org/stw/template.html.

advocates: First, to have a "place at the table" as state standards are rapidly developed and implemented, and second, to advocate for comprehensive approaches to career development in an era in which school curricula are becoming more narrowly focused. Not all state standards include career development goals, and many states are linking high-stakes consequences only to English and math test scores, making all other subjects, including career development, of lower priority to many schools whose funding and prestige are increasingly linked primarily to their students' performance on the English and mathematics tests. Professionals involved in career development thus must continue to fight for comprehensive career development initiatives and also to find ways to link these efforts with the politics of the day, which may or may not be supportive of the latest in career development research. The ways in which this balance can best be reached varies by community, making a local needs assessment of critical importance to the long-term survival and effectiveness of a career development program.

Local Needs Assessment

Career development teams do not work in a vacuum. Different communities will have different career development needs and possibilities. In other words, a career development team can work very hard to devise a program that is steeped in the national literature and appears to be very solid on paper, but if this program is not a good fit with available resources and is devised in such a way that no feedback has been obtained from the local community (the eventual consumers of the program), the career development team may find that their well-intentioned and well-researched efforts are met with significant resistance. An effective local needs assessment is therefore essential to the long-term success of a career development program.

The first and perhaps most important step in conducting the needs assessment is selecting the areas to be assessed. Due to time limitations, it is impossible to do a good job of assessing all possible career development needs; therefore, the team, in consultation with its stakeholders, must set assessment priorities. Attempting to assess too many areas is a common mistake that results in collecting data that inspires little confidence in its trustworthiness. For example, if the principal concern in a high school is the adequacy of the students' career decision-making skills, the needs assessment might focus on the relevant types of these skills.

After the team has identified the assessment priorities, it needs to choose the appropriate data collection method. Direct observation, review of records, interviews, or questionnaires can be used. The area(s) targeted for assessment, the people providing the data, and available resources will all have a bearing on the type(s) of collection methods selected. For example, if the team wanted to obtain parental opinions about the need for a career awareness program, it might make sense to prepare a brief questionnaire that is mailed to each household or at least to a representative sample of the households.

Direct observation involves recording the behavior as it occurs. Although it can be a highly objective approach to collecting data, direct observation takes a considerable amount of time in terms of developing a reliable observation system and carrying out the observations. It should therefore be used sparingly. In a sheltered workshop for individuals with developmental disabilities, for example, the instructor might systematically observe the clients at periodic intervals to determine the development of their interpersonal skills. The observation should focus on clearly defined behaviors. A review of records can also be highly objective, but records might not exist for many potential targets of a needs assessment, such as people's perceptions of the quality of career services in a school system. The following is a brief example of how a review of records might be used in a needs assessment: An inspection of the annual records for Hypothetical Careers Center showed that 75% of the students used only 38 different occupational briefs, whereas the *Occupational Outlook Handbook* (U.S. Department of Labor, 2002) describes 250 occupations, which consist of 85% of all jobs in the United States. These data indicate a possible service delivery problem and may mean that students are not being challenged regarding awareness of a wide variety of jobs.

Interviews and questionnaires are well-suited to assessing individuals' interests, perceptions, and opinions; however, both of these approaches rely on people reporting their own thoughts or behaviors. As such, they can be vulnerable to lapses in memory and deliberate distortions. Interviews may offer opportunities for in-depth probing of specific needs, whereas questionnaires can be used to survey large groups in a time-efficient manner. An interview of a principal, for instance, might reveal the source of his or her resistance to expanding certain types of career development services. A hypothetical principal, who was opposed to inviting parents, guardians, and local business people to visit classrooms to offer talks about specific careers and local opportunities said, "Once you open the floodgate, everybody wants to come into the classroom to 'advertise,' and it is disruptive to the schedule." This information might be used to devise a program that is less disruptive to the schedule and addresses the principal's concern about self-promotion.

An example of a needs assessment questionnaire is presented in Figure 14.2. The intent of the questionnaire is to collect worthwhile data on school personnel's perceptions of (a) the importance of different types of career development needs and (b) students' current achievement levels with respect to these needs. People who use survey data or data generated from other instruments to make important programmatic decisions must realize that all data collection methods

CAREER GUIDANCE AND COUNSELING NEEDS ASSESSMENT

POSITION (Please circle one): Administrator Teacher Counselor Student Parent
Other (please specify) _____

GRADE LEVEL (Please circle one): Sixth   Seventh   Eighth   Ninth

INSTRUCTIONS: We are conducting a survey of the career guidance needs of our students. This survey lists attitudes, skills, and knowledge that are related to effective career awareness and exploration. Read each item and give it **two types of ratings:** (1) **importance** for students in our school, and (2) **student achievement:** your perceptions of how many students in our school already have the attitude, skills, or knowledge.

Circle your choice for each item below using the following **importance** scale:

Of Little Importance		Of Moderate Importance		Of Great Importance
1	2	3	4	5

Circle your choice for each item below using the following student **achievement** scale:

Few or No Students (0% to 20%)	Some (21% to 40%)	About half (41% to 60%)	Most (61% to 80%)	All or Almost All (81% to 100%)
1	2	3	4	5

You may add an additional indicator in the space at the end of each competency if you think it is (1) important for our students, (2) relevant to the competency listed, and (3) not addressed by those indicators already listed.

Competency II: Skills for interacting with others.

The student will . . .

1. Demonstrate concern and respect for feelings and interest of others.

	Importance					Perceived Achievement			
1	2	3	4	5	1	2	3	4	5

2. Demonstrate coping skills acceptable to self and others.

	Importance					Perceived Achievement			
1	2	3	4	5	1	2	3	4	5

3. Distinguish between self-characteristics and group characteristics in interrelationships.

	Importance					Perceived Achievement			
1	2	3	4	5	1	2	3	4	5

4. Demonstrate an appreciation for the similarities and differences among people.

	Importance					Perceived Achievement			
1	2	3	4	5	1	2	3	4	5

(*continues*)

Figure 14.2. Example of a needs assessment questionnaire.

Competency II. *Continued.*

5. Demonstrate tolerance and flexibility in interpersonal relationships and group participation.

Importance	Perceived Achievement
1 2 3 4 5	1 2 3 4 5

6. Demonstrate skills in dealing with criticism.

Importance	Perceived Achievement
1 2 3 4 5	1 2 3 4 5

7. Contribute to group activities by demonstrating competencies in interrelating with group members.

Importance	Perceived Achievement
1 2 3 4 5	1 2 3 4 5

8. Relate one's beliefs and attitudes to the process of interpersonal communication and begin to identify one's own value system.

Importance	Perceived Achievement
1 2 3 4 5	1 2 3 4 5

9. Demonstrate effective social skills.

Importance	Perceived Achievement
1 2 3 4 5	1 2 3 4 5

10. Additional indicator? _____

Importance	Perceived Achievement
1 2 3 4 5	1 2 3 4 5

Figure 14.2. *Continued.*

are imperfect; therefore, all data have some degree of error. For example, in the survey presented in Figure 14.2, care must be taken so that people do not confuse ratings of importance with ratings of achievement.

Regardless of the type of data collection method used, an overriding concern should be the attainment of a representative sample of data, that is, data that accurately reflect the range of needs being targeted in the needs assessment. In addition, team members should attempt to anticipate the type of data they will obtain from each type of data collection method (as well as the specific items on each measure) and whether the data will truly meet their program planning needs.

If surveys do not already exist for the areas to be assessed, then the team might want to develop its own needs assessment instruments. The decision to develop a survey should be given careful consideration. Although it is easy to conduct an interview or create a questionnaire, it is a far more daunting task to develop a high-quality interview format or questionnaire that will generate meaningful needs assessment data. The team that wants to develop its own survey instrument should either have a team member with the requisite expertise or work collaboratively with a consultant to develop an instrument.

If the planning team develops its own data collection instruments, they must be critiqued by relevant others and revised prior to dissemination. This procedure should be followed regardless of whether a consultant has helped the team develop an instrument. Multiple perspectives are valuable in detecting possible flaws that might be overlooked by those intimately involved in the development process. Moreover, the feedback might help the team avoid potential political controversies with which they might not be prepared to cope.

An issue closely related to the selection or development of data collection instruments concerns which people will provide the data. Sometimes it is advantageous to obtain the perceptions of multiple groups in regard to the same needs. This approach can point to areas of consensus as well as disagreement, and these areas can be the focus of program planning discussions. For some groups participating in the needs assessment, it might be relatively easy to obtain a high percentage of responses. Helpers, for instance, are usually highly motivated to participate in a survey that might affect their work. In contrast, lower response rates can be expected from other groups, such as parents and guardians. To obtain a representative sample of data from a group that typically does not respond in high percentages to surveys, it is advisable to take a systematic approach to maximizing response (see, e.g., Salant & Dillman, 1994). It is better to obtain a high response rate by tenaciously pursuing the responses of a random sample of a large group than it is to obtain the same number of responses by surveying the entire group. The former approach is more likely to result in responses that are representative of the entire group. A consultant can be of help in determining the appropriate sampling strategy.

After the needs assessment has been conducted, the team should have a strategy for analyzing and summarizing the data. This is often a very critical task, for a team that is able to measure the right variables at the right time will be in a much better position to create a targeted career development program that meets community needs. Although the method of summarization may vary as a function of the audience, descriptive statistics and charts are most often used. Commonly employed descriptive statistics are means, standard deviations (or ranges), frequencies, and ranks. If the team wants to investigate the relationship among different needs and other factors (e.g., obstacles to addressing the needs), they might require outside technical assistance in how to use inferential statistics (e.g., regression analysis). Commonly used graphs are bar (including Pareto), pie, and line. A visual display of data can be effective in focusing people's attention on the aspects of the data that are especially salient for decision

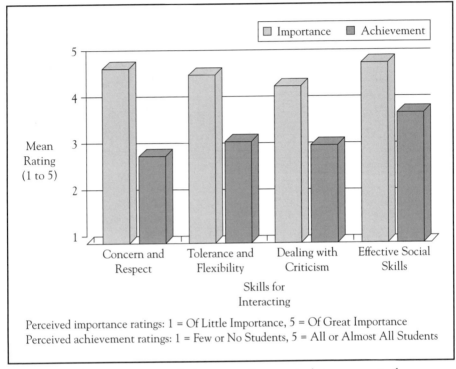

Figure 14.3. Competency areas with the greatest discrepancies between perceived importance and achievement.

making. Figure 14.3 is an example of a bar graph based on hypothetical data derived from the previously presented needs assessment questionnaire (shown in Figure 14.2). The graph depicts the competency areas with the largest mean discrepancies between perceived importance and perceived achievement. Mean discrepancies illustrated in the graph are 1.9 for concern and respect, 1.4 for tolerance and flexibility, 1.3 for dealing with criticism, and 1.1 for effective social skills. Armed with these data, team members and relevant stakeholders can set priorities for the middle-school guidance program.

After the data have been analyzed and summarized, the team prepares a report. This report should contain (a) an abstract or overview of the needs assessment, (b) a description of the service delivery setting, (c) the goals of the needs assessment, (d) the process by which instruments were developed and/or selected, (e) how data were collected and who collected the data, (f) results of the needs assessment, (g) conclusions or main patterns of results, and (h) recommendations. The team should solicit feedback from trusted individuals before more widely disseminating the report. Recommendations can be added to the report after the team has received this feedback.

Designing the Career Development Program

Purpose and Goals

The needs assessment report is used to develop the program's purpose (also referred to as a mission statement) and goals. A purpose is intended to provide a brief overview of the program's intent. At minimum, it delineates the program rationale, the broad intention, and the service recipients and providers. In addition, it might include the primary services and program philosophy. The statement of purpose is a major vehicle for communicating the nature and scope of the program to a variety of constituents. For this reason, considerable care should be taken in writing statements of purpose. Goals are more specific than the purpose and exclusively describe intended outcomes. As stated previously in this chapter, the competencies listed in the appendixes at the end of the book can be consulted for suggestions on how to develop written descriptions of goal areas.

Purpose and goals are arguably the most important aspects of program design. They provide the direction for the other elements of the program design. They can convince people about the importance of the program and motivate helpers. In addition, goals can provide a focus for evaluation efforts. It thus seems advisable for the team to use a structured process in developing the purpose and goals. One such process is the nominal group technique (NGT; Delbecq, Van de Ven, & Gustafson, 1975). In regard to setting goals with the NGT, the following steps could be used:

1. Team members privately record their proposed goals for the program.

2. Each member's proposed goals are presented one at a time in round-robin format, without any critiques or comments.

3. Each proposed goal is recorded in a visible place (e.g., a chart).

4. Sharing is continued until all members have presented all their proposed goals.

5. Each proposed goal is discussed and evaluated by the participants.

6. Members privately rank proposed goals.

7. Rankings are discussed.

8. Members reach consensus or vote on goals.

The team's setting of goals might be expedited if team members ask themselves several interrelated questions while using the NGT:

- Is the goal consistent with the organization's mission and goals?

- Is the goal consistent with the program's purpose?

- Is the goal important to attain?

- Is the goal sufficiently specific so that progress can be potentially evaluated?

- Does the organization have the resources or is the organization likely to obtain the resources needed to attain the goal?

- Do helpers have the time to attain the goal?

The NGT attempts to capitalize on the potentially diverse perspectives of individual members as well as on the group's ability to make decisions based on the collective wisdom of its members. Diverse perspectives are more likely to be expressed when group pressure on minority opinions is minimized, as is the case when each member shares his or her opinions without criticism from others. Also, the NGT makes use of group decision making by providing time for group discussion and feedback after all the privately generated ideas have been shared.

The purpose and goals developed by the planning team should be viewed as preliminary statements awaiting feedback from key constituencies. Following any needed revisions to the purpose and goal statements, the team should again use a structured decision-making process to develop a program to meet the goals. A decision matrix, similar to the one illustrated in Figure 14.4, might facilitate the selection of a program. As indicated in the matrix, the program options can be examined with respect to three criteria: (a) the extent to which the organization has the resources to implement the program, (b) the probability that the program will result in goal attainment, and (c) the extent to which the program protects the clients' well-being and rights. Although the program options can be rated on each of the criteria, basing a decision solely on the sum of the ratings of all team members might lead to a poor choice. Instead, ratings should be used heuristically to facilitate group discussion and attain consensus on the most desirable choice.

Program Design

Once a career development program has been selected, a comprehensive description of a program can be developed that includes the following six components (Maher & Bennett, 1984):

	Criteria for Evaluating Alternate Programs		
INSTRUCTIONS:	Rate each program with respect to the three criteria. Use the following scale: 3 = high, 2 = moderate, 1 = low. Place your ratings in each respective rectangle below.		
Program Option	Resources Available?	Probability of Goal Attainment?	Protects Welfare and Rights of Clients?

Figure 14.4. Sample worksheet for evaluating alternate career development programs with respect to three criteria.

1. Resources for program
    1.1. People: number of staff needed as well as their qualifications
    1.2. A budget
    1.3. Information, in particular, written policies
    1.4. Equipment
2. Methods or activities used to attain goals
3. Roles and responsibilities
4. Sequence of activities
5. Location(s)
6. Evaluation plan

The literature also can be consulted for guidelines on structuring roles and responsibilities. Although many different school professionals can be involved in team-oriented planning and evaluating of career development programs, school counselors often have primary roles. In this regard, the focus often has been on the suggested distribution of the counselor's time with respect to major job functions (e.g., small-group counseling) without that time being tied to an accountability system. Recently, a shift has occurred, and school systems increasingly are being held accountable through high-stakes state testing programs. As a result, counselors must document their activities and accomplishments. In the context of this new accountability and emphasis on student outcomes, Gysbers and Henderson (2000) advocated that counselors keep track of their time for the purposes of improving their efficiency and their programs. This methodology can be linked to monitoring the implementation and enhancement of content-based guidance programs. The first step in this process is for the counselor to record time spent in various activities, such as program management, guidance, counseling, consultation, coordination, assessment, and staff development. These data can be summarized in percentages for the different activities. For example, the results of time monitoring can be compared to program-related goals in order to determine if a counselor is spending the appropriate amount of time on activities linked to important goals. If there is a large discrepancy between the importance of an activity and the amount of time spent on it, the counselor might need to develop a strategy for narrowing the gap. Such an analysis also may help counselors justify how they spend their time.

Discussing an entire design for a career development program is beyond the scope of this chapter; however, we can provide a brief example of the components for one programmatic goal, social development. Methods of accountability are included in the design.

1. Resources for goal of social development

    1.1. One helper with group-intervention training and at least 1 year of experience

    1.2. Training manual with exercises

    1.3. School policies: confidentiality rules of disclosure in grading of experiential involvements

    1.4. Video equipment for providing performance feedback on specific skills

2. Methods and activities—Table 14.3 offers examples of methods and activities that might be used to attain the social development goal

3. Roles and responsibilities—Group facilitator and assessor of student competence within a classroom setting

TABLE 14.3
Methods and Activities That Might Be Used To Help High School Students Attain Competency in Social Development

Subgoal	Method: The counselor will assist the students to . . .	Activities: The student will . . .
Develop and maintain effective interpersonal skills	Experience opportunities for deeper interpersonal relationships and increase their appreciation for the individuality of others Experience a variety of opportunities for group interaction and develop social skills appropriate for group activities	Be able to be involved in a peer counseling program Participate in small groups where students can receive feedback from peers Experience small-group work Engage in role-playing activities
Understand the roles and responsibilities of others in school, family, and community	Understand the importance of individual members to a group	Be part of small groups where peer interactions can occur Observe presentations of local professionals/workers
Acquire a knowledge of and respect for individual differences in abilities, interests, attitudes, and backgrounds	Promote effective cooperation among the various components of the school population	Have opportunities to observe or celebrate diverse cultural events Be provided the opportunity to serve on a committee whose purpose is to reduce tensions among components of the school population

Note. Adapted from *Arkansas Scope and Sequence K-12, Guidance and Counseling Curriculum Guide*, by Arkansas Department of Education, 1987, Little Rock: Author.

4. Sequence of activities

    4.1. Students learn important skills in a safe environment (e.g., practice role playing with other students)

    4.2. Students use social skills in the context of school activities (e.g., serving on school-wide committee)

5. Location — Town high school

6. Evaluation plan

    6.1. Assess extent to which each activity was implemented

    6.2. Use questionnaires to assess teachers' and students' perceptions of the students' competence in each subgoal area

    6.3. Conduct evaluations before winter and summer vacations

> 6.4. Hold focus group interviews of students, teachers, and helpers after each of the two evaluations for the purpose of obtaining their reactions to the questionnaire data

Developing a design, such as the one just described, can be time-consuming. An alternative is to purchase a commercially available curriculum for social skills that is tied to career development (see, e.g., www.realgame.com). The planning team should carefully scrutinize any commercial package to ensure that it is consistent with the local school system's needs and goals.

Incorporating Technology into the Program Design

Technology increasingly is being used as a resource in career development programs. Technology, including computers, can be used for many different goals, such as career exploration, identification of interests, and skill development. The use of technology, regardless of type, should be influenced by several important guidelines.

First, it should be viewed as a means to an end. All too often, people become enamored by what the technology can do and are distracted from their original goals. Educational goals must drive the use of technology, not the converse.

Second, technology should be used to individualize the learning experience. One of the most powerful features of computers is that software programs can be modified to meet the specific needs of different students. This strength should be capitalized upon. For example, after a student explores alternative career options with a computer program, the software should have the capacity to "save" the individual's preferences so that the next time the student uses the program, he or she doesn't have to start from the beginning. Avoiding this time-consuming scenario is particularly important for students with special needs who have a low threshold for frustration.

Third, the use of technology should increase, not decrease, the opportunities for collaboration. Many students with special needs have weak social skills; the last thing they need is to be further isolated from others. Sitting at a computer is a potentially isolating experience; therefore, a collaborative component should be part of using the computer. O'Neill (2001) provided an excellent example of how collaboration can be enhanced by means of a "telementoring" program. In this approach, students were "yoked" by means of e-mail with a professional in the field who had expertise in the subject area that the students were studying in class. The students had a knowledgeable mentor as well as a model for a future possible career.

Fourth, when possible, the technology should link academic experiences with real-world applications. These applications can be directly related to types of problem-solving skills that are needed in work settings. The Workplace Literacy Project (Woodward, 2001) has provided examples of how this linkage can be developed by using technology as simple as a calculator or computer spreadsheet. For example, one teacher gave his students an assignment of estimating the company-wide financial implications of just adding a few more French fries to each bag sold by a fast-food restaurant chain.

Fifth, the appropriate use of technology should be taught to students in the same systematic manner that any subject matter is approached. This entails (a) providing an explanation and a rationale for its use, (b) modeling appropriate use, (c) guiding the students' practice, (d) and providing feedback. Often the use of computer programs and Web sites requires multiple steps and successive decisions. Many students with special needs might become confused or frustrated with such demands without appropriate, structured guidance.

Sixth, the ecological context should be considered when using technology with students who have special needs. For example, a student's family culture can have a major impact on the student's successful use of computer technology, especially if there is an expectation that computer use at home will complement the use of computers in school (Parette & Anderson, 2001).

Seventh, the use of technology should be consistent with ethical principles and legal requirements, particularly in regard to safeguarding privacy. For example, if a student has the ability to save his or her preferences or performance on a computer, other students should not have access to this information. The implication is that privacy features should be a consideration in software purchases and staff should know how to use these privacy features. These seven guidelines are not intended to be exhaustive of all possible considerations relative to using technology with students who have special needs, but they do highlight the important factors to take into consideration when using technology in career development programs.

Evaluating the Design of the Program

Evaluating the design of the career development program prior to implementation can help the team identify flaws that otherwise might go undetected and interfere with either implementation or goal attainment. More specifically, five criteria can be used: comprehensiveness, theoretical soundness, internal consistency, clarity, and compatibility with other programs and routines. *Comprehensiveness* refers to the scope of the program: Whether it encompasses all the intended goals. For example, if a program is intended to address all major facets of career development, it should contain activities for each facet. A program is *theoretically sound* if design elements, such as methods and activities, are based on empirically supported strategies for meeting the clients' needs.

Internal consistency is concerned with the extent to which the elements of the program are logically connected to another. For instance, if one of the goals is to learn decision-making skills, there should be methods or activities that address this goal. A program is *clear* if staff understand the elements of the program and how they are interrelated. A lack of clarity, for example, would be indicated by staff members providing widely different descriptions of a program's goals. *Compatibility* refers to the extent to which the program does not conflict with other programs and services. One possible cause for incompatibility is scheduling. The design of the program usually is assessed by means of reviewing the written program and interviewing or administering questionnaires to staff. One approach to surveying staff is to ask them to rate different program elements with respect to the aforementioned criteria. A second approach is to use open-ended questions for the purpose of determining whether staff members share a common understanding of a program. If a career development program is found deficient in one or more of the above criteria, attention should be directed toward improving the area(s) prior to implementation.

Implementing the Program

Based on a review of the literature, McDaniels and Gysbers (1992) described attitudes and practices that might enhance the implementation of career development programs for individuals with special needs. Their guidelines encompass (a) personal concerns, (b) professional interventions, and (c) theoretical considerations:

Personal Concerns

1. Helpers should consider how their own values and prejudices might affect their work with special populations.

2. Helpers should strive to seek a deeper level of understanding of the various population groups with special needs.

3. Helpers should have a philosophy of continuous professional development.

Professional Interventions

1. Helpers must take initiative with family members in promoting better career development for populations with special needs.

2. Helpers should promote the visibility of career models wherever and whenever possible.

3. It is important to find career mentors for individuals from special populations.

4. Helpers should try to act as advocates of career development for everyone in special population groups.

Theoretical Considerations

1. It is desirable to view career development for individuals with special needs in the largest possible context, such as the context of life-span development.

2. Helpers should grasp the full meaning of the following concept: career = work + leisure.

3. Helpers should take a career information systems approach to the problems of career development for populations with special needs. Although information from local individuals can be valuable, any single source of information should be used cautiously. In general, it is helpful to rely on accurate databases that might be available in print, on computer, on microfiche, or via telephone.

A first step in implementation is assessing the organization's readiness for the program. Failure to assess readiness can lead to increased resistance and incomplete implementation. Furthermore, a readiness assessment might suggest strategies for increasing individuals' receptivity to the program. Davis and Salasin (1975) identified seven factors, represented in the acronym A VICTORY, that should be considered in assessing an organization's readiness for change. (See Table 14.4 for the readiness questions linked to the seven factors.) If planning team members have strong concerns about the organization's readiness for a program, a formal survey of people's perceptions of readiness can be conducted. (For an example of a survey instrument intended to assess readiness, see Illback, 1984.) If a lack of readiness exists with respect to one or more of these factors, actions can be taken to improve it. An organization's staff, for instance, might be skeptical about whether the potential benefits of implementing a

TABLE 14.4
A VICTORY: Is the Organization Ready for the Program?

Factor	Readiness Question
Ability	To what extent does the organization have the resources to implement the program?
Values	Are the values of the staff consistent with the purpose and operating procedures of the program?
Idea	Do staff clearly understand the nature and purpose of the program?
Circumstances	Are organizational conditions and routines conducive to the development of a program?
Timing	Is the time propitious for the development of the program?
Obligation	Are staff motivated to implement change?
Resistance	To what extent are staff resistant to change?
Yield	Do staff believe that the time and effort put into the program will produce positive changes?

portfolio approach to assessing career development needs of high school students outweigh the potential scheduling problems (a question related to Yield; see Table 14.4). To increase readiness, supporters of the program might plan a presentation to illustrate the potential advantages of the program and how scheduling and other difficulties can be resolved.

Program implementation can be facilitated by means of the empirically validated DURABLE approach (Kruger, Fagley, Maher, & Parad, 1987; Maher, 1984). This acronym denotes several different activities that can be carried out by individuals interested in the program's success. These activities are defined in Table 14.5. It is important to note that the order of the letters in the acronym does not represent a prescribed sequence for these activities. For example, teams will often adapt (A) the program after they have learned (L) about obstacles to its implementation. The evaluation (E) part of the DURABLE approach is sufficiently important to warrant more detailed discussion.

Evaluating Implementation and Outcomes

Evaluation is critical to making data-based decisions about how to develop and improve the program. In our experiences, the lack of a systematic evalua-

TABLE 14.5
DURABLE: Approach to Facilitating Program Implementation

Activity	Definition
Discuss	The purpose, implementation, and/or expected outcomes of the program are discussed with staff members and key constituencies.
Understand	Concerns or misgivings about the program are shared and understood.
Reinforce	Encouragement, positive feedback, or other reinforcement is provided to those who contribute to the program's implementation.
Adapt	The plan is adapted or altered as a result of reviewing the implementation or receiving feedback about the program.
Build	Attempts are made to build and maintain positive expectations about the potential success of the program.
Learn	Efforts are made to learn about potential obstacles to implementing the program.
Evaluate	Program implementation and goal attainment are evaluated.

tion plan is a major flaw of many programs. The absence of trustworthy evaluation data can lead to diminished stakeholder support for the program and confusion about how it can be improved. Although we agree that a primary consideration in any evaluation is whether the potential benefits of the evaluation will exceed its costs, more often than not, organizations put insufficient resources into evaluation efforts.

Evaluating Implementation

A successful evaluation is driven by questions that are practical to answer. Questions must be raised about both program implementation and outcomes. Typically, attention is devoted to outcomes and rightly so; positive outcomes can help support the merit of the program; however, the planning team needs to know how to improve the program. This knowledge can be derived only by examining implementation data in tandem with outcome data. For example, knowing only that students are doing poorly with respect to a program objective, such as understanding how physical development affects career decision making, does not indicate a clear direction for program improvement. However, knowing that students are doing poorly with respect to this objective, and realizing that staff did not implement activities to facilitate attaining this objective because of their lack of expertise in the area, might lead to staff training. In regard to implementation, five broad questions can be considered:

1. To what extent did implementation deviate from the program?
2. What are the reasons for the deviations?
3. Are the deviations justifiable?
4. What problems occurred during implementation?
5. How were the problems dealt with?

Although these questions are important starting points for evaluating program implementation, the planning team should seek to further specify their concerns, thereby providing a clearer focus for data collection. For instance, what deviations are of the greatest concern to the planning team? From a program improvement perspective, knowledge of these deviations is most valuable when they are examined with respect to program outcomes.

Evaluating Outcomes

Obtaining clarity and consensus on the questions that the team and the stakeholders want answered is a necessary first step in evaluating program outcomes. The particular questions have implications for the overall design of the evaluation, as well as the data collection procedures. Several possible outcome questions might be posed (Maher & Kruger, 1985):

1. To what extent has the program attained its goals?
2. In addition to goal attainment, has the program had any other positive or negative outcomes?
3. What are the stakeholders' reactions to the program?
4. Is the program cost-effective?
5. To what extent was the program responsible for the outcomes?

Rarely does an organization have the resources to evaluate all these questions. More typically, one or two questions become the primary focus of outcome evaluation efforts. Regardless of the questions addressed, the team should guard against "devaluing" a program by setting impossibly high standards or carrying out the evaluation process in an unfair manner.

Goal attainment is a common focus of evaluations. It presupposes that staff have delineated clear program goals. Even with clearly defined goals, it is often difficult to quantify outcomes without specific goal indicators. These indicators, also known as objectives, are the measurable outcomes of the program. A single goal might be specified by multiple objectives. For example, in regard to the subgoal area of "Understand the roles and responsibilities of others in school, family, and community," the following two objectives (among others) might be set: (a) to understand the three most important aspects of a teacher's role and (b) to understand the four most important responsibilities of being a parent or guardian. Assessment of goal attainment involves comparing the desired attainment level with the obtained level. If a discrepancy exists, it is important to know why. Program implementation data might be helpful in this regard. For example, why did 80% of the students fail to verbalize one of the three most important aspects of the teacher's role? Perhaps, this objective was not met because of circumstances beyond the control of the staff, such as an excessive number of snowstorms that substantially reduced the amount of time given to lessons related to the teacher's role. In this case, it would be misleading to state that the program was unsuccessful.

Programs often have important outcomes that are not encompassed by the goals. These are referred to as the program's related outcomes; that is, outcomes that might be related to the program's implementation but were unanticipated by the stakeholders. These unintended outcomes can be positive, negative, or both. For example, a program might succeed in helping students become aware of the wide variety of possible occupations, but such knowledge might make career decision making a more anxiety-provoking task for some students. These data might lead program planners to ask, how can we inform students about their career choices without overwhelming them and still accomplish our goals? Sometimes, the identification and assessment of possible related outcomes might be as helpful or even more helpful in improving the program than the assessment of goal attainment. In fact, the assessment of related outcomes can lead in future years to the inclusion of one or more related outcomes as goals.

During the last two decades, increased attention has been directed toward how stakeholders think and feel about programs. This has been driven by the realization that programs are ultimately meant to serve people; therefore, satisfaction with a program provides an important source of data for individuals who want to assess and improve programs. As trends in education reform change, maintaining a strong connection to stakeholders is important for the long-term effectiveness and survival of any school-based program, lest the program fall prey to broader societal movements that lead to reduced support. Within career development programs specifically, it is particularly important to obtain feedback for stakeholders because local career needs and the outlets for obtaining these needs can change yearly (or even monthly) in our rapidly changing economy. The use of open-ended questions to obtain individuals' reactions (e.g., "What was the least satisfying aspect of the program?") in an interview or questionnaire can illuminate aspects of the program that might otherwise go unnoticed.

Evaluating cost-effectiveness involves assessing program benefits relative to costs. Cost-effectiveness is a frequently articulated concern; however, conducting a meaningful evaluation of it is fraught with difficulties. One common approach to evaluating cost-effectiveness is to identify another program with similar goals and then to compare costs of the two programs. A problem with this approach is that it might be difficult to find a similar program. The Internet does afford new opportunities for locating such information. For example, a member of the planning team might send a query to an Internet discussion group composed of school counselors in an attempt to find a similar career development program. Another difficulty with cost-effectiveness evaluations is that even small differences between programs might result in very different effects. Because of these pitfalls and the possible damage that can be done to a program with an unfavorable cost-effectiveness evaluation, this type of evaluation should be pursued with the utmost caution and with a high level of expertise. Indeed, an external consultant is often needed.

The final evaluation question might be even more difficult to address than the cost-effectiveness one. It focuses on whether the program caused the observed outcomes. As any student in an introductory research methods course can verbalize, the fact that goals were attained after the program was implemented does not necessarily mean that the program was the cause. There are other competing explanations, such as concurrent educational experiences. A definitive answer to the cause-and-effect question requires an experimental design, something that is neither practical nor ethical to implement in most instances. Some insight into the probability that the program was responsible for the outcomes can be gained by using quasi-experimental designs (see, e.g., Trochim, 2002), which allow the evaluators to control for some of the competing explanations for the observed outcomes. In one type of quasi-experimental design referred to as *time-series* (Barlow & Hersen, 1984), for example, data on outcomes are collected at multiple points in time, including prior to implementation, during implementation, and after the termination of the program. This approach helps rule out the possibility that events not associated with the program might have been responsible for the changes in the clients because the effects of these events presumably also would be evident prior to the program's implementation. Thus, if the program was successful in producing change, one would expect changes during implementation that were above and beyond those observed during the preimplementation phase. Even when using a quasi-experimental design, stakeholders and the planning team must scrupulously avoid the use of words such as "caused," "affected," or "influenced" that imply that a definitive causal link exists between the program and goal attainment. This language is misleading and can precipitate unwarranted blame of the program if, sometime in the future, circumstances beyond the control of helpers or stakeholders result in problems or perceived failures.

Conclusion

This chapter has provided an overview of the important aspects of the process in delivering career planning services. We have advocated for a data-based team approach to planning. Despite the potential problems associated with teams, such as interpersonal and coordination difficulties, they offer unparalleled advantages in tackling complex tasks such as career planning. Chief among these is a flexible approach to problem solving. No set of guidelines, regardless how comprehensive, can anticipate all the decisions and obstacles that local stakeholders will confront in planning career services; however, the multiple perspectives and complementary skills of a well-composed team can adapt to an ever-changing set of demands. To bring the metaphor at the beginning of this chapter full circle, a cohesive team not only can successfully traverse dangerous rapids, it can give the other stakeholders in the school system the knowledge and confidence they need to ford the same river. In this way, the team can provide leadership in career planning for the entire school system.

References

Arkansas Department of Education. (1987). *Arkansas scope and sequence K-12: Guidance and counseling curriculum guide*. Little Rock: Author.

Bales, R. F. (1958). Task roles and social roles in problem solving groups. In E. E. Maccoby, T. M. Newcomb, & E. L. Hartley (Eds.), *Readings in social psychology* (3rd ed.). New York: Holt, Rinehart & Winston.

Barlow, D. H., & Hersen, M. (1984). *Single case experimental designs: Strategies for studying behavior change* (2nd ed.). Elmsford, NY: Pergamon Press.

Cannon-Bowers, J. A., Tannenbaum, S. I., Salas, E., & Volpe, C. E. (1995). Defining competencies and establishing team training requirements. In R. A. Guzzo & E. Salas (Eds.), *Team effectiveness and decision-making in organizations* (pp. 333–380). San Francisco: Jossey-Bass.

Davis, H. T., & Salasin, S. E. (1975). The utilization of evaluation. In E. L. Struening & M. Guttentag (Eds.), *Handbook of evaluation research* (Vol. 1, pp. 621–666). Beverly Hills, CA: Sage.

Delbecq, A. L., Van de Ven, A. H., & Gustafson, D. H. (1975). *Group techniques for program planning: A guide to nominal group and delphi processes*. Glenview, IL: Scott, Foresman.

Dorn, S. (1998, January 2). The political legacy of school accountability systems. *Education Policy Analysis Archives*. Retrieved December 4, 2001, http://olam.ed.asu.edu/epaa/v6n1.html

Gysbers, N., & Henderson, P. (2000). *Developing and managing your school guidance program* (3rd ed.). Alexandria, VA: American Counseling Association.

Heubert, J. P. (2001). High-stakes testing: Opportunities and risks for students of color, English-language learners, and students with disabilities. In M. Pines (Ed.), *The continuing challenge: Moving the youth agenda forward.* (Policy Issues Monograph 00-02, Sar Levitan Center for Social Policy Studies). Baltimore: Johns Hopkins University Press. Retrieved December 4, 2001, from http://www.cast.org/ncac/index.cfm?=920

Illback, R. J. (1984). Assessing and facilitating school readiness for microcomputers. *Special Services in the Schools, 1*(1), 91–105.

Janis, I. L. (1982). *Groupthink: Psychological studies of policy decision and fiascoes* (2nd ed.). Boston: Houghton Mifflin.

Kazis, P., & Pennington, H. (1999). *What's next for school-to-career?* Boston: Jobs for the Future.

Kiesler, S., & Sproull, L. (1992). Group decision making and communication technology. *Organizational Behavior and Human Decision Processes, 52,* 96–123.

Kobylarz, L. (Ed.). (2001). *National career development guidelines: K–adult handbook.* Des Moines, WA: National Training Support Center.

Kruger, L. J., Cohen, S., Marca, D., & Matthews, L. (1996). Using the INTERNET to extend training in team problem solving. *Behavior Research Methods, Instruments, and Computers, 28,* 248–252.

Kruger, L. J., Fagley, N. S., Maher, C. A., & Parad, H. (1987). Implementing individualized counseling programs: Staff perceptions of important activities. *Professional Psychology: Research and Practice, 18,* 71–77.

Kruger, L. J., & Kaplan, S. (1994, March). *Multi-modal team leadership skills.* Paper presented at the annual conference of the National Association of School Psychologists, Seattle, WA.

Maher, C. A. (1984). Implementing programs and systems in organizational settings: The DURABLE approach. *Journal of Organizational Behavior Management, 6*(3), 69–98.

Maher, C. A., & Bennett, R. E. (1984). *Planning and evaluating special education services.* Englewood Cliffs, NJ: Prentice Hall.

Maher, C. A., & Kruger, L. J. (1985). Evaluating educational programs. In J. Grimes & A. Thomas (Eds.), *Best practices in school psychology.* Washington, DC: National Association of School Psychologists.

McDaniels, C., & Gysbers, N. C. (1992). *Counseling for career development*. San Francisco: Jossey-Bass.

McLaughlin, M. W. (1989, March). *The RAND change agent study ten years later: Macro perspectives and micro realities*. Paper presented at the annual meeting of the American Educational Research Association, San Francisco.

O'Neill, D. K. (2001). Enabling constructivist teaching through telementoring. In L. J. Kruger (Ed.), *Computers in the delivery of special education and related services: Developing collaborative and individualized learning environments*. Binghamton, NY: Haworth Press.

Parette, H. P., & Anderson, C. L. (2001). Family and related service partnerships in home computer decision making. In L. J. Kruger (Ed.), *Computers in the delivery of special education and related services: Developing collaborative and individualized learning environments* (pp. 97–113). Binghamton, NY: Haworth Press.

Salant, P., & Dillman, D. A. (1994). *How to conduct your own survey*. San Francisco: Jossey-Bass.

Shriberg, A., Lloyd, C., Shriberg, D., & Williamson, M. L. (Eds.). (1997). *Practicing leadership: Principles and applications*. New York: Wiley.

Shriberg, A. J., Shriberg, D., & Lloyd, C. (Eds.). (2001). *Practicing leadership: Principles and applications* (2nd ed.). New York: Wiley.

Trochim, W. M. (2002). *The research methods knowledge base* (2nd ed.). Retrieved December 4, 2001, from http://trochim.human.cornell.edu/kb/quasiexp.htm

U.S. Department of Labor. (2002). *Occupational outlook handbook*. Washington, DC: U.S. Government Printing Office.

Vaill, P. B. (1989). *Managing as a performing art*. San Francisco: Jossey-Bass.

Woodward, J. (2001). Constructivism and the role of skills in mathematics instruction for academically at-risk secondary students. In L. J. Kruger (Ed.), *Computers in the delivery of special education and related services: Developing collaborative and individualized learning environments* (pp. 15–31). Binghamton, NY: Haworth Press.

A P P E N D I X

ELEMENTARY SCHOOL STUDENT COMPETENCIES AND INDICATORS

Self-Knowledge

Competency I: Knowledge of the Importance of Self-Concept

Describe positive characteristics about self as seen by self and others.

Identify how behaviors affect school and family situations.

Describe how behavior influences the feelings and actions of others.

Demonstrate a positive attitude about self.

Identify personal interests, abilities, strengths, and weaknesses.

Describe ways to meet personal needs through work.

Competency II: Skills to Interact with Others

Identify how people are unique.

Demonstrate effective skills for interacting with others.

Demonstrate skills in resolving conflicts with peers and adults.

Note. From *The National Career Development Guidelines K–Adult Handbook,* by the National Occupational Information Coordinating Committee, 1996, Washington, DC: Author. Reprinted with permission.

Demonstrate group membership skills.

Identify sources and effects of peer pressure.

Demonstrate appropriate behaviors when peer pressures are contrary to one's beliefs.

Demonstrate awareness of different cultures, lifestyles, attitudes, and abilities.

Competency III: Awareness of the Importance of Growth and Change

Identify personal feelings.

Identify ways to express feelings.

Describe causes of stress.

Identify and select appropriate behaviors to deal with specific emotional situations.

Demonstrate healthy ways of dealing with conflicts, stress, and emotions in self and others.

Demonstrate knowledge of good health habits.

Educational and Occupational Exploration

Competency IV: Awareness of the Benefits of Educational Achievement

Describe how academic skills can be used in the home and community.

Identify personal strengths and weaknesses in subject areas.

Identify academic skills needed in several occupational groups.

Describe relationships among ability, effort, and achievement.

Implement a plan of action for improving academic skills.

Describe school tasks that are similar to skills essential for job success.

Describe how the amount of education needed for different occupational levels varies.

Competency V: Awareness of the Relationship Between Work and Learning

Identify different types of work, both paid and unpaid.

Describe the importance of preparing for occupations.

Demonstrate effective study and information-seeking habits.

Demonstrate an understanding of the importance of practice, effort, and learning.

Describe how current learning relates to work.

Describe how one's role as a student is like that of an adult worker.

Competency VI: Skills to Understand and Use Career Information

Describe work of family members, school personnel, and community workers.

Identify occupations according to data, people, and things.

Identify work activities of interest to the student.

Describe the relationship of beliefs, attitudes, interests, and abilities to occupations.

Describe jobs that are present in the local community.

Identify the working conditions of occupations (e.g., inside/outside, hazardous).

Describe ways in which self-employment differs from working for others.

Describe how parents, relatives, adult friends, and neighbors can provide career information.

Competency VII: Awareness of the Importance of Personal Responsibility and Good Work Habits

Describe the importance of personal qualities (e.g., dependability, promptness, getting along with others) to getting and keeping jobs.

Demonstrate positive ways of performing working activities.

Describe the importance of cooperation among workers to accomplish a task.

Demonstrate the ability to work with people who are different from one's self (e.g., race, age, gender).

Competency VIII: Awareness of How Work Relates to the Needs and Functions of Society

Describe how work can satisfy personal needs.

Describe the products and services of local employers.

Describe ways in which work can help overcome social and economic problems.

Career Planning

Competency IX: Understanding How to Make Decisions

Describe how choices are made.

Describe what can be learned from making mistakes.

Identify and assess problems that interfere with attaining goals.

Identify strategies used in solving problems.

Identify alternatives in decision-making situations.

Describe how personal beliefs and attitudes affect decision making.

Describe how decisions affect self and others.

Competency X: Awareness of the Interrelationship of Life Roles

Describe the various roles an individual may have (e.g., friend, student, worker, family member).

Describe work-related activities in the home, community, and school.

Describe how family members depend on one another, work together, and share responsibilities.

Describe how work roles complement family roles.

Competency XI: Awareness of Different Occupations and Changing Male/Female Roles

Describe how work is important to all people.

Describe the changing life roles of men and women in work and family.

Describe how contributions of individuals both inside and outside the home are important.

Competency XII: Awareness of the Career Planning Process

Describe the importance of planning.

Describe skills needed in a variety of occupational groups.

Develop an individual career plan for the elementary school level.

APPENDIX

B

MIDDLE/JUNIOR HIGH SCHOOL STUDENT COMPETENCIES AND INDICATORS

Self-Knowledge

Competency I: Knowledge of the Influence of a Positive Self-Concept

Describe personal likes and dislikes.

Describe individual skills required to fulfill different life roles.

Describe how one's behavior influences the feelings and actions of others.

Identify environmental influences on attitudes, behaviors, and aptitudes.

Competency II: Skills to Interact with Others

Demonstrate respect for the feelings and beliefs of others.

Demonstrate an appreciation for the similarities and differences among people.

Demonstrate tolerance and flexibility in interpersonal and group situations.

Note. From *The National Career Development Guidelines K–Adult Handbook,* by the National Occupational Information Coordinating Committee, 1996, Washington, DC: Author.

487

Demonstrate skills in responding to criticism.

Demonstrate effective group membership skills.

Demonstrate effective social skills.

Demonstrate understanding of different cultures, lifestyles, attitudes, and abilities.

Competency III: Knowledge of the Importance of Growth and Change

Identify feelings associated with significant experiences.

Identify internal and external sources of stress.

Demonstrate ways of responding to others when under stress.

Describe changes that occur in the physical, psychological, social, and emotional development of an individual.

Describe physiological and psychological factors as they relate to career development.

Describe the importance of career, family, and leisure activities to mental, emotional, physical, and economic well-being.

Educational and Occupational Exploration

Competency IV: Knowledge of the Benefits of Educational Achievement to Career Opportunities

Describe the importance of academic and occupational skills in the work world.

Identify how the skills taught in school subjects are used in various occupations.

Describe individual strengths and weaknesses in school subjects.

Describe a plan of action for increasing basic educational skills.

Describe the skills needed to adjust to changing occupational requirements.

Describe how continued learning enhances the ability to achieve goals.

Describe how skills relate to the selection of high school courses of study.

Describe how aptitudes and abilities relate to broad occupational groups.

Competency V: Understanding the Relationship Between Work and Learning

Demonstrate effective learning habits and skills.

Demonstrate an understanding of the importance of personal skills and attitudes to job success.

Describe the relationship of personal attitudes, beliefs, abilities, and skills to occupations.

Competency VI: Skills to Locate, Understand, and Use Career Information

Identify various ways that occupations can be classified.

Identify a number of occupational groups for exploration.

Demonstrate skills in using school and community resources to learn about occupational groups.

Identify sources to obtain information about occupational groups, including information on self-employment.

Identify skills that are transferable from one occupation to another.

Identify sources of employment in the community.

Competency VII: Knowledge of Skills Necessary to Seek and Obtain Jobs

Demonstrate personal qualities (e.g., dependability, punctuality, getting along with others) that are needed to get and keep jobs.

Describe terms and concepts used in describing employment opportunities and conditions.

Demonstrate skills to complete a job application.

Demonstrate skills and attitudes essential for a job interview.

Competency VIII: Understanding How Work Relates to the Needs and Functions of the Economy and Society

Describe the importance of work to society.

Describe the relationship between work and economic and societal needs.

Describe the economic contributions that workers make to society.

Describe the effects that societal, economic, and technological change have on occupations.

Career Planning

Competency IX: Skills to Make Decisions

Describe personal beliefs and attitudes.

Describe how career development is a continuous process with series of choices.

Identify possible outcomes of decisions.

Describe school courses related to personal, educational, and occupational interests.

Describe how the expectations of others affect career planning.

Identify ways in which decisions about education and work relate to other major life decisions.

Identify advantages and disadvantages of various secondary and post-secondary programs for the attainment of career goals.

Identify the requirements for secondary and postsecondary programs.

Competency X: Knowledge of the Interrelationship of Life Roles

Identify how different work and family patterns require varying kinds and amounts of energy, participation, motivation, and talent.

Identify how work roles at home satisfy needs of the family.

Identify personal goals that may be satisfied through a combination of work, community, social, and family roles.

Identify personal leisure choices in relation to lifestyle and the attainment of future goals.

Describe advantages and disadvantages of various life role options.

Describe the interrelationships among family, occupational, and leisure decisions.

Competency XI: Knowledge of Different Occupations and Changing Male/Female Roles

Describe advantages and problems of entering nontraditional occupations.

Describe the advantages of taking courses related to personal interests, even if these courses are most often taken by members of the opposite gender.

Describe stereotypes, biases, and discriminatory behaviors that may limit opportunities for women and men in certain occupations.

Competency XII: Understanding the Process of Career Planning

Demonstrate knowledge of exploratory processes and programs.

Identify school courses that meet tentative career goals.

Demonstrate knowledge of academic and vocational programs offered at the high school level.

Describe skills needed in a variety of occupations, including self-employment.

Identify strategies for managing personal resources (e.g., talents, time, money) to achieve tentative career goals.

Develop an individual career plan, updating information from the elementary-level plan and including tentative decisions to be implemented in high school.

HIGH SCHOOL STUDENT COMPETENCIES AND INDICATORS

Self-Knowledge

Competency I: Understanding the Influence of a Positive Self-Concept

Identify and appreciate personal interests, abilities, and skills.

Demonstrate the ability to use peer feedback.

Demonstrate an understanding of how individual characteristics relate to achieving personal, social, educational, and career goals.

Demonstrate an understanding of environmental influences on one's behaviors.

Demonstrate an understanding of the relationship between personal behavior and self-concept.

Competency II: Skills to Interact Positively with Others

Demonstrate effective interpersonal skills.

Demonstrate interpersonal skills required for working with and for others.

Note. From *The National Career Development Guidelines K–Adult Handbook,* by the National Occupational Information Coordinating Committee, 1996, Washington, DC: Author.

Describe appropriate employer and employee interactions in various situations.

Demonstrate how to express feelings, reactions, and ideas in an appropriate manner.

Competency III: Understanding the Impact of Growth and Development

Describe how developmental changes affect physical and mental health.

Describe the effect of emotional and physical health on career decisions.

Describe healthy ways of dealing with stress.

Demonstrate behaviors that maintain physical and mental health.

Educational and Occupational Exploration

Competency IV: Understanding the Relationship Between Educational Achievement and Career Planning

Demonstrate how to apply academic and vocational skills to achieve personal goals.

Describe the relationship of academic and vocational skills to personal interests.

Describe how skills developed in academic and vocational programs relate to career goals.

Describe how education relates to the selection of college majors, further training, and/or entry into the job market.

Demonstrate transferable skills that can apply to a variety of occupations and changing occupational requirements.

Describe how learning skills is required in the workplace.

Competency V: Understanding the Need for Positive Attitudes Toward Work and Learning

Identify the positive contributions workers make to society.

Demonstrate knowledge of the social significance of various occupations.

Demonstrate a positive attitude toward work.

Demonstrate learning habits and skills that can be used in various educational situations.

Demonstrate positive work attitudes and behaviors.

Competency VI: *Skills to Locate, Evaluate, and Interpret Career Information*

Describe the educational requirements of various occupations.

Demonstrate use of a range of resources (e.g., handbooks, career materials, labor market information, and computerized career information delivery systems).

Demonstrate knowledge of various classification systems that categorize occupations and industries (e.g., *Dictionary of Occupational Titles*).

Describe the concept of career ladders.

Describe the advantages and disadvantages of self-employment as a career option.

Identify individuals in selected occupations as possible information resources, role models, or mentors.

Describe the influence of change in supply and demand for workers in different occupations.

Identify how employment trends relate to education and training.

Describe the impact of factors such as population, climate, and geographic location on occupational opportunities.

Competency VII: *Skills to Prepare to Seek, Obtain, Maintain, and Change Jobs*

Demonstrate skills to locate, interpret, and use information about job openings and opportunities.

Demonstrate academic or vocational skills required for a full- or part-time job.

Demonstrate skills and behaviors necessary for a successful job interview.

Demonstrate skills in preparing a résumé and completing job applications.

Identify specific job openings.

Demonstrate employability skills necessary to obtain and maintain jobs.

Demonstrate skills to assess occupational opportunities (e.g., working conditions, benefits, and opportunities for change).

Describe placement services available to make the transition from high school to civilian employment, the armed services, or postsecondary education/training.

Demonstrate an understanding that job opportunities often require relocation.

Demonstrate skills necessary to function as a consumer and manage financial resources.

Competency VIII: Understanding How Societal Needs and Functions Influence the Nature and Structure of Work

Describe the effect of work on lifestyles.

Describe how society's needs and functions affect the supply of goods and services.

Describe how occupational and industrial trends relate to training and employment.

Demonstrate an understanding of the global economy and how it affects each individual.

Career Planning

Competency IX: Skills to Make Decisions

Demonstrate responsibility for making tentative educational and occupational choices.

Identify alternatives in given decision-making situations.

Describe personal strengths and weaknesses in relationship to postsecondary education/training requirements.

Identify appropriate choices during high school that will lead to marketable skills for entry-level employment or advanced training.

Identify and complete required steps toward transition from high school to entry into postsecondary education/training programs or work.

Identify steps to apply for and secure financial assistance for postsecondary education and training.

Competency X: Understanding the Interrelationship of Life Roles

Demonstrate knowledge of life stages.

Describe factors that determine lifestyles (e.g., socioeconomic status, culture, values, occupational choices, work habits).

Describe ways in which occupational choices may affect lifestyle.

Describe the contribution of work to a balanced and productive life.

Describe ways in which work, family, and leisure roles are interrelated.

Describe different career patterns and their potential effect on family patterns and lifestyle.

Describe the importance of leisure activities.

Demonstrate ways that occupational skills and knowledge can be acquired through leisure.

Competency XI: Understanding the Continuous Changes in Male/Female Roles

Identify factors that have influenced the changing career patterns of women and men.

Identify evidence of gender stereotyping and bias in educational programs and occupational settings.

Demonstrate attitudes, behaviors, and skills that contribute to eliminating gender bias and stereotyping.

Identify courses appropriate to tentative occupational choices.

Describe the advantages and problems of nontraditional occupations.

Competency XII: Skills in Career Planning

Describe career plans that reflect the importance of lifelong learning.

Demonstrate knowledge of postsecondary vocational and academic programs.

Demonstrate knowledge that changes may require retraining and upgrading of employees' skills.

Describe school and community resources to explore educational and occupational choices.

Describe the costs and benefits of self-employment.

Demonstrate occupational skills developed through volunteer experiences, part-time employment, or cooperative education programs.

Demonstrate skills necessary to compare education and job opportunities.

Develop an individual career plan, updating information from earlier plans and including tentative decisions to be implemented after high school.

APPENDIX

ADULT COMPETENCIES AND INDICATORS

Self-Knowledge

Competency I: Skills to Maintain a Positive Self-Concept

Demonstrate a positive self-concept.

Identify skills, abilities, interests, experiences, values, and personality traits and their influence on career decisions.

Identify achievements related to work, learning, and leisure and their influence on self-perception.

Demonstrate a realistic understanding of self.

Competency II: Skills to Maintain Effective Behaviors

Demonstrate appropriate interpersonal skills in expressing feelings and ideas.

Identify symptoms of stress.

Demonstrate skills to overcome self-defeating behaviors.

Demonstrate skills in identifying support and networking arrangements (including role models).

Demonstrate skills to manage financial resources.

Note. From *The National Career Development Guidelines K–Adult Handbook*, by the National Occupational Information Coordinating Committee, 1996, Washington, DC: Author.

Competency III: Understanding Developmental Changes and Transitions

Describe how personal motivations and aspirations may change over time.

Describe physical changes that occur with age and adapt work performance to accommodate these.

Identify external events (e.g., job loss, job transfer) that require life changes.

Educational and Occupational Exploration

Competency IV: Skills to Enter and Participate in Education and Training

Describe short- and long-range plans to achieve career goals through appropriate educational paths.

Identify information that describes educational opportunities (e.g., job training programs, employer-sponsored training, graduate and professional study).

Describe community resources to support education and training (e.g., child care, public transportation, public health services, mental health services, welfare benefits).

Identify strategies to overcome personal barriers to education and training.

Competency V: Skills to Participate in Work and Lifelong Learning

Demonstrate confidence in the ability to achieve learning activities (e.g., studying, taking tests).

Describe how educational achievements and life experiences relate to occupational opportunities.

Describe organizational resources to support education and training (e.g., remedial classes, counseling, tuition support).

Competency VI: Skills to Locate, Evaluate, and Interpret Career Information

Identify and use current career information resources (e.g., computerized career information systems, print and media materials, mentors).

Describe information related to self-assessment, career planning, occupations, prospective employers, organizational structures, and employer expectations.

Describe the uses and limitations of occupational outlook information.

Identify the diverse job opportunities available to an individual with a given set of occupational skills.

Identify opportunities available through self-employment.

Identify factors that contribute to misinformation about occupations.

Describe information about specific employers and hiring practices.

Competency VII: Skills to Prepare to Seek, Obtain, Maintain, and Change Jobs

Identify specific employment situations that match desired career objectives.

Demonstrate skills to identify job openings.

Demonstrate skills to establish a job search network through colleagues, friends, and family.

Demonstrate skills in preparing a résumé and completing job applications.

Demonstrate skills and attitudes essential to prepare for and participate in a successful job interview.

Demonstrate effective work attitudes and behaviors.

Describe changes (e.g., personal growth, technological developments, changes in demand for products or services) that influence the knowledge, skills, and attitudes required for job success.

Demonstrate strategies to support occupational change (e.g., on-the-job training, career ladders, mentors, performance ratings, networking, continuing education).

Describe career planning and placement services available through organizations (e.g., educational institutions, business/industry, labor, and community agencies).

Identify skills that are transferable from one job to another.

Competency VIII: Understanding How the Needs and Functions of Society Influence the Nature and Structure of Work

Describe the importance of work as it affects values and lifestyle.

Describe how society's needs and functions affect occupational supply and demand.

Describe occupational, industrial, and technological trends as they relate to training programs and employment opportunities.

Demonstrate an understanding of the global economy and how it affects the individual.

Career Planning

Competency IX: Skills to Make Decisions

Describe personal criteria for making decisions about education, training, and career goals.

Demonstrate skills to assess occupational opportunities in terms of advancement, management styles, work environment, benefits, and other conditions of employment.

Describe the effects of education, work, and family decisions on individual career decisions.

Identify personal and environmental conditions that affect decision making.

Demonstrate effective career decision-making skills.

Describe potential consequences of decisions.

Competency X: Understanding the Impact of Work on Individual and Family Life

Describe how family and leisure functions affect occupational roles and decisions.

Determine effects of individual and family developmental stages on one's career.

Describe how work, family, and leisure activities interrelate.

Describe strategies for negotiating work, family, and leisure demands with family members (e.g., assertiveness and time-management skills).

Competency XI: Understanding the Continuing Changes in Male/Female Roles

Describe recent changes in gender norms and attitudes.

Describe trends in the gender composition of the labor force and assess implications for one's own career plans.

Identify disadvantages of stereotyping occupations.

Demonstrate behaviors, attitudes, and skills that work to eliminate stereotyping in education, family, and occupational environments.

Competency XII: Skills to Make Career Transitions

Identify transition activities (e.g., reassessment of current position, occupational changes) as a normal aspect of career development.

Describe strategies to use during transitions (e.g., networks, stress management).

Describe skills needed for self-employment (e.g., developing a business plan, determining marketing strategies, developing sources of capital).

Describe the skills and knowledge needed for pre-retirement planning.

Develop an individual career plan, updating information from earlier plans and including short- and long-range career decisions.

APPENDIX

AMERICAN COUNSELING ASSOCIATION CODE OF ETHICS

Section A: The Counseling Relationship

A.1. *Client Welfare*

A.2. *Respecting Diversity*

A.3. *Client Rights*

A.4. *Clients Served by Others*

A.5. *Personal Needs and Values*

A.9. *Group Work*

A.10. *Fees and Bartering*

  a. Advance Understanding. Counselors clearly explain to clients, prior to entering the counseling relationship, all financial arrangements related to professional services including the use of collection agencies or legal measures for nonpayment. (A.11.c.)

Note. Adapted from the American Counseling Association Code of Ethics. Retrieved December 18, 2002, from the American Counseling Association Web site (www.counseling.org/resources/ethics.htm). Copyright 2002 by American Counseling Association. Adapted with permission.

    b. Establishing Fees. In establishing fees for professional counseling services, counselors consider the financial status of clients and locality. In the event that the established fee structure is inappropriate for a client, assistance is provided in attempting to find comparable services of acceptable cost. (See A.10.d., D.3.a., and D.3.b.)

A.11. Termination and Referral

    a. Abandonment Prohibited. Counselors do not abandon or neglect clients in counseling. Counselors assist in making appropriate arrangements for the continuation of treatment when necessary, during interruptions such as vacations, and following termination.

    b. Inability to Assist Clients. If counselors determine an inability to be of professional assistance to clients, they avoid entering or immediately terminate a counseling relationship. Counselors are knowledgeable about referral resources and suggest appropriate alternatives. If clients decline the suggested referral, counselors should discontinue the relationship.

A.12. Computer Technology

    a. Use of Computers. When computer applications are used in counseling services, counselors ensure that (1) the client is intellectually, emotionally, and physically capable of using the computer application; (2) the computer application is appropriate for the needs of the client; (3) the client understands the purpose and operation of the computer applications; and (4) a follow-up of client use of a computer application is provided to correct possible misconceptions, discover inappropriate use, and assess subsequent needs.

Section B: Confidentiality

B.1. Right to Privacy

    a. Respect for Privacy. Counselors respect their clients' right to privacy and avoid illegal and unwarranted disclosures of confidential information. (See A.3.a. and B.6.a.)

    f. Minimal Disclosure. When circumstances require the disclosure of confidential information, only essential information is revealed. To the extent possible, clients are informed before confidential information is disclosed.

h. Subordinates. Counselors make every effort to ensure that privacy and confidentiality of clients are maintained by subordinates including employees, supervisees, clerical assistants, and volunteers. (See B.1.a.)

B.4. Records

a. Requirement of Records. Counselors maintain records necessary for rendering professional services to their clients and as required by laws, regulations, or agency or institution procedures.

b. Confidentiality of Records. Counselors are responsible for securing the safety and confidentiality of any counseling records they create, maintain, transfer, or destroy whether the records are written, taped, computerized, or stored in any other medium. (See B.1.a.)

c. Permission to Record or Observe. Counselors obtain permission from clients prior to electronically recording or observing sessions. (See A.3.a.)

d. Client Access. Counselors recognize that counseling records are kept for the benefit of clients, and therefore provide access to records and copies of records when requested by competent clients, unless the records contain information that may be misleading and detrimental to the client. In situations involving multiple clients, access to records is limited to those parts of records that do not include confidential information related to another client. (See A.8., B.1.a., and B.2.b.)

B.5. Research and Training

a. Data Disguise Required. Use of data derived from counseling relationships for purposes of training, research, or publication is confined to content that is disguised to ensure the anonymity of the individuals involved. (See B.1.g. and G.3.d.)

Section C: Professional Responsibility

C.1. Standards Knowledge

C.2. Professional Competence

a. Boundaries of Competence. Counselors practice only within the boundaries of their competence, based on their education, training, supervised experience, state and national professional credentials, and appropriate professional experience. Counselors will demonstrate a commitment to gain knowledge, personal awareness, sensitivity, and skills pertinent to working with a diverse client population.

b. New Specialty Areas of Practice. Counselors practice in specialty areas new to them only after appropriate education, training, and supervised experience. While developing skills in new specialty areas, counselors take steps to ensure the competence of their work and to protect others from possible harm.

c. Qualified for Employment. Counselors accept employment only for positions for which they are qualified by education, training, supervised experience, state and national professional credentials, and appropriate professional experience. Counselors hire for professional counseling positions only individuals who are qualified and competent.

d. Monitor Effectiveness. Counselors continually monitor their effectiveness as professionals and take steps to improve when necessary. Counselors in private practice take reasonable steps to seek out peer supervision to evaluate their efficacy as counselors.

f. Continuing Education. Counselors recognize the need for continuing education to maintain a reasonable level of awareness of current scientific and professional information in their fields of activity. They take steps to maintain competence in the skills they use, are open to new procedures, and keep current with the diverse and/or special populations with whom they work.

C.3. Advertising and Soliciting Clients

a. Accurate Advertising. There are no restrictions on advertising by counselors except those that can be specifically justified to protect the public from deceptive practices. Counselors advertise or represent their services to the public by identifying their credentials in an accurate manner that is not false, misleading, deceptive, or fraudulent. Counselors may only advertise the highest degree earned which is in counseling or a closely related field from a college or university that was accredited when the degree was awarded by one of the regional accrediting bodies recognized by the Council on Postsecondary Accreditation.

C.4. Credentials

    a. Credentials Claimed. Counselors claim or imply only professional credentials possessed and are responsible for correcting any known misrepresentations of their credentials by others. Professional credentials include graduate degrees in counseling or closely related mental health fields, accreditation of graduate programs, national voluntary certifications, government-issued certifications or licenses, ACA professional membership, or any other credential that might indicate to the public specialized knowledge or expertise in counseling.

    b. ACA Professional Membership. ACA professional members may announce to the public their membership status. Regular members may not announce their ACA membership in a manner that might imply they are credentialed counselors.

Section D:
Relationships With Other Professionals

D.1. Relationships With Employers and Employees

    a. Role Definition. Counselors define and describe for their employers and employees the parameters and levels of their professional roles.

    b. Agreements. Counselors establish working agreements with supervisors, colleagues, and subordinates regarding counseling or clinical relationships, confidentiality, adherence to professional standards, distinction between public and private material, maintenance and dissemination of recorded information, work load, and accountability. Working agreements in each instance are specified and made known to those concerned.

    c. Negative Conditions. Counselors alert their employers to conditions that may be potentially disruptive or damaging to the counselor's professional responsibilities or that may limit their effectiveness.

    d. Evaluation. Counselors submit regularly to professional review and evaluation by their supervisor or the appropriate representative of the employer.

    e. In-Service. Counselors are responsible for in-service development of self and staff.

    f. Goals. Counselors inform their staff of goals and programs.

Section E:
Evaluation, Assessment, and Interpretation

E.1. General

a. Appraisal Techniques. The primary purpose of educational and psychological assessment is to provide measures that are objective and interpretable in either comparative or absolute terms. Counselors recognize the need to interpret the statements in this section as applying to the whole range of appraisal techniques, including test and nontest data.

E.2. Competence to Use and Interpret Tests

E.3. Informed Consent

E.7. Conditions of Test Administration

a. Administration Conditions. Counselors administer tests under the same conditions that were established in their standardization. When tests are not administered under standard conditions or when unusual behavior or irregularities occur during the testing session, those conditions are noted in interpretation, and the results may be designated as invalid or of questionable validity.

b. Computer Administration. Counselors are responsible for ensuring that administration programs function properly to provide clients with accurate results when a computer or other electronic methods are used for test administration. (See A.12.b.)

c. Unsupervised Test Taking. Counselors do not permit unsupervised or inadequately supervised use of tests or assessments unless the tests or assessments are designed, intended, and validated for self-administration and/or scoring.

E.8. Diversity in Testing

E.9. Test Scoring and Interpretation

a. Reporting Reservations. In reporting assessment results, counselors indicate any reservations that exist regarding validity or reliability because of the circumstances of the assessment or the inappropriateness of the norms for the person tested.

E.10. Test Security

Section F:
Teaching, Training, and Supervision

F.2. Counselor Education and Training Programs

a. Orientation. Prior to admission, counselors orient prospective students to the counselor education or training program's expectations, including but not limited to the following: (1) the type and level of skill acquisition required for successful completion of the training, (2) subject matter to be covered, (3) basis for evaluation, (4) training components that encourage self-growth or self-disclosure as part of the training process, (5) the type of supervision settings and requirements of the sites for required clinical field experiences, (6) student and supervisee evaluation and dismissal policies and procedures, and (7) up-to-date employment prospects for graduates.

F.3. Students and Supervisees

b. Self-Growth Experiences. Counselors use professional judgment when designing training experiences conducted by the counselors themselves that require student and supervisee self-growth or self-disclosure. Safeguards are provided so that students and supervisees are aware of the ramifications their self-disclosure may have on counselors whose primary role as teacher, trainer, or supervisor requires acting on ethical obligations to the profession. Evaluative components of experiential training experiences explicitly delineate predetermined academic standards that are separate and do not depend on the student's level of self-disclosure. (See A.6.)

d. Clients of Students and Supervisees. Counselors make every effort to ensure that the clients at field placements are aware of the services rendered and the qualifications of the students and supervisees rendering those services. Clients receive professional disclosure information and are informed of the limits of confidentiality. Client permission is obtained in order for the students and supervisees to use any information concerning the counseling relationship in the training process. (See B.1.e.)

Section G: Research and Publication

G.2. Informed Consent

a. Topics Disclosed. In obtaining informed consent for research, counselors use language that is understandable to research participants and that (1) accurately explains the purpose and procedures to be followed; (2) identifies any procedures that are experimental or relatively untried; (3) describes the attendant discomforts and risks; (4) describes the benefits or changes in individuals or organizations that might be reasonably expected; (5) discloses appropriate alternative procedures that would be advantageous for subjects; (6) offers to answer any inquiries concerning the procedures; (7) describes any limitations on confidentiality; and (8) instructs that subjects are free to withdraw their consent and to discontinue participation in the project at any time. (See B.1.f.)

c. Voluntary Participation. Participation in research is typically voluntary and without any penalty for refusal to participate. Involuntary participation is appropriate only when it can be demonstrated that participation will have no harmful effects on subjects and is essential to the investigation.

Section H: Resolving Ethical Issues

H.1. Knowledge of Standards

H.2. Suspected Violations

c. Organization Conflicts. If the demands of an organization with which counselors are affiliated pose a conflict with the Code of Ethics, counselors specify the nature of such conflicts and express to their supervisors or other responsible officials their commitment to the Code of Ethics. When possible, counselors work toward change within the organization to allow full adherence to the Code of Ethics.

d. Informal Resolution. When counselors have reasonable cause to believe that another counselor is violating an ethical standard, they attempt to first resolve the issue informally with the other counselor if feasible, providing that such action does not violate confidentiality rights that may be involved.

e. Reporting Suspected Violations. When an informal resolution is not appropriate or feasible, counselors, upon reasonable cause, take action such as reporting the suspected ethical violation to state or national ethics committees, unless this action conflicts with confidentiality rights that cannot be resolved.

AUTHOR INDEX

Field, S., 386, 408, 409
Finn, L. L., 213
Fioretti, S., 117
Fisch, R., 91
Fischer, J., 171
Fitzgerald, L., 29, 103, 419, 432
Fitzgerald, S., 122
Florian, V., 123
Fogg, N. P, 315–337, 379
Folsom, B., 23
Forest, M., 188
Fossey, M., 120, 360
Fouad, N., 30–31
Francis, F., 123
Frank, A., 374
Freeman, B., 230
Fremont, T. S., 171
French, S., 147, 151
Fried, J., 46, 137, 350
Friesen, W., 47
Fry, R., 199
Fuhrer, M. J., 122

Gainer, L. J., 214
Gajar, A., 48
Garcia, J. G., 140
Garriga, O., 142, 143
Gaskins, P., 169
Gastonis, C., 166
Gati, I., 22, 102
Gaylord-Ross, L., 127
Gerber, S., 48
Gerson, R., 418
Getzel, E., 364
Gibbons, F. X., 124
Gibbons, M. B., 429
Gibson, K. R. C., 112
Gill, C., 150, 419, 431
Gilmore, D. S., 149
Ginzberg, E., 13, 179
Giordano, J., 138
Gitten, J. C., 115
Givan, M., 22
Glaser, C. H., 117
Glasser, W., 89, 103, 104
Gliedman, J., 419, 430, 431
Global School Psychology Network, 453–454

Gloria, A., 31
Glover, R. W., 190, 191
Goldberg, R., 111, 124, 126
Gomez, R., 141
Goodrick, G., 348
Gordon, L. B., 374
Gordon, M., 367
Gordon, T., 48
Gordon, W., 125
Gottfredson, L. S., 10, 13–15
Graham, P., 164
Green, P., 300
Greenwalt, B., 262
Grieco, E. M., 136
Griffin, S. L., 126
Grossman, P. D., 120
Grubb, W. N., and Associates, 209
Gullotta, T. P., 169
Guralink, D. B., 39
Gurney, A. G., 417–443
Gussel, L., 345, 347
Gustafson, D. H., 465
Gysbers, N., 434, 468
Gysbers, N. C., 472

Hackbarth, J. S., 262
Hackett, G., 10, 29, 30, 103, 143, 150, 151
Hackney, G., 39
Hagner, D., 433
Hahn, H., 122, 148, 150
Hale, T. W., 322, 323, 325, 326
Haley, J., 418, 421–422, 441
Halleck, S. L., 176
Halloran, W., 208
Halpern, A. S., 374, 375–376, 378, 379, 386, 387
Hampson, R., 430
Hanley-Maxwell, C., 200
Harasymiw, S., 125
Hare-Mustin, R. T., 143, 147
Harney, J. Y., 211
Harrington, J. C., 230, 257
Harrington, T. F., 3–40, 77–106, 229–264, 267–312, 315–337, 379

Harris, R., 342
Harry, B., 122, 140, 143, 144
Hartman, R., 366
Hartoonian, M., 167
Harway, M., 428, 430
Hasazi, S. B., 374
Hasselbring, R. S., 117
Hauck, C., 212
Hauser, S. T., 164
Haveman, R., 315
Hayghe, H. V., 322, 323, 325, 326
HEATH Resource Center. See Higher Education and Adult Training for People with Disabilities (HEATH) Resource Center
Hebbeler, K., 379
Hebel, S., 342, 346
Hecker, D. E., 335
Helms, J. E., 136, 137, 138, 140–144, 146
Henderson, C., 210
Henderson, P., 468
Henggler, S. W., 169
Heppner, M., 102, 434
Hernandez, B., 122, 123
Herr, E. L., 8, 9
Hersen, M., 171, 478
Hershenson, D., 33–34
Heubert, J. P., 457
Heyward, S., 212, 345, 346–347
Higher Education and Adult Training for People with Disabilities (HEATH) Resource Center, 212, 357, 366
Hill, J. L., 212
Hird, J., 31
Hirshberg, L. M., 435
Hitchings, W. E., 364, 418
Hoffman, A., 409
Hoffman, L., 212, 213
Hohenshil, T. H., 46
Holdern, L., 121
Holland, J. L., 15–21, 34, 84, 231, 236, 283, 380

SUBJECT INDEX

About the Editor

Thomas F. Harrington, PhD, is a counseling psychologist and a practioner with a theoretical orientation in the broad field of vocational development. He teaches in Northeastern University's Department of Counseling and Applied Educational Psychology, and since 1975 has been a psychological consultant to the Massachusetts Rehabilitation Commission. Currently he works with Northeastern's Center for Labor Market Studies. He has been a visiting scholar, fellow, and professor in Australia, the United Kingdom, South Africa, Israel, and Jamaica. Dr. Harrington has coauthored four books, two psychological tests, four films, and numerous articles.

DATE DUE

JAN 1 8 '05 G		
FEB 1 0 2005		
GAYLORD		PRINTED IN U.S.A.